UNDERSTANDING CONFLICT OF LAWS

REVISED THIRD EDITION

William M. Richman
Distinguished University Professor
University of Toledo College of Law

William L. Reynolds
Professor of Law
University of Maryland

LexisNexis

Library of Congress Cataloging-in-Publication Data

Library of Congress Cataloging-in-Publication Data
Richman, William M.
Understanding Conflict of Laws / by William M. Richman, Willam L. Reynolds. 3rd ed.
p. cm.
Includes bibliographical references and index.
ISBN 0–8205–5807–9 (softbound)
1. Conflict of Laws — United States. I. Reynolds, William L., 1945-. II. Title.
KF411.R53 2002
340.9'0973--dc21

2002072921

ISBN: 978-1-4224-8381-7

Editorial Offices
744 Broad Street, Newark, NJ 07102 (973) 820-2000
201 Mission St., San Francisco, CA 94105-1831 (415) 908-3200
701 East Water Street, Charlottesville, VA 22902-7587 (804) 972-7600
www.lexis.com

(Pub.127 Rel.3R)

DEDICATION

For Carol.

W.M.R.

To My Parents, Roy and Doris.

W.L.R.

PREFACE TO THE THIRD EDITION

In the decade since the publication of the Second edition of this book, there have been steady changes in most of the areas covered. None has been revolutionary on its own, but together the developments have had a substantial impact; those changes are reflected throughout this edition. We have also reorganized and supplemented Chapter IV, part C in order to better show the great importance of the Second Conflicts Restatement in choice of law in the courts today. Finally, we have added a new section on cyberspace jurisdiction.

During the preparation of this edition, David Vernon, our co–author on a Conflicts casebook, died. David was a fine scholar, and an even better person. Also, between the second and third editions, we suffered the losses of Roy L. Reynolds, Bernice C. Richman, and Jacob L. Richman — all of blessed memory. We will miss them.

We deeply appreciate the work of our research assistants Amanda Lesher and Karin Clarkson.

Once again, thanks to our families for their support: Carol, Emily and Nathan Richman, and Teddy, Bill, Catherine, and Sarah Reynolds.

July 2002

Toledo, Ohio

Baltimore, Maryland

TABLE OF CONTENTS

CHAPTER 1 INTRODUCTION

CHAPTER 2 DOMICILE

CHAPTER 3 JURISDICTION OF COURTS

Part A. INTRODUCTION

TABLE OF CONTENTS

Page

TABLE OF CONTENTS

Page

TABLE OF CONTENTS

Page

TABLE OF CONTENTS

Page

Part A. SOME PERVASIVE PROBLEMS

Part B. THE FIRST RESTATEMENT

Page

TABLE OF CONTENTS

Page

TABLE OF CONTENTS

TABLE OF CONTENTS

Page

Chapter 1

INTRODUCTION

§ 1 The Nature of the Subject

The study of conflict of laws centers on disputes and transactions that have legal implications involving more than one sovereign.[1] Conflicts problems, therefore, can involve questions that go to the very heart of relations between governments. The proper adjustment and balance of those relations requires a high degree of sensitivity on the part of decision–makers. Because conflicts questions generally arise in the context of litigation, because they pose a vast array of different fact patterns, and because many of the problems resist the application of inflexible rules, the solutions to conflict of laws questions in American law generally, although not always, have been the province of the judiciary.

This treatise examines the common questions raised in multi–state disputes and transactions. The focus is almost exclusively on relations among the sovereigns in the American federal system: the national and state governments. Within that category, the focus is generally directed to horizontal relations among the states.

Two major areas of concern touched upon only briefly in this book are international conflicts problems and problems created when state law conflicts with federal law. Because the Federal Constitution limits in many ways the exercise of state power, we also discuss the impact of the Constitution on conflicts problems. That impact is sometimes quite significant (*e.g.*, jurisdiction and judgments) and sometimes hardly evident at all (*e.g.*, choice of law).[2]

Conflicts, like Caesar's Gaul, is generally said to be divided into three parts: jurisdiction, choice of law, and judgments. In addition to these subjects, this book examines at the start the problem of domicile and concludes with an analysis of conflicts problems in domestic relations, an area where specialized treatment is necessary. Each of these five Chapters is discussed briefly below.

[a] Domicile

The question of a person's "domicile" (something close to, but not identical with, "residence") is a recurrent problem in the field of conflicts. Domicile, in particular, has significant implications in jurisdiction and choice of law.

[1] This definition is circular; it is not possible, after all, to know the legal implications of a problem until you know the rules that will be applied to it.

[2] There is also a short discussion of the *Erie* decision and its impact on choice of law.

Because of this, we have broken domicile out as a separate chapter, using it to begin our discussion of the whole subject of conflicts.

[b] Jurisdiction

"Jurisdiction" concerns the power of courts to adjudicate with respect to a person or thing.[3] If a court has jurisdiction over a person, for example, it can exercise power over her, and adjust her legal relations with others. A court, for example, might order that a defendant pay money to a plaintiff for a breach of contract; the court must have personal jurisdiction for that order to be valid. In contrast, a court might exercise jurisdiction over a piece of property (real or personal), adjudicating the rights of the whole world in it (in rem jurisdiction), or adjudicating the rights in it of certain named individuals only (quasi–in rem jurisdiction). Examples of the former include Torrens land registration systems and decrees of probate and admiralty courts; quasi–in rem jurisdiction is typified by a suit to quiet title or an attachment action by a creditor against a piece of a debtor's property.

To exercise jurisdiction properly, a court must have enough connection with a problem to satisfy both constitutional and statutory requirements. There must be a sufficient nexus between the defendant or the res on the one hand and the state on the other to justify the exercise of power. This does not mean that the defendant, for example, necessarily must be present in the jurisdiction; it may be that her activities (such as selling goods in the state) will make it reasonable for the state to exercise jurisdiction over her even though she is not within the state's territory. When that happens, the state's "long–arm" jurisdiction can bring the defendant before the court. The chapter on jurisdiction examines the development of modern jurisdictional concepts, problems involving specific types of jurisdiction, and conceptual difficulties with modern doctrine, particularly with regard to new developments in electronic communication and commerce.

[c] Choice of Law

Whenever a legal problem involves incidents or issues concerning more than one state, a court must determine which state's legal rules should control. The development of current approaches to choice of law has been revolutionary. The story begins with the vested rights/territorial approach, which dominated thinking until well past mid–century. Then, under the guidance of the American Law Institute and of a brilliant band of judges and professors led by Brainerd Currie, conflicts analysis began to examine the "interests" involved in any particular legal problem. The chapter on choice of law explores the development of modern theories, as well as the counter–revolution in vogue in some quarters. The chapter also includes a unit on the restraints imposed by the Constitution on choice–of–law analysis, and concludes with a discussion of the impact of the Supreme Court's decision in *Erie R.R. v. Tompkins* on choice–of–law questions.

[3] This is known as "jurisdiction to adjudicate," in contrast to "legislative jurisdiction" discussed in § 94, *infra*.

[d] The Effect of a Judgment

A defendant who prevails in a case may find that her troubles are not over; the losing plaintiff, for example, may sue again in another jurisdiction, and the victor in the first case will seek to interpose that judgment as a defense to the second claim. Or, to illustrate from the other perspective, if the plaintiff wins the first time around, she may try to satisfy her judgment by levying on assets of the loser located in another state. In each case, what effect must the second court give to the decision by the first court? These problems are examined in Chapter Five of this book. The focus of the chapter is the Full Faith and Credit Clause of the Constitution of the United States, one device used by the Framers to unify the nation.

[e] Domestic Relations

The last chapter in the book deals with the special case of domestic relations. Family problems receive special treatment because of their unique features. Judgments in family matters, for example, often can be reopened time after time in contrast to the rule of finality that prevails in other litigation. And although choice–of–law questions are virtually non–existent in this area, jurisdictional questions can become quite complex because a judgment may affect both personal rights (alimony) as well as status (divorce).

Because general conflicts rules do not apply neatly, domestic relations typically is treated as a discrete subject in conflicts analysis. Because it is both like and unlike other problems in this book, a concluding chapter on family issues provides a good summary and review.

§ 2 Bibliography

Conflicts scholarship is enormous and varied in scope, content, and quality. Many of these articles and books will be cited in the text. Some of the works are referred to often enough, however, to warrant a shorthand citation form. The list below gives the full citation for each work, followed by the manner in which we cite it in footnote references:

1. Treatises

Robert Casad and William Richman, Jurisdiction in Civil Actions (3d ed. 1998) — Casad & Richman.

Brainerd Currie, Selected Essays on the Conflict of Laws (1963) — Currie, Essays.

Robert Leflar, Luther McDougal, and Robert Felix, American Conflicts Law (4th ed. 1986) — Leflar, McDougal & Felix.

Eugene Scoles, Peter Hay, Patrick Borchers, and Symeon Symeonides, Conflict of Laws (3d ed. 2000)
— Scoles, Hay, Borchers & Symeonides.

Gene R. Shreve & Peter Raven–Hansen, Understanding Civil Procedure (3d ed. 2002) — Shreve & Raven–Hansen.

Russell Weintraub, Commentary on the Conflict of Laws (4th ed. 2001) — Weintraub.

2. The Restatements

Restatement (First) of Conflict of Laws (1934) — Restatement (First) of Conflict of Laws.

Restatement (Second) of Conflict of Laws (1971) — Restatement (Second) of Conflict of Laws.

Restatement (Second) of Judgments (1982) — Restatement (Second) of Judgments

3. Casebook

David Vernon, Louise Weinberg, William Reynolds, and William Richman, Conflict of Laws: Cases, Materials and Problems (2d ed 2002) — Vernon, Weinberg, Reynolds & Richman

Chapter 2
DOMICILE

§ 3 Domicile: Generally[1]

Where a person is domiciled can be of great practical significance in our law. The concept has a large number of uses and is employed by judges and scholars in a variety of contexts. Domicile of either spouse, for example, is the basis for divorce jurisdiction in most states;[2] also, a defendant in an ordinary civil action is always amenable to the general jurisdiction of a court of her domicile.[3] Domicile commonly provides the basis for jurisdiction to tax incomes and estates, as well as for determining which state's law of intestate succession applies. One might think that a concept so widely used would be subject to a hard–and–fast test about which there could be no mistake in application, but that is not the case. Determining domicile can be a subtle and elusive task, and the result may easily be one about which reasonable persons — and judges — might disagree. This chapter examines the legal definition of domicile, some problems associated with the term, and some alternative concepts.

§ 4 The Definition: Presence

"Domicile," in Holmes' phrase, is a person's "pre–eminent headquarters."[1] The relationship between a person and his domicile must be close enough to justify the reciprocal right/duty status denoted by the term; hence, the focus on the "headquarters" of the individual. Thus, each person has one and only one domicile at any one time for any one purpose. To fix a person's domicile, all that is necessary is to establish his physical presence in the jurisdiction and his intent "to make that place his home for the time at least."[2] "Home," in turn, is where a person lives and is the center of his life.[3]

For most of us that definition presents little problem; but, as might be expected in the law, there are occasional difficulties. This section examines the requirement of presence in the domicile; the next section explores the intent requirement. In order to acquire a new domicile, it is necessary

---

[1] *See generally* Scoles, Hay, Borchers & Symeonides, Ch. 4. We have adopted the more common spelling of "domicile"; it is occasionally spelled without the "e" — *viz.* "domicil." The latter spelling is used by the Restatement (Second) of Conflict of Laws.

[2] *See* § 120, *infra.* For a critique of the rule, see Rhonda Wasserman, *Domicile and Divorce: Time to Sever the Knot*, 39 Wm. & Mary L. Rev. 1 (1997).

[3] *See* § 29, *infra.*

[1] Bergner & Engel Brewing Co. v. Dreyfuss, 172 Mass. 154, 51 N.E. 531, 532 (1898).

[2] Restatement (Second) of Conflict of Laws §§ 15, 18.

[3] *Id.,* § 12.

actually to be present, at least for a while, in that jurisdiction. The presence requirement serves a useful purpose by providing an objective confirmation of subjective intent.

Presence need not be of long duration, as the famous case of *White v. Tennant*[4] illustrates. Michael and Lucinda White, life–long domiciliaries of West Virginia, decided to move to Pennsylvania. They sold their West Virginia farm and set off with their belongings for a new farm in Pennsylvania. That farm was part of a much larger tract, straddling the West Virginia/Pennsylvania border which Michael's family owned. The couple arrived at their new abode; but Lucinda became ill, and her husband, on the very day that they arrived, took her a few hundred yards back into West Virginia so that she could be cared for properly at the family home. Michael also became ill and died two weeks later. He was found to be a Pennsylvania domiciliary for purposes of determining intestate succession. The court reasoned that because Michael had abandoned his West Virginia home with no intention of returning, intending instead to make his home in Pennsylvania "for an indefinite time," he had acquired a Pennsylvania domicile when he entered Pennsylvania. If he had not, then he "was in the anomalous position of being without a domicile anywhere, which is a legal impossibility." It was irrelevant that he went back into his former state and never returned to his new domicile, because he never intended to re–establish a West Virginia domicile. The holding of *White,* then, is that even momentary presence at the new domicile is sufficient to satisfy the presence requirement.

Presence cannot be dispensed with entirely, however, as *In Re Estate of Jones*[5] shows. Jones, a native of Wales, left his homeland to escape a paternity suit. He settled in Iowa where he lived for a third of a century. After World War I broke out, Jones decided to return to Wales to live. He sold his property in Iowa, leaving the proceeds there with a banker until he got to Wales. He then embarked on the Lusitania and became a part of a larger story when that ill–fated ship was torpedoed in May of 1915.

The money left behind in Iowa was claimed by Jones' siblings and by his illegitimate daughter. Had Jones been a British domiciliary at death, his illegitimate daughter would have no legal claim on the estate; Iowa, on the other hand, would have awarded her an interest. The question was whether Jones at death was domiciled in Wales. His intent was clear: He wished to abandon Iowa for Wales. But was his physical presence in Wales necessary? The court held that it was. After rejecting the old notion that a person returning to his domicile of origin[6] regains it the moment he abandons his domicile of choice, the court based its decision on the "general rule that a domicile once legally acquired is sustained until a new domicile

---

[4] 31 W. Va. 790, 8 S.E. 596 (1888).

[5] 192 Iowa 78, 182 N.W. 227 (1921).

[6] A domicile of origin is that domicile one acquires at birth; it is derived from the parental domicile. It is contrasted with a domicile of choice, one acquired by volition.

is secured." Jones, a long–time domiciliary of Iowa, never set foot in Wales, so he never acquired a domicile there.[7]

Presence, in short, cannot be dispensed with no matter how good the evidence of intent. *Estate of Jones* demonstrates the reluctance of courts to find a change of domicile without physical presence in the jurisdiction. The question of constructive presence sometimes arises when a spouse goes ahead into the intended new domicile to select and prepare the family home. The few cases appear to be divided on the question of whether the wife's presence, for example, in the new place is sufficient to change the husband's domicile.[8]

§ 5 The Definition: Intent

More difficult to establish is the intent necessary to constitute domicile. The old rule required that an individual intend to make the new location her home for an indefinite period.[1] The Second Restatement requires only that it be "his home for the time at least."[2] That definitional shift is in accord with modern case law, especially that aspect dealing with the constitutional right of a new or transient resident to vote.[3] But intent of some sort is still required, and thus a court must decide a question whose answer can be elusive and subjective.

Historically, the answer was easy in some cases. Changing domicile is a matter of choice; because one who moved under physical or legal compulsion had no "choice," older cases held that she could not acquire a new domicile.[4] The classic examples were military personnel and prisoners.[5] Even here, however, the general statement on intent now must be qualified, for a soldier can acquire a new domicile,[6] and a state cannot constitutionally deny the vote to her.[7] Even a prisoner, the classic example of a compelled "domiciliary," has been permitted to establish a residence for voting in the place where she has been incarcerated.[8] The Second Restatement now creates only a rebuttable presumption against the acquisition of a new domicile by one who moves under compulsion.[9]

---

[7] The alert reader will note that justice was probably served by this result. The reader may also wonder why setting foot on a ship flying the British flag (the Lusitania, as all World War I buffs know, was a Cunard liner) did not amount to constructive presence on British soil. The court did not address that issue.

[8] Restatement (Second) of Conflict of Laws § 16, Reporter's Note to comment f. The Restatement expressly takes no position on the issue. Caveat to § 16.

[1] Restatement (First) of Conflict of Laws § 18.

[2] Restatement (Second) of Conflict of Laws § 18.

[3] *See generally* Seymour W. Wurfel, *Jet Age Domicil: The Semi–Demise of Durational Residence Requirements,* 11 Wake Forest L. Rev. 349 (1975).

[4] Restatement (Second) of Conflict of Laws § 17.

[5] *Id.,* comments c–d.

[6] *Id.,* Reporter's Note to comment d.

[7] Carrington v. Rash, 380 U.S. 89 (1965) (military personnel).

[8] Dane v. Board of Registrars, 374 Mass. 152, 371 N.E.2d 1358 (1978); *cf.* Stifel v. Hopkins, 477 F.2d 1116 (6th Cir. 1973) (diversity jurisdiction).

[9] Restatement (Second) of Conflict of Laws § 18 (1988 Revision).

[a] Derivative Domicile

For some persons, domicile is determined by the relevant intent of another. A child's domicile, for example, is that of her parents (or the parent with whom she lives).[10] At common law, a wife could not establish a domicile apart from that of her husband.[11] The original Second Restatement modified that rule and provided that a married woman living apart from her husband may acquire a separate domicile, but that, absent special circumstances, she took her husband's domicile as long as she lived with him.[12] Although it is true that the vast majority of husbands and wives who live together share the same domicile, it is also quite likely that it is unconstitutional generally to derive a wife's domicile by referring to that of her husband. Cases decided in the past decade have made it clear that legal rules which fail to treat a woman as an individual violate the Equal Protection Clause.[13] The revision of the Restatement in 1988 reflects this change.[14]

[b] Proving Intent: The *Dorrance* Cases

Proof of the intent requirement can be a difficult task. Classic illustrations of that difficulty are the two *Dorrance* cases. Dr. Dorrance was the long–time head of the Campbell Soup Company. He died in 1930, leaving an estate of $115,000,000. The size of his holdings prompted both Pennsylvania and New Jersey to claim Dorrance as a domiciliary in order to levy a tax upon his estate.

Each state had facts to support its claim. Until 1925, Dorrance was clearly a New Jersey domiciliary. That year he purchased Woodcrest, a magnificent estate near Philadelphia, but he also maintained his former residence in Cinnaminson, New Jersey. Dorrance wished for tax reasons to be considered a New Jersey domiciliary, and in documents and conversations he referred to himself as such. On the other hand, he spent most of his time in Pennsylvania and sent his children to school from the Woodcrest estate. Pennsylvania struck first. A divided court held that Dorrance had abandoned his New Jersey domicile to settle at Woodcrest.[15] The court emphasized the fact that Woodcrest was clearly the decedent's primary residence: "We may readily believe that in his heart Dr. Dorrance knew 'Woodcrest' to be his personal home." As for the expressed intent of Dorrance, the majority believed it to be relevant but not conclusive: "a person's expression of domicile may not supersede the effect of his conduct."

Not surprisingly, New Jersey reached a different conclusion.[16] The court emphasized the decedent's long relationship and many contacts with New

---

[10] Restatement (Second) of Conflict of Laws § 22(1).

[11] *Id.* § 21, comment d.

[12] *Id.* § 21(1).

[13] *E.g.*, Craig v. Boren, 429 U.S. 190 (1976). The Supreme Court, however, has not addressed directly this aspect of the domicile issue.

[14] Restatement (Second) of Conflict of Laws § 21 (1988 Revision).

[15] In Re Dorrance's Estate, 309 Pa. 151, 163 A. 303 (1932).

[16] In Re Dorrance's Estate, 115 N.J. Eq. 268, 170 A. 601 (Prerog. Ct. 1934).

Jersey, his intent — expressed continually — that New Jersey be his home, and the fact that when his last illness began he went to New Jersey to die. Those facts persuaded the court that Dorrance had never abandoned his New Jersey domicile and that only family expediency kept him temporarily in Pennsylvania. Thus, the Dorrance estate was forced to pay an estate tax in two states because a legal impossibility — his simultaneous domicile in more than one state for the same purpose — became a practical reality due to the inconsistent holdings of the two cases.[17]

The *Dorrance* cases show the sometimes slippery nature of domicile, as well as the perils of trying to outwit the tax collector. Intent is crucial in determining domicile,[18] but courts generally will find that actions speak louder than words.

[c] Intent Versus Motive

The law of domicile focuses on intent — not motive.[19] The distinction, though subtle, is easy to illustrate with an example. Suppose husband, a lifelong domiciliary of Nebraska, moves to Maine, intending to make it his permanent home in order to avoid his obligation to support his wife and children. Although his motive is blameworthy and perhaps criminal, his intent is nevertheless to make Maine his new home and it is sufficient to result in a change of domicile.

Motive, however, is not entirely irrelevant because it may supply *evidence* of intent.[20] Suppose the dissatisfied Nebraska husband moves instead to Nevada, intending to stay only long enough to obtain a divorce under Nevada's liberal divorce laws before moving on. Here the husband's motive along with other, more objective evidence (living in a motel, not registering to vote, etc.) can be used to show that he did not intend to make Nevada his new home.

§ 6 Related Concepts[1]

Legislatures sometimes use concepts other than domicile to establish the requisite link between an individual and the state. The most common are citizenship and residence, but other tests are used as well.

[a] Citizenship

The connections of nationality and citizenship can be very important in conflicts law. American citizenship, for example, confers a great many rights and privileges; in turn, the national government exacts certain

17 The multiple domicile problem is discussed in more detail in § 7, *infra*.

18 *See generally* Restatement (Second) of Conflict of Laws § 18, comments f and g.

19 *See id.* § 18, comment f.

20 *Id.*

1 *See generally* Willis L. M. Reese & Robert S. Green, *That Elusive Word, "Residence,"* 6 Vand. L. Rev. 561 (1953).

duties. Thus, an American citizen living abroad can be required to return to her country to testify.[2] Choice of law may also be affected by a party's citizenship, although citizenship is likely to be far more important in cases involving citizens of nations with a unitary legal system (*e.g.*, France). In our federal system, the relation between an individual and her state is likely to be more important in conflicts matters than the relationship between an individual and her country. Thus, case law and statutes usually refer to the state of a person's domicile or residence rather than to the state where she is a citizen.[3]

[b] Residence

Residence and domicile are not synonymous. A lawyer practicing in Detroit may live in Michigan most of the year, but spend four months in a vacation home in Florida. The lawyer surely is a Michigan domiciliary, because that state is the "headquarters" of her professional and personal life, even though she apparently has two residences. "Residence" is a term favored by legislators seeking to establish rights and duties on the basis of a person's link with a location. The term is used in a number of different ways.[4]

At times it is synonymous with domicile, as in statutes providing for judicial jurisdiction, eligibility for office, and liability for inheritance taxes. Sometimes residence means less than domicile, as in statutes prescribing liability for income taxation and eligibility to attend school. Sometimes residence means more than domicile in that it focuses on the place where a person actually lives, as in homestead exemption laws.[5] Because the term has been given so many meanings, judges and lawyers must be careful to avoid confusion when using it.

[c] Habitual Residence[6]

The Hague Convention on Private International Law chose the phrase "habitual residence" to define the connection between an individual and a jurisdiction, in place of the common law concept of "domicile." Habitual residence has the advantage of apparent objectivity in that it does not focus on intent, a concept easily manipulated by all concerned. But the term is inadequate in some instances, because some individuals are so peripatetic that it cannot fairly be said that they have a habitual residence anywhere; a student attending law school in a state different from her parents' residence provides a good example. Despite widespread use of the habitual

[2] Blackmer v. United States, 284 U.S. 421 (1932) (upholding contempt citation of an American citizen living in France for failure to testify as required by 28 U.S.C. §§ 1783–84).

[3] "Citizenship" in states does exist, *see* Jonathan D. Varat, *State "Citizenship" and Interstate Equality,* 48 U. Chi. L. Rev. 487 (1981), but it is a concept generally ignored in conflicts law.

[4] *See* Restatement (Second) of Conflict of Laws § 11, comment k.

[5] Domicile, because it is a technical requirement, may be a less demanding concept to satisfy than residence. Thus, a child's technical domicile is that of his parents, although he may have relatively little connection with that state.

[6] *See* David F. Cavers, *"Habitual Residence": A Useful Concept?,* 21 Am. U. L. Rev. 475 (1972).

residence concept in international matters, it seems unlikely that American courts (and scholars) will forego the hard–won common understandings associated with domicile and replace it with the new term.

§ 7 The Multiple Domicile Problem

Because domicile provides the normal basis for jurisdiction to tax decedents' estates, it is not surprising that the amorphous nature of the concept has led to conflicting attempts by states to tax the estates of the wealthy. The notorious double taxation by New Jersey and Pennsylvania of the Dorrance estate, discussed in Section 5, inspired attempts to alleviate the problem.

The Federal Interpleader Statute of 1936[1] was thought by its chief proponent, Professor Zechariah Chafee, to be an ideal way of providing a forum in which conflicting state claims of domicile could be resolved.[2] Unfortunately, the Supreme Court quickly held in *Worcester County Trust Co. v. Riley*[3] that the Eleventh Amendment barred a federal interpleader action against a state. Two years later, the Court did accept original jurisdiction of a complaint filed by Texas "in the nature of an interpleader," but the circumstances were extraordinary. In that case, *Texas v. Florida,*[4] the Court found jurisdiction because the claims of four states and the federal government against the estate of a Colonel Green exceeded the value of the estate. So matters stood until the death of billionaire recluse Howard Hughes. As might have been expected with a man whose life was so controversial, his death and the claims on his vast estate produced yet another dispute. Two states, California and Texas, claimed Hughes as a domiciliary and sought to tax his property. In order to avoid the multiple taxation problem, California sought to file an original action against Texas in the Supreme Court. The Court, however, without comment, denied leave to file the complaint.[5] Four Justices concurred, suggesting that the proper course would have been for the administrator of the estate to file an interpleader action, because the holding of *Worcester County* — that the Eleventh Amendment bars a federal interpleader action against a state — had been eroded by later decisions.[6]

Heeding that suggestion, the administrator of the Hughes estate filed an interpleader action in federal district court, naming the taxing officials of California and Texas as defendants. The Court of Appeals held that diversity jurisdiction existed. The Supreme Court, however, reaffirmed

[1] 28 U.S.C. § 1335 (1976). *See generally* Charles A. Wright, The Law of Federal Courts 493–501 (4th ed. 1983).

[2] *See* Zechariah Chafee, *Federal Interpleader Since the Act of 1936,* 49 Yale L.J. 377, 379 (1940).

[3] 302 U.S. 292 (1937).

[4] 306 U.S. 398 (1939).

[5] California v. Texas, 437 U.S. 601 (1978).

[6] Especially by Edelman v. Jordan, 415 U.S. 651 (1974).

Worcester County, and held that the Eleventh Amendment barred the action.[7]

Interpleader, therefore, is not available to resolve conflicting claims of domicile. This leaves only the original jurisdiction of the Supreme Court — the route approved in *Texas v. Florida* — which may be available when the claims against the estate exceed its value. Ironically, that route was available to the Hughes estate. The same day that the Court rejected the interpleader filed by the administrator, it permitted California to file an original action against Texas[8] because the claims on the Hughes estate exceeded its value. Thus, the Court has provided an escape route for conflicting claims, but one available only for very large estates. In the absence of effective federal procedures, the beneficiaries of more modest estates must hope that their states have adopted one of the uniform acts that lead to arbitration of such disputes.[9]

§ 8 Domicile: Does It Always Mean the Same Thing?[1]

Judicial expressions about domicile tend to treat it as a unitary concept: that is, it has the same meaning for all purposes in all common law courts. In a debate going back to the First Restatement, scholars have argued that the term "domicile" bears a different meaning according to the context in which it is used; the general definition of the term is flexible enough to permit considerable stretching when a highly subjective factor, such as intention, must be ascertained. The flexibility of the concept permits its manipulation — perhaps unconsciously — in order to avoid harsh results in particular cases. A court deciding whether domicile is present so that it can assert jurisdiction in a divorce case, for example, is likely to be less demanding of proof of domicile than is a court exercising personal jurisdiction over an absent domiciliary where questions of fairness are more likely to be raised.

The Second Restatement recognizes the problem and addresses the question quite sensibly: A person has one and only one domicile at a time, "at least for the same purpose."[2] The trend in case law is toward the Restatement position, although resistance surfaces at times. That trend is a good one. In passing on questions of domicile, a court should remember that the precedents consulted may reflect the multi–faceted nature of the concept. Judicial inquiry into the problem here, as always, should be guided by the purpose behind the inquiry. The "core concept" of domicile remains the same in all cases, but its application in different contexts may depend upon the purpose for which domicile is to be used.[3]

---

[7] Cory v. White, 457 U.S. 85 (1982).

[8] California v. Texas, 457 U.S. 164 (1982).

[9] Uniform Interstate Arbitration of Death Taxes Act, 8A U.L.A. 521 (1943) (adopted in 15 states).

[1] *See generally* Willis Reese, *Does Domicil Bear a Single Meaning?,* 55 Colum. L. Rev. 589 (1955).

[2] Restatement (Second) of Conflict of Laws § 11(2).

[3] *See* Moffatt Hancock, *The Fallacy of the Transplanted Category,* 34 Can. B. Rev. 535 (1959).

Chapter 3
JURISDICTION OF COURTS

Part A

INTRODUCTION

§ 9 Overview

The term "jurisdiction" is used in several different ways in the study of conflicts law. The two basic uses of the term are to describe legislative jurisdiction on the one hand and judicial (or adjudicatory) jurisdiction on the other. Legislative jurisdiction refers to the state's authority to apply its law, whether statutory or judge–made, to a dispute — choice of law, in other words. The constitutional limits on a state's legislative jurisdiction are discussed in Chapter 4, Part E. Judicial jurisdiction is the subject of this chapter.

Part A of this chapter is a general introduction to the concept of territorial jurisdiction (jurisdiction over the person or property of the litigants). Territorial jurisdiction is defined and compared with two related concepts — subject matter jurisdiction and venue. In the next two sections, the text discusses the constitutional consequences of the lack of jurisdiction and the requirement of adequate notice.

Part B then traces the history of the due process restrictions on state–court jurisdiction, beginning with the Supreme Court's establishment of the territorial power theory of jurisdiction, proceeding through the theoretical and practical problems with that view, and ending with the Court's rejection of it in favor of the minimum contacts standard of *International Shoe* and its progeny. Part C brings the discussion up to date with a treatment of the Supreme Court's modern jurisdiction opinions.

The law of jurisdiction is not, however, purely constitutional law, because a court cannot exercise jurisdiction unless it is empowered by state law; the state law bases for jurisdiction (traditional case law and long–arm statutes), are the subject of Part D.

The goal of Part E is to summarize and synthesize the main themes of the Supreme Court's treatment of personal jurisdiction. Unlike Parts B and C, it is not organized chronologically; instead it proceeds from the current perspective, ending with an analytical schema for attacking any personal jurisdiction problem.

Part F treats jurisdiction over property. After comparing in personam and in rem jurisdiction, it discusses the distinctions between in rem jurisdiction, quasi–in–rem jurisdiction and attachment jurisdiction. Next, Part F explains the development of attachment jurisdiction, which resulted in a serious unfairness to defendants. After a brief discussion of the limited appearance, a small concession to defendant, the text explains the in rem revolution wrought by *Shaffer v. Heitner*[1] and the current state of the law of jurisdiction over property.

Part G concludes Chapter 3 with a potpourri of jurisdictional topics. It begins with the traditional limits on state court jurisdiction, a topic producing much current litigation, and then proceeds to discuss several procedural problems relevant to the jurisdiction of American courts. Its final section treats the territorial jurisdiction of the United States District Courts.

§ 10 Selecting the Proper Court — Jurisdiction and Related Concepts

Judicial jurisdiction in the most inclusive sense refers to the power or ability of a court to hear a dispute and render a valid judgment — valid in the sense that it will be recognized by other courts. Courts and scholars have used the word "jurisdiction" as a label for several different questions: Does the state have sufficient connections with the defendant to render a judgment against him? Has the state given this particular court the authority to hear actions of this type? Is the court properly located to hear the action?

Of these questions, only the first is properly the subject of a text in conflict of laws, because it concerns the allocation of the judicial business among the several states. But as the other questions indicate, the enterprise of allocating judicial business or selecting the proper court is a good deal more complicated than simply determining which state is the proper one in which to bring suit. Accordingly, before embarking on an extended discussion of the first question — territorial jurisdiction (jurisdiction over person and property) — it is useful to consider that issue in a preliminary and general way (§ 11) and to distinguish it from the other two questions — jurisdiction over the subject matter (§ 12) and venue (§ 13).

§ 11 Territorial Jurisdiction — Jurisdiction Over Person and Property

[a] The Need for a Jurisdictional Basis

The question to be asked here is: Can the state, acting through any of its courts, exert power over the particular person or property in question? The familiar case of *Buchanan v. Rucker*[1] strikingly illustrates this fundamental question. Plaintiff sued defendant in an English court seeking to

[1] 433 U.S. 186 (1977).

[1] 9 East. 192 (K.B. 1808).

enforce a judgment of the Island Court in Tobago. Defendant had been served in Tobago by nailing a copy of the declaration and summons to the courthouse door; there was no proof that defendant had ever been on the island of Tobago or had had any connection with the island whatsoever. Lord Ellenborough read the Tobago statute as not permitting the exercise of jurisdiction, and then expressed indignation about Tobago's attempt to assert power over this defendant:

> Supposing however that the Act had said in terms, that though a person sued in the island had never been present within the jurisdiction, yet that it should bind him upon proof of nailing up the summons at the Court door; how could that be obligatory upon the subjects of other countries? Can the island of Tobago pass a law to bind the rights of the whole world? Would the world submit to such an assumed jurisdiction?

The source of Lord Ellenborough's indignation is not hard to understand. The Island court had attempted to exercise jurisdiction (or power) over a person who had no connection of any sort with Tobago. Thus, *Buchanan* teaches one of the fundamental principles of jurisdiction: The state must have some connection or relationship with defendant or his property to exercise power over him.[2] The kinds of connections which suffice for jurisdiction are referred to by courts and scholars as jurisdictional bases (or predicates) and are the subject of Parts C, D, E, and F of this chapter.

[b] Categories of Jurisdiction

The type of connection that exists between the state and the defendant determines the category of jurisdiction that the court can exercise and the type of judgment it may render. If the defendant has personal contacts with the state (the sort that are discussed in Parts C, D, and E, below), the court may exercise in personam jurisdiction over the defendant. A court with that sort of jurisdiction may render a personal judgment against the defendant, which can be satisfied out of *any* property of hers within the state. A personal judgment creates a judgment debt against her which may also be enforced in other states (against her property in those states) by operation of the Full Faith and Credit Clause.[3] By contrast, if the state asserts its power because of a connection with defendant's *property* (the sort of connection discussed in Part F) and not with her person, the court exercises some form of in rem jurisdiction.[4] The only sort of judgment the court can render then is one that affects only that particular piece of defendant's property.

---

[2] *See also* Restatement (Second) of Conflict of Laws, Ch. 3, Introductory Note.

[3] Weintraub § 4.1.

[4] Restatement (Second) of Conflict of Laws, Ch. 3, Introductory Note. In rem jurisdiction is further divided into in rem jurisdiction, quasi–in–rem jurisdiction, and attachment jurisdiction. *See* § 41, *infra*, for a complete discussion.

[c] Consequences of Lack of Jurisdiction

Absent a jurisdictional basis (or predicate), the court has no jurisdiction over the defendant and cannot proceed to hear the action. If it does, its judgment will not be valid.[5] But a mistaken exercise of jurisdiction is not like any other legal mistake that a court makes. A typical mistake of law (for instance, application of the wrong substantive rule or misallocation of the burden of proof) must be corrected, if at all, on appeal — a direct attack. If the mistake is incorporated into a judgment and all appeals are exhausted, however, the error may not be asserted in a separate proceeding — a collateral attack.[6]

A jurisdictional error, however, may be the subject of a collateral attack. Suppose, for example, that a California court exercises jurisdiction over a New Yorker who has had no connection with California. If the New York defendant defaults, the victory may be an empty one for the California plaintiff since it is likely that the defendant has no property in California out of which to satisfy the judgment. The plaintiff may decide to sue the defendant in New York to enforce the California judgment. In that action, the defendant will certainly raise the lack of jurisdiction of the California court as a defense. The assertion of lack of jurisdiction of the F–1–first forum — (California) court as a defense to a subsequent suit on that judgment in F–2 (New York) is the classic form of collateral attack.[7]

§ 12 Subject Matter Jurisdiction — Competence

[a] Distinct from Jurisdiction Over Person and Property

Jurisdiction over the subject matter (often called "competence") differs from jurisdiction over person and property, i.e., territorial jurisdiction, in two principal respects. First, jurisdiction over the person or property is concerned with whether the state, through any of its courts, has power to hear the case and render a judgment. But once it is clear that a state has power to hear a case, another question arises. Which court within the state has been given the competence to hear this type or class of case?[1] States customarily divide up the judicial business among their several courts according to subject matter. A typical division would result in: (1) a court of general jurisdiction (often called a court of common pleas, a circuit court, or a superior court) which is competent to hear most civil matters; (2) a group of inferior courts (often called municipal courts or district courts) which have limited jurisdiction of cases where the matter in controversy does not exceed a certain dollar amount; and (3) a group of specialized

[5] Restatement (Second) of Judgments § 1.

[6] For a careful treatment of the distinction between direct and collateral attack, *see* Restatement (Second) of Judgments, Ch. 5, Introductory Note.

[7] *Id.*

[1] For more on the distinction between competence or subject matter jurisdiction and jurisdiction over person and property, *see* Restatement (Second) of Judgments, Ch. 2, Introductory Note; Weintraub § 4.1.

courts which have competence in such areas as probate, domestic relations, and appeals from regulatory agencies. Whether a case falls within the class of cases that the state has assigned to the particular court that plaintiff has chosen is a question of subject matter jurisdiction or competence.

A second distinction concerns the notion of waiver. A defendant can always waive her objection to jurisdiction over her person.[2] If she is willing to submit to the jurisdiction of a state with which she lacks a connection sufficient to constitute a jurisdictional basis, she may do so. The only interest at stake is her right not to be compelled to litigate in a distant forum; and if she is willing to forego the assertion of that interest, the court will not raise it on its own motion.

The situation is different with regard to subject matter jurisdiction or competence. The litigants, of course, have an interest in having their dispute heard by a competent court, but the state has an interest as well. It has determined how the judicial business is to be divided up among its courts, and the agreement of the parties cannot thwart that scheme. Thus, it is often said that jurisdiction over the subject matter cannot be conferred on a court by the agreement of the parties. Further, lack of competence, even if not raised by the parties, must be noticed by the court on its own motion.[3]

[b] Subject Matter Jurisdiction of the Federal Courts

The term "subject matter jurisdiction" (or "competence"), in addition to its use to describe the allocation of judicial business within a state, is also used to describe the rules (constitutional and statutory) that control the jurisdiction of federal courts. The federal courts are courts of limited jurisdiction; if jurisdiction over a case cannot be found in Article III of the Constitution and the Judicial Code,[4] it does not exist. Because the jurisdiction of federal courts is limited, the party who invokes that jurisdiction must plead its source and, if called upon, prove its existence.[5] Many state courts, by contrast, are courts of general jurisdiction; they have jurisdiction over most kinds of civil cases, and their jurisdiction is assumed until questioned.

The principal categories of federal jurisdiction are federal question jurisdiction (cases arising under the laws of the United States) and diversity jurisdiction (cases in which citizens of different states are adverse parties).[6] In some kinds of federal question cases — admiralty, antitrust, and patents, for instance — federal courts have *exclusive* jurisdiction; the state courts may not hear such cases. But most cases that fall within the jurisdiction of the federal courts can also be heard by state courts; in those cases federal jurisdiction is *concurrent* with that of state courts.

---

[2] *See* § 30, *infra.*

[3] *See* Fed. R. Civ. P. 12(h)(3); Restatement (Second) of Judgments § 12, comment a.

[4] 28 U.S.C. §§ 1251 *et. seq.*

[5] *See* Fed. R. Civ. P. 8(a)(1).

[6] 28 U.S.C. §§ 1331, 1332. For a short and very lucid discussion of these, *see* Shreve & Raven–Hansen, Ch. 5.

§ 13 Venue

Whether a state has a sufficient contact or relationship with a dispute so that any of its courts can hear it is a question of jurisdiction over person and property.[1] But even after plaintiff has established that there is some court within a state that can hear a dispute, he must still answer the question: which court? This question is partially answered by considerations of subject matter jurisdiction — the way in which states divide the judicial business among their courts according to the type or class of litigation involved. States also divide up the judicial business geographically by rules that indicate which county or judicial district within the state is the appropriate place to bring the action. These are rules of venue. A typical set of venue provisions might require, for instance, that the action be brought in the county or district where defendant lives, or where the cause of action arose, or where the property is located.[2]

Venue differs fundamentally from jurisdiction over the person and from subject matter jurisdiction. Rules of venue give the defendant a privilege not to be sued in an inconvenient forum; they do not affect the power or competence of the court.[3] This rather abstract sounding distinction can be rendered more concrete by considering the question of waiver. A venue objection, unlike an objection based upon lack of subject matter jurisdiction, can always be waived by defendant. Furthermore, unlike an objection to jurisdiction over the person, a venue objection can be raised only if defendant appears and seasonably asserts it.[4] If defendant defaults, he may raise the defense of lack of jurisdiction over his person in a collateral attack, but he has lost his venue objection forever.

§ 14 Selecting the Proper Court — A Summary

Of the concepts discussed in sections 11, 12, and 13, *supra*, conflicts is concerned mainly with territorial jurisdiction (jurisdiction over person and property), although subject matter jurisdiction and venue are often discussed in conflicts opinions. The three concepts together determine the permissible choice of forum for plaintiff. A particular court is not the appropriate one in which to bring suit unless it satisfies all three requirements.

A litigant might go about choosing the proper court as follows: She could first ask whether the case belongs in state or federal court. This is a question of subject matter jurisdiction. If the case is within the limited subject matter jurisdiction of the federal courts, the question becomes: which

---

[1] *See* § 11, *supra*.

[2] *See, e.g.*, 28 U.S.C. § 1391, the general federal venue statute. In the federal system, venue controls the district and division in which the action may be brought.

[3] For more on the distinction between venue and jurisdiction, *see* Casad & Richman § 1-3, Fleming James, Jr., Geoffrey C. Hazard, Jr. & John Leubsdorf, Civil Procedure § 2.1 (5th ed. 2001).

[4] *Id.*

federal court?[1] This is a problem of territorial jurisdiction and venue. The appropriate federal court will be one that has a jurisdictional basis and is specified as proper by the federal venue statutes. If the case is not within the subject matter jurisdiction of the federal courts, it can be heard only in a state court. But which state, and which court within the state? The way to attack those questions is first to determine which state or states have a sufficient jurisdictional basis. The next issue is which court within the state has been given the competence or subject matter jurisdiction to hear the class of cases in which plaintiff's action fits. Finally, the plaintiff must ask the venue question to determine which county or district within the state is appropriate.[2]

§ 15 Jurisdiction and the Constitution: Due Process and Full Faith and Credit

In the United States, there are limits upon the jurisdiction of state and federal courts imposed by the Due Process Clauses of the Fifth and Fourteenth Amendments. A court that exercises jurisdiction over a defendant in the absence of a proper jurisdictional basis has violated her right not to be deprived of property without due process, and, therefore, its judgment is invalid. The kind of connection or relationship between defendant and the state that suffices to support an exercise of jurisdiction is a question of federal law, and the Supreme Court is the final arbiter.[1]

Just as the Due Process Clause limits the states' exercise of judicial jurisdiction, the Full Faith and Credit Clause controls the states' obligations to recognize and enforce the judgments of the courts of sister states.[2] Subject to only a few controversial exceptions, the two constitutional clauses are co–extensive; thus, if a state has a jurisdictional basis sufficient to satisfy the Due Process Clause, the judgment of its courts will be entitled to full faith and credit in other states.

To understand fully the impact of the Constitution on the jurisdiction and judgments of the states, it is helpful to compare the states with totally independent sovereigns. Suppose that the law of Japan regards residence of the plaintiff as a sufficient basis upon which to exercise jurisdiction over the defendant but that Australian law does not. If a Japanese court exercises jurisdiction over a defendant on that basis, its judgment will not

[1] Of course, plaintiff usually can choose a state court even though the action is within the subject matter jurisdiction of the federal courts because, with regard to most federal cases, the federal courts' jurisdiction is concurrent with the state court's and not exclusive.

[2] This paragraph indicates how a litigant might choose the proper court. A separate question, of course, is why the litigant might prefer one court to another. The answer usually depends on considerations of litigation strategy: the identity and quality of the bench, the reputation of local juries for high or low damage awards, the length of the court's docket, and, of course, the substantive law and choice–of–law principles of the various possible jurisdictions. For a brief discussion of these factors, *see* Shreve & Raven–Hansen, 19–21.

[1] *See* Parts C–F, *infra*, for a discussion of the constitutional limits on jurisdiction.

[2] *See* Ch. 5, *infra*, for a discussion of the Full Faith and Credit Clause and the exceptions to its mandate.

be recognized in Australia. The Australian court will not feel itself bound by comity to enforce a foreign judgment based upon a jurisdictional connection that would not support the judgment of an Australian court.[3] Nevertheless, although unenforceable abroad, the Japanese judgment is perfectly valid at home. Because the Australian and Japanese courts recognize no common superior sovereign, they can agree only to disagree.

This problem cannot occur between states of the United States. There is one constitutional standard that limits state court jurisdiction and one final decisionmaker on the contents of that standard — the Supreme Court. Thus, a judgment that perfectly satisfies the law of the rendering state, but fails to meet the due process standard, is invalid both at home and in other states.[4]

§ 16 Notice

[a] Relation of Notice to Jurisdictional Basis

The Due Process Clause requires not only an acceptable jurisdictional basis but also adequate notice to the defendant of the action and an opportunity for him to be heard.[1] It is important to understand that the requirement for adequate notice is entirely separate from the requirement for a jurisdictional basis.[2] No matter what sort of jurisdictional basis exists, and no matter whether jurisdiction is exercised in personam or in rem, the judgment will be invalid if defendant has not been given adequate notice. Similarly, no matter how adequate the notice defendant receives, the judgment will be invalid absent a satisfactory jurisdictional basis.

It is easy to understand how the two requirements came to be confused by the courts. According to early jurisdictional theory, personal service of process was the only adequate basis for personal jurisdiction over a non–domiciliary defendant. In–hand service amply satisfied the notice requirement as well, because even the most stouthearted defendant was likely to have at least his attention arrested by the marshall's hard knock at the door and the classic recitation: "I have something for you." Thus, at one stroke, the notice and basis requirements were satisfied, leading courts to confuse the two. Now that other bases for jurisdiction are constitutionally acceptable, it is crucial to distinguish between the two requirements.[3]

---

[3] The hypothetical is a variation on the facts of Schibsby v. Westenholz, L. R. [1870], 6 Q.B. 155.

[4] Some scholars question this very fundamental premise. For a strong argument that the Due Process clause should place no restrictions on state–court jurisdiction, *see* Patrick J. Borchers, *The Death of the Constitutional Law of Personal Jurisdiction: From Pennoyer to Burnham and Back Again*, 24 U.C.Davis L. Rev. 19 (1990).

[1] Restatement (Second) of Judgments § 1, Restatement (Second) of Conflict of Laws § 25.

[2] See Casad & Richman § 2-7[1]. Notice is not really a conflict–of–laws problem, because the requirement exists and problems may arise even when only one state is involved.

[3] *See* Parts C, D, and E of this Chapter for a discussion of those other bases.

[b] The Standard for Adequate Notice — *Mullane*

What is adequate notice under the Due Process Clause? The Supreme Court went a long way toward answering the question in *Mullane v. Central Hanover Bank and Trust Co.*[4]

The case involved a New York statute which provided for the existence and administration of common trust funds. Those funds were formed by pooling numerous small trust estates into one fund for purposes of investment administration. The accounts of the common fund were to be settled from time to time by a judicial proceeding called an accounting; beneficiaries of the constituent trusts (some of whose interests, names, and addresses were known to the corporate trustee and others not) were to be notified of the accounting by publication. The Court held that notification by publication was *adequate* for the *unknown* beneficiaries but *inadequate* for the *known* beneficiaries and announced this general standard for measuring the adequacy of notice:

> The means employed must be such as one desirous of actually informing the absentee might reasonably adopt to accomplish it. The reasonableness and hence the constitutional validity of any chosen method may be defended on the ground that it is itself reasonably certain to inform those affected . . . or, where conditions do not reasonably permit such notice, that the form chosen is not substantially less likely to bring home notice than other of the feasible and customary substitutes.

The test seems to require a two–part inquiry:

1. Is the method of notice chosen reasonably likely to reach those affected?

2. If conditions do not permit such notice, is the method chosen about as good as any other?

On this standard the result in *Mullane* was clear. Notice by publication failed the first part of the test for both known and unknown beneficiaries. For known beneficiaries, publication failed the second test as well, because notice by mail (possible because their names and addresses were known), was clearly more likely to inform them than notice by publication. For the unknown beneficiaries, notice by publication was adequate, not because it was likely to inform them, but because it passed the second part of the test; no other technique was more likely to give them actual notice.

[c] Methods of Giving Notice

There are numerous ways of giving constitutionally adequate notice. Most are justified because they comply with part 1 of the *Mullane* test; they are reasonably likely to inform the persons affected. The paradigm, of course, is personal service of process by an official of the court or a private process server.[5] Also adequate are service upon an authorized agent;[6] service by

---

[4] 339 U.S. 306 (1950).

[5] *See* Fed. R. Civ. P. 4(c)(2).

mail;[7] and substituted personal service, where the process server leaves the summons and complaint at defendant's house with "some person of suitable age and discretion then residing therein."[8]

Notice by publication is much more troublesome. It clearly fails part 1 of the *Mullane* test. In the words of the Court:

> It would be idle to pretend that publication alone . . . is a reliable means of acquainting interested parties of the fact that their rights are before the courts. . . . Chance alone brings to the attention of even a local resident an advertisement in small type inserted in the back pages of a newspaper, and if he makes his home outside the area of the newspaper's normal circulation the odds that the information will never reach him are large indeed.

If publication is ever to be considered constitutionally adequate notice, it must be because it satisfies part 2 of the *Mullane* test. When the identity, interest, or address of persons affected by legal action are unknown, notice by publication, although not likely to reach them, is no less likely to give actual notice than any other method. It is only in those situations that publication alone is constitutionally adequate.

A finding of constitutional adequacy does not end the inquiry into the sufficiency of notice. Each court system has technical statutes and rules of court that specify the form of process and the way in which it must be served. A method of notification that satisfies due process standards may yet fail to satisfy these technical requirements and may result in an invalid judgment.[9] Service by certified mail is a constitutionally acceptable means of giving notice, for example, but not every state permits it. In a state that does not, a judgment based upon certified mail service will be invalid if state law deems the defect sufficiently serious; and if the judgment is invalid according to the law of the rendering state, it is not entitled to full faith and credit in sister states.

[d] Notice in In Rem Actions

The measure of adequate notice does not change when the court exercises power over defendant's property instead of her person. There is language in older cases that indicates that, because property is deemed to be in possession of its owner, seizing the property or posting the notice upon it (especially if accompanied by publication) constitutes adequate notice to its

[6] The agent may be one actually appointed by defendant for the purpose, or one appointed by operation of law, Wuchter v. Pizzuti, 276 U.S. 13 (1928), or one appointed by an obscure clause in an adhesion contract, National Equipment Rental v. Szukhent, 375 U.S. 311 (1964). When service is upon an agent who was not actually appointed by defendant, due process may require that the agent be obligated to transmit actual notice to the defendant. *Compare Wuchter* with *Szukhent.*

[7] In some systems, service by mail is the preferred and regular method. *See, e.g.*, Ohio Rules of Court 4.1(1). *See also* Fed. R. Civ. P. 4(d), permitting plaintiff to mail to the defendant a request to waive service of process.

[8] *See* Fed. R. Civ. P. 4(e)(2).

[9] *See* Casad & Richman § 3-1.

owner.[10] After *Mullane*, however, the Supreme Court explicitly rejected this notion.[11] The measure of adequate notice for in rem as well as in personam actions is the two–part *Mullane* test. Posting property and publication in local newspapers will rarely pass part 1 since they are unlikely to give actual notice to defendant. Nor will such forms of notice satisfy part 2 of the *Mullane* test because typically they are not the best means of notice available. The names and addresses of property owners are usually available from public records, and notice by mail (considerably more reliable than posting or publication) often will be possible. Based on this analysis, the Court has rejected notice by publication and posting in a wide variety of contexts.[12]

---

[10] Pennoyer v. Neff, 95 U.S. 714 (1878).

[11] Schroeder v. City of New York, 371 U.S. 208 (1962); Walker v. City of Hutchinson, 352 U.S. 112 (1956).

[12] *See* Tulsa Professional Collection Service Inc. v. Pope, 485 U.S. 478 (1988)(published notice of probate proceeding insufficient notice to creditors of the estate); Mennonite Board of Missions v. Adams, 462 U.S. 791 (1983)(notice of tax sale by publication and posting of property inadequate as to mortgagee); Green v. Lindsey, 456 U.S. 444 (1982)(posting notice on tenant's apartment door insufficient notice in eviction action).

Part B

HISTORY: FROM POWER AND TERRITORIALITY TO CONTACTS AND FAIRNESS

§ 17 Early Dogma

In *Pennoyer v. Neff*,[1] the Supreme Court announced a theory of state–court jurisdiction that was to hold sway for nearly seventy years.[2] It is this analytical framework, rather than the holding of *Pennoyer*, that is important here.[3] The theory, which may be labelled conveniently "the territorial power theory" relied on a conception of the states as nearly independent sovereigns.[4] In the words of Justice Field:

> The several States of the Union are not, it is true, in every respect independent, many of the rights and powers which originally belonged to them being now vested in the government created by the Constitution. But, except as restrained and limited by that instrument, they possess and exercise the authority of independent States, and the principles of public law to which we have referred are applicable to them. One of these principles is, that every State possesses exclusive

---

[1] 95 U.S. 714 (1878).

[2] International Shoe v. Washington, 326 U.S. 310 (1945), was decided sixty–eight years after *Pennoyer*.

[3] The case arose when Mitchell sued Neff in Oregon for $300 in attorney's fees. Neff was neither domiciled in Oregon, nor was he personally served with process there. Pursuant to Oregon statute, notice of the action was published in a local newspaper. Neff did not appear, and Mitchell took a default judgment. To satisfy the judgment, a piece of land belonging to Neff was sold at a sheriff's sale to Pennoyer. Neff later sued Pennoyer for the land. Pennoyer's right to the land depended upon the validity of the judgment in *Mitchell v. Neff* and, therefore, upon the court's jurisdiction to render that judgment. The Oregon court lacked personal jurisdiction over Neff because he was neither domiciled in Oregon nor served with process while present in Oregon. The Supreme Court held that the Oregon court also lacked attachment jurisdiction over the land because it was not attached at the commencement of the action. *Pennoyer* is discussed in greater detail in § 42, *infra*.

[4] Traditionally, the commentators have not been kind to *Pennoyer*'s framework, faulting its mechanical division of jurisdiction into in rem and in personam categories and its use of an international law model to control jurisdiction in a federal union. *See, e.g.*, Geoffrey C. Hazard, Jr., *A General Theory of State–Court Jurisdiction*, 1965 Sup. Ct. Rev. 241. Other historical work has attempted to rehabilitate the decision. *See* Terry S. Kogan, *A Neo–Federalist Tale of Personal Jurisdiction*, 63 S. Cal. L. Rev. 257 (1990).

A rather intriguing commentary suggests that *Pennoyer* announced *no* general theory of the due process limits on state jurisdiction; instead, it held only that the due process clause guaranteed defendants the opportunity to attack state court jurisdiction in the rendering state just as the Full Faith and Credit Clause gave them the right to challenge the rendering state's jurisdiction in another state. On this view the substantive law actually creating the jurisdictional limits would be the state's own jurisdictional statutes and decisions — not the Due Process Clause. *See* Patrick J. Borchers, *The Death of the Constitutional Law of Personal Jurisdiction: From Pennoyer to Burnham and Back Again*, 24 U. Cal. Davis. L. Rev. 19, 40 (1990).

> jurisdiction and sovereignty over persons and property within its territory. . . . The other principle of public law referred to follows from the one mentioned; that is, that no State can exercise direct jurisdiction and authority over persons or property without its territory.

The result of these two "principles of public law" was that physical power over the defendant or his property was *necessary* for a constitutional exercise of jurisdiction. In other words, an exercise of jurisdiction could not be sustained, no matter how close defendant's ties were with the state, *unless* the state had some sort of physical power. Further, physical power was *sufficient* for the constitutional exercise of jurisdiction; in other words, power would *always* justify the exercise of jurisdiction no matter how weak defendant's ties with the state were.

In practice, only two jurisdictional bases perfectly satisfied the theory.[5] A state court could exercise some form of *in rem* jurisdiction if it seized a piece of defendant's property within the state's borders, and it could exercise *in personam* jurisdiction if defendant had been served with process while present within the state. This second basis for jurisdiction followed not literally, but only metaphorically from the territorial power theory. Personal service traced its ancestry to the English writ of *capias ad respondendum*, according to which the sheriff arrested the defendant and held him to await the sovereign's pleasure. Service of process, where the sheriff is physically situated to seize the defendant, is simply the modern and civilized analogue of the arrest.

The opinion in *Pennoyer* recognized three additional bases for *in personam* jurisdiction that could be derived from the territorial power theory with only a bit more stretching:[6] (1) Jurisdiction based upon appearance or consent made some sense under the theory. If a defendant actually appeared in court, she could be said to be within the court's power; and if she consented to the exercise of jurisdiction, she could be held to have submitted to the court's power. (2) Domicile within the state did not guarantee that the defendant was at any given moment subject to the court's power, but it did mean that she had a permanent territorial affiliation with the state and was regularly subject to its laws. (3) Jurisdiction over a corporation based upon its incorporation within the state also seems consistent with the territorial power theory. A corporation is not only a "domiciliary" of its charter state, but also owes its legal life to that state's laws. Further, a state could require a corporation's consent to judicial

[5] Another jurisdictional basis was carefully preserved by the *Pennoyer* court even though it did not fit the territorial power theory very well. In a long dictum, the Court indicated that its opinion should not be read to question the jurisdiction of the state of domicile over the marital status of its domiciliaries. The fiction used to legitimate such jurisdiction over status was that the marriage was a thing or *res* that had a situs at the domicile of the parties. Thus the state of domicile could exercise some form of *in rem* jurisdiction. *See* Casad & Richman § 2-2[3][b]. For a modern critique of the exception, see Rhonda Wasserman, *Parents, Partners, and Personal Jurisdiction,* 1995 U. Ill. L. Rev. 813. Jurisdiction over the marital status is discussed fully at § 120, *infra.*

[6] Dicta in *Pennoyer* ratified these bases for jurisdiction even though they did not fit perfectly under the theory. *See also* Casad & Richman § 2-2[2].

jurisdiction in return for allowing its existence as a limited liability association.

In summary, the Supreme Court's adoption in *Pennoyer* of the territorial power theory limited jurisdictional practice to a very few jurisdictional bases — known in the literature today as the "traditional bases" for jurisdiction.[7] A court could exercise some form of *in rem* jurisdiction if there was some piece of defendant's property located within the state; it could exercise *in personam* jurisdiction if the defendant was personally served with process while present in the state, if she was a domiciliary of the state, or if she consented to the court's jurisdiction. Similarly a court could exercise *in personam* jurisdiction over a corporation if it was chartered in the state.

§ 18 Stretching the Dogma by Fictions

[a] The Problem: Natural Persons

The territorial power theory and the exceedingly narrow jurisdictional practice that it required proved too confining for the courts as modern methods of transportation, communication, and commerce made interstate litigation more common. For example, a simple interstate automobile accident could produce a very distressing result under the traditional theory. If a defendant from Pennsylvania drove his car to Massachusetts, injured plaintiff there, and returned to Pennsylvania,[1] plaintiff might well find herself without a remedy in Massachusetts because defendant was not a domiciliary of Massachusetts, was not served with process in Massachusetts, and had not consented to the jurisdiction of Massachusetts. Similarly a foreign (out–of–state) corporation could send its products into the forum state and derive substantial revenue from the sales, yet not be amenable in a suit by a consumer in the state's courts.

[b] Implied Consent and the Early Long–Arm Statutes

Burdened with a jurisdictional theory that ill fit the realities of modern transportation and commerce, the courts and legislatures faced a choice; they could scrap the outmoded theory or stretch it to reach more out–of–state defendants. Initially they chose the second, more conservative strategy, stretching the traditional theory with the doctrine of implied consent. The consent implied, of course, was fictional. Defendant did not actually consent to the court's jurisdiction; rather he conducted certain activities in the forum, and his consent was inferred from those activities. Thus, for example, some early long–arm statutes declared that by operating a motor vehicle upon the roads of the state, the non–resident motorist was deemed to have appointed the registrar of motor vehicles his agent for receipt of

[7] The traditional bases for personal jurisdiction are discussed fully in Part D, *infra*.

[1] This hypothetical is based on Hess v. Pawloski, 274 U.S. 352 (1927).

service of process.[2] By driving into the state, the non–resident "consented" to the jurisdiction of the state's courts.

The Supreme Court upheld such statutory fictions on the argument that the state had the right to exclude a motorist (resident or non–resident) from the use of its highways. It could therefore condition permission to drive its roads upon the execution of an actual consent to jurisdiction.[3] Finally, if it could extort an actual consent in return for the privilege of using its highways, it could infer a consent from the non–resident's exercise of the privilege.

The same fiction could be used to support jurisdiction over a defendant who engaged in any sort of closely regulated activity within the state.[4] It would not serve, however, to reach an out–of–state defendant whose in–state conduct was more mundane. In *Flexner v. Farson*,[5] the Supreme Court held that a state could not exclude non–residents from simply traveling through or conducting ordinary business in the state because natural persons (unlike corporations) are entitled to the privileges and immunities of national citizenship, one of which is the right to travel through and conduct ordinary business in any of the states. Because the state could not exclude non–resident natural persons, it could not extract a consent from them or infer their consent to jurisdiction from their activities within the state.

[c] Foreign Corporations

The territorial theory of *Pennoyer v. Neff*, although adequate to explain jurisdiction over domestic corporations,[6] encountered real problems when used to justify jurisdiction over an entity incorporated in another state. Under *Pennoyer*, a defendant could be served whenever it could be "found" in the forum, but early theory held that a corporation could be "found" only where it was incorporated. As the Supreme Court said in *Bank of Augusta v. Earle*, "[A] corporation can have no legal existence out of the boundaries of the sovereignty by which it is created. . . . [I]t must dwell in the place of its creation, and cannot migrate to another sovereignty."[7] If transient

---

[2] *See, e.g.*, Hess v. Pawloski, 274 U.S. 352 (1927).

[3] *See* Kane v. New Jersey, 242 U.S. 160 (1916).

[4] *See* Henry L. Doherty & Co. v. Goodman, 294 U.S. 623 (1935). *See Developments in the Law: State–Court Jurisdiction*, 73 Harv. L. Rev. 909, 945–946 (1960), for a brief discussion of *Hess, Doherty*, and the implied consent theory.

[5] 248 U.S. 289 (1919).

[6] Even before the decision in *International Shoe*, there were ample bases upon which to exercise jurisdiction over the domestic corporation. A corporation is a domiciliary of its state of incorporation. Indeed, a particularly close relationship exists between a corporation and its home state because the laws of that state make the corporation's existence possible. Another traditional basis that applies without much stretching is the notion of consent. In return for giving it life, the state can require the corporation's consent to the jurisdiction of the state's courts. *See Developments in the Law: State–Court Jurisdiction*, 73 Harv. L. Rev. 909, 919 (1960). Whatever the rationale, and often there was no felt need to articulate any, courts have traditionally assumed jurisdiction over the domestic corporation.

[7] 38 U.S. (13 Pet.) 519 (1839).

service could not be used as a jurisdictional basis, neither could domicile, for a corporation's domicile was only in its state of incorporation.

Once again, the Court used the fiction of implied consent. The Privileges and Immunities Clause does not apply to corporations,[8] so a state could prohibit a corporation from conducting any activities within its territory.[9] If the state could exclude the foreign corporation completely, it could also condition the corporation's right to enter on an express consent to the jurisdiction of the state's courts. And, if the state could extort an actual consent, it could infer the corporation's consent from the entity's decision to engage in business in the forum.[10]

The courts also used the fiction of corporate "presence" as another doctrine–stretching device to justify the exercise of jurisdiction over foreign corporations. The idea was that if a corporation was conducting activities in the forum, it could be deemed to be "present" there. In the words of Justice Brandeis: "A foreign corporation is amenable to process to enforce a personal liability, in the absence of consent, only if it is doing business within the State in such a manner and to such an extent as to warrant the inference that it is present there."[11]

The fictions of "consent" and "presence" provided the theoretical justifications for the exercise of jurisdiction over foreign corporations. The remaining question was how much contact between the defendant and the state was required in order to find that the corporation "consented" to jurisdiction or to find that it was "present" in the forum. Under both theories, the courts settled upon the practical test of "doing business." If the defendant was doing business in the forum, jurisdiction existed; otherwise, it did not.

Exactly what activities constituted "doing business" was not entirely clear; it is clear, however, that by modern standards the "doing business" test required a fairly substantial connection between the defendant and the forum. If the defendant's forum related activities were continuous and systematic, the courts were likely to find it amenable; otherwise not.[12]

[8] Paul v. Virginia, 75 U.S. (8 Wall.) 168 (1868).

[9] Lafayette Ins. Co. v. French, 59 U.S. (18 How.) 404 (1855).

[10] The theoretical basis for the doctrine of implied consent suffered a serious blow when the Supreme Court began to expand the definition of "commerce among the several states." A state could not prevent a corporation from conducting "interstate commerce" within its borders, International Text Book Co. v. Pigg, 217 U.S. 91 (1910), and as the definition of "interstate commerce" expanded, it became doubtful that a state could constitutionally exclude a corporation from its territory. Lacking the ability to exclude the corporation, the state could not require an express or implied consent as a condition of inclusion. By the 1940's, therefore, the basic premise of the theory of implied consent had eroded considerably.

[11] Philadelphia & Reading Ry. Co. v. McKibbin, 243 U.S. 264 (1917). The "presence" theory had two major problems. Theoretically it was inconsistent with the Supreme Court's well known dictum in Bank of Augusta v. Earle, *see* note 7, *supra*, and the accompanying text. Practically, it failed to justify jurisdiction in cases where a corporation conducted activity in the forum that gave rise to a cause of action but ceased activity before suit was brought.

[12] Minimal or isolated contacts within the forum did not constitute doing business. Even regular but intermittent activities — such as a retailer's periodic buying trips into the forum — were not enough. Rosenberg Bros. & Co. v. Curtis Brown Co., 260 U.S. 516 (1923). The presence in the forum of a corporate agent and the maintenance of an office were factors to

§ 19 Inadequacy of the Territorial Theory

By the middle of the twentieth century, the territorial theory of jurisdiction had proved to be seriously inadequate. The theory, as formulated in *Pennoyer v. Neff,*[1] held that a state could exercise jurisdiction only when it had physical power over the defendant or his property. The roots of the theory lay in an outdated conception of the United States as a federation of relatively independent states. On this international law model, it might make sense to limit a state's jurisdiction so that it could issue only those judgments which it could enforce by its own power. The Constitution, however, made a single nation of the several states, and the international law model of *Pennoyer* was thus inadequate to explain jurisdiction in a unified nation.[2]

The inadequacy of the territorial theory manifested itself in two principal ways. First, its limited reach caused it to fall out of step with the commercial realities of the twentieth century. Improved transportation made it possible for individuals to travel and conduct business in several states over a relatively short period of time. The increasing sophistication and complication of commercial life resulted in chains of distribution which began in commercial and industrial centers and ended in retail outlets in every small town throughout the country. These changes resulted in more and more claims by state citizens against non–resident individuals and corporations, but often the territorial theory would not justify jurisdiction over such defendants. Absent in–state service, courts upheld jurisdiction over non–domiciliary natural persons only if they could infer consent from the defendant's engaging in activities that were closely regulated by the state.[3] If defendant caused personal or economic injury as a result of simply travelling through the state or engaging in unregulated business activity in the state, the state courts could not compel him to appear and defend. The resident plaintiff was forced to travel to defendant's home to litigate.

The ability of the territorial theory to reach the corporate defendant was similarly limited; if the corporation was not doing business locally, the state could not exercise jurisdiction. "Doing business" meant activity of a systematic and continuous nature,[4] but a corporation by dint of a modern chain of distribution could derive very substantial economic benefit from a state without doing business there.

The second major defect of the territorial theory was that it required a great deal of fictional talk to reach even as far as it did. Applied literally

---

be considered but were not determinative. Green v. Chicago, Burlington & Quincy Ry. Co., 205 U.S. 530 (1907). Mere solicitation of business in the forum was also deemed insufficient, although "solicitation plus" some additional activity might be enough. Hutchinson v. Chase & Gilbert, Inc., 45 F.2d 139 (2d Cir. 1930).

[1] 95 U.S. 714 (1878).

[2] *See* Philip B. Kurland, *The Supreme Court, the Due Process Clause and the In Personam Jurisdiction of State Courts — From Pennoyer to Denckla: A Review*, 25 U. Chi. L. Rev. 569, 585 (1958), for a more complete statement of this argument.

[3] *See* § 18, *supra.*

[4] *Id.*

and consistently, the theory could justify jurisdiction only in a narrow band of cases. Jurisdiction in most other cases was based on defendant's "implied" consent,[5] and the fictional nature of that consent was quite apparent. Thus, the theory lacked power in that it failed to reach many defendants, and it lacked elegance in that it needed a good deal of stretching and manipulation to reach many others.

By the 1940's, the defects of the territorial power theory had rendered it obsolete, and the law of jurisdiction was ready for a major overhaul. The doctrinal overhaul that began in *International Shoe v. Washington*[6] and that continues today is best viewed as a shift in the conceptual basis of state–court jurisdiction from power toward fairness. State–court jurisdiction is no longer based on physical power over the person or property of the defendant. Today the law is much more concerned with fairness, convenience and the justified expectations of the parties. Nevertheless, remnants of power and territoriality recur in the Supreme Court's opinions. The beginning of the shift from power to fairness is the subject of the next section. The current state of the law is explored in Parts C, D, and E, *infra*, of this Chapter.

§ 20 The Revolution in Personal Jurisdiction: Contacts and Fairness

[a] *International Shoe Co. v. Washington*[1]

International Shoe marked the beginning of the change in the conceptual framework of jurisdiction. It not only changed the factual test that courts apply, but also the way they think and speak about jurisdictional problems. Accordingly, it would be difficult to overstate its importance.

The facts of the case are ordinary and uncomplicated. Defendant, a Delaware corporation with its principal place of business in Missouri, manufactured and sold shoes. It employed about a dozen salesmen in the state of Washington to solicit orders for shoes from prospective purchasers. The salesmen lived in Washington and conducted all their business activities there. Occasionally, they rented permanent or temporary sample rooms to display defendant's merchandise, but they did not enter into contracts with buyers in Washington. Instead, they transmitted offers to purchase to defendant's offices in St. Louis, where the offers were accepted or rejected. Defendant shipped shoes from Missouri to Washington and received payment in Missouri. Aside from the salesmen, defendant had little connection with Washington; it did not have an office in the state nor did it maintain a stock of merchandise there.

The state of Washington sued defendant for failure to contribute to the state unemployment compensation fund. Process was served on one of the

---

[5] *Id.*

[6] 326 U.S. 310 (1945).

[1] *Id.*

salesmen and was also mailed to defendant in Missouri. Defendant appeared specially, but its jurisdictional objection was overruled by both the unemployment office and the Washington courts.

The Supreme Court could have upheld jurisdiction on these facts based on the traditional doctrine. Because defendant's Washington activities were systematic and continuous, it was likely that defendant met the doing business test.[2] But the Court had bigger fish to fry. In three sentences, it ended almost a century of reliance on physical power as the basis for jurisdiction and announced a new standard based upon fairness and defendant's contacts with the forum.

> Historically the jurisdiction of courts to render judgment *in personam* is grounded on their de facto power over the defendant's person. Hence his presence within the territorial jurisdiction of a court was prerequisite to its rendition of a judgment personally binding him. But now that the *capias ad respondendum* has given way to personal service of summons or other form of notice, due process requires only that in order to subject a defendant to a judgment *in personam*, if he be not present within the territory of the forum, he have certain minimum contacts with it such that the maintenance of the suit does not offend "traditional notions of fair play and substantial justice."

Having destroyed the need to ground jurisdictional theory on physical power, the Court was in a position to do some long–needed doctrinal house–cleaning. Since the theories of presence and consent were simply elaborate fictions to permit jurisdiction over foreign corporations under the power theory, those fictions were now expendable; and the Court lost no time in debunking them. Of "presence" it said:

> To say that the corporation is so far "present" there as to satisfy due process requirements . . . is to beg the question to be decided. For the terms "present" or "presence" are used merely to symbolize those activities of the corporation's agent within the state which courts will deem to be sufficient to satisfy the demands of due process.

As for "consent":

> True, some of the decisions holding the corporation amenable to suit have been supported by resort to the legal fiction that it has given its consent to service and suit, consent being implied from its presence in the state through acts of its authorized agents. But more realistically it may be said that those authorized acts were of such a nature as to justify the fiction.

With the old doctrine discarded, the Court began to give some content to the new formula. Under what circumstances could it be said that defendant had "certain minimum contacts with [the forum] such that the maintenance of the suit does not offend 'traditional notions of fair play and substantial justice' "? The facts of *International Shoe* did not help much, because they were too easy. Defendant's activities were much more than

[2] *See* § 18, *supra.*

required to satisfy the standard. Nevertheless, the Court indicated how the new test was to be applied. Courts should no longer simply total up contacts, as they did under the doing business test, to determine whether defendant's activity is "a little more or a little less." The new test is not "mechanical or quantitative." Whether a state has jurisdiction depends rather on the "quality and nature" of defendant's forum related activities. Courts are to make an "estimate of the inconveniences" which would result to defendant as a consequence of a trial away from its home. Further, they should determine whether defendant exercised "the privilege of conducting activities within [the] state" and "enjoy[ed] the benefits and protection of the laws of that state." Later decisions and analytical commentaries have reiterated these themes, first announced in *International Shoe*, and have used them to flesh out and solidify the new standard.[3]

While the opinion in *International Shoe* gives some content to the new theory of jurisdiction, it does not resolve a crucial ambiguity in the "minimum contacts . . . fair play and substantial justice" test. One reading of the famous formula focuses on "minimum contacts" and has led courts to require some sort of physical pre–litigation connection between the defendant and the forum.[4] Another plausible reading focuses on "fair play and substantial justice". Decisions using that approach[5] have considered a wide range of factors (the inconvenience to the defendant of defending in the forum, the inconvenience to the plaintiff of bringing the action elsewhere, the interest of the forum state in the litigation, the relative wealth of the parties, the location of witnesses and evidence) to determine whether the exercise of jurisdiction is "fair."[6]

Rather than resolving the ambiguity, the Court's next two decisions highlighted the tension between the "contacts" and "fairness" approaches.

[b] *McGee v. International Life Insurance Co.*[7]

In *McGee v. International Life Insurance Co.*, the Court strongly endorsed the "fairness" interpretation of *International Shoe* and upheld an exercise of jurisdiction based on the most tenuous connection that it has ever approved. Franklin, a California resident, purchased a life insurance policy

---

[3] *See* Part C, *infra*, for a discussion of the decisions which elucidate the International Shoe formulation.

[4] *See, e.g.*, Hanson v. Denckla, 357 U.S. 235 (1958)(discussed in § 20[c], *infra*.

[5] *See, e.g.*, McGee v. International Life Ins. Co., 355 U.S. 220 (1957)(discussed in § 20[b], *infra*).

[6] The opinion in *International Shoe* contains numerous passages that support one interpretation or the other. For a more complete discussion of the two approaches and numerous citations to cases using each one, *see* Casad & Richman § 2-3 [1][b]. *See, also* Kevin M. Clermont, *Restating Territorial Jurisdiction and Venue for State and Federal Courts*, 66 Cornell L. Rev. 411, 416–418 (1981). In addition to the courts, the commentators regularly do battle over the issue of contacts versus fairness. *Compare, e.g.*, Arthur M. Weisburd, *Territorial Authority and Personal Jurisdiction*, 63 Wash. U.L.Q. 377, 422 (1985), *with* Russell J. Weintraub, *Due Process Limitations on the Personal Jurisdiction of State Courts: Time for a Change*, 63 Or. L. Rev. 485, 486 (1984).

[7] 355 U.S. 220 (1957).

from the Empire Mutual Insurance Company. Defendant later assumed Empire's insurance obligations and mailed a reinsurance certificate to Franklin in California. The certificate contained an offer to insure Franklin upon the same terms as the policy he held with Empire. Franklin accepted the offer and mailed his policy premiums from California to defendant's offices in Texas. Apart from this one contact, the record revealed no other connection between defendant and California. Plaintiff, Franklin's mother (the beneficiary of the policy) claimed the death benefit after Franklin's death; but defendant refused to pay on the ground that Franklin had committed suicide.

Plaintiff sued on the policy in California, serving defendant by mail in Texas pursuant to the California Unauthorized Insurers Process Act. When defendant failed to appear, plaintiff took a default judgment and sued defendant in Texas to enforce that judgment. The Texas courts refused to give full faith and credit to the California judgment on the ground that the California court lacked jurisdiction.

The Supreme Court reversed, holding that California's exercise of jurisdiction was proper. The Court was not daunted by the fact that defendant had so few connections with California: "It is sufficient for purposes of due process that the suit was based on a contract which had substantial connection with that State." That language is strong medicine; read in light of the facts in *McGee*, it means that a single transaction — say, a contract or a tort — is sufficient to support an exercise of jurisdiction provided only that the one transaction has a "substantial" connection with the state. Such connections between a transaction and the forum are not hard to come by. In a tort action, for instance, it would probably be enough to show that injury to a forum resident occurred within the forum's territory. Later Supreme Court cases have not been as liberal,[8] and *McGee* has proved to be the high–water mark of permissible state court jurisdiction.

The Court justified its expansive view of jurisdiction by relying on changing patterns of business and commerce:

> [A] trend is clearly discernible toward expanding the permissible scope of state jurisdiction. . . . In part this is attributable to the fundamental transformation of our national economy over the years. Today many commercial transactions touch two or more States and may involve parties separated by the full continent. With this increasing nationalization of commerce has come a great increase in the amount of business conducted by mail across state lines. At the same time modern transportation and communication have made it much less burdensome for a party sued to defend himself in a State where he engages in economic activity.

The opinion is also remarkable for its emphasis on the "fair play and substantial justice" component of the *International Shoe* test:

---

[8] It may be that the Court was willing to go so far in *McGee* because it involved life insurance — an area where the Court has been particularly sensitive to the states' interests in protecting their citizens.

> It cannot be denied that California has a manifest interest in providing effective means of redress for its residents when their insurers refuse to pay claims. These residents would be at a severe disadvantage if they were forced to follow the insurance company to a distant State in order to hold it legally accountable. When claims were small or moderate individual claimants frequently could not afford the cost of bringing an action in a foreign forum — thus in effect making the company judgment proof. Often the crucial witnesses — as here on the company's defense of suicide — will be found in the insured's locality. Of course there may be inconvenience to the insurer if it is held amenable to suit in California where it had this contract but certainly nothing which amounts to a denial of due process.

The Court's concern with the relative inconvenience of the parties, the regulatory interest of the forum state, and the ease of access to sources of proof makes it clear that *McGee* is a "fairness" case. After *McGee*, it appeared that the Supreme Court would adopt the "fairness" approach decisively and steadily expand the limits on state court jurisdiction. The court's next jurisdictional decision, however, moved in quite the opposite direction.

[c] *Hanson v. Denckla*[9]

In 1935 Mrs. Donner, a Pennsylvania domiciliary, created a trust in Delaware, naming a Delaware trustee. She directed that the income be paid to her during her life and reserved a power of appointment over the corpus. Mrs. Donner moved to Florida where, in 1949, she executed both her will and the power of appointment. The appointment directed that $400,000 from the trust go to the children of her daughter Elizabeth; the rest of her estate — about one million dollars — she left to her other two daughters, who were the legatees in her will.

After Mrs. Donner's death, the residuary legatees brought an action in Florida, naming as defendants (among others) Elizabeth (the executrix) and the Delaware trustee. They sought a determination that the trust corpus passed to them through the residuary clause. The Florida Supreme Court held that Florida had jurisdiction over the Delaware trustee and that under Florida law the trust was invalid because the settlor had retained too much power over the trustee and the trust corpus. The result was that nearly all of Mrs. Donner's estate (the $400,000 appointed to her grandchildren plus the one million bequeathed to the two daughters) passed through the residuary clause to the two daughters.

After the Florida suit began, but before the Florida judgment, Elizabeth, the executrix, began a declaratory judgment proceeding in Delaware to determine who was entitled to the trust assets. When the Florida decree was entered, the residuary legatees urged it as res judicata in Delaware, but the Delaware courts refused full faith and credit on the ground that the Florida court lacked jurisdiction over the Delaware trustee. The

9 357 U.S. 235 (1958).

Supreme Court granted certiorari in both cases; it held that Florida lacked jurisdiction over the Delaware trustee and that Delaware was justified in refusing to give full faith and credit to the Florida judgment.

The Delaware trustee had had some contact with Florida; during the eight years Mrs. Donner lived in Florida, the trustee had communicated with her about trust administration and had earned fees for its duties. Its position was not unlike that of a commercial enterprise in one state with a single customer in another state; in other words, it was in a position very much like that of the defendant in *McGee*. Accordingly, the Court tried hard to distinguish *McGee*. A significant difference in the eyes of the Court was that in *McGee*, defendant, by mailing the reinsurance certificate into California, initiated contact with the state. By contrast, in *Hanson* the trustee's contact with Florida came not as a result of its doing or soliciting business in Florida, but rather as a result of one of its clients moving there:

> [T]he Court [in *McGee*] upheld jurisdiction because the suit "was based on a contract which had substantial connection with that State." In contrast, this action involves the validity of an agreement that was entered without any connection with the forum State. The agreement was executed in Delaware by a trust company incorporated in that State and a settlor domiciled in Pennsylvania. The first relationship Florida had to the agreement was years later when the settlor became domiciled there.

Other factual distinctions can be drawn, as well;[10] but the real difference between the two cases is one of approach. While *McGee* relied on the "fairness" reading of the *International Shoe* test, *Hanson* emphasized the "contacts" interpretation and, in doing so, resurrected *Pennoyer*'s territorial power theory.[11]

> In *McGee* the Court noted the trend of expanding personal jurisdiction over nonresidents. . . . But it is a mistake to assume that this trend heralds the eventual demise of all restrictions on the personal jurisdiction of state courts. *Those restrictions are more than a guarantee of immunity from inconvenient or distant litigation. They are a consequence of territorial limitations on the power of the respective States.* However minimal the burden of defending in a foreign tribunal, a defendant may not be called upon to do so unless he has had the "minimal contacts" with that State that are a prerequisite to its exercise of power over him [emphasis added].

---

[10] The Court pointed out that California had enacted a special long–arm statute to reach out–of–state insurers; Florida had no similar statute for out–of–state trustees. This point is curious. Because Florida had as great an interest in the estates and trusts business as California had in the insurance business, a distinction based on the strength of the state interests in the disputed transaction will not hold water. It may be that the Court was relying on the fact that California expressed its interest through a special long–arm statute while Florida did not. That distinction is unsatisfactory; it would produce the odd consequence of a state's being able to increase the constitutional range of its judicial jurisdiction simply by passing a statute.

[11] *See* § 17, *supra*. *See, also* Harold S. Lewis, *The Three Deaths of "State Sovereignty" and the Curse of Abstraction in the Jurisprudence of Jurisdiction*, 58 Notre Dame L. Rev. 699, 709–711 (1983).

Thus the Court held that the "unilateral activity" of one (in this case, Mrs. Donner) who has some relationship with the defendant cannot satisfy the minimum contacts requirement. Rather "it is essential in each case that there be some act by which the defendant purposely avails itself of the privilege of conducting activities in the forum State, thus invoking the benefits and protection of its laws."

As part of its rejection of *McGee*'s fairness approach, the Court drew a clear distinction between the Constitutional limitations on jurisdiction and choice of law: "[a state] does not acquire . . . jurisdiction by being the 'center of gravity' of the controversy or the most convenient location for the litigation. The issue is personal jurisdiction, not choice of law."[12]

Given this clear distinction, it is ironic that choice of law may have been the hidden motive behind the Court's decision. The Florida courts had applied Florida law to determine that the trust and the power of appointment were invalid and that the corpus thus passed to the residuary legatees. The Delaware courts instead applied Delaware law and concluded that the trust and power of appointment were valid and that the corpus passed to Mrs. Donner's grandchildren. In order for the Supreme Court to permit an equitable *per stirpes* distribution of Mrs. Donner's estate (and give the grandchildren their fair share), the Court had to reverse the Florida judgment and affirm the Delaware judgment. The direct route would have been to hold unconstitutional the Florida courts' choice–of–law decision, but that path was precluded by recent decisions of the Court that minimized the constitutional restrictions on state court choice–of–law decisions.[13] The Court was forced to use the constitutional restrictions on jurisdiction to do the dirty work instead.

The obvious ulterior motive for the decision led many to believe that *Hanson* was bad law (made by a hard case), a jurisdictional oddity that went against the national trend.[14] In fact, however, the later decisions of the Supreme Court have relied heavily on *Hanson* and its requirement that "there be some act by which the defendant purposely avails itself of the privilege of conducting activity in the forum State." Thus the lasting lesson of *Hanson* was that modern commerce and transportation and the trend toward looser limits on state–court jurisdiction did not "herald . . . the eventual demise of all restrictions on personal jurisdiction. . . ." Even after the doctrinal revolution of *International Shoe*, the Court was still committed to a theory of jurisdiction based, at least in part, on territory and power.

[12] For a discussion of the constitutional limitations on state choice–of–law decisions, *see* Chapter 4, Part E.

[13] *See* Alaska Packers Ass'n v. Industrial Acc. Comm'n., 294 U.S. 532 (1935); Pacific Employers Ins. Co. v. Industrial Accident Comm'n, 306 U.S. 493 (1939).

[14] *See* Geoffrey C. Hazard, *A General Theory of State–Court Jurisdiction*, 1965 Sup. Ct. Rev. 241, 244 (1965).

Part C

JURISDICTION AFTER 1977 — THE RECENT CASES

For two decades, between *Hanson v. Denckla*[1] and *Shaffer v. Heitner*,[2] the Supreme Court issued no major decisions on the constitutional limitations upon state court jurisdiction. After 1977, the Court ended its twenty year silence with a vengeance — issuing ten major decisions in the next ten years. Part C considers that decade of extraordinary productivity.

§ 21 *Shaffer v. Heitner*

Shaffer v. Heitner is most famous, of course, for its unification of in personam and in rem jurisdictional analysis under the *International Shoe* standard,[1] but the opinion also contains a significant discussion of the power, contacts and fairness themes we have been considering.

Plaintiff, a shareholder of Greyhound — a Delaware corporation with its principal place of business in Arizona — brought a derivative action in Delaware against several of Greyhound's officers and directors. He claimed that they had violated their duties to Greyhound by causing it to incur substantial civil and criminal antitrust liabilities based on activities that took place in Oregon. The Delaware court asserted attachment jurisdiction over defendants, based not on their minimum contacts with Delaware, but on their ownership of Greyhound stock with a situs in Delaware according to a unique Delaware statute. The Supreme Court invalidated the exercise of jurisdiction and held that all attempts to exercise jurisdiction must satisfy the minimum contacts test of *International Shoe*.

From the point of view of the development of jurisdictional theory, the opinion in *Shaffer* is a mixed bag. Several passages bode well for a jurisdictional theory based largely on fairness; others do not. On the one hand, the opinion clearly rejects the territorial power theory of *Pennoyer*: "Thus, the relationship among the defendant, the forum, and the litigation, rather than the mutually exclusive sovereignty of the States on which the rules of *Pennoyer* rest, became the central concern of the inquiry into personal jurisdiction." A footnote to this passage also dismisses the brief resurgence of the territorial power theory in the Court's opinion in *Hanson*.

> Nothing in *Hanson v. Denckla* is to the contrary. The *Hanson* Court's statement that restrictions on state jurisdiction "are a consequence of territorial limitations on the power of the respective States," simply makes the point that the States are defined by their geographic territory. After making this point, the Court in *Hanson* determined that

---

[1] 357 U.S. 235 (1958).

[2] 433 U.S. 186 (1977).

[1] *See* § 44, *infra*, for a discussion of this aspect of the opinion.

> the defendant over which personal jurisdiction was claimed had not committed any acts sufficiently connected to the State to justify jurisdiction under the *International Shoe* standard.[2]

Further, in a sweeping dictum, the Court asserted that "all assertions of state–court jurisdiction must be evaluated according to the standards set forth in *International Shoe* and its progeny." This proposition, if rigorously applied, could result in the abandonment of transient service and technical domicile as a sufficient jurisdictional bases, since it is difficult to argue that they satisfy the *International Shoe* standard. After the Court's ruling in *Burnham v. Superior Court,*[3] however, these traditional jurisdictional bases appear secure.

On the other hand, other parts of the opinion are not as supportive of a theory of jurisdiction based on fairness. Part IV contains a very restrictive view of Delaware's ability to exercise jurisdiction over the absent officers and directors. Because defendants had no other contacts with Delaware and the cause of action was based on activities in Oregon, the issue resolved itself into one narrow question: Can the state in which a corporation is chartered exercise jurisdiction in a derivative action over directors of the corporation even if there is no other contact between the directors and the forum? Plaintiff first argued that personal jurisdiction would have been proper because Delaware had a strong interest in regulating the supervision and management of Delaware corporations; Delaware law, after all, established the corporation and set up the duties owed by officers and directors. Plaintiff's second argument was that by accepting positions as directors, defendants received considerable benefit from Delaware's corporation law; in return for that benefit they could be required to respond to Delaware's summons in a cause of action related to their fiduciary duties. The Court rejected both arguments:

> [T]his line of reasoning establishes only that it is appropriate for Delaware law to govern the obligations of appellants to Greyhound and its stockholders. It does not demonstrate that appellants have "purposefully avail[ed themselves] of the privilege of conducting activities within the forum State" . . . in a way that would justify bringing them before a Delaware tribunal. Appellants have simply had nothing to do with the State of Delaware.[4]

---

[2] Several commentators have noted this second death of the territorial power theory in the *Shaffer* footnote. *See* David E. Seidelson, *Recasting World–Wide Volkswagen as a Source of Longer Jurisdictional Reach*, 19 Tulsa L.J. 1, 8 (1983); Harold S. Lewis, *The Three Deaths of "State Sovereignty" and the Curse of Abstraction in the Jurisprudence of Personal Jurisdiction*, 58 Notre Dame L. Rev. 699, 711 (1983).

[3] 495 U.S. 604 (1990). The traditional bases and the impact on them of *Shaffer* and *Burnham* are discussed in Part D, *infra*.

[4] This passage reinforces the distinction in Hansen v. Denckla, 357 U.S. 235 (1958), between the constitutional limits on jurisdiction and choice of law. Justice Brennan in a strong dissent argued that the Court has been too rigid in separating the questions of jurisdiction and choice of law. He found the same considerations of fairness and party expectations important for both inquiries and further argued that merging the two questions would have the practical benefit of minimizing the number of cases in which the governing law will be applied by a court that is unfamiliar with it and unsympathetic to its policies.

This passage suggests that the Court is looking for some actual physical contact between defendants and the forum. Arguably it is asking for too much. After all, Delaware had created an entity and allowed certain people (defendant directors) to have power and control over it. Delaware ought to be able to monitor their conduct by asserting jurisdiction over them in a cause of action arising out of their duties.[5] Regardless of whether we approve of the Court's holding, it is clear that this passage seems committed to the "contacts" rather than the "fairness" interpretation of *International Shoe*.[6]

§ 22 *World-Wide Volkswagen Corp. v. Woodson*[1]

In *World-Wide*, the Supreme Court had the opportunity to apply the minimum contacts analysis to a subject that has produced considerable jurisdictional litigation — products liability.[2] The area is a natural source of such disputes because in many cases the deepest pocket available — the manufacturer — does no *direct* in-state business. In this respect *World-Wide* was slightly unusual because jurisdiction over the manufacturer was not the bone of contention. Rather the issue was jurisdiction over a regional distribution and a local retail dealer.

Plaintiffs had purchased an Audi from Seaway Volkswagen in upstate New York; the car had been manufactured by Audi, imported by Volkswagen of America (Volkswagen), and distributed by World-Wide Volkswagen (World-Wide). Seaway did business only in New York, and World-Wide only in New York, New Jersey, and Connecticut, while both Audi and Volkswagen had nationwide sales. Plaintiffs left New York to establish a home in Arizona. On the way, in Oklahoma, their auto was struck from the rear by another car and caught fire. Plaintiffs, severely injured in the fire, brought a products liability action in Oklahoma against Audi, Volkswagen, Seaway, and World-Wide. Seaway and World-Wide[3] challenged the jurisdiction of

[5] After *Shaffer*, Delaware passed an in personam long-arm statute to reach absent corporate directors. In Armstrong v. Pomerance, 423 A.2d 174 (Del. 1980), the Delaware court upheld the statute based on the argument that defendant directors had accepted the benefits of their directorships with explicit statutory notice that they could be required to answer Delaware's process.

[6] *See* Earl M. Maltz, *Reflections on a Landmark: Shaffer v. Heitner Viewed from a Distance*, 1986 B.Y.U. L. Rev. 1043, 1058–60.

[1] 444 U.S. 286 (1980).

[2] Before *World-Wide*, the issue had been dealt with in several influential state court opinions. *See, e.g.*, Gray v. American Radiator & Standard Sanitary Corp., 22 Ill. 2d 432, 176 N.E. 2d 761 (1961); Buckeye Boiler Co. v. Superior Court of Los Angeles City, 17 Cal. 2d 893; 80 Cal. Rptr. 113, 458 P.2d 57 (1969). For more on this issue, *see* § 37[g], *infra*.

[3] Volkswagen also made a special appearance, but did not seek review of the trial court's ruling in the Oklahoma Supreme Court. Jurisdiction over Volkswagen and Audi, therefore, was not an issue in the Supreme Court. A puzzle then in *World-Wide* (noted in Justice Blackmun's dissent) is why the plaintiffs were so insistent that the retailer (Seaway) and the distributor (World-Wide) be joined as defendants. The manufacturer (Audi) and the importer (Volkswagen of America) were clearly amenable and had deep pockets. A possible motive was that the plaintiffs were afraid that the manufacturer and the importer would assert in their defense that the defect in the car resulted from wrongdoing by the dealer or the distributor.

the Oklahoma courts, but the state courts ruled against them; the Supreme Court granted certiorari and reversed.

The most remarkable feature of the majority opinion in *World–Wide* was not its elaboration of the "minimum contacts . . . fair play and substantial justice" standard, but rather its explanation of the source of that standard. According to the majority, fairness to the defendant is not the only reason for the minimum contacts test. The requirement is also justified by "principles of interstate federalism embodied in the Constitution." The Court made it quite clear that the relationship of the states *to each other* (as constituent sovereigns in a federation) places a limit on their adjudicatory jurisdiction that is separate and distinct from any restriction based on fairness to the defendant.[4]

The opinion went on to make it clear that "interstate federalism" is nothing more than a revival of the territorial power theory.

> But the Framers also intended that the States retain many essential attributes of sovereignty, including, in particular, the sovereign power to try causes in their courts. The sovereignty of each State, in turn, implied a limitation on the sovereignty of all of its sister States — a limitation express or implicit in both the original scheme of the Constitution and the Fourteenth Amendment.[5]

The Court's reliance on reasoning of this sort caused significant consternation. If the restrictions on jurisdiction were based not only on fairness to the defendant but also on the rights of other states, how could the defendant waive a jurisdictional objection? Certainly, individuals cannot waive the rights of states. The problem of waiver surfaced quickly and caused the

---

In fact, however, plaintiffs' motive was concerned more with choice of forum than litigation strategy. The state court in Creek County, Oklahoma has a reputation for sympathy for plaintiffs and high damage awards; the federal court in Tulsa is a much less favorable forum for personal injury plaintiffs. Plaintiffs' counsel believed that plaintiffs retained a technical domicile in New York. Because they were not yet present in Arizona and had no intention of remaining in Oklahoma, they had not abandoned their New York domicile. By joining the dealer and the distributor, both New York corporations, he hoped to prevent removal of the case to federal court by destroying the "complete" diversity required for removal. *See* Weintraub 153. For a lively and highly detailed account of the facts of the case and its progress through the courts, see Charles Adams, *World–Wide Volkswagen v. Woodson — The Rest of the Story*, 72 Neb. L. Rev. 1122 (1993).

[4] In the Court's words:

> The concept of minimum contacts . . . perform[s] two related, but distinguishable, functions. It protects the defendant against the burdens of litigating in a distant or inconvenient forum. And it acts to ensure that the States, through their courts, do not reach out beyond the limits imposed on them by their status as coequal sovereigns in a federal system.

In other words, even if the forum's exercise of jurisdiction causes no unfairness to the defendant, it may yet be unconstitutional because of its infringement upon the sovereignty of the other states.

[5] For more on "interstate federalism," *see* § 35, *infra*.

Supreme Court to abandon decisively its reliance on "interstate federalism" as a source of the constitutional limitations on jurisdiction.[6]

Although "interstate federalism" proved to be a doctrinal blind alley, other aspects of the majority's *World–Wide* opinion have retained vitality. The Court laid the foundation for its developing resolution of the contacts/fairness ambiguity of *International Shoe*. That resolution has taken the form of a weighted two–stage test.[7] The first (and, by far, the more important) step[8] is the requirement that defendant establish purposeful contacts with the forum. If that threshold test is satisfied, the next step requires a weighing of the overall fairness of the exercise of jurisdiction — considering such factors as the inconvenience to the defendant, the plaintiff's interest in a ready forum, the state's regulatory interest in the cause of action, and the ease of access to sources of proof.

Having recited its general view of the due process limits on jurisdiction, the Court applied the standard to the facts at hand. The Court held that defendants had essentially no contact with Oklahoma; neither made any sales there either directly or indirectly (through a chain of distribution).

---

[6] In Insurance Corp. of Ireland v. Compagnie Des Bauxites De Guinee, 456 U.S. 694 (1982), defendants objected to the exercise of personal jurisdiction by a United States District Court, and plaintiff attempted to use discovery to establish defendants' minimum contacts. The defendants refused to comply with the court's discovery orders, and the Supreme Court held that their refusal constituted a waiver of their jurisdictional objections. The Court abandoned its reliance on interstate federalism as a foundation for the minimum contracts requirement — focusing exclusively instead on defendant's liberty interest. "The personal jurisdiction requirement recognizes and protects an individual liberty interest. It represents a restriction on judicial power not as a matter of sovereignty, but as a matter of individual liberty." In footnote 10 the Court added: "[The Due Process] Clause is the only source of the personal jurisdiction requirement and the Clause itself makes no mention of federalism concerns."

The cyclic waxing and waning of the territorial power theory, including its recent rise and fall in the guise of "interstate federalism," is discussed in Allen R. Stein, *Styles of Argument and Interstate Federalism in the Law of Personal Jurisdiction*, 65 Tex. L. Rev. 689 (1987); Harold S. Lewis, *The Three Deaths of "State Sovereignty" and the Curse of Abstraction in the Jurisprudence of Personal Jurisdiction*, 58 Notre Dame L. Rev. 699 (1983); David E. Seidelson, *Recasting World–Wide Volkswagen as a Source of Longer Jurisdictional Reach*, 19 Tulsa L.J. 1, 5–10 (1983); John N. Drobak, *The Federalism Theme in Personal Jurisdiction*, 68 Iowa L. Rev. 1015 (1983). For more on the *Bauxites* case, *see* § 30[b], *infra*.

[7] The *World–Wide* majority did not adopt the two–stage analysis explicitly, as have more recent cases. *See* Burger King Corp. v. Rudzewicz, 471 U.S. 462 (1985), Asahi Metal Industry Company Ltd. v. Superior Court, 480 U.S. 102 (1987). *See* Vernon, Weinberg, Reynolds & Richman 62; Shreve & Raven–Hansen § 3.12[2].

[8] A famous passage of the opinion reveals the primacy of contacts over fairness:

> Even if the defendant would suffer minimal or no inconvenience from being forced to litigate before the tribunals of another State; even if the forum State has a strong interest in applying its law to the controversy; even if the forum State is the most convenient location for litigation, the Due Process Clause, acting as an instrument of interstate federalism, may sometimes act to divest the State of its power to render a valid judgment.

Some commentators approve of *World–Wide*'s emphasis on contacts over fairness. *See, e.g.*, Martin B. Louis, *The Grasp of Long Arm Jurisdiction Finally Exceeds its Reach: A Comment on World–Wide Volkswagen Corp. v. Woodson*, 58 N.C.L. Rev. 407 (1980). The majority, however, favor greater emphasis on the fairness approach. *See, e.g.*, Martin H. Redish, *Due Process, Federalism and Personal Jurisdiction: A Theoretical Evaluation*, 75 Nw. U.L. Rev. 1112 (1981).

Neither advertised, solicited, or carried on any other activity in Oklahoma. Oklahoma could not base jurisdiction "on one, isolated occurrence . . .the fortuitous circumstance that a single Audi automobile, sold in New York to New York residents, happened to suffer an accident while passing through Oklahoma."

The Court next addressed plaintiff's argument that it was foreseeable that the car would cause injury in Oklahoma because of its inherently mobile nature. The Court rejected foreseeability[9] as an adequate substitute for purposefully established minimum contacts; if foreseeability were the test, every seller of chattels would be amenable in every state, since it is foreseeable that highly mobile consumers will take their purchases all over the country. In the Court's words: "Every seller of chattels would in effect appoint the chattel his agent for service of process." Foreseeability, the Court concluded, is significant only if defendant should have been aware of its minimum contacts with the forum so that it could "reasonably anticipate being haled into court there." In other words, defendant is amenable to jurisdiction in the forum if defendant could foresee being amenable to jurisdiction in the forum. The Court did not explain how this circular admonition advanced the jurisdictional inquiry.[10]

Finally, the Court dealt with the chain of distribution problem. Is a manufacturer or distributor amenable wherever the product turns up or only where it is sent deliberately?[11] The Court concluded that a state may exercise jurisdiction over everyone in the chain of distribution of a product *purchased within* the state, but that jurisdiction will not necessarily exist when the product enters the state as a result of the foreseeable action of a consumer who *purchased* it *elsewhere*. According to this standard, there was no jurisdiction over Seaway and World–Wide. The chain of distribution of which they were a part ended with the retail sale in New York. Only the independent action of the plaintiff/consumer took the product to Oklahoma. The Court's solution to the chain of distribution problem makes sense and is a very significant contribution. By rejecting the notion that jurisdiction can be based solely on injury within the forum, the Court allows distributors and manufacturers to have some control over the scope of their amenability by controlling the scope of their commercial operations.[12]

---

[9] For more on foreseeability, *see* § 37[e], *infra*; Katherine Sheehan, *Predicting the Future: Personal Jurisdiction for the Twenty–First Century*, 66 U. Cin. L. Rev. 385, 435–436 (1998). Leonard Ratner, *Procedural Due Process and Jurisdiction to Adjudicate,* 75 Nw. U.L. Rev. 363, 379 (1980).

[10] *See*, Vernon, Weinberg, Reynolds & Richman 64, Leonard G. Ratner, *Procedural Due Process and Jurisdiction to Adjudicate*, 75 N.W. U.L. Rev. 363, 379 (1980). In addition to circularity, the Court's use of foreseeability is problematic because it relies on an untested empirical assumption about the defendant's state of mind. Indeed, very little empirical research has been done in the entire area of jurisdiction. *But see* Michael Solimine, *The Quiet Revolution in Personal Jurisdiction*, 73 Tul. L. Rev. 1 (1998)

[11] For more on the stream of commerce, *see* §§ 27 and 37[g], *infra*.

[12] In sharp contrast to this sensible treatment of the stream of commerce is the disastrous limitation added by the plurality opinion in Asahi Metal Industry Co. v. Superior Court of California, 480 U.S. 102 (1987). For more on *Asahi*, *see* § 27, *infra*.

World–Wide is also remarkable for its three dissenting opinions. Those of Justices Marshall and Blackmun were directed to the particular facts of *World–Wide*. Justice Marshall thought jurisdiction existed because both World–Wide and Seaway were part of a nationwide network for sales and service of Audi cars. Without such a network, the cars would have considerably less worth, so Seaway and World–Wide profited from the network. Further, the existence of the network made it virtually certain that some of defendants' cars would end up in Oklahoma, so it would be reasonable to make defendants respond to process there. Blackmun's dissent focused even more narrowly on the nature of the automobile — an inherently mobile product. He expressly limited his opinion to the distribution and retailing of cars, leaving other cases to be dealt with as they arise.

Justice Brennan's disagreement with the majority was more fundamental. He urged the rejection of the minimum contacts standard in favor of an approach based more on fairness. His two–step test would focus on the forum's interest and the potential inconvenience for the defendant; first, plaintiff must show that the forum has a "sufficient interest in the litigation (or sufficient contacts with the defendant)"; second, if plaintiff makes such a showing, defendant can defeat jurisdiction by showing that the exercise of jurisdiction is "unfair for some reason other than that a state boundary must be crossed."

That last phrase isolates the heart of the dispute between Brennan and the majority. The majority has retained enough territorialism in its jurisdictional doctrine that state boundaries have independent significance; for jurisdictional purposes, the states do not resemble departments in France or counties in Missouri. For Brennan, however, state boundaries have no significance unless forcing a defendant to cross one involves an unfair inconvenience to him in the conduct of his defense.[13]

§ 23 *Keeton v. Hustler Magazine*[1]

Kathy Keeton, a resident of New York, brought a libel action against Hustler Magazine, an Ohio corporation, in the United States District Court in New Hampshire. Her claim was based on photographs and comments published in five issues of Hustler in 1975 and 1976. Hustler's contact with New Hampshire consisted of monthly sales of 10,000 to 15,000 copies of its magazine. Keeton's only connection with the forum was the circulation there of copies of several magazines ("Penthouse," "Viva," and "Omni") for which she had worked as corporate officer, staff member, or editor. Initially Keeton had sued Hustler in Ohio where her claims were dismissed as barred by the relevant statutes of limitations. She chose the New Hampshire forum for this action because New Hampshire was the only state remaining in which her claims were not time–barred. The district court

---

[13] For commentary on Brennan's view of territoriality, see Sheehan, *supra* note 9, at 433–435. Brennan's views also color his majority opinion in Burger King v. Rudzewicz, 471 U.S. 462 (1985), but there he was required to moderate them to maintain a majority. For more on *Burger King*, *see* § 26, *infra*.

[1] 465 U.S. 770 (1984).

dismissed for lack of personal jurisdiction over Hustler, and the Circuit Court of Appeals affirmed. The Supreme Court reversed.

The Supreme Court's opinion first assessed Hustler's contacts with New Hampshire and concluded easily that its regular circulation of magazines in the forum was sufficient to justify the exercise of jurisdiction in a libel action based on the contents of the magazine. Regular sales of that volume could not be characterized as "random, isolated or fortuitous."

Next the Court addressed the three fairness factors that had troubled lower courts: the operation of the "single publication" rule, the application of New Hampshire's extremely long limitations period, and the plaintiff's lack of contacts with the forum.

The problem with the single publication rule was that it permitted plaintiff to recover for all her damages nationwide in the single action in New Hampshire,[2] a state that had relatively little interest in the dispute. In the words of the Court of Appeals, "the New Hampshire tail is too small to wag so large an out–of–state dog."[3]

The Supreme Court disagreed and found several, somewhat anemic, New Hampshire interests to be sufficient. According to the Court, New Hampshire had an interest in redressing injuries suffered in New Hampshire by out–of–state defamation victims, as well as an interest in protecting New Hampshire consumers. "False statements of fact harm both the subject of the falsehood *and* the readers. . . ." Further, New Hampshire had an interest in cooperating with other states — via the single publication rule — in furnishing a forum where a plaintiff can recover in one action for all the harm caused by multi–state defamation.

The Court's marshalling of these New Hampshire interests is quite curious; they are hardly the sort of compelling state concerns that figure in some of the Court's other jurisdiction decisions.[4] It may be that the forum state's interest in a dispute should not count for much in the jurisdictional calculus; but if it does, it seems disingenuous to hold that these make-weights are sufficient.[5]

---

[2] *See* Restatement (Second) of Torts § 577A(4) (1977).

[3] Keeton v. Hustler Magazine, 682 F.2d 33, 36 (1982).

[4] *See, e.g.*, McGee v. International Life Insurance Co., 355 U.S. 220 (1957) (forum's interest in protecting its residents from being bilked by out–of–state insurers/consumers); World–Wide Volkswagen v. Woodson, 444 U.S. 286 (1980)(State's interest in providing a forum for non-resident accident victims not sufficient). *McGee* is discussed *supra* at § 20(b); *World–Wide* at § 22. For more on state interest, *see* § 38[b], *infra*.

[5] The Court's ambivalence in *Keeton* about the relevance of state interests is apparent in its willingness to consider them only as a "surrogate" for other factors. After *Bauxites'* rejection of "interstate federalism," some commentators have contended that the forum's regulatory interest in the dispute should be irrelevant. They argue that the two concepts are very closely related, and that the rejection of "interstate federalism" requires that the Court eliminate all consideration of the forum's interest. William J. Knudsen, Jr., *Keeton, Calder, Helicopteros and Burger King — International Shoe's Most Recent Progeny*, 39 Miami L. Rev. 809, 813 (1985); Harold S. Lewis, *The Three Deaths of "State Sovereignty" and the Curse of Abstraction in the Jurisprudence of Personal Jurisdiction*, 58 Notre Dame L. Rev. 699, 701 (1983). For the contrary argument, *see* Vernon, Weinberg, Reynolds & Richman 69.

The second "fairness" concern of the Court of Appeals centered on New Hampshire's six–year statute of limitations. The Supreme Court dismissed the issue summarily. Echoing a theme it had announced in *Hanson v. Denckla*[6] and *Shaffer v. Heitner*,[7] the Court held that a potentially unfair choice–of–law result should have little, if any, effect on the jurisdictional decision:

> "The issue is personal jurisdiction, not choice of law." *Hanson v. Denckla*, 357 U.S. 235, 254 (1958). The question of the applicability of New Hampshire's statute of limitations to claims for out–of–state damages presents itself in the course of litigation only after jurisdiction over respondent is established, and we do not think that such choice–of–law concerns should complicate or distort the jurisdictional inquiry.[8]

The final "fairness" issue treated by the Supreme Court was the very limited connection between the *plaintiff* and the forum. The Court held that minimum contacts between the plaintiff and the forum has never been a jurisdictional prerequisite. While not irrelevant, the plaintiff's residence in or contacts with the forum are important only insofar as they "enhance the defendant's contact with the forum." For instance, plaintiff's residence in the forum may be the "focus of the activities of the defendant out of which the suit arises."[9]

Although the Court's holdings on the last two issues are not remarkable under orthodox minimum contacts analysis, their interplay has an effect worth noting. If choice–of–law unfairness and plaintiff's minimal forum connections are together insufficient to oust jurisdiction, then a plaintiff suing a multi–state defendant has almost complete license to shop for the forum with the most attractive substantive law and choice–of–law principles. Apparently that result does not perturb the Supreme Court.[10]

---

6 357 U.S. 235, 254 (1958), discussed in § 20(c), *supra*.

7 433 U.S. 186, 204 (1977), discussed in § 21, *supra* and § 44, *infra*.

8 Recall that in both *Hanson* and *Shaffer*, the Court held that the fact that a forum's law might apply to a dispute was not a good reason to hold that the forum had adjudicatory jurisdiction. In *Keeton* the Court holds the converse: that the fact that the forum's law should not be applied to a dispute is not a good ground to defeat the forum's adjudicatory jurisdiction. In other words, the applicability of the forum's law to a dispute is neither a necessary nor a sufficient condition for the exercise of adjudicatory jurisdiction. Allen Stein, *Styles of Argument and Interstate Federalism in the Law of Personal Jurisdiction*, 65 Tex. L. Rev. 689, 729 (1987). For more on the relevance of choice of law to jurisdiction, *see* § 38, *infra*.

9 The Court gives the example of Calder v. Jones, 465 U.S. 783 (1984), treated at § 24, *infra*.

10 In the Court's words: "The victim of a libel, like the victim of any other tort, may choose to bring suit in any forum with which the defendant has 'certain minimum contacts . . . such that the maintenance of the suit does not offend' traditional notions of fair play and substantial justice."

§ 24 *Calder v. Jones*[1]

Offended by an article in the National Enquirer, plaintiffs, Shirley Jones and her husband, sued the magazine in the state of California for libel, invasion of privacy, and intentional infliction of emotional distress. They also joined as defendants the Enquirer's local distributing company, the author of the article, and the Enquirer's editor. The Enquirer had very substantial contacts with California, as did the distributor; about 600,000 copies of the weekly magazine were sold in the state, and it was the Enquirer's largest single market. The author and the editor, both citizens of Florida, had fewer contacts with California, consisting mostly of telephone calls and business and pleasure trips. Both, however, worked on the offending article. The Enquirer and its distributor raised no objection to California's jurisdiction; the individual defendants, however, objected, basing their challenge on their status as employees and on the protection supplied them by the First Amendment.

With little difficultly, the Supreme Court concluded that California had jurisdiction over the individual defendants because their Florida actions caused "effects" in California.[2] The unanimous opinion pointed out that the article relied on California sources, and caused injury in California to the professional reputation of a California resident, whose career was centered in California.

The defendants argued that, as employees, they had no direct economic stake in the magazine's sales in California, nor were they able to control their employer's marketing activities. They compared themselves to a welder employed in Florida who works on a boiler that is later shipped to California, where it explodes causing injuries. The welder, they claimed, should not be amenable in California simply because her employer chose to market the product there.[3] The Court was not impressed.

> [Defendants'] . . . analogy does not wash. Whatever the status of their hypothetical welder, [defendants] are not charged with mere untargeted negligence. Rather, their intentional, and allegedly tortious, actions were precisely aimed at California.[4]

The Court held that the defendants' status as employees was not especially relevant to the jurisdictional calculus. Employees should not be held amenable simply because their employer has contacts with the forum; but, by the same token, their status as employees does not insulate them either. Each defendant's contacts with the forum should be evaluated individually.

---

[1] 465 U.S. 783 (1984). It is important for conflicts scholars to distinguish between Shirley Jones and Florence Hendersen; Jones was the female lead in the Partridge Family; Hendersen, in the Brady Bunch.

[2] *See* Restatement (Second) of Conflict of Laws § 37 (1971).

[3] The analogy is drawn from two well–known long–arm cases; *see* Buckeye Boiler Co. v. Superior Court, 17 Cal. 2d 893, 458 P.2d 57, 80 Cal. Rpt. 113 (1969); Gray v. American Radiator & Standard Sanitary Corp., 22 Ill.2d 432, 176 N.E.2d 761 (1961).

[4] The Court's distinction here is somewhat ambiguous; is it based on the difference between negligent and intentional tortious conduct, or on the geographical "targeting," or both? For more discussion, *see* William J. Knudsen, Jr., *Keeton, Calder, Helicopteros and Burger King — International Shoe's Most Recent Progeny*, 39 U. Miami L. Rev. 809, 821 (1985).

The defendants' other major argument was that the First Amendment requires a more rigorous standard of amenability for out–of–state publishers than for other out–of–state defendants;[5] otherwise, publishers might be chilled from circulating magazines or newspapers in distant markets.[6] The Court rejected this argument emphatically. For one thing, consideration of First Amendment concerns would "needlessly complicate an already imprecise inquiry." And, for another, the possible chilling effect of defamation actions on protected speech is taken into account already in the elaboration of the constitutional limits on the states' substantive law of libel and slander. "To reintroduce those concerns at the jurisdictional stage would be a form of double counting."[7]

The "double counting" argument is a weak one. The Court is correct that consideration of First Amendment concerns at the jurisdictional stage and on the merits would be double counting, but the opinion never indicates why double counting is objectionable. Sometimes our law requires double counting in the form of procedural/substantive redundancy,[8] and sometimes it does not. Absent some principled standard for determining when the maneuver is appropriate, and when not, the Court's invocation of double counting is a conclusion, not an argument.

§ 25 *Helicopteros Nacionales de Colombia v. Hall*[1]

Defendant, Helicol, was a Columbian corporation engaged in the business of providing helicopter transportation for oil and construction companies in South America. Plaintiffs were the survivors and representatives of four American citizens, who died in a crash of one of defendant's helicopters in Peru. The decedents, none of whom was a Texan, had been hired in Texas by Consorcio, a Peruvian consortium. Consorcio was the alter ego of a joint venture composed of three American corporations. Headquartered in Houston, Texas, it was formed to construct a pipeline for Petro Peru, the Peruvian state–owned oil company.[2]

---

[5] This argument succeeded in one influential lower court holding. *See* New York Times Co. v. Connor, 365 F.2d 567 (5th Cir. 1966); *but see* Buckley v. New York Post Corp., 373 F.2d 175 (2d Cir. 1967).

[6] Professor Levine suggests that the publishers most likely to be chilled by the possibility of libel actions in a distant forum are major daily newspapers such as the Atlanta Constitution or the Detroit Free Press, which distribute only a few newspapers in distant states. A sensible reaction for such publishers might well be to stop such marginally beneficial distributions — an outcome that does raise serious First Amendment concerns. *See* David I. Levine, *Preliminary Procedural Protection for the Press from Jurisdiction in Distant Forums After Calder and Keeton*, 1984 Ariz. St. L.J. 459.

[7] The central issue, of course, is whether the substantive law controlling the claim should affect the jurisdictional issue. *See* Vernon, Weinberg, Reynolds & Richman 72; Paul D. Carrington and James A. Martin, *Substantive Interests and the Jurisdiction of State Courts*, 66 Mich. L. Rev. 227 (1967).

[8] *See e.g.*, Fed. R. Civ. P. 9(b) (requiring specificity in pleading fraud and mistake).

[1] 466 U.S. 408 (1984). *See generally* Vernon, Weinberg, Reynolds & Richman 81–87.

[2] Peruvian law required that work on the pipeline be performed by Peruvian entities.

At Consorcio's request, the chief executive officer of Helicol travelled to Houston and negotiated a deal with the joint venturers to supply them with helicopter transportation in Peru. The parties formally executed the contract in Peru some time after Helicopteros had begun performing. Consorcio paid for Helicol's services with checks of more than $5,000,000 drawn on Consorcio's account with a Texas bank.

In addition to this contract, Helicol had other contacts with Texas. For eight years it had purchased $4,000,000 worth of helicopters and spare parts from Bell Helicopter in Forth Worth. It had sent pilots and maintenance and management employees to Fort Worth for training and to transport helicopters to South America. Bell helicopters constituted about 80% of Helicopteros' fleet.

Plaintiffs brought wrongful death actions against Helicol, Bell Helicopter, and Consorcio in state court in Texas. The trial court denied Helicol's jurisdictional challenge and awarded plaintiffs a $1,141,200 judgment. Helicol appealed the jurisdictional ruling through the appellate courts, and ultimately the Texas Supreme Court upheld jurisdiction. The Supreme Court of the United States reversed.[3]

In order to assess the defendant's contacts with Texas, the Court adopted the distinction between general jurisdiction and specific jurisdiction.[4] General jurisdiction exists when the defendant's connections with the state are substantial enough to justify jurisdiction over the defendant based on any claim — even one that is completely unrelated to the defendant's forum contacts. The paradigm is the forum's power to exercise jurisdiction over one of its domiciliaries based upon an out–of–state tort. By contrast, "specific jurisdiction" exists when the defendant has relatively few contacts with the forum, but the claim arises directly out of those contacts. The classic case is the forum's ability to exercise jurisdiction over an out–of–state defendant who has committed a tort within the state.

After summarily eliminating the possibility of specific jurisdiction,[5] the Court set itself the relatively easy task of determining whether there was general jurisdiction over Helicol. Preliminarily, the Court pointed out that Helicol did not have a place of business in Texas and was not licensed to do business there. Next, the court evaluated the three contacts Helicol did have with Texas. First, it determined that the negotiation in Texas of the

[3] The progress of the case through the Texas courts is discussed in detail in Dennis G. Terez, *The Misguided Helicopteros Case: Confusion in the Courts Over Contacts*, 37 Baylor L. Rev. 913 (1985).

[4] The distinction was proposed in Arthur T. von Mehren & Donald T. Trautman, *Jurisdiction to Adjudicate: A Suggested Analysis*, 79 Harv. L. Rev. 1121 (1966). It is refined in Mary Twitchell, *The Myth of General Jurisdiction*, 101 Harv. L. Rev. 610 (1988). *See* § 37[b], *infra*, for further discussion of the distinction.

[5] In the words of the Court, "[a]ll parties to the present case concede that respondents' claims against Helicol did not 'arise out of,' and are not related to, Helicol's activities within Texas." Saying it does not make it so, however. There is some discussion of specific jurisdiction in the parties' briefs and in the lower court opinions. *See* Justice Brennan's dissenting opinion, n. 3; William M. Richman, *Review Essay*, 72 Cal. L. Rev. 1328, 1339, n. 46 (1984).

contract for helicopter services was not sufficiently "continuous and systematic" to support general jurisdiction. Second, the opinion concluded quite sensibly that the fact that Helicol accepted checks drawn on a Texas bank was "of little consequence" to Helicol and was jurisdictionally irrelevant.

That left the purchases of helicopters, parts, and personnel training by Helicol from a Texas supplier. The Court found them insufficient. Citing *Rosenberg Bros. & Co. v. Curtis Brown Co.*,[6] it held that "mere purchases, even if occurring at regular intervals, are not enough to warrant a[n] . . . assertion of . . . jurisdiction over a non–resident . . . in a cause of action not related to those purchase[s]. . . ."[7]

The Court's narrow holding — no general jurisdiction over Helicol[8] — is plausible. Helicol's contacts with Texas were not sufficient to support jurisdiction based on a claim totally unrelated to those contacts. To see the point clearly, consider a claim that really is completely unrelated to Helicol's Texas contacts. Suppose a Louisianan flew to Columbia and loaned Helicol money to finance a fuel purchase from a Columbian supplier. In the event of Helicol's default, should the lender be able to sue Helicol in Texas? If not, the holding of no general jurisdiction is correct.

Although the general jurisdiction holding is correct, the opinion is nevertheless unfortunate and problematic for several reasons. For one thing the resurrection of the once moribund *Rosenberg* case is a legal–process blunder. The case was decided some twenty–two years *before International Shoe*, under the territorial power regime of *Pennoyer v. Neff*. But after *Rosenberg*, fundamental changes in American business, travel, and communications prompted the Supreme Court to jettison the territorial power theory in favor of the contacts and fairness approach of *International Shoe*.[9] Thus, precedent from before the jurisdictional revolution should be nearly irrelevant to modern jurisdictional analysis.

Another serious problem with the Court's decision is its exceedingly harsh result. While Helicol could have managed a credible defense in Texas,[10]

---

[6] 260 U.S. 516 (1923).

[7] The United States and the Motor Vehicle Manufacturers Association filed amicus briefs in *Helicopteros*, arguing that holding a foreign purchaser amenable to general jurisdiction would discourage foreign firms from purchasing American goods — a result which is especially troubling given the current balance of trade deficit.

If the Supreme Court considered the argument, it did not say so. If the foreign trade problem affected the Court, *Helicopteros* would be a classic example of a case where the abstract manipulations in the opinion have nothing to do with the real reason for the decision. For a discussion of that possibility, *see* Louise Weinberg, *The Helicopteros Case and the Jurisprudence of Jurisdiction*, 58 S.Cal. L. Rev. 913 (1985).

[8] *But see* Justice Brennan's dissent: "As a foreign corporation that has actively and purposefully engaged in numerous and frequent commercial transactions in . . . Texas, Helicol clearly falls within the category of nonresident defendants that may be subject to that forum's general jurisdiction." For commentary on the general jurisdiction issue in *Helicopteros, see* Weintraub 161–163; William J. Knudsen, Jr., *Keeton, Calder, Helicopteros and Burger King — International Shoe's Most Recent Progeny*, 39 U. Miami L. Rev. 809, 826–832 (1985).

[9] For a discussion of the territorial theory, its inability to keep pace with modern advances in communications, business and travel, and its ultimate displacement by the contacts and fairness theory, *see* Part B, *supra*.

[10] Helicol did manage to make and capably argue its jurisdictional objection in three levels of courts in Texas and in the United States Supreme Court.

the plaintiffs' burden in the courts of Peru or Columbia might well have been insuperable. The contingent fee arrangement, relied on by American personal injury plaintiffs, is not permitted in many foreign systems; and South American limits on wrongful death damage awards might well make the plaintiffs' claims futile to pursue there. Based on those considerations, one commentator has concluded that "a dismissal on jurisdictional grounds in a case like *Helicopteros* is tantamount to a dismissal for all purposes."[11]

A third serious problem with the opinion is its failure to treat the problem of specific jurisdiction at all. Clearly the wrongful deaths did not occur in Texas, but that does not mean that plaintiffs' claims were entirely unrelated to Helicol's Texas contacts. The event that brought the four decedents and Helicol together was the meeting and negotiation between Helicol and Consorcio in Houston. Had it not occurred, the deaths would not have occurred either. Further, the helicopter that crashed was made in Texas, and its pilot was trained in Texas.

The Court's stated reason for not dealing with specific jurisdiction was that the parties had not briefed the issue. That point is debatable, but the Court's failure to treat the issue in a case like *Helicopteros* may be read to imply a very strict definition of specific jurisdiction — one requiring that some element of plaintiff's claim (injury, for example) occur within the forum.[12]

On this question, Justice Brennan's dissent is much better. He argued that specific jurisdiction should exist not only in cases where the claim "arises out of" defendant's forum connections, but also in cases where the claim "relates to" those contacts. *Helicopteros*, he maintained, was just such a case, and the Court should have held Helicol amenable to specific jurisdiction in Texas.[13]

As a result of its decision to ignore specific jurisdiction, the Court missed an opportunity to elaborate the general/specific jurisdiction dichotomy. *Helicopteros* posed the problem of the case that falls between the two paradigms. Helicol had significant contacts with Texas, but not enough for general jurisdiction; and plaintiffs' claims, while not arising directly out of

---

[11] *See* Louise Weinberg, *The Helicopter Case and the Jurisprudence of Jurisdiction*, 58 S. Cal. L. Rev. 913, 934 (1985). Based on considerations of that sort, plaintiffs made an argument for jurisdiction by necessity. If Texas had no jurisdiction, the plaintiffs would be denied any forum for practical purposes. The Court rejected the argument in footnote 13, finding that plaintiffs had "failed to carry their burden of showing that all three defendants could not be sued together in a single forum." Jurisdiction by necessity is also discussed in §§ 39 and 45, *infra*.

[12] Some commentators see this as the only correct basis for specific jurisdiction. *See* Lea Brilmayer, *How Contacts Count: Due Process Limitations on State Court Jurisdiction*, 1980 Sup. Ct. Rev. 77, 82. *But see* Mary Twitchel, *The Myth of General Jurisdiction*, 101 Harv. L. Rev. 610, 727–741 (1988).

[13] In footnote 10, the majority responded to Justice Brennan's dissent with an explicit disclaimer: "[W]e decline to reach the questions (1) whether the terms 'arising out of' and 'related to' describe different connections with a forum and (2) what sort of tie between a cause of action and a defendant's contacts with a forum is necessary to a determination that either connection exists." The issue dividing Justice Brennan and the Court is discussed also § 37[b], *infra. See also* William M. Richman, *Review Essay*, 72 Cal. L. Rev. 1328, 1336–1346 (1984).

defendant's Texas contacts, were nevertheless closely related to them. Should there be jurisdiction in such cases, cases that fail to satisfy completely the requirements for general or specific jurisdiction, but partially satisfy the requirements for both?

Some commentators have argued that there should not be. They view the relationship between plaintiff's claim and defendant's forum connections as an all–or–nothing affair, an electrical switch that is either on or off. Either the claim arises out of defendant's forum connections or it does not; if not there must be enough contacts to justify general jurisdiction.[14] Justice Brennan, of course, disagreed and argued for a third discrete category where plaintiff's claim does not "arise out of" the defendant's forum contacts, but is nevertheless "related" to them.

In fact, the relationship between the plaintiff's claim and the defendant's forum connections does not fit well into two or even three discrete categories; rather, it is a continuum. At one extreme are cases where an element of the plaintiff's claim consists of some act by the defendant purposefully done in the forum.[15] At the other extreme are cases where the plaintiff's

[14] *See* Lea Brilmayer, *How Contacts Count: Due Process Limitations on State Court Jurisdiction*, 1980 Sup. Ct. Rev. 77; Lea Brilmayer, Jennifer Haverkamp, Buck Logan, Loretta Lynch, Steve Neuwirth and Jim O'Brien, *A General Look at General Jurisdiction*, 66 Tex. L. Rev. 721, 738 (1988). *But see* Mary Twitchell, *The Myth of General Jurisdiction*, 101 Harv. L. Rev. 1444 (1988); William M. Richman, *Review Essay*, 72 Cal. L. Rev. 1328, 1336 (1984). For general discussion of the issue, see Scoles, Hay, Borchers & Symeonides, 343–346; Casad & Richman § 2-5[4][c].

Without guidance from the Supreme Court, the lower courts also have divided on the issue. Some refuse to find specific jurisdiction unless the claim arises from defendant's activity in the forum, *see, e.g.,* Pizarro v. Hoteles Concorde Int'l C.A., 907 F. 2d 1256, 1259 (1st Cir. 1990). Others find specific jurisdiction more readily, using Justice Brennan's disjunctive formulation, which requires only that the claim "arise out of" *or* "be related to" defendant's forum contacts, *see* Ruston Gas Turbine Inc. v. Donaldson Co., 9 F. 3d 415, 418 (5th Cir. 1993). Still others permit specific jurisdiction over a claim that has "a substantial relation to," *see* Third Nat'l Bank v. WEDGE Group, Inc, 882 F.2d 1087, 1091 (6th Cir. 1989), *cert. denied,* 493 U.S. 1058 (1990) "is made possible by," *see* Lanier v. v. American Board of Endodontics, 843 F.2d 901, 908–909 (6th Cir.), *cert. denied* 488 U.S. 926 (1988) or "lies in the wake of," see Deluxe Ice Cream Co v. R. C. H. Tool Corp., 726 F. 2d 1209, 1215–1216 (7th Cir. 1984), defendant's activities in the forum state.

Among the federal courts one issue is whether a "but for" relationship is sufficient for specific jurisdiction. Some federal appellate panels uphold specific jurisdiction when the plaintiff's claim — although not arising out of defendant's activities in the forum — would not have arisen "but for" those activities. *See* Trinity Indus., Inc. v. Myers & Assocs, Ltd., 41 F.3d 229, 231–232 (5th Cir.), *cert. denied* 516 U.S. 807 (1995), Creech v. Roberts, 908 F.2d 75, 80 (6 Cir. 1990), *cert. denied* 499 U.S. 975 (1991), Deluxe Ice Cream Co v. R. C. H. Tool Corp., 726 F. 2d 1209, 1215–1216 (7th Cir. 1984), Ballard v. Savage, 65 F.3d 1495, 1500 (9th Cir. 1995). Others reach results inconsistent with the "but for" test. *See* Kelly v. Shell Petroleum, 213 F.3d 841 (5th Cir. 2000), Pizarro v. Hoteles Concorde Int'l C.A., 907 F. 2d 1256, 1259 (1st Cir. 1990), Sybaritic, Inc. v. Interport Int'l, Inc., 957 F.2d 522, 525 (8th Cir. 1992). For more on the lower court cases *see* Casad and Richman § 2-5[4][c], Mark Maloney, *Note, Specific Jurisdiction and the "Arise From or Relate To" Requirement . . .What Does It Mean?*, 50 Wash. & Lee L. Rev. 1265 (1993).

[15] A classic example is Hess v. Pawloski, 274 U.S. 352 (1927) (jurisdiction in Massachusetts over defendant, a Pennsylvania domiciliary, for a tort claim based on an auto accident in Massachusetts).

claim simply has nothing to do with the defendant's forum contacts.[16] In between, the variations and gradations are too numerous to catalogue. For instance, some portion of the plaintiff's claim might be closely connected with the defendant's forum contacts while another portion might be unconnected.[17] Or the plaintiff's claim might arise from activities outside the forum that breached a duty created by a relationship centered in the forum.[18] Or the plaintiff's claim might arise from an extra–forum act of the defendant that nevertheless is part of an on–going activity that is significantly connected to the forum.[19] It bears repetition; the variations seem endless.

Seeing the relationship between plaintiff's claim and defendant's forum contacts as a continuum allows us to plot it against another variable — the extent of defendant's forum contact — that is also a continuum. The relationship between the two should be thought of as a *sliding scale*. As the quantity and quality of the defendant's forum contacts increase, a weaker connection between the plaintiff's claim and those contacts is permissible; as the quantity and quality of the defendant's forum contacts decrease, a stronger connection between the plaintiff's claim and those contacts is required. The concepts of general jurisdiction and specific jurisdiction are simply the two opposite ends of this sliding scale.

The significant advantage of the sliding scale model is that it permits jurisdiction in cases that do not satisfy either of the two paradigms completely but partially satisfy both. It also allows us to see that "general jurisdiction" and "specific jurisdiction" are just useful analytical tools that identify two sorts of cases in which the basic underlying factors — the defendant's benefit from the forum, the foreseeability of forum litigation, lack of serious inconvenience, defendant's initiation of the transaction — in one mix or another — make jurisdiction fair. It is rigid and wrongheaded to suggest that no intermediate mixtures are permissible. So far, however, the Supreme Court has not adopted the sliding scale; in *Helicopteros* it missed an important opportunity to do so.

---

[16] *See* Perkins v. Benguet Consolidated Mining Co., 342 U.S. 437 (1957), discussed in § 37[c], *infra*.

[17] *See, e.g.*, Keeton v. Hustler Magazine, 465 U.S. 770 (1984). (A small portion of plaintiff's defamation injury resulted from defendant's publication of the defamation in New Hampshire, the forum; most of the injury, however, resulted from publication in other states.) *Keeton* is treated more fully in § 23, *supra*.

When the plaintiff brings two claims against a defendant, one of which would qualify for specific jurisdiction and the other not, a possible solution lies in the doctrine of "pendent personal jurisdiction." *See* Linda S. Simard, *Exploring the Limits of Specific Jurisdiction,* 62 Ohio St. L.J. 1619 (2001).

[18] *See, e.g.*, Shaffer v. Heitner, 433 U.S. 186 (1977). (Defendant–directors' activities in Oregon breached their fiduciary duty to a corporation incorporated in Delaware, the forum state.)

[19] *See, e.g.*, Cornelison v. Chaney, 16 Cal. 3d 143, 545 P.2d 264 (1976).

§ 26 *Burger King Corp. v. Rudzewicz*[1]

Ian McShara approached John Rudzewicz about the possibility of their obtaining a Burger King franchise in the Detroit area; McShara was to provide his services as manager and Rudzewicz (an accountant) would provide the capital. They applied to Burger King's Michigan district office, which forwarded the application to headquarters in Miami, Florida. After considerable negotiation with headquarters and with the district office, McShara and Rudzewicz agreed to assume operation of an existing restaurant in Drayton Plains, Michigan. The final agreement provided for a 20–year franchise relationship during which the franchisees agreed to pay $1 million in franchise fees, rent, and advertising and promotional fees and to submit to Burger King's regulation of many facets of the restaurant's operation. The contract also contained a choice–of–law clause calling for the application of Florida law.

After some preliminary success, the restaurant's business declined, and Rudzewicz and McShara fell behind on the payments to Burger King. The difficulties occasioned a series of long, but ultimately unsuccessful, negotiations between the franchisees and Burger King's Michigan district office and Miami headquarters. Ultimately Burger King terminated the franchise and ordered the franchisees to vacate the restaurant. They refused and continued the business as a Burger King restaurant.

Burger King sued Rudzewicz and McShara in federal district court in Miami alleging breach of contract and tortious infringement of its trademarks and service marks. The trial court held the defendants amenable to the Court's personal jurisdiction and entered judgment against them for over a quarter of a million dollars. The Eleventh Circuit reversed the district court, and the Supreme Court, in turn, reversed the Eleventh Circuit and upheld the district court's jurisdiction.

In his opinion for the majority, Justice Brennan was obviously constrained by the two–stage (contacts plus fairness) analysis adopted by the Court in its recent jurisdiction opinions.[2] But, just as clearly, he had his own view of the matter, which he had articulated so forcefully in his dissent in *World–Wide Volkswagen v. Woodson.*[3] *Burger King* gave him the opportunity to reformulate subtly the two–stage test to bring it closer to his own expansive, fairness–oriented theory.

The contacts portion of the opinion did not depart significantly from the Court's recent analyses. Justice Brennan noted that jurisdiction is not proper unless the defendant has had "fair warning" that his actions would render him amenable in the forum. That requirement is satisfied if the defendant has "purposefully established 'minimum contacts' in the forum state." Defendant's physical entry into the forum is not required; it is

---

[1] 471 U.S. 462 (1985).

[2] *See, e.g.*, World–Wide Volkswagen v. Woodson, 444 U.S. 286 (1980), discussed in § 22, *supra*; Keeton v. Hustler Magazine, Inc., 465 U.S. 770 (1984), discussed in § 23, *supra*.

[3] For a discussion of Justice Brennan's *World–Wide* dissent, *see* § 22, *supra*.

sufficient if the defendant has "purposefully directed" his activities toward forum residents.[4]

While the contacts portion of Justice Brennan's opinion is relatively conventional, his contribution to the second stage — the fairness stage — of the analysis is more innovative. After identifying the five factors that should be considered in the fairness inquiry,[5] he directed his attention to the question of burden of proof. Once the plaintiff has shown that defendant has purposefully established minimum contacts with the forum, the burden of persuasion[6] on the fairness issue is on the defendant, who "must present a compelling case that the presence of some other considerations would render jurisdiction unreasonable." This burden shift is a significant reformulation of the *World–Wide* two–step analysis, which seemed to place the persuasion burden on both the contacts and the fairness issues on plaintiff.

Even more surprising is Justice Brennan's treatment of the relationship between the contacts and fairness tests. Somehow he got five of his colleagues to agree that fairness considerations could "sometimes serve to establish the reasonableness of jurisdiction upon a lesser showing of minimum contacts than would otherwise be required." This passage is the strongest support in recent memory for the fairness interpretation of the *International Shoe* formula; coming from a Court that has consistently emphasized contacts over fairness, it is remarkable indeed.[7]

After subtly reworking the Court's jurisdictional theory, Justice Brennan next turned to the application of that theory to John Rudzewicz. First, assessing contacts, Brennan concluded that Rudzewicz had eschewed the option of establishing a local independent restaurant and reached out beyond Michigan to negotiate with a Florida franchisor in hopes of securing the benefits of affiliating with a nationwide organization. Harking back to an earlier contract case, *McGee v. International Life Insurance Co.*,[8] Justice

[4] The observation concerning physical entry is more a clarification than a reformulation, since other recent Supreme Court opinions have upheld exercises of jurisdiction when the defendant had not physically entered the forum. *See, e.g.*, Keeton v. Hustler Magazine, Inc., discussed in § 23, *supra*. The reason why physical entry is not a requirement is the "inescapable fact of modern commercial life that a substantial amount of business is transacted solely by mail and wire communication across state lines." For commentary on this portion of the opinion, *see* Margaret G. Stewart, *A New Litany of Personal Jurisdiction*, 60 U. Colo. L. Rev. 5, 38–40 (1989).

[5] The factors identified are: the burden on the defendant, the forum state's interest in adjudicating the dispute, the plaintiff's interest in obtaining convenient and effective relief, the interstate judicial system's interest in obtaining the most efficient resolution of controversies, and the shared interest of the several states in furthering fundamental substantive social policies. For discussion of the factors, *see* § 38, *infra*.

[6] For more discussion of the burden of persuasion on the issue of amenability, *see* Lea Brilmayer, *Three Themes in the Law of Personal Jurisdiction*, 44 Rutgers L.J. 561, 564–565 (1991).

[7] Justice Brennan's re–tooling of *World–Wide*'s two–stage test has led some commentators to conclude that at least this once he was able to have it "his way" and that his opinion is indeed a "whopper." Rex R. Perschbacher, *Minimum Contacts Reapplied: Mr. Justice Brennan Has It His Way in Burger King Corp. v. Rudzewicz*, 1986 Ariz. St. L. J. 585; Pamela J. Stephens, *The Single Contract as Minimum Contacts: Justice Brennan "Has It His Way,"* 28 Wm. & Mary L. Rev. 89 (1986).

[8] 355 U.S. 220 (1957). *See* § 20[b], *supra* for a discussion of *McGee*. It is no accident that

Brennan determined that the dispute between the parties arose directly out of a "contract that had a *substantial* connection" with Florida.

Next he rejected the Court of Appeals' argument that the Michigan district office was the embodiment of Burger King for Rudzewicz and that his dealings with the district office gave him no reason to expect to be sued in Miami. That conclusion, wrote Justice Brennan, ignored substantial record evidence showing that Rudzewicz knew that the real decision–making power was in Miami and that the Michigan office was merely a conduit.

In the final portion of the contacts analysis, Justice Brennan turned his attention to the choice–of–law clause, which the court of appeals had held irrelevant to the jurisdictional analysis. The lower court's ruling was not surprising given the Supreme Court's holdings in several recent cases that the forum's ability to apply its own law to a dispute was neither a necessary nor a sufficient condition for it to exercise adjudicatory jurisdiction.[9] Justice Brennan, however, distinguished between the relevance of choice–of–law analysis, on the one hand, and a choice–of–law clause, on the other. Choice–of–law analysis, which considers all elements of the case, might have little import for the issue of jurisdiction, which focuses on the defendant's purposeful connection to the forum. But a choice–of–law clause, the opinion argued, is relevant because it shows that the defendant has "purposefully invoked the benefits and protections" of forum law and that he could reasonably foresee litigation in the forum.

The first argument is very weak because the function of the clause, inserted by Burger King, was to "protect" and "benefit" the franchisor — not its franchisees.[10] The second point, however, does make some sense; a franchisee who signs a contract calling for the application of Florida law should foresee the possibility of litigation in Florida.

After his lengthy treatment of the contacts test, Justice Brennan dealt only briefly with the fairness analysis. Rudzewicz was not able to show that Florida had no interest in hearing the case, nor that litigation in Florida was so inconvenient for him that it impaired his ability to defend the law suit. Further, Justice Brennan rejected the Court of Appeals' conclusion

---

Burger King and *McGee* — both contracts cases — involve expansive views of state–court jurisdiction. Because contractual transactions involve planning that is absent in tort cases, it makes sense for the contract cases to produce more liberal jurisdictional rulings. For more on jurisdiction in contract cases, see Martin Louis, *Jurisdiction Over Those Who Breach Their Contracts: The Lessons of Burger King*, 72 N.C. L. Rev. 55 (1993).

[9] *See, e.g.*, World–Wide Volkswagen v. Woodson, 444 U.S. 286 (1980) (the fact that Oklahoma law would apply did not guarantee that Oklahoma would have jurisdiction); Keeton v. Hustler Magazine, Inc., 465 U.S. 770 (1984)(New Hampshire had jurisdiction even though it might not be able to apply its own law). *World–Wide* and *Keeton* are treated in §§ 22 & 23, *supra*.

[10] It seems odd that *Burger King*, with its superior bargaining power, failed to insert a consent–to–jurisdiction clause as well. Professor Weintraub points out, however, that consent–to–jurisdiction clauses were forbidden by the Michigan Franchisee Investment Act, while choice–of–law clauses were not. *See* Weintraub 167. Justice Brennan's ingenious but perhaps disingenuous use of the choice–of–law clause allowed *Burger King* to accomplish indirectly what it could not have done directly.

that *Burger King* used its superior bargaining power to victimize the franchisees via an adhesion contract. He pointed out that Rudzewicz, an experienced accountant himself, had advice of counsel throughout his dealings with Burger King, and that, by dint of able negotiating, he was able to secure modest concessions from Burger King.

The majority's fairness analysis provoked a strong dissent by Justice Stevens and Justice White who adopted a portion of the Court of Appeals' opinion. That opinion, emphasizing Rudzewicz's extensive dealings with the Michigan district office and limited contact with the Miami headquarters, had concluded that Rudzewicz had reason to anticipate litigation in Michigan, not Florida. Further it found the franchisees were unready for the added cost of litigation away from home:

> [The] typical franchise store is a local concern serving at best a neighborhood or community. Neither the revenues of a local business nor the geographical range of its market prepares the average franchise owner for the cost of distant litigation.

Finally, the opinion cited the "characteristic disparity of bargaining power" between franchisors and franchisees, which can be used to impose adhesion contracts that impair the franchisee's ability to defend a lawsuit away from home.[11]

§ 27 *Asahi Metal Industry Co. Ltd. v. Superior Court*[1]

Gary Zurcher and his wife, Ruth Ann Moreno, were riding on Zurcher's motorcycle in California when he lost control and the bike collided with a tractor; Zurcher was injured, and Moreno was killed. Alleging that a sudden deflation of the motorcycle's rear tire caused the collision, Zurcher and his children brought a product liability claim in California against Cheng Shin,

---

[11] The Court of Appeals and Justices Stevens and White were concerned that the majority's holding would result in oppressive contract clauses imposed on powerless litigants — consumers and franchisees — by their more powerful opponents — mail order sellers and franchisors. The concern about such clauses being used against mail order consumers has been termed "the mail order specter;" it is discussed in detail in Casad & Richman § 8-1[2][b]. In response, to the dissent, the majority pointed out that:

> jurisdiction may not be grounded on a contract whose terms have been obtained through "fraud, undue influence, or overweening bargaining power" and whose application would render litigation "so gravely difficult and inconvenient that [a party] will for all practical purposes be deprived of his day in court."

After the holding in *Burger King*, however, it seems clear that special jurisdictional protection for the powerless litigant may be limited to mere small fry, such as mail order consumers. After *Carnival Cruise Lines v. Shute*, 111 S. Ct. 39 (1991), it may not exist at all. *See* William M. Richman, *Carnival Cruise Lines and Forum–Selection Clauses in Adhesion Contracts,* 40 Am. J. Comp. L. 977 (1993).

[1] 480 U.S. 102 (1987). For Commentary on *Asahi*, *see* Mollie A. Murphy, *Personal Jurisdiction and the Stream of Commerce: A Reappraisal and a Revised Approach*, 77 Ky. L.J. 243 (1989); Symposium, 39 S.C.L. Rev. 729–896 (1988) (articles by Professors Howard Stravitz, Mark Weber, and Gregory Gelfand), William Van Dercreek, *Jurisdiction over the Person — the Progeny of Pennoyer and the Future of Asahi*, 13 Nova L. Rev. 1287 (1989); Bruce M. Morton, *Contacts, Fairness and State Interests: Personal Jurisdiction After Asahi*, 9 Pace L. Rev. 451 (1989).

the Taiwanese manufacturer of the tire tube and several other defendants. Cheng Shin then impleaded Asahi, the Japanese manufacturer of the tube's valve, seeking indemnification. Asahi moved to quash service, arguing that California lacked personal jurisdiction over it.

The trial court denied the motion based on the following information about Asahi's contacts with Cheng Shin and California: Asahi sold between 100,000 and 500,000 valves annually to Cheng Shin, those sales accounting for a very small percentage of Asahi's income. A survey of one California motorcycle shop conducted by counsel for Cheng Shin revealed that about 20 per cent of the tire valves were manufactured by Asahi. Further, a representative of Cheng Shin's maintained in an affidavit that he had told representatives of Asahi that Cheng Shin tires containing Asahi valves were sold in California. The president of Asahi, however, weighed in with an affidavit of his own declaring that Asahi "never contemplated that its limited sales . . . to Cheng Shin in Taiwan would subject it to lawsuits in California."

While the case proceeded through the California courts, plaintiffs settled their claims, leaving only the claims among the original defendants and Asahi. Ultimately the Supreme Court of California upheld the trial court's jurisdiction over Asahi.

[a] The Reasonableness Analysis

In a troubling trio of opinions, the United States Supreme Court reversed. Eight of the justices agreed that California's exercise of jurisdiction failed the fairness or reasonableness step of the Court's two–stage jurisdictional analysis.

As it had in *Burger King*, the Court enumerated the factors to be considered in the reasonableness calculus: the burden on the defendant, the interests of the forum state, the plaintiff's interest in a convenient forum, the interstate judicial system's interest in the efficient resolution of controversies, and the shared interest of the states in furthering fundamental substantive social policies.

Then the opinion, authored by Justice O'Connor, weighed the interests and found the exercise of jurisdiction unreasonable. First, the burden on Asahi was severe. It was an alien defendant, who must not only traverse the distance between Japan and California but also submit to a foreign nation's judicial system. Further, the interests of other nations and the federal government's interest in foreign relations counselled against burdening a foreign defendant unless the interests of the plaintiff and the forum were substantial.

The Court concluded they were not. The opinion discounted Cheng Shin's interest in a California forum because Cheng Shin had not demonstrated that California was a more convenient forum than Taiwan. Further, California's interest in the transaction was diminished because, after the settlement, the Californian was no longer a party.

The Court's reasonableness holding breaks new ground. Since *World–Wide*, the Court has been committed to the two–step jurisdictional test: minimum contacts plus fairness or reasonableness. Further, dictum in *Burger King* suggested that "fair play and substantial justice" may defeat the reasonableness of jurisdiction even if the defendant has purposefully engaged in forum activities. Until *Asahi*, however, the Supreme Court had never *held* that an exercise of jurisdiction could fail the reasonableness test even though defendant had minimum contacts with the forum.[2]

Although not controversial within the Court, the reasonableness holding nevertheless is questionable. Its problems stem from the Court's heavy reliance on the settlement of the claims of the dead and injured Californians, leaving only Cheng Shin's indemnity claim against Asahi. First, the Court's use of the settlement to discount Cheng Shin's interest in a California forum seems inconsistent with the holding in *Keeton v. Hustler Magazine*[3] that plaintiff's (now Chen Shin) lack of residence in the forum will not defeat jurisdiction established on the basis of defendant's contacts.[4]

Second, the opinion's reliance on the settlement to minimize California's interest in exercising jurisdiction is misplaced. The Supreme Court of California had argued that exercising jurisdiction over Asahi would advance California's strong interest in deterring the flow of defective component parts into the state. Justice O'Connor countered, arguing that asserting jurisdiction over the final–product manufacturer would accomplish the same result:

> The possibility of being haled into a California court as a result of an accident involving Asahi's components undoubtedly creates an additional deterrent to the manufacture of unsafe components; however, similar pressures will be placed on Asahi by the purchasers of its components as long as those who use Asahi components in their final products, and sell those products in California, are subject to the application of California tort law.

The argument, like other recent efforts of the Court relying on economic analysis of law,[5] is conclusory. It may well be that Asahi's customers who

---

[2] Some commentators argue that it is unwise to insist on a separate reasonableness inquiry once the contacts test is passed. The fairness holding of *Asahi*, they argue, will produce more litigation on the threshold issue of jurisdiction. Further, the reasonableness test merely duplicates at the constitutional level an inquiry mandated under state law by the doctrine of forum non conveniens. Weintraub 173, Linda Silberman, *"Two Cheers" for International Shoe (and None for Asahi): An Essay on the Fiftieth Anniversary of International Shoe*, 28 U. C. Davis L. Rev. 755 (1995). *But see* Courtland H. Peterson, *Jurisdiction and Choice of Law Restated*, 59 U. Colo. L. Rev. 37, 50 (1988).

[3] 465 U.S. 770 (1984), discussed in § 23, *supra*.

[4] *See* Earl M. Maltz, *Unraveling the Conundrum of the Law of Personal Jurisdiction: A Comment on Asahi Metal Industry Co., Ltd. v. Superior Court of California*, 1987 Duke L. J. 669, 686.

[5] *See, e.g., Carnival Cruise Lines v. Shute*, 111 S.Ct. 1522 (1991); William M. Richman, *Carnival Cruise Lines and Forum Selection Clauses in Adhesion Contracts,* 40 Am. J. Comp. L. 977 (1993). The Court upheld a forum–selection clause in an adhesion contract (a ticket for passage on a cruise ship) relying in part on the financial benefit of the clause to the cruise line. The opinion concluded quite superficially that "it stands to reason" that the cruise line's savings would be passed on to passengers in the form of lower prices.

are subject to the adjudicatory and legislative jurisdiction of California will be able to force Asahi to make higher quality parts, but merely saying it does not make it so. To rely confidently on that argument, the Court would need to know more about the relative bargaining strength of Asahi and its customers, the availability to those customers of alternative suppliers, and Asahi's willingness to agree to a lower price in return for its customer's willingness to shoulder the entire risk of California litigation. Absent information about the economic realities, it makes little sense to rely on Asahi's customers to exert "similar pressures" on Asahi.

Finally, the Court's reliance on the settlement gives the wrong message to finished–product manufacturers sued by American consumers. On the one hand, if the finished–product manufacturer does not settle with the American consumer, then the consumer's liability claim and the finished–product manufacturer's indemnity claim against the component part maker both will be decided in an American forum. On the other hand, if the finished–product manufacturer does settle, *Asahi* means that the indemnity claim probably will not be decided in the same American forum as the consumer's liability claim. With the indemnity claim relegated to a foreign forum, the finished–product maker might well suffer from inconsistent results, particularly if the foreign forum's law is less favorable to product liability claims. Thus *Asahi* gives the finished–product maker a strong incentive *not to settle* with the injured American consumer[6] — certainly not the result we seek from the law of jurisdiction.

[b] The Contacts Analysis

While the reasonableness test produced near unanimity[7] on the Court, the contacts test generated three opinions and no majority on the stream of commerce issue. Originating in several influential state court opinions,[8] the stream of commerce test upholds jurisdiction in products liability actions over everyone (manufacturer, wholesaler, retailer) who participates in the chain of distribution that brings the product into the state. In *World-Wide Volkswagen v. Woodson*,[9] the Supreme Court added an important limitation: while a state may exercise jurisdiction over everyone in the chain if the product is purchased by the consumer *in the state*, jurisdiction might not exist when the chain ends outside the forum and the product enters the state as a result of the foreseeable action of a consumer who purchased it elsewhere.

In *Asahi*, Justice O'Connor, writing for a four–Justice plurality, urged yet another and tighter limitation on the theory. There must be some act

[6] *See* David E. Seidelson, *A Supreme Court Conclusion and Two Rationales That Defy Comprehension*, 53 Brooklyn L. Rev. 563, 584 (1987).

[7] Only Justice Scalia did not join in the fairness analysis, presumably because he thought it unnecessary given his view (expressed in Justice O'Connor's plurality opinion) that jurisdiction over Asahi failed the contacts test.

[8] *See, e.g.*, Grey v. American Radiator & Standard Sanitary Corp., 22 Ill. 2d 432, 176 N.E.2d 761 (1961). The theory is also discussed in § 37[g], *infra*.

[9] 444 U.S. 286 (1980). The case is discussed in § 22, *supra*.

by the defendant, she wrote, that is "purposefully directed" at the forum. The mere act of placing a product into the stream of commerce is not enough, even if the defendant was aware that the stream would carry the product into the forum. The opinion went on to indicate what other contacts might be sufficient to show purposeful direction:

> Additional conduct of the defendant may indicate an intent or purpose to serve the market in the forum State, for example, designing the product for the market in the forum State, advertising in the forum State, establishing channels for providing regular advice to customers in the forum State, or marketing the product through a distributor who has agreed to serve as the sales agent in the forum State. But a defendant's awareness that the stream of commerce may or will sweep the product into the forum State does not convert the mere act of placing the product into the stream into an act purposefully directed toward the forum State.

Since Asahi had not engaged in any of these additional activities, Justice O'Connor concluded that jurisdiction over Asahi did not pass her reformulation of the stream of commerce test.

Justice Brennan, writing for another plurality of four, disagreed sharply. He rejected Justice O'Connor's requirement of "additional conduct," maintaining instead that the manufacturer's awareness of its product's ultimate destination should be sufficient.

> I see no need for . . . a showing [of additional conduct]. . . . The stream of commerce refers not to unpredictable currents or eddies, but to the regular and anticipated flow of products from manufacturer to distribution to retail sale. As long as a participant in this process is aware that the final product is being marketed in the forum State, the possibility of a lawsuit there cannot come as a surprise. Nor will the litigation present a burden for which there is no corresponding benefit.

That corresponding benefit (profit from the eventual sale in the forum), it can be argued, accrues to the manufacturer whether it merely relies on the stream of commerce or more actively engages in "additional conduct." Because the manufacturer's benefit does not depend upon the existence of "additional conduct" its amenability in the forum should not either.

Justice Stevens joined neither plurality on the stream of commerce issue. Because jurisdiction over Asahi failed the fairness or reasonableness step, there was no need, he wrote, to reach a conclusion on the contacts step. Accordingly, he expressed no opinion on whether the manufacturer's "mere awareness" of the product's destination was sufficient or whether instead "additional conduct" was necessary.

Stevens did argue, however, that Justice O'Connor had misapplied her own standard. Asahi's conduct had exceeded "mere awareness" that its products would reach the California market. In his words, "Asahi [in its dealings with Cheng Shin] has arguably engaged in a higher quantum of conduct than '[t]he placement of a product into the stream of commerce, without more. . . .' " He was not prepared to say whether Asahi's conduct amounted to "purposeful availment;" that issue would turn on "the volume, the value and the hazardous character of the components" sent to California. He did acknowledge, however, that in most cases, "a regular course of dealing that results in deliveries of over 100,000 units annually over . . . several years would constitute purposeful availment."[10]

Justice O'Connor's reformulation of the stream of commerce theory is extremely troubling.[11] To appreciate fully the harmful potential of her view, it is important to note that the stream of commerce test applies at the contacts stage of the analysis — not at the fairness stage. At the contacts stage, Zurcher's settlement — so important to the fairness analysis — would be irrelevant. Thus, in *Asahi*, Justice O'Connor's version of the stream of commerce test would have required dismissal not only of Cheng Shin's indemnity claim but also of any direct products liability claim by Zurcher against Asahi. Further, the type of distribution chain in *Asahi* is not at all unusual in our economy. Very often, the component part manufacturer has not engaged in any "additional conduct" beyond selling to a finished–product maker, knowing full well that the latter would ship the product into the forum.[12]

Were Justice O'Connor's view to prevail, consumers often would not be able to sue foreign component–part makers in an American forum. Typically they would be able, of course, to obtain jurisdiction over downstream actors such as finished–product manufacturers, wholesalers, and retailers; and often that would be enough. In some cases, however, the component–part maker might be the only deep pocket or the only defendant with adequate insurance. In those cases, Justice O'Connor's reformulation of the stream of commerce test would deprive the American consumer of an American forum, which, in many cases, would be tantamount to depriving the consumer of *any* forum. It would, in other words, take us back to the pre–*International Shoe* period when an out–of–state businesses could reap substantial financial rewards from the sales of its products in the forum and yet remain beyond the reach of the forum's jurisdiction in products liability claims by injured forum residents. Indeed, one commentator has referred to Justice O'Connor's specification of "additional conduct" as simply "a primer for a non–resident defendant seeking to enjoy economic benefits of a forum state's market while retaining immunity from jurisdiction in the state."[13] About the best thing to be said for Justice O'Connor's view is that it is not the law.

---

[10] For discussion of Justice Stevens' brief opinion, *see* R. Lawrence Dessem, *Personal Jurisdiction After Asahi: The Other (International) Shoe Drops*, 55 Tenn. L. Rev. 41, 74–77 (1987).

[11] The arguments that follow are developed in greater detail in Weintraub 176–179. See also Christine Wiseman, *Reconstructing the Citadel: The Advent of Jurisdictional Privity*, 54 Ohio St. L.J. 403 (1993).

[12] Note also her analysis seemingly applies to foreign manufacturers of *finished products* who sell to wholesalers or distributors but who do not engage in "additional conduct" and who exert no control over the subsequent downstream course of the product.

[13] *See* Seidelson, *supra* note 6, at 578.

Part D

BASES FOR JURISDICTION

Part C of this Chapter dealt with the constitutional restrictions on the territorial jurisdiction of the American courts. The United States Constitution, however, is not the only source of law governing the jurisdiction of state courts. The mere fact that an exercise of jurisdiction does not violate the Due Process Clause does not mean that it is permissible. A state court can exercise jurisdiction only if state law (decisional or statutory) gives it the authority to do so.

Traditionally, state decisional law has authorized jurisdiction when (1) the defendant is served with process while present within the state's territory, (2) the defendant is a domiciliary of the state, or (3) the defendant consents to the state's exercise of jurisdiction. These three relationships between the defendant and the forum state, referred to as traditional bases for jurisdiction, are treated in §§ 28–30. Sections 31 and 32 deal with bases for jurisdiction over business entities. After *International Shoe Co. v. Washington*,[1] all states enacted statutes that extended their courts' jurisdiction beyond the traditional bases toward the constitutional limits. These provisions, known as long–arm statutes, are treated in § 33.

§ 28 Personal Service Within the State

[a] Basics

The oldest and most common way of acquiring personal jurisdiction over a natural person is by serving him with process within the state.[1] Because service of process also gives defendant constitutionally adequate notice, the notice–giving and jurisdiction–creating functions of service should be distinguished at the outset. Personal service gives notice no matter where accomplished, but it serves as a jurisdictional basis only if it is accomplished *within the state*. Thus, service from a California court upon a New York defendant vacationing in Mexico gives perfectly adequate notice, but it may not be used as a jurisdictional basis; to perform that function, service must be accomplished in California.

Another important point to bear in mind is that service of process is a basis for *general*[2] jurisdiction. That means that it serves as a jurisdictional basis for any claim against the defendant — even one that has no relationship to the forum state or defendant's transitory presence and receipt of process there. Suppose, for instance, a California defendant injures a New

[1] 326 U.S. 310 (1945), discussed in § 20[a], *supra*.

[1] Weintraub § 4.10; Leflar, McDougal & Felix § 27.

[2] *See* § 25, *supra*, and § 37[b], *infra*, for a more complete explanation of the term.

York plaintiff in an automobile collision in California. If the defendant later visits New York and is served with process there, New York will have personal jurisdiction over the defendant, even though his visit to New York was completely unrelated to the plaintiff's claim.

[b] History: *Pennoyer, International Shoe*, and *Shaffer*

The remote historical background of service as a jurisdictional basis is a matter of some dispute. The predominant view (espoused by Justice Story) is that service has respectable English antecedents. Originally, the English courts exercised jurisdiction over a defendant by arresting him on the writ of *capias ad respondendum*;[3] service of process, where the sheriff is physically situated to seize the defendant, is the modern and civilized analogue of the arrest. More modern scholars have argued vigorously to the contrary — that service alone was never a sufficient jurisdictional basis in England.[4] Also a subject of debate is the status of transient service in 1868, when the Fourteenth Amendment was adopted.

If the remote history of service as a jurisdictional predicate is controversial, its recent history is clear. In *Pennoyer v. Neff*,[5] the Supreme Court adopted the territorial theory of jurisdiction which held that "every State possesses exclusive jurisdiction and sovereignty over persons and property within its territory" and "no State can exercise direct jurisdiction . . . over persons or property without its territory."

Translated into practice, the territorial theory meant that personal service within the state was always a *sufficient* condition for the exercise of personal jurisdiction and, absent defendant's consent or appearance, it was a *necessary* condition as well. In other words, the state could *always* exercise personal jurisdiction over anyone who could be served within its borders, and it could exercise jurisdiction *only* over people who could be so served.

The consequences of the second branch of the rule were out of step with the expansion of interstate commerce and travel that occurred in the first half of the twentieth century. Thus, the Supreme Court jettisoned it in *International Shoe Co. v. Washington*, requiring only that a non–present defendant have "certain minimum contacts with [the state] . . . such that maintenance of the suit does not offend 'traditional notions of fair play and substantial justice.' "[6]

The first branch of the rule — maintaining service of process as a *sufficient* basis for jurisdiction — however, survived the Supreme Court's opinion in *International Shoe*. In 1977, however, it too seemed imperiled by the Court's grand dictum in *Shaffer v. Heitner*,[7] requiring that "all

[3] *See* Fleming James, Jr., Civil Procedure § 12.2 (1965).

[4] *See, e.g.*, Albert Ehrenzweig, *The Transient Rule of Personal Jurisdiction: The "Power" Myth and Forum Conveniens*, 65 Yale L.J. 289 (1956).

[5] 95 U.S. 714 (1878). *See* § 17, *supra* for a more complete discussion of the theory.

[6] 326 U.S. 310 (1945). The decision is discussed in detail in § 20[a], *supra*.

[7] 433 U.S. 186 (1977). The decision is discussed in § 21, *supra*, and § 44, *infra*.

assertions of state–court jurisdiction . . . be evaluated according to the standards set forth in *International Shoe*. . . ." Based on *Shaffer*, many commentators urged and predicted the demise of service of process as a sufficient jurisdictional basis.[8]

[c] *Burnham v. Superior Court*[9]

The Supreme Court in *Burnham v. Superior Court* opted to resuscitate the doctrine instead. Desiring to separate, Dennis and Francie Burnham, a New Jersey couple, agreed in July of 1987 that Francie would take custody of their two children and move to California. They also agreed that she would file for divorce on grounds of irreconcilable differences. In October, Dennis filed for divorce in New Jersey on the grounds of desertion. After demanding unsuccessfully that Dennis honor the agreement to submit to an "irreconcilable differences" divorce, Francie sued Dennis for divorce in California in January of 1988.

In late January Dennis made a business trip to southern California and then went north to visit his children in the San Francisco Bay area, where Francie lived. During that visit he was served with process in Francie's California divorce action. Dennis made a special appearance and moved to quash service on the ground that California lacked personal jurisdiction over him. The trial court denied the motion, and the appellate court denied Dennis' petition for mandamus.

The Supreme Court affirmed unanimously, holding that service of process was an adequate basis for general jurisdiction. The Justices split hopelessly, however, on the rationale. One group of four,[10] led by Justice Scalia, relied on the historical pedigree of jurisdiction based on transient personal service; another,[11] led by Justice Brennan, relied on the current fairness of the practice. Complicating matters further, each group emphatically rejected the other's rationale, and Justice White and Stevens each wrote short separate opinions.

[d] Justice Scalia and Historical Pedigree

Justice Scalia began by surveying the history of service of process as a jurisdictional basis from the eighteenth century to the present, finding the rule well–supported by cases and commentators. Further he found no cases

[8] *See, e.g.*, David H. Vernon, *Single–Factor Bases of In Personam Jurisdiction — A Speculation on the Impact of Shaffer v. Heitner*, 1978 Wash. U. L.Q. 273, 303. A few of the lower courts agreed that jurisdiction based on transient service could not survive after *Shaffer*; most, however, continued to uphold it as a constitutionally adequate basis for jurisdiction. The cases are noted in Casad & Richman § 2-4[a] at note 160.

[9] 495 U.S. 604 (1990). *Burnham* has produced a wealth of scholarly comment. *See, e.g., The Future of Personal Jurisdiction: a Symposium on Burnham v. Superior Court*, 22 Rutgers L. J. 559–699 (1991)(articles by Professors Lea Brilmayer, Linda Silberman, Allan R. Stein, Terry S. Kogan, Mary Twitchell, Martin H. Redish, Russell J. Weintraub, and Earl M. Maltz).

[10] Justices Scalia, Rehnquist, Kennedy, and White.

[11] Justices Brennan, O'Connor, Marshall, and Blackmun.

or traditional commentary that rejected the doctrine. Finally, he concluded that the rule remained in practice in nearly all federal and state courts.[12]

He next addressed the argument that the jurisdictional revolution of *International Shoe* required the rejection of service of process as a jurisdictional basis. That revolution, based on modern advances in travel and communications, had established that service of process was not a necessary condition for jurisdiction (long–arm bases were adequate); it did not follow, he argued, that service was no longer a sufficient condition for jurisdiction.[13] Revealing his complete dependence on historical pedigree, Justice Scalia observed:

> The short of the matter is that jurisdiction based on physical presence alone constitutes due process because it is one of the continuing traditions of our legal system that define the due process standard of "traditional notions of fair play and substantial justice." That standard was developed by *analogy* to "physical presence," and it would be perverse to say it could now be turned against that touch–stone of jurisdiction.

Relying so heavily on tradition, Justice Scalia found *Shaffer v. Heitner* to be an uncomfortable precedent. In *Shaffer*, the Court said that "all assertions of state–court jurisdiction must be evaluated according to the standards set forth in *International Shoe*" and that due process "can be as readily offended by the perpetuation of ancient forms that are no longer justified as by the adoption of new procedures." In the weakest part[14] of his opinion, Scalia attempted to avoid *Shaffer*'s difficult dicta. The "all assertions" language, he argued, needed to be seen in the context of the immediately preceding sentences concerning attachment jurisdiction. Based on context, he concluded that the "all assertions" passage should be read to say only that the minimum contact requirement applied to attachment (quasi–in–rem) jurisdiction as well as personal jurisdiction.[15] He then turned to the "perpetuation of ancient forms" passage and concluded that *Shaffer* might invalidate the "ancient form" if it were followed by only a

---

[12] He allowed for a few exceptions — those cases that had held the practice unconstitutional after the Court's decision in Shaffer v. Heitner. *See, e.g.*, Nehemiah v. Athletics Congress of the USA, 765 F.2d 42 (3d Cir. 1985); Duehring v. Vasquez, 490 So.2d 667 (La. App. 1986). For commentary on the role of tradition in the jurisprudence of jurisdiction, see James Weinstein, *The Early American Origins of Territoriality in Judicial Jurisdiction*, 37 St Louis U. L. J. 1 (1992); L. Benjamin Young, *Justice Scalia's History and Tradition: the Chief Nightmare in Professor Tribes Anxiety Closet*, 78 Va. L. Rev. 581 (1992).

[13] Quoting from the Court's opinion in *International Shoe*, he added that the requirement of minimum contacts applied only when the defendant "be not present within the territory of the forum." For a sympathetic evaluation of this portion of the opinion, *see* Earl M. Maltz, *Personal Jurisdiction and Constitutional Theory — A Comment on Burnham v. Superior Court*, 22 Rutgers L.J. 689, 695 (1991).

[14] In this portion of his opinion, Justice Scalia wrote only for three of his colleagues; Justice White did not concur in Scalia's remarks on *Shaffer*.

[15] For commentary critical of Justice Scalia's "disingenuous" distinction of *Shaffer*, *see* Martin H. Redish, *Tradition, Fairness and Personal Jurisdiction; Due Process and Constitutional Theory After Burnham v. Superior Court*, 22 Rutgers L.J. 675, 680 (1991).

few states but could not be used to invalidate a practice that "is both firmly approved by tradition and still favored" in all the states.[16]

While not casting doubt upon the holding of *Shaffer*,[17] Scalia did acknowledge that its basic approach was different from his own. Although *Shaffer* conducted an independent inquiry into the fairness of attachment jurisdiction, that was not necessary for service of process; "its validation is its pedigree, as the phrase '*traditional notions* of fair play and substantial justice' makes clear."

[e] Justice Brennan and Contemporary Notions of Due Process

Justice Brennan, writing for Justices Marshall, Blackmun and O'Connor, concurred only in the result. Preliminarily, he rejected Justice Scalia's reading of the history of service of process; he found it "a stranger to the common law" and "rather weekly implanted in American jurisprudence" at the time of the adoption of the Fourteenth Amendment. More important, he disagreed with Justice Scalia on the *role* of history in the due process inquiry. The Court's decisions in *International Shoe* and *Shaffer v. Heitner* precluded justification of any jurisdictional practice purely by historical pedigree: "The critical insight of *Shaffer* is that all rules of jurisdiction, even ancient ones, must satisfy contemporary notions of due process. . . ."[18] Accordingly, he undertook the independent inquiry into the fairness of transient jurisdiction that Scalia had thought unnecessary.

Based on expectations, benefits, and convenience, Justice Brennan concluded that service of process satisfied contemporary notions of due process. First, a defendant who ventures into the forum has assumed the foreseeable risk that it may exercise jurisdiction over him. Despite the confusion about the remote history of service of process, the recent history — the fact that American courts have followed the rule for a century —

---

[16] There is an arguable distinction between attachment jurisdiction and personal jurisdiction based on service of process, but that distinction works against Justice Scalia's view rather than for it. The practice that *Shaffer* struck down is in one respect more defensible than the one Scalia sought to uphold. Defendant's ownership of some types of property in the forum often indicates a more substantial affiliation with that state than does temporary personal presence there. *See* Bruce Posnak, *A Uniform Approach to Judicial Jurisdiction After World-Wide and the Abolition of the "Gotcha" Theory*, 30 Emory L.J. 729, 745–746 (1981). Further attachment jurisdiction jeopardizes only one piece of defendant's property, while transient jurisdiction — since it can result in a personal judgment — threatens all of defendant's property in every state.

[17] For a discussion of whether *Burnham* overrules, or at least undermines, *Shaffer*, *see* Russell J. Weintraub, *An Objective Basis for Rejecting Transient Jurisdiction*, 22 Rutgers L.J. 611 (1991).

[18] The disagreement between Justices Scalia and Brennan on the role of history and tradition as opposed to contemporary mores in the due process calculation is not limited to the context of personal jurisdiction. *See, e.g.*, Michael H. v. Gerald D., 491 U.S. 110 (1989) (traditional versus contemporary views of the conflicting parental rights of wife's adulterous lover (child's biological father) and wife's husband with respect to a child born to wife during the marriage).

provides a defendant with notice that he is subject to service while in the forum.[19]

Further, the defendant who visits the forum receives the benefits and protections of its laws. His health and safety are protected by state and local fire, police, and medical services. He is able to use state highways and waterways, benefits from the state's economy, and has access to the state's courts. These benefits make it fair for the defendant to be held amenable to service of process in the state.

Finally, Justice Brennan argued, the burdens on a transient defendant are minimal. The defendant's one visit to the forum (when he was served there) shows that travel to the forum and defense of a lawsuit there would not be "prohibitively inconvenient." Likewise, modern procedural devices could be used to diminish any inconveniences that do occur.[20]

[f] Justice Scalia's Rejoinder

Just as Justice Brennan rejected Justice Scalia's pedigree argument, Justice Scalia returned the favor and responded convincingly to Justice Brennan's fairness arguments. He had two general objections to the use of contemporary notions of due process as the constitutional yardstick. First, the test is wholly subjective and relies on each judge's idiosyncratic view of fairness.[21] Second, it is extremely fact–specific and requires a separate balance of a plethora of fairness factors (benefits, burdens, procedural conveniences, length of stay, purpose of visit, etc.) in every case.

Next Justice Scalia turned to Justice Brennan's specific fairness arguments. The "benefits and burdens" rationale was an easy mark:

> Three days' worth of these benefits . . . [are] powerfully inadequate to establish . . . that it is "fair" for California to decree the ownership of all of Mr. Burnham's worldly goods acquired during the ten years of his marriage, and the custody of his children.

Adding the "modern procedural devices" rationale to the "benefits and burdens" justification did not help much. Scalia found both vulnerable to a powerful *reductio ad absurdum* attack. He pointed out that those arguments justified jurisdiction over Mr. Burnham *whether he was served with*

---

[19] Brennan's "expectations" argument is quite problematic. It is not at all clear that ordinary people (like Dennis Burnham) have any expectations at all about what will and will not render them amenable. The literature on personal jurisdiction reveals not a shred of evidence one way or the other. *See* Vernon, Weinberg, Reynolds & Richman 121. Further, the argument is circular. "A defendant will expect to be subjected to jurisdiction where the Supreme Court says she is amenable to jurisdiction." Allan Stein, *Burnham and the Death of Theory in the Law of Personal Jurisdiction*, 22 Rutgers L.J. 597, 604–605 (1991). It makes no sense then to use those Supreme Court–generated expectations to justify the Supreme Court's decision.

[20] Justice Brennan had in mind Fed. R. Civ. P. 12(b)(6) and 56, which permit prompt dismissal of frivolous claims; discovery devices, which permit long distance discovery and limit discovery abuse; and federal and state transfer and forum non–conveniens doctrines, which provide for change of venue to a more convenient forum.

[21] *But see* Russell J. Weintraub, *An Objective Basis for Rejecting Transient Jurisdiction*, 22 Rutgers L.J. 611 (1991)(arguing that civil law traditions and international law provided *objective* grounds for rejection of the transient service rule).

process in California or not. But in that case, they proved too much, since it was obvious that California could not have exercised general jurisdiction over Mr. Burnham if he had not been served with process there.

Justice Scalia did approve of one of Justice Brennan's "fairness" arguments. He acknowledged that a transient defendant does have a reasonable expectation that travelling through the forum subjects him to the risk service of process and, thus, general jurisdiction. He denied, however, that the "reasonable expectation" rationale was really based on fairness. Instead it was based on tradition or pedigree "masquerading as 'fairness.' "

> The only reason for charging Mr. Burnham with the reasonable expectation of being subject to suit is that the States . . . have always asserted . . . jurisdiction over the person by serving him with process during his temporary presence in their territory. . . . Justice Brennan's long journey is a circular one, leaving him, at the end of the day, in complete reliance on the very factor [tradition] he sought to avoid. . . .

[g] Justice White[22]

Justice White's odd little opinion contains less than 250 words but, nevertheless, raises several interesting questions. He started out by concurring in Justice Scalia's "justification by pedigree" argument, but he did not concur in Scalia's attempt to distinguish *Shaffer*, nor in his attack on Justice Brennan's fairness arguments.

The major theme of his opinion, however, is the need in transient jurisdiction cases to avoid the "endless fact–specific litigation" of minimum contacts that now occurs in long–arm cases.[23] Accordingly, he adopted a "presumptive constitutionality" test. Jurisdiction based on service within the state is presumptively constitutional; unless the defendant can show that the rule is "arbitrary and lacking in common sense" in *most* cases, there is no need to consider the fairness of the practice in each defendant's *particular* case.[24]

[22] For commentary on Justice White's opinion, *see* Mary Twitchell, *Burnham and Constitutionally Permissible Levels of Harm*, 22 Rutgers L.J. 659 (1991).

[23] Commentators are split on the question of whether the administrative convenience of a bright–line rule in service–of–process cases is worth tolerating the occasional unfairness that may occur in unusual cases. *Compare* Linda Silberman, *Reflections on Burnham v. Superior Court: Toward Presumptive Rules of Jurisdiction and Implications for Choice of Law*, 22 Rutgers L.J. 569, 578, 583 (1991), Winton Woods, *Burnham v. Superior Court: New Wine, Old Bottles*, 13 Geo. Mason L. Rev. 199, 204 (1990), *with* Erwin Chemerinsky, *Assessing Minimum Contacts: A Reply to Professors Cameron and Johnson*, 28 U. C. Davis L. Rev. 863, 867 (1995), Mary Twitchel, *Burnham and Constitutionally Permissible Levels of Harm, supra*, note 22, at 672.

[24] Professor Hay argues that international cases may fit Justice White's test; an alien defendant might be able to show that tag jurisdiction is "arbitrary and lacking in common sense" in *most* cases involving aliens. *See* Peter Hay, *Transient Jurisdiction, Especially Over International Defendants: Critical Comments on Burnham v. Superior Court of California*, 1990 U. of Ill. L. Rev. 593.

One final facet of Justice White's opinion warrants mention. He limited his presumptively–constitutional approach to cases where the defendant's presence in the forum is intentional and thus eliminated a class of cases where jurisdiction based solely on service of process is most objectionable.[25]

[h] Justice Stevens: Easy Cases and Bad Law

In an extremely brief opinion Justice Stevens concurred in the result but refused to join either Justice Scalia or Justice Brennan because of their opinions' "unnecessarily broad reach." He did, however, ratify in part each of his colleagues' justifications for the rule of transient jurisdiction, concluding that:

> the historical evidence and consensus identified by Justice Scalia, the considerations of fairness identified by Justice Brennan, and the common sense displayed by Justice White, all combine to demonstrate that this is a very easy case.

In a footnote to the quoted passage, however, Justice Stevens revealed his reservations about the overbreadth of the other opinions and observed that easy cases, like hard ones, sometimes make bad law.[26]

[i] Evaluation and Prediction

There is something to admire in both of the major *Burnham* opinions; unfortunately, the admirable part of each opinion is the part that demolishes the rationale of the other.[27] Thus, Scalia was right when he poked fun at Brennan's benefits and burdens analysis. The "benefits" Mr. Burnham got from his brief stay in California are trivial in comparison to the burden of general jurisdiction. Further, Scalia was right to point out that the "modern procedural devices" argument is more an argument for nationwide jurisdiction generally than for jurisdiction based on service of process particularly. Finally, he probably was right when he pointed out that the "reasonable expectations" argument is just a tradition argument in disguise; and if it's not, it is surely circular. It makes little sense to rely on

[25] For years, Grace v. MacArthur, 170 F.Supp. 442 (E.D. Ark. 1959), has been the favorite bete noire of jurisdiction scholars; the court upheld jurisdiction over a defendant who was served with process while on a commercial airline flight over Arkansas. *Grace* may no longer be good law after *Burnham*. Probably, the Brennan group would not approve, and Justice White's insistence on "intentional" presence may disqualify cases like *Grace*. The result may hinge on what Justice White means by that legendary legal weasel–word.

[26] For an insightful evaluation of Justice Stevens' opinion, *see* Stanley E. Cox, *Would that Burnham Had Not Come to be Done Insane! A Critique of Recent Supreme Court Personal Jurisdiction Reasoning, An Explanation Why Transient Presence Jurisdiction is Unconstitutional, and Some Thoughts About Divorce Jurisdiction in a Minimum Contacts World*, 58 Tenn. L. Rev. 497, 531–537 (1991)(title only a bit shorter than Stevens' opinion).

[27] Also worth noting is that both opinions attempt to link the jurisprudence of jurisdiction to more general constitutional doctrine. Until *Burnham*, the Court had treated personal jurisdiction doctrine as an entity unto itself. *See* Patrick J. Borchers, *The Death of the Constitutional Law of Personal Jurisdiction: From Pennoyer to Burnham and Back Again*, 24 U.C. Davis L. Rev. 19 (1990).

expectations to justify the Court's decisions when those decisions are the basis for the expectation.

Similarly Justice Brennan's critiques of Justice Scalia's tradition–based arguments were right on target. The *International Shoe* and *Shaffer v. Heitner* opinions preclude the ratification of any jurisdictional practice on the basis of tradition or pedigree alone. Justice Scalia's attempts to distinguish *Shaffer* and explain away its dicta are petty, literal, and formalistic. To maintain that *Shaffer*'s "all assertions" passage referred only to attachment jurisdiction, and that the "perpetuation of ancient forms" passage applies only to procedures that are now unpopular among the states[28] is disingenuous and unprincipled.[29]

What remains, then, of *Burnham* is a clear holding — transient jurisdiction is constitutionally adequate — and two troubling rationales, each rejected by a Supreme Court majority. Perhaps, however, that is only the inevitable result of the Court's chronic inability to choose between a jurisprudence of jurisdiction based on territoriality and one based on fairness.

Muddled jurisdictional theory, however, is not the only unfortunate legacy of *Burnham*; the decision, combined with modern choice of law developments, may have a lamentable effect on jurisdictional practice as well. Modern choice of law theory, adopted by most states, is forum–favoring, and the Supreme Court has chosen to exert very little constitutional control over a state's ability to choose its own law. All that is required is "a significant contact or significant aggregation of contacts, creating state interests, such that the choice of its law is neither arbitrary nor fundamentally unfair."[30] In particular, the Court has held that the forum always can apply its own statute of limitations.[31]

Given these developments, the decision in *Burnham* presents plaintiffs with strong incentives and attractive opportunities to forum shop. *Burnham* holds that service is a basis for *general* jurisdiction; plaintiff's claim need not be related to defendant's presence in the forum. A plaintiff, therefore, with a stale claim or one disfavored by most states can simply lie in ambush for the defendant and "tag" him in *any* state with more favorable law.[32]

---

[28] The "current unpopularity" argument would have precluded not only the result in *Shaffer* (many states permitted attachment jurisdiction) but also the result in Mullane v. Central Hanover Bank and Trust, 339 U.S. 306 (1950), (notice by publication), D. H. Overmeyer v. Frick, 405 U.S. 174 (1972)(cognovit notes); Schroeder v. City of New York, 371 U.S. 208 (1962)(notice by posting of property).

[29] There is one clear distinction between *Burnham* and *Shaffer*, but it seems to work against Justice Scalia's view rather than for it. *See* note 16, *supra*.

[30] *See* Allstate Insurance Co. v. Hague, 449 U.S. 302 (1981). For a full discussion of *Allstate, see* § 97, *infra*.

[31] *See*, Sun Oil Company v. Wortman, 486 U.S. 717 (1988), discussed *infra*, in § 97.

[32] Two traditional defenses provide some protection for the ambushed defendant. Service of process does not confer jurisdiction if plaintiff has brought defendant into the forum by force or fraud; and defendants who enter the forum for certain reasons are immune from service. For discussion of these two doctrines, *see* § 48, *infra*.

This is hardly the sort of jurisdictional practice the Supreme Court should encourage.

Ironically, the questionable rationales and pernicious consequences of the Court's decision in *Burnham* were unnecessary, for the facts presented a plausible case for specific long–arm jurisdiction. Defendant agreed with his wife that she and the children should live in California and that he would submit to an "irreconcilable differences" divorce. He breached the agreement by suing for divorce based on desertion. He may also have engaged in fraud or at least overreaching to obtain his wife's consent to the agreement. His tortious conduct and breach of contract outside California therefore, arguably caused foreseeable injury inside California.[33]

§ 29 Domicile — Residence — Citizenship

Defendant's domicile within a state provides an adequate basis for the exercise of general jurisdiction.[1] If jurisdiction is based on domicile, the cause of action need not arise out of defendant's connection with the state; in other words, a defendant can be sued in his domicile upon any cause of action no matter where it arises. When domicile operates as a basis for general jurisdiction, the time to assess defendant's domicile is the time the action is commenced. Thus, if defendant had lived his entire life in Maryland, married and raised a family there, and moved only yesterday to Ohio, Maryland could not exercise general jurisdiction over him.

Domicile also can serve as a basis for specific jurisdiction however, and then the time to measure is the time the claim arose. Many state long–arm statutes, for example, use domicile as a basis for specific jurisdiction in domestic relations cases.[2] Thus, in the preceding example, if defendant's wife brings a support action against him in Maryland, jurisdiction will exist, but it will be specific jurisdiction limited to claims based on defendant's past actions in Maryland.

General jurisdiction based on domicile makes sense for the most part.[3] One justification relies on considerations of fairness. A defendant would find it difficult to argue that she is somehow denied "fair play and substantial justice" by being sued conveniently in her home state, which has an interest in her economic well being.[4] Jurisdiction based on domicile is also

[33] *See* Mary Twitchell, *Burnham and Constitutionally Permissible Levels of Harm*, 22 Rutgers L. J. 659 (1991). *But see* Kulko v. Superior Court, 436 U.S. 84 (1978)(rejecting specific long–arm jurisdiction in a case similar to *Burnham*). *Kulko* is discussed in § 127, *infra*.

[1] Milliken v. Meyer, 311 U.S. 457 (1940); Restatement (Second) of Conflict of Laws § 29 Casad & Richman § 2-4[2]. Domicile however, satisfies only the jurisdictional basis requirement; it does not satisfy the requirement of adequate notice. Thus, if defendant, a domiciliary of Texas, is absent from the state in Missouri, a Texas court may exercise personal jurisdiction over him; but if it employs an inadequate notification procedure (say publication), its judgment will be constitutionally invalid.

[2] *See, e.g.*, Ohio R. Civ. P. 4.3(A)(8).

[3] *See generally* Vernon, Weinberg, Reynolds & Richman 123–124; Lea Brilmayer, Jennifer Haverkamp, Buck Logan, Loretta Lynch, Steve Neuwirth and Jim O'Brien, *A General Look at General Jurisdiction*, 66 Tex. L. Rev. 721, 728–33 (1988).

[4] *See* Hall v. Hall, 585 S.W.2d 384 (Ky., 1979).

easy to justify based on the reciprocal rights and duties of the citizen and the state. If the citizen is entitled to the benefits and protections of the state's laws, one of her duties is to assist its administration of justice by answering its summons.[5] Finally, jurisdiction based on domicile has a justification based on necessity; there should always be some place where defendant is continuously amenable to suit on any cause of action.[6] Absent such a jurisdictional basis, a defendant might slip through the cracks of state long–arm statutes, avoid personal service, and thus leave plaintiff with no forum or only an inconvenient forum.[7]

Despite these arguments, technical rules about domicile occasionally make it an inappropriate basis for jurisdiction. Members of the armed services and prisoners, for example, usually do not choose where they will live;[8] relatively arbitrary rules assign them a domicile in a state where they may have very little current contact. It could be quite unfair for a state to exercise general jurisdiction in such circumstances.

Another troublesome situation involves a defendant who has left her home permanently but has not yet established a new one. Suppose a domiciliary of New York leaves the state with all her belongings to seek her fortune in the West. On the trip her car collides in Wyoming with one driven by another New Yorker. Some months later, while still wandering from one western state to another, and before settling on one as her new home, she is served with process from the New York court based on the Wyoming accident. Because she has not yet acquired a new domicile of choice,[9] her domicile remains in New York. New York will be able to exercise jurisdiction over her based on this technical domicile even though she has no present connection with the state and even though the cause of action arose outside the state.

It is tempting to conclude that general jurisdiction based on technical domicile is unconstitutional[10] — particularly after the Supreme Court's dictum in *Shaffer v. Heitner*[11] requiring all exercises of jurisdiction to pass the minimum contacts test. In *Burnham v. Superior Court*,[12] however, a plurality of the Supreme Court upheld transient service jurisdiction based on its historical pedigree alone; and that same historical argument might also be used to justify jurisdiction based on technical domicile.

---

[5] *See* Milliken v. Meyer, 311 U.S. 457 (1940); Blackmer v. United States, 284 U.S. 421 (1932).

[6] *See* Restatement (Second) of Conflict of Laws § 29 (comment a); Mary Twitchel, *The Myth of General Jurisdiction*, 101 Harv. L. Rev. 610, 631 (1988).

[7] Suppose, for instance, a suit by a Michigan plaintiff against an Ohio defendant based on a cause of action arising in California or Japan. The action would not be covered by the Ohio long–arm statute because the cause of action has nothing to do with Ohio. If the Michigan plaintiff cannot sue defendant in his domicile (the neighboring state of Ohio), she would be forced to litigate in California or abroad.

[8] *See* Restatement (Second) of Conflict of Laws (1986 Revisions) § 17 (comments b and c).

[9] *See* §§ 4 and 5, *supra*.

[10] *See, e.g.*, Weintraub §§ 2.15, 2.15A, 2.15B.

[11] 433 U.S. 186 (1977). *Shaffer* is discussed *infra* in § 44 and *supra* in § 21.

[12] 495 U.S. 604 (1990). For discussion of *Burnham*, *see* § 28, *supra*.

Residence is a weaker connecting factor than domicile because it does not require an intention to make a relatively permanent home. Furthermore, a person can have more than one residence, while she can have only one domicile. Nevertheless, residence suggests a connection between a person and a state that is often strong enough to support the exercise of personal jurisdiction. Although the Supreme Court has never passed on the question, commentators have argued, and state courts have typically held, that residence by itself provides a sufficient jurisdictional basis.[13]

Jurisdiction based on citizenship is a redundant notion as far as the states of the United States are concerned; a citizen of a state will always be a domiciliary of that state,[14] and jurisdiction can always be based on domicile. The situation is different with regard to the federal government because domicile in the United States is not required for American citizenship. Indeed, many United States citizens are domiciled abroad. Can the federal courts exercise judicial jurisdiction over such absentees based on their American citizenship? In *Blackmer v. United States*,[15] the Supreme Court, relying on the reciprocal obligations arising between a nation and its citizens, held that they could.

Citizenship or nationality as a jurisdictional basis comes up in one other context. Will courts in the United States enforce a judgment of a foreign nation which is based on defendant's citizenship or nationality? There is no constitutional compulsion that they do so, since the Full Faith and Credit Clause does not apply to foreign–nation judgments.[16] Nevertheless, courts typically do recognize and enforce the judgments of a foreign country against citizens of that country. Recognition may be refused, however in compelling circumstances — for instance, when defendant has been absent from her native land for many years and seeks to renounce her citizenship.[17]

§ 30 Appearance and Consent

[a] General Appearance

Suppose a Californian who has had no contact with Delaware is sued in that state. She has three options. She might choose to default, to appear specially to object to the court's jurisdiction, or to appear generally and litigate the action in Delaware. If she takes the last course, she has consented to the jurisdiction of the Delaware court; her general appearance,

[13] Restatement (Second) of Conflict of Laws § 30; the Restatement hedges its bet by stating that residence is an adequate jurisdictional basis unless the defendant's connection with the state is "so attenuated as to make exercise of such jurisdiction unreasonable."

[14] *See* Scoles, Hay, Borchers & Symeonides § 6.4.

[15] 284 U.S. 421 (1932).

[16] *See* § 112, *infra*, for a discussion of the recognition of foreign nation judgments by American courts.

[17] *See* Restatement (Second) of Conflict of Laws § 31, comment c, for a discussion of other factors which would prompt an American court to refuse to recognize a judgment of a foreign country against one of its citizens.

without any other contact with the state, is a sufficient basis for the exercise of general jurisdiction.[1] That means that the Delaware court can hear *any* claim against the defendant — even one that has no connection with Delaware.

What kinds of action by defendant constitute an appearance sufficient to grant judicial jurisdiction? First, it does not matter whether defendant appears personally or by an authorized attorney; she need not set foot in the courthouse or even in the state to appear and, therefore, consent. Second, *any* sort of participation in the action is *constitutionally* sufficient as a jurisdictional basis. The right to make a special appearance[2] — the right to appear for the sole purpose of objecting to the court's jurisdiction — is a right which must be granted, if at all, by the states.

The scope of the jurisdiction generated by an appearance is not entirely clear. Certainly there is jurisdiction over the defendant on the cause of action in which he appears, and it is equally certain that an appearance in one action is not a jurisdictional basis for a totally unrelated suit.[3] The troublesome case occurs when the defendant appears in an action, and plaintiff amends the complaint to add an additional claim.[4] The authorities divide on the question of whether defendant's appearance to defend the original action is an adequate jurisdictional basis for the claims added by the subsequent amendment.[5]

The concept of general appearance applies to plaintiffs, as well. Suppose a plaintiff having no connection with the forum state sues a defendant there, and defendant counterclaims against plaintiff. The forum has judicial jurisdiction over the plaintiff on the original claim as well as the counterclaim.[6] By resorting to the state's courts, plaintiff has supplied a reasonable basis for the state's exercise of jurisdiction. If the rule were otherwise, an out–of–state plaintiff would have a considerable advantage over in–state litigants because he could use the courts to press his own claims without fear of a counterclaim.

[b] Special Appearance[7]

Consider again the hypothetical California defendant sued in Delaware. Instead of making a general appearance, the defendant might choose simply

[1] Restatement (Second) of Conflict of Laws § 33. *See generally* Casad & Richman § 3-1[5]. Appearance, while a basis for exercising jurisdiction over the person, is irrelevant to the question of subject matter jurisdiction, because an objection on that ground cannot be waived.

[2] *See* subsection [b], *infra*.

[3] Furthermore, if defendant is present in a state for the sole purpose of defending in one action, she is likely to be immune from process served on her in some other action. *See* § 48, *infra*.

[4] *See, e.g.*, Fed. R. Civ. P. 15 (permitting amendment liberally).

[5] *Compare* Chapman v. Chapman, 284 A.D. 504, 132 N.Y.S.2d 707 (1954), *with* Everitt v. Everitt, 4 N.Y. 2d 13, 171 N.Y.S.2d 836, 148 N.E.2d 891 (1958). The Restatement also seems confused. *Compare* Restatement (Second) of Conflict of Laws § 26, comment d, *with* § 34, comment c.

[6] Adam v. Saenger, 303 U.S. 59 (1938).

[7] *See generally* Weintraub § 4.37; Leflar, McDougal & Felix §§ 28–29.

to default. Plaintiff, if unable to enforce the judgment in Delaware, might choose to sue the defendant in California, where she has property. As a defense to plaintiff's action on the Delaware judgement, defendant will answer that the judgment is not entitled to full faith and credit because there was no jurisdiction over her person in Delaware. Defendant's maneuver is a "collateral attack" on the Delaware judgment.

Default and collateral attack is an effective way of challenging the Delaware court's jurisdiction, but it is very risky. If the collateral attack fails — if the California court determines that Delaware did have jurisdiction over defendant — California will enforce the Delaware judgment without further ado. Defendant will never have an opportunity to litigate the merits of plaintiff's claim.

A less risky maneuver for defendant is to make a special appearance. That device permits a defendant to appear for the purpose of litigating the court's jurisdiction over her without making a general appearance and thereby consenting to the court's exercise of jurisdiction. The right to appear specially is not a constitutional right,[8] but all states permit some form of special appearance.[9]

If defendant makes a special appearance and loses her jurisdictional challenge in the trial court, a few courts require her to appeal the decision immediately. If she fails to do so and litigates the merits, she is held to have made a general appearance and cannot later assert the lack of jurisdiction on appeal.[10] According to most courts, however, a defendant whose jurisdictional challenge has failed in the trial court can plead to the merits without losing the right to assert the jurisdictional objection on appeal.[11]

The Federal Rules of Civil Procedure deal with the problems of appearance and jurisdictional objections in a more liberal and elegant manner. There is no longer a requirement for a special appearance. Defendant simply includes the jurisdictional objection in the answer or in a Rule 12 motion to dismiss.[12] Defendant does not waive the jurisdictional objection and submit to the court's jurisdiction by answering on the merits. Waiver does occur, however, if defendant fails to assert the jurisdictional objection seasonably in the proper pleading or motion.[13]

The Supreme Court has held that the defendant also can waive a jurisdictional objection by refusing to participate in discovery directed to

[8] York v. Texas, 137 U.S. 15 (1890).

[9] The last holdouts, Texas and Mississippi, capitulated by the mid–1960's. *See* Tex. R. Civ. P. 120a (Vernon's Supp. 1962); Mladinich v. Kohn, 250 Miss. 138, 164 So.2d 785 (1964).

[10] *See, e.g.*, Corbett v. Physicians' Casualty Ass'n, 135 Wis. 505, 115 N.W. 365 (1908).

[11] *See, e.g.*, Harkness v. Hyde, 98 U.S. 476 (1878).

[12] Fed. R. Civ. P. 12.

[13] In the words of Rule 12(b): "No defense or objection is waived by being joined with one or more other defenses or objections in a responsive pleading or motion." Defendant waives her jurisdictional objection only if (1) she makes a Rule 12 motion but does not include in it the objection to personal jurisdiction or, (2) she does not make a Rule 12 motion and she fails to include the jurisdictional objection in her answer. *See* Fed. R. Civ. P. 12(b), (g), (h)(1). For a careful discussion of the special appearance and Rule 12, *see* Casad & Richman § 3-1(5)(a).

the jurisdictional issue. In *Insurance Corporation of Ireland, Ltd. v. Compagnie des Bauxites de Guinee*[14] the defendants — foreign insurance companies — objected to the assertion of jurisdiction over them by the United States District Court in Pennsylvania. Plaintiffs attempted to use the discovery devices to show the defendants' minimum contacts with Pennsylvania, but the defendants were recalcitrant. After their repeated refusals to comply with the court's discovery orders, the district judge finally warned them that if they did not comply, he would rule (as a discovery sanction under rule 37(b)) that the court had jurisdiction over them. The insurers did not comply, and the court invoked the threatened sanction.

The Supreme Court upheld the district courts ruling. Justice White's opinion made a clear distinction between subject matter jurisdiction, which the parties cannot waive, and personal jurisdiction, which they can. Just as the jurisdictional objection can be waived under Rule 12, it can be forfeited by failure to comply with discovery orders. "The expression of legal rights," wrote Justice White, is "often subject to certain procedural rules," and "[t]he failure to follow those rules may well result in a curtailment of the rights." The insurers had argued that they had no obligation to obey the district court's discovery orders because the court lacked jurisdiction over them. The Court rejected this argument as an attempt "to create a logical conundrum out of a fairly straightforward matter." The defendants initially had the option of default; instead they submitted to the jurisdiction of the court for the limited purpose of challenging jurisdiction, and thus agreed to abide by that court's orders on that issue.

Issue preclusion is another procedural rule that can restrict the defendant's assertion of the jurisdictional objection. If the defendant attacks the court's jurisdiction and the court erroneously finds against her, that erroneous finding has issue preclusion effect, unless reversed by the appropriate appellate court. The issue cannot be re–litigated in a subsequent collateral attack. Accordingly, a defendant who loses a jurisdictional challenge is well advised to stay in the forum and litigate the merits of the action. Otherwise, plaintiff will win a default judgment that can be enforced in any state where defendant has property. In an action on the judgment, defendant has no defense: The jurisdictional issue is precluded by the prior litigation, and the merits are merged into a judgment that is entitled to full faith and credit.[15]

[c] Consent

[1] Statutory

Defendant's general appearance is essentially a consent after the fact. After the court asserts jurisdiction, defendant consents by appearing to

[14] 456 U.S. 694 (1982). For commentary critical of the reasoning in Bauxites, see Lea Brilmayer, *Consent, Contract and Territory,* 74 Minn. L. Rev. 1, 27 (1989).

[15] Baldwin v. Iowa State Traveling Men's Ass'n, 283 U.S. 522 (1931).

litigate the merits. But a defendant may also consent in advance. His consent may take the form of a document (often a power of attorney) nominating a particular state official or private person as his agent to accept service of process.[16] Sometimes a state regulatory scheme or corporation code compels such a consent in return for granting the privilege of conducting activities or engaging in business within the state. In *Kane v. New Jersey*,[17] for example, the Supreme Court upheld a regulatory scheme which conditioned an out–of–state driver's permission to drive on New Jersey's highways on his executing an instrument appointing the Secretary of State his agent for receipt of service of process. Such provisions are now largely unnecessary since modern long–arm statutes allow the exercise of jurisdiction over defendants who engage in activities within the state without resort to the conceptual expedient of an extorted or implied consent.[18]

[2] Contractual

The defendant also may consent by contract to the court's jurisdiction. Consent–to–jurisdiction clauses, fairly common in commercial contracts, sometimes specify the jurisdiction of an arbitration panel in a particular forum rather than that of the forum's courts. Jurisdiction consent clauses serve a valuable purpose. When combined with choice–of–law clauses, they permit sophisticated contracting parties considerable freedom to plan for and bargain over the place and the manner in which their disputes will be resolved. These considerations have prompted courts to find an adequate jurisdictional basis in such contractual consents.

Contractual consents to the exercise of jurisdiction can also be used in consumer contracts, and here they cause more concern than in the commercial setting. A commercial enterprise in New York, for instance, dealing extensively with consumers in California, might include in its standard contract a clause which requires the consumer's consent to jurisdiction in New York. The problem is that the consent is largely a fiction; rarely does the consumer actually bargain with the seller over the inclusion of the clause. Should these jurisdiction consent clauses render consumers amenable to suit in New York even though they have no other contacts with the

[16] For a succinct statement of the various ways in which defendant may consent to jurisdiction, *see* Casad & Richman § 3-1 [5][c].

[17] 242 U.S. 160 (1916). More typical is a state corporate code requiring that out–of–state corporations be licensed to do business in the state and then conditioning the grants of such a license upon the corporation's consent to the jurisdiction of the state's courts.

[18] Early long–arm statutes also relied on the doctrine of "implied consent." The consent implied, of course, was fictional. The statutory schemes did not require an extorted actual consent as in *Kane*; rather they provided that the defendant's conducting of certain activities in the forum (driving a car, for instance) constituted "implied consent" to the jurisdiction of the forum's courts for any cause of action arising out of those activities. *See, e.g.*, Hess v. Pawloski, 274 U.S. 352 (1927).

Once again, the decision in *International Shoe* rendered the doctrine of implied consent obsolete. Legislatures were free to enact long–arm statutes providing for jurisdiction over defendants based directly on their activities in the forum without the need to infer from those activities a fictional consent. For a more complete account of the use of express and implied consent to expand state court jurisdiction in the pre–*International Shoe* era, *see* § 18, *supra*.

state? The Supreme Court went a long way towards a positive response to this question in *National Equipment Rental, Ltd. v. Szukhent.*[19] Defendants, Michigan farmers, contracted with a New York equipment leasing firm. The form contract included a consent to jurisdiction clause, which made one Florence Weinberg, wife of an officer of National Equipment Rental, defendants' agent to receive service of process in New York. Plaintiff sued defendants in New York, alleging that the periodic lease payments had not been made; service was made on Florence, who transmitted it to defendants. In a 5–4 decision, the Court held the consent clause valid; Justice Black dissented vigorously, emphasizing the "take it or leave it" nature of the contract and the unequal bargaining power of the parties.

Szukhent seems to indicate that jurisdiction consent clauses, even in consumer adhesion contracts, are valid. For a time it seemed that *Shaffer v. Heitner*,[20] required a reexamination of *Szukhent*,[21] because *Shaffer* required that all assertions of jurisdiction meet the "fair play and substantial justice" standard of *International Shoe*. Now, however, *Burnham v. Superior Court* has cast doubt on this aspect of *Shaffer* and has suggested that the traditional bases for personal jurisdiction are constitutional by virtue of their historical pedigree alone.[22]

Nevertheless, the *Szukhent* rule is unfortunate. It permits circumvention of carefully worded state long–arm statutes and Supreme Court opinions that require some basis in contacts or fairness to support an exercise of jurisdiction. Furthermore, the rule helps the corporate plaintiff (the contract drafter), who often can more easily sustain the burden of interstate litigation, and hurts the consumer–defendant, who almost always cannot.

A consent–to–jurisdiction clause operates to vest a court with jurisdiction. A forum–selection clause goes further and binds the parties to litigate *only* in a particular forum. A court willing to enforce such a clause would dismiss the lawsuit unless it was the contractually designated forum.[23] Traditionally, common law courts have been reluctant to enforce such clauses, seeing them as an attempt to "oust the court of jurisdiction."

In *The Bremen v. Zapata Offshore Co.*,[24] the Supreme Court took the opposite view. Plaintiff an American corporation, contracted with

[19] 375 U.S. 311 (1964).

[20] 433 U.S. 186 (1977).

[21] The argument is made in Rudolph B. Schlesinger, *Jurisdictional Clauses in Consumer Transactions: A Multifaceted Problem of Jurisdiction and Full Faith and Credit*, 29 Hastings L.J. 967, 974 (1978).

[22] 495 U.S. 604 (1990). *Burnham*, however, can be distinguished. The practice it sustained, jurisdiction based on service of process, has a much older historical pedigree than does the jurisdiction–consent clause, the practice upheld in *Szukhent*.

[23] The contractual designation of a forum, acting as a consent to jurisdiction, is referred to as "prorogation." The exclusion of all other forums is referred to as "derogation." *See* Michael E. Solimine, *Forum Selection Clauses and the Privatization of Procedure*, 25 Cornell Int'l L. J. 51 (1992); Linda S. Mullenix, *Another Choice of Forum, Another Choice of Law: (Consensual Adjudicatory Procedure in Federal Court*, 57 Fordham L. Rev. 291 (1989).

[24] 407 U.S. 1 (1972). For discussion of the case, *see* Harold G. Maier, *The Three Faces of Zapata: Maritime Law, Federal Common Law, Federal Courts Law*, 6 Vand. J. Trans. L. 387 (1973).

defendant, a German entity, to tow plaintiff's drilling rig from the Gulf of Mexico to Italy. The rig was damaged in a storm, and defendant's tug put in at Tampa. There plaintiff sued the defendant despite a forum–selection clause in the towing contract, requiring any dispute to be litigated in London.

Relying on current commercial realities and expanding foreign trade, the Supreme Court held that forum–selection clauses are prima facie valid and should be enforced unless the clause is unreasonable or unjust, it was procured by fraud or overreaching, it violates the forum's strong public policy, or litigation in the designated forum would be seriously inconvenient. Not explicitly part of the holding but, nevertheless, important for the Court, were several key facts in *The Bremen*: The contract was freely negotiated at arms–length by experienced and sophisticated parties from different countries; the forum selected (London) was "neutral;" and the towage contract contemplated performance in international waters and in the territorial waters of several different countries, a circumstance that made forum choice quite uncertain in the absence of a forum–selection clause.

The rule of *The Bremen* makes good sense; it permits sophisticated parties to plan the resolution of their disputes and to take the risk of distant litigation into account when they set the other terms of their agreement. But should a forum–selection clause prevail when one of the parties is not a sophisticated business entity, but rather a consumer, who signed an adhesion contract? The Supreme Court gave a positive answer in *Carnival Cruise Lines v. Shute.*[25] Mr. and Mrs. Shute, residents of Washington state, purchased a cruise on one of defendant's ships through a Washington travel agent. In fine print, on the back of their "passage contract tickets" was a clause requiring all disputes to be litigated in Florida. Mrs. Shute was injured on the ship in international waters, and the Shutes sued Carnival in federal court in Washington.

The Supreme Court upheld the clause. Despite the obvious distinction between the freely–negotiated commercial contract in *The Bremen* and the consumer adhesion contract in *Carnival Cruise Lines*, the Court found three reasons to support enforcement. First, a cruise ship often carries passengers from several different states and foreign nations; so, without a forum–selection clause, a single incident could subject the carrier to litigation in several different forums. Second, a forum–selection clause would save the parties and the courts considerable time and expense by minimizing pre–trial litigation over jurisdictional issues. Finally, the Court concluded that "it stands to reason" that cruise lines save money by using forum–selection clauses and that the savings are passed on to passengers in the form of reduced fares. Justice Stevens dissented, relying on the hostility of traditional contract law toward forum–selection clauses and adhesion contracts.

[25] 111 S. Ct. 1522 (1991). For commentary on *Carnival Cruise Lines, see* Patrick J. Borchers, *Forum Selection Agreements in the Federal Courts After Carnival Cruise: A Proposal For Congressional Reform*, 67 Wash. L. Rev. 55 (1992), Linda S. Mullenix, *Another Easy Case, Some More Bad Law: Carnival Cruise Lines and Contractual Personal Jurisdiction*, 27 Tex. Int'l L.J. 324 (1992).

The dissent has the better of the argument. The majority's reasons are weak. Litigation in several different forums would not cripple the cruise line, and it was in a position to insure against the risk and to adjust its prices accordingly. The Court was right to note the expense of pre–trial jurisdictional litigation, but a forum–selection clause offers no cure; the validity of the clause is tested by a standard that is as subtle and fact–specific as the minimum contacts formula has turned out to be. Finally, the Court's reliance on law and economics is more a conclusion than an argument. In order to be confident that Carnival would save money because of the clause and that it would pass the savings on to its passengers, the Court would need to know a great deal more about the microeconomics of the cruise industry than is revealed in its brief and conclusory discussion of the issue.[26]

Not only are the Court's reasons weak, but its result is also unfortunate. Passengers with small and medium–sized claims will not be able to sue the cruise line far from their homes; thus, an entire industry will be able to insulate itself jurisdictionally from the standards of care decreed by the substantive law. Together, *Szukhent* and *Carnival Cruise Lines* reveal the Court's deference to freedom of contract in matters of jurisdiction. That deference is misplaced; plaintiff's right to a reasonable forum and defendant's due process protection from distant and inconvenient litigation should not be so easily defeated by sharp drafting practices.

[3] Class Action Plaintiffs

In *Phillips Petroleum v. Shutts*,[27] the Supreme Court dealt with the application of consent doctrine to absent class action plaintiffs. Phillips produced natural gas from leased land in eleven different states. It made regular payments to the owners of royalty rights in the leases and then sold the gas to its customers. There were over 30,000 royalty owners spread throughout the fifty states. Only a small percentage of the royalty owners were Kansans, and only a few of the leases were located in Kansas.[28]

The Federal Power Commission[29] regulated the price Phillips could charge its gas customers and ruled on Phillips' periodic requests for rate increases. During its review, the Commission permitted Phillips to charge its customers the higher rate; if denied the increase, Phillips had to refund to its customers the higher payments plus interest. However, Phillips did not pay the higher rate to the royalty owners during the review period.[30]

[26] For commentary on the Court's use of economics in *Carnival Cruise Lines*, *see* Russell Weintraub, *Conference on Jurisdiction, Justice and Choice of Law for the Twenty–First Century: Case One: Choice of Forum Clauses*, 29 N. Eng. L. Rev. 517, 555 (1995), Lee Goldman, *My Way and the Highway: the Law and Economics of Choice of Forum Clauses in Consumer Form Contracts*, 86 Nw. U. L. Rev. 700, 7140–716 (1992), William M. Richman, *Carnival Cruise Lines: Forum Selection Clauses in Adhesion Contracts*, 40 Am. J. Comp. L. 977, 979 (1993).

[27] 472 U.S. 797 (1985).

[28] Shutts v. Phillips Petroleum, 235 Kan. 195, 679 P.2d 1159, 1166 (1984).

[29] Now, the Federal Energy Regulatory Commission.

[30] Phillips would pay the higher rate to royalty owners who provided a bond to cover amount of the higher rate plus interest.

Three named plaintiffs, residents of Kansas and Oklahoma, brought a state class action against Phillips in Kansas on behalf of all the royalty owners seeking interest on the rate increase during the review period. After the trial court certified the class, the named plaintiffs provided each of the royalty owners with first–class mail notice of the action. The notice explained the action and offered each class member the opportunity to "opt–out" by executing and returning a "request for exclusion," which was contained in the mailed notice. Ultimately, 3400 potential class members opted out, leaving a class of over 28,000 plaintiffs. The trial court applied Kansas law to all claims and found Phillips liable for the interest payments; the Kansas Supreme Court affirmed.

In the United States Supreme Court, Phillips argued that Kansas lacked jurisdiction over the absent plaintiff class members (those who did not opt–out) and that Kansas could not apply its own law to the claims of the royalty owners who had no connection with Kansas. The jurisdiction issue is treated here; the choice–of–law question, in Chapter 4, Part E.[31]

The Court first held that Phillips had standing to challenge the Kansas court's jurisdiction over the absent class members. As a class–action defendant, Phillips had a "distinct and personal" interest in making sure that there was jurisdiction over all members of the plaintiff class. Otherwise, Phillips would be bound by the Kansas court's judgment, but the absent class members might not. Thus, they would be able to bring separate suits against Phillips in Kansas or elsewhere.[32] The only way Phillips could assure itself that the absent class members would be bound by the result was to make sure of the court's jurisdiction over them; and the only way it could do that was to challenge the court's jurisdiction and provoke a ruling.

With the standing problem out of the way, the Court addressed the merits of the jurisdictional issue. Here was the problem: the absent class members had a property interest at stake and a state cannot take away a litigant's property without jurisdiction. For civil defendants, jurisdiction requires minimum contacts with the state, but in *Shutts* it was quite clear that many members of the plaintiff class had no contact with Kansas.

The Court countered that argument by drawing a sharp distinction between the litigational burdens of the out–of–state defendant and the absent class–action plaintiff.[33] Absent class–action plaintiffs need not hire

---

[31] *See* § 97, *infra*.

[32] Of course, Phillips could not insure completely against multiple actions because opt–out class members clearly would be able to bring separate actions.

[33] One commentator argues forcefully that the application of the label "plaintiff" to non–opt–out class members is misleading. Such individuals bear little relationship to the traditional civil plaintiff. It is better to treat them as *sui generis*, as a type of litigant that did not exist in the relatively simple legal world that gave us the terms "plaintiff" and "defendant." John E. Kennedy, *The Supreme Court Meets the Bride of Frankenstein: Phillips Petroleum Co. v. Shutts and the State Multistate Class Action*, 34 U. Kan. L. Rev. 255, 280 (1985). The author also argues that the opt–out class action reveals a fundamental change in the court's role from a passive non–initiating umpire to a quasi–administrative agency actively prosecuting the claims of persons who fail to object. *Id.* at 284.

counsel, travel to the forum, or submit to expensive and time–consuming discovery. Nor are they normally subject to damages or injunctive relief — counterclaims and cross–claims against plaintiff classes being quite rare.[34] Further the absent class–member is protected in ways the typical civil defendant is not. The court, the named plaintiffs, the rules of procedure,[35] and occasionally the defendant (as in *Shutts*) show solicitude for the rights of the class members.

The Court also rejected the argument that, absent minimum contacts, a state can exercise jurisdiction only over those absent plaintiffs who affirmatively consent by "opting–in." The Federal Rules of Civil Procedure and most state statutes and rules use the "opt–out" procedure; a constitutionalization of the "opt–in" requirement would invalidate those rules. Further, the Court argued that the fact that over 3,400 class members in *Shutts* exercised their right to the "opt out" shows that the procedure is not merely *pro forma*.

The result in *Shutts* is clearly correct, but reliance on the consent rationale is problematic. The inference of the consent of class members who do not opt–out is based entirely on their ability to understand the notice and its explanation of their rights and options. But much of what lawyers write and say is incomprehensible to non–lawyers, and there are well-known examples — some rather amusing — of the misreading of legal notices by non–lawyers.[36]

Arguably, the real justification for the result in *Shutts* is a form of jurisdiction by necessity, similar to the doctrine which justifies jurisdiction over the interests of all the world in an in rem action.[37] A multi–state class action would be virtually impossible without some way to assert jurisdiction over absent class members. Why, then, did the Court fail to articulate that rationale? Possibly the Court was concerned about the scope and implications of such a doctrine. It has rejected arguments for jurisdiction based

[34] One commentary argues that the Court has dismissed too cavalierly the possibility that members of a class might be subject to genuine burdens — discovery requests, counterclaims, cross claims, and court costs. *See* Arthur F. Miller & David Crump, *Jurisdiction and Choice–of–law in Multistate Class Actions After Phillips Petroleum Co. v. Shutts*, 96 Yale L.J. 1, 26 (1986).

The Court's broad view of state class action jurisdiction (with no minimum contacts requirement) also poses other questions: What if two or more state courts certify the same nationwide class? Would the result depend upon a race to judgment? Could the defendant manipulate the result by dilatory tactics in some states and cooperative acceleration in its favored state? *See id.* at 24.

[35] *E.g.*, Fed. R. Civ. P. 23(e), prohibiting dismissal or compromise of a class action without notice to all class members.

[36] *See, e.g.*, Miller & Crump, *supra* note 34, at 22. Note that the consent rationale, dependant as it is on the class members' prerogative to opt-out, works only for Rule 26(b)(3) class actions; in class action under Rules 26(b)(1) and (2) class members have no opt-out right. The implication is that in such actions there must be some other justification for exercising jurisdiction over members of the plaintiff class. For commentary see Linda Mullenix, *Class Actions, Personal Jurisdiction, and Plaintiffs' Due Process: Implications for Mass Tort Litigation*, 28 U. C. Davis L. Rev. 871 (1995).

[37] *See* § 44, *infra*, for a discussion of the rationale for in rem jurisdiction. Jurisdiction by necessity is discussed in § 38, *infra*. That rationale would work in all class actions, not just those that provide class members with an opt-out right. *See* note 36, *supra*.

on necessity in some rather egregious cases, in which plaintiffs really had no other practical forum.[38]

[d] Appearance, Consent, Waiver, and Jurisdictional Theory

In both *Bauxites*, and *Shutts*, the Supreme Court sanctioned exercises of jurisdiction without relying at all on minimum contacts. In *Bauxites* it relied on waiver, and in *Shutts*, on consent. But why are waiver and consent adequate substitutes for minimum contacts? Probably because waiver and consent are based on fairness. If so, these cases suggest that fairness may be the ultimate jurisdictional goal and that waiver and consent in some cases, and minimum contacts in other cases, are simply instruments to guarantee fairness.

If "minimum contacts" is simply a device to ensure fairness, why not routinely permit jurisdiction in cases where defendant lacks minimum contacts with the forum, but could not be subject to any unfair burden in defending there? Consider a Michigan defendant who has no pre–litigation contacts with Ohio, but lives so close to the border that the Ohio court is actually closer to his home than the appropriate Michigan court. Why would it be unfair to require him to defend in the Ohio court?[39] Perhaps the unfairness would be in the Ohio court's propensity to apply its own law. If that is the real problem, why not deal with it through meaningful constitutional restrictions on state court choice–of–law decisions rather than by clinging to the minimum contacts requirement?[40]

§ 31 Traditional Bases for Jurisdiction over Corporations

[a] Domestic Corporations

Jurisdiction over the domestic corporation was not a problem, under the restrictive territorial theory. Even before *International Shoe*[1] there were ample bases upon which to exercise jurisdiction over the domestic corporation. A corporation is a domiciliary of its state of incorporation. Indeed, a particularly close relationship exists between a corporation and its home state because the laws of that state make the corporation's existence possible. Another traditional basis, which applies without much stretching, is consent. In return for giving it life, the state can require the corporation's consent to the jurisdiction of the state's courts.[2] Whatever the rationale,

---

[38] *See* Helicopteros Nacionales de Colombia v. Hall, 466 U.S. 408 (1984), discussed *supra* at § 25.

[39] *See* Robert T. Mills, *Personal Jurisdiction Over Border State Defendants: What Does Due Process Require?*, 13 S. Ill. U.L. Rev. 919 (1989).

[40] For a discussion of the minimal constitutional restrictions on state–court choice–of–law decisions, *see* § 97, *infra*.

[1] International Shoe v. Washington, 326 U.S. 310 (1945).

[2] *See Developments in the Law, State Court Jurisdiction*, 73 Harv. L. Rev. 909, 919 (1960).

and often there was no felt need to articulate any, courts traditionally have assumed jurisdiction over domestic corporations.

Under current jurisdictional theory, incorporation within the state remains a constitutionally adequate basis for jurisdiction over a corporation; and every state has statutes or rules that permit its courts to exercise jurisdiction on that basis.[3] Further incorporation within the state usually will support an exercise of general jurisdiction; thus the forum can adjudicate any claim against the corporate defendant, not merely those that arise in the forum.

The current state of the law is consistent with *International Shoe*'s command to safeguard "fair play" and "substantial justice." The only troublesome case is the one where the corporation has no contact with the state beyond the purely formal connection of its charter of incorporation. But even in such a case, jurisdiction seems reasonable. Because corporate officers and directors make a completely voluntary choice in selecting the state of incorporation, it is difficult to find a violation of "fair play" or "substantial justice" in the exercise of jurisdiction by that state. Furthermore, there is much to be said for a corporation, like a natural person, having some place where it can be sued on any cause of action.[4]

[b] Foreign Corporations[5]

Every state provides conditions that an out–of–state corporation must satisfy in order to "qualify" to operate within the state. One such condition is that the foreign corporation consent to the jurisdiction of the state's courts. The consent usually is not limited to claims arising within the state. The use of "qualification" as a basis for *general jurisdiction* is not entirely uncontroversial. Arguably, the forum court should look beyond the formal "consent" and exercise general jurisdiction only if the defendant's connections with the state are sufficiently substantial to warrant it without regard to the defendant's extorted submission.[6]

Before the jurisdictional revolution of *International Shoe* and the advent of modern long–arm statutes, states exercised jurisdiction over foreign, non–qualifying corporations based upon "doing business" statutes. Many states retain such statutes, but their function has changed over the years. Once they provided a basis for specific jurisdiction, but in that capacity the statutes have been superseded largely by the "transacting business" provisions of modern enumerated act long–arm statutes.[7] The new provisions

[3] *See* Restatement (Second) of Conflict of Laws § 41 (1971); Casad & Richman § 3-2[1].

[4] The Supreme Court's decision in Burnham v. Superior Court, 495 U.S. 604 (1990), provides strong support for the rule even if current notions of fairness were to suggest an opposite result. The Court upheld transient service jurisdiction based in part on its historical pedigree, a consideration that works just as well to justify jurisdiction based on incorporation in the state.

[5] The problem of jurisdiction over the foreign corporation was very difficult under the territorial power theory. In order to justify the practice, the courts used the fictions of corporate "consent" and "presence." The history is discussed in § 18[c], *supra*.

[6] *See* Casad & Richman § 3-2[2][a][ii].

[7] Those provisions are discussed in § 33, *infra*.

require much less contact between the defendant and the forum than do the older "doing business" statutes. Often a single transaction is sufficient.

No longer needed for specific jurisdiction, the emerging modern role of the "doing business" statutes is as a basis for general jurisdiction. When used as a basis for general jurisdiction, the "doing business" statutes have been construed to require fairly significant contacts between the defendant and the forum. In the words of the Restatement (Second) of Conflict of Laws, the foreign corporation's in–state activites must be "so continuous and substantial" that the exercise of general jurisdiction is "reasonable."[8]

Thus, mere solicitation of orders does not meet the standard. Even if a corporation has agents in the state who solicit orders and even if products are then shipped into the state to fill those orders, the corporation is not "doing business" according to most courts. "Solicitation plus" some additional activity, such as maintaining a showroom or office in the state, however, may be sufficient.[9] Cases involving regular but intermittent contact with the state, such as a retailer's periodic buying trips or a professional sports team's road trips, have produced inconsistent results.[10]

[c] Parents and Subsidiaries

Judicial jurisdiction over a subsidiary corporation does not guarantee judicial jurisdiction over the subsidiary's parent corporation. Similarly, jurisdiction over the parent does not guarantee jurisdiction over the subsidiary.[11] If, however, the parent so controls the subsidiary that its separate legal existence is a mere fiction, courts will "pierce the corporate veil" for purposes of jurisdiction, as well as substantive law, and attribute the forum contacts of the subsidiary to the parent. Thus, if the subsidiary is found to be "doing business" in the forum, the parent will be also.[12]

Even if the entities are not so close as to permit piercing the corporate veil, jurisdiction over the parent might still be available on an agency theory. Suppose, for instance, a national retailer conducts buying and other corporate business through a parent corporation but accomplishes its retail distribution through ten subsidiaries, each of which has a separate geographical territory. If the subsidiaries are each separately capitalized and separately controlled, piercing the veil will be extremely difficult; but if a

---

[8] Restatement (Second) of Conflict of Laws § 47(2)(1971).

[9] *See* B. Glenn George, *In Search of General Jurisdiction*, 64 Tul. L. Rev. 1097, 1129 (1990).

[10] Professor Weintraub points out that the trend toward the expansive use of a "doing business" statute as a basis for general jurisdiction may have stalled as a result of the Supreme Court's very restrictive view of general jurisdiction in Helicopteros Nacionales de Colombia v. Hall, 466 U.S. 408 (1984)(discussed *supra* at § 25); Weintraub 214. A very careful and complete study of "doing business" statutes and cases appears in Casad & Richman § 3-2(2)(b). For additional commentary on "doing business" and its relationship to the general/specific jurisdiction distinction, see Mary Twitchell, *Why We Keep Doing Business With "Doing–Business Jurisdiction,"* 2001 U. Chi. Legal F. 171.

[11] *E.g.*, Cannon Mfg. Co. v. Cudahy Packing Co., 267 U.S. 333 (1925); Restatement (Second) of Conflict of Laws § 52, comment b.

[12] *Id.*

subsidiary acts as the parent's agent in the forum, jurisdiction over the parent may be permissible upon that basis.[13]

§ 32 Traditional Bases for Jurisdiction Over Partnerships and Unincorporated Associations[1]

Traditionally, partnerships and unincorporated associations lacked the separate legal existence of corporations. What that meant for jurisdictional purposes was that the forum had to obtain personal jurisdiction over each defendant partner or member in order to render a valid judgment. Now, most states have statutes that permit a partnership or association to be sued in its own name based on its activities in the forum. A judgment in such an action can be satisfied only out of the property of the entity, unless, of course, the court obtains personal jurisdiction over the partners or members as well as the entity.[2]

§ 33 Long–Arm Statutes

[a] In General

The preceding section examined traditional bases for personal jurisdiction. These bases, incorporated in state law, were adequate to extend the forum's jurisdiction as far as the Constitution would permit under the Supreme Court's restrictive territorial power theory of jurisdiction. When the Court jettisoned that theory in *International Shoe*, however, new state legislation was required to extend state court jurisdiction towards the new and expanded constitutional limits. State legislatures responded to the challenge by enacting long–arm statutes.

Long–arm statutes take two basic forms. The simpler type — the California statute is the paradigm — directs the court to exercise jurisdiction whenever permitted by the Constitution.[1] The more complicated statutes, often called "enumerated act" statutes, direct the court to exercise jurisdiction over any defendant who commits one of several enumerated acts in the forum. With these statutes, Illinois, and later Wisconsin and New York, were the pioneers.[2] The most influential formulation is probably the one adopted by the Commissioners on Uniform State Laws in the Uniform Interstate and International Procedure Act.[3]

---

[13] *See* Weintraub § 4.21; Casad & Richman, § 3-2[b][ix], Lea Brilmayer & Kathleen Paisley, *Personal Jurisdiction and Substantive Legal Relations: Corporations, Conspiracies, and Agency*, 74 Calif. L. Rev. (1986).

[1] *See generally* Casad & Richman § 3-3.

[2] *Id.*

[1] Cal. Civ. Proc. Code § 410.10.

[2] A more detailed treatment of the comparison and of the early history of long–arm statutes appears in Casad & Richman § 4-1. *See also* David Currie, *The Growth of the Long Arm: Eight Years of Extended Jurisdiction in Illinois*, 1963 U. Ill. L. F. 533 (1963).

[3] Uniform Interstate and International Procedure Act § 1.03, 13 U.L.A. 361 (1986).

The following two subsections treat the two types of long–arm statutes.

[b] The California Style Long–Arm Statute

California's long–arm statute provides that: "A court of this state may exercise jurisdiction on any basis not inconsistent with the Constitution of this state or of the United States."[4] The statute tells the state courts to exercise jurisdiction to the fullest extent possible without violating the Due Process Clause. In other words, it puts no state law generated limits on the jurisdiction of state courts.

The argument for the California style statute is based on its simplicity and thoroughness. Because of the statute's simplicity, the court need not engage in any statutory construction at all. When faced with a jurisdictional challenge, it proceeds directly to the due process issue. If jurisdiction is constitutionally permissible, the statutory test is also satisfied. The thoroughness of the California type statute becomes apparent when compared to a typical enumerated act statute. The latter may fail to reach some defendants, who would be amenable under the Due Process Clause, because the defendant has not committed one of the statute's enumerated acts. Even careful legislative drafting cannot foresee all the possible constitutionally permissible jurisdictional bases. To rectify this, some states with enumerated act statutes have added catchall "any constitutional basis" provisions to the list of specific statutory bases.[5]

The argument against the California style statute is based on vagueness and notice. The statute does not notify potential defendants specifically of the types of conduct that will render them amenable to the forum's jurisdiction. That, however, should not be a serious concern; jurisdictional rules probably have little effect on potential defendants' primary conduct. On the other hand, the Supreme Court has indicated that the foreseeability of defendant's being haled into court is a crucial constitutional yardstick.[6]

[c] Enumerated Act Statutes

Most states have enacted more specific statutes, which restrict jurisdiction to certain kinds of cases. Section 1.03 of the Uniform Interstate and International Procedure Act[7] is an example. It provides:

(a) A court may exercise personal jurisdiction over a person, who acts directly or by an agent, as to a [cause of action][claim for relief] arising from the person's

(1) transacting any business in this state;

---

[4] Cal. Civ. Proc. Code 410.10 (West 1973).

[5] *See* Casad & Richman § 4-1, n. 14.

[6] *See* World–Wide Volkswagen v. Woodson, 444 U.S. 286 (1980), discussed *supra* at § 22. For arguments for and against the California style statute, *see* Weintraub § 4.9A; Robert Leflar, *Barely Fair, Not Grossly Unjust*, 25 S.C. L. Rev. 177 (1973).

[7] 13 U. L. A. 361 (1986). The provisions of this statute as well as other long–arm issues are treated exhaustively in Casad & Richman, Ch. 4.

(2) contracting to supply services or things in this state;

(3) causing tortious injury by an act or omission in this state;

(4) causing tortious injury in this state by an act or omission outside this state if he regularly does or solicits business, or engages in any other persistent course of conduct, or derives substantial revenue from goods used or consumed or services rendered, in this state; or

(5) having an interest in, using, or possessing real property in this state; or

(6) contracting to insure any person, property, or risk located within this state at the time of contracting.

(b) When jurisdiction over a person is based solely upon this section, only a [cause of action][claim for relief] arising from acts enumerated in this section may be asserted against him.

The complexity of a statute such as the Uniform Act ensures that statutory construction will be an issue in every jurisdiction problem. With a California–style statute, the court can pass directly to the constitutional question; under the Uniform Act, in contrast, the court must first determine if the case fits into one of the specified categories. If the court determines that the statute provides a basis for jurisdiction, it must then ask whether the resulting exercise of jurisdiction violates defendant's rights under the Due Process Clause.

The relationship between sections (a) and (b) is central to the Act. Section (a) lists certain kinds of contacts which may be the basis for an exercise of jurisdiction. Section (a)(3), for instance, provides that if defendant causes tortious injury in the state, the state's courts may exercise jurisdiction over her. Section (b) then limits the claims that can be asserted against defendant to those which *arise out of* the contacts listed in section (a). Thus, if jurisdiction is based on Section (a)(3) (defendant's causing tortious injury in the forum), only a cause of action based on that tort may be asserted against her. A cause of action based on an unrelated business transaction, for example, could not be asserted against defendant, absent some independent jurisdictional basis. Section (b) thus makes it clear that the statute provides for specific, rather than general, jurisdiction.[8]

Some courts have held that statutes patterned on the Uniform Act were intended by the legislature to extend the state's jurisdiction to the outer limits of the Due Process Clause.[9] For those courts, jurisdictional analysis is a one–step procedure; ignoring the language of the statue, they simply proceed to test the court's jurisdiction under the Supreme Court's constitutional standards.[10]

---

[8] *See* § 25, *supra*, and § 37[b], *infra*, for a discussion of specific and general jurisdiction.

[9] For an exhaustive treatment of this reading of long–arm statutes, *see* David S. Welkowitz, *Going to the Limits of Due Process: Myth, Mystery and Meaning*, 28 Duq. L. Rev. 233 (1990). *See also* Casad & Richman § 4-1[1].

[10] *See, e.g.*, Mun. Mtg. & Equity, LLC v. Southfork Apartments, Ltd. Partnership, 93 F. Supp. 2d 622 (D.Md. 2000), Davis v. American Family Mut. Ins. Co., 861 F.2d 1159 (9th Cir. 1988)(interpreting Montana statute); Dwyer v. District Court, 188 Colo. 41, 532 P. 2d 725 (1975).

As a matter of statutory construction, this one–step analysis make no sense. Why would a legislature use a complicated enumerated act statute to achieve the same result that the California statute reaches with only 24 words? One commentary suggests that opinions that interpret an enumerated act statute to reach to the limits of due process should not be read too literally. They may mean only that the specific provisions of the statute (the enumerated acts) should be very broadly construed.[11]

With these general questions out of the way, what remains to be considered are the individual contacts listed in section (a):

(1) *Transacting business in the state*

The statutory phrase "transacting any business" should not be confused with the earlier traditional formula "doing business." "Doing business" has been defined traditionally as activity of a systematic and continuous nature; because of the extensive contact required, it may be sufficient as a basis for general jurisdiction. "Transacting business," by contrast, serves only as a basis for specific jurisdiction; consequently it requires significantly less contact between the defendant and the forum.

Exactly how much forum–directed activity is required for defendant to be transacting business? Some courts have taken an extremely expansive view. In *Parke–Bernet Galleries, Inc. v. Franklyn,*[12] for example, the court held that a California defendant had "transacted business" in New York by making long–distance telephone bids in an auction held in New York. Not all courts have been so liberal. Some have found no transaction of business even when defendant had significant business dealings with a plaintiff based in the forum.[13]

A fact pattern that occurs frequently involves a forum–based buyer who has commercial dealings with an out–of–state seller, primarily by telephone and mail. Are such contacts by the seller sufficient to constitute "transacting business in the forum"? Based on a survey of the cases, the leading study on long–arm jurisdiction concludes that the key variables are whether the seller or its agents have physically entered the forum during negotiations and whether the seller initiated contact with the buyer or vice versa.[14]

Another common pattern poses the question whether advertising in the forum constitutes "transacting business" there. Suppose defendant, a Missouri seller, advertises goods or services in Kansas. Plaintiff, a resident of Kansas, travels to Missouri and purchases an item that turns out to be defective. Can plaintiff maintain a warranty action against defendant in

[11] *See* Leflar, McDougal & Felix 103.

[12] 26 N.Y.2d 13, 256 N.E.2d 506, 308 N.Y.S.2d 337 (1970).

[13] *See, e.g.*, Scullin Steel v. National Ry. Utilization Corp., 676 F.2d 309 (8th Cir. 1982).

[14] Casad & Richman § 4-2[1] (isolating these variables, among others, and citing numerous cases). The authors pose the question whether courts should be more willing to find "transaction of business" when the out–of–state defendant is the seller rather than the buyer. They conclude that the standards should be the same: "Transacting should be transacting . . . whether done by buyer or seller." *Id.* [1][a][ii].

Kansas based on the theory that defendant's advertising there constitutes transacting business? The cases seem to be split.[15]

It might be tempting to try to interpret "transacting business" in terms of formal commercial law. One might think, for instance, that in a transcontinental mail or telephone deal, it would be important to decide where the contact was made or where title passed. Such formalism, however, should not control the interpretation of a jurisdictional statute. As one court observed, the only meaningful inquiry is "whether a foreign purchaser has produced effects in the forum state of such significance that it is not manifestly unfair to require him to resolve a resulting legal dispute in this state."[16]

(2) *Contracting to supply services or things in this state*[17]

There is a fair amount of overlap between this section and the preceding provision. Often a defendant who contracts to supply services or things in the forum does so by transacting business there. The present section, however, also reaches the defendant who makes an agreement outside the state to supply goods or services within the state. Thus, under the language of the statute, it is not fatal that the contract was negotiated or executed elsewhere.[18]

Further, the statute does not require that performance be rendered in the forum.[19] Indeed, there is no requirement that defendant or his agents have entered the state. Consider an in–state buyer who travels several thousand miles to seller's place of business and contracts for seller to supply widgets in buyer's state: even if no widgets have been delivered and even if the seller's only contact with buyer's state is the widget contract, the statute grants jurisdiction over seller. This extreme application of the section probably would be held unconstitutional, but in the routine case where defendant has other contacts with the state or where the goods are actually sent into the state, exercise of jurisdiction under the statute clearly passes constitutional muster.

(3) *Causing tortious injury by an act or omission in this state*

This straightforward provision is the lineal descendant of the old non–resident motorist statutes upheld in cases like *Hess v. Pawloski.*[20] It is

[15] *Compare* Osage Homestead, Inc. v. Sutphin, 657 S.W. 2d 346 (Mo. App. 1983) *with* Shoppers Food Warehouse v. Moreno, 715 A. 2d 107 (D.C. App 1998), Slocum v. Sandestin Beach Resort Hotel, 679 F. Supp. 899 (E.D. Ark. 1988); Acme Equipment Co. v. Metro Auto Auction of Kansas City Inc., 484 F. Supp. 219 (W.D. Okla. 1979). These cases, among others, are analyzed in Casad & Richman § 4-2 [1][a][ix].

[16] State ex rel. White Lumber Sales Inc. v. Sulmonetti, 252 Or. 121, 123–124, 448 P. 2d 571, 572–573 (1968).

[17] *See generally* Casad & Richman, Chapter 8 (90 pages of discussion of this provision, including exhaustive case citations, organized by subject matter).

[18] *E.g.*, Droukas v. Divers Training Academy, Inc., 375 Mass. 149, 376 N.E.2d 548, 553 (1978). While physical presence in the state during negotiation and execution is not necessary, ordinarily it is sufficient. Casad & Richman § 8-1[2][c][i].

[19] *E.g., Snyder v. Hampton Indus., Inc.*, 521 F. Supp. 130, 145 (D. Md. 1981). Delivery in the forum does make a holding of jurisdiction more likely, however. *See* Casad & Richman §§ 8-1[2][c][i] & [ii].

[20] 274 U.S. 352 (1927), discussed *supra*, § 18[a].

designed to reach a defendant who drives a car into the forum and causes tortious injury there. The statute does not require, however, that the injury occur in the forum; thus, the statute reaches a defendant whose tortious act in the forum (say negligent manufacture of a product) causes injury *outside of the forum*. Here also it is uncontroversial, since the doing of the act in the forum will nearly always satisfy the minimum contacts test.

Although the statute uses the phrase "tortious injury," its application has not been limited strictly to common law torts. Rather, some courts have read it to cover other wrongs such as copyright and patent infringement and antitrust violations. Note also that the statute applies to an "act or omission." Less precise statutes refer only to "tortious acts," leaving the courts with the question whether tortious nonfeasance constitutes a tortious act.[21]

(4) *Causing tortious injury in this state by an act or omission outside this state if he regularly does or solicits business, or engages in any other persistent course of conduct, or derives substantial revenue from goods used or consumed or services rendered, in this state*

This section is quite complex and requires substantial explanation. First, it is clear that it covers a defendant who performs an act outside the state that causes injury inside the state.[22] Thus it reaches the typical products liability case in which defendant manufactures a defective product outside the state, and sends it either directly or through middle–men to the forum where it injures plaintiff, a consumer.[23]

The reason that the statute is so precise in separating the tort into the *foreign act* and *local injury* is that earlier statutes, which were less careful, produced problems of interpretation. In *Gray v. American Radiator & Standard Sanitary Corp.*,[24] the statute provided for jurisdiction over a defendant who "commits a tortious act within the State." *Gray* involved a foreign act (manufacture of a defective product) that produced a local injury, creating a difficult problem of statutory construction. Was the "tortious act" committed in Ohio where the product was made or Illinois where the defective product caused injury? The court dealt with the problem by using the venerable choice–of–law rule that "the place of a wrong is where the last event takes place which is necessary to render the actor liable."[25] Thus,

---

[21] These issues of statutory interpretation are treated in detail in Casad & Richman § 4-2[2][a].

[22] This fact pattern has produced many of the knotty constitutional problems the Supreme Court has had to deal with. *See* World–Wide Volkswagen v. Woodson, 444 U.S. 286 (1980); Calder v. Jones, 465 U.S. 783 (1984); Keeton v. Hustler Magazine, Inc., 465 U.S. 770 (1984); Asahi v. Superior Court, 480 U.S. 102 (1987). The cases are discussed in detail in §§ 22–24, 27, *supra*.

[23] In a modern products liability action, it is common for a plaintiff to plead breach of warranty as well as tort theories. Therefore some state long–arm statutes also have sections which provide for jurisdiction based on "causing injury in this state to any person by breach of warranty expressly or impliedly made in the sale of goods outside this state. . . ." *e.g.*, Ohio Rev. Code § 2307.382.

[24] 22 Ill. 2d 432, 176 N.E. 2d 761 (1961).

[25] *See* § 65, *infra*, for a discussion of that choice–of–law rule.

the defendant "committed a tortious act" in Illinois because plaintiff's injury there was the last event necessary to produce liability.

Not all courts followed the approach in *Gray*, however. For example, in *Feathers v. McLucas*,[26] the Court of Appeals of New York held that New York's long–arm statute, which required a "tortious act within the state," could not reach the foreign act/local injury situation. The statutory construction issue that split the *Gray* and *Feathers* courts is eliminated by the more careful wording of § 4. By separating the tort into the foreign act and local injury, the statute removes the need to ask the question: Where was the tort?

With the ambiguity thus removed, the first clause of the section is very expansive; it grants jurisdiction over a defendant whose acts *anywhere* cause injury in the forum. This first clause standing alone surely would produce unconstitutional results. Consider a manufacturer in Maine who makes fishing lures for the local market only. One of its products is purchased by a citizen of Maine and given as a gift to a Marylander, who loses it while fishing in Canada. It is found by a visiting Californian who takes it back to California where, because of a defective design, it injures plaintiff. The first clause of § 4, standing alone, would make the Maine defendant amenable in California, even though it had no contact with California or any other state but Maine, and even though its product arrived in California through pure happenstance.

To avoid unconstitutional results such as this one, the statute requires that there be one of three "additional affiliations." For jurisdiction to exist under the section, the defendant must either (1) regularly do or solicit business, (2) engage in any other persistent course of conduct, or (3) derive substantial revenue from goods used in the forum.[27] The requirement for an "additional affiliation" eliminates cases like the Maine Fishing Lure Maker since it satisfies none of the three specified contacts. Thus, the requirement assures the constitutionality of the statute.

A change in the hypothetical shows how the statute can work. Suppose the Maine Fishing Lure Maker has a fishing lodge in California where it tests new products for one month every year. The statute arguably generates jurisdiction. According to the original hypothetical, the defendant has committed an act in Maine which caused injury in California. It does not regularly do or solicit business in California or derive substantial revenue from California, but it does "engage in any other persistent course of conduct" there. It tests products there for one month every year. Thus, it satisfies one of the additional affiliations and, therefore, is covered by the statute.

An interesting variation on the foreign act-local injury theory involves the defendant's foreign act that causes the death of a forum resident outside

[26] 15 N.Y. 2d 443, 209 N.E.2d 68, 261 N.Y.S. 2d 8, *cert. denied*, 382 U.S. 905 (1965).

[27] The opinion of the Supreme Court of Oklahoma in *World–Wide* provides an expansive treatment of the "derives substantial revenue" clause; *see* World–Wide Volkswagen v. Woodson, 585 P.2d 351 (Okla. 1978).

the forum. Can the plaintiff, the victim's spouse, successfully assert jurisdiction over defendant in a wrongful death action in the forum on the theory that defendant committed a tortious act outside the forum that caused financial injury and loss of companionship in the forum? Most cases do not interpret the statute to assert jurisdiction in such cases, but some do.[28]

(5) *Having an interest in, using, or possessing real property in this state*[29]

Section 5 is straightforward and very broad. It provides for jurisdiction in a wide variety of cases having to do with land: cases dealing with conveyances including sale, purchase, lease and mortgage; cases sounding in contract such as real estate listing agreements, and contracts to perform work or services on the property; and tort cases such as those involving injury to persons on the property (slip and fall) or misrepresentations made surrounding the sale of the property.[30]

Although the statute deals with cases involving land, it is important to note that it grants *personal*, rather than in rem, jurisdiction. A prevailing plaintiff will obtain a personal judgment that can be enforced against any of defendant's property (inside the state or out), not just the piece of property that provides the jurisdictional basis.[31]

An exercise of jurisdiction under this section almost always will be constitutional; an absentee landowner normally can anticipate being "haled into court" in the situs state to defend a claim relating to the land.[32] Further, such a defendant avails himself of the benefits and protections of situs law, which provides an extensive set of rights and privileges to landowners. Finally, the state's strong interest in the regulation of title, use, and possession of land within its borders also argues strongly for jurisdiction.[33]

(6) *Contracting to insure any person, property, or risk located within this state at the time of contracting*

This provision, sometimes referred to as a foreign insurers process act, appears in many states' long–arm statutes. Note that the contract may be negotiated and executed elsewhere, and by interstate or international communication, so long as the risk insured is within the forum. Further jurisdiction can be sustained even if the defendant has insured only one risk in the forum.[34]

---

28 See Casad & Richman § 4-2[3][b] for citations to cases on both sides of the issue.

29 *See generally* Casad & Richman § 9-1.

30 A useful collection of cases construing the reach of the statute appears in Leflar, McDougal & Felix § 40.

31 Of course, the statute grants only specific, not general, jurisdiction so the plaintiff's claim must relate to the particular piece of defendant's property that provides the jurisdictional basis.

32 *See* § 37[e], *infra*, for a discussion of the importance of foreseeability to the jurisdictional calculus.

33 *See* § 38[b], *infra*, for a discussion of the relevance of state interests in justifying jurisdiction.

34 A collection of cases liberally applying this provision can be found in Casad & Richman § 8-8.

Why is it constitutionally permissible for jurisdiction to be so expansive here? Surely one who insures a risk in the forum can "anticipate being haled into court there;" that basically is what the insurance business is all about. Also, the forum state has a strong interest in regulating out–of–state insurers to make sure that its citizens are not bilked by them. This latter argument carried the day in *McGee v. International Life Insurance Co.*,[35] the most expansive exercise of jurisdiction ever permitted by the Supreme Court.

§ 34 Long–Arm Jurisdiction in Federal Courts

[a] Constitutional Power

The constitutional limitation on Congress' power to confer territorial jurisdiction on a federal court comes from the fifth amendment, not the fourteenth, and requires that the defendant have minimum contacts with the United States as a whole, rather than with the forum state.[36] Further, the fifth amendment, like the fourteenth, also prohibits the assertion of jurisdiction if the forum is so inconvenient to the defendant as to constitute a denial of "fair play and substantial justice" in spite of the defendant's minimum contacts with the United States.[37] Subject to these limits, Congress probably could confer nationwide personal jurisdiction on the district courts.

[b] Rule 4(k)

In fact, however, Congress generally has not done so,[38] and Rule 4(k) of the Federal Rules of Civil procedure restricts the territorial jurisdiction of the federal courts well short of the constitutional limits. The current version of Rule 4, unlike its predecessors, clearly separates the issues of basis and notice. The notice provisions of the rule — rules 4(d), 4(e), and 4(f) — permit service on or solicitation of a waiver of service from a defendant anywhere in the world. Rule 4(k) then provides that service or waiver is sufficient to establish jurisdiction over a defendant only in the circumstance specified in subsections 4(k)(1)(A)–(D) and 4(k)(2).

Rule 4(k)(1)(A) permits a federal court to exercise jurisdiction over the person of a defendant "who could be subjected to the jurisdiction of a court

[35] 355 U.S. 220 (1957). *McGee* is discussed in § 20[B], *supra.*

[36] See Mississippi Pub. Corp. v. Murphree, 326 US 438 (1946).

[37] See Casad & Richman § 5-1[2]. Fullerton, *Constitutional Limits on Nationwide Personal jurisdiction in the Federal Courts,* 79 N.W. L. Rev. 1 (1984). Another possible limit on congressional power to extend the range of a federal court's jurisdiction beyond that of the courts of the state in which the federal court sits may come from *Erie Railroad v. Tompkins,* 304 U.S. 64 (1938), *see* § 104[a][2], *infra. See* Gerald Abraham, *Constitutional Limitations Upon the Territorial Reach of Federal Process,* 8 Vill. L. Rev. 520 (1963).

[38] There are some special kinds of cases for which Congress has expressly provided for nationwide — or even worldwide — service of process. See Casad & Richman § 5-3.

of general jurisdiction in the state in which the district court is located." This language confers jurisdiction over a defendant who is served within the state, who would be subject to general jurisdiction in the state courts, or who would be subject to long–arm (specific) jurisdiction in the state courts. Thus under Rule 4(k)(1)(A), state law controls the application of both traditional and long–arm jurisdictional bases to both individual and corporate defendants. The constitutional test for an exercise of jurisdiction under this provision is also the same as would apply to an action in state court, the minimum contacts test of *International Shoe,* with the court measuring the contacts between the defendant *and the forum state.* Thus it is not sufficient that the defendant has minimum contacts with the United States as a whole. Further, there is no difference in the way the rule applies to federal question and diversity cases. Thus Rule 4(k)(1) eliminates several difficult issues that had plagued earlier versions of Rule 4.[39]

Rule 4(k)(1)(B)[40] permits the court to exercise personal jurisdiction over a party impleaded under Rule 14 or joined pursuant to Rule 19 as a person needed for a just adjudication if the party is served (or waives service) in the United States and within 100 miles of the federal courthouse where the action is pending. The bulge provision applies whether the case rests on federal question, diversity, or admiralty jurisdiction. The constitutional test for jurisdiction under the bulge provision is minimum contacts with either the forum state or the bulge state.

Rule 4(k)(1)(D) provides that service or waiver of service is effective to establish jurisdiction over the person of a defendant "when authorized by a statute of the United States." This provision refers to federal statutes that provide for nation–wide or world–wide territorial jurisdiction for particular types of cases. Subdivision (C), which provides for jurisdiction over a defendant "who is subject to the federal interpleader jurisdiction under 28

[39] Under earlier versions of the rule it was not clear whether the court was to apply a federal or state law standard of amenability to foreign corporations and whether the corporation's contacts with the state or the nation were controlling. The Supreme Court explicitly declined to rule on these issues in Omni Capital Int'l v. Rudolph Wolf & Co., Ltd., 484 US 97, 102, n. 5 (1987).

The lower courts seemed to agree that in federal question cases, federal rather than state law would control. *See* Note, *Alien Corporations and Aggregate Contacts: A Genuinely Federal Jurisdictional Standard*, 95 Harv. L. Rev. 470 (1981). However, they were unable to come to consensus on whether to measure the defendant's contacts with the state or the nation as a whole. *Compare* United Rope Distributors, Inc. v. Seatriumph Marine Corp., 930 F 2d 532 (7th Cir 1991)(contacts with nation sufficient), *with* Point Landing, Inc. v. Omni Capital Int'l, Ltd., 795 F 2d 415 (5th Cir 1986), aff'd sub nom Omni Capital Int'l, Ltd. v. Rudolph Wolff & Co., 484 US 97 (1987)(contacts with state required).

Diversity cases initially produced some controversy in the lower courts, and two of the Second Circuit's best known judges, Clark and Friendly, disagreed vigorously. *See* Jaftex Corp. v. Randolph Mills Inc., 282 F.2d 508 (2nd Cir.1960); Arrowsmith v. United Press Int'l, 320 F.2d 219 (2nd Cir.1963). In the latter case, the Court of Appeals for the Second Circuit sitting *en banc* agreed with Judge Friendly's view that the corporation's amenability to jurisdiction in a diversity case is governed by the law of the state where the court sits. That view was later been adopted by all the circuits. *See* 4 Wright & Miller, Federal Practice and Procedure, § 1075, at 489–491.

[40] Fed. R. Civ. P. 4(k)(1)(B). *See generally* Casad & Richman § 5-2[4][b].

USC § 1335," is thus superfluous. Interpleader jurisdiction is permitted, after all, by the Federal Interpleader Act, which is a federal statute and so comes within the terms of subsection (D). Presumably either subsection is satisfied by minimum contacts with the United States as a whole.[41]

Rule 4(k)(2) provides for jurisdiction in cases "arising under federal law," over defendants who are not subject to personal jurisdiction in any state court, provided that the assertion of jurisdiction is consistent with the due process clause. It applies principally to aliens that have diffuse contacts with the United States as a whole but lack sufficient minimum contacts with any one state, and to aliens that have sufficient contacts with a state but fall outside the terms of the state's long–arm statute.[42] The other main category of defendants affected is American citizens living abroad, whose national citizenship renders them amenable to jurisdiction in federal court regardless of their minimum contacts with the forum state or the United States as a whole.[43]

The constitutional limitation on an assertion of jurisdiction under Rule 4(k)(2) comes from the fifth amendment, not the fourteenth, and requires minimum contacts with the United States as a whole, rather than with the forum state. Further, the fifth amendment, like the fourteenth, also prohibits the assertion of jurisdiction if the forum is so inconvenient to the defendant as to constitute a denial of "fair play and substantial justice" in spite of the defendant's minimum contacts with the United States.[44]

---

[41] *See generally id.* at § 5-2[4][c], [d], David D. Seigel, Supplementary Practice Commentaries, Fed. R. Civ. P. 4, 28 U.S.C.A. 83–84 (1998 Pocket Part).

[42] *See generally* Casad & Richman § 5-2[4][e]. Presumably, it would also apply to an alien with negligible national contacts who is personally served with process, in the territory of a state that has abolished transient service as a jurisdictional basis. *See* Burnham v. Superior Court, 495 U.S. 604 (1990), discussed at § 28, *supra.*

[43] *See* Blackmer v. United States, 284 U.S. 421 (1932), discussed in § 29, *supra.*

[44] *See* Asahi Metal Indus. v. Superior Court, 480 U.S. 102 (1987), discussed in § 27, *supra.*

Part E

UNDERSTANDING PERSONAL JURISDICTION

Personal jurisdiction is a complicated topic addressed by numerous and sometimes conflicting Supreme Court decisions, and it can be difficult for the student or practitioner to grasp it all at once. Organization and synthesis are the key tools to promote understanding. This part of Chapter 3 aims toward that goal by synthesizing, summarizing, and reorganizing the main themes of personal jurisdiction. Because much of the material in Parts B and C is organized chronologically, Part E takes a different tack and treats the Supreme Court's jurisprudence of jurisdiction from the current perspective.

§ 35 Constitutional Source and Underlying Policy

[a] The Source

The Supreme Court has been relatively consistent in identifying the constitutional source of the restrictions on judicial jurisdiction. Since *Pennoyer v. Neff*,[1] it has relied almost exclusively on the Due Process Clause.[2] Its one significant detour came in *World–Wide Volkswagen v. Woodson*,[3] where it relied in part on "principles of interstate federalism embodied in the Constitution." The Court suggested that the rights of sister states placed a limit on the forum's adjudicatory jurisdiction that was completely distinct from any limit based on fairness to the defendant. The jurisdictional limitations "act to ensure that the States through their courts do not reach out beyond the limits imposed on them by their status as coequal sovereigns in a federal system."

---

[1] 95 U.S. 714 (1878). For an extremely thorough discussion of the Court's views before *Pennoyer*, *see* Terry S. Kogan, *A Neo–Federalist Tale of Personal Jurisdiction*, 63 S. Cal. L. Rev. 257 (1990).

[2] Recently commentators have begun to question the Court's reliance on the due process rationale. *See* Jay Conison, *What Does Due Process Have to Do With Jurisdiction*, 46 Rutgers L. Rev. 1071 (1994), Roger H. Transgrud, *The Federal Common Law of Personal Jurisdiction*, 57 Geo. Wash. L. Rev. 849 (1989)(arguing that the limits on jurisdiction should be based on the Full Faith and Credit Clause and federal legislation or common law); Patrick J. Borchers, *The Death of the Constitutional Law of Personal Jurisdiction: From Pennoyer to Burnham and Back Again*, 24 U.C. Davis L. Rev. 19 (1990)(arguing that there should be almost no constitutional limits on state–court jurisdiction and that the Court's use of the Due Process Clause for the purpose is historically unjustified and currently unwise). *See also* Patrick J. Borchers, *Jurisdictional Pragmatism: International Shoe's Half–Buried Legacy*, 28 U.C. Davis L. Rev. 561 (1995). For critical commentary see John B. Oakley, *The Pitfalls of "Hint and Run" History: A Critique of Professor Borchers' "Limited View" of Pennoyer v. Neff*, 28 U.C. Davis L. Rev. 591 (1995).

[3] 444 U.S. 286 (1980). *World–Wide* is treated more completely in § 22, *supra*.

The Court's reliance on "interstate federalism," however, did not make sense in light of the traditional procedural rules that permit a defendant to waive any defect of adjudicatory jurisdiction. The defendant could waive her own rights, but how could she waive the rights of other states? The waiver problem, surfaced quickly in *Insurance Corp. of Ireland v. Campagnie des Bauxites de Guinee*[4] and forced the Court to retreat from its stance on interstate federalism.

In *Bauxites*, the Court held that the personal jurisdiction requirement "represents a restriction on judicial power not as a matter of sovereignty, but as a matter of individual liberty." In footnote 10 the Court was even more explicit:

> The restriction on state sovereign power described in *World–Wide* . . . must be seen as ultimately a function of the individual liberty interest preserved by the Due Process Clause. That Clause is the only source of the personal jurisdiction requirement and the Clause itself makes no mention of federalism concerns.

Another possible source for jurisdictional restrictions — the First Amendment — figured in several lower court opinions. In *New York Times Co. v. Connor*,[5] the Fifth Circuit held that a libel action against The Times by "Bull" Connor — an Alabama official who had actively opposed the civil rights movement — should be dismissed for lack of jurisdiction. Despite The Times' minimum contacts with Alabama, the court determined that holding it amenable there might impede the free flow of information throughout the country. Accordingly, it held that "First Amendment considerations surrounding the law of libel require a greater showing of contact" than is needed in other cases.

In *Calder v. Jones*[6] — a libel action by actress Shirley Jones against the National Enquirer and two of its employees — the Supreme Court rejected the defendants' free–speech arguments and held that the First Amendment does not require a special jurisdictional standard for libel cases. It reasoned that First Amendment considerations would "needlessly complicate" the already difficult and fact–specific minimum contacts inquiry. Further, the chilling effect of libel actions in distant forums had been taken into account already by the constitutional limitations on the states' substantive law of

---

[4] 456 U.S. 694 (1982). *Bauxites* is discussed in detail in § 30[b], *supra*.

[5] 365 F.2d 567 (5th Cir. 1966). Not all lower court cases agreed. *See, e.g.*, Buckley v. New York Post Corp., 373 F.2d 175 (2d Cir. 1967).

An additional potential source for legal limits on territorial jurisdiction would be future international treaties entered into by the United States. For commentary on the possible effect of such a treaty on the law of jurisdiction see Walter Heiser, *A "Minimum Interest" Approach to Personal Jurisdiction*, 35 Wake Forest L. Rev. 915, 942 (2000), Kevin Clermont, *Jurisdictional Salvation and the Hague Treaty*, 85 Cornell L. Rev. 89 (1999), Symposium, 61 Albany L. Rev. 1159 (1998) (articles by Professors Borchers, Cox, Meyer, Strauss, Weintraub, and Zekoll), Ronald Brand, *Tort Jurisdiction in a Multilateral Convention: The Lessons Of Due Process Clause and the Brussels Convention*, 24 Brooklyn J. Int'l L. 125 (1998), Friedrich Juenger, *American Jurisdiction: A Story of Comparative Neglect*, 65 U. Colo. L. Rev. 1 (1993).

[6] 465 U.S. 783(1984). *Calder* and the First Amendment argument are discussed more fully in § 24, *supra*.

defamation; there was no need to take account of those considerations again at the jurisdictional stage.

Having disqualified "interstate federalism" and the First Amendment, the Court has made it clear that the Due Process Clause is the only constitutional source for the limitations on the judicial jurisdiction of American courts. The Court has not been clear, however, whether the jurisdictional limitation is grounded in "substantive" or "procedural" due process. There is reason, however, to believe that it is neither, and that there is a separate third category of "jurisdictional" due process. Procedural due process guarantees a party the right to be heard at a meaningful time and in a meaningful manner.[7] It is possible that an exercise of jurisdiction could violate that right if the forum is so distant and the defendant's witnesses, evidence, etc. so difficult to transport that, as a practical matter, trial at the forum amounts to no process at all.[8] But jurisdictional limits based only on defense–crippling inconvenience would be very minimal indeed, and many of the Court's negative jurisdictional holdings cannot be explained on this basis.[9]

Substantive due process works no better. *United States v. Carolene Products*,[10] sets out the generally applicable "rational basis" standard, requiring no more than a state interest to justify state action. Once again, however, jurisdictional limits based only on the rational basis test would be very minimal, and many of the Court's negative holdings would not be justified. In *Shaffer v. Heitner*,[11] for instance, Delaware had a state interest in monitoring the performance of a Delaware corporation's officers and directors, so litigation in Delaware would not be irrational. And in *World–Wide Volkswagen v. Woodson*,[12] Oklahoma had an interest in arranging for the compensation of a product liability victim injured in Oklahoma, so it would not be irrational to exercise jurisdiction there over all possible tortfeasors.[13] Because neither "substantive" nor "procedural" due process doctrine explains the Supreme Court's jurisdiction decisions, it makes sense to view those decisions as creating a third category — jurisdictional due process.

[b] Policies and Justifications

While the Court has been relatively clear about the constitutional source of the limitations on judicial jurisdiction, it has been neither clear nor consistent in identifying and applying the policies that stand behind the

[7] Mathews v. Eldridge, 424 U.S. 319 (1976).

[8] *See* Wendy C. Perdue, *Personal Jurisdiction and the Beetle in the Box*, 32 B. C. L. Rev. 529, 562 (1991).

[9] *E.g.*, World–Wide Volkswagen v. Woodson, 444 U.S. 286 (1980), Hanson v. Denckla, 357 U. S. 235 (1958).

[10] 304 U.S. 144, 152 n.4 (1938).

[11] 433 U.S. 186 (1977).

[12] 444 U.S. 286 (1980).

[13] *See* Patrick J. Borchers, *The Death of the Constitutional Law of Personal Jurisdiction: From Pennoyer to Burnham and Back Again*, 24 U.C. Davis L. Rev. 19, 90 (1990).

restriction. The problem is not that the court says too little, but rather that it says too much. Thus, it has advanced and rejected territorial sovereignty repeatedly.[14] Defendant's inconvenience, a major theme in some opinions[15] gets short shrift in others.[16] Sometimes protecting the defendant from jurisdictional surprise — a law suit in an unforeseeable forum — is an important consideration;[17] other times, not.[18] The Court has distinguished choice of law from jurisdiction repeatedly, yet it has also used jurisdiction to police state choice–of–law decisions.[19]

The Court has done no better with the policies that justify a state in exercising jurisdiction.[20] Sometimes state interest is a crucial factor; other times, not.[21] Necessity, an adequate justification in some cases, is not in others;[22] the same is true of tradition.[23] Defendant's receipt of benefits from association with the forum state similarly has and has not been a key determinant.[24]

---

[14] *See* Pennoyer v. Neff, 95 U.S. 714 (1878)(advanced), discussed *supra* in § 17; International Shoe Co. v. Washington, 326 U.S. 310 (1945) (rejected), discussed *supra* in § 20[a]; Hanson v. Denkla, 357 U.S. 235 (1958) (advanced), discussed *supra* in § 20[c]; Shaffer v. Heitner, 433 U.S. 186 (1977) (rejected), discussed *supra* in § 21; World–Wide Volkswagen Corp. v. Woodson, 444 U.S. 286 (1980) (advanced), discussed *supra* in § 22; Insurance Corp. of Ireland Ltd., v. Campagnie des Bauxites de Guinee, 456 U.S. 694 (1982) (rejected), discussed *supra* in § 30[b].

[15] *See, e.g.*, Asahi Metal Industry Co., Ltd. v. Superior Court, 480 U.S. 102 (1987), discussed *supra* in § 27.

[16] Burger King Corp. v. Rudzewicz, 471 U.S. 462 (1985), discussed *supra* in § 26.

[17] World–Wide Volkswagen v. Woodson, 444 U.S. 286 (1980), discussed *supra* in § 22.

[18] Keeton v. Hustler Magazine, 465 U.S. 770 (1984), discussed *supra* in § 23.

[19] In Hanson v. Denkla, 357 U.S. 235 (1958) and Shaffer v. Heitner, 433 U.S. 186 (1977), the Court went to great pains to make clear that judicial jurisdiction should be distinguished from choice of law. The considerations relevant to one ought not control the other. ***But see*** Walter Heiser, *A "Minimum Interest" Approach to Personal Jurisdiction*, 35 Wake Forest L. Rev. 915, 955 (2000)(advocating similar atandards). Nevertheless, it seems fairly clear that the Court's hidden agenda in *Hanson* was to prohibit Florida from applying its law to generate an intuitively unjust result. *Hanson* is discussed *supra* in § 20[c]. For more on the Court's hidden motives in recent jurisdiction decisions, *see* Hayward D. Reynolds, *The Concept of Jurisdiction: Conflicting Legal Ideologies and Persistent Formalist Subversion*, 18 Hastings Const. L. Q. 819 (1991).

[20] Lately, some scholars, realizing that a Court's taking jurisdiction is, after all, a governmental exercise of coercion, have sought a theoretical justification for jurisdiction in the ancient and continuing debate among moral and political philosophers over the legitimacy of governmental authority generally. Thus citations to Locke, Hume, Jefferson, Rawls and Nozick have begun to appear in the current debate on jurisdiction. *See* Lea Brilmayer, *Jurisdictional Due Process and Political Theory*, 39 U. Fla. L. Rev. 293 (1987); Roger H. Transgrud, *The Federal Common Law of Personal Jurisdiction*, 57 Geo. Wash. L. Rev. 849 (1989); Wendy C. Perdue, *Personal Jurisdiction and the Beetle in the Box*, 32 B.C.L. Rev. 529 (1991). *See also* Kevin C. McMunigal, *Desert, Utility, and Minimum Contacts: Toward a Mixed Theory of Personal Jurisdiction*, 108 Yale L.J. 189 (1998)(seeking a justification for the jurisdictional restriction in the basic philosophical justifications for the criminal law).

[21] *Compare* McGee v. International Life Insurance Co., 355 U.S. 220 (1957), discussed *supra* in § 20[b], *with* Shaffer v. Heitner, 433 U.S. 186 (1977), discussed *supra* in § 21.

[22] *Compare* Mullane v. Central Hanover Bank and Trust Co., 339 U.S. 306 (1950), *with* Helicopteros Nacionales de Colombia v. Hall, 466 U.S. 408 (1984), discussed *supra* in § 25.

[23] *Compare* Burnham v. Superior Court, 495 U.S. 604 (1990), discussed *supra* in § 28, *with Shaffer, supra* note 11.

[24] *Compare* Burger King v. Rudzewicz, 471 U.S. 462 (1985), discussed *supra* in § 26, *with Shaffer, supra* note 11, *Helicopteros*, discussed *supra* in § 25.

Perhaps this critique of the Court is unfair, and no single overarching theory of jurisdiction is possible or even desirable. It may be that both the exercise of and restrictions on jurisdiction are justified by multiple policies whose relative importance changes from one case to another. Even if that is true, however, the Court's performance still has been weak; it has not been able to assign weights or priorities to the various policies, nor has it given lower courts, lawyers, or scholars much of an explanation why and when some should prevail over others.

§ 36 The Two–Part Test: "Minimum Contacts . . . Fairplay and Substantial Justice"

Although the Court has not done well in articulating the policies behind the jurisdictional restriction, it has been relatively clear about the two–step test for measuring it. The test originates, of course, in the Court's pronouncement in *International Shoe Co. v. Washington*[1] that defendant must have "certain minimum contacts with . . . [the state] such that the maintenance of the suit does not offend 'traditional notions of fair play and substantial justice.' " There was ambiguity built into this formulation: Some decisions emphasized the "minimum contacts" language, concentrating on the defendant's pre–litigation connections with the forum state.[2] Others focused more on the "fair play and substantial justice" passage and tested an exercise of jurisdiction by its overall fairness or reasonableness.[3]

The Supreme Court resolved this ambiguity in the more recent cases, particularly *World–Wide Volkswagen Corp. v. Woodson*[4] and *Burger King Corp. v. Rudziewicz*,[5] by combining the two interpretations into a single, two–stage test. First the court must measure the defendant's pre–litigation connections with the state. Then it must assess the overall fairness or reasonableness of the exercise of jurisdiction. The following sections address the components of the two–part test.

§ 37 Measuring Contacts

[a] Contacts Required

The Supreme Court has made it clear that pre–litigation contacts between the defendant and the forum are a prerequisite for long–arm jurisdiction.[1]

---

[1] 326 U.S. 310 (1945). *International Shoe* is treated in detail in § 20[a], above.

[2] *See* Hanson v. Denkla, 357 U.S. 235 (1958), discussed *supra* in § 20[c].

[3] *See* McGee v. International Life Insurance Co., 355 U.S. 220 (1957), discussed *supra* in § 20[b].

[4] 444 U.S. 286 (1980), discussed in § 22, *supra*.

[5] 471 U.S. 462 (1985), discussed in § 26, *supra*.

[1] An exercise of jurisdiction pursuant to a traditional basis does not seem to require pre–litigation connections. This is most clear in the cases of consent and waiver. *See* National Equipment Rental, Ltd. v. Szukhent, 375 U.S. 311 (1964)(jurisdiction based on defendants'

In the words of the Court:

> [T]he Due Process Clause "does not contemplate that a state may [exercise jurisdiction over] . . . an individual . . . with which the state has no contacts, ties, or relation." Even if the defendant would suffer minimal or no inconvenience . . .; even if the forum State has a strong interest in applying its law to the controversy; even if the forum State is the most convenient location for the litigation, the Due Process Clause . . . may sometimes divest the State of its power to render a valid judgment.

Exactly why the Court insists on pre–litigation contacts is not clear. The requirement may be designed to assure fairness to the defendant, but the second stage of the Court's two–step test seems to make that assurance without the need for contacts. It may be that the contacts requirement is a device to make the fairness requirement more concrete — a bright–line test to keep judges from running amok in expansive discussions of fairness. Another possibility is that contacts are required because primary actors in our federal system really do have expectations about the jurisdictional significance of state lines. The most likely answer, however, is that the contacts requirement is simply a vestige of the Court's territorial power theory and has no modern, functional justification.[2]

[b] General Jurisdiction, Specific Jurisdiction and the Sliding Scale

In *Helicopteros Nacionales de Colombia v. Hall*,[3] the Court adopted the distinction between general and specific jurisdiction — a device that helps in assessing the defendant's contacts with the forum.[4] If a defendant is amenable to general jurisdiction in a state, the state can exercise jurisdiction over her based on any claim, even one that is unrelated to her contacts with the State. Usually, general jurisdiction exists only when defendant's forum connections are numerous and substantial. [5] Thus Ohio can exercise

contractual consent even though they had no contacts with the forum); Phillips Petroleum Co. v. Shutts, 472 U.S. 797 (1985)(jurisdiction over absent class–action plaintiffs based on their failure to "opt–out" even though they had no contact with forum), Insurance Corp. of Ireland v. Compagnie des Bauxites de Guinee, 456 U.S. 694 (1982)(jurisdiction based on defendants' waiver of their rights to object; defendant's contacts with forum not required). *Szukhent, Shutts*, and *Bauxites* are discussed fully in § 30, *supra. See also* Burnham v. Superior Court, 495 U.S. 604 (1990) (four justices saw no need to examine contacts when defendant had been served with process within the forum state). *Burnham* is discussed in § 28, *supra.*

[2] *See* Weintraub § 4.8, Louise Weinberg, *The Place of Trial and the Law Applied: Overhauling Constitutional Theory*, 59 U. Colo. L. Rev. 67,102 (1988).

[3] 466 U.S. 408 (1984), discussed *supra* in § 25.

[4] The distinction was first suggested in Arthur von Mehren & Donald Trautman, *Jurisdiction to Adjudicate: A Suggested Analysis*, 79 Harv. L. Rev. 1121 (1966).

[5] Thus, the forum will have jurisdiction over natural persons who are domiciliaries of the state and corporations that are incorporated in the state. General jurisdiction may also exist over out–of–staters if their forum connections are very substantial; for example, most states will have general jurisdiction over McDonald's. For more on general jurisdiction, *see generally* Linda Silberman, *"Two Cheers" for International Shoe (and None for Asahi): An Essay on the*

general jurisdiction over one of its domiciliaries based on an automobile tort in Florida; even though the claim has nothing to do with the defendant's contacts with Ohio, those contacts are sufficiently substantial to justify general jurisdiction.

By contrast, if the defendant is amenable to specific jurisdiction, the state can exercise jurisdiction over her based only on claims that arise out of her forum contacts. Specific jurisdiction may be available when the defendant has very few contacts with the state; thus, in the preceding hypothetical, Florida could exercise specific jurisdiction over the Ohio defendant based on the Florida tort. The defendant had only one connection with Florida — the one automobile trip — but the claim arises directly out of that one Florida contact.

To round out the possibilities, it is useful to consider two additional variations of the Florida automobile accident hypothetical. In these, assume the same accident in Florida, but suppose that the Ohioan sues the Floridian. A Florida court would have general *and* specific jurisdiction over the Florida defendant. Not only does she have extensive contact with Florida, but also the claim arises directly out of those contacts. An Ohio court, by contrast, could exercise *neither* general *nor* specific jurisdiction over the Florida defendant; she has no contacts with Ohio, and the claim does not arise in Ohio.

Some cases fall between the paradigms of general and specific jurisdiction. The defendant has substantial contacts with the forum, but not enough for general jurisdiction; further, the claim, although not arising directly out of defendant's forum contacts, is nevertheless closely related to them. *Helicopteros Nacionales de Colombia v. Hall*[6] is an example: The defendant, Helicol, a Colombian corporation, had significant, but not overwhelming, contacts with Texas; it had negotiated a deal in Texas, with a Texas company to provide helicopter transportation in Peru. It had also purchased most of its helicopter fleet in Texas and sent its pilots to be trained there as well. The claim against Helicol resulted from a helicopter accident in Peru, not Texas; but the downed aircraft was bought in Texas, the pilot trained there, and the accident victims, American employees of the Texas company, would not have been in one of Helicol's helicopters if Helicol had not negotiated the transport deal in Texas. *Helicopteros* thus fails to satisfy completely the requirements for general or specific jurisdiction, yet it partially satisfies the requirements for both.

Jurisdiction should exist in cases like *Helicopteros*; the general/specific distinction should not eliminate the possibility of amenability in cases that

Fiftieth Anniversary of International Shoe, 28 U.C. Davis L. Rev. 755 (1995), Harold Maier & Thomas McCoy, *A Unifying Theory for Personal Jurisdiction and Choice of Law*, 39 Am. J. Comp. L. 249, 271 (1991), B. Glenn George, *In Search of General Jurisdiction*, 64 Tul. L. Rev. 1097 (1990).

There is one important exception to the principle that general jurisdiction requires extensive forum contacts. Personal service within the State, permits general jurisdiction, even if defendant had no pre–litigation forum contacts. *See* Burnham v. Superior Court, 495 U.S. 604 (1990), discussed *supra* in § 28.

[6] 466 U.S. 408 (1984).

fall between the two paradigms. To encompass all the proper cases, the dichotomy should be supplemented by a sliding scale. As the extent and importance of defendant's forum contacts increase, a weaker connection between the claim and defendant's contacts is permissible; as the extent and importance of defendant's forum contacts decrease, a stronger connection between the claim and defendant's contacts is required. Thus far, the Supreme Court has not adopted such a sliding scale.[7]

[c] How Much Contact?

Exactly how much contact must there be between the forum and defendant? For general jurisdiction, it is clear that very substantial contact is necessary. Certainly domicile is sufficient for a natural person, as is incorporation within the state for a corporation.[8] Also, if the defendant, though not incorporated in the forum, conducts nearly all its activities there, general jurisdiction will be proper. *Perkins v. Benguet Consolidated Mining Co.*[9] is a good example. Defendant was a Philippine corporation conducting operations "in exile" in Ohio during the Japanese occupation of the Philippines. Its activities in Ohio were fairly extensive: the president and chief stockholder lived there; he kept corporate funds in Ohio banks, drew and distributed salary checks there, and generally conducted corporate business in Ohio. Plaintiff's cause of action, however, bore no relation to defendant's Ohio contacts; rather, it arose out of defendant's mining operations in the Philippines. Despite the lack of relation between the cause of action and the forum, the Court upheld jurisdiction, relying on the very substantial nature of defendant's contact with Ohio.

Connections that are weaker than those in *Perkins* probably will not support general jurisdiction. Thus, in *Helicopteros Nacionales de Colombia v. Hall*,[10] general jurisdiction did not exist even though the defendant frequently sent employees and agents into the forum and purchased most of its helicopter fleet there. Beyond *Perkins* and *Helicopters*, the Court has provided little guidance on the issue of general jurisdiction.

In contrast, the Court has flooded the market with decisions on the issue of specific jurisdiction. In *Hansen v. Denckla*,[11] the Court announced that "it is essential in each case that there be some act by which the defendant purposefully avails itself of the privilege of conducting activities within the forum State, thus invoking the benefits and protections of its laws." The

[7] The sliding scale was proposed in William M. Richman, *Review Essay*, 72 Cal. L. Rev. 1328, 1336 (1984). For commentary critical of the idea, see Linda Simard, *Hybrid Personal Jurisdiction: It's Not General Jurisdiction, Or Specific Jurisdiction, But Is It Constitutional?*, 48 Case W. L. Rev. 559 (1998), Flavio Rose, *Related Contacts and Personal Jurisdiction*, 82 Cal. L. Rev. 1545 (1994). The courts and commentators are divided on whether there should be jurisdiction in cases that fall between the paradigms of general and specific jurisdiction. *See supra*, § 25, note 14.

[8] *See* §§ 28–31, *supra*, for a discussion of these traditional bases for jurisdiction.

[9] 342 U.S. 437 (1952).

[10] 466 U.S. 408 (1984).

[11] 357 U.S. 235 (1958), discussed *supra* in § 20[c].

passage suggests that the defendant's physical entry into the forum is necessary, but that is clearly false. The Court has realized that "it is an inescapable fact of modern commercial life that a substantial amount of business is transacted solely by mail and wire communication across state lines, thus obviating the need for physical presence. . . ."[12] It is enough if defendant's conduct is "purposefully directed" at the forum. Thus jurisdiction may exist when the defendant has sent into the state, a contract offer,[13] a partner,[14] or a defamatory magazine article.[15] Also, defendant may be amenable when her actions outside the state have foreseeable effects inside the state. Indeed, if the defendant's out–of–state activity is purposeful and geographically targeted at the forum state, jurisdiction can be based on a single transaction or occurrence — the most minimal of minimum contacts.[16]

[d] Whose Contacts?

The Court has been emphatic that the contacts that count are those of the defendant, not plaintiff or a third party. In *Keeton v. Hustler Magazine*,[17] the plaintiff had no contact with the forum beyond the fact that a magazine on which she worked, and another in which she was defamed, were distributed there. The Court was not perturbed: "[W]e have not to date required a plaintiff to have 'minimum contacts' with the forum. . . . On the contrary, we have upheld . . . jurisdiction where such contacts were entirely lacking. . . ." The Court went on to add, however, that plaintiff's residence or contacts might be relevant insofar as they are the focus of defendant's forum related activities and thus enhance defendant's contacts with the forum.

One of the Court's earliest pronouncements on the question occurred in *Hanson v. Denckla*.[18] The issue there was whether the contacts of a third party could be attributed to the defendant. Settlor was a Pennsylvania domiciliary who set up a trust, using a Delaware corporate trustee. Later she moved to Florida, continuing to have regular dealings with the Delaware trustee. The Court held Florida could not exercise personal jurisdiction over the trustee, explaining that "[t]he unilateral activity of those who claim some relationship with a non–resident defendant cannot satisfy the requirement of contact with the forum State."

Of course, defendant's agent's contacts with the forum may enhance defendant's contacts. Thus, if the defendant has employees that work regularly in the forum[19] or a partner who conducts partnership business

---

[12] Burger King v. Rudzewicz, 471 U.S. 462 (1985), discussed *supra* in § 26.

[13] McGee v. International Life Insurance Co., 355 U.S. 220 (1957), discussed *supra* at § 20[b].

[14] *Burger King, supra* note 12.

[15] Keeton v. Hustler Magazine, Inc., 465 U.S. 770 (1984), discussed *supra* in § 23.

[16] McGee v. International Life Insurance Co., *supra* note 13.

[17] 465 U.S. 770 (1984); *see* § 23, *supra*.

[18] 357 U.S. 235 (1958); *see* § 20[c], *supra*.

[19] International Shoe Co. v. Washington, 326 U.S. 310 (1945); *see* § 20[a], *supra*.

in the forum,[20] those activities will count toward defendant's minimum contacts.

A related problem is whether there is jurisdiction over the employee in such cases. Initially some courts had held that a corporate employee, who acted in a fiduciary capacity in the forum, acted for the corporation and not for herself; thus long–arm jurisdiction over the employee could not be based on those acts.[21] This view, known as the fiduciary shield doctrine, surfaced in *Calder v. Jones*,[22] but the Supreme Court rejected it emphatically. Defendants, Florida–based employees of the National Enquirer, were the author and editor of an article that defamed the California plaintiff. They argued that they should be shielded from California's jurisdiction because their California–directed activities were undertaken to benefit their employer and because they were not responsible for the circulation of the magazine there. The Court was not impressed:

> [Defendants] are correct that their contacts with California are not to be judged according to their employer's activities there. On the other hand, their status as employees does not somehow insulate them from jurisdiction. Each defendant's contacts with the forum State must be assessed individually.

In summary, the Court's view on this issue is clear. The defendant's agent's contacts in the forum may be attributed to the defendant; but, otherwise, the only contacts that count are the defendant's. The forum connections of plaintiff or a third party matter only to the extent that they result in forum–directed activity by the defendant.

[e] Foreseeability

Because the exercise of judicial jurisdiction is based in part upon fairness and reasonableness, foreseeability ought to be relevant. If defendant could not have foreseen that her activities would cause injury in the forum state, she ought not be compelled to defend there. In the words of Justice White, "The Due Process Clause . . . gives a degree of predictability to the legal system that allows potential defendants to structure their primary conduct with some minimum assurance as to where that conduct will and will not render them liable to suit."[23]

In *World–Wide Volkswagen v. Woodson*,[24] the Court made it clear, however, that foreseeability cannot act as a substitute for minimum contacts. In other words, foreseeability that defendant's activities might cause harm in the forum is not sufficient for jurisdiction. A hypothetical case, posed by Judge Sobeloff in *Erlanger Mills v. Cohoes Fibre Mills*,[25] shows the problem with foreseeability.

---

20 Burger King Corp. v. Rudzewicz, 471 U.S. 462 (1985); *see* § 26, *supra*.

21 Casad & Richman, § 4-3.

22 465 U.S. 783 (1984), *see* § 24, *supra*.

23 World–Wide Volkswagen v. Woodsen, 444 U.S. 286 (1980).

24 *Id.*

25 239 F.2d 502 (4th Cir. 1956).

Suppose a California filling station owner, who has never ventured outside his native state. One day a Pennsylvania tourist drives into the station and purchases a tire. Back home in Pennsylvania, the tire ruptures and causes the tourist severe injury. Should the California filling station owner be amenable to suit in Pennsylvania? Surely it was foreseeable to him that his sale of the tire could cause injury there; the license plates on the tourist's car clearly made Pennsylvania a likely destination. Yet it seems unfair and perhaps counterproductive to require this very "local" person to travel to Pennsylvania to defend. He did nothing to encourage out of state business. The only way he could "structure his primary conduct" to avoid effects in Pennsylvania is deliberately to be inhospitable to out–of–state drivers — hardly a result that the law of jurisdiction should encourage.

Although the *World–Wide* majority held that foreseeability is not a sufficient condition for jurisdiction, it did indicate that foreseeability is a relevant concept. The foreseeability that is crucial is the defendant's anticipation (given its forum–related activity) that it could be "haled into court" in the forum. In other words, a defendant is amenable to jurisdiction in the forum if it could foresee being amenable to jurisdiction in the forum. It is hard to foresee how that circular dictum could be helpful either to lower courts or potential defendants.[26]

[f] Initiation — Who Went to Whom

A second look at the California Filling Station Owner hypothetical suggests another concept that has figured in the Court's minimum contacts calculations. Perhaps what was objectionable about holding the California defendant amenable in Pennsylvania is that he did not initiate the contact with Pennsylvania or seek business with its citizens; it was the Pennsylvania tourist who came to him and initiated the transaction. The test suggested by the hypothetical may be conveniently termed the "Initiation" or the "Who Went to Whom" test. If defendant goes to plaintiff's home state and seeks her business, he ought to be amenable there. If plaintiff goes to defendant, however, and initiates the contact with him, defendant ought not be amenable in plaintiff's home state.

The initiation test has played a part in several of the Supreme Court's modern cases.[27] It was one of the elements the Court used to distinguish

---

[26] For further discussion of foreseeability, *see* Vernon, Weinberg, Reynolds & Richman 64, Leonard Ratner, *Procedural Due Process and Jurisdiction to Adjudicate*, 75 Nw.U. L. Rev. 363, 379 (1980).

[27] The test has figured prominently in some state–court decisions. In Conn v. Whitmore, 9 Utah 2d 250, 342 P.2d 871 (1959), plaintiff, a resident of Illinois, who raised and sold Arabian horses, mailed to defendant in Utah a list of horses for sale. Defendant purchased a horse, and a dispute developed over its condition. Plaintiff recovered a default judgment against defendant in Illinois, but the Utah court denied that judgment full faith and credit on the ground that the Illinois court lacked jurisdiction over defendant. Said the court: "It is important to bear in mind that it was not the defendant Utah resident who took the initiative by going into Illinois to transact business. . . . Quite the contrary, it was the plaintiff resident of Illinois who proselyted for business in Utah. . . ." The Court then suggested that, if the initiation test were ignored, mail order sellers would be able to advertise for business all over the country yet conduct all litigation against customers in the seller's home state.

between *McGee v. International Life Insurance Co.*[28] and *Hanson v. Denckla*.[29] In *McGee*, the defendant solicited the insured by sending an offer of a life insurance policy to him in California — the forum state. By contrast, in *Hanson* the Delaware trustee did not seek out business in Florida; its contact with the forum began when its customer — the settlor — moved there. More recently in *Burger King v. Rudzewicz*,[30] the Court relied in part on the initiation test to uphold Florida's jurisdiction over a Michigan franchisee who, "[e]schewing the option of operating an independent local enterprise, . . . 'reach[ed] out beyond' Michigan and negotiated with a Florida corporation for the purchase of a long–term franchise. . . ."

The initiation test does not always prevail, however. In *National Equipment Rental, Ltd. v. Szukhent*,[31] the New York plaintiff initiated contact with the Michigan defendants; nevertheless, the Court, relying on a contractual consent–to–jurisdiction clause, upheld New York's jurisdiction over the Michigan defendants.

In other cases, the initiation test yields no result. Those are cases where neither the plaintiff nor the defendant initiates the contact. Suppose a consumer purchases a camping stove from defendant in Maine and then travels to Montana — a state with which the seller has no contact. There, a defect in the stove causes a fire in which a third person — a Montana domiciliary — is injured. The initiation test gives no answer here, but the result under the stream–of–commerce test is almost certain to favor the defendant–seller.

[g] Purposefulness and the Stream of Commerce[32]

Defendant's contacts with the forum justify personal jurisdiction only if defendant has established them purposefully.[33] If, instead, the contacts result from chance or the acts of others, jurisdiction will not exist.[34] In most cases, the purposefulness requirement presents no difficulty; thus if defendant drives her car into the forum[35] and negligently injures the plaintiff, or sends defamatory material into the forum, the requirement is clearly satisfied.[36]

The difficult cases involve an out–of–state enterprise whose products or services cause injury in the forum. In the period following the jurisdictional revolution of *International Shoe Co. v. Washington*,[37] state courts developed

28 355 U.S. 220 (1957).

29 357 U.S. 235 (1958). *McGee* and *Hanson* are discussed in §§ 20[b], [c], *supra*.

30 471 U.S. 462 (1985); *see* § 26, *supra*.

31 375 U.S. 311 (1964), discussed *supra* in § 30[c].

32 *See generally* Vernon, Weinberg, Reynolds & Richman 63, 106–107.

33 The clearest cases involve an intentional act of defendant geographically targeted at plaintiff in the forum. *See, eg.*, Calder v. Jones 465 U.S. 783 (1984), discussed in § 24, *supra*.

34 *See* World–Wide Volkswagen v. Woodson, 444 U.S. 286 (1980), discussed in § 22, *supra*.

35 *See* Hess v. Pawloski, 274 U.S. 352 (1927); *see* § 18[c], *supra*.

36 *See* Calder v. Jones, *supra* note 33.

37 326 U.S. 310 (1945).

the stream of commerce theory[38] to deal with such cases. The doctrine held that a manufacturer, distributor, or retailer of defective goods should be amenable to jurisdiction wherever those goods are distributed, either directly or indirectly, through the chain of distribution or stream of commerce. The theory allowed the expansion of jurisdictorial doctrine to match the expansion of interstate and international commerce; without it, an out–of–state enterprise could reap substantial rewards from goods sold in the forum yet insulate itself from amenability by the use of middlemen.

But what if the product ends up in the state not as a direct result of the chain of distribution but rather as a result of the foreseeable action of a consumer. In *World–Wide Volkswagen Corp. v. Woodson*,[39] the Supreme Court addressed the issue and added a significant limitation to the stream of commerce theory. The opinion suggested that if a consumer purchased the product in the forum, that state could exercise jurisdiction over everyone in the chain of distribution, but that jurisdiction might not exist when the product entered the state as a result of the foreseeable action of a consumer who purchased it elsewhere. The *World–Wide* limitation makes sense; an enterprise should not be held amenable wherever its product happens to turn up regardless of its efforts to limit distribution.

In *Asahi Metal Industry Co., Ltd v. Superior Court*,[40] Justice O'Connor, writing for a four–vote plurality, endorsed a much more ominous limitation on the theory. The defendant, a Japanese component part maker, was aware that the final product would arrive in the forum but took no action to direct it there beyond selling the part to the Taiwanese final product manufacturer. Justice O'Connor argued that the mere act of placing the product into the stream of commerce should not be sufficient even though the defendant knew that the stream would carry the product into the state. Additional conduct "purposefully directed" at the forum should be required, such as designing the product for the market in the forum–state, advertising there, establishing a customer–advice service there, or marketing through a distributor who had agreed to serve as a sales agent there.

Justice Brennan, leading another group of four, disagreed, rejecting the requirement of "additional conduct"; he argued that the defendant's knowledge that the stream would carry the product into the state should be enough. Justice Stevens, the ninth vote, saw no need to reach the issue.

The Court should reject Justice O'Connor's position. If it does not, the American consumer injured by a defective component part often would not be able to sue the foreign component–part maker in the United States. Because of the expense and choice–of–law disadvantages of foreign litigation, it is seldom a practical alternative. Of course, the consumer would be able to reach other defendants, such as finished–product makers, distributors and retailers, and usually that would be enough. In some cases,

---

[38] *See, e.g.*, Gray v. American Radiator & Standard Sanitary Corp., 22 Ill. 2d 432, 176 N.E.2d 761 (1961); Buckeye Boiler Co. v. Superior Court of Los Angeles City, 17 Cal.2d 893, 458 P.2d 57, 80 Cal. Rptr 113 (1969).

[39] 444 U.S. 286 (1980); discussed fully in § 22, *supra*.

[40] 480 U.S. 102 (1987); discussed fully in § 27, *supra*.

however, the other defendants may be judgment proof or may have substantive–law defenses, and the consumer could end up without a remedy.

§ 38 Measuring Fairness or Reasonableness

[a] Fairness Required

World–Wide Volkswagen Corp. v. Woodson[1] and *Burger King Corp v. Rudzewicz*[2] indicated that fairness or reasonableness is a required component of the two–stage test for jurisdiction; even if the defendant's contacts with the forum are sufficient, an exercise of jurisdiction might yet fail if found to be unreasonable or unfair. In *Asahi Metal Industry Co., Ltd. v. Superior Court,*[3] the Court backed up its dicta with a holding. Although the Justices were unable to agree on the contacts issue, they voted 8–1 to strike down California's exercise of jurisdiction based on its unfairness. If there was doubt before *Asahi,* there is none now; a separate inquiry into fairness is required.

[b] The Fairness Factors

In several recent opinions the Court has listed five factors to be taken into account at the fairness stage of the two–step jurisdiction inquiry: the burden on the defendant, the forum state's interest in adjudicating the dispute, the plaintiff's interest in obtaining convenient and effective relief, the interstate judicial system's interest in obtaining the most efficient resolution of controversies, and the shared interest of the several states in furthering fundamental substantive social policies.

While the Court has lavished attention on the contacts issues, its treatment of the fairness factors has been more perfunctory.[4]

[1] The Burden on the Defendant

According to the Court, the burden on the defendant is "always a primary concern," yet it has said little on the topic. In *Burger King Corp. v. Rudzewicz,*[5] the Court had the opportunity to develop the theme because the defendant was not a corporate litigant and so had limited resources to litigate in Florida, 1,000 miles from his home in Michigan. The Eleventh Circuit was troubled that litigation in Florida might severely impair the

[1] 444 U.S. 286 (1980), discussed in § 22, *supra.*

[2] 471 U.S. 462 (1985), discussed in § 26, *supra.*

[3] 480 U.S. 102 (1987), discussed in § 27, *supra.*

[4] The lower courts have had to wrestle with the factors. *See* Leslie W. Abramson, *Clarifying "Fair Play and Substantial Justice": How the Courts Apply the Supreme Court Standard for Personal Jurisdiction,* 18 Hastings Const. L.Q. 441 (1991).

[5] 471 U.S. 462 (1985), discussed in § 26, *supra.*

defendant's ability to call Michigan witnesses, but the Supreme Court found that concern to be "wholly without support in the record."[6]

The Court has made more of the defendant's burden when the defendant is an alien. In *Asahi Metal Industry Company, Ltd. v. Superior Court,*[7] the Court found the burden on the Japanese defendant to be severe. Not only would Asahi have to traverse the distance between Japan and California, but it also would have to submit its dispute to a foreign nation's judicial system. The "unique burdens" on the alien defendant, said the Court, "should have significant weight in assessing the reasonableness of extending personal jurisdiction over national borders."

Occasionally, the Court has justified an exercise of jurisdiction based on the minimal burden placed on a litigant. Thus in *Phillips Petroleum Co. v. Shutts,*[8] it upheld jurisdiction over absent class–action plaintiffs who had no contact with the forum; unlike a typical defendant, they did not have to hire counsel, travel to the forum, participate in discovery, or pay damages if they lost. Further, their interests were protected by other actors: the defendant, the named plaintiff, and the Court. In other cases, however, the Court has ignored the "minimal burden" factor. Thus in *Hanson v. Denckla,*[9] Florida could not exercise jurisdiction over a Delaware trustee even though it was merely a stakeholder and stood to gain or lose nothing in the case.

[2] The Forum State's Interest in Adjudicating the Dispute

The Court has paid considerable attention to this factor, and evaluated several different kinds of state interests. A common theme is the state's interest in providing a forum for state residents to pursue claims against outsiders. Thus in *McGee v. International Life Insurance Co.,*[10] the Court relied on California's interest in allowing its citizens to sue non–resident insurers, and in *Burger King Corp. v. Rudzewicz,*[11] it pointed to Florida's "manifest interest" in supplying a convenient forum for Florida residents.

Occasionally, the Court has been willing to take account of less pressing interests, such as the state's interest in providing a forum for a non–resident plaintiff's injured in the forum; in *Keeton v. Hustler Magazine, Inc.,*[12] for

---

[6] At the "fairness" stage, the relative wealth and power of the parties is directly relevant since conducting litigation away from home can be prohibitively expensive for consumers or small business enterprises. *See* Walter Heiser, *A "Minimum Interest" Approach to Personal Jurisdiction,* 35 Wake Forest L. Rev. 915, 935 (2000) (suggesting that the fairness attack on jurisdiction should be reserved for such defendants), Russell Weintraub, *A Map Out of the Personal Jurisdiction Labyrinth,* 28 U.C. Davis L. Rev. 531, 547 (1995)(same). Based on its ability to rouse judicial disagreement at several stages of the litigation, the factual setting in *Burger King* must be close to the line.

[7] 480 U.S. 102 (1987), discussed in § 27, *supra.*

[8] 472 U.S. 797 (1985), discussed in § 30[c][3], *supra.*

[9] 357 U.S. 235 (1958), discussed in § 20[c], *supra.*

[10] 355 U.S. 220 (1957); discussed in § 20[b], *supra.*

[11] 471 U.S. 462 (1985); discussed in § 26, *supra.*

[12] 465 U.S. 770 (1984); discussed in § 23, *supra.*

instance, the Court recognized New Hampshire's interest in hearing the claims of a non–resident who had been defamed in a magazine circulated in New Hampshire. Another somewhat minimal state goal recognized in *Keeton* was New Hampshire's interest in "cooperating with other States, through the 'single publication rule', to provide a forum for efficiently litigating all issues and damage claims arising out of a libel in a unitary proceeding."

On the other hand, the Court has ignored or discounted some fairly important state interests. In *Asahi Metal Industry Company, Ltd. v. Superior Court,*[13] it minimized California's interest in deterring foreign component–part makers from making defective parts for finished products to be sold in California. While such an interest might be important in a suit by a consumer against the manufacturer, it was not in *Asahi*, where the consumer's claim had been settled and all that remained was an indemnity claim by the finished product maker against the maker of the component part.

In *Shaffer v. Heitner*[14] the Court used two interest–minimizing strategies. Plaintiff had argued that Delaware had an interest in exercising personal jurisdiction over officers and directors of a Delaware corporation to supervise their management and control of the entity. The Court rejected the argument. First it disputed the existence of the state interest, pointing out that Delaware had no special long–arm statute directed toward officers and directors of Delaware corporations. Then it suggested that even if the Delaware interest did exist, it could support only the choice of Delaware law to govern the issue, not Delaware's jurisdiction to hear the dispute.

The Court has offered no general principle to explain its seemingly divergent views of the importance of state interests. It is worth noting, however, that in the cases where state interest figures importantly, the Court's resolution of that issue is consistent with its ultimate holding on jurisdiction.[15] It may be that state interests are so easy to manufacture, magnify, or discount that the Court can reach its result first and then always find a state interest argument — positive or negative — to support it.

[3] Plaintiff's Interest in Obtaining Convenient and Effective Relief

Long before the Court adopted the two–step test, it had indicated that plaintiff's interest in a ready forum was an important consideration. In *McGee v. International Life Insurance Co.,*[16] the Court upheld jurisdiction over an out–of–state insurer based in part on the inability of potential claimants to pursue small claims against insurers away from home. Later

[13] 480 U.S. 102 (1987); discussed in § 27, *supra*.

[14] 433 U.S. 186 (1977), discussed in § 44, *infra*, and § 21, *supra*.

[15] This seems to be true in the lower courts as well; *see* Abramson, note 4, *supra*.

[16] 355 U.S. 220 (1957); *see* § 20[b], *supra*.

in *Shaffer v. Heitner*,[17] the Court suggested that property–based jurisdiction might be appropriate "when no other forum is available to plaintiff."

Without minimum contact, however, even the plaintiff's dire necessity is not enough. Thus, in *Helicopteros Nacionales de Columbia v. Hall*,[18] the plaintiffs' lack of a convenient forum did not count for much at all. Plaintiffs, widows and orphans of passengers killed in Peru in one of the Colombian defendant's helicopters, sued the defendant in Texas. The Texas forum was probably the plaintiffs' only realistic choice; litigation in South America would have been expensive and probably futile, given the unfavorable substantive and procedural law of the available forums there. Nonetheless, the Supreme Court reversed because Texas' exercise of jurisdiction over the defendant failed the contacts test.

Finally, plaintiff's option of a ready and convenient alternative forum can count against jurisdiction in the fairness calculation. In *Asahi Metal Industry Company, Ltd. v. Superior Court*,[19] plaintiffs brought an action in California against Cheng Shin, a Taiwanese corporation, who then filed an indemnity claim against Asahi, a Japanese corporation. When the plaintiffs' claims were settled, only the indemnity claim remained. The Supreme Court, relying on the ready availability to Cheng Shin of a convenient forum in Japan or Taiwan, held that California's exercise of jurisdiction over Asahi failed the fairness test.

[4] The Interstate Judicial System's Interest in Obtaining the Most Efficient Resolution of Controversies

Neither the Supreme Court nor the lower courts[20] have said much about this fairness factor. Presumably, the proximity of the forum to witnesses, physical evidence, and other forms of proof should matter. Choice of law should be an issue also, with the need for the forum to apply difficult and unfamiliar law counting against jurisdiction. A final concern should be the court's ability to exercise jurisdiction over all parties and all issues in a dispute.[21] If it can, the interstate judicial system benefits because repetitious, piecemeal litigation and inconsistent results are avoided. An example, is *Keeton v. Hustler Magazine, Inc.*,[22] where the Court relied in part on this factor. Cutting in favor of jurisdiction was New Hampshire's cooperation with other states in the "single publication rule," which reduced the possibility of multiple law suits based on a defamatory article in a nationally circulated magazine.

---

[17] 433 U.S. 186 (1977); the case is discussed in detail in §§ 21 and 44.

[18] 466 U.S. 408 (1984); *see* § 25, *supra*.

[19] 480 U.S. 102 (1987); *see* § 27, *supra*.

[20] *See* Abramson, *supra* note 4.

[21] *Id.*; the author expands considerably on these themes.

[22] 465 U.S. 770 (1984); *see* § 23, *supra*.

[5] The Shared Interest of the Several States in Furthering Substantive Social Policies

Once again, the Supreme Court and the lower courts have said very little.[23] The Court's only substantial discussion occurred in *Asahi Metal Industry Company, Ltd. v. Supreme Court,*[24] where it relied in part on this factor to conclude that California's exercise of jurisdiction over an alien defendant failed the fairness test. When a state court exercises jurisdiction over an alien, *Asahi* requires extra caution and consideration of the substantive and procedural interests of other nations, as well as the Federal government's interest in foreign relations. These interests suggest, said the Court, that state courts should be reluctant to conclude that "serious burdens on an alien defendant are outweighed by minimal interests . . . of the plaintiff or the forum State."

[c] Balancing Fairness Against Contacts

Writing for the Court in *Burger King v. Rudzewicz,*[25] Justice Brennan indicated how fairness and contacts should be balanced against one another:

> Once it has been decided that a defendant purposefully established minimum contact within the forum State, these contacts may be considered in light of other [fairness] factors to determine whether the assertion of personal jurisdiction would comport with "fair play and substantial justice. . . ." [The fairness] factors sometimes serve to establish the reasonableness of jurisdiction upon a lesser showing of minimum contacts than would otherwise be required. On the other hand, where a defendant who purposefully has directed his activities at forum residents seeks to defeat jurisdiction, he must present a compelling case that the presence of some other considerations would render jurisdiction unreasonable.

The passage is quite clear. The contacts step is by far the more important. The fairness inquiry plays a subsidiary role.

The Court's jurisdictional holdings reinforce the dominance of contacts over fairness. That trend is clearest where the contacts and fairness tests suggest opposite results — one supporting jurisdiction, the other not. Usually in such cases, the ultimate result has been consistent with the contacts ruling. In *World–Wide Volkswagen v. Woodsen,*[26] for example, the defendants, a New York automobile wholesaler and a New York automobile dealer, had very little contact with Oklahoma; but the fairness factors supported jurisdiction. Plaintiffs, who purchased the car in New York, were

---

[23] *See* Abramson, *supra* note 4.

[24] 480 U.S. 102 (1987). The Court's only other mention of the issue is in Burger King Corp. v. Rudzewicz, 471 U.S. 462 (1985), where it said that the interests of other states can usually be accommodated by means short of a jurisdictional dismissal. Often the forum's choice–of–law rules will provide for adequate consideration of the interests of other states.

[25] 471 U.S. 462 (1985), discussed in § 26, *supra*.

[26] 444 U.S. 286 (1980), discussed in § 22, *supra*.

injured in Oklahoma, and most of the evidence was there, as well. Oklahoma had a strong state interest in hearing the case, and Oklahoma law probably would govern. Nevertheless, the Supreme Court struck down Oklahoma's jurisdiction because of defendants' negligible contacts there.[27]

Keeton v. Hustler Magazine,[28] a defamation case, is *World–Wide*'s mirror image. The contacts analysis favored jurisdiction because defendant regularly distributed its magazine in New Hampshire. The fairness issue was less clear: Plaintiff had no real connection with New Hampshire, but picked the forum because of New Hampshire's six–year statute of limitations for defamation claims. Moreover, despite the Court's desperate attempt to create one,[29] New Hampshire had no real interest in hearing the case. Nevertheless, the Court, greatly impressed by defendant's New Hampshire contacts, upheld jurisdiction.[30]

Asahi Metal Industry Co., Ltd. v. Supreme Court[31] is the Court's lone exception to the contacts–over–fairness trend. Regardless of the contacts analysis, the Court held 8–1 that California's jurisdiction over the Japanese defendant failed the fairness test. Originally, the case involved a California plaintiff's product liability claim against Cheng Shin, a Taiwanese tire maker, who then brought an indemnity claim against Asahi, the Japanese valve maker. When the plaintiff's claim settled, only the indemnity action remained. In support of its fairness holding, the Court cited California's minimal interest, the substantial burden of California litigation on Asahi, and the ready availability to Cheng Shin of alternative forums.

§ 39 Jurisdiction Without Contact and Fairness

In *Shaffer v. Heitner*,[1] the Supreme Court announced that "all assertions of state–court jurisdiction must be evaluated according to the standards set forth in *International Shoe*. . . ." Despite that magnificent dictum, not every permissible exercise of jurisdiction fits well into the "minimum contacts . . . fair play and substantial justice" rubric. In some cases the

[27] Helicopteros Nacionales de Columbia v. Hall, 466 U.S. 408 (1984), *see* § 25, *supra*, is another example. Although the defendant had substantial contact with Texas, the case failed the contacts test because it fit neither the general nor specific jurisdiction paradigm. Relying on the contacts test the Court struck down the Texas court's jurisdiction despite the powerful fairness argument that plaintiffs had no alternative forum.

[28] 465 U.S. 770 (1984), discussed in § 23, *supra*.

[29] The Court decided that New Hampshire had an interest in protecting non–residents from defamatory statements published in New Hampshire and an interest in cooperating with other sates through the use the "single publication rule" to provide a forum for efficiently litigating all defamation claims arising from a single publication of a nationally circulated magazine.

[30] Another case where the Court's contacts–over–fairness preference supports jurisdiction is Burger King Corp. v. Rudzewicz, 471 U.S. 462 (1985). Defendant, a Michigan franchisee, had substantial contact with Florida, home of the franchisor, but litigation away from home was much more difficult for the franchisee than the franchisor. Nevertheless, the Court upheld Florida's jurisdiction, emphasizing defendant's ties to Florida and minimizing the inconvenience to him of litigating there.

[31] 480 U.S. 102 (1987), discussed in § 27, *supra*.

[1] 433 U.S. 186 (1977); discussed in § 21, *supra*, and § 44, *infra*.

Supreme Court has upheld jurisdiction without requiring the familiar two–step assessment of contacts and fairness.

The clearest examples are the cases involving a litigant's appearance, waiver, or consent.[2] Thus, without an inquiry into contacts and fairness, the Court has upheld jurisdiction when the defendant waived its jurisdictional objection by refusing to engage in discovery concerning the issue.[3] Similarly, contacts were not necessary when defendants signed an adhesion contract with a jurisdiction consent clause.[4] And finally, in a state court class action, the Court was willing to ignore the contacts problem and permit personal jurisdiction over absent class members who did not "opt out" of the class.[5]

In other cases, the Court's willingness to approve of jurisdiction without contacts and fairness is less clear. Thus, it has given conflicting signals on whether tradition is a sufficient substitute for minimum contacts. In *Shaffer v. Heitner*,[6] the Court held that the venerable history of attachment jurisdiction did not shield it from modern jurisdictional analysis because " '[t]raditional notions of fair play and substantial justice' can be as readily offended by the perpetuation of ancient forms that are no longer justified as by the adoption of new procedures that are inconsistent with the basic values of our constitutional heritage." In *Burnham v. Superior Court*,[7] however, tradition got a warmer reception; the Justices split 4–4 on whether jurisdiction based upon service of process could be justified by its historical pedigree alone or instead required a contemporary contacts and fairness analysis.

Another possible justification for personal jurisdiction without minimum contacts is necessity. Occasionally, the Court has suggested that it might furnish an independent basis for jurisdiction when plaintiff has no alternate forum available.[8] More recently, however, the Court has treated plaintiff's lack of an alternative forum simply as one factor to be taken into account at the fairness stage of contacts and fairness inquiry.[9] Thus, without

[2] These, of course, are traditional bases for personal jurisdiction. Domicile is also, *see* § 29, *supra*; but it is not discussed in this section because jurisdiction based on domicile passes both the contacts and fairness tests.

[3] *See* Insurance Corporation of Ireland, Ltd. v. Compagnie des Bauxites de Guinee, 456 U.S. 694 (1982). *See* § 30[b], *supra*.

[4] *See* National Equipment Rental, Ltd., v. Szukhent, 375 U.S. 311 (1964) discussed in § 30[c], *supra*.

[5] Phillips Petroleum Co. v. Shutts, 472 U.S. 797 (1985); *see* § 30[c], *supra*.

[6] 433 U.S. 186 (1977), discussed in § 44, *infra*.

[7] 495 U.S. 604 (1990), discussed in § 28, *supra*.

[8] *See* Mullane v. Central Hanover Bank and Trust Co., 339 U.S. 306 (1950). A New York statute permitted the creation of common trust funds by pooling the funds of numerous small trusts. The accounts of the common fund were to be settled at regular intervals by a judicial procedure called an accounting, which, according to the New York statute, was binding on all interested persons regardless of their contacts with New York. The Supreme Court upheld the statute based on the practical necessity for personal jurisdiction over all interested persons. Without it, common trust funds would be impossible because no trustee would be willing to undertake such an open–ended risk.

[9] In Helicopteros Nacionales de Colombia v. Hall, 466 U.S. 408 (1984), discussed *supra* in § 25, the Court found the defendant's contacts with Texas inadequate and thus never reached plaintiffs' compelling argument based upon necessity.

minimum contacts between the defendant and the forum, it is quite unlikely that jurisdiction can be based on necessity alone.

§ 40 Analytical Summary: Attacking a Personal Jurisdiction Problem

Sections 35 through 38 discuss the considerations and issues relevant to solving a personal jurisdiction problem. But how should those issues be organized when attacking a particular case? This section supplies a plan of attack — a plan that will provide the organization for any personal jurisdiction discussion, whether that discussion occurs in a pre–trial memorandum, an appellate brief, or a law school examination.

First, determine whether jurisdiction over defendant exists because of a traditional basis. If defendant is a natural person, was she served with process in the forum, is she domiciled in the forum, did she consent to jurisdiction? If defendant is a corporation, is it incorporated in the forum, is it doing business in the forum, did it consent? If a traditional basis exists, it is quite likely defendant can be constitutionally haled into court.

If no such basis exists, examine the forum's long–arm statute. If it is a California–style statute, it raises no separate issues of statutory construction; proceed to consider the constitutional question. If it is an enumerated act long–arm statute, determine whether any of its sections provides for jurisdiction over defendant.

Finally, determine whether exercising jurisdiction will violate defendant's right to due process. The long–arm statute may reach too far, and even the traditional bases may raise a constitutional question.[1] To answer the constitutional question, use the Supreme Court's two–stage (contacts plus fairness) test.

First, does the defendant have minimum contacts with the state? The best place to begin is with the general/specific jurisdiction distinction. If the defendant has very substantial contacts with the forum (*e.g.*, defendant is a domiciliary of the forum or a corporation incorporated in the forum), general jurisdiction may exist. If not, the case must fit the specific jurisdiction paradigm, and plaintiff's claim must "arise out of" or "relate to" defendant's forum contacts.

Next, assess the quantity and quality of defendant's forum contacts. For general jurisdiction, of course, a great deal of contact is required. For specific jurisdiction, much less will suffice; indeed, one contact may be

---

1 The Supreme Court has considered the constitutionality of one of the traditional bases recently. In Burnham v. Superior Court, 495 U.S. 604 (1990), the Court upheld the constitutionality of personal service as a jurisdictional basis. The Justices disagreed, however, on the reasons for their holding. One group of four, led by Justice Scalia was willing to approve of the practice based on its historical pedigree alone. Another group of four, whose spokesman was Justice Brennan, insisted on a complete due process inquiry even if the jurisdictional basis is well grounded in tradition. It is unclear which view ultimately will prevail and, therefore, unclear whether the traditional bases are *per se* constitutional. *See* § 28, *supra*, for a complete discussion of *Burnham*.

enough if it is intentionally established by the defendant. Further, the one contact need not involve defendant's physical entry into the forum; if she has purposefully directed her conduct at the forum, mail or telephone contact, or sending a product into the state is enough.

When assessing contacts, remember that the ones that count are those established by the defendant or her agents. The unilateral activity in the forum of one who claims some relationship to the defendant is not enough. By the same token, the only contacts required are defendant's; there is no requirement that plaintiff be a forum resident or have minimum contacts with the forum. Plaintiff's contacts, however, or those of a third party may be relevant insofar as they are the focus of defendant's forum–directed activity.

Next consider foreseeability and initiation. Are defendant's forum–directed activities such that she should be able to anticipate being "haled into court" in the forum? The mere foreseeability that defendant's out–of–state activities might cause an effect in the forum is not enough. If the case involves dealings between an in–state plaintiff and an out–of–state defendant, apply the initiation test to determine who went to whom. Jurisdiction is much more likely if the defendant initially contacted the plaintiff rather than vice versa.

Finally, determine whether the defendant's contacts have been established purposefully. If a manufacturer purposefully creates a chain of distribution that directs its products into the forum, it will be amenable to a products liability action there. If, however, the defendant merely delivers its products into the stream of commerce with knowledge that they will end up in the forum, jurisdiction may or may not exist.[2] Finally, if the stream ends outside the forum and the product enters the forum because of the foreseeable conduct of the consumer, the manufacturer probably will not be amenable in the forum.

After measuring defendant's minimum contacts with the forum, assess the overall fairness or reasonableness of exercising jurisdiction. Consider first the burden on the defendant, particularly if it is an alien. Then determine whether the forum state has an interest in adjudicating the case. Usually it will — the interest in providing a forum for state residents to pursue claims against out–of–state defendants. Plaintiff's interest in a ready and convenient forum should also be considered, but even plaintiff's dire necessity will not support jurisdiction in the absence of contacts. Finally, factor in the interstate judicial system's interest in the efficient resolution of controversies and the shared interest of the several states in furthering substantive social policies.

A consideration of these issues in this order should produce a complete discussion of nearly any personal jurisdiction question and should satisfy

[2] This was the issue that divided the Court in Asahi v. Superior Court, 480 U.S. 102 (1987). One group of four, led by Justice O'Connor, held that the manufacturer's mere awareness that the stream would take the product into the forum was not enough. Another group of four, led by Justice Brennan, held that it was. Justice Stevens joined neither group. *Asahi* is discussed in detail in § 27 *supra*.

the judge, the lawyer who requested the memorandum, or even the law professor who drafted the examination question. But even summaries can be summarized, so consider the following personal jurisdiction checklist:

1. Does a traditional basis give jurisdiction over defendant?

a. Natural Persons

(1) Was defendant served with process in the forum?

(2) Is defendant a domiciliary of the forum?

(3) Did defendant consent to jurisdiction?

b. Corporations

(1) Is defendant incorporated in the forum?

(2) Is defendant doing business in the forum?

(3) Did defendant consent to jurisdiction?

2. If jurisdiction is not available under item 1 above, consider the forum's long–arm statute.

a. If it is a California–style statute, proceed directly to the constitutional question (item 3).

b. If it is an enumerated–act statute, does one of its sections apply in this case?

3. If jurisdiction is available under items 1 or 2, is the resulting exercise of jurisdiction constitutional?

a. Does the defendant have minimum contacts with the forum?

(1) Are defendant's contacts sufficient to support the exercise of general jurisdiction? If not, does specific jurisdiction exist because plaintiff's claim arises out of defendant's forum contacts?

(2) Are the contacts relied upon to support jurisdiction of those of the defendant or her agent?

(3) Could the defendant anticipate being "haled into court" in the forum?

(4) Did the out–of–state defendant initiate the contact with the in–state plaintiff or vice–versa?

(5) Did the defendant "purposefully establish" her contacts with the forum?

(6) Did the stream of commerce carry the defendant's products into the state?

b. Is the exercise of jurisdiction fair or reasonable?

(1) Will the burden on defendant be severe?

(2) Does the forum have an interest in adjudicating the case?

(3) Does plaintiff have a convenient alternative forum for the claim?

(4) Will jurisdiction further the interstate judicial system's interest in the efficient resolution of controversies?

(5) Will jurisdiction advance the shared interest of the several states in furthering substantive social policies?

Part F

JURISDICTION OVER PROPERTY

Part F of this Chapter examines jurisdiction over things — or more precisely, jurisdiction over the interests of persons in things. Section 41 compares in rem jurisdiction with in personam jurisdiction and describes the three traditional ways of exercising jurisdiction over property. After these preliminaries, § 42 discusses the traditional learning on attachment jurisdiction, with emphasis on *Pennoyer v. Neff*, *Harris v. Balk*, and *Seider v. Roth*. Section 43 discusses the limited appearance, a device that provides some protection to defendants from the unfairness of attachment jurisdiction. The last three sections treat the revolution in in rem thinking generated by *Shaffer v. Heitner*.

§ 41 The Traditional Taxonomy

[a] Jurisdiction in Rem and Jurisdiction In Personam

The territorial power theory of *Pennoyer v. Neff*,[1] distinguished strictly between in personam jurisdiction and in rem jurisdiction.[2] A court with in personam jurisdiction could bind the persons who were before it, while a court with in rem jurisdiction could bind only the property before it. This way of speaking is somewhat misleading, since every exercise of jurisdiction or power by a court affects the interests of persons.[3] The distinction between in personam and in rem jurisdiction, then, is really a way of describing two quite different methods by which a court can affect persons' interests.

---

[1] 95 U.S. 714 (1878).

[2] Under the traditional approach, real consequences turned on this formal distinction. Notice requirements for in rem actions were considerably more lenient, and a court could exercise jurisdiction over a piece of defendant's property in the forum even though the defendant had no other contact with the state.

The formal distinction lost some of its significance as jurisdictional theory matured. It became clear that every exercise of jurisdiction, whether styled "in rem" or "in personam" affects the interests of persons. *See* Restatement (Second) of Judgments § 5, Comment b (1982). Accordingly, the Supreme Court held in Mullane v. Central Hanover Bank & Trust Co., 339 U.S. 306 (1950), and its progeny (discussed in § 16, *supra*) that the constitutional adequacy of notice–giving provisions does not depend on whether the action is in rem or in personam. Further in Shaffer v. Heitner, 433 U.S. 186 (1977), the Court held that every exercise of jurisdiction — in personam or in rem — must satisfy the "minimum contacts . . . fair play and substantial justice" standard of *International Shoe*.

Despite these developments, the in rem–in personam distinction retains descriptive as well as historical significance. It describes two very different ways in which a court can affect the interests of persons. *See* Restatement (Second) of Conflict of Laws, Ch. 3, Topic 2, Introductory Note.

[3] *Id.*

The best way to understand the distinction is to concentrate on the different effects of in rem[4] and in personam judgments. A court exercising personal jurisdiction over a defendant can issue a judgment against him for any kind of legal or equitable relief. If plaintiff's claim is for damages, the court can issue a general money judgment that plaintiff can satisfy out of any property of defendant's within the forum. Further, the Full Faith and Credit Clause permits plaintiff to sue on the judgment debt in any other state and satisfy it out of defendant's property there.[5] If, on the other hand, plaintiff's claim is for equitable relief, a court with personal jurisdiction over the defendant can order him to do or refrain from doing any act on pain of contempt. Thus, a court exercising personal jurisdiction can affect defendant profoundly and can give plaintiff any type of relief available under the substantive law.

A court with in rem jurisdiction can act only in a much more limited way. It can affect defendant only by terminating his interest in the particular property over which it has jurisdiction. It cannot issue a general money judgment against him, nor can it grant equitable relief against him. From plaintiff's point of view, in rem jurisdiction will nearly always be a second choice, because the only relief an in rem judgment can grant plaintiff is to establish her title to the property or to order the property sold and the proceeds paid to her. Thus, if the value of plaintiff claim exceeds the value of the property seized, an in rem judgment can grant plaintiff only partial relief.

[b] Jurisdiction In Rem, Jurisdiction Quasi–In–Rem and Attachment Jurisdiction

The traditional learning divided jurisdiction over property into three sub classes: "true in rem" (often called, simply "in rem"), "quasi–in–rem type I," and "quasi–in–rem type II" (now usually called "attachment jurisdiction").[6]

In a true in rem action, the court determines the interests of everyone, whether named in the proceedings or not, in the particular res or thing. In essence, the action is one "against all the world."[7] The practical effect of such a proceeding is to establish relatively unassailable title in the thing because no one, whether named as a party or not, can later claim exemption from the effect of the judgment on the ground that the court lacked personal jurisdiction.[8]

---

[4] The words "in rem" in this sub–section are used to refer generally to any sort of jurisdiction based on property. The concept is refined and broken down into several categories in sub–section [b], *infra*.

[5] The Full Faith and Credit Clause is discussed in detail in § 110, *infra*.

[6] For a discussion of the three categories of in rem jurisdiction, *see* Restatement (Second) of Conflict of Laws, Ch. 3 Topic 2, Introductory Note.

[7] Restatement (Second) of Judgments § 6, Comment a (1982).

[8] Restatement (Second) of Conflict of Laws, Ch 3, Topic 2, Introductory Note (1971). A latecomer could, however, assert the lack of proper notice. *See* Mullane v. Central Hanover Bank and Trust Co., 339 U.S. 306 (1950); Schroeder v. City of New York, 371 U.S. 208 (1962). Notice in in rem actions is treated in § 16, *supra*.

Traditional examples of in rem actions are admiralty, forfeiture, eminent domain, probate, and land title registration. For these it is crucial that the court be able to extinguish the interests of persons who may be outside the forum's territory or whose interests, or even existence, may be unknown. The captions of such actions may reflect their effect on all the world, since often no parties are named; rather the case is known by the name of the thing. Thus, a probate proceeding in which a statutory heir contests a will against the testamentary devisee may be captioned "*In re Decedent's Estate*" and not "*Heir v. Devisee*." Similarly, a forfeiture action is typically captioned "*State v. 17 Cases of Scotch Whiskey*" rather than "*State v. Owner*."

In a quasi–in–rem type I action, plaintiff asserts a preexisting interest in a particular thing against certain named individuals only, and the judgment affects only the interests of the named parties, not those of "all the world." An example of such an action is a suit to remove a cloud on title, an action where plaintiff seeks to establish the right to the land against a particular person's rival claim.

The analytical significance of the distinction between in rem and quasi–in–rem jurisdiction has all but vanished. The constitutional prerequisites are the same. In both instances, there must be a relationship between the forum and the *res* or thing sufficient to make the exercise of jurisdiction reasonable.[9] And in both, all persons likely to be affected are entitled to adequate notice. Thus, apart from any consequences state law attaches to the labels, the distinction between in–rem and quasi–in–rem type I jurisdiction has only historical significance.[10]

Quasi–in–rem type II jurisdiction (now more commonly called "attachment jurisdiction") is quite different. In both a true in rem action and in a quasi–in–rem type I action, plaintiff has a pre–existing claim to the *res* or thing, and that claim is the subject of the action. In other words, plaintiff asserts an interest in the thing, and the court adjudicates that claim. By contrast, in an attachment action, plaintiff does not assert a pre–existing interest in the thing; indeed the claim often has nothing at all to do with the attached property. Rather, plaintiff asserts a personal claim against defendant (a tort or contract claim, for example) and simply uses the property or res as a device to obtain jurisdiction.[11]

A few examples illustrate the distinction. Suppose plaintiff purchases a piece of land from owner. Defendant tells plaintiff that he (defendant) has an easement to haul logs across plaintiff's land. Plaintiff sues defendant to remove this cloud on her title. The action is a quasi–in–rem type I action because plaintiff's claim is an assertion of title (free of defendant's purported easement) in the land. Now consider an ordinary tort claim. Defendant injures Plaintiff with his automobile. For some reason, not important

---

[9] Restatement (Second) of Judgments § 6, Comment a (1982). (Usually the presence of the thing in the state will suffice.)

[10] The American Law Institute has abandoned the distinction completely. *See* Restatement (Second) of Conflict of Laws § 6, Comment a (1986 Revisions).

[11] For more on the distinction, *see* Restatement (Second) of Conflict of Laws § 66, Comment a (1986 Revisions).

here, plaintiff cannot acquire personal jurisdiction over defendant in the forum state. However, defendant owns a piece of land in that state. Plaintiff sues the defendant and the court attaches defendant's land to gain jurisdiction. The suit is an attachment (quasi–in–rem type II) action. Plaintiff does not have a pre–existing claim of title in defendant's land. She concedes that defendant owns the property. In fact, the suit has nothing to do with the land; it is about a completely unrelated tort. The property is used simply as a device to obtain jurisdiction when personal jurisdiction over defendant is unavailable.

Remember that in each of the three types of in rem jurisdiction the only relief that the court can grant is either to award plaintiff the property or order the property sold and the proceeds paid to plaintiff.[12] Thus, in the second example posed above, if plaintiff prevails, the court will order defendant's land sold and the proceeds paid to plaintiff up to the amount of her damages. If her damages exceed the value of the property, plaintiff's claim will be satisfied only in part. For complete satisfaction she would have to sue defendant again where she can get personal jurisdiction over him or where she can get attachment jurisdiction over some other piece of defendant's property.[13]

True in rem jurisdiction and quasi–in–rem type I jurisdiction have proved relatively uncontroversial. Not so attachment jurisdiction. The next section considers the major cases in the development of attachment jurisdiction. As that evolution unfolds, note how the notion of property becomes more and more attenuated; and as it does, note how the exercise of attachment jurisdiction becomes more and more unfair to defendant. It was this unfairness that led to the doctrinal revolution in in rem jurisdiction wrought by *Shaffer v. Heitner*.[14]

§ 42 The Development of Attachment Jurisdiction[1]

[a] *Pennoyer v. Neff*[2]

Pennoyer v. Neff is the source for much of the traditional learning on jurisdiction. The opinion provided an early statement of the territorial theory of jurisdiction,[3] and established personal service as a basis for exercising personal jurisdiction.[4] It also set out the theoretical basis for attachment jurisdiction.

---

[12] *See* § 41[a], *supra*, for a discussion of the limited relief available when a court has in rem jurisdiction.

[13] *See* Restatement (Second) of Conflict of Laws § 66, comment h (1986 Revisions).

[14] 433 U.S. 186 (1977). *See* § 44, *infra*, for a discussion of *Shaffer*.

[1] A full treatment of the historical development appears in Joseph J. Kalo, *Jurisdiction as an Evolutionary Process: The Development of Quasi–in–Rem and In Personam Principles*, 1978 Duke L.J. 1147.

[2] 95 U.S. 714 (1878).

[3] *See* § 17, *supra*.

[4] *Id.*

The case arose when Mitchell sued Neff in Oregon for $300 in attorney's fees. Neff was neither domiciled in Oregon, nor was he personally served with process there. Pursuant to Oregon statute, notice of the action was published in a local newspaper. Neff did not appear, and Mitchell took a default judgment. To satisfy the judgment, a piece of land belonging to Neff was sold at a sheriff's sale to Pennoyer. Neff later sued Pennoyer for the land. Pennoyer's right to the land depended upon the validity of the judgment in *Mitchell v. Neff* and, therefore, upon the court's jurisdiction to render that judgment.

The Oregon court lacked personal jurisdiction over Neff because he was neither domiciled in Oregon nor served with process there. But might the judgment and the judicial sale be sustained because of Oregon's ability to exercise jurisdiction over Neff's land? On the way to answering that question, the Supreme Court announced the principle that a nonresident's land in the forum state might provide the basis for litigating against the owner a personal claim unrelated to the land:

> Every State owes protection to its own citizens; and, when non–residents deal with them, it is a legitimate and just exercise of authority to hold and appropriate any property owned by such non–residents to satisfy the claims of its citizens. It is in virtue of the State's jurisdiction over the property of the non–resident situated within its limits that its tribunals can inquire into that non–resident's obligations to its own citizens. . . .

Despite this broad language, the Supreme Court held the Oregon judgment invalid. The difficulty was that the trial court had not attached Neff's land *at the commencement* of the action. Rather, it had treated the case as an ordinary in personam action and had seized Neff's land only after rendering judgment against him. The opinion suggested that such a procedure was based on a fundamental misunderstanding about the nature of attachment jurisdiction:

> [T]he jurisdiction of the court to inquire into and determine [defendant's] obligations at all is only incidental to its jurisdiction over the property. Its jurisdiction in that respect cannot be made to depend upon facts to be ascertained [whether defendant has property in the forum state] after it has tried the cause and rendered the judgment.

Because the court did not attach Neff's land at the beginning of the suit, it could not exercise attachment jurisdiction. Thus, the narrow holding of *Pennoyer* was that the presence of defendant's property within the forum and its attachment at the commencement of the action are absolute prerequisites to a proper exercise of attachment jurisdiction.

Despite the narrow holding, a more general and more significant principle emerged over time from *Pennoyer* and defined the traditional scope of attachment jurisdiction. The *Pennoyer* principle permitted a court, if it attached real property of the defendant at the commencement of the action, to adjudicate a personal claim against the defendant even though there was no personal jurisdiction over him and even though the claim had no relation to the attached property. The main limitation was that a court with attachment jurisdiction could not issue a personal judgment against the defendant; its power was limited to the authority to award the property to plaintiff or order the property sold and the proceeds paid to satisfy the claim.

The *Pennoyer* principle seems to fly in the face of the teachings of *International Shoe*, with its emphasis on fairness and substantial justice.[5] Yet there is an argument to be made for the principle, or at least for its application in cases like *Pennoyer*, where real property was involved. It is difficult to have land in Oregon without having minimum contact with that state. Even if the land is idle, there are taxes to pay, and state regulations to comply with. Furthermore, anyone who owns land in the forum enjoys the benefits and protections of the forum's law. Thus, in the case of real property, the *Pennoyer* principle may be justified.[6]

The argument for the rule is weaker with tangible personal property. Personal property is not permanently located, so it is much easier for it to be temporarily within the state without its owner having minimum contacts with the state. Further, it sometimes wanders into the forum without the consent or knowledge of its owner. In such cases, the assertion of jurisdiction is unfair. The real possibilities for unfairness multiply dramatically when the *Pennoyer* principle is applied to *intangible* personal property.

[b] *Harris v. Balk*[7] — Intangibles

An attempt to exercise jurisdiction over intangible property, such as a debt, generates a question not raised when jurisdiction is asserted over real or tangible personal property: What is the *situs* of the intangible? Or, in plainer terms, where is it?[8] The question does not arise with respect to land or tangible personal property, because its answer there is so obvious. We can see and feel where such property is, but with intangible property, our senses don't help us. The *situs* must be determined on other grounds. Further, the question is one that matters, because the *situs* of the intangible determines which state can exercise jurisdiction over it. Thus, the issue of *situs* provided an opportunity to expand or contract the scope of attachment jurisdiction. In *Harris v. Balk*, the Supreme Court opted clearly for expansion.

In *Harris*, a Maryland plaintiff (Epstein) sued a North Carolina defendant (Balk) in Maryland for $344. The Maryland court acquired jurisdiction

[5] The Supreme Court in Shaffer v. Heitner, 433 U.S. 186 (1977). discarded the *Pennoyer* principle because of its unfairness to defendants and its inconsistency with the holding of *International Shoe*. *See* § 44, *infra*, for a discussion of *Shaffer*.

[6] In Shaffer v. Heitner, 433 U.S. 186 (1977), Justices Powell and Stevens suggested in separate opinions that the case for attachment jurisdiction is considerably stronger when the property is land in the forum than when the property is more ephemeral. *See* § 45, *infra*, for a discussion of those opinions.

[7] 198 U.S. 215 (1905).

[8] For a modern treatment of the situs problem, *see* Andreas F. Lowenfeld, *In Search of the Intangible: A Comment on Shaffer v. Heitner*, 53 N.Y.U. L. Rev. 102 (1978).

by personal service upon Harris, who owed Balk a debt from a prior transaction. By serving Harris, the court garnished the debt ($180) that Harris owed Balk; in other words, the court attached some intangible personal property of Balk's. Pursuant to the court's order, Harris gave up the property (paid the $180 to Epstein) and returned to his residence in North Carolina.

When Balk sued Harris in North Carolina for the $180 debt, Harris answered that he had already paid the money to Epstein and should not have to pay twice. This response raised the issue of the Maryland court's jurisdiction. If the Maryland court had jurisdiction over Balk's property, then Harris gave up the property pursuant to a valid court order and should not have to pay Balk; but if the court lacked jurisdiction, then Harris' payment to Epstein was purely voluntary and did not extinguish his obligation to pay Balk.

The jurisdictional issue turned on the *situs* of the debt Harris owed Balk; if it was "located in" Maryland, then the Maryland court, under the *Pennoyer* principle, had jurisdiction; otherwise not. The Supreme Court held that "[t]he obligation of the debtor to pay his debt clings to and accompanies him wherever he goes." That obligation represents intangible personal property of the *creditor* (Balk), which can be attached (according to the *Pennoyer* principle) to provide a basis for attachment jurisdiction, even though the creditor has no connection with the forum state. To picture the holding, it might help to think of Harris actually carrying a piece of Balk's property, say a bag of $180 in cash, into Maryland. There, that property can be attached as could any other piece of Balk's property.

The *Harris* corollary of the *Pennoyer* rule proved to be a very potent instrument of unfairness;[9] its practical effect was to make every debtor his creditor's agent for receipt of service of process. The creditor had to be prepared to defend an attachment action in any forum where the debtor could be found, even though the creditor had no contact with the forum and even though the attached property (the debt) had no relationship to plaintiff's claim. For example, a person who had a savings account in a bank in a distant state could be forced to defend any cause of action in the distant state. In the commercial context, a supplier was amenable to attachment jurisdiction in the home state of any customer who purchased on credit terms. Nevertheless, some courts pushed the concept even further.

[c] *Seider v. Roth*[10]

In *Seider v. Roth*, the Court of Appeals of New York extended the rule of *Harris v. Balk*[11] to its logical extreme. Plaintiff, a New Yorker, was injured in Vermont in an automobile accident with Lemiux, a resident of Quebec. Lemiux had no contact with New York sufficient to support an exercise of personal jurisdiction, nor did he have any real or tangible

[9] *See Developments in the Law — State–Court Jurisdiction*, 73 Harv. L. Rev. 909, 960 (1960).

[10] 17 N.Y.2d 111, 216 N.E.2d 312, 269 N.Y.S.2d 99 (1966).

[11] 198 U.S. 215 (1905), discussed in subsection [b], *supra*.

personal property in New York upon which to base an attachment action. Lemiux did have, however, a liability insurance policy with the Hartford Accident and Indemnity Company, and Hartford was doing business in New York.

The Court of Appeals held that Hartford's obligation to defend and indemnify Lemiux constituted a "debt" to Lemiux and was, therefore, "property" of his, which could be garnished by service on Hartford to provide the basis for an attachment action. Note that this obligation is an even more minimal sort of property than the debt in *Harris*. In *Harris*, at least the debt was an unconditional obligation, while in *Seider*, the "debt" was conditioned upon the existence of Lemiux's liability, a fact not yet determined.

The practical effect[12] of the *Seider* doctrine was to make the carefully worked out limits on personal jurisdiction somewhat beside the point in any action in which insurance figured. As long as defendant had an insurer who did business in all fifty states he was amenable to suit in any of those states, no matter where the injury occurred. Thus, to take only one example, a California defendant who injured a New Yorker on a California highway could be forced to defend the claim in New York even though he had not the slightest connection with New York. The *Seider* doctrine thus could be used to circumvent all the policies of fairness that are embodied in the limits on personal jurisdiction and make every vacationing New York motorist a rolling transcontinental summons to a New York courtroom.[13]

Comparing *Seider* to *Harris* and comparing both to *Pennoyer* shows how the exercise of attachment jurisdiction expanded from tangible property to intangible property to property whose existence and location was uncertain. This steadily attenuating notion of property created a substantial possibility of unfairness to defendant.[14] A temporary response was the limited

[12] *Seider* also provoked the theoretical criticism that it was based upon a "bootstraps" argument. Under traditional theory, a court could exercise attachment jurisdiction only if some piece of defendant's property was found within the state and attached at the beginning of the action. In a *Seider* action, the attached intangible property was the "debt" that the insurer owed the defendant–insured; but the "debt," the insurer's obligation to defend and indemnify the defendant, did not exist until the defendant had been sued. In other words, the *res* that formed the basis for attachment jurisdiction could not come into existence until the action was commenced, and the action could not be commenced without the res to exercise jurisdiction over. *See* David D. Siegel, *Jurisdiction Ad Infinitum: New York's "Rem" Seizure of the Insurance Policy for Jurisdiction in Accident Cases*, 20 Int. & Comp. L.Q. 99 (1971).

[13] *Seider* did not catch on in many states. Only New York and Minnesota adopted the doctrine completely. New Hampshire followed the doctrine only if defendant resided in a *Seider* jurisdiction. Most other courts rejected it. *See* Rush v. Savchuk, 444 U.S. 320 n. 10–13 (1980) (notes containing a complete listing of the courts which had considered the *Seider* question).

[14] In the years before *International Shoe* the expansive reach of attachment jurisdiction may have been worth that price because the concept operated as a proto–long–arm statute, allowing plaintiffs to sue out–of–state defendants who could not be reached under the restrictive territorial power theory. *See* Linda J. Silberman, *Commentaries on Shaffer v. Heitner: The End of an Era*, 53 N.Y.U. L. Rev. 33, 48 (1978). But after *International Shoe* and the rise of state long–arm statutes, the expansive view of attachment jurisdiction was no longer necessary to assure fairness to plaintiffs. The remaining possibility of unfairness to defendants eventually attracted the attention of the Supreme Court. *See* § 44, *infra*.

appearance — a judicially or legislatively created procedural device that ameliorated the unfairness to the defendant of attachment jurisdiction. The conclusive resolution of the problem was the Supreme Court's decision in *Shaffer v. Heitner*.[15] The next two sections treat those two developments.

§ 43 A Partial Measure: The Limited Appearance

Traditional attachment practice under *Pennoyer*,[1] *Harris*,[2] and *Seider*[3] produced a substantial possibility of unfairness to defendants. They could be sued in distant states with which they had no real contact. The limited appearance developed as a device for mitigating the impact of that unfairness.[4] To appreciate the value of the limited appearance, it is necessary to understand the predicament of a defendant sued in a traditional attachment action. At the commencement of that action, a court in the forum attached a piece of defendant's property within the state. Defendant then faced a dilemma. Failure to appear and defend the action resulted in default; the property was then sold and the proceeds paid to plaintiff. On the other hand, an appearance to defend on the merits could be considered a consent to the court's personal jurisdiction.

The limited appearance concept removed one of the horns of the dilemma by permitting the defendant to appear and litigate the merits of plaintiff's claim without submitting to the personal jurisdiction of the court. In other words, defendants could defend their interest in the property that was "held hostage" without risking a personal judgment. Thus, the limited appearance was a valuable dispensation for defendants.

The argument for the limited appearance was that forcing the defendant either to appear generally or to forfeit the property is so unfair as to violate fundamental notions of fair play. Accordingly, it was argued that the limited appearance was constitutionally required.[5] The case against the limited appearance was based on judicial economy. Suppose defendant were permitted to make a limited appearance in an attachment action, and the parties fully litigated the merits of their claims and defenses. Further, suppose plaintiff prevailed, but the attached property was not worth enough to satisfy plaintiff's claim completely. To obtain complete relief, plaintiff would have to sue defendant again (where in personam or attachment jurisdiction was available), and the parties would again litigate the merits of the action.[6] That duplication of effort is wasteful and contravenes the important policies underlying the doctrine of res judicata.

---

[15] 433 U.S. 186 (1977).

[1] Pennoyer v. Neff, 95 U.S. 714 (1878).

[2] Harris v. Balk, 198 U.S. 215 (1905).

[3] Seider v. Roth, 17 N.Y.2d 111, 269 N.Y.S.2d 99, 216 N.E.2d 312 (1966).

[4] The cases that have permitted the limited appearance are collected in Casad & Richman § 6-4. That section also lists cases disapproving the practice, as well as citations to the commentaries on both sides of the issue.

[5] *See Developments in the Law — State-Court Jurisdiction*, 73 Harv. L. Rev. 909, 954 (1960).

[6] Issue preclusion (collateral estoppel) may preclude subsequent re–litigation of issues even when defendant has been permitted to make a limited appearance. *See* § 111, *infra*, for a discussion of issue preclusion in attachment actions.

The decision in *Shaffer v. Heitner*[7] made it much less important to settle the argument over the limited appearance.[8] Since *Shaffer*, a court can exercise attachment jurisdiction over defendant's property only if maintenance of the suit would not offend traditional notions of fair play and substantial justice. In such cases, it is very likely that some basis for personal jurisdiction will also be available, and questions about attachment jurisdiction and limited appearances may not arise. Further, if those questions do arise, an assertion of attachment jurisdiction that can pass the *Shaffer* test usually will not produce the sort of unfairness to defendant that characterized traditional practice. Absent that unfairness, the need for the limited appearance is considerably reduced.

The limited appearance should be distinguished from another device — the special appearance.[9] In a special appearance, defendant comes into the forum for the sole purpose of attacking the court's jurisdiction.[10] By proper motion, she suggests, for instance, that the local long–arm statute does not cover her conduct or that it would be unconstitutional to exercise jurisdiction over her. Thus, the defendant may appear specially in any sort of action — either in personam or in rem[11] — and the only questions she may address are those relevant to the court's jurisdiction. By contrast, defendant can make a limited appearance only in an attachment action; and in a limited appearance she *does* litigate the merits of plaintiff's claim. The appearance is "limited" only in the sense that defendant's risk is limited to the property attached.

§ 44 The In Rem Revolution: *Shaffer v. Heitner*

Attachment doctrine was in an unsatisfactory state by the 1970's. A distant court could exercise jurisdiction over a defendant's important interests even though the defendant had no contact with the state and regardless of defendant's inconvenience. The only requirement was that the defendant have "property" in the forum. That requirement became less and less restrictive as the notion of property became more and more attenuated. Nearly all courts were willing to base attachment jurisdiction on "property" that consisted only of a debt owed defendant by a person who could be served in the forum.[1] A few courts went even further and exercised

[7] 433 U.S. 186 (1977), discussed *infra* in § 44.

[8] *See* Restatement (Second) of Judgments § 8, comment g.

[9] *See* § 30[b], *supra*, for a discussion of the special appearance.

[10] In other words, defendant may make a motion to dismiss only; a demurrer or an answer or any other plea to the merits constitutes consent to the in personam jurisdiction of the court.

[11] Before the decision in Shaffer v. Heitner, 433 U.S. 186 (1977), a special appearance in an attachment action was nearly useless. The only facts relevant to jurisdiction under *Pennoyer* and *Harris* were the existence of defendant's property within the forum state and its seizure prior to the action. Defendant could appear to litigate these facts, but her prospects were poor. Since *Shaffer*, a special appearance in an attachment action makes more sense. The parties would litigate the issue of minimum contacts, much as they would in an in personam action.

[1] *See* § 42[b], *supra*, for a discussion of this principle as expounded in Harris v. Balk, 198 U.S. 215 (1905).

jurisdiction over an insurer's obligation to its insured, rendering the insured amenable to an attachment action in any state where the insurer did business.[2] This extension of attachment jurisdiction proved very unfair to defendants, and in some types of litigation substantially reduced the significance of the carefully elaborated limits on personal jurisdiction.

In *Shaffer v. Heitner*,[3] the Supreme Court overhauled traditional in rem doctrine, much as it had reworked personal jurisdiction thirty years earlier in *International Shoe Co. v. Washington*.[4] Each decision is a major jurisdictional watershed. While *International Shoe* expanded the scope of jurisdiction and *Shaffer* contracted it, the two cases have this feature in common: Each changed the conceptual foundation of jurisdiction from an emphasis on power and territoriality to a more practical emphasis on fairness. *Shoe* began the jurisdictional revolution by abandoning one tenet of the territorial power theory. After *Shoe*, territorial power was no longer a *necessary* condition for a constitutional exercise of jurisdiction. Three decades later, the Court held the converse in *Shaffer*; territorial power is not a *sufficient* condition either.[5]

Shaffer was a shareholder's derivative action. Plaintiff, owner of one share of stock in Greyhound (a Delaware corporation with its principal place of business in Arizona), brought the action in a Delaware court, naming as defendants Greyhound, a subsidiary, and several officers and directors of both corporations. He claimed that these officers and directors had violated their duties to Greyhound and had subjected the corporation to substantial antitrust penalties arising out of corporate operations in Oregon.

Plaintiff did not attempt to obtain personal jurisdiction over the individual defendants. Rather, he arranged for the Delaware court to "seize" shares of Greyhound stock belonging to the defendant directors and officers, thus procuring attachment jurisdiction over their property. The "seizure" was only constructive because the stock certificates were not physically present in Delaware. It was accomplished by placing "stop transfer" orders on the books of the corporation. That maneuver was possible because of a Delaware statute that made Delaware the situs of all stock in Delaware corporations.[6]

The defendants entered a special appearance and argued that Delaware's assertion of jurisdiction over their property violated the Due Process

[2] *See* § 42[c], *supra*, for a discussion of Seider v. Roth, 17 N.Y.2d 111, 216 N.E.2d 312, 269 N.Y.S.2d 99 (1966).

[3] 433 U.S. 186 (1977).

[4] 326 U.S. 310 (1945), discussed § 20[a], *supra*.

[5] Donald J. Werner, *Dropping the Other Shoe: Shaffer v. Heitner and the Demise of Presence-Oriented Jurisdiction*, 45 Brook. L. Rev. 565 (1979). *Shaffer*'s power–is–not–sufficient holding may be jeopardized by the decision in Burnham v. Superior Court, 495 U.S. 604 (1990), validating personal service as an adequate jurisdictional basis. Justice Scalia's opinion suggests that physical (or metaphorical) power may be sufficient for jurisdiction in cases where the power–based practice is firmly rooted in tradition. *See* § 28, *supra*, for a discussion of *Burnham*.

[6] Del. Code Ann., Tit. 8, § 169.

Clause. The Delaware courts rejected this contention and held explicitly that minimum contacts between the defendant and the forum were not a prerequisite for the exercise of attachment jurisdiction.

The Supreme Court reversed. Justice Marshall's majority opinion began with a fairly complete history of the doctrinal change in personal jurisdiction from a basis in power to a basis in fairness. After noting that "[n]o equally dramatic change has occurred in the law governing jurisdiction *in rem*," the Court then proceeded to make that dramatic change. In a single short paragraph, the Court re-conceptualized property-based jurisdiction and held that it should be subject to the same constitutional restrictions that govern personal jurisdiction.

> The phrase, "judicial jurisdiction over a thing," is a customary elliptical way of referring to jurisdiction over the interests of persons in a thing. . . . This recognition leads to the conclusion that in order to justify an exercise of jurisdiction in rem, the basis for jurisdiction must be sufficient to justify exercising "jurisdiction over the interests of persons in a thing." The standard for determining whether an exercise of jurisdiction over the interests of persons is consistent with the Due Process Clause is the minimum-contacts standard elucidated in *International Shoe*.

The importance of the holding would be hard to overestimate. It means, of course, that the presence of defendant's property in the forum is no longer a sufficient condition for exercise of jurisdiction over defendant's interest in that property. *Shaffer* requires, instead, a sufficient relationship among "the defendant, the forum and the litigation." But *Shaffer* did not merely change a rule about jurisdiction over property; it altered that very concept with the realization that "jurisdiction over property" is merely a "customary elliptical way of referring to jurisdiction over the interests of persons" in the property. *Shaffer* thus establishes a "unified field theory" of jurisdiction with all exercises to be based on the standards of *International Shoe*.[7]

It might be tempting to conclude that *Shaffer* eliminates property-based jurisdiction totally, but that would be a great mistake. The opinion is carefully drafted to avoid that outcome; it fairly bristles with qualifications that indicate how much of traditional property-based jurisdiction should survive the doctrinal revolution. The next two sections address those qualifications.

§ 45 In Rem Jurisdiction After *Shaffer v. Heitner*

After a significant shift in doctrine, it is necessary to take stock and consider how much traditional practice survives the theoretical revolution. So after *Shaffer v. Heitner*[1] it became important to determine which of the old rules concerning in rem jurisdiction were still good.[2] This section examines that question using the opinion in *Shaffer* as the principal guide.

---

[7] *See* Geoffrey C. Hazard, Jr., *A General Theory of State — Court Jurisdiction*, 1965 Sup. Ct. Rev. 241, 281, for an early argument that a unified theory was required.

[1] 433 U.S. 186 (1977).

[2] *See generally* Casad & Richman § 2-6[3] Weintraub § 4.27-4.29

[a] True In Rem Jurisdiction and Quasi–In–Rem Type I Jurisdiction

True in rem jurisdiction and quasi–in–rem type I jurisdiction involve an attempt by plaintiff to assert a preexisting claim to the property that is the basis for jurisdiction. In other words, the property itself is the subject of the dispute. The opinion in *Shaffer* indicates that these two forms of jurisdiction over property survive the in rem revolution intact:

> [T]he presence of property in a State may bear on the existence of jurisdiction by providing contacts among the forum State, the defendant, and the litigation. For example, when claims to the property itself are the source of the underlying controversy between the plaintiff and the defendant, it would be unusual for the State where the property is located not to have jurisdiction.[3]

The Court cited several reasons why jurisdiction in rem and quasi–in–rem should survive the conceptual revolution of *Shaffer*. First, defendant's claim to the property suggests that he hopes to benefit from the protection of the state's law. Second, the state has "strong interests in insuring the marketability of property within its borders"; that interest is well served by conducting litigation affecting that property in the state's courts. Finally, the situs of the property will generally be the most convenient place to conduct the litigation. Important records and witnesses will be found nearby, and the law of the situs is likely to control.

Although the reasons are weighty, they seem to address primarily the fairness and reasonableness portion of the *International Shoe* formulation, not the contacts portion. *World–Wide Volkswagon v. Woodson*[4] and its progeny clearly indicate that both tests must be passed. The theoretical problem becomes most apparent in justifying the "against all the world" feature of in rem jurisdiction. Clearly the situs does not have minimum contacts with the whole world. It may be that the presence of the property in the forum is enough of a "contact"; or perhaps, this is one of those cases where fairness "considerations . . . serve to establish the reasonableness of jurisdiction upon a lesser showing of minimum contacts than would otherwise be required."[5] But, if convenience, state interest, and defendants' expectation of benefit can overcome the lack of pre–litigation connections in the in rem context, it is odd that they cannot in other contexts, such as *Helicopteros Nacionales de Colombia v. Hall*,[6] where defendant's lack of contacts with Texas meant that the plaintiffs, for practical purposes, would have no forum.

---

[3] For commentary on this facet of the Court's opinion, *see* Donald W. Fyr, *Shaffer v. Heitner: The Supreme Court's Latest Last Words on State Court Jurisdiction*, 26 Emory L.J. 739 (1977).

[4] 444 U.S. 286 (1980), discussed in § 22, *supra*.

[5] *See* Burger King v. Rudzewicz, 471 U.S. 462 (1985). Another possibility is that, after the Court's tradition–bound holding in Burnham v. Superior Court, 495 U.S. 604 (1990), there is no need for contemporary contacts and fairness arguments to justify in rem jurisdiction.

[6] 466 U.S. 408 (1984), discussed at § 25, *supra*.

[b] Attachment Jurisdiction

Shaffer has the greatest impact on this type of jurisdiction. The opinion requires an adequate relationship among the defendant, the forum, and the litigation that is often absent in the typical attachment action. Thus, jurisdictional landmarks like *Harris v. Balk*[7] have been overruled. But *Shaffer* did not wipe out attachment jurisdiction entirely; the opinion indicated six types of cases in which it survives.

[1] A Close Relation

Dictum in *Shaffer* indicates quite clearly that attachment jurisdiction survives in cases where plaintiff's claim is closely related to the attached property. Immediately after the passage legitimizing in rem and quasi–in–rem–type I jurisdiction, the Court stated that:

> [t]he presence of property may also favor jurisdiction in cases such as suits for injury suffered on the land of an absentee owner, where the defendant's ownership of the property is conceded but the cause of action is otherwise related to rights and duties growing out of that ownership.[8]

The survival of attachment jurisdiction in such cases[9] makes sense. The situs state has a strong interest in the safety of property and the protection of people within its borders. Further, litigation there often will be convenient because of ready access to witnesses and evidence. Finally, the defendant benefits from state law protecting the property and should be able anticipate litigation there.[10]

[2] Minimum Contacts

Another circumstance in which attachment jurisdiction survives *Shaffer* is where the defendant has minimum contacts with the forum. The obvious question here is why a plaintiff would use attachment jurisdiction when

[7] 198 U.S. 215 (1905), discussed, *supra*, in § 42[b]. *Harris* stood for the proposition that a court could exercise attachment jurisdiction over a defendant's intangible personal property even though the defendant had no contact with the state and even though plaintiff's claim was unrelated to the attached property. *Shaffer* clearly overturns that proposition. Whether *Harris*, on its facts, is overruled is not completely clear; Balk, the defendant, in fact may have had minimum contacts with Maryland. *See* Andreas F. Lowenfeld, *In Search of the Intangible: A Comment on Shaffer v. Heitner*, 53 N.Y.U. L. Rev. 102 (1978).

[8] Although the opinion does not say so, it is clear that its hypothetical is a case of attachment jurisdiction because plaintiff is not asserting a pre–existing claim of title in defendant's property. *See* § 41, *infra*, for a discussion of the differences between attachment jurisdiction and in rem jurisdiction.

[9] Because the claim arises out of the attached property, these are cases of "specific jurisdiction." *See* § 37[b], *supra*.

[10] *See* David H. Vernon, *Single–Factor Bases of In Personam Jurisdiction — A Speculation on the Impact of Shaffer v. Heitner*, 1978 Wash. U. L.Q. 273, 296. Defendant's ability to anticipate litigation in the forum is clear when the attached property is land or personal property that defendant knew was in the forum. When the attached property is intangible or tangible property defendant did not know was in the forum, the anticipation argument does not work.

defendant had minimum contacts with the forum, contacts which would support an exercise of personal jurisdiction.[11] One answer is that the forum's in personam long–arm statute might not reach plaintiff's case, even though the Due Process Clause would permit the exercise of jurisdiction. Attachment jurisdiction, in other words, might be used to extend an unambitious long–arm statute.[12]

Another answer recognizes that "minimum contacts" may mean different things in different contexts. *Shaffer* held that all assertions of jurisdiction must be measured by the *International Shoe* test, but it did not hold that that test must produce the same result no matter what type of jurisdiction is asserted. The contacts required to support an exercise of attachment jurisdiction (where only one piece of defendant's property is at stake) might be more minimal than the contacts required to support an exercise of personal jurisdiction (where all of defendant's property is affected). Thus, plaintiff might settle for attachment jurisdiction because defendant's connections with the state are too attenuated to support personal jurisdiction.[13]

[3] Attachment to Enforce

One use of attachment jurisdiction that must survive *Shaffer* is a suit to enforce a sister–state judgment. The typical case occurs when plaintiff obtains a personal judgment in the rendering state — one where defendant has minimum contacts but no property to satisfy the judgment. Plaintiff then sues on the judgment in the enforcing state where defendant has property but no other contacts. The Court provided for just this case in footnote 36 of its opinion:

> Once it has been determined by a court of competent jurisdiction that the defendant is a debtor of the plaintiff, there would seem to be no unfairness in allowing an action to realize on that debt in a State where the defendant has property, whether or not that State would have jurisdiction to determine the existence of the debt as an original matter.

But how can the enforcing state's exercise of attachment jurisdiction be justified under the *Shoe / Shaffer* test when, by hypothesis, there are no minimum contacts with the defendant?[14] An obvious, and correct, answer

---

[11] *See* § 41, *supra*, on why plaintiff will usually prefer personal jurisdiction.

[12] *See, e.g.*, Banco Ambrosiano v. Artoc Bank & Trust Ltd., 62 N.Y.2d 65, 464 N.E.2d 432, 476 N.Y.S.2d 64 (1984). *See also* Joseph P. Zammit, *Reflections on Shaffer v. Heitner*, 1978 Hastings Const. L.Q. 15, 20. In such cases, the defendant has a potential counter–argument: If the case is not covered by the state's enumerated act statute, the omission may be purposeful and the use of attachment jurisdiction would frustrate the legislative intent. *See* Restatement (Second) of Conflict of Laws § 66, comment c (1986 Revisions).

[13] *See* Weintraub, 256; Stefan A. Riesenfeld, *Shaffer v. Heitner: Holding, Implications, Forebodings*, 30 Hastings L.J. 1183, 1204 (1979).

[14] Usually, of course, defendant will have minimum contacts in the enforcing state, but the presence of defendant's property in the state is no guarantee. The enduring lesson of Harris v. Balk, 195 U.S. 215 (1905), discussed in § 42[b], *supra*, is that defendant can have intangible property in a state where he has no minimum contacts. *See also* Berger v. Berger, 138 Vt. 367, 417 A.2d 921 (1980)(defendant's only contact with Vermont was an undistributed one–quarter of his mother's estate).

is that attachment jurisdiction is justified by fairness, necessity, and the national policy favoring interstate enforcement of judgments.[15] Otherwise, defendant could make herself judgment proof by the simple device of removing all her property to a state where plaintiff could not obtain personal jurisdiction over her.

Although relatively obvious, the justification for attachment jurisdiction in the enforcing state reveals something important about the Supreme Court's theory of jurisdiction. In some contexts — interstate enforcement of judgments, for example — fairness, necessity, and national policies are important enough to trump defendant's right not to be sued in a state with which she has no pre–litigation connections. But in other cases — cases like *World–Wide* and *Helicopteros* — they are not. Thus far, the Supreme Court has not been able, nor has it really tried, to explain why. Addressing that question might take the Court beyond its current contacts–for–contacts–sake theory of jurisdiction.

[4] Attachment as Security

Another instance of attachment jurisdiction that is rooted in practical necessity occurs when plaintiff attaches defendant's property in one state to secure a judgment being sought in another. Suppose plaintiff has a claim against defendant and can obtain personal jurisdiction over him only in the rendering state. Defendant, although not amenable to personal jurisdiction in the enforcing state, does have a valuable piece of property there. Plaintiff would like to attach that property as security for her judgment should she prevail in the main action. The opinion in *Shaffer* permits this use of attachment jurisdiction, even though defendant would not be amenable to personal jurisdiction in the enforcing state;[16] if the result were otherwise, defendant would be able to remove or liquidate the property before the rendering court proceeded to judgment, and thus before plaintiff could commence ordinary enforcement proceedings in the enforcing state.

[5] Land

The concurring opinions of Justices Powell and Stevens suggest that attachment jurisdiction should survive when the attached property is real estate — "property whose situs is indisputably and permanently located within a state." This is a valuable suggestion. The unfairness inherent in traditional practice resulted largely from the application of attachment

[15] *See* David H. Vernon, *State–Court Jurisdiction: A Preliminary Inquiry into the Impact of Shaffer v. Heitner*, 63 Iowa L. Rev. 997, 1008 (1978). One commentator argues, however, that in at least some cases attachment jurisdiction in the enforcing state can be unfair to the defendant. *See* Earl M. Maltz, *Reflections on a Landmark: Shaffer v. Heitner Viewed from a Distance*, 1986 B.Y.U.L. Rev. 1043, 1046–1048.

[16] It might be argued, in fact, that attachment jurisdiction should require a lesser showing of contacts in this context than in others because here what is taken, at least immediately, from defendant is only possession of the property, not title to it. *See* Carolina Power & Light Co. v. Uranex, 451 F.Supp. 1044, 1047–8 (N.D. Cal. 1977). Note, however, that defendant may be entitled to a hearing before pre–judgment attachment. *See* North Georgia Finishing Inc. v. Di–Chem Inc., 419 U.S. 601 (1975); Fuentes v. Shevin, 407 U.S. 67 (1972).

jurisdiction to highly attenuated notions of property — intangibles that could have a situs within a state even though their owner had nothing to do with the state. This situation, however, is not likely with real property; it would be very difficult for a person to have real property in a distant state and yet have no connection with the state. Justice Powell also suggested that the maintenance of traditional attachment practice in the case of real property would have the additional virtue of avoiding "the uncertainty of the general *International Shoe* standard" in cases where fair play and substantial justice could not really be an issue.

[6] No Other Forum

In footnote 37 of the opinion, the Court left open the question whether attachment jurisdiction should exist in a state where the defendant has property but no minimum contacts, "when no other forum is available to plaintiff." Such an exception to *Shaffer*'s minimum contact requirement, a form of jurisdiction necessity, certainly makes sense.[17] *Shaffer*'s holding is based on fairness, and its whole reason for being is to avoid oppressing defendants. But fairness is a two–way street; and a plaintiff ought not go without a remedy simply because no available forum has personal jurisdiction over the defendant. A court with power over defendant's property should be able to apply that property to plaintiff's claim in those circumstances.

Footnote 37 also left open the question of what "no other forum" means exactly. Does it mean no other forum in the United States, or no other forum in the world?[18] And does it take into account the particular plaintiff's resources or lack thereof to litigate in the "available" forum? In the personal jurisdiction context, the Court has answered those questions. In *Helicopteros Nacionales de Colombia v. Hall*,[19] the Court held that Texas could not exercise jurisdiction over a Columbian defendant, even though no alternative forum in the United States was available to plaintiffs and even though proceeding in a South American court was likely to be futile, given plaintiffs' resources and the procedural and substantive law of the available foreign forums. It may be that the Court would reach a more humane result in an action based on attachment jurisdiction, but it seems unlikely.[20]

---

[17] Jurisdiction by necessity is treated in § 39, *supra*. For a more complete discussion *see* Vernon, Weinberg, Reynolds and Richman 172–173.

[18] *Compare* Louring v. Kuwait Boulder Shipping Co., 455 F. Supp. 630 (D. Conn. 1977) (attachment jurisdiction exercised over defendant who lacked minimum contacts with Connecticut but had fair warning that its activities might subject it to suit somewhere in the United States), *with* Leathers, *Forum Juridicum: The First Two Years After Shaffer v. Heitner*, 40 La. L. Rev. 907, 916 (1980)(critical of *Louring* and suggesting that the "no other forum" language in footnote 37 should be read literally).

Another open question is the meaning of "no other forum" in a case with multiple defendants. Suppose plaintiff can reach all defendants only by suing them separately in several different states. Should the "no other forum" passage permit one state to exercise jurisdiction over all defendants? *See* Donald W. Fyr, *Shaffer v. Heitner: The Supreme Court's Latest Last Words on State Court Jurisdiction*, 26 Emory L.J. 739, 771–772 (1977).

[19] 466 U.S. 408 (1984), discussed in § 25, *supra*.

[20] In the meantime, cautious litigators should hedge their bets and attempt to attach defendant's property, as well as proceeding against her personally when lack of jurisdiction in an American court would consign plaintiff to the tender mercies of a foreign, plaintiff–hostile judicial system.

§ 46 The *Seider* Doctrine Today

The most recent vestige of traditional attachment practice to succumb to the in rem revolution was the *Seider* doctrine.[1] Recall that in a *Seider* case, plaintiff sues a defendant who is not amenable to in personam jurisdiction by attaching the obligation of defendant's insurer to defend and indemnify the defendant. According to *Seider*, that obligation constitutes property of the defendant which may form the basis for an attachment action. After *Shaffer v. Heitner*[2] required that all exercises of jurisdiction satisfy the minimum contacts standard of *International Shoe*,[3] there was a split of opinion on whether the *Seider* procedure should survive.[4] The Supreme Court conclusively settled that dispute in ***Rush v. Savchuk***.[5]

In ***Rush***, plaintiff and defendant, both residents of Indiana, were involved in a single car automobile accident in Indiana; plaintiff was a guest in defendant's car. Plaintiff moved to Minnesota after the accident and sued defendant there. Since defendant had no contacts with Minnesota, plaintiff obtained attachment jurisdiction by garnishing defendant's insurance policy with the State Farm Insurance Company. After the Minnesota courts approved the exercise of jurisdiction based on the *Seider* doctrine, defendant appealed to the Supreme Court, and the case was remanded for further consideration in light of *Shaffer*. On remand, the Minnesota Supreme Court again upheld the exercise of jurisdiction, this time on the ground that the case passed the *Shaffer* test because the insurance policy, the property attached, was closely related to the automobile tort litigation. On a second appeal, the Supreme Court reversed, rejecting both of the major justifications for *Seider* practice.

[a] *Seider* and the *Shaffer* Test

The Court first measured the *Seider* procedure according to the *Shaffer* test, asking whether in ***Rush*** there was an adequate "relationship among the defendant, the forum, and the litigation." It concluded that State Farm's presence in Minnesota did not demonstrate any connection between the *defendant* and the forum. State Farm's decision to serve the market in Minnesota was "completely adventitious" as far as defendant was concerned. The Court also rejected the reasoning of the Minnesota Supreme Court, finding no significant connection between the *litigation* and the forum. The insurance policy (defendant's "property" in the forum) related only to the conduct of the litigation and not to the substance of the claim, so it could not be said that the property attached was closely related to the cause of action. The Court concluded its application of the *Shaffer* test by rejecting completely the theoretical foundation for the *Seider* doctrine:

[1] Seider v. Roth, 17 N.Y.2d 111, 216 N.E.2d 312, 269 N.Y.S.2d 99 (1966), is discussed in § 42[c], *supra*.

[2] 433 U.S. 186 (1977).

[3] International Shoe Co. v. Washington, 326 U.S. 310 (1945), discussed in § 20[a], *supra*.

[4] *Compare* O'Connor v. Lee–Hy Paving Corp., 579 F.2d 194 (2d Cir.), *cert. denied* 439 U.S. 1034 (1978), *with* Robert A. Leflar, American Conflicts Law § 25 (3d ed. 1977).

[5] 444 U.S. 320 (1980).

> To say that "a debt follows the debtor" is simply to say that intangible property has no actual situs. . . . State Farm is "found" . . . in all 50 States and the District of Columbia. Under appellee's theory, the "debt" owed to Rush would be "present" in each of those jurisdictions simultaneously. It is apparent that such a "contact" can have no jurisdictional significance.

[b] The "Direct Action" Argument

Another suggestion that had been advanced to support *Seider* jurisdiction was that the attachment practice is simply a judicially created direct action procedure[6] — much like the statutory direct action procedure approved by the Supreme Court in *Watson v. Employer's Liability Assurance Corp.*[7] According to that argument, minimum contacts between defendant and the forum are unnecessary because defendant really has nothing at stake in the action; the insurer is the only one with a real stake if (as was the case in *Seider* practice) plaintiff's judgment is limited to the value of the policy.

The *Rush* court rejected this argument as well. The Court distinguished *Watson* on the ground that a direct action procedure simply substitutes the insurer for the insured; it does not affect jurisdiction or violate the minimum contacts test. Because the accident and injury in *Watson* occurred in the forum, defendant would have been amenable there without regard for the direct action statute. In a *Seider* action, by contrast, the litigation takes place in a forum which is not the place where the cause of action arose — a forum where defendant would not be amenable absent the direct action device.

Further, the Court found that the "nominal" defendant (the insured) in a *Seider* action does not have an insignificant stake in the outcome. Footnote 20 identified several situations where the insured has a great deal to lose. Economically, a *Seider* defendant might suffer significant harm if the forum action is only one of several lawsuits (some in other states) pending against him, and the *aggregate* demands of those suits exceed the policy limits. If the *Seider* action exhausts the fund, defendant would have significant non–insured liability in other states. Further, a *Seider* action might harm defendant economically by rendering him uninsurable or by drastically increasing his premiums. Finally, the Court recognized that defendant may have an important non–economic stake in a *Seider* action; in a professional malpractice suit, for example, his professional standing and reputation may hang in the balance.[8]

---

[6] The suggestion was made first in Minichiello v. Rosenberg, 410 F.2d 106 (2d Cir.), *cert. denied*, 396 U.S. 844 (1969).

[7] 348 U.S. 66 (1954).

[8] Another unfairness produced by *Seider*–type attachment jurisdiction is caused by its use in combination with modern forum–favoring choice–of–law methodologies. *E.g.*, Weintraub 257. Plaintiff in *Rush* was an Indiana domiciliary at the time of the accident, and his injury occurred in Indiana. The Indiana court almost certainly would have applied Indiana law, which included two serious obstacles for plaintiff — a guest statute and a common law contributory negligence rule. The Minnesota forum, however, applying Robert Leflar's "better rule of law"

In sum, the *Rush* Court held that *Seider* practice does not pass the minimum contacts test, nor can it be justified by the direct action argument. Having destroyed each of the two main lines of argument which justified *Seider* practice, the Court made it quite clear that the *Seider* doctrine did not survive the in rem revolution wrought by *Shaffer v. Heitner*.

---

choice–of–law method (*see* § 81, *infra*), most likely would have applied Minnesota law, which did not have a guest statute and which had a more plaintiff–favoring comparative negligence rule. The inter–play of *Seider*–style attachment theory and forum–favoring choice–of–law methodologies had raised forum shopping into an art form.

Part G

ADDITIONAL PROBLEMS IN JURISDICTION

§ 47 Limits: Forum Non Conveniens[1]

[a] The Common Law Notion

The system of jurisdiction outlined in this chapter gives plaintiff a very wide choice of courts. She can maintain an action against defendant in any state with which defendant has minimum contacts. Many factors can affect that choice. She may be influenced by geographical convenience, by choice–of–law factors (choosing a forum whose law is hospitable to her claim), and by the likelihood of finding a sympathetic jury. These are all legitimate reasons to pick one forum over another, and our system gives plaintiff the considerable strategic advantage of being able to choose her arena based upon them. On the other hand, that choice might have been motivated, not by the legitimate concerns already mentioned, but by a less worthy desire to harass the defendant, provoke a high settlement offer, or force the defendant to default. The doctrine of forum non conveniens permits a court to refuse to exercise jurisdiction[2] if it is a seriously inconvenient forum for the action, and if another more convenient forum is available to the plaintiff.[3]

Forum non conveniens does not give defendant a *right* to avoid suit in an inconvenient forum; rather, its application depends heavily on the exercise of sound discretion by the trial judge. In *Gulf Oil Corp. v. Gilbert,*[4] the Supreme Court indicated the two interests which should be relevant to the trial court's decision. First, "an interest to be considered and the one likely to be most pressed, is the private interest of the litigant." Important to the interest of the litigant are such factors as: the proximity and accessibility of tangible evidence, the availability of compulsory process for unwilling witnesses, the travel costs for willing witnesses, the possibility of viewing the relevant property, and the enforceability of any possible judgment. The second interest is that of the public. The relevant factors are: the caseload pressures which can develop if litigation is shunted to certain popular centers rather than being handled at its origin, the burden

---

[1] *See, generally* William L. Reynolds, *The Proper Forum for a Suit: Transnational Forum Non Conveniens and Counter–Suit Injunctions in the Federal Courts*, 70 Texas L. Rev. 1663 (1992).

[2] The doctrine has no application when jurisdiction does not exist or when venue is improper. In those situations, defendant is entitled to a dismissal as of right; he is not dependent on the discretionary doctrine of forum non conveniens. Many courts, however, will exercise forum non conveniens without deciding contested issues of jurisdiction or venue.

[3] This statement of the doctrine is adapted from Restatement (Second) of Conflict of Laws § 84.

[4] 330 U.S. 501 (1947).

of jury duty on the citizens of a community having no relationship to the cause of action, the local interest in having cases decided where they arose, and the difficulties in having the court decide a case according to unfamiliar principles of substantive law. After identifying the considerations that must be weighed, the Supreme Court stated that the balance must tilt heavily in favor of defendant in order to disturb plaintiff's choice of forum.

If the trial judge determines that the balance does favor defendant, what should she do? Although she cannot transfer the case directly to the courts of another state,[5] she does have several options.[6] The simplest option is to dismiss the case outright and assume that plaintiff will bring suit in a more convenient forum. Another possibility is to condition a dismissal upon defendant's waiver of any objection (jurisdiction over the person, venue, statute of limitations) he may have to suit in a more convenient forum. Finally, the court may stay the action pending plaintiff's demonstrated ability to bring suit against defendant in a more convenient forum.

[b] Federal Transfer[7]

Within the federal court system, the doctrine of forum non conveniens has been supplanted largely by statute. 28 U.S.C. § 1404(a) provides: "For the convenience of the parties and witnesses, in the interest of justice, a district court may transfer any civil action to any other district or division where it might have been brought." The remedy under the statute is not dismissal, as it is under the common law; rather, the federal court simply transfers the case to a more appropriate federal forum.[8] Another difference between the statute and the common law doctrine lies in the amount of inconvenience which defendant must show to justify relief; the statute permits transfer on a lesser showing of inconvenience.[9]

In *Hoffman v. Blaski,*[10] defendant contended that the statutory clause, "where it might have been brought," permitted transfer to any district in which defendant was willing to be sued. Defendant had argued that if he was willing to waive his venue and jurisdiction objections to suit in a different forum, then that court was one in which the action "might have been brought." The Supreme Court rejected that argument, and in a controversial opinion[11] held that the statute permitted transfer only to a district where plaintiff initially would have been able (without regard to defendant's waiver) to bring the action.

---

[5] *See* subsection [b] of this section for a discussion of the federal transfer statute.

[6] *See* Restatement (Second) of Conflict of Laws § 84, comment e.

[7] *See generally* Charles Alan Wright, Law of Federal Courts § 44 (5th ed. 1994).

[8] *Contrast* 28 U.S.C. § 1406 (a) which provides for transfer or dismissal when suit is filed in the wrong venue.

[9] Norwood v. Kirkpatrick, 349 U.S. 29 (1955).

[10] 363 U.S. 335 (1960).

[11] The commentators have been critical of *Hoffman*. *See* C. Wright, *supra,* note 7, at § 44.

[c] Forum Non Conveniens, Federal Transfer, and Choice of Law

A serious choice–of–law problem can be generated by the use of forum non conveniens or the federal transfer statute. The difficulty is that the new forum may have choice–of–law principles or substantive law rules less favorable to plaintiff's claims than the law of the original forum. Should this problem play a role in the forum non conveniens calculation?

The Supreme Court has dealt with this question three times — twice in the context of federal transfer and once in the context of forum non conveniens — and has given two quite different answers. In *Van Dusen v. Barrack,*[12] defendants sought to transfer several wrongful death actions from the Eastern District of Pennsylvania to the District of Massachusetts. Plaintiffs argued that the transfer was improper because it would produce a change in the applicable choice–of–law principles and substantive law rules which would be very prejudicial to their claims. The Supreme Court dealt with the problem not by invalidating the transfer, but by requiring the transferee court to apply the substantive law that the transferor court would have applied. In the words of the Court, the defendant should not "get a change of law as a bonus for a change of venue."[13] The Court addressed the reverse problem in *Ferens v. John Deere Co.*[14] There, the plaintiff, who had been injured in Pennsylvania, did not file suit until limitations had expired in that state. Suit was filed, therefore, in Mississippi, which had a longer limitations period. Plaintiff then moved for a § 1404(a) transfer to Pennsylvania. The Court permitted both the transfer and the application of the longer Mississippi statute of limitations. Thus, any transfer of jurisdiction under § 1404 (a) carries to the new forum the law of the state where suit was filed originally.

Piper Aircraft Co. v. Reyno[15] raised the problem of choice of law in the context of forum non conveniens. The suit, based on the fatal crash of a small commercial airplane in Scotland, pitted the representative of the estates of several passengers (citizens of Scotland) against two American corporations — Piper, the manufacturer of the plane, and Hartzell, the manufacturer of the propeller. Both defendants moved to dismiss the action in the Middle District of Pennsylvania on the ground of forum non conveniens, contending that a Scottish forum would be much more convenient. Plaintiff opposed the dismissal. She contended that it would result in her claims being tried under Scottish law, which was much less favorable to her. Her theory, endorsed by the Third Circuit, was that forum non conveniens should not produce a change in the governing substantive law.

---

[12] 376 U.S. 612 (1964).

[13] The Court quoted this language from Justice Jackson's dissent in Wells v. Simonds Abrasive Co., 345 U.S. 514 (1953). A related question is whether the *Van Dusen* rule applies when transfer is from one federal circuit to another and the two differ on the interpretation of federal law. *See* Robert Ragazzo, *Transfer and Choice of Federal Law: The Appellate Model*, 93 Mich. L. Rev. 703 (1995).

[14] 494 U.S. 516 (1990).

[15] 454 U.S. 235 (1981).

The Supreme Court reversed. It held that "a change in substantive law should ordinarily not be given conclusive or even substantial weight in the forum non conveniens inquiry."[16]

Van Dusen and *Ferens* are not inconsistent with *Piper Aircraft*. *Van Dusen* and *Ferens* clearly indicates that when the Supreme Court has control of the transferee court, it will ensure that a change of courts does not result in a change of law. But the *Van Dusen* solution was not available in *Piper Aircraft* because the Court could not require the Scottish courts to apply American law.[17]

Accordingly, the Court was faced squarely with the choice between an inconvenient forum and an unfavorable change in substantive law — a choice it was able to avoid in *Van Dusen* and *Ferens*. Read together, the three cases indicate the Court's value preferences. Its first choice is a trial in a convenient court which must employ the law that would have been applied by the plaintiff's chosen forum. Its second choice is a trial in a convenient forum applying its own substantive law. The result the Court seems most anxious to avoid is a trial in an inconvenient forum.[18]

§ 48 Limits: Force, Fraud, and Immunity[1]

A court will not exercise jurisdiction over a defendant or his property if jurisdiction has been obtained by force or fraud.[2] Thus, state courts will not assert personal jurisdiction over a defendant who is served with process in the state after having been brought into the state by kidnapping. Similarly, if a defendant is tricked into entering the state by a plaintiff[3] or by a third person[4] and is then served with process, the state will not exercise jurisdiction. The classic and amusing case of *Wyman v. Newhouse*[5] illustrates the principle. Defendant, a married man, had a love affair with plaintiff. Apparently it was not proceeding smoothly, because plaintiff decided to sue defendant for "seduction under promise of marriage." From Florida, she wrote him endearing letters, explaining that she had to return to Ireland to care for her dying mother and wished to see him once more

[16] The Court reasoned that plaintiffs will ordinarily choose the forum whose law is most favorable to their claims. Thus, if an unfavorable change in substantive law were conclusive on the issue of forum non conveniens, the doctrine would rarely apply.

[17] The Court found it relevant that the real parties in interest in the case were citizens of Scotland. It held that a foreign plaintiff's choice of an American forum is entitled to less deference than is a citizen's choice of such a forum.

[18] The value preference between the second and third choices changes if the remedy offered by the convenient forum "is so clearly inadequate or unsatisfactory that it is no remedy at all." This limit, however, has had little effect in practice.

[1] *See generally* Fleming James, Geoffrey Hazard, and John Leubsdorf, Civil Procedure § 2.17 (5th ed. 2002).

[2] Restatement (Second) of Conflict of Laws § 82.

[3] E/M Lubricants, Inc. v. Microfral, S.A.R.L., 91 F.R.D. 235 (N.D. Ill. 1981); Wyman v. Newhouse, 93 F.2d 313 (2d Cir. 1937).

[4] Blandin v. Ostrander, 239 F. 700 (2d Cir. 1917). *But see* Ex parte Taylor, 29 R.I. 129, 69 A. 553 (1908).

[5] 93 F.2d 313 (2d Cir. 1937).

before they parted forever. When he arrived at the airport in Florida, she greeted him in the company of a deputy sheriff who served him with process. Defendant returned to his home in New York, and plaintiff took a default judgment in Florida. She later sued defendant on the Florida judgment in a federal court in New York. That court refused to grant full faith and credit to the Florida default judgment, upon the ground that jurisdiction over defendant had been procured by plaintiff's fraud.

An analogous case occurs when the plaintiff lures defendant's property into the state in order to establish in rem, quasi–in–rem, or attachment jurisdiction. The result ought to be the same as in *Wyman,* but not all courts have agreed.[6]

A topic closely related to force and fraud is immunity from service. For policy reasons, courts typically have held some defendants immune from service and refused to exercise jurisdiction over them.[7] Foreign sovereigns and their representatives, for instance, have been held immune for reasons of comity. Other defendants are immune from service because exercising jurisdiction over them would impede the forum's administration of justice. Thus, if a person enters the state to serve as a witness in a proceeding in the state's courts, he typically will be immune from service.[8] Similarly, a person who enters the state to appear as a defendant in a criminal or civil proceeding has immunity.[9]

The limits on jurisdiction based upon force, fraud, and immunity are less important today than they once were. When transient service of process was the principal basis for acquiring jurisdiction over non–resident defendants, the rules were a significant limitation upon the jurisdiction of state courts. Today, however, modern jurisdictional theory[10] and modern long–arm statutes[11] permit state courts to exercise jurisdiction over non–residents without in–state service. Accordingly, the problems of force, fraud, and immunity have much less impact today than they once did. Had the Supreme Court in *Burnham v. Superior Court*[12] struck down transient service as a sufficient basis for jurisdiction, these once crucial doctrines would have had interest for historians only. After *Burnham,* however, they have a renewed lease on life.

---

[6] *See* Siro v. American Express Co., 99 Conn. 95, 121 A. 280 (1923).

[7] Restatement (Second) of Conflict of Laws § 83.

[8] *See* Higgins v. Garcia, 522 So.2d 95 (Fla. App. 1988).

[9] What of a defendant who enters the state for reasons of his own, accidentally injures a state resident, and is incarcerated to await trial for criminal negligence? While in jail, should he be immune from service in a tort action based on the same accident? In State *ex rel.* Svinksty v. Duffield, 137 W.Va. 112, 71 S.E.2d (1952), the court held defendant had no immunity.

[10] *See* §§ 20–27, *supra.*

[11] *See* § 33, *supra.*

[12] 495 U.S. 604 (1990), discussed in § 28, *supra.*

§ 49 Limits: Local Actions[1]

Our law has long distinguished between local and transitory actions.[2] Although virtually any problem might be designated "local," today the label is reserved for land cases. Actions involving land — "local" actions — can be heard only by a court in the situs state. The rule is an old one in American law, dating back at least to Chief Justice Marshall's opinion in *Livingston v. Jefferson.*[3]

There is little to commend the rule. As we discuss elsewhere in more detail,[4] there is no reason why the forum should refuse to entertain an action based on foreign land. To be sure, an action based on in rem jurisdiction requires the presence of the res in the forum; but not all "local" actions are in rem. A suit in trespass is an in personam action, for example, but it nevertheless has been classified as "local" by many courts.[5] This is not nearly the problem it once was because modern long–arm statutes typically permit personal jurisdiction in the situs state.

No good policy supports the refusal of a court with personal jurisdiction over the parties to hear their action.[6] The interests of the situs can be recognized adequately through normal choice–of–law rules and the protection afforded by the recording statutes of the situs. Indeed, it is hard to discover any justification for the continued existence of the local action rule other than the mystique afforded real property by the common law. The trend, both scholarly and judicial, is toward elimination of the distinction between local and transitory actions. Courts today routinely enforce contracts to convey foreign land, and the Restatement (Second) recommends that courts entertain actions for trespass to land and actions on a covenant running with land located in another state.[7] Thus, it can be said that today, "the true distinction between a local action and a transitory action is the distinction between an action in rem and an action in person."[8] In short, the real difference centers on the relief that can be granted[9] — relief involving the res itself can only be granted, of course, if the court has jurisdiction over the res. Any other relief should be available in any court with personal jurisdiction over the defendant.

---

[1] *See generally* Leflar, McDougal & Felix § 47.

[2] Designation of an action as "local" depends on forum law.

[3] 15 F. Cas. 660, 663 (C.C.D. Va. 1811) (No. 8,411). *See generally* Ronan Degnan, *Livingston v. Jefferson — A Footnote,* 75 Cal. L. Rev. 115 (1987).

[4] *See* § 115[e], *infra.*

[5] Occasionally, real problems have been generated by the existence of in personam actions which are nevertheless considered "local." Suppose a defendant from Arkansas damages plaintiff's land in Missouri, but that defendant is not amenable to in personam jurisdiction in Missouri. Plaintiff cannot sue in Missouri because of lack of jurisdiction over the defendant, and he cannot sue in Arkansas because the suit is a local action. *See* Reasor–Hill Corp. v. Harrison, 220 Ark. 521, 249 S.W.2d 994 (1952), for an opinion avoiding this bizarre result.

[6] Leflar, McDougal & Felix § 47.

[7] Restatement (Second) of Conflict of Laws §§ 87, 88.

[8] 13 Charles A. Wright, Arthur R. Miller & Edward H. Cooper, Federal Practice and Procedure § 3822.

[9] Ely v. Smith, 764 F. Supp. 1413, 1415 (D. Kans. 1991).

§ 50 Limits: Penalties, Taxes, and Public Policy

Another set of limitations on jurisdiction involves claims that the forum will not entertain based on "policy" reasons. Here, too, scholars and judges have been chipping away at the bases for those rejections. This section examines three such areas.

[a] Penal Laws[1]

A dictum by Chief Justice Marshall has long dominated this area: "The courts of no country execute the penal laws of another."[2] The trick, of course, lies in determining what constitutes a "penal law." Although that term may be defined broadly (it might include, for example, punitive damages in tort, a rule generally designed to deter rather than to compensate), the modern tendency clearly is to define the term narrowly; both courts and commentators have followed the definition of "penal" given by the Supreme Court in the landmark case of *Huntington v. Attrill:*[3]

> Whether it [the law under consideration] appears to the tribunal which is called upon to enforce it to be, in its essential character and effect, a punishment of an offense against the public.

The jurisdictional limitation on penal actions today, therefore, is usually limited to efforts to enforce the criminal law of another state; indeed, it is difficult to find a case in the past few decades which denies jurisdiction on any other ground. This result makes good sense. There are a number of reasons why a prosecution based upon a state's criminal law should be confined to that state: The discretionary elements involved in prosecuting and sentencing, the need of the sovereign to redress the wrong done its own citizens, constitutional and other fair play considerations based on the right to a jury trial of one's peers, all suggest strongly that a state is justified in refusing to enforce another state's criminal law.[4]

The considerations are altogether different when the foreign "penal" statute is "civil" in nature and designed both to deter and to compensate. Cases involving statutory penalties for failure to perform a corporate director's duty, a minimum recovery in a wrongful death, or punitive damages in tort do not call into play the special considerations present in criminal prosecutions. Hence, the courts justifiably have given the jurisdictional limitation on "penal" claims a narrow construction.

---

[1] *See generally* Robert Leflar, *Extrastate Enforcement of Penal and Governmental Claims,* 46 Harv. L. Rev. 193 (1932).

[2] The Antelope, 23 U.S. (10 Wheat.) 66, 123 (1825).

[3] 146 U.S. 657, 683 (1892). *Huntington* involved enforcement of a foreign "penal" judgment; the definition, however, has been used in jurisdictional cases, as well as in full faith and credit cases. *See* Restatement (Second) of Conflict of Laws § 89. *See also* § 116, *infra.*

[4] *See* Leflar, *supra,* note 1.

[b] Taxes[5]

One strand of American conflicts law holds that a state will not entertain an action brought by a sister state to enforce the sister state's tax laws. That limitation resembles the one involving penal claims, but is less defensible. No good policy supports the tax limitation rule; the only conceivable policy — concern that exercising jurisdiction would offend the sovereignty of the other state[6] — does not apply here, because it is the other sovereign which brings the suit. Moreover, refusal to entertain the action means the forum "offers a legally respectable asylum to the tax dodger."[7] In recent years, a number of state courts have enforced tax claims made by other states,[8] and many states have adopted reciprocal tax enforcement statutes. It is doubtful that any American court today would refuse to entertain a claim to collect back taxes.[9]

[c] Public Policy[10]

The issue posed in this section is limitation on jurisdiction based on public policy. Both the penal and tax claim limitations on the exercise of jurisdiction are but parts of a larger category of limitations premised on the notion that the law upon which the cause of action is based offends the public policy of the forum. The classic analysis of this more general limitation comes from Cardozo's opinion in *Loucks v. Standard Oil Co.*[11]

Plaintiffs' intestate in *Loucks* had been killed by defendant's employees in an accident in Massachusetts. The victim's wife and children, New York residents, sued in New York under the Massachusetts wrongful death statute. The court held that it would not offend New York policy to hear the case, even though there were substantial differences between the wrongful death statutes of the two states:[12]

> The courts are not free to refuse to enforce a foreign right at the pleasure of the judges, to suit the individual notion of expediency or

[5] *See generally* Leflar, *supra* note 1.

[6] *See* Learned Hand's concurring opinion in Moore v. Mitchell, 30 F.2d 600, 604 (2d Cir. 1929), *aff'd on other grounds,* 281 U.S. 18 (1930).

[7] Oklahoma *ex rel.* Oklahoma Tax Comm'n v. Neely, 225 Ark. 230, 282 S.W.2d 150 (1955).

[8] *E.g., id.*; City of Detroit v. Gould, 12 Ill.2d 297, 146 N.E.2d 61 (1957). Restatement (Second) of Conflict of Laws § 89, concurs.

[9] In Milwaukee County v. M.E. White Co., 296 U.S. 268 (1935), the Court held that a judgment based on a tax claim must be accorded full faith and credit, but that it was an "open question" whether a court had to hear a tax claim brought by a sister state.

[10] *See generally* Monrad G. Paulsen & Michael I. Sovern, *"Public Policy" in the Conflict of Laws*, 56 Colum. L. Rev. 969 (1956). The issue posed in this section is limitation on jurisdiction based on public policy. A court, because it despises the policy on which the claim is based, refuses to hear the claim. The issue of public policy can also arise in the *choice–of–law* context. There, a court, for policy reasons, seeks to apply its own rule of law rather than the law which its choice–of–law principles would otherwise dictate. *See* § 60, *infra.*

[11] 224 N.Y. 99, 120 N.E. 198 (1918).

[12] The court also rejected a claim that the Massachusetts wrongful death act was "penal." That act provided a recovery of between $500 and $10,000, based on "the degree of [defendant's] culpability."

> fairness. They do not close their doors, unless help would violate some fundamental principle of justice, some prevalent conception of good morals, some deep–rooted tradition of the common weal.

Because New York also recognized the "fundamental policy that there shall be atonement for the wrong," the New York courts could not refuse to hear the action, even though there were substantial differences between the two statutes.

The public policy exception to jurisdiction makes a great deal of sense when a court is asked to enforce a claim founded on the law of a less than civilized jurisprudence. No one would expect an American forum to enforce a foreign claim based on slavery or de jure racism. The argument for the public policy exception becomes much weaker when the law said to be offensive is that of a sister state.[13] Because federal and state constitutional guarantees insure that state law does not violate basic notions of decency and fair play, the only reason not to hear such a claim is simply that the forum does not like the substance of the policy upon which the claim is based. Such a parochial reason should not be sufficient for the forum to refuse to hear a claim based on the law of another state which has a legitimate interest in the problem.[14]

The utility of the public policy limitation was that it provided a way of avoiding unjust results created by a territorially–based choice–of–law regime. "Public policy," in short, was a convenient escape device.[15] It should have little application, therefore, in a forum which has adopted modern choice–of–law analysis. The continued application of a public policy exception in such a forum is unnecessary, and it carries the added drawback of substituting reflex action pigeonholing the problem for careful analysis of the competing interests implicated by the problem.

§ 51 Limits: Forum Selection Clauses

Many contracts today routinely include forum–selection clauses.[1] Courts today enforce them just as routinely. Indeed, as *Carnival Cruise Lines, Inc. v. Shutte*[2] makes clear, at least in federal court, it will be difficult not to enforce them. A valid forum–selection clause can be seen as yet another limit on the exercise of jurisdiction. A court may otherwise have jurisdiction over the defendant, but may choose not to exercise that jurisdiction by enforcing the clause.

---

[13] State courts must hear federal claims if Congress has so directed. Testa v. Katt, 330 U.S. 386 (1947).

[14] The constitutionality of a refusal to entertain an action based on the law of a sister state is questionable. *See* Hughes v. Fetter, 341 U.S. 609 (1951), discussed *infra* at § 101. *See also* Paulsen & Sovern, *supra* note 10.

[15] Public policy in the area of choice of law is discussed at § 60, *infra*.

[1] Forum–selection clauses are discussed, *supra,* § 30[c].

[2] 499 U.S. 585, 111 S.Ct. 1522 (1991).

§ 52 Procedure: Continuing Jurisdiction[1]

Once a court has jurisdiction over a defendant or his property, it retains that jurisdiction for all proceedings which arise out of the original cause of action.[2] An issue hidden in this formulation is the dimensions of a single "cause of action." Surely plaintiff can make minor changes in his claim by amendment; however, he cannot — without an independent jurisdictional basis — add an entirely new claim.

It does not matter that the original basis for the exercise of jurisdiction no longer exists. Jurisdiction obtained over a defendant based upon service of process within the state is not ousted when the defendant leaves the state, and jurisdiction based on defendant's domicile does not evaporate when defendant moves her home. A contrary rule would be impossible, because it would permit a defendant to divest the court of jurisdiction by her own voluntary action after the commencement of the suit. The same rule for the same reason applies to jurisdiction based on property. A court's jurisdiction over property within the state is not ousted when the property is removed.

Lapse of time — even many years — between stages of the litigation is irrelevant. *Michigan Trust Co. v. Ferry,*[3] the leading case in the area, illustrates the principle. Decedent had died domiciled in Michigan, and defendant was appointed his executor in 1867. Defendant moved to Utah in 1878. In 1903, decedent's residuary legatees and devisees petitioned the Michigan court to remove defendant from his office as executor, and to require him to account for the unadministered portion of the estate. The Supreme Court ruled that the Michigan court's jurisdiction over defendant continued, despite his twenty–five year absence from the state and the long hiatus in the proceedings.

Continuing jurisdiction has particular relevance to domestic relations cases. Alimony, support, and custody decrees are typically modifiable, and courts often retain jurisdiction for years after the parties have left the forum and all jurisdictional bases have ceased to exist.[4] On the other hand, a court may refuse to hear a case over which it maintains jurisdiction. In a child support case, for example, the court which issued the original order might decline to hear a modification petition if a) the parents and children have moved elsewhere, and b) some other convenient forum has jurisdiction over the defendant.[5]

The concept of continuing jurisdiction satisfies only the requirement of a jurisdictional basis; it does not satisfy the constitutional requirement of notice. This means that a party is entitled to adequate notice of each new stage in the litigation which might affect her interests.

---

1 *See generally* Scoles, Hay, Borchers & Symeonides 327; Leflar, McDougal & Felix § 31.

2 Restatement (Second) of Conflict of Laws § 26.

3 228 U.S. 346 (1913).

4 *See* §§ 120, 127, 130, *infra,* for a discussion of jurisdictional problems in family law cases.

5 *E.g.,* Helen B.M. v. Samuel F.D., 479 A.2d 852 (Del. Fam. Ct. 1984).

§ 53 Procedure: Multidistrict Litigation

A legal problem can affect persons in many states. An antitrust conspiracy, for example, may harm competitors in every state. If each person who claims she was injured by the conspiracy were to sue, enormous practical and logistical problems would arise; in addition, the possibility of inconsistent rulings and judgments would be very real. Congress attempted to deal partially with this problem by adopting in 1968 the Multidistrict Litigation Act.[1]

That Act permits a special panel to transfer civil cases which involve a common question of fact to one district judge for all pre–trial proceedings. Thus, the transferee judge supervises discovery, rules on motions to dismiss, determines the preclusive effect of prior litigation, chooses the law to be applied in each action,[2] and passes on any other matter that can be disposed of before trial. The cases are then transferred for trial to the districts in which they were filed.

The Multidistrict Litigation Act has been employed in a wide variety of legal settings: antitrust, securities fraud, products liability, and breach of contract. Perhaps the most common use has been in tort litigation involving mass disasters, such as bridge collapses and aircraft accidents. The crash of a DC–10 near Chicago in May, 1979, illustrates the working of the Act.[3]

Plaintiffs (and their decedents) lived in eleven states and three foreign countries. After suits were filed against the airline and the manufacturer of the plane in federal courts in five states and Puerto Rico, the cases were transferred by the panel on multidistrict litigation to the Northern District of Illinois. That court ruled, *inter alia*, that under the choice–of–law rules of those six jurisdictions, liability would be determined under Illinois law, while compensatory damages would be determined by the law of the domiciles of plaintiffs or their decedents. The court then ruled on whether punitive damages would be available against the defendants. It analyzed the conflicts rules of the transferor states and concluded that the airline could not be subject to punitive damages, but that the manufacturer, in some circumstances, might be forced to pay such claims.[4] That decision was appealed to the Seventh Circuit. In an elaborate opinion covering most of the choice–of–law issues, that court held that punitive damages could not be assessed against either the airline or the manufacturer.[5]

---

[1] 28 U.S.C. § 1407(a).

[2] The court will apply the choice–of–law rules of the state where the action originally was filed, In Re Air Crash Disaster Near Chicago, 644 F.2d 594 (7th Cir. 1981), *cert. denied,* 454 U.S. 878 (1982), just as it would in a transfer case under 28 U.S.C. § 1404 (1976). *See* § 47, *supra,* for a discussion of forum non conveniens and § 1404.

[3] *See* In Re Air Crash Disaster Near Chicago, 500 F. Supp. 1044 (N.D. Ill. 1980).

[4] This was a complex undertaking. The court found that Illinois applied the "most significant relationship" test; California applied "comparative impairment‘; New York used the "government interest" approach; Michigan followed "interest analysis‘; and Puerto Rico and Hawaii still followed *lex loci delicti*. *See* Chapter 4, *infra,* for an explanation of these choice–of–law theories.

[5] In Re Air Crash Disaster Near Chicago, 644 F.2d 594 (7th Cir. 1981), *cert. denied,* 454 U.S. 878 (1982).

Thus, consolidation for pre–trial purposes enabled one court to coordinate and supervise all discovery and pre–trial motions. Further, the court was able to establish the legal rules that would be followed when the cases were transferred back for trial. That procedure, although incomplete, saved a great deal of litigant and judicial effort while helping to insure against inconsistent rulings.

§ 54 A Note on Complex Litigation[1]

Recent years have seen an explosion of what has become known as "complex litigation." There are two types of cases. First, there are single–incident problems, typically torts, which involve a large number of claimants; examples include airplane crashes, hotel fires, and toxic waste spillage. The other type of complex litigation involve mass torts in which large numbers of people claim to have been injured over a long period of time. Examples include asbestos and DES litigation.

Both types of cases place enormous stress on the legal system. They often have hundreds or even thousands of plaintiffs and defendants, and involve innumerable cross–claims. The causes of action themselves may extend back several decades, and, as a result, present incredibly difficult problems of causation; those factors make these cases true monsters. Further complications are created by the broad jurisdictional sweep of American courts and the great latitude they have in deciding what law to apply. The federal system has gradually learned to cope with the single–incident tort. The asbestos cases have proven to be close to intractable, however. Tens of thousands of cases are pending in virtually every jurisdiction, state and federal in this country. Many courts have become badly congested as a result, and many litigants have to wait much too long for justice.

The American Law Institute's Complex Litigation Project is an ambitious set of proposals for state and federal legislation designed to facilitate the consolidation of related cases in the state and federal systems.[2] The touchstone of the Project might be a quote from Professor Zachariah Chafee: "In matters of justice. . .the benefactor is he who makes one lawsuit grow where two grew before."[3]

The Project's first major proposal is a federal statute to expand the current multidistrict litigation regime by providing for transfer and consolidation in *one district* (for trial as well as pretrial proceedings) *of actions pending in several federal districts* if they involve common factual or legal questions and if transfer and consolidation would promote the just, fair and efficient conduct of the actions.[4] The consolidation decision would be entrusted to a special Complex Litigation Panel of federal judges, which

---

[1] *See generally* the on–going ALI Project on Complex Litigation; Linda Mullenix, *Federalizing Choice of Law for Mass Tort Litigation,* 70 Texas L. Rev. 1623 (1992).

[2] *See Complex Litigation: Statutory Recommendations and Analysis* (1994).

[3] *Id.* at 23, quoting Zachariah Chafee, *Bills of Peace with Multiple Parties,* 45 Harv. L. Rev. 1297 (1932).

[4] *Id.*, § 3.01

could act sua sponte, on motion of any party, or at the suggestion of the court in which one of the actions is pending. Liberalized venue provisions and nationwide personal jurisdiction would permit transfer to any district or districts "where the just and efficient resolution of the actions will be promoted and fairness to individual litigants will be facilitated."[5]

Another proposal is designed to consolidate in a *single state court multiple actions pending in different state and federal courts.* It recommends: (1) a federal statute permitting transfer of cases from federal courts for consolidation in a state court if other pending state cases and the events giving rise to the controversy are centered in one state, fairness and the interests of justice would be advanced, and the state court is more appropriate than other possible transferee forums; and (2) an interstate compact or uniform act to facilitate the transfer and consolidation in one state court of related cases pending in the courts of different states.[6]

A third proposal is for federal legislation that would facilitate the consolidation of *state court actions in a federal court* in which related litigation is pending. The proposal would significantly liberalize removal and supplemental jurisdiction in the context of complex multiforum litigation.[7]

The most controversial provisions of the project deal with antisuit injunctions, involuntary consolidation, and choice of law in consolidated cases. Section 5.04 permits a transferee court to enjoin related proceedings in any state or federal court. Even more radically, § 5.05 permits a transferee court to enter an order informing nonparties that they may intervene and, even if they do not, will be bound by its determinations to the same extent as a party. Finally Chapter 6 proposes a code of federal choice–of–law rules to govern in complex consolidated cases.

Several features of the ALI project have proved quite controversial. It trenches significantly on the plaintiff's traditional prerogative in our system to choose *where* she wants her case tried. (Remember that the forum she chose is a perfectly proper one; it only becomes "inconvenient" because of a rash of related litigation elsewhere.) The mandatory intervention or binding of nonparties who refuse to intervene is also quite a radical departure. The ALI proposals would also increase the current tendency to concentrate major litigation in a few urban centers. Probably most transfers will be made to large metropolitan areas that have the courtroom facilities, extra staff, and travel conveniences to handle mass litigation. The law and its practice may lose much of its richness, it has been argued, if certain types of very important cases are handled only in, say, Los Angeles and New York.

The ALI Project has had little practical impact; none of its legislative proposals have been implemented, and most of the commentary has been critical (especially of its choice–of–law proposals).[8]

---

[5] *See id.,* § 3.04.

[6] *Id.,* §§ 4.01, 4.02.

[7] *Id.,* 5.01, 5.03.

[8] For commentary see *Symposium,* 1995 B.Y.U. L. Rev. 731–1155 (1995), *Symposium,* 54 La. L. Rev. 843–1160 (1994).

§ 55 The Challenge of the Future: Jurisdiction in Cyberspace

[a] Introduction to Cybertalk

Before considering the jurisdictional problems posed by the information revolution, it is helpful to learn the lay of the land. In *Reno v. ACLU*, the Supreme Court provided this explanation for the cyber–challenged:

> The Internet. . . .began in 1969 as a military program called "ARPANET". . . ., [and] provided an example for the development of a number of civilian networks that, eventually, linking with each other, now enable tens of millions of people to communicate with one another and to access vast amounts of information from around the world. . . .
>
> The Internet has experienced "extraordinary growth." The number of "host" computers. . .increased from about 300 in 1981 to approximately 9,400,000 by 1996. Roughly 60%. . .are located in the United States. . . .
>
> Individuals can obtain access to the Internet from many different sources,. . . [e.g., colleges and universities, corporations, local libraries, storefront "computer coffee shops" and major national "online services" such as America Online, CompuServe, the Microsoft Network, and Prodigy].
>
> Anyone with access to the Internet may take advantage of a wide variety of communication and information retrieval methods. . . .[including] electronic mail ("e-mail"), automatic mailing list services (. . ."listservs"), "newsgroups," "chat rooms," and the "World Wide Web." [T]hese methods can be used to transmit text. . . sound, pictures, and moving video images. Taken together, these tools constitute a unique medium — known. . .as "cyberspace."
>
> [T]he World Wide Web. . .allows users to search for and retrieve information stored in remote computers. . .[and] to communicate back to designated sites. . . . Each [site]has its own address — "rather like a telephone number. . ."
>
> [F]rom the readers' viewpoint, [the web is comparable]to both a vast library including millions of readily available and indexed publications and a sprawling mall offering goods and services. . . .
>
> From the publishers' point of view, it constitutes a vast platform from which to address and hear from a world-wide audience of millions of readers, viewers, researchers, and buyers. . . . Publishers include government agencies, educational institutions, commercial entities, advocacy groups, and individuals. . . .[1]

[1] 521 U.S. 844, 849–53 (1997). A more complete treatment of the basics can be found in David Wille, *Personal Jurisdiction and the Internet — Proposed Limits on State Jurisdiction over Data Communications in Tort Cases*, 87 Ky. L.J. 95, 183–201 (1998).

[b] Jurisdiction and the Internet

"Just as the automobile challenged and exposed the weaknesses in the power theory of jurisdiction, so the internet is challenging modern jurisdiction theory."[2] The automobile stressed the power theory because it minimized distances and thus contracted space. The internet creates a whole new type of space and thus poses a more fundamental challenge to the territorialist elements of current doctrine. A theory adequate for a world defined by state and national borders is likely to founder in one where those familiar concepts are increasingly irrelevant.

[1] Easy Cases

Nevertheless, many internet cases fit easily within current jurisdiction theory. E-mail, for example, is no more problematic than ordinary ("snail") mail or the telephone because the sender is aware of and can limit the geographical target of the message.[3] The Worldwide Web lacks those features, yet current doctrine is still adequate for many cases involving web sites. In breach of contract and product liability cases, there usually will be contacts between the defendant and the forum beyond defendant's mere construction of a web page that can be accessed in the forum. Typically there will be individual negotiations between the plaintiff and the defendant and often the delivery of a product or a service into the forum. While such cases will not always support jurisdiction, the extra contacts make them relatively easy to analyze under current theory.[4]

Even less problematic for current jurisdictional doctrine are assertions of general jurisdiction. Maintenance of a web site that can be accessed by users in the forum should not render the defendant amenable to general jurisdiction there. Not surprisingly, the few cases that have faced the issue have agreed. In *Weber v. Jolly Hotels*[5] , for example, a federal court in New Jersey refused to exercise jurisdiction over an Italian hotel that maintained a web site that could be accessed in the forum because the plaintiff's claim involved an injury in Italy, and the plaintiff had neither learned of the hotel nor made arrangements to stay there through the web site.

[2] The Hard Case

The difficult issue for current jurisdictional theory is whether the author of a web page should be amenable to specific jurisdiction based *solely* on the fact that the page can be accessed in the forum. Cases posing the hard question, *i.e.*, cases involving no contact beyond creation of the web site,

---

[2] Casad & Richman § 2-5[7] (3d ed. 1999).

[3] *See* Katherine Sheehan, *Predicting the Future: Personal Jurisdiction for the Twenty-first Century*, 66 U. Cinn. L. Rev. 385, 412 (1998).

[4] For a case dealing with contacts beyond the defendant's mere creation of a forum–accessible web page, *see* CompuServe, Inc. v. Patterson, 89 F.3d 1257 (6th Cir.1996). For commentary on cases of this type, *see* Martin Reddish, *Of New Wine and Old Bottles: Personal Jurisdiction, the Internet, and the Nature of Constitutional Evolution,* 38 Jurimetrics 575, 595 (1998).

[5] 977 F. Supp. 327, 333 (D.N.J. 1997).

often involve a tort theory, most often one involving intellectual property. So far the most typical fact pattern involves a defendant that has chosen an internet domain name that allegedly violates the plaintiff's trade name or service mark.[6] The emerging answer to the question seems to be that the defendant's maintenance of a web site that can be accessed from the forum is not enough, by itself, to generate jurisdiction over the defendant in the forum.[7] A contrary result would expose every web page owner to nationwide (or worldwide) jurisdiction, in and threaten to "chill" activity on the web.

Instead the courts arrange internet contacts along a continuum. At one end courts usually find jurisdiction in cases where the defendant regularly does business with forum residents via its web site.[8] At the other end of the continuum, courts usually refuse to exercise jurisdiction when the defendant's web site, accessible in the forum, just passively advertises the defendant's product or service.[9] In the middle, along a sliding scale, are cases where the defendant's web site is "interactive," and the degree of interactitvity controls the likelihood of an exercise of jurisdiction.[10] Even

[6] *See, e.g.,* Cybersell, Inc. v. Cybersell, Inc, 130 F.3d 414 (9th Cir. 1997).

[7] *See, e.g.,* Cybersell, Inc. v. Cybersell, Inc, 130 F.3d 414 (9th Cir. 1997), Zippo Mfg. Co. v. Zippo Dot Com, Inc., 952 F. Supp. 1119, 1124 (W.D. Pa. 1997), Bensusan Restaurant Corp. v. King, 937 F. Supp. 295 (S.D.N.Y. 1996), *aff'd,* 126 F.3d 25, (2d Cir. 1997). *But see* Inset Systems, Inc. v. Instruction Set, Inc., 937 F. Supp. 161 (D. Conn. 1996). For commentary on Zippo and Bensusan, see Note, *Personal Jurisdiction and the Internet, An Introduction*, 13 Berkeley Tech. L. J. 263 (1998).

[8] *See* CompuServe, Inc. v. Patterson, 89 F.3d 1257 (6th Cir.1996), Euromarket Designs, Inc. v. Crate & Barrel, Ltd., 96 F. Supp.2d 824 (N.D. Ill. 2000) (actively doing business over the net with consumers in the forum); Colt Studio, Inc. v. Badpuppy Enterprise, 75 F. Supp.2d 1104 (C.D. Cal. 1999); Stomp, Inc. v. Neatco, 61 F. Supp.2d 1074 (C.D. Cal. 1999). One or very few such transactions, however, may not suffice. Butler v. Beer Across America, 83 F. Supp. 2d 1261 (N.D. Ala. 2000).

[9] *See, e.g.,* CompuServe, Inc. v. Patterson, 89 F.3d 1257 (6th Cir.1996), Euromarket Designs, Inc. v. Crate & Barrel, Ltd., 96 F. Supp.2d 824 (N.D. Ill. 2000), Nutrition Physiology Corp. v. Enviros Ltd., 87 F. Supp.2d 648 (N.D. Tex. 2000), GTE New Media Services Inc. v. BellSouth Corp., 199 F.3d 1343 (D.C. Cir. 2000) (passive web site accessible from the forum did not constitute "persistent course of conduct" or "transacting business" within meaning of long–arm statute). Some cases find amenability based even upon a passive cite based on the number of "hits" the cite receives from forum users. *See, e.g.,* Heroes, Inc. v. Heroes Found., 958 F. Supp. 1 (D.D.C. 1996); Pres-Kap, Inc. v. System One, Direct Access, Inc., 636 So. 2d 1351 (Fla. Dist. Ct. App. 1994).

[10] GTE New Media Services Inc. v. BellSouth Corp., 199 F.3d 1343 (D.C. Cir. 2000) (passive web site accessible from the forum did not constitute "persistent course of conduct" or "transacting business" within meaning of long–arm statute), Soma Medical Internat'l v. Standard Chartered Bank, 196 F.3d 1292 (10th Cir. 1999) (passive web site insufficient for specific jurisdiction), JB Oxford Holdings, Inc. v. Net Trade, Inc., 76 F.Supp2d 1363 (SD Fla. 1999) (same), LFG, LLC v. Zapata Corp., 78 F. Supp.2d 731 (N.D. Ill. 1999) ("portal" web site is not merely passive).

Purely territorial solutions to the problem are particularly inapposite in cyberspace; thus the location of the server for the web page ought to be irrelevant. *See* Katherine Sheehan, *Predicting the Future: Personal Jurisdiction for the Twenty–first Century*, 66 U. Cinn. L. Rev. 385, 417 (1998).

a relatively passive site can generate jurisdiction however if it geographically targets the forum.[11]

Not surprisingly, some jurisdiction scholars see the cyberspace cases as a welcome occasion for the general reexamination of current jurisdiction theory.[12] Presumably those cases suggest a greater emphasis on litigational convenience and a reduced reliance on contacts. If so purposeful availment may become increasingly irrelevant in cyberspace. If the law of jurisdiction generally moves in that direction, it may prompt the Court to place more meaningful restrictions on state–court choice–of–law decisions.[13]

Another radical solution to the problem of jurisdiction in cyberspace draws on the historical analogy of the law merchant and would involve a separate set of cyber–courts enforcing a separate law of cyberspace. This option would eliminate much of the inconvenience associated with out-of-state litigation.[14]

---

[11] The geographical targeting argument relies on Calder v. Jones, 465 U.S. 783 (1984), *see* § 24, *supra*, and has proved influential in some decisions. *See* Inset Systems, Inc. v. Instruction Set, Inc., 937 F. Supp. 161,165 (D.Conn. 1996).

Perhaps initiation should be relevant as well. In non–electronic jurisdiction cases, the courts have found the concept of initiation to be especially useful. Courts tend to find jurisdiction more readily when defendant has initiated contact with the plaintiff in the forum than when plaintiff seeks out the defendant in its home state. *See* § 37[f], *supra*. Unfortunately the test does not apply as neatly in Web transactions as in non–electronic contexts. Thus it is unclear whether a Web page author initiates the transaction by creating the page, or the user initiates the transaction by accessing it. The actual electronics of the transaction occur as follows:

> When an accessor "visits" a web site. . .the accessor does not make a visit analogous to a physical visit. A web site access involves a two–way data communication in a request/response protocol. The accessor's computer sends a request to the web site operator's computer, and the web server, in response to the request sends a copy of the web page to the accessor's computer. . . . A web site access is analogous to the. . . accessor sending a post card . . . requesting a free copy of a newspaper published by the web site operator, followed by the sending of the newspaper. . . . Of course,. . . the web site operator does not know exactly where the newspaper is being sent; the web site operator has instead employed automatic equipment for the distribution.

David Wille, *Personal Jurisdiction and the Internet — Proposed Limits on State Jurisdiction Over Data Communications in Tort Cases*, 87 Ky. L.J. 95, 109. But how far does the purely electronic explanation go toward answering the legal question of initiation?

[12] *See* Redish, *supra* note 4, at 601–610; Wille, *supra* note 1 at 115–139.

[13] *See* § 97, *infra*.

[14] For discussion of the possibility, see David Johnson and David Post, *Law and Borders — The Rise of Law in Cyberspace*, 48 Stan. L. Rev. 1367 (1996), I. Trotter Hardy, *The Proper Legal Regime for "Cyberspace,"* 55 U. Pitt. L. Rev. 993, 1019 (1974); Henry Perritt, Jr., *Jurisdiction in Cyberspace*, 41 Vill. L. Rev. 1 (1996).

Chapter 4
CHOICE OF LAW

OVERVIEW

§ 56 Overview

A court called upon to resolve a dispute with multi–state aspects must choose a law to apply to the problem. That choice often is not easy to make, and the task is further complicated by the need to select a method to use in choosing the appropriate law. It is not surprising, therefore, that the search for a system for choice of law has occupied a great deal of judicial and academic time and effort. The discussion, especially among the scholars, sometimes seems as though it were being conducted by Byzantine theologians.

Choice of law as a discipline in this country began with the monumental treatise by Justice Joseph Story, published in 1834.[1] Story, heavily influenced by the territorial concepts of earlier Dutch thinkers, emphasized the right of a state to control what went on in its courts, subject to notions of comity. American conflicts law in the first half of this century centered on the work of Professor Joseph Beale of the Harvard Law School, an effort culminating in the Restatement (First) of Conflict of Laws in 1934 and Beale's own treatise published in the following year.[2] A territorial imperative lies at the core of Beale's work, for it is based on the idea that at the moment a cause of action arises, rights vest according to the law of the place where the crucial event occurred. In tort law, for example, *lex loci delicti* ("the law of the place of the wrong") held sway, on the theory that the victim's cause of action had vested according to the law of the place where the injury occurred. This "vested rights" approach was enormously influential.

The seeds of the demise of Beale's Restatement, however, had been planted even before it was written. Beginning at the turn of this century Sociological Jurisprudence, and then Legal Realism, had taught that law was and should be functional, and that legal rules should be tailored to serve societal goals. Because Beale's territorial system did not inquire into the purposes behind the competing substantive law rules, the system did not satisfy the mandate of twentieth–century jurisprudence. This problem was recognized by a young professor, David Cavers, in a path–breaking article in 1933,[3] as well as by Walter Wheeler Cook in a series of articles

[1] Joseph Story, Conflict of Laws (1834).

[2] Joseph H. Beale, A Treatise on the Conflict of Laws (1935).

[3] David F. Cavers, *A Critique of the Choice–of–Law Problem*, 47 Harv. L. Rev. 173 (1933).

ending in his masterpiece, The Legal and Logical Bases of the Conflict of Laws (1942).

The approach advocated by those and other writers led to the drafting of the Restatement (Second). Work on the project began in 1952 and was essentially complete by 1963, although final publication did not occur until 1971. The Reporter was Professor Willis Reese of Columbia. The Restatement (Second) generally eschews hard–and–fast rules in favor of the general principle that the law of the state with the "most significant relationship" to a transaction should control. The goal of that formula is to ensure that the law of the state most concerned with the problem will be applied and lead thereby to a sensible outcome to the litigation. This approach is sometimes called looking for the "proper law."

While work progressed on the Second Restatement, Professor Brainerd Currie of Duke argued that the choice–of–law process should focus on the policies behind state substantive law rules; whether a rule should be applied should depend upon whether the policy underlying that rule would be advanced by its application. Currie's approach, known as "interest analysis," has appeared in various forms and has been incorporated (some would say, co-opted) by the Restatement (Second). Some combination of the two systems has been adopted by most courts and commentators in the half century since Currie's first articles appeared.[4]

Recent years have seen a partial withdrawal from interest analysis. The specific worry is that the apparently indefinite, almost formless nature of Currie's process has led — perhaps ineluctably — to ad hoc decision–making. To counter that problem, some judges and scholars have suggested that our experience with modern forms of choice–of–law analysis is broad enough to permit the promulgation of new "rules" that will be both functional and certain.

One way to look at alternative methods of choosing the applicable law is to distinguish between jurisdiction–selecting systems on the one hand, and content or policy selecting systems on the other. Jurisdiction–selecting systems choose a state whose law will be applied, regardless of its content or motivating policy. By contrast, content–selecting systems focus on the policy behind competing substantive laws in making the choice–of–law decision. The First Restatement used jurisdiction–selecting rules. The rules prescribed a jurisdiction whose law was to be invoked once the problem had been properly characterized (as, say, one sounding in tort). The many varieties of interest analysis, on the other hand, are content–selecting systems. choice–of–law decisions in those systems are functional, in that they seek to assess the impact of a choice on the goals of the substantive law. Of course, the First Restatement and interest analysis are the polar opposites; intermediate positions also exist. An illustration is the Second Restatement, which combines presumptive jurisdiction–selecting rules with statements of concern which can be used to focus on policy considerations.

This Chapter examines the various techniques used today in choosing the law in multi–state problems. We begin by discussing several recurring

[4] These are collected in Currie, Essays.

problems in choice of law generally. Next we turn our attention to the two Restatements, describing them generally and then detailing their treatments of tort, contract, and property matters. We then examine other forms of choice of law analysis and special emphasis is placed on "interest analysis." The next part discusses certain common problems in choice of law law today. The last two parts explore the impact of the federal Constitution on choice of law, and choice of law in the federal courts.

Part A

SOME PERVASIVE PROBLEMS

A number of conceptual issues recur in discussions of choice–of–law problems. Topics such as characterization, renvoi, and the substance/procedure distinction occur frequently enough that Conflicts literature generally refers to them as "pervasive problems." These concepts often serve as "escape devices," because they can be (and, apparently, often are) manipulated to "escape" the otherwise inflexible regime imposed by traditional choice–of–law rules. Part A examines generally each of these escape devices and discusses the relevance of each to various choice of law theories. The last two sections of this part discuss two other recurring themes in choice of law: depeçage and proof of foreign law.

§ 57 Characterization[1]

The jurisdiction–selecting rules of the First Restatement required that each case be labeled in order to determine which choice–of–law rule applied. If the case were labeled a "contract" problem, for example, then the law of the place of making or performance would be applied; if the case sounded in "tort," then the system specified application of the law of the place of injury (the place of the last event necessary to the cause of action). Obviously, the result could turn on which label the court chose for the problem. Often it was not clear why the court picked one name tag rather than another. The leading casebook example is *Alabama Great Southern Railroad v. Carroll.*[2]

The parties in that case — a brakeman and the railroad for which he worked — were from Alabama, and the contract of employment had been made in that state. While working on a train running from Alabama into Mississippi, plaintiff was injured as a result of the negligence of a fellow servant. The negligent act occurred in Alabama, but plaintiff's injury occurred in Mississippi. Plaintiff filed suit against the railroad in Alabama, and the defendant argued that, under the law of the place of injury (Mississippi) the fellow servant rule provided a complete defense.

Plaintiff tried to counter with the contention that the Alabama worker's compensation statute, which had abolished the fellow servant defense, had become part of the contract of employment which gave rise to the claim sued upon. Hence, Alabama law should be applied as the law of the place of making. Although the court observed that plaintiff's argument "would lead to conclusions astounding to the profession," it did not bother to explain

[1] *See generally* Weintraub at 49–55. *See also* Moffatt Hancock, *The Fallacy of the Transplanted Category*, 37 Can. B. Rev. 535 (1959).

[2] 97 Ala. 126, 11 So. 803 (1892).

why such "astounding" consequences would follow. Thus, without giving any real reasons for doing so, the court simply characterized the case as a tort problem rather than a contract question, and produced a victory for defendant rather than for plaintiff.

Another well–known example of characterization is *Levy v. Daniels' U-Drive Auto Renting Co.*[3] Defendant, a car–rental company, had rented a car in Connecticut to a man named Sack; the car was driven to Massachusetts, where an accident occurred. Plaintiff, a passenger in Sack's car, based his resulting claim on a Connecticut statute providing for liability of car rental agencies. Massachusetts lacked a comparable law, and defendant argued that the law of the place of injury — Massachusetts — should be applied. The court, however, characterized the problem as one in contract, thereby enabling it to apply the liability rule of Connecticut, where the contract was made. Why was the problem contractual? Because the statutory liability became "a part of every contract of hiring" made in Connecticut. Thus, the right sued on by plaintiff was created by contract and he could recover as the third party beneficiary of the contract between Sack and defendant. A wave of the characterization wand was all that was necessary to avoid the inconvenient result reached by the place of injury rule; the result certainly can be defended,[4] but not on the conclusory ground adopted by the court.

Although characterization is probably an inescapable part of thinking conceptually about any problem, its use entails a substantial risk. Such "decision–making by pigeon–hole" avoids the reasoning necessary to explain why a particular pigeon–hole should be chosen. Characterization encourages reflexive, mechanical choices rather than reflective inquiry into the reasons *why* a particular result is proper.[5]

Unfortunately, the sort of characterization required by the First Restatement was not conducive to such careful inquiry. Instead, the characterizer apparently used some intuitive process — perhaps asking what law school course might have addressed the problem. In those circumstances, manipulation by both judge and lawyer was all too possible — and all the more vexing because it was done sub silentio.

One way to understand the use and ultimate futility of recharacterization under the First Restatement is to ask the questions: why, how and where.[6] First consider why the court felt the need to escape from the traditional lex loci rule. In *Levy*, for example, the court wanted to compensate the plaintiff, deter the defendant from renting to irresponsible drivers, and place the risk of loss on the growing and profitable industry of automobile rental. Probably, the court also felt justified in applying Connecticut law to a case where all relevant contacts except the place of injury were in Connecticut.

---

[3] 108 Conn. 333, 143 A. 163 (1928).

[4] *See* George W. Stumberg, Principles of Conflict of Laws 202–03 (3d ed. 1963).

[5] *See* William L. Reynolds, Judicial Process in a Nutshell 62–65 (2d ed. 1991).

[6] This method of analyzing First Restatement escape device cases figures prominently in Vernon, Weinberg, Reynolds, and Richman, § 4.11.

How to accomplish the escape was a different matter. Because the systematics of the First Restatement did not permit stating frankly the reasons for applying Connecticut law, the court needed to use an escape device instead. The limits of the First Restatement also controlled the where of the escape, limiting the possibilities to another lex loci rule, place of contracting.

The difficulty, of course, is the precedent established. What will the court do in the next case when the Massachusetts driver rents a car in Massachusetts (from a lessor doing business in both states), drives it into Connecticut, and injures a Connecticut resident? Most of the reasons for applying Connecticut law in *Levy* apply in the hypothetical case, but the precedent of *Levy* gives the wrong result, exonerating the defendant lessor under law of Massachusetts, the place of the contract. Will a future court feel bound by the characterization precedent of *Levy*, or will it be able to look behind the mechanics of the result for the real reasons that motivated the court? The recharacterization maneuver virtually guarantees that the reasons for the decision will not be revealed in the reasoning of the opinion, thus leaving future courts to choose unpredictably between the two and confounding any attempt to predict the result.[7]

Characterization plays a less prominent role in modern theories, which have tried to focus on the policies that legal rules are designed to serve. Interest analysts, such as Currie, have very little regard for this device.[8] Because the Second Restatement employs a number of jurisdiction-selecting presumptions,[9] characterization cannot be avoided when using that system. Today, however, virtually everyone agrees that characterization, although perhaps inescapable, should not be employed in the thoughtless manner displayed in *Carroll* and *Levy*. At the very least, the crass characterization of cases by the type of cause of action displayed in those two opinions can be replaced by a more careful examination of the several issues presented in each decision.

§ 58 Substance or Procedure[1]

A subset of the characterization problem involves the choice between substance and procedure. Under the traditional approach, procedural problems (those dealing with the process of litigation) were controlled by forum law; substantive issues (those involving claims of right) were determined by the law of another jurisdiction. This obviously made labeling the cause of action a very important, albeit still partially intuitive, game.[2]

---

[7] For a historical example of this phenomenon see *infra* § 64[b][1] the discussion of the Arkansas telegraph cases.

[8] *See* § 78, *infra*.

[9] *See* § 71, *infra*.

[1] The classic articles are: Walter Wheeler Cook, *"Substance" and "Procedure" in the Conflict of Laws*, 42 Yale L. J. 333 (1933); Edmund M. Morgan, *Choice of Law Governing Proof*, 58 Harv. L. Rev. 153 (1944).

[2] The substance/procedure dichotomy does not appear in the conflicts literature until the turn of the century. D. Michael Risinger, *"Substance" and "Procedure" Revisited*, 30 U.C.L.A. L. Rev. 189, 195 (1982). The entry of that dichotomy coincides with the rise of the vested rights methodology.

The substance/procedure dichotomy arises because the forum has strong reasons for seeing its law applied to issues concerning pleading, motion practice, the presentation of evidence, and so forth. There are really two interests at stake here. First, the forum's own substantive policy may be implicated, at least on some "procedural" issues. Thus, the scope of a testimonial privilege may be very important to the public policy of a forum. Today, we might say that the forum has an interest in the application of its own law on that issue; calling the issue "procedural" is merely a shorthand way of insuring that the interest will be protected. The second justification for the procedural rubric is the need to protect scarce judicial resources by ensuring that the law of another state need not be considered on every point that might arise at trial. Think how awkward it would be, for example, if an Indiana court had to consult South Carolina law every time a question at a trial (where South Carolina law was being applied to "substantive" issues) was objected to as calling for hearsay.

Forum interest and convenience, therefore, should dictate the classification of an issue as "procedural." Expressed differently, if neither the forum's interest nor judicial convenience is involved, no reason exists to treat the problem as "procedural." The focus should be on whether the reasons which gave rise to the substance/procedure distinction are involved in the problem, not on the judge's vague intuition or on a precedent which addressed the issue in a different setting and is, therefore, of questionable application.

Students of the *Erie* problem are well aware that the labels "substance" and "procedure" are used in several different areas in the law, and bizarre results can be reached by using precedent from one area to solve a problem in another.[3] A famous series of cases from Massachusetts involving burden of proof on the issue of contributory negligence illustrates the problem. The first case, *Duggan v. Bay State Street Railway*,[4] held that a statute allocating burden of proof on contributory negligence was procedural. The court did this in the context of upholding the constitutionality of retroactive application of the act — a much easier thing to do if the act is called procedural. The following year, the court was asked to decide whether the Massachusetts law (imposing the burden of proof on the defendant) was "procedural" in a conflicts case. In *Levy v. Steiger*,[5] a plaintiff from Massachusetts was injured in an automobile accident in Rhode Island; that state allocated to plaintiff the burden of proof on the issue of contributory negligence. The court found the question routine — it had already classified the statute as procedural (in *Duggan*), and procedural it would remain. Thus, the law of the forum (Massachusetts), rather than that of the place of injury (Rhode Island), should be applied. No matter that the question of retroactivity (*Duggan*) on the one hand and choice of law (*Steiger*) on the other differ starkly. Procedure is procedure is procedure.

---

[3] The problems associated with the rule in Erie R.R. Co. v. Tompkins, 304 U.S. 64 (1938), are discussed in §§ 103–105, *infra*.

[4] 230 Mass. 370, 119 N.E. 757 (1918).

[5] 233 Mass. 600, 124 N.E. 477 (1919).

The issue became even more complicated when it arose later in a federal court. Judge Magruder, in *Sampson v. Channell*,[6] had before him a diversity action in Massachusetts based on an auto accident in Maine. The question was whether the burden of proof was to be determined by Massachusetts law, Maine law, or federal law. Magruder determined that, under *Erie*, he was bound to apply state law rather than federal law, because the burden of proof rules were "substantive" because they could "determine the outcome of the case." Although Massachusetts choice–of–law decisions (*e.g.*, *Duggan*) had classified these questions as procedural, Magruder realized that the reasons for the substance/procedure distinction in the *Erie* context were different from the reasons for it in choice–of–law cases. Next came the state choice–of–law issue: Should the court apply the law of Maine or Massachusetts? Magruder, following *Duggan*, held that the issue was "procedural" for choice–of–law purposes and thus applied Massachusetts law. Magruder, in other words, classified the issue as substantive for *Erie* purposes and procedural for choice–of–law purposes, thereby demonstrating that different policies motivate the distinction in different contexts.

The Massachusetts burden of proof cases illustrate the difficulties that can arise from mindless labeling. The most absurd example, however, comes from the pen of Timothy Dwight, a law professor acting as referee in a New York case. The question in *Marie v. Garrison*[7] was whether an oral agreement was barred by the Statute of Frauds of either Missouri or New York. In an opinion that has bedeviled generations of law students, the founder of Columbia Law School[8] held that neither statute applied. He reached this curious result by finding the New York statute substantive because it declared that contracts in violation of the statute were "void." Hence, the New York rule could not, under "accepted rules, be applied to contracts made in other states, and accordingly not to the present case." The Missouri Statute of Frauds, on the other hand, merely made oral agreements "unenforceable"; it was, therefore, a procedural statute, and not to be given extraterritorial effect in a New York forum. The agreement, Dwight concluded, "whether treated by the law of New York or Missouri, does not trench upon any provision of the Statute of Frauds," and, therefore, was valid because neither Statute of Frauds applied to it. In short, Dwight, using a little substance/procedure magic, enforced an agreement that probably could not have been enforced in either state.

The modern trend away from characterization (discussed in the preceding section) has been carried over into the substance/procedure area. The Second Restatement expressly disclaims attempts to classify issues as substantive or procedural, encouraging courts instead to face directly the question of whether to apply forum law.[9] This trend is clearly conducive

[6] 110 F.2d 754 (1st Cir. 1940).

[7] 13 Abb. N. Cas. 210 (N.Y. Sup. Ct. 1883).

[8] Lawrence Friedman, A History of American Law 419 (1976).

[9] Restatement (Second) of Conflict of Laws, § 122, comment b. *See also* comment a, which provides four factors that should guide the court: (1) Is the issue one about which the parties may have planned? (2) Is the issue outcome–determinative in the case? (3) Do the precedents classify the issue as "procedural"? and (4) Would application of foreign law place an undue burden on the judicial administrations of the forum?

to rational and predictable results. Horrors such as *Marie v. Garrison* confirm vividly the wisdom of the modern approach. Still, the distinction lives on, often in theory and usually in practice. Generally treated as procedural today, and thus governed by the local law of the forum are:[10] service, pleading, motion practice, burden of proof, presumptions, set–off or counterclaim problems, the methods used in enforcing a judgment, exemptions from execution, and requirements concerning proof of foreign law. Although most evidentiary questions are controlled by forum law,[11] some are considered substantive. Among this last group are questions of privilege,[12] the parol evidence rule,[13] and problems involving the Statute of Frauds.[14] Statute of limitations issues, which are traditionally considered procedural, are discussed in detail in a later section.[15]

§ 59 Renvoi[1]

In American conflicts law, a reference to the law of another jurisdiction almost always is a reference to the law that the foreign state would apply to a purely domestic problem. American courts rarely look to the conflicts law of the other jurisdiction as an aid to solving a choice–of–law problem. The focus, in conflicts parlance, is not on the "whole law" of the other state (that is, its substantive law plus its choice–of–law rules), but rather on its "internal law" (that is, the rules which the other state would use to decide a purely domestic problem).

[a] Two Examples

Occasionally, however, common law courts have looked at a foreign state's whole law to decide a question. This procedure, known as "renvoi," can be illustrated by two well–known cases. The first, *University of Chicago v. Dater*,[2] involved a guarantee of a mortgage note by a married woman domiciled in Michigan. She signed the guarantee in Michigan and mailed it to Illinois, where the lender and property were located. Several years later, when the borrower defaulted, the mortgagee sought to collect on the guarantee and brought suit in Michigan. Michigan choice–of–law rules referred to the law of the place of making — arguably, Illinois. The majority noted, however, that, under Illinois precedent, if an Illinois court had been faced with this case, it would have applied Michigan's internal law.[3]

---

[10] *See* Restatement (Second) of Conflict of Laws §§ 122–36.

[11] *See id.* §§ 137–38.

[12] *See id.* § 139.

[13] *See id.* § 140.

[14] *See id.* § 141.

[15] *See* § 93, *infra*.

[1] *See generally* Larry Kramer, *Return of the Renvoi*, 66 N.Y.U. L. Rev. 979 (1991); Erwin N. Griswold, *Renvoi Revisited*, 51 Harv. L. Rev. 1165 (1938).

[2] 277 Mich. 658, 20 N.W. 175 (1936).

[3] *See* Burr v. Beckler, 264 Ill. 230, 106 N.E. 206 (1914).

In other words, if the Michigan court looked to the whole law of Illinois to resolve the case (Illinois was, arguably, the place where the contract was made), the Michigan court would find that Illinois, rather than looking to its own law, would refer to the domestic law of the state where the woman executed the guarantee (here, Michigan). The Michigan court decided to "accept" the renvoi and apply forum law. As a result, the guarantee was held invalid because a married woman in Michigan lacked the capacity to make such a guarantee. *Dater* illustrates the use of renvoi in a contract case. A more typical use of renvoi occurs in property cases. The common illustration is *In re Schneider's Estate.*[4]

There, an American citizen of Swiss birth died domiciled in New York. Included in the assets of his estate was certain real property located in Switzerland. Schneider's will attempted to dispose of the Swiss property in a manner arguably forbidden by Swiss law. The property had been sold by the administrator of the estate, and the proceeds had been transmitted to New York. The court was faced, therefore, with an unusual situation; normally, as the Surrogate recognized, "[a]ctions concerning realty are properly litigable only before the courts of the situs." He ruled, therefore, that the issue should be decided by the law of the situs. The question then became what it meant to apply "the law of the situs": Should the court apply Swiss internal (*i.e.,* substantive) law, or should it apply the "whole" law of Switzerland (including Swiss choice-of-law principles). The Surrogate determined that he should decide the case as it would have been decided absent the fortuity of the sale and transmittal of the funds to New York. If the land had not been sold, only a Swiss court would have had the power to issue a decree concerning local land. Because a Swiss court could not address the issue (due to the inadvertent conversion of the land), the Surrogate ruled that he should decide the case as a Swiss court would have decided it. The Swiss court, he found, would apply the whole law of Switzerland and would refer the case to the internal law of New York. He, therefore, accepted the renvoi and applied New York law.[5]

[b] Renvoi Terminology

Renvoi terminology can be as complex as the concept. The forum can either "accept" or "reject" the "remission" from foreign law; the acceptance can be either "total" or "partial." Thus, when the *Schneider* court followed the Swiss reference to New York law, it "accepted" the renvoi. If the court had refused to follow that reference, it would have "rejected" the renvoi. Because the Surrogate accepted the renvoi and applied New York internal law, the renvoi was "partial"; if he had found that Swiss law referred to New York's whole law, the renvoi would have been "total." The reference of the Swiss conflicts law to New York law is referred to as a "remission."

---

[4] 198 Misc. 1017, 96 N.Y.S.2d 652 (N.Y. Supp. Ct. 1950).

[5] A more complicated version of *Schneider* is In re Annesley, (1926) Ch. 692, where the court applied a total renvoi. If a total renvoi had been used in *Schneider*, the New York court would have referred the matter back to Swiss internal law.

If the Swiss conflicts law had referred to a third jurisdiction, the result would have been a "transmission."

[c] The Uses of Renvoi[6]

The First Restatement had little use for renvoi. There were only two exceptions to the ordinary rule against renvoi: Questions concerning title to land or the validity of a divorce were to be decided under the whole law of the appropriate state.[7] The Restatement does not explain the reasons for these exceptions, but their very limited scope suggests substantial hostility toward the doctrine. That hostility, typical of proponents of the territorial theory of choice of law, is difficult to understand; there is nothing necessarily incompatible between that theory and renvoi. Perhaps the problem under the territorial theory was the difficulty of breaking a potentially endless circle of reference when policy analysis was not available to turn the trick.

The current Restatement accords renvoi a somewhat more hospitable reception, although it also provides for only two circumstances in which the normal reference to foreign internal law should be displaced. The first occurs when there is a disinterested forum and the courts of all interested states would reach the same result.[8] Renvoi, in this situation, insures that no law will be applied which does not further the policy of an interested jurisdiction. The second use of renvoi is less straightforward, occurring when "the objective of the particular choice–of–law rule is that the forum reach the same result on the very facts involved as would the courts of another state."[9]

This is not very helpful unless the Restatement helps delineate when uniformity is so important that the normal reference to internal law should not operate. A comment suggests that this occurs in two situations: (1) when the other state "clearly has the dominant interest in the issue and its interest would be furthered by having the issues decided in the way that its courts would have done"; and (2) "where there is an urgent need that all states should apply a single law in resolving a certain question."[10]

As an illustration of the first situation, the comment suggests questions concerning the validity and effect of transfers of interests in land, which are to be decided by the whole law of the situs. An example of the second situation is the use of the whole law of decedent's domicile at death to secure uniformity in the distribution of movables.

Modern approaches to choice–of–law focus on the various state policies implicated by the problem and whether those policies would be advanced

---

[6] *See generally* Comment, *Renvoi and the Modern Approaches to Choice of Law*, 30 Am. U. L. Rev. 1048 (1981).

[7] Restatement (First) of Conflict of Laws § 8.

[8] Restatement (Second) of Conflict of Laws § 8(3).

[9] *Id.* § 8(2).

[10] *Id.* comment h. The two situations where renvoi is contemplated are title records, *see* § 77[b][2], *infra*, and intestate succession to movables, see § 77[c][3], *infra*

by a particular choice.[11] Renvoi, because it sheds light on the question of how each state views the desirability of applying its own law (and, therefore, its own policy), should have a good deal to offer to modern interest analysts. Consider the situation in the *Dater* case discussed earlier. Before that case arose, the Illinois court had held that, if such a case were brought in Illinois, the law of the place of making (here, Michigan) would be applied. Thus, Illinois had disclaimed its own interest in *Dater*-type situations, so no policy of Illinois would be advanced by applying its internal law. In short, the Michigan court was faced with what we today call a false conflict.[12]

The use of renvoi insured not only that the result would be uniform regardless of whether suit was brought in Illinois or Michigan, but also that the law of the only state which had retained an interest in the problem (Michigan) would be applied.

Although the marriage between modern analysis and renvoi is a natural one, cases employing the technique are still relatively rare. In part, that may be due to a lack of familiarity with renvoi in the legal profession. Lack of use may also stem from the retention of the territorial theory in some states. Because that theory does not rely on policy analysis, renvoi should not be used to determine how a state which adheres to the territorial theory views its own interests. Nevertheless, a few cases have employed renvoi to sort out the problem when both states use interest analysis.[13] More typical, however, is the comment by one court that renvoi is an "ancient, disfavored doctrine . . . [which] is not, and should not become, part of our law."[14]

A final important use of renvoi today is in cases brought under the Federal Tort Claims Act.[15] That Act makes the United States liable "under circumstances where a private person would be liable in accordance with the law of the place where the act or omission occurred." The Supreme Court has held that, in order to produce uniformity between cases where the United States is a defendant and cases where defendant is a private person, the whole law of the place of injury must be applied to a claim under the Act.[16]

[d] The Vices of Renvoi

A number of arguments have been advanced opposing the use of renvoi. Two will be discussed here. Perhaps the weaker argument involves the fear that the court will be caught in an endless circle of references. In *Schneider*,

[11] *See, e.g.*, Larry Kramer, *Return of the Renvoi*, 66 N.Y.U. L. Rev. 979 (1991).

[12] *See* § 78, *infra*. If the Michigan court had held initially that the case should be referred to the internal law of Illinois, then Michigan would also have disclaimed an interest. It would then have been an "unprovided for" case. *See id.*

[13] A number of cases are discussed in Comment, *supra*, note 6.

[14] Maroon v. State Dept. of Mental Health, 411 N.E. 2d 404, 413 (Ind. App. 1980).

[15] 28 U.S.C. § 1346(b).

[16] Richards v. United States, 369 U.S. 1 (1962). For a forceful and plausible exposition of the argument that the *Richards* decision is wrong, *see* James A. Shapiro, *Choice of Law Under the Federal Tort Claims Act: Richards and Renvoi Revisited*, 70 No. Car. L. Rev. 641 (1992).

for example, if Swiss law had referred to the whole law of New York, and if New York referred to the whole law of Switzerland, which referred back to New York, etc., no resting point for the decision would ever be found. It is easy enough to break the circle, however, because the forum can always employ its own law or, alternatively, the forum could use modern choice–of–law theories (such as comparative impairment) to end the deadlock. In any event, the theoretical possibility of endless circles generally should not preclude the use of renvoi. And, indeed, courts seem to have had little difficulty with what appears to be a purely theoretical problem.

A more telling objection centers on the difficulty of determining the choice–of–law rules of another state — a task generally more difficult than ascertaining foreign substantive law (which can be hard enough). Indeed, it has been argued that Swiss law was misapplied in *Schneider*.[17] But, again, the forum can control the situation; if another state's choice–of–law rules are that difficult to figure out, then it is hard to see what purpose would be served by referring to them.

§ 60 Public Policy[1]

Courts confined by the rules of the First Restatement had an ultimate escape device available to avoid an unpalatable result. By invoking "public policy," a court could magisterially sweep away the results called for by traditional rules and, usually without much explanation, apply its own law to achieve the desired result. "Public policy," as every law student well knows, however, is all too often employed as a talisman to avoid reasoning on the underlying issues. We have already discussed this phenomenon in connection with jurisdictional questions.[2]

This section explores the use of public policy in choice of law. The leading case is *Kilberg v. Northeast Airlines, Inc.*[3] Plaintiff's intestate, a New York domiciliary, purchased a ticket in New York for a New York–to–Massachusetts airline flight. He was killed when the plane crashed in Massachusetts. Plaintiff, also a New York domiciliary, filed suit in New York under the Massachusetts wrongful death act. The Act contained a $15,000 limitation on recovery for wrongful death. The New York Court of Appeals refused to abide by that limit on the ground that it violated New York public policy — a policy derived from an express provision in the New York Constitution.[4]

---

[17] John D. Falconbridge, *Renvoi in New York and Elsewhere*, 6 Vand. L. Rev. 708, 725–31 (1953).

[1] *See generally* Monrad G. Paulsen & Michael I. Sovern, *"Public Policy" in the Conflict of Laws*, 56 Colum. L. Rev. 969 (1956).

[2] *See* § 50, *supra*.

[3] 9 N.Y.2d 34, 211 N.Y.S.2d 133, 172 N.E.2d 526 (1961).

[4] The court refused to characterize the claim as one in contract, but it did hold, in the alternative, that damage issues are procedural and, therefore, controlled by New York law. This latter holding was repudiated the following year in Davenport v. Webb, 11 N.Y.2d 392, 183 N.E.2d 902 (1962).

Unfortunately, the court gave no standard for determining when that policy should be invoked. New York public policy may be hostile to limits on recovery for wrongful death, but when does New York have enough contact with a dispute to permit its policy to overcome the Massachusetts policy expressed in its statute? Would it matter if, for example, the plaintiff had moved away from New York following the accident?[5] What if the ticket had been bought in New Jersey, or what if the plane had taken off from there? In the absence of any reasoning indicating how to analyze those cases, *Kilberg* merely grants courts a crude tool to do rough justice — but not necessarily justice under law.[6]

The uneven approach of the Court of Appeals of New York in applying the public policy exception can be seen in a case decided only three years after *Kilberg*. In *Intercontinental Hotel Corp. v. Golden*,[7] a Puerto Rican gambling casino brought an action in New York against one of its patrons, a New York domiciliary, to recover on I.O.U.s which the patron had used to cover his gambling debts. New York legislation provided that a losing gambler could sue a winner to recover losses; in addition, gambling was a crime in New York. Despite this apparently clear expression of public policy from the legislature, the Court of Appeals held the debt could be enforced. Why? Because the legalization of racetrack and bingo gambling showed that the public policy of New York would not be offended if the agreement were enforced. The court argued that a gambling debt was not "immoral" per se. The Court of Appeals, therefore, reversed the court below and ruled that the case should be heard.[8]

Intercontinental shows the potential for selectivity inherent in the public policy escape device.[9] Fortunately, both the Restatement (Second) and other modern forms of choice–of–law analysis (more or less) successfully direct attention to the real questions that a court should ask in this area: How do we know what our policy is here, and why does a foreign law offend that policy? The question, in other words, should not be "what is our policy," but "why should our policy prevail over that of another state in this particular inter–state case?"

Wong v. Tenneco[10] provides an example of the chary use a court, which generally employs modern choice–of–law analysis, should make of the

---

[5] *Compare id.* (post–accident move defeats the public policy argument, but only pre–judgment interest was at stake), *with* Gore v. Northeast Airlines, Inc., 373 F.2d 717 (2d Cir. 1967) (post–accident move is irrelevant under New York conflicts law).

[6] The reader should compare Cardozo's statement in Loucks v. Standard Oil Co. of New York, 224 N.Y. 99, 120 N.E. 198 (1918), that "there is nothing in the Massachusetts [wrongful death] statute that outrages the public policy of New York."

[7] 15 N.Y.2d 9, 254 N.Y.S.2d 527, 203 N.E.2d 210 (1964).

[8] For more on public policy, gambling contracts, and judicial disagreement on how they work, *see* Vernon, Weinberg, Reynolds and Richman 285.

[9] A dramatic example of this kind of selectivity is the rule of "dissimilarity" under which the Texas courts had refused to apply Mexican law. In Gutierrez v. Collins, 583 S.W.2d 312 (1979), however, the court rejected Texas law in favor of the Restatement (Second) approach and discarded the rule of "dissimilarity."

[10] 39 Cal. 3d 126, 216 Cal. Rptr. 412, 702 P.2d 570 (1989).

public policy escape route. *Wong* decided a dispute involving a Californian farming in Mexico. To avoid Mexican restrictions of foreign ownership of Mexican land, Wong ran his operation through a Mexican front. The Supreme Court of California found his subterfuge illegal, and refused to enforce it on grounds of comity. The court refused to apply a public policy exception to the comity doctrine even though the California constitution expressly provides that non–citizens may own California land. This disparity between the two sovereigns over land ownership did not set up an insuperable policy conflict. "Mexico's history," the court reasoned, "has led to a different approach. That California public policy regarding land ownership differs from the equivalent Mexican policy, does not suggest that long–established conflicts principles should be abandoned." The law elsewhere may be radically different, in other words, but that does not make it wrong.

§ 61 Depeçage[1]

Traditional choice–of–law analysis led to the selection of a jurisdiction whose rules would determine the outcome of a case: The law of the place of wrong, for example, would govern the substantive issues involved in an automobile accident. But not all issues were controlled by the lex loci; some were treated separately. The most common examples were procedural issues which would be decided under the forum law. This treatment of issues in a case, by referring to the laws of more than one state is known as "depeçage" (from the French "depeçer" meaning "to dissect" or "to take to pieces"). A substantive example of depeçage from the First Restatement is its dual reference in contract cases to (1) the law of the place of making "to determine the binding nature of the promise," and (2) the law of the place where performance is to take place for issues concerning performance.[2]

An example of depeçage by a court using traditional analysis is *Maryland Casualty Company v. Jacek.*[3] That case involved a New Jersey couple who had an automobile accident in New York. New Jersey prohibited suits between spouses; New York, the place of the wrong, permitted them. New York law, however, expressed a compromise which required an insurance company to pay liability arising from a suit between spouses only if the insurance policy contained an express provision to that effect; the New York combination of liability and strict construction of insurance policies clearly had been adopted by the legislature as a compromise package. Using a vested rights approach, the court held that the question of immunity (a tort issue) was controlled by New York law (where the accident occurred), and that the contract construction problem should be determined by New Jersey law (where the insurance contract was made). Thus, the insurance company

[1] *See generally* Willis Reese, *Depeçage: A Common Phenomenon in Choice of Law*, 73 Colum. L. Rev. 58 (1973).

[2] Restatement (First) of Conflict of Laws § 322, comment a.

[3] 156 F.Supp. 43 (D.N.J. 1957).

was held liable, even though it would not have been liable in either jurisdiction in a purely domestic case.

The *Jacek* decision has been criticized trenchantly on the ground that both states, concerned about collusion in suits brought by one spouse against another, had significantly limited the availability of these actions (as in New York) or else prohibited them altogether (as in New Jersey). The decision, by combining the law of the two states, frustrated the policy of both without advancing the interests of either. The result, as one commentator noted, was "grotesque,"[4] and shows in particular the danger of using depeçage in a case where the law of one state (here, New York) was itself a compromise between the two policies involved. The *Jacek* result also neatly illustrates a comment by Brainerd Currie on the use of depeçage: "It is one thing to fall between two stools; it is quite another to put together half a donkey and half a camel, and then ride to victory on the synthetic hybrid."[5]

Nevertheless, scholarly commentary on depeçage is very favorable. Because modern choice–of–law analysis focuses on individual issues (and policies) rather than on large subject areas (*e.g.*, torts, contracts), proponents of both interest analysis and the Restatement (Second) approach believe that depeçage will be more common under their systems than under the vested rights theory. Although those beliefs seem well founded in theory, explicit use of depeçage in case law is quite rare. Indeed, in order to illustrate the concept, scholarly discussion has been forced to rely on hypotheticals or cases decided under the territorial theory.[6]

Several reasons may explain the paucity of case law in this area. First, it is likely that significant differences among the substantive laws of the several states are rare, at least rare enough so that multiple issue choice–of–law problems in the same case are few in number. Second, discussion in most multi–issue cases centers on only one aspect of the case; resolution of what law to apply to the other issues is so "obvious" that analysis is rarely thought necessary. This last point is most apparent in the routine application of forum law on procedural issues. Another example occurs in accident cases where a major opinion might be written on whether to apply a guest statute, but the court has no difficulty in applying the law of the place of wrong to determine the driver's negligence.[7]

Thus, it would require an unusual case to force the court to consider the wisdom of depeçage. It is not surprising, therefore, to find that one of the few express judicial considerations of depeçage is a piece of multi–district litigation involving multiple defendants and possible application of the laws of several states.[8]

---

[4] Comment, *False Conflicts*, 55 Cal. L. Rev. 74, 114 (1967). Professor Reese, however, approved of *Jacek*; *see supra* note 1 at 67–68.

[5] Quoted in David F. Cavers, The Choice–of–Law Process 39 (1965).

[6] *E.g.*, Reese, *supra* note 1.

[7] *E.g.*, Babcock v. Jackson, 12 N.Y.2d 473, 191 N.E.2d 279, 240 N.Y.S.2d 743 (1963).

[8] In Re Air Crash Disaster Near Chicago, Ill., 644 F.2d 594 (7th Cir. 1981), *cert. denied* 454 U.S. 878 (1982) (depeçage applied to question of punitive damage in actions brought against

An illustration of how depeçage might work under modern analysis is *Sabell v. Pacific Intermountain Express Co.*[9] Plaintiff was injured in a collision in Iowa with one of defendant's trucks. Both drivers were from Colorado. Under Iowa law, the truck had been illegally parked and, thus, its driver had been negligent per se. Plaintiff, on the other hand, was also found negligent and, therefore, could not recover under Iowa's rule of contributory negligence; under Colorado's doctrine of comparative negligence, however, plaintiff could recover even though his negligence was held to have been the "primary cause" of the accident. The Colorado court held that Iowa law should control the issue of defendant's negligence, because that state had an "overriding interest" in regulating conduct on its highways. On the issue of plaintiff's fault, however, the court applied Colorado law, because Colorado had the more significant contacts with that issue.

Although the court did not use the term depeçage, the holding clearly applies the concept. The effect was to permit recovery by plaintiff, even though he could not have recovered in a purely domestic litigation in either state. It is this type of apparently anomalous result which led to Currie's comment quoted earlier. And yet the result is correct: Iowa's interest in highway safety was furthered; Colorado had no interest in that issue. In addition, Colorado had a valid interest in the question of whether comparative or contributory negligence was applied in Colorado litigation between two Colorado residents; Iowa had no interest in the resolution of that issue.

Judicious use of depeçage makes sense, for it recognizes that a multi–state problem should not necessarily be decided the same way as a purely domestic case. Addition of a foreign element often injects different interests and policies into the choice–of–law equation. Depecage permits the court to accommodate the interests of several states and, thus, helps to ease the stress that choice–of–law problems place upon our federal system. The result in *Sabell*, therefore, is both internally consistent and correct.

§ 62 Proof of Foreign Law[1]

A decision to apply foreign law to a problem means that a court must learn the content of that law. The process by which that is done, and what happens when it is not done, is the subject of this section.

[a] Judicial Notice

Proof of foreign law, until recently, was treated as a question of fact. That meant that the foreign law was argued to the jury and could not generally be reviewed by an appellate court. In this century, however, "judicial notice" statutes or rules have changed that absurd practice. Federal Rule of Civil

---

airline and manufacturer). An interesting example of depeçage is Corporacion Venezolana de Fomento v. Vintero Sales, 629 F.2d 786 (2d Cir. 1980), where the two laws applied by the court came from New York and federal common law.

[9] 36 Colo. App. 60, 536 P.2d 1160 (1975).

[1] *See generally* Gregory S. Alexander, *The Application and Avoidance of Foreign Law in the Law of Conflicts*, 70 Nw. L. Rev. 602 (1975).

Procedure 44.1, for example, provides that the court shall treat an issue concerning the law of a foreign country as a question of law which may be reviewed on appeal.[2]

The court "may consider any relevant material or source" in determining the content of that law. Two uniform acts, the Uniform Judicial Notice of Foreign Law Act[3] and the Uniform Interstate and International Procedure Act,[4] provide a similar procedure for state courts, although the former permits judicial notice only of the law of another state. The judicial notice procedure is very useful and generally presents little trouble when the law of another state is in question. When the law of another nation is at issue, however, courts should be wary of making assumptions about legal systems which bear a surface similarity to ours, but which, on closer analysis, are quite different; foreign law must be understood as well as recited. Nevertheless, American courts have managed to apply the law of some rather exotic places.[5]

[b] Failure to Prove Foreign Law

Judicial notice statutes typically require the parties to give timely notice (usually in the pleadings) of their reliance on foreign law. But what should a court do when the parties fail to argue foreign law, even though it appears relevant? May the court refuse to notice the foreign law because it has not been assisted by counsel? Some courts have so held. In *Walton v. Arabian American Oil Co.*,[6] for example, the Second Circuit, in an opinion by Judge Frank, ruled that it would be an abuse of discretion to take judicial notice of foreign law unless the party relying on it "has in some way assisted the court in learning it."

Although some states make judicial notice permissible in this situation,[7] the cases generally (and, because of the difficulty, understandably) do not suggest that a searching inquiry should be made *sua sponte*. How then do courts handle the situation? Several alternatives are available. The court simply may dismiss the case, as was done in *Walton*. Dismissal fits in nicely with the vested rights theory: If a tort plaintiff can recover only under the law of the place of injury, then failure to prove that law should doom her claim, as would failure to prove any other essential part of the claim. Dismissal seems harsh, however, in those cases where the expense of proving foreign law may approach the value of the claim. Not surprisingly,

[2] *See* Arthur Miller, *Federal Rule 44.1 and the "Fact" Approach to Determining Foreign Law: Death Knell for a Die-Hard Doctrine*, 65 Mich. L. Rev. 617 (1967).

[3] Superseded by the Uniform Interstate and International Procedure Act. The Uniform Judicial Notice of Foreign Law Act remains in effect, however, in many states.

[4] 13 U.L.A. 459 (1962) (adopted in 6 states).

[5] *E.g.*, Poncotto v. Sociedade de Safaris de Mozambique, S.A.R.I., 422 F. Supp. 405 (N.D. Ill. 1976) (Mozambique law of negligence); Kunstsammlungen Zu Weimar v. Elicofon, 678 F.2d 1150 (2d Cir. 1982) (*inter alia*, 19th century German dynastic law, modern German property law, and Allied military law during the German occupation).

[6] 233 F.2d 541 (2d Cir.), *cert. denied*, 352 U.S. 872 (1956).

[7] *E.g.*, N.Y.R. Civ. Prac. 3016(e).

courts have developed escape devices to avoid that result. First, some courts will presume that forum law and foreign law are the same. Often this presumption is restricted only to "rudimentary" legal principles (such as the role of negligence in automobile accidents), or to the common law unmodified by statute, or to the law of jurisdictions which follow the common law. The difficulty here is that the presumption may be doubtful.[8] In one case, for example, a court in a divorce action presumed that Chinese law dealing with marital property was the same as California's community property law[9] — certainly a very strange presumption.

A better escape device is to treat the parties' failure to prove foreign law as showing their acquiescence in having forum law applied.[10] This was the method used by Chief Justice Vanderbilt in *Leary v. Gledhill*,[11] where he applied New Jersey law to a loan agreement made in France between two Americans. Vanderbilt refused to assume that forum law and French law were the same, because he believed it would be presumptuous to assume congruence between civil and common law. He argued that it was better to hold that "the parties by failing to prove the law of France have acquiesced in having their dispute determined by the law of the forum." Acquiescence does present some difficulties as the court struggles to accommodate domestic law and foreign facts. *Loebig v. Larucci*[12] nicely illustrates the problem. Although both parties were Americans, the case involved a motorcycle accident in Nuremberg, Germany. The substantive issue was the cyclist's negligence. Neither party presented proof of German law, and the court held that New York law should apply. The court further held that "New York courts would assume that the general negligence standard of care would be applicable." The parties' attempts to introduce evidence concerning New York statutory law on subjects such as reckless driving, making a left–hand turn, and the appropriate speed entering an intersection were rebuffed by the court because "strict statutory requirements in New York should not be held binding as the standard of care for operation of a vehicle in Germany." Thus, the court held it proper to submit the case to the jury on a general charge of negligence (that is, under the common law of New York).[13]

The acquiescence approach is preferable to the presumption theory because it comports more readily with litigative reality. The problem is that the device may ignore the substantial interests of another jurisdiction. In

---

[8] Scoles & Hay § 12.19.

[9] Louknitsky v. Louknitsky, 123 Cal.App.2d 406, 266 P.2d 910 (1954). Alexander, *supra* note 63, at 610 n.41, comments: "California community property law is peculiar even in the United States. How likely is it, then, that it is the same as Chinese law?"

[10] *Id.* at 610–11.

[11] 8 N.J. 260, 84 A.2d 725 (1951).

[12] 572 F.2d 81 (2d Cir. 1978).

[13] Acquiescence and depeçage may be combined in a single case. An example is In re Oil Spill by the Amoco Cadiz, 954 F.2d 1279 (7th Cir. 1992). There, the court applied French substantive law to the issue of liability. The case also had a significant issue concerning contribution; the court applied American admiralty law to that question because the parties had not given the court sufficient information about the French law of contribution.

Loebig, for example, Germany arguably had an interest in seeing its law applied to determine what constitutes safe driving on its roads. Such neglect of another jurisdiction's interests may be unavoidable. Our legal system tends to rely on private litigants to advance governmental interests before the court. If neither side feels it advantageous to do so, perhaps the foreign sovereign's interests are not sufficiently threatened to create concern. The acquiescence notion, with dismissal and/or judicial notice held in reserve for rare cases, may represent the best approach to the problem presented by the litigants' failure to prove foreign law.

[c] Certified Questions

Difficult problems involving proof of foreign law arise when no controlling precedent exists on the issue in the foreign state. A partial solution is provided by the Uniform Certification of Questions of Law Act.[14] The Act permits a federal court or a state appellate court to certify a question of law to the highest court of another state. Certification is permitted only if there is no "controlling precedent" from the foreign court, and if the certifying court believes that the issue "may be determinative" of the case. Certification is a wonderful device for getting foreign law interpreted correctly.[15] It may cost time and money and result in quasi–advisory opinions divorced from the discipline imposed by the real facts of an actual case; nevertheless, certification helps to achieve uniformity and should be used more often.

---

[14] 12 U.L.A. 49 (1967) (adopted in 31 states). *See generally* John B. Corr & Ira P. Robbins, *Interjurisdictional Certification and Choice of Law*, 41 Vand. L. Rev. 411 (1988).

[15] Judge Meyer of the Court of Appeals of New York suggested that there should be a certification process from state to federal courts for federal issues. Bernard Meyer, *Justice, Bureaucracy, Structure, and Simplification*, 42 Md. L. Rev. 659, 673 (1983).

Part B

THE FIRST RESTATEMENT

The traditional system for choice of law in the United States was the system embodied in the First Restatement. Based on the vested rights theory, the system consisted of a few broad, hard and fast rules coupled with an array of escape devices. Although most conflicts scholars have by now abandoned the First Restatement system, it retains surprising popularity among the courts. The following section examines the historical and theoretical underpinnings of the First Restatement. The next four sections then discuss practice under the First Restatement — first generally and then in three specific areas: torts, contracts, and property. A final section contains a critique of the First Restatement.

§ 63 The First Restatement — Theory

[a] A Bit of History

In order to understand the First Restatement system for choice of law and the vested rights theory, upon which it was based, it is important to consider a bit of the history of choice–of–law theory. Early conflicts theorists asked a question that modern writers are inclined to ignore: When an Ohio court decides a conflicts case using a principle found in Michigan law, exactly what is it doing? Is it "applying" the Michigan law, is it enforcing a Michigan "right," or is it creating an Ohio right which is modeled on a Michigan right which would have existed had the case been a wholly Michigan case?[1]

Joseph Story, the first American writer to treat the question,[2] thought that the forum court "applied" the foreign law based on the theory of comity — the respect that one sovereign owes another.[3] Because comity was a discretionary doctrine, the forum court was not *required* to apply the foreign law, but did so as a matter of courtesy. Dissatisfaction with this account of the choice–of–law process spawned the vested rights theory.

---

[1] *See* Elliot E. Cheatham, *American Theories of Conflict of Laws: Their Role and Utility*, 58 Harv. L. Rev. 361, 365–367 (1945), for a discussion of this question and the three competing theories which American courts have used to answer it. Today, the question has only historical interest. Modern choice–of–law theory is less concerned with the formalistic account of the choice–of–law process and more concerned with the practical questions of why and when the forum should apply foreign law. *See also* Vernon, Weinberg, Reynolds and Richman 217–219.

[2] Choice of law did not begin in America, of course. For a discussion of the early developments in Italian, Dutch and German law, *see* Scoles et al. §§ 2.2, 2.3.

[3] Joseph Story, Commentaries on the Conflict of Laws, Foreign and Domestic (1883).

[b] Vested Rights

Some turn–of–the–century choice–of–law theorists objected to the notion of comity. There were two criticisms. First, comity suggested that in a conflicts case the forum court might "apply" foreign law, thus implying that the foreign law operated outside the territory of the foreign sovereign. This notion conflicted with the then–current territorial dogma that no law could have any effect outside the territory of the sovereign that promulgated it.[4] Second, the theory of comity allowed too much rein to judicial discretion. It seemed to suggest that a judge was free to decide on his own whether justice and convenience required the application of foreign law. This expanded view of judicial discretion was at odds with the prevalent notion of formalism, the view that judges had little freedom and that their decisions were the inevitable result of applying certain, relatively unchanging legal rules.[5]

The vested rights theory provided an alternate view of the choice–of–law process, a view which was more acceptable to the territorialist and formalist jurisprudence of the early twentieth century. The main proponents of vested rights, Joseph H. Beale[6] in this country and A. V. Dicey in England,[7] held that foreign law could never operate outside the territory of the foreign sovereign. Rather, the forum's use of foreign law could be explained in terms of the creation and enforcement of vested rights. In their view, when an event (a tort, for example) occurred in a foreign territory, a right was created. Because the only law that *could* operate in the foreign territory was the law of the foreign sovereign, the existence and content of any such right was determined by the foreign law. The forum court simply enforced the *right* which had *vested* in the foreign territory according to the foreign law.

Under the theory, it was important to know when and where a particular right vested, because the law of the place where the right vested would control the content of the right. The practical result was a system of a few, broad, relatively rigid choice–of–law rules. Each governed a major area of the law (*e.g.*, torts, contracts, property) by identifying a particular contact (the tortious injury, the making of the contract, the situs of the land) as the trigger for the vesting of a right. Thus, questions in tort were decided by the law of the place of injury; questions in contract, by the law of the place of making; and questions in property, by the law of the situs of the land.

---

[4] *See* Cheatham, *supra* note 1, at 365.

[5] *See* 3 Joseph H. Beale, A Treatise on the Conflict of Laws, 1964–1965 (1935).

[6] *See* Beale, *supra* note 5, at 1967–1970.

[7] *See* A.V. Dicey, A Digest of the Law of England with Reference to the Conflict of Laws, 17–25 (5th ed. 1932).

[c] Critique of the Vested Rights Theory

Even before the adoption of the Restatement in 1934, the vested rights theory was the target of a vigorous attack led by Walter Wheeler Cook.[8] Cook's attack was based on the American Legal Realist[9] notion that a legal right is simply a prediction that a court will grant plaintiff relief.[10] According to the predictive theory, rights are not objects or things in the world that exist independently before courts later enforce them; thus it made no sense to speak of "enforcing vested rights" in choice–of–law cases. Until the court decided, there simply was no "right" for it to enforce.[11]

Cook also argued that the vested rights theory failed to explain adequately how courts actually treat choice–of–law problems. Once again, he used the predictive theory to show that courts do not enforce "foreign rights." A "foreign right" is simply a prediction about what a foreign court would do if faced with the exact facts of plaintiff's case. To make such a prediction, the forum court would have to apply the foreign choice–of–law rules as well as the foreign internal rule; in other words, the court would have to apply the doctrine of renvoi.[12] Because courts do not routinely apply the doctrine of renvoi to all choice–of–law problems, Cook concluded that the vested rights theory was not an accurate description of actual practice in the courts.[13]

Cook proposed an alternate description which came to be called the local law theory.[14] According to that view, the forum court does not "apply" foreign law, nor does it enforce a "foreign right." Rather, it applies forum law (the only law it can apply); in a case with foreign elements that law, for reasons of fairness and party expectations, may incorporate a principle or rule of decision drawn from the legal system of a sister state. In the words of Learned Hand:

> However, no court can enforce any law but that of its own sovereign, and, when a suitor comes to a jurisdiction foreign to the place of the tort, he can only invoke an obligation recognized by that sovereign. A foreign sovereign under civilized law imposes an obligation of its own as nearly homologous as possible to that arising in the place where the tort occurs.[15]

---

[8] The finest statement of Cook's view is Walter W. Cook, *The Logical and Legal Bases of the Conflict of Laws,* 33 Yale L.J. 457 (1924). Cook was not alone in his attack on the theory. *See also* Ernest G. Lorenzen, *Territoriality, Public Policy and the Conflict of Laws,* 33 Yale L.J. 736 (1924); Hessel Yntema, *The Hornbook Method and the Conflict of Laws,* 37 Yale L.J. 468 (1928).

[9] American Legal Realism was a jurisprudential movement of the early and middle twentieth century. Its leading lights were Karl Llewellyn and Jerome Frank. *E.g.,* Karl N. Llewellyn, The Bramble Bush (1950); Jerome E. Frank, Law and the Modern Mind (1930). *See generally,* R.M.W. Dias, Jurisprudence 619–639 (1976).

[10] Oliver W. Holmes, *The Path of the Law,* 10 Harv. L. Rev. 457 (1897), is the most famous exposition of the predictive theory of law.

[11] *See* Walter W. Cook, The Logical and Legal Bases of the Conflict of Laws 29–31 (1942).

[12] *See* § 59, *supra,* for a discussion of renvoi.

[13] *See* Cook, *supra* note 11, 31–33.

[14] *Id.* 20–21.

[15] Guinness v. Miller, 291 Fed. 769 (S.D.N.Y. 1923).

Cook's view is more economical than the vested rights theory[16] because it can explain the forum's use of a foreign rule of law without the need to postulate a "foreign right" which exists prior to any court's enforcement of it. More important, it shifts the focus of the discussion away from a formalistic account of the choice–of–law process toward the more practical question: What reasons justify the forum's use of a principle found in another state's law to resolve a dispute?

§ 64 The First Restatement in Practice — Broad Rules and Escape Devices

In spite of the conceptual difficulties with the vested rights theory, it was adopted by the American Law Institute and incorporated into the First Restatement. This traditional system of choice–of–law rules prevailed in most American courts until the work of a new generation of judges and scholars began to supplant it in the 1950's and 1960's. Even today, the First Restatement system retains a good deal of vitality. In perhaps a third of the states, it is alive and well as the dominant general choice–of–law methodology.[1] Furthermore, even the states that have abandoned the First Restatement for most choice–of–law problems retain it for issues involving interests in land.[2]

The First Restatement system for choice of law consists of a few broad, single–contract, jurisdiction–selecting rules coupled with an array of escape devices. Each of these characterizations requires a brief comment. At first glance, the rules do not appear to be few or broad; the Restatement contains over 300 sections on choice of law.[3] Most of the sections, however, can be condensed into a few general summary rules. Nearly all questions in tort, for example, are governed by the law of the place of injury, and nearly all questions about property are governed by the law of the situs.

The rules of the First Restatement are jurisdiction–selecting rules.[4] They pick between competing states, not between competing rules. The court does not consider the scope, content, or policy of the substantive rule of law until

[16] Lately, rights–based approaches to choice of law seem to be making a come–back. *See, e.g.,* Lea Brilmayer, Conflict of Laws: Foundations and Future Directions (1991), reviewed in Patrick J. Borchers, *Professor Brilmayer and the Holy Grail*, 1991 Wisc. L. Rev. 465; Perry Dane, *Vested Rights, "Vestedness," and Choice of Law*, 96 Yale L.J. 1191 (1987); Terry S. Kogan, *Toward a Jurisprudence of Choice of Law: The Priority of Fairness Over Comity*, 62 N.Y.U. L. Rev. 651 (1987).

[1] For a list of the states at various times,, *see* Symeon Symeonides, *Choice of Law in the American Courts in 2000: As the Century Turns*, 49 Am. J. Comp. L. 1 (2001); Fitts v. Minnesota Mining & Manufacturing Co., 581 So.2d 819 (1991) (listing 15 states using the First Restatement in tort cases); Gregory E. Smith, *Choice of Law in the United States*, 38 Hastings L.J. 1172–1174 (1987); Herma H. Kay, *Theory into Practice: Choice of Law in the Courts*. 34 Mercer L. Rev. 521, 582 (1983).

[2] *See* § 89, *infra,* for a discussion of the property choice–of–law rules used by most courts today.

[3] Restatement (First) of Conflict of Laws §§ 119–428.

[4] For a discussion of the distinction between jurisdiction–selecting rules and content–selecting rules, *see* § 56, *supra. See also* David F. Cavers, The Choice–of–Law Process 9 (1965).

after the state is chosen. Thus, in making the initial choice,[5] the First Restatement rules are not concerned with which substantive rule is "better," or which validates the parties' intentions, or which is motivated by a policy that can be advanced by its application in this case; rather, they are concerned only with identifying a particular event and the jurisdiction (state) in which that event occurred.

Another feature of the First Restatement rules is that, unlike other choice–of–law systems, they rely upon *only one* salient connection between the dispute and the state. On the issue of the validity of a contract, for example, the Center of Gravity Theory[6] might look to several important contacts: the domicile of the parties, the place where the contract was made, the place where it was to be performed, the place where financial injury from breach might be felt. The First Restatement considers only one contact: the place of making.

The courts that applied the First Restatement were not always satisfied with the results produced by the simple, hard–and–fast rules. When faced with a rule that required choice of X's law when justice and common sense favored the law of Y, the judges found ways to avoid the rule. Typically, they did not articulate the considerations of policy, fairness, and party expectations that motivated their decisions; conflicts theory of the time was too rigidly formalistic to permit so frank a strategy. Rather, they invented escape devices — highly conceptual maneuvers which permitted them to avoid an undesirable outcome without breaking faith with the traditional system.[7] Thus, they could recharacterize a property issue as a tort problem and escape the law of the situs in favor of the law of the place of injury, or characterize a tort problem as a question of procedure and escape the law of the place of injury in favor of the law of the forum. Another possibility was renvoi; if the forum's choice–of–law rule directed the choice of X's law and the result was offensive, the court could read "X's law" to mean X's whole law — including its choice–of–law rules — which might refer the issue back to forum law. Finally, courts occasionally took the bull by the horns and refused for reasons of "public policy" to apply the law suggested by the First Restatement's rigid rules.

The three sections that follow examine the Restatement's treatment of three substantive areas of law: torts, contracts, and property. Each section discusses first the hard–and–fast rule and then the escape devices.

---

5 Courts using the First Restatement rules did concern themselves with the content of substantive rules of law when they used the public policy escape device. *See* § 60, *supra,* for a general discussion of public policy. *See* §§ 65 and 66, *infra,* for examples.

6 *See* § 70, *infra,* for a discussion of the Center of Gravity Theory.

7 *See generally* Vernon, Weinberg, Reynolds & Richman 247–292.

§ 65 Torts

[a] The Law of the Place of the Wrong[1]

The First Restatement specifies the law of the place of the wrong for nearly all issues in torts. Thus, the law of the place of the wrong controls: the existence of a legal injury (§ 378), defendant's standard of responsibility (§ 381), causation (§ 383), contributory negligence (§ 385), the fellow-servant rule (§ 386), vicarious liability (§ 387), defenses to liability (§ 388), survival of actions (§ 390), and the measure of damages (§ 412).

According to § 377, the place of the wrong is "in the state where the last event necessary to make an actor liable for an alleged tort takes place."[2] In almost all circumstances, the "last event" is the injury to the plaintiff, so the "place of the wrong" really means the place of injury or, in the words of the Restatement, "the place where the harmful force first takes effect on the body."[3] To put the matter flippantly, "look for the blood." Typically, it does not matter that defendant's conduct may have occurred in another state. Thus, if defendant standing in state A shoots plaintiff standing in state B, the law of B will control.[4] Similarly, if defendant negligently manufactures a product in state A which injures plaintiff in state B, the law of B will control.

The First Restatement contains a few fairly limited exceptions to the "place of the wrong" rule. Section 387 provides that the vicarious liability of defendant for the acts of another is determined by the place of the wrong *only if* defendant *authorized* the person to act for him in that state.[5] Section 382 shields from liability a person who acts in state X pursuant to a legal

---

[1] *See generally* Vernon, Weinberg, Reynolds & Richman 222–225; Scoles et al. §§ 17.1–17.7; Leflar, McDougal & Felix §§ 132, 133. Although few scholars admire the rule, there is still lively controversy among the courts. *Compare* Fitts v. Minnesota Mining & Manufacturing Co., 581 So.2d 819 (1991) (discussing the rule, as well as more modern choice–of–law theories, and determining to retain the traditional approach) *with* Hataway v. McKinley, 830 S.W.2d 53 (1992) (same, but determining to abandon it). The scholars do not have kind words for the courts that retain the rule. *See, e.g.,* Doug Rendleman, *McMillan v. McMillan: Choice of Law in a Sinkhole*, 67 Va. L. Rev. 315 (1981), commenting on McMillan v. McMillan, 219 Va. 1127, 253 S.E.2d 662 (1979).

[2] Restatement (First) of Conflict of Laws § 377. The rule is really a deduction from the premises of the vested rights theory. *See* § 63[b], *supra*. According to that theory, the forum court enforces a right which has vested in a foreign state. The right can vest only when all the elements of plaintiff's claim have been satisfied. Accordingly, the right vests where the last event takes place. There are, however, inconsistencies in the application of the theory. The "last event" in a wrongful death action would seem to be the death of plaintiff's decedent; thus, if defendant acted wrongfully in A, decedent was injured in B, and he died in C, the theory seems to suggest that the law of C should be applied. The Restatement, however, directs the choice of B's law because B is the place where the harmful force first took effect upon decedent's body. *See* Restatement (First) of Conflict of Laws § 377, note 1.

[3] *Id.*

[4] *Id.* § 377, illustration 1.

[5] *Id.* § 387. Comment a explains that if defendant does not authorize his agent to enter the state, he (defendant) has not submitted himself to the law of that state. *See also* Scheer v. Rockne Motors Corp., 68 F.2d 942 (2d Cir. 1934).

duty or privilege and causes injury actionable in state Y.[6] Section 380(2) provides that one who acts in state X in reliance upon a very particular standard of care will not be liable if the act causes injury in state Y where the relevant standard is higher.[7] The argument for each of these exceptions to the "place of the wrong" rule is that the actor in each case justifiably relies upon the law of the state where he acts; his reasonable expectations about the results of his conduct should not be frustrated because of the fortuity of an out–of–state injury. Nevertheless each exception is inconsistent with the vested rights theory, which would hold in each case that a right would vest as long as plaintiff is injured in a state that would permit a recovery.

The fourth exception is an *ad hoc* solution to a macabre problem. Suppose defendant in state X mails poisoned candy to plaintiff in state Y. Plaintiff eats the candy in Y, falls ill in Z, and dies in W. The law of Z controls.[8] Why? Who knows? Certainly the Restatement provides no explanation.

Aside from these exceptions, the "place of the wrong" rule is hard and fast. *Alabama Great Southern R.R. Co. v. Carroll*[9] illustrates what unfortunate results such a rigid, one–dimensional analysis can produce. Plaintiff, a resident of Alabama, worked as a brakeman for defendant railroad — an Alabama entity. Employees of the railroad negligently failed to inspect car links in Alabama, and plaintiff was injured in Mississippi where a defective link broke. Under the law of Mississippi, plaintiff could not recover because Mississippi had the common law fellow–servant rule; plaintiff could recover under the law of Alabama because Alabama had a statute abrogating the fellow–servant rule. The Supreme Court of Alabama applied the law of Mississippi because that state was the place of injury, even though every other important contact (plaintiff's residence, defendant's residence, the contract of employment, and the negligent act) was located in Alabama and even though it was purely fortuitous that the injury occurred in Mississippi rather than a few miles earlier in Alabama. The court's mechanical and one–dimensional approach to choice–of–law is illustrated in this passage:[10]

> It is admitted . . . that negligence of duty unproductive of damnifying results will not authorize or support a recovery. Up to the time the train passed out of Alabama no injury had resulted. For all that occurred

[6] Restatement (First) of Conflict of Laws § 382. Comment a, illustration 1, gives the example of a health officer in state X who is required by X law to burn infected rags in a particular place. He is not liable even if the burning causes a nuisance in state Y.

[7] *Id.* § 380(2), comment b, illustration 1, provides an example: By the law of both X and Y, a railroad is liable for fire if it acts negligently. In Y, failure to equip a locomotive with a spark arrester is negligence *per se;* in X it is not. If a railroad operates a locomotive carefully in X without a spark arrester and causes a fire which damages property in Y, the railroad is not liable.

[8] *Id.* § 377, comment a, illustration 2.

[9] 97 Ala. 126, 11 So. 803 (1892).

[10] The passage also demonstrates, of course, that the court was firmly entrenched in the vested rights theory. *See* § 63[b], *supra.* The decision is criticized in J.H.C. Morris, *The Proper Law of a Tort,* 64 Harv. L. Rev. 881, 888 (1951).

in Alabama, therefore, no cause whatever arose. The fact which created the right to sue, the injury . . . transpired in the state of Mississippi. It was in that state, therefore, necessarily that the cause of action, if any, arose; and whether a cause of action arose and existed at all, or not, must in all reason be determined by the law which obtained at the time and place when and where the fact which is relied on to justify a recovery transpired.

If the First Restatement rule for torts can produce untoward results in a simple negligence action like *Carroll,* its application in more complicated cases can be baffling indeed. Where, for instance, is the "place of injury" in a case of defamation published by a national magazine? Every state where plaintiff's reputation suffers?[11] Plaintiff's domicile? The place where the magazine is composed and edited? The place where it is published?[12] The point of the illustration is simply that some torts involve non–physical injuries, and locating such injuries spatially is not always easy. Defamation is only one example. The place of injury is also hard to locate with invasion of privacy, fraud, alienation of affections, and interference with contractual relations.

[b] Escaping the Law of the Place of Injury

[1] Characterization

Decisions like *Carroll* reveal how arbitrary and unjust the place of injury rule can be. Without abandoning the rule, courts often were able to avoid the most egregious results by employing several conceptual escape devices. The most fruitful was characterization.[13] The ploy was to reclassify the issue for decision as a non–tort issue and thus use another First Restatement rule to generate a better result. In *Grant v. McAuliffe*[14] the court used the substance/procedure distinction to recharacterize the issue. Plaintiffs and decedent — all residents of California — were involved in an auto accident in Arizona. Decedent died shortly after the accident, and plaintiffs sued the administrator of his estate in California. Tort actions did not survive the death of the tortfeasor under Arizona law, but they did survive according to the law of California. Justice Traynor, writing for the Supreme Court of California, avoided the application of the Arizona law and saved

[11] This seems to be the answer given by Restatement (First) of Conflict of Laws § 377, comment a, illustration 7.

[12] Dean Prosser identified ten possibilities for choice of law in multistate defamation cases. *See* William L. Prosser, *Interstate Publication,* 51 Mich. L. Rev. 959, 971–978 (1953). *See* Dale System, Inc. v. Time, Inc., 116 F. Supp. 527 (D. Conn. 1953), for a case which struggles with the problem and selects the law of plaintiff's domicile.

[13] *See* § 57, *supra;* Leflar, McDougal & Felix § 134. Results reached under the regime of the First Restatement depended on how a problem was characterized — as a tort, as a contract, and so on. The First Restatement, however, did not explain how a court was to know what label to attach. This is not an insignificant problem. After all, as even first–year students know, legal problems do not come in tidy and neatly–labelled packages. It is exceedingly curious, therefore, that the Restatement failed to deal with this critical issue.

[14] 41 Cal.2d 859, 264 P.2d 944 (1953).

plaintiff's cause of action by classifying the issue of survival of actions as a procedural question to be referred to the law of the forum rather than a tort issue to be decided by the law of the place of injury.[15]

A more typical use of characterization as an escape device involves changing the substantive law category in which the case belongs. A well–known example is *Haumschild v. Continental Casualty Co.*[16] Plaintiff, a Wisconsin domiciliary, sued her ex–husband, also a domiciliary of Wisconsin, for injuries which she received from his negligent driving in California. California, the place of injury, had an interspousal immunity rule; Wisconsin did not. Had the Wisconsin Supreme Court followed the law of the place of injury, as dictated by Wisconsin precedent, plaintiff would have been denied a recovery — a result the court found unpalatable. Instead, the court was able to recharacterize the issue as a problem of status to be governed by the law of the marital domicile — Wisconsin.

Perhaps the most remarkable examples of recharacterization are the Arkansas telegraph cases. Arkansas, unlike its neighboring states, had a statute that permitted plaintiff to recover for "mental anguish and suffering" when the telegraph company's negligence resulted in mis–delivery or late delivery of the message. The cases are poignant; often the message concerned the death of a loved one, and the company's negligence caused the plaintiff to miss the funeral. When the message was sent from Arkansas, the court, sympathetic to plaintiff, characterized the case as a contract problem and applied the law of Arkansas, the place of making.[17] When the message was sent into Arkansas, however, a contract characterization would preclude plaintiff's recovery. To avoid that result the court characterized the issue as one in tort and applied the law of the place of injury — Arkansas.[18] Remarkably, the court decided eight cases in five years, characterizing each as contract or tort depending upon which label resulted in the application of Arkansas law to allow plaintiff's recovery.[19]

---

[15] The Restatement disagreed. *See* Restatement (First) of Conflict of Laws § 390.

[16] 7 Wis.2d 130, 95 N.W.2d 814 (1959). Another famous example is Levy v. Daniels U–Drive Auto Renting Co., 108 Conn. 333, 143 A. 163 (1928). Lessee rented a car from defendant in Connecticut. He drove it into Massachusetts where plaintiff, a passenger in the car, was injured as a result of lessee's negligence. Had the court characterized the issue as one sounding in tort, plaintiff could not have recovered against lessor under the law of Massachusetts. Instead, the court saw the case as a contract problem and looked to the law of Connecticut (the place of making), which contained a statute providing for the liability of car lessors to persons injured by lessees. It ruled that the statute was incorporated into every leasing contract made in Connecticut and that plaintiff was an intended beneficiary of that contract.

[17] *See, e.g.,* Western Union Telegraph Co. v. Griffin, 92 Ark. 219, 122 S.W. 489 (1909).

[18] *See, e.g.,* Western Union Telegraph Co. v. Chilton, 100 Ark. 296, 140 S.W. 26 (1911).

[19] *See* Leflar, McDougal & Felix 258. The Arkansas telegraph cases reveal that recharacterization is a very crude tool for achieving conflicts justice. When a court uses recharacterization to escape a First Restatement choice–of–law rule its only possible escape is another over–broad jurisdiction–selecting rule. Subsequently, of course, the new characterization can produce an unfortunate result in the very next case. That is exactly what happened in the Arkansas telegraph cases. The results in those cases make sense; Arkansas had a strong policy at stake, and it had substantial connection with each case, whether the message was sent into or out of Arkansas. The court could not articulate those reasons, however; to achieve the desired results, it had to shift back and forth between contract and tort characterization, leaving Arkansas choice–of–law precedent in an unprincipled shambles. *See*, Vernon, Weinberg, Reynolds & Richman 269–270.

[2] Renvoi

Although courts have rarely used renvoi as an escape device in tort cases, there are notable exceptions. In *Haumschild v. Continental Casualty Co.,*[20] Justice Fairchild wrote a concurring opinion based on the doctrine. Earlier Wisconsin precedents had considered interspousal immunity in tort cases to be governed by the law of the place of injury — in this case, California. California, however, viewed the issue as a status problem to be decided by the law of the marital domicile. Fairchild, used renvoi as an expedient to generate the right result without overruling Wisconsin's prior tort characterizations. His solution for the case was to construe Wisconsin's place of injury rule to refer to the *whole law* of California, which then referred the issue back to the internal law of Wisconsin — the marital domicile.

[3] Public Policy

Under the First Restatement, the boldest and most candid method for escaping the law of the place of injury was to hold that that law violated the forum's public policy. The public policy exception was supposedly quite narrow; in order to refuse to apply foreign law on public policy grounds, the court would need to find that law "vicious, wicked or immoral, and shocking to the prevailing moral sense."[21] Nevertheless, First Restatement courts managed on public policy grounds to escape the law of the place of injury in some rather mundane circumstances. In *Mertz v. Mertz,*[22] for example, the New York Court of Appeals refused to apply Connecticut's rule permitting interspousal tort liability. And in *Kilberg v. Northeast Airlines*[23] that same court denied application to Massachusetts' limit on wrongful death damages.

Cases like *Mertz* and *Kilberg* reveal that, although public policy was the most candid of the traditional escape devices, it was still not very candid. The judges could not conclude honestly that interspousal tort liability and wrongful death damage limitations were barbarous, shocking, wicked, and immoral. What the judges found so disturbing was not the foreign law but rather New York's own choice–of–law principle — the place–of–injury rule;[24] it required application of foreign law in cases where New York had a strong interest in the result. In order to avoid the application of the rule the judges had to disparage the foreign law.

---

[20] *See* note 16, *supra*.

[21] Intercontinental Hotels Corp. v. Golden, 15 N.Y.2d 9, 254 N.Y.S. 2d 527, 203 N.E.2d 210 (1964). Another formulation permits refusal to apply foreign law that violates "good morals or natural justice." Ramsey v. County of McCormick, 412 S.E.2d 408 (1991). *See generally* § 60, *supra*.

[22] 271 N.Y. 466, 3 N.E.2d 597 (1936).

[23] 9 N.Y.2d 34, 211 N.Y.S. 2d 133, 172 N.E. 2d 526 (1961). *Kilberg* is discussed in § 60, *supra*.

[24] *See* Monrad G. Paulsen & Michael I. Sovern, *Public Policy in the Conflict of Laws*, 56 Colum. L. Rev. 969, 981 (1956).

§ 66 Contracts

[a] The Place of Making

Before the first Restatement, American jurisdictions were divided over the proper choice–of–law rule to govern the validity of contracts. Three principles[1] could claim some support: (1) the validation rule, which held that the validity of a contract is controlled by the law that the parties presumably intended to govern their dealings; (2) the place–of–performance rule, and; (3) the place–of–making rule. Professor Beale rejected the first two candidates and settled on the third as required by the vested rights theory.[2] The validation principle was unsatisfactory because it "involves permission to the parties to do a legislative act. It practically makes a legislative body of any two persons who choose to get together and contract."[3] He rejected the place–of–performance rule as inconsistent with the vested rights theory and its territorial assumptions: "Any attempt to make the law of the place of performance govern the act of contracting is an attempt to give to that law exterritorial effect."[4]

In addition to these theoretical arguments, Beale also suggested practical reasons for choosing the place–of–making rule. For one thing, he claimed, it was certain of application. Also, it was easier for the parties to ascertain and follow. Parties meeting at the place of making to negotiate their contract can seek legal counsel there to determine that state's governing law. The parties are unlikely to return to their respective domiciles to get legal advice, and they might not be able to find legal counsel expert in the law of the place of performance.

Under the influence of Beale, the First Restatement adopted the place–of–making rule. Section 332 provides that the law of the place of making controls such issues of contract validity as capacity, formalities, consideration, and defenses (illegality or fraud, for example) which might make the contract void or voidable.[5] Determination of the place of making, therefore, is very important. Section 311, comment d indicates that the place of making is the place where "the principal event necessary to make a contract occurs."[6] For a formal contract (§ 312), the principal event is delivery; for an informal unilateral contract (§ 323), the offeree's performance;[7] for an

---

[1] *See* 2 Joseph H. Beale, A Treatise on the Conflict of Laws § 332.1 (1935).

[2] *Id.*

[3] Joseph H. Beale, *What Law Governs the Validity of a Contract*, 23 Harv. L. Rev. 1, 260 (1909).

[4] *Id.* at 267.

[5] Restatement (First) of Conflict of Laws § 332.

[6] Restatement (First) of Conflict of Laws § 311, comment d. Professor Beale specified the place where "the final act was done which made the promise . . . binding." 2 J. Beale, *supra* note 1, at § 311.1. For a more readable discussion of the place of making problems, *see* Herbert F. Goodrich, Handbook of the Conflict of Laws § 107 (3d ed. 1949).

[7] The Restatement appears to hedge somewhat here for it speaks of "the event . . . which makes the promise binding." The illustrations, however, make it apparent that the event contemplated is the offeree's performance. *See* Restatement (First) of Conflict of Laws § 323 (illustrations 1–5).

informal bilateral contract (§ 325), the offeree's promise. The Restatement goes into considerable detail on the question of a bilateral contract made by an offer in one state and an acceptance in another. Section 326 adopts the mailbox rule and provides that the state where the acceptance was transmitted is the place of contracting.[8] The section then provides four illustrations, indicating specific results when the acceptance is transmitted by mail, telegraph, telephone, and word of mouth.

Milliken v. Pratt illustrates the working of the place–of–making rule.[9] Husband, a Massachusetts domiciliary, sought to purchase goods on credit from plaintiffs, merchants domiciled in Maine. Before extending credit to the husband, plaintiffs required him to obtain a guarantee from his wife. She executed a written guarantee at her home in Massachusetts, and husband mailed it to plaintiffs in Maine. Plaintiffs then sold goods to the husband on credit. When the goods were not paid for, plaintiffs sued wife on the guarantee in a Massachusetts court. According to the law of Massachusetts, a married woman could not guarantee her husband's debts, but under Maine law she could contract as if she were unmarried. The Massachusetts court applied Maine law and held for plaintiffs. It found the contract to be a unilateral one — completed in Maine when plaintiffs sold goods on credit to the husband in reliance on his wife's guarantee. "The contract between the defendant [wife] and the plaintiffs was complete when the guaranty had been received and acted on by them at Portland, and not before . . . It must therefore be treated as made and to be performed in the State of Maine."

There is only one major exception to the place–of–making rule. Section 358 provides that questions concerning issues of performance are to be governed by the law of the place of performance. Such questions include the manner of performance, the time and place of performance, the persons by and for whom performance shall be rendered, the sufficiency of performance, and excuses for non–performance.[10] Although § 358 is the only major exception to the place of making rule, it is an exception so large that it threatens to swallow the rule.[11] The Restatement was sensitive to this difficulty. Comment b to § 358 hedges by suggesting that the law of the place of performance "is not applicable to the point where the substantial obligation of the parties is materially altered." Further, the Restatement acknowledges that it will not always be easy to separate issues of validity from issues of performance.[12]

---

[8] Restatement (First) of Conflict of Laws § 326(b). For criticism of the Restatement's use of the mailbox rule as a choice–of–law principle, *see* Walter W. Cook, The Logical and Legal Bases of the Conflict of Laws 361–362 (1942); Ian R. MacNeil, *Time of Acceptance: Too Many Problems for a Single Rule*, 112 U. of Pa. L. Rev. 947, 950–951 (1964).

[9] 125 Mass. 374 (1878). A more recent example is Solomon v. FloWarr Management, Inc., 777 S.W.2d 701 (Tenn. App. 1989).

[10] Restatement (First) of Conflict of Laws § 358.

[11] *See* Arthur Nussbaum, *Conflict Theories of Contract: Cases Versus Restatement*, 51 Yale L.J. 893, 915–916 (1942).

[12] Restatement (First) of Conflict of Laws § 332, comment c. From the point of view of the First Restatement, this is a rather astounding admission, especially since the principal virtues

Difficult as it may be, however, line drawing between issues of validity and issues of performance is not the major problem with the First Restatement rules on contracts. The really serious difficulty with the place–of–making rule is that it can produce arbitrary results; it relies on a single factual contact which may point toward the law of a state which has little interest in the resolution of the dispute.[13] To illustrate the point, reconsider *Milliken v. Pratt,* but suppose that the parties had met face to face in New York to execute the guarantee. By the place–of–making rule, New York law would control the wife's capacity even though it is quite clear that Massachusetts and Maine have the greatest interest in the determination of the issue.

[b] Escaping the Place of Making

Courts developed several techniques for escaping the place–of–making rule. Two (manipulation of the place of making and use of the making/performance distinction) are specialized devices, useful only in contract actions. Three others (characterization, renvoi, and public policy) are the standard escape techniques that courts have used in all sorts of cases.

[1] Manipulation of the Rule

One of the principal arguments for the place–of–making rule is certainty of application. According to Professor Beale, a contract can be made in only one place and there can never be "great or serious doubt" as to where that place is.[14] Beale could scarcely have been more wrong. In a modern commercial transaction conducted by telephone or by mail, it can be quite difficult to determine exactly which piece of correspondence is an offer and which is an acceptance. Indeed, one of the plagues of the first year of law school is the contracts exam which requires the student to deal with a long series of communications beginning with invitations to negotiate and ending with an agreement. The point of the exercise is for the student to learn that the words "offer" and "acceptance" are legal conclusions and that there are no "right answers." In practice, it is often a question of art (or at best craft) and never science to determine when preliminary negotiating stops and an offer occurs.[15] Similarly, distinguishing a counter–offer from an acceptance can be a tricky business. This inherent flexibility in contract theory provides a method by which a clever court can easily manipulate the notions of offer and acceptance to relocate the place of making and thus change the choice of law in a contract case.

---

claimed for the First Restatement are its certainty and its deduction via pure logic from the axioms of the vested rights theory. *See* Walter W. Cook, The Logical and Legal Bases of the Conflict of Laws 360–361 (1942).

[13] *See* Brainerd Currie, *Married Women's Contracts: A Study in Conflict–of–Laws Methods,* 25 U. Chi. L. Rev. 227 (1958).

[14] 2 Joseph H. Beale, *supra* note 1, § 332.4.

[15] Indeed, a contract may exist under the Uniform Commercial Code "even though the moment of its making is undetermined." U.C.C. § 2–204(2).

The unilateral/bilateral contract distinction is also manipulable. Recall that in *Milliken v. Pratt,* the court determined that the wife had made an offer which was accepted by the performance of plaintiffs in Maine. The agreement, in other words, was classified as a unilateral contract. Equally plausible would have been a bilateral characterization. On that theory, plaintiffs made a promise in Maine to sell to the husband on the condition that his wife promise to guarantee the debt. That deal would have been a bilateral contract with the wife's promise in Massachusetts constituting the acceptance. Thus, by tinkering with the bilateral/unilateral distinction, the court could have chosen Massachusetts law instead of Maine's and produced a victory for the wife instead of the plaintiffs.

[2] Issues of Making and Issues of Performance

The distinction between issues of validity and issues of performance gives a court the opportunity to avoid application of the law of the place of making by characterizing the issue as one of performance. A well known example is *Louis–Dreyfus v. Paterson Steamships, Ltd.*[16] Shipper contracted with carrier in Duluth, Minnesota, for the transportation of wheat from Duluth to Montreal. The contract provided that the carrier would unload the wheat in Port Colbourne, Ontario, and reload it onto smaller ships for the voyage to Montreal. One of these ships ran aground and sank due to a navigational error. The shipper then sued the carrier in federal court for damage to the wheat.

Learned Hand, writing for the Second Circuit, faced an interesting predicament. Under American admiralty law (the law of the place of making), the carrier was liable for damage to cargo caused by errors of navigation.[17] The Harter Act[18] had changed that rule by giving carriers a defense; if the carrier exercises due diligence to make the ship seaworthy and to insure that she is properly manned, he is relieved of liability for errors of navigation. The Act applied, however, only to voyages "to or from any port in the United States." The trip from Port Colbourne to Montreal was not such a voyage, and Hand assumed that the Harter Act did not apply. Canada had a statute which was in pertinent part identical to the Harter Act.

Here, then, was Hand's predicament. Both Canadian and American policy limited the carrier's responsibility for errors of navigation. The place–of–making rule pointed to American admiralty law; but because the Harter Act did not apply, the relevant American law was common law, which provided for the carrier's liability. In other words, the place–of–making rule provided a recovery for the shipper even though the policy of the only two states involved opposed that recovery. Hand's solution to the dilemma was to characterize the issue of limitation of liability as an issue of performance: "All we need say here is that the same law which determines what liabilities

---

[16] 43 F.2d 824 (2d Cir. 1930). For commentary on the decision, *see* J.H.C. Morris, *The Eclipse of the Lex Loci Solutionis — A Fallacy Exploded,* 6 Vand. L. Rev. 505, 506–507 (1953).

[17] Grant Gilmore & Charles L. Black, Jr., The Law of Admiralty § 3.22 (2d ed. 1975).

[18] 46 U.S.C. § 192.

shall arise upon nonperformance, must determine any excuses for nonperformance, which are no more than exceptions to those liabilities." The result, of course, was that the Canadian act applied and the carrier was entitled to the seaworthiness defense.

[3] The Standard Escape Devices

In addition to the specialized contracts escape devices, courts also used the familiar tricks of characterization, renvoi, and public policy. In *Preine v. Freeman*[19] the problem was the effect of a release upon tort liability, and the court had to choose between contract and tort characterizations. Plaintiffs, injured in an automobile accident in Virginia, released from liability two of five alleged joint tortfeasors by agreements made in other states. According to the law of Virginia, the release of one joint tortfeasor released all; but according to the law of the states where the releases were executed, it did not. The court characterized the effect of the release as a tort problem rather than a contract issue and applied the law of Virginia — the place of injury.

Although the Restatement did not approve of renvoi in contract cases,[20] traditionalist courts occasionally resorted to the concept to escape the place–of–making rule. In *University of Chicago v. Dater*,[21] defendant, a married woman, and her husband executed a note in Michigan and mailed it to the lender in Illinois. The lender made the loan by check delivered to defendant and her husband in Chicago. The husband later died, the defendant defaulted, and the lender sued her in Michigan. Under Michigan law, defendant had no contractual capacity; under Illinois law she did. Both jurisdictions used the place–of–contracting rule; and that circumstance would ordinarily preclude an escape via renvoi. Illinois and Michigan, however, interpreted the rule differently. Michigan law held the place of contracting to be the place where the loan was actually made (Illinois), while Illinois had held in *Burr v. Beckler*,[22] that the place of making was the place where the note was executed (Michigan). The Supreme Court of Michigan was able to use the *Burr* holding to escape the result of its own "law of the place of contracting" rule. It determined that the "law" of Illinois included Illinois' choice–of–law rules which, as interpreted in *Burr*, selected Michigan law.

"Public policy" can also be employed to avoid application of the law of the place of making. In two famous contract cases, the argument was made but did not win the day. In *Intercontinental Hotels Corp. v. Golden,*[23] plaintiff, a casino operator in Puerto Rico sued the defendant, a New Yorker, for gambling debts incurred in Puerto Rico. The Court of Appeals of New York showed considerable restraint in interpreting the public policy of New York. Although casino gambling was illegal in New York, other types

[19] 112 F. Supp. 257 (E.D. Va. 1953).

[20] *See* Restatement (First) of Conflict of Laws § 7.

[21] 277 Mich. 658, 270 N.W. 175 (1936). The case is discussed in greater detail in § 59, *supra*.

[22] 264 Ill. 230, 106 N.E. 206 (1914).

[23] 15 N.Y.2d 9, 203 N.E.2d 210, 254 N.Y.S. 2d 527 (1964).

of gambling were legal and approved of by "[i]nformed public sentiment." Accordingly, the court held that enforcement of gambling debts, incurred legally in Puerto Rico, would not be inherently immoral or wicked and vicious; it refused, therefore, to apply the public policy exception to aid defendant.[24]

The refusal to use the public policy device in *Holzer v. Deutsche Reichsbahn–Gesellschaft*[25] is hard to justify. Plaintiff, a German Jew, was discharged by defendant, his employer, pursuant to a German law, which required forced retirement of non–Aryans. Plaintiff sued defendant in New York claiming damages as a result of the discharge. Defendant raised the German law as an affirmative defense, and plaintiff moved to strike it. The Court of Appeals of New York held that "[d]efendants did not breach their contract with plaintiff. They were forced by operation of law to discharge him."[26] This result is difficult to square with accepted pronouncements about the use of public policy to void transactions which are "inherently vicious, wicked or immoral, and shocking to the prevailing moral sense."[27] If that cumbersome characterization does not apply to a case of *de jure* racism, it is hard to justify its application in any case.

§ 67 Property

It has been traditional in conflicts law to distinguish between immovable and movable property. The distinction is generally comparable to that drawn between real and personal property, except that a leasehold interest is classified as an interest in immovable property in conflicts parlance, while in general property parlance, it is considered personal rather than real property.[1] The organization of this Section follows the distinction drawn by the First Restatement between interests in land and other sorts of property.

[a] Land

The First Restatement requires application of the law of the situs (the location of the land) to nearly all questions concerning interests in land. The rule applies to conveyances of land (§§ 214–222), adverse possession (§ 224), mortgages and liens (§§ 225–231), marital property (§§ 237–238), trusts (§ 241), and succession by will or intestacy (§§ 245–254). Indeed, the

[24] *Accord* Kramer v. Bally's Park Place, Inc., 311 Md. 387, 535 A.2d 466 (1988); *but see* The Cassanova Club v. Bisharat, 189 Conn. 591, 458 A.2d 1 (1983). For commentary on public policy and gambling, *see* Vernon, Weinberg, Reynolds & Richman 285–286.

[25] 277 N.Y. 474, 14 N.E.2d 798 (1938).

[26] In the second count of his complaint, plaintiff claimed damages under a contract clause which required defendant to pay plaintiff $50,000 if he "should die or become unable, without fault on his part, to serve during the period of the contract." The Court of Appeals held that this second count did state a cause of action against defendant.

[27] The quotation is from Intercontinental Hotels Corp. v. Golden, 15 N.Y.2d 9, 254 N.Y.S.2d 527, 203 N.E.2d 210 (1964).

[1] Restatement (First) of Conflict of Laws § 208, Special Note.

situs rule is among the broadest of the First Restatement choice–of–law principles; it retains much of its authority today,[2] even though many modern courts have abandoned the First Restatement in other areas.

The Restatement devotes very little attention to justifying the situs rule, perhaps because it seemed so self–evident to thinkers raised on the territorial theory. Slightly more surprising is the short shrift which First Restatement apologists gave to those reasons. In one brief sentence Beale suggested that the law of the situs must be applied because "any contrary provision would be given no effect" in the situs state.[3] In an equally terse passage, Goodrich suggested that a reason for the situs rule is concern for the integrity of the recording system of the situs state.[4]

Modern commentators have given much more attention to reasons for the situs rule.[5] Three arguments are made frequently. First, only the courts of the situs can directly affect title to land in that state.[6] A non–situs court may bind the *litigants* before it with respect to their *interests* in situs land, *but it may not act in rem on that land.* Thus, the argument goes, the forum should apply the situs law to ensure that courts in the situs state will willingly enforce the forum court's decree. A second argument for the situs rule relies on recording statutes. Title searching should be made as simple as possible; the searcher should be able to examine conveyances in the chain of title and easily determine their effect. That she can do only if their effect is controlled by the law of the situs. If the validity of a conveyance were determined by the law of the grantor's domicile, for example, the searcher would have to ascertain that domicile, and it might not appear on the face of the recorded conveyance. Further, instead of being able to rely upon the situs law with which she is familiar, the searcher would need to research the land law of the grantor's domicile. The situs rule, therefore, helps keep title searching from becoming a significantly more complicated process. The third argument for the situs rule relies on the strong interest which the state and its people have in land within the state's borders. Questions affecting that land should be determined by the law of the state with the strongest interest in their resolution.[7]

Whatever the reasons for the situs rule, First Restatement courts applied it with rigid zeal. The well–known probate case, *In re Barrie's Estate,*[8] provides an excellent example. Decedent died domiciled in Illinois, owning real property in Iowa and real and personal property in Illinois. Her will was denied probate in Illinois because she had revoked it by cancellation.

---

[2] *See, e.g.,* Matter of Estate of Reed, 768 P.2d 566 (Wyo. 1989); Manderson & Associates, Inc. v. Gore, 193 Ga. App. 723, 389 S.E.2d 251 (1989).

[3] 2 Joseph H. Beale, A Treatise on the Conflict of Laws § 214.1 (1935).

[4] Herbert F. Goodrich, Handbook of the Conflict of Laws 455 (3d ed. 1949).

[5] *See generally* Scoles et al. § 19.1; Weintraub § 8.2.

[6] *See* § 115, *infra,* for a discussion of the faith and credit due F–1 decrees affecting F–2 land.

[7] A more thorough discussion of the reasons for the situs rule appears in § 89, *infra.*

[8] 240 Iowa 431, 35 N.W.2d 658 (1949). A more recent endorsement of the situs rule appears in Manderson & Associates, Inc. v. Gore, 193 Ga. App. 723, 389 S.E.2d 251 (1989).

One of the testamentary beneficiaries later offered the will for probate in Iowa. Decedent's heirs objected to the petition for probate. The first question for the Supreme Court of Iowa was whether the Illinois decree denying probate should bind the Iowa courts on the same issue. The court held it should not because a probate decree in one state can not bind real property in another state.[9] With the full faith and credit question removed, the court was left with a pure choice–of–law problem. Decedent had clearly attempted to revoke her will by writing the word "Void" on it in several places. That action was sufficient to constitute a revocation under Illinois law, but not under Iowa law. The Iowa court held, in accordance with the situs rule, that the law of Iowa should control and that the testamentary beneficiaries should take under the unrevoked will.

The mechanical (and perverse) quality of much First Restatement choice–of–law thinking is illustrated by a closer look at the opinions in *Barrie.*[10] The dissent relied upon an Iowa statute that provided that a will executed outside Iowa in the manner prescribed by either the law of the place of execution or the law of decedent's domicile should be deemed to be validly executed under Iowa law. The dissent argued that the statute should apply to *revocation* as well as *execution,* but the majority disagreed, holding that the statute (because it modified the common law) should be strictly

---

[9] This rule is just an instance of the general rule of Fall v. Eastin, 215 U.S. 1 (1909), that an F–1 court does not have jurisdiction to act in rem upon land in F–2. *See* § 115, *infra,* for a discussion of *Fall.*

[10] *Barrie* also demonstrates an important flaw in the reasons for the situs rule. The problem is not that the reasons are inconsequential; they make sense and justify the situs rule in many cases. The problem is rather that the scope of the rule and the scope of the reasons are a mismatch; the reasons justify the rule only in *some* cases, but the rule applies to *all* property choice–of–law issues.

In *Barrie,* for instance, the rule applied even though none of the reasons justified it. The exclusive–power–over–land rationale makes sense only when the forum court has to rely on the situs courts for enforcement of its decree, but in *Barrie,* the forum *was* the situs. The Iowa court could have applied either Illinois or Iowa law in perfect confidence that its judgment could be enforced; after all, it had power over the res.

The recording–statute argument did not apply either. The rationale makes sense in cases where a bona fide purchaser has relied on land records in the situs, but that was not the case in *Barrie.* The contest was between the decedent's heirs and devisees, none of whom had any occasion to consider or rely on Iowa land records. Nor could application of Illinois law deceive future purchasers relying on Iowa land records. The Iowa court could have applied Illinois law and then ordered a master to draft a valid Iowa deed conveying the property to the heirs. That deed would have been recorded, and future title searches would not be misled.

The final rationale — the situs has the greatest interest in situs land — also makes no sense in *Barrie.* That argument certainly applies in cases where some environmental or perpetuities issue arises. The situs does have the greatest interest in preservation of its natural resources and in maintaining the marketability of situs land. In *Barrie,* however, it is hard to see how the contest between the heirs and devisees had any relevance at all to land–use or alienability concerns.

For more on the reasons for the rule, *see* Weintraub, § 8.2; Moffatt Hancock, *Conceptual Devices for Avoiding the Land Taboo in Conflict of Laws: The Disadvantages of Disingenuousness,* 20 Stan. L. Rev. 1, 22–23 (1967); Moffatt Hancock, *Full Faith and Credit to Foreign Laws and Judgments in Real Property Litigation: The Supreme Court and the Land Taboo,* 18 Stan. L. Rev. 1299 (1966). More succinct discussions appear in § 89, *infra,* and in Vernon, Weinberg, Reynolds & Richman, 240–43.

construed. The majority's decision is hard to justify. The statute, as the dissent points out, was clearly designed to "minimize confusion and conflict between states in the matter of handling wills." It also seems to have been directed toward the validation of the expectations and intentions of the prudent decedent. If these policies are important with regard to execution, they are similarly crucial to the closely related issue of revocation. The majority decision radically discounted the importance of the policy or purpose behind the statute; it seemed to be motivated instead by a mechanical devotion to the literal language of the statute. That sort of rigidly conceptualistic jurisprudence was characteristic of many courts that followed the First Restatement.

[b] Movables — Personal Property

[1] Inter Vivos Transactions

For nearly all[11] inter vivos transactions of movables, the First Restatement prescribes the law of the place where the movable was located at the time of the transaction. Thus, the situs rule applies to conveyances (§§ 255–258), adverse possession (§ 259), mortgages (§ 265), conditional sales (§ 272), liens and pledges (§ 279), powers of appointment (§ 283), and trusts (§ 294).

It is immaterial that the parties to the transaction are domiciled elsewhere, or that the agreement to make the transaction occurs elsewhere, or that the movable arrived at the situs only by chance. *Cammell v. Sewell*[12] illustrates these points very well. That action involved lumber shipped on a Prussian vessel from a Russian port to England. The ship ran aground in Norwegian waters, and the cargo was unloaded and sold at auction pursuant to the request of the ship's master. The purchaser resold the lumber to defendants in England where plaintiff, the insurer of the cargo, sued them for the it. According to Norwegian law the auction sale gave good title to a bona fide purchaser; under English law it did not. The English court ruled that the law of Norway — the situs of the lumber at the time of the auction — should be applied to validate the sale. Said the court:

> "[I]f personal property is disposed of in a manner binding according to the law of the country where it is, that disposition is binding everywhere." And we do not think that it makes any difference that the goods were wrecked, and not intended to be sent to the country where they were sold.[13]

The argument for the situs rule was based upon convenience and party expectations. Judge Goodrich,[14] a proponent of the First Restatement–

---

[11] The rules dealing with rights of married persons in each other's property were a notable exception. *See* Restatement (First) of Conflict of Laws §§ 289 & 290, which refer such questions to the parties' domicile.

[12] 5 Hurl. & N. 728, 157 Eng. Rep. 1371 (1860).

[13] The first sentence is set off by quotation marks, because the appellate court is quoting from the proceedings below.

[14] Goodrich, *supra* note 4, at 470–478.

suggested that the situs rule made a good deal more sense than the older notion that conveyances of movables should be controlled by the law of the domicile of the parties. Several obvious objections can be made to that rule. First, the parties to a commercial sale may have different domiciles; whose then should control? Further, much modern business is conducted by corporations, and corporate domicile is often a mere legal technicality. Finally, corporations as well as individuals often conduct business far from their domiciles; a party to a sale of property far from home would not naturally expect the validity of the sale to be governed by the law of his domicile.[15] With the domicile rule thus disqualified, the situs rule was the natural choice for the First Restatement.[16]

[2] Succession on Death

The First Restatement refers questions concerning testamentary disposition of movables and intestate succession of movables to the law of decedent's domicile at the time of death.[17] The result is partially inconsistent with the territorial theory since it permits the law of decedent's domicile to operate extra–territorially on movables located elsewhere. The rationale for this major exception to the situs rule is that it is desirable to have an entire estate pass according to a single plan. If each item of a decedent's estate were distributed according to the law of its situs, no single plan could control. If decedent died intestate, for example, each piece of his property would be distributed according to the intestacy laws of its situs. If decedent died leaving a will, the will might be valid according to the law of the situs of some property and invalid according to the law of the situs of other property. In order to avoid this lack of uniformity, the reference for the entire estate is to the law of decedent's domicile.[18]

[c] Escaping the Law of the Situs

Courts have used several techniques to avoid the iron hand of the situs rule. Three discussed below are equitable conversion, renvoi, and characterization.

---

[15] For more on the justifications for the situs rule, *see* Wendell Carnahan, *Tangible Property and the Conflict of Laws*, 2 U. Chi. L. Rev. 345 (1935).

[16] A modern flexible treatment of property issues based on the policies behind the competing internal rules was not a realistic option for First Restatement thinkers.

[17] *See* Restatement (First) of Conflict of Laws §§ 303, 306. Matter of Estate of Rivas, 233 Kan. 898, 666 P.2d 691 (1983).

[18] *See* Goodrich, *supra* note 4, at 501. The rationale for the rule seems so convincing that one might well wonder why the domicile rule was not applied to the decedent's land as well. In light of the First Restatement's strong commitment to territorialism, however, a reference to any law other than that of the situs to solve a real property problem would be quite surprising.

[1] Equitable Conversion[19]

Equitable conversion is really a specialized characterization device which permits a court to recharacterize real property as personal property.[20] In a decedent's estate case, the recharacterization can change the reference from the law of the situs to the law of decedent's domicile. The most typical instance of equitable conversion occurs when decedent leaves instructions by will that her land be sold and the proceeds paid to her legatee; whether the conversion occurs and the recharacterization is permissible is, under the First Restatement, a question to be decided by the law of the situs.[21]

The decision in *Duckwall v. Lease*[22] provides an example of equitable conversion. Testatrix died in Ohio owning real property in Indiana. Her will left a life estate in the Indiana land to her husband and directed that the land be sold at his death and the proceeds paid to her brother and sister. The brother and sister pre–deceased the testatrix, however. When her husband died and his life estate terminated, the question was whether the land should pass to the heirs of the brother and sister or whether their deaths caused the gift to lapse, in which case the land would go to the husband's devisees. According to Indiana law, the gift to the brother and sister lapsed at their death; according to Ohio law it did not. The Indiana court ruled in favor of the brother's heirs. It held that the testatrix's will had effected an equitable conversion of the land and that the gift, as personalty, was governed by the anti–lapse statute of Ohio — her domicile. The result makes sense because the anti–lapse statute helped to effectuate the probable intentions of the testatrix.[23] A First Restatement court, however, could not rely on so practical and untechnical a rationale; the fictional magic of equitable conversion did the dirty work instead.

---

[19] *See generally* Leflar, McDougal & Felix § 167. The most comprehensive discussion of the topic is Moffat Hancock, *Equitable Conversion and the Land Taboo in Conflict of Laws,* 17 Stan. L. Rev. 1095 (1965).

[20] The concept of equitable conversion did not originate in the choice–of–law context. Its original use was in English common law where different rules governed the descent of personal and real property; personal property passing to the personal representatives and real property passing by the rule of primogeniture to the heir. Suppose that testator's will ordered land sold and the proceeds paid to beneficiary, but that the beneficiary died intestate before the sale. Is his interest in the land real property that goes to his heir or personal property that goes to his personal representative? Equity courts held that the will caused an equitable conversion of the land into personal property, which then went to the beneficiary's personal representative. *See* Austin W. Scott, Abridgment of the Law of Trusts §§ 130–131 (1960).

In choice of law, equitable conversion performs the same transformation of real to personal property, but with a very different consequence; it changes the choice from the law of the situs (the rule for real property) to the law of decedent's domicile (the rule for personal property). It can be dangerous, of course, to pick a concept, category, or distinction from one context and use it in another without being aware that it serves very different functions in the new setting. *See* Moffatt Hancock, *Fallacy of the Transplanted Category,* 37 Can. B. Rev. 535 (1959).

[21] Restatement (First) of Conflict of Laws § 209.

[22] 106 Ind. App. 664, 20 N.E.2d 204 (1939). A famous example of a refusal to apply the doctrine is Toledo Soc'y for Crippled Children v. Hickok, 152 Tex. 578, 261 S.W.2d 692 (1953), *cert. denied,* 347 U.S. 936 (1954).

[23] For commentary on the decision, *see* Vernon, Weinberg, Reynolds & Richman 263–264; Hancock, *supra* note 19.

[2] Renvoi

Renvoi has already been explained and illustrated in several places in this text, so a general discussion is not warranted here.[24] It is appropriate, however, to indicate the specific view of the First Restatement on renvoi in land cases. Although First Restatement courts used renvoi as an escape device in contract and tort cases, the Restatement did not sanction that use of the doctrine. The Restatement did, however, approve of renvoi in cases involving title to land.[25] The reason for the exception is that the situs court is the only one with direct power over the land, so a non–situs forum, in order to ensure the enforceability of its decree, should decide questions involving land exactly as a situs court would. In order to do that, the forum would have to employ the choice–of–law rules of the situs; the forum, in other words, would have to apply the doctrine of renvoi.[26]

The opportunity to use renvoi in property cases is very restricted because nearly all American jurisdictions have the same choice–of–law rules for property cases. Renvoi has no practical implications if all relevant jurisdictions have identical choice–of–law rules. Thus, most property cases in which renvoi has been used have been cases involving an American state and a foreign country.[27]

[3] Characterization

Another strategy available to a court dissatisfied with the law of the situs, is to recharacterize the case so that the reference is to the law of another state. The contract/conveyance distinction[28] is a specialized property characterization device. The idea is that a contract to convey land should be governed by the law of the place of making even though the validity of the conveyance (deed) itself should be governed by the law of the situs.[29] The distinction makes sense in light of the reason for the situs rule. Only the situs courts can act directly to affect title to the land, but any court with personal jurisdiction over defendant can order him to pay damages for breach of contract. Thus, if the main rationale for the situs rule[30] is the unique power of the situs' courts, there is no reason to apply the situs rule to contracts concerning land.

---

[24] *See* §§ 59, 65, and 66, *supra*.

[25] Restatement (First) of Conflict of Laws § 8.

[26] 1 Joseph H. Beale, *supra* note 3, at § 8.1.

[27] *See, e.g.,* In re Schneider's Estate, 198 Misc. 1017, 96 N.Y.S. 2d 652 (1950) (choice between law of New York and Switzerland), discussed in § 59, *supra*.

[28] *See* Leflar, McDougal & Felix § 170 for a general discussion of the distinction between contract and conveyance.

[29] Courts also used the contract/conveyance dichotomy to distinguish a note from the mortgage securing it and covenants personal to the parties from those running with the land. *See generally* Weintraub, § 8.16; Note, *Choice of Law Governing Land Transactions: The Contract–Conveyance Dichotomy*, 111 U. Pa. L. Rev. 482 (1963).

[30] *See* notes 4–7 and accompanying text for a discussion of the other reasons for the situs rule.

Polson v. Stewart[31] is an example of the intelligent use of the distinction. A husband contracted with his wife in North Carolina (their domicile) to release all his rights in her land in Massachusetts. Under North Carolina law, the wife had capacity to make such a contract, but according to Massachusetts law she did not. After the wife's death, her administrator sued the husband in Massachusetts for specific performance. The Massachusetts court characterized the issue as a contract problem and applied the law of North Carolina to produce a victory for the administrator. The result makes good sense.[32] Massachusetts' incapacity rule was outmoded, and it frustrated the intentions of the parties, who had acted at arms length. Further, North Carolina had a greater interest in the issue than did Massachusetts. The decision is just one of many examples where a court was able to manipulate First Restatement categories to produce the sort of result that modern choice–of–law theories would favor.

Another possible escape from the situs rule is a tort characterization. Suppose a debtor attempts to frustrate his creditors by executing a conveyance in state X of land in state Y. Can creditor's claim of fraud be referred to the law of X — the place of the wrong — instead of the law of Y — the situs? Some courts have permitted the recharacterization, others have not.[33] The answer should depend upon an assessment of the interests of X and Y and of the policies that motivate each state's rules on fraudulent conveyances rather than on a mechanical gimmick like the tort/property characterization device.

§ 68 The First Restatement — A Critique

The principal benefits claimed for the First Restatement system for choice of law are ease of administration, predictability, and forum neutrality. By the use of a few, simple rules, the Restatement sought to generate a system that was easy to apply, certain of outcome, and not subject to change depending upon where the suit was brought. The first goal was clearly attained; the rules are (at least on the surface) easy to understand and apply. Predictability and forum neutrality are another matter. If the rules were applied "right out of the box" perhaps these ends could be reached, but the system of escape devices substantially undermines predictability and forum neutrality.[1] Further, the importance of ease of application, predictability, and forum neutrality can be overstated easily.[2] A choice–of–law system which achieves those ends much more efficiently than the First

---

[31] 167 Mass. 211, 45 N.E. 737 (1897).

[32] The opinion in Polson, however, has been subject to serious criticism. *See* Moffat Hancock, *Conceptual Devices for Avoiding the Land Taboo in Conflict of Laws: The Disadvantages of Disingenuousness,* 20 Stan. L. Rev. 1 (1967).

[33] *Compare* Irving Trust Co. v. Maryland Casualty Co., 83 F.2d 168 (2d Cir. 1936), *with* James v. Powell, 19 N.Y.2d 249, 225 N.E.2d 741, 279 N.Y.S.2d 10 (1967). *See generally* Albert A. Ehrenzweig & Peter K. Westen, *Fraudulent Conveyances in the Conflict of Laws: Easy Cases May Make Bad Law,* 66 Mich. L. Rev. 1679 (1968).

[1] *See* text accompanying notes 5–8, *infra,* for more criticism of the system of escape devices.

[2] *See* Vernon, Weinberg, Reynolds & Richman 223.

Restatement is one which directs the application of the law of the state which is first (or last) in alphabetical order, yet no one has seriously argued for such a system.[3]

A preliminary problem with the First Restatement is its very simplicity. That simplicity is bought at the price of insisting on a few broad rules which lump together cases and issues that appear quite unrelated. In tort cases, for example, the Restatement prescribes the law of the place of injury for all torts, from defamation to battery to misrepresentation. It seems improbable that such diverse legal actions, restricted by widely different defenses and qualifications, could all be covered profitably by a single choice–of–law rule. On the other hand, the Restatement's categories sometimes separate problems that should be closely linked. A products liability plaintiff will typically plead a count of strict liability in tort and a count in warranty. The two theories, one descended from tort and the other from contract, seek to compensate the same injury, yet the First Restatement will apply the law of the place of injury to one theory and the law of the place of making to the other. That hardly passes an intuitive test of rationality.

A far more serious problem with the First Restatement is that it often chooses the law of a state with no interest in the resolution of the dispute. Suppose a contract is negotiated in Connecticut for the delivery of goods in Connecticut by a Connecticut seller to a Connecticut buyer. Although Connecticut is the only state with a real interest in the transaction; if the parties had concluded their negotiation at a trade convention in Florida, the Restatement would apply the law of Florida to the contract. Surely that is a triumph of form over substance.

The reason for such anomalies is that the First Restatement rules are almost entirely (and deliberately) blind to the content of and the policies behind the competing internal laws. Consider an automobile accident between two Californians, plaintiff and defendant, which occurs about two miles south of the border between California and Mexico. Suppose that plaintiff is seriously injured — about $200,000 worth. Further suppose that Mexico, desiring not to impoverish tortfeasors, has established a negligence damage limitation of $6,000 but that California does not limit damages because it favors full compensation for tort victims.[4] According to the Restatement, the law of Mexico should apply because Mexico is the place of injury. But note how applying Mexican law seriously frustrates California's policy of compensation without advancing Mexico's goal in the least. If Mexico is concerned about impoverishing tortfeasors, surely that concern does not extend to Californians. Thus, the application of the First Restatement's mechanical formula produces a foolish result here for the simple reason that the formula totally ignores the purposes behind Mexico's and California's tort rules. Such blind adherence to the letter of the law, while ignoring its spirit, would not be tolerated in a purely domestic case; why then should it be the rule for conflicts cases?

[3] *See* Currie, Essays, 609, for the ironic suggestion that such a system would be satisfactory if the conflicting internal laws expressed no governmental policies.

[4] The hypothetical is suggested by the facts of Victor v. Sperry, 163 Cal. App. 2d 518, 329 P.2d 728 (1958).

A final problem with the First Restatement is the system of escape devices. Basically the devices work to give some flexibility to the mechanical choice–of–law rules. Because the rules by and large ignore government interests, the policies behind legal rules, the parties' expectations, and justice in the individual case, the escape devices have been used to import those considerations into the choice–of–law process. In the hands of able and reflective judges, the escape devices have been potent weapons for good. In *Polson v. Stewart,*[5] for instance, then–Judge Holmes was able to avoid the law of the situs and decide the issue (a wife's capacity to contract with her husband regarding his rights in her property) according to the law of the marital domicile — the state with the most concern for the resolution of the issue. Similarly, in *Louis–Dreyfus v. Paterson Steamships, Ltd.,*[6] Judge Hand used the making/performance distinction to make sure that the common policy (limiting the liability of carriers) of Canada and the United States would be furthered.

But even in the hands of able judges, the escape devices can be dangerous. The danger is that First Restatement courts articulate only the technical rationales for the escape devices — not the real policy interests and considerations of justice that have, in fact, motivated them. In other words, the escape device assures that the reasons for the court's *decision* will have little to do with the reasons announced in the court's *opinion.*[7] The result is that the court has a freedom to indulge in unprincipled decision–making, a freedom incompatible with the rule of law. Judges in our system have extraordinary power; the requirement that their decisions be reasoned and public is one of the only real constraints on that power. Devices that effectively hide the real reasons for decisions considerably weaken that constraint and take our judicial system far from the common law model of principled decision–making.[8]

Despite its defects, the First Restatement has proved remarkably resilient in the courts. The most recent recent exhaustive survey of American choice–of–law decisions found that eleven jurisdictions still follow the traditional method in contract or tort cases.[9]

That total both over and understates the influence of the First Restatement today. The understatement involves real property cases. The quoted total deals only with contract and tort conflicts cases; in real property cases, courts of all choice–of–law persuasions apply the situs rule almost universally. The overstatement involves the level of commitment that First Restatement courts show to the traditional lex loci methodology.

[5] 167 Mass. 211, 45 N.E. 737 (1897), discussed in § 67, *supra.*

[6] 43 F.2d 824 (2d Cir. 1930), discussed in § 66, *supra.*

[7] The American Realists noted this tendency in our jurisprudence generally, not just in conflicts. *See* Jerome Frank, Law and the Modern Mind, 100–104 (1931).

[8] *See* William L. Reynolds & William M. Richman, *The Non–Precedential Precedent — Limited Publications and No–Citation Rules in the United States Courts of Appeals,* 78 Colum. L. Rev. 1167 (1978).

[9] *See* Symeon Symeonides, *Choice of Law in the American Courts in 2000: As the Century Turns,* 49 Am. J. Comp. L. 1 (2001).

Traditionalist courts routinely deviate from the lex loci rules in insurance, usury, workers' compensation, and contract choice–of–law clause cases.[10]

Another difficulty with the quoted total is that it reflects in part the absence of recent choice–of–law decisions in some states. Part of the total, however, represents a sizeable number of jurisdictions where recent decisions have rejected the modern choice–of–law systems in favor of the comfortingly familiar black letter rules of the First Restatement. In other words, in spite of its inadequacies, the First Restatement retains considerable practical importance today.

[10] William M. Richman and David Riley, *The First Restatement of Conflict of Laws on the Twenty-fifth Anniversary of its Successor: Contemporary Practice on Traditional Courts*, 56 Md. L. Rev. 1196 1213–1217, 1226 (1997).

Part C

MODERN CHOICE OF LAW

§ 69 Introduction[1]

Although theory has always been important in choice–of–law literature, its role in the past third of a century has been truly remarkable. Indeed, conflicts today positively blossoms with theory. The sections in this Part examine the dominant positions, beginning with the Second Restatement and its spiritual antecedent, the center of gravity test (§§ 70–77). Next, we examine interest analysis, the extremely influential method of analyzing choice–of–law problems developed by Brainerd Currie (§§ 78–80). Sections 81–84 describe alternative modern methods of looking at choice of law, and the last section (§85) gives a perspective on choice–of–law theory today.

§ 70 Center of Gravity

The theoretical bases of the First Restatement were under challenge even before the project was finished,[1] and its promulgation was followed by a devastating attack on the territorial theory by Walter Wheeler Cook in 1942.[2] Judicial resistance to Bealean dogma, however, primarily took the form of resort to characterization and other escape devices.[3] Beginning with *Auten v. Auten*,[4] however, a frontal attack began in the courts as they started to experiment with new approaches to choice–of–law problems.

Plaintiff in *Auten* sought to enforce a separation agreement. The couple had married in England and lived there until the husband deserted his wife and moved to New York.

They entered into a separation agreement in New York, and the wife then returned to England. Fourteen years later, she sued her husband in New York on the agreement for unpaid support. He defended on the ground that while in England she had sued him for a divorce, in violation of the separation agreement. That defense, invalid under English law, succeeded in the lower New York courts. The Court of Appeals reversed.

Judge Fuld's opinion began by noting the general conflicts rule that questions concerning performance of a contract are controlled by the law of the place of performance. Fuld then observed that some recent cases had

---

1 *See generally* Lea Brilmayer, Conflict of Laws: Foundations and Future Directions (1991).

1 David F. Cavers, *A Critique of The Choice–of–Law Problem*, 47 Harv. L. Rev. 173 (1933).

2 Walter W. Cook, The Logical and Legal Bases of the Conflict of Laws (1942).

3 Several decisions, however, had suggested a more modern approach. In Val Blatz Brewing Co. v. Industrial Comm., 201 Wis. 474, 479, 230 N.W. 622, 624 (1930), for example, the court abandoned territorial analysis in order that "the whole beneficent purpose of the workmen's compensation act would [not] be frustrated."

4 308 N.Y. 155, 124 N.E.2d 99 (1954).

adopted the "center of gravity" or "grouping of contacts" theory, which looks not to the place of making or performance, but emphasizes the law of the place "which has the most significant contacts with the matter in dispute."[5]

Although Fuld recognized that the center of gravity test afforded "less certainty and predictability than the rigid general rules," he adopted the new theory because its focus on specific legal issues (as opposed to large areas of subject matter) permitted application of the "policy" of the jurisdiction "most intimately connected" with the case. The approach not only enabled the court to consider the "relative interests" involved, but also gave it the flexibility to consider party intent and achievement of "the best practical result." The center of gravity test, in short, permitted the court to consider both party and governmental interests in its quest for justice. Determination of the center of gravity in *Auten* was straightforward. England had all the "truly significant contacts" — the marital and family domicile had been there, the wife and children were still domiciled there, and all the parties were British subjects. New York's nexus with the case was "entirely fortuitous," arising only because the husband lived there after deserting his wife. Fuld further justified his selection of English law on the ground that England had a great concern in the financial well–being of its domiciliaries, and that the result squared more closely with the intention of the parties when they executed the agreement.

Auten marked an important change in the law.[6] Written by a respected jurist for an influential court, *Auten* was handed down at a time when conflicts law was ripe for revolution.[7] The most important effect of the case was its influence on the drafting of the Second Restatement, which adopted "the most significant relationship test" (discussed in the next Section).[8] Although its primary effect was transitional, the center of gravity formulation has some force today, because some states treat the center of gravity test as more or less the same as the most significant relationship standard.[9]

§ 71 The Second Restatement: History and Theory[1]

[a] The Drafting History

Holmes' famous aphorism that a page of history is worth a volume of logic applies with special force to the Second Restatement. It is difficult to

[5] *Id.*, quoting Rubin v. Irving Trust Co., 305 N.Y. 288, 305, 113 N.E.2d 424, 431 (1953).

[6] Work on the Second Restatement began the year before the decision in *Auten.*

[7] *E.g.*, Schmidt v. Driscoll Hotel, Inc., 249 Minn. 376, 82 N.W.2d 365 (1957) (rejection of the *lex loci delicti* in dramshop cases). The New York cases after *Auten* are discussed *infra* in § 78.

[8] Judge Fuld was one of the Advisers to the drafting of the Second Restatement.

[9] *See* Vernon, Weinberg, Reynolds, & Richman at 296. North Dakota, however, specifically follows the center of gravity test rather than the Second Restatement; New York no longer uses the center of gravity. *Id.*

[1] *See generally* Willis Reese, *Conflict of Laws and the Restatement (Second)*, 28 Law & Contemp. Probs. 679 (1963). *See also* Willis Reese, *The Second Restatement of Conflict of Laws Revisited,* 34 Mercer L. Rev. 501 (1983).

understand the document and its hybrid method without some understanding of its eighteen-year drafting history. The project began in 1953 as an attempt to respond to the withering academic criticism of the First Restatement and to accommodate the beginnings of a conflicts revolution that was occurring in the courts. It ended in 1971 as a complex, negotiated settlement among several warring factions of choice–of–law revolutionaries. As a descriptive "restatement," it was doomed to failure from the outset because it is impossible to "restate" a revolution that is in progress and whose outcome is in doubt. As a normative "pre-statement," it has proved to be a huge success among the courts, but an object of academic derision.

Repudiating the dogma of vested rights, the early drafts nevertheless retained the First Restatement's strong territorial bias but broadened its scope.[2] Thus they contained a multitude of specific jurisdiction-selecting rules, but they also incorporated the "center of gravity" or "grouping of contacts" approach that had begun to appear in progressive judicial opinions. Conspicuously absent, however, was any serious attempt at policy analysis or consideration of the content of competing internal rules. The predictable result of those omissions was scathing criticism from the academic proponents of the more modern theories, particularly Brainerd Currie and Albert Ehrenzweig. The response of the drafters and their leader, Professor Willis Reese, was to attempt to co-opt the critics by incorporating many of their ideas in the choice–of–law Principles of § 6. Three drafts were considered between 1967 and 1969, when the Institute adopted the version which was finally published in 1971.[3] As a result of the drafting history, the final document is depending upon your point of view, either a balanced and sophisticated amalgam or an incoherent mishmash.[4]

[b] An Overview

The Restatement (Second) of Conflict of Laws is a complex approach to choice of law that borrows from the wide array of traditional and modern choice–of–law methodologies discussed in the preceding and succeeding Parts of Chapter 4.[5] Like its predecessor, it is comprehensive and detailed, containing hundreds of territorial choice–of–law rules divided by subject

[2] The Second Restatement differs significantly from its predecessor in this respect; the First Restatement rules chose one jurisdiction whose laws applied to all substantive issues in the case; the Second Restatement presumes the application of a law for each *issue* in a case.

[3] The Second Restatement was modified slightly in 1986, primarily to reflect changes in Constitutional law.

[4] For more on the history of the drafting process, see William L. Reynolds, *Legal Process and Choice of Law*, 56 Md. L. Rev. 1376, 1391 (1997), Patrick J. Borchers, *Courts and the Second Conflicts Restatement: Some Observations and an Empirical Note*, 56 Md. L. Rev. 1233, 1236 (1997), Jeffrey M. Shaman, *The Vicissitudes of Choice of Law: The Restatement (First, Second) and Interest Analysis*, 45 Buff. L. Rev. 329, 357 (1997), Michael S. Finch, *Choice-of-Law Problems in Florida Courts: A Retrospective on the Restatement (Second)*, 24 Stetson L. Rev. 653, 656 (1995).

[5] Especially influential are the First Restatement, see Part B, *supra*; the center of gravity, see § 70, *supra*; interest analysis, see §§ 78–80, *infra*; and new territorialism, see § 83, *infra*.

matter (torts, contracts, property, etc.). It also incorporates, however, much modern learning from the choice–of–law revolution including grouping-of-contacts, interest analysis, validation, and party autonomy. To complicate matters further, the reception of the Second Restatement has varied widely. Excoriated by commentators, it has proved to be extremely popular among the courts. Adopted by more than half of the states and influential, as well, in the federal system, the Second Restatement is by far the most popular choice-of-law regime in the country today.[6] The courts have added a final level of complexity with divergent interpretations of the Restatement's basic approach, some of which seem at odds with the intentions of the drafters.

Three basic elements define the choice–of–law approach of the Second Restatement: (1) § 6 and the most significant relationship, (2) a few grouping–of–contacts sections and (3) numerous sections that provide choice–of–law rules for specific legal claims and issues. These are the subject of subsections [c]–[e].

[c] Section 6 and The Most Significant Relationship

[1] Statutory Directive

Section 6 (1) uncontroversially directs a court to follow a statutory directive of its own state on choice of law. Although the subsection is uncontroversial, its range of application is fairly narrow, as statutory directives on choice of law are quite rare. As the comments suggest, "legislatures usually legislate. . .only with the local situation in mind." There are, however, a few exceptions; the Uniform Commercial Code, for example, contains choice–of–law provisions, as do many no-fault automobile accident compensation statutes.[7]

[2] The Most Significant Relationship

In the absence of a choice–of–law statute, § 6 (2) counsels a choice based on a series of factors that capture many of the themes of the choice–of–law revolution:[8]

(a) the needs of the interstate and international systems,

(b) the relevant policies of the forum,

(c) the relevant policies of other interested states and the relative interests of those states in the determination of the particular issue,

---

[6] *See* Symeon Symeonides, *Choice of Law in the American Courts in 2000: As the Century Turns,* 49 Am. J. Comp. L. 1 (2001).

[7] Restatement (Second) § 6, comment c.

[8] The drafters deliberately chose to list the factors in no particular order of importance and acknowledged that "varying weight will be given to a particular factor, or to a group of factors, in different areas of choice of law." *See* Restatement (Second) § 6, comment c. Although the list of factors first appeared in an article co-authored by the reporter for the Second Restatement, *see* Elliott E. Cheatham and Willis L. M. Reese, *Choice of the Applicable Law,* 52 Colum. L. Rev. 959, 962–981 (1952), it also reveals a debt to Professors Currie and Leflar, the several true-conflict-resolution devices, and even the First Restatement.

(d) the protection of justified expectations,

(e) the basic policies underlying the particular field of law,

(f) certainty, predictability and uniformity of result, and

(g) ease in the determination and application of the law to be applied.[9]

Section 6 (2) and the concept of the most significant relationship form the heart of the Restatement (Second). They appear in section after section, sometimes as a general residual choice–of–law directive to be used when no specific section applies (*e.g.*, § 145), sometimes as a check, such as a limit on party autonomy in contract (*e.g.*, § 187), and sometimes as an escape device used to avoid the irrational result of a presumptive reference section (*e.g.*, § 149, comment c).

The Restatement contains no explicit definition of the concept of "most significant relationship," but clearly implies that the state of the most significant relationship is the state whose law would be applied by a court committed to the choice–of–law Principles of § 6 (2).

[d] The Factors of § 6 (2)

[1] The Needs of The Interstate and International Systems

Although listed first, this factor may be the least important on the list for the resolution of individual conflicts cases. Comment d suggests that the goals here are "to further harmonious relations between states and to facilitate commercial intercourse between them."[10] Important to achieving these goals are choice–of–law rules that are likely to be adopted by most states and that further the values of certainty, predictability and uniformity of result. Judicial opinions rarely give strong consideration to this factor, and commentators, including the reporter for the Second Restatement acknowledge that, "it is difficult to see in the ordinary case how these needs would be affected by a decision one way or the other."[11]

[2] The Policy Analysis Factors

Factors (b) the relevant policies of the forum, (c) the relevant policies of other interested states and the relative interests of those states in the determination of the particular issue, and (e) the basic policies underlying the particular field of law reveal the Restatement's debt to Currie and the central place of interest analysis in the Restatement's choice–of–law methodology. So does the commentary of the drafters

[9] Restatement (Second) of Conflict of Laws § 6(2). Copyright © 1971 by the American Law Institute. Reprinted with the permission of the American Law Institute.

[10] Id. at comment d.

[11] Willis L. M. Reese, *The Second Restatement of Conflict of Laws Revisited*, 34 Mercer L. Rev. 501, 509 (1983). *See also* Michael S. Finch, *Choice–of–Law Problems in Florida Courts: A Retrospective on the Restatement (Second),* 24 Stetson L. Rev. 660, 653 (1995).

> The purpose sought to be achieved by the relevant tort rules of the interested states and the relation of these states to the occurrence and the parties, are important factors to be considered in determining the state of most significant relationship. This is because the interest of a state in having its. . .rule applied in the determination of a particular issue will depend upon the purpose sought to be achieved by that rule and by the relation of the state to the occurrence and the parties.[12]

The drafters intended factors (b) and (c) to incorporate not only the basics of interest analysis, but also some of its refinements, as well. Thus the comments show that the drafters also had in mind the true conflict resolution devices of comparative impairment and relative commitment.

> [T]he forum should give consideration. . . also to the relevant policies of all other interested states. The forum should seek to reach a result that will achieve the best possible accommodation of these policies. The forum should also appraise the relative interests of the states involved in the determination of the particular issue. In general, it is fitting that the state whose interests are most deeply affected should have its local law applied. . . .[13]

The inclusion of factor (e) (basic policies) also makes it clear that the drafters were familiar with and intended to incorporate much of the true conflict resolution literature. It explains the rule of validation used in the usury, rule against perpetuities, and statute of frauds sections. Professor Reese also remarks upon the role of this factor in tort cases, where the basic policy, compensation for the plaintiff, helps to explain the pro-plaintiff tendency of many modern tort choice–of–law decisions.[14]

[3] Factor d: The Protection of Justified Expectations

The drafters indicate that this factor is responsible for the party autonomy and validation provisions in the Restatement, but that it should have little impact on negligence issues.[15]

[4] Factor f: Certainty, Predictability and Uniformity of Result

The comment explaining this factor, reveals more than any other the conservative/revolutionary tension in the drafters:

> These are important values in all areas of the law. To the extent that they are attained in choice of law, forum shopping will be discouraged. These values can, however, be purchased at too great a price. In a rapidly developing area, such as choice of law, it is often more important that good rules be developed than that predictability and

[12] *Id.*, § 145, comment c.

[13] *Id.*, § 6, comment f.

[14] *See* Reese, *supra* note 9, at 513.

[15] *Id.* § 6, comment g. Note also that the protection of justified expectations has been used by some courts as a device for resolving true conflicts (*see* § 78, *infra*); the inclusion of this factor in the § 6 list suggests that the drafters approve this use of the concept.

uniformity of results should be assured through continued adherence to existing rules.[16]

[5] Factor g: Ease in the Determination and Application of the Law to Be Applied

Again tension is evident in this factor, but here the tension is between rule and approach,[17] a theme that recurrently occupied the Reporter.

> Ideally, choice of law rules should be simple and easy to apply. This policy should not be overemphasized, since it is obviously of greater importance that choice–of–law rules lead to desirable results. The policy does, however, provide a goal for which to strive.[18]

Oddly, the comments do not cite this factor as an explanation for the forum's use of its own procedural rules, but the connection is fairly obvious. It would be massively inconvenient, for example, for the forum to determine and apply foreign pleading and evidence rules whenever it adjudicated a claim based upon foreign law.

[e] The Specific Sections: A Wide Variety of Approaches

[1] Territorial Presumptions

The specific sections of the Second Restatement use a wide variety of choice–of–law strategies. Most, by far, are territorial references, although, they differ from the single contact, jurisdiction–selecting rules of the First Restatement in one significant respect. Nearly all are presumptive references that may be overcome by use of the most significant relationship device of § 6 and the grouping of contacts sections (§§ 145 and 188) to be discussed in the next subsection.

The strength of the presumption varies widely. In some cases, the presumption is nearly absolute. Thus nearly all issues of procedure and evidence,[19] except for limitations,[20] burden of proof,[21] and privilege[22] are referred to the law of the forum with no "most significant relationship" exception clause. Similarly, and much more controversially, the sections dealing with real property point absolutely to the law that would be applied by the courts of the situs,[23] and most of those dealing with the succession

[16] Id., comment i. The comment indicates that this factor helps to explain the validity and party autonomy rules as well as the decedent's–domicile rule for the distribution of movables, which is incorporated in §§ 260 and 263.

[17] Id., comment j.

[18] *See* Willis L. M. Reese, *Choice of Law: Rules or Approach*, 57 Cornell L. Rev. 315 (1972).

[19] Restatement (Second) §§ 122–133, 138.

[20] *Id.,* § 142 (1988).

[21] *Id.,* §§ 133, 134.

[22] *Id.,* § 139.

[23] *Id.,* §§ 223–240.

on death of personal property refer, without an exception clause, to the law that would be applied by the courts of decedent's domicile.[24]

The language of other sections reveals less confidence in the presumptive reference. Thus for many types of tort claims[25] and for many types of contracts,[26] the Second Restatement refers to a particular territorial contact, "unless, with respect to the particular issue, some other state has a more significant relationship under the principles stated in § 6" to the claim and the parties. Sections treating particular contract and tort issues are even more tentative, suggesting only that the supplied territorial reference will "usually" control.[27]

Finally some sections include no presumptive territorial reference at all, referring instead to the appropriate general grouping–of–contacts section, which, of course, incorporates by reference the choice–of–law principles of § 6.[28]

[2] Non-Territorial Sections

In addition to its territorial presumptive references, the Second Restatement also uses other choice–of–law methodologies in several of its specific sections. Party autonomy figures importantly in the Restatement provisions governing consensual, planned transactions.[29] Thus, the drafters give the parties total control over the construction of wills,[30] trusts,[31] and

[24] *Id.*, §§ 260, 263.

[25] *See, e.g., id.*, §§ (§§ 146, 147, 152, 154, 155, 175).

[26] *See, e.g., id.*, §§ 189–197. The substantive law has changed in the decades since the Restatement was drafted, and some of the presumptive choices no doubt would be different today. Joseph William Singer, *A Pragmatic Guide to Conflicts*, 70 B.U. L. Rev. 731, 736 (1990). Others, however, have stood the test of time and have become the nearly universal solution to the problem they address. *See, e.g.* §§ 192, 193 (contracts of insurance referred to the law of the place that the parties understood to be the principle location of the risk). *See* William Richman and William Reynolds, *Prologomenon to an Empirical Restatement of Conflicts,* 75 Ind. L. J. 417, 433 (2000).

[27] *See, e.g.,id.*, §§ 156–160, 164–166, 169, 172, 198, 199. The use of the most significant relationship device builds flexibility into the system, providing an honest escape device for judges by giving them the opportunity to select another law without the need to disguise the fact that they are doing so. This method of escaping from the presumptive choices has a great advantage over the escape devices employed under the vested rights theory. Although the most significant relationship standard may lead to some ad hoc decision making, at least a judge who "escapes" by using that standard must justify her decision in terms of the framework provided by the Restatement.

[28] *See, e.g.*, §§ 145,175, 188. For more discussion of the Restatement's territotial presumptions, see Symeon C. Symeonides, *Exception Clauses in American Conflicts Law,* 42 Am. J. Comp. L. 601 (1994), Jeffrey M. Shaman, *The Vicissitudes of Choice of Law: The Restatement (First, Second) and Interest Analysis,* 45 Buff. L. Rev. 329, 357–358 (1997).

[29] On the party autonomy provisions, *see* Larry Kramer, *Choice of Law in the American Courts in 1990: Trends and Developments*, 39 Am. J. Comp. L. 465 (1991); Andreas Lowenfeld, *"Tempora Mutantur. . ." — Wills and Trusts in the Conflicts Restatement*, 72 Colum. L. Rev. 382 (1972).

[30] *Id.*, § 268.

[31] *Id.*, §§ 269, 271, 272, 277.

contracts,[32] and substantial control over the validity of contracts,[33] and inter vivos trusts of movables.[34]

Substantivism — choosing law by the result that it produces — informs at least a few specific sections of the Restatement.[35] The clearest examples are the validating provisions affecting usurious contracts,[36] powers of appointment,[37] testamentary trusts,[38] foreign incorporations,[39] and contract formalities.[40] Another example is § 139, which provides for the admission into evidence of a communication if it is admissible according to the privilege law of either the forum or the state that has the most significant relationship with the communication.[41]

Finally, a few of the specific sections of the Second Restatement are purely interest-analytic. The best examples are the sections on presumptions,[42] as well as those on burdens of production and persuasion,[43] which refer to the law of the forum "unless the primary purpose of the relevant rule of the state of the otherwise applicable law is to affect decision of the issue rather than to regulate the conduct of the trial."

[f] The Grouping-of-Contacts Sections:

The grouping-of-contacts sections, §§ 145 (2) and 188 (2), serve a residual function; thus when an issue or a claim in tort is not treated by a specific choice–of–law directive, the forum should resort to the general rule of § 145.

The early drafts of these sections, are the lineal descendants of the "center of gravity" opinions that appeared early in the choice–of–law revolution, especially in New York.[44] Later drafts, however, incorporated the insights

---

[32] *Id.* § 187(1).

[33] *Id.* § 187(2).

[34] *Id.* § 270.

[35] On substantivism as a choice–of–law strategy, *see* Gene Shreve, A Conflict–of–Laws Anthology 139–152 (1997).

[36] *Id.*, § 203.

[37] *Id.*, § 274.

[38] *Id.*, § 269(b)(ii).

[39] *Id.*, § 297.

[40] *Id.* § 199.

[41] *Id.*, § 139.

[42] *Id.* § 134.

[43] *Id.* §§ 133, 134.

[44] *See* § 70, *supra*. That approach, which dominated the early drafts of the Second Restatement, is vulnerable to two fundamental criticisms. *See* Michael S. Finch, *Choice–of–Law Problems in Florida Courts: A Retrospective on the Restatement (Second),* 24 Stetson L. Rev. 653, 656 (1995). First, like the hard–and–fast rules of the First Restatement, it is jurisdiction-selecting; it does not take into account the contents of the competing internal rules. Second, it offers no way of measuring the significance of contacts, and, without a measure of significance, the center of gravity system amounts to little more than contract counting. *See* Jeffrey M. Shaman, *The Vicissitudes of Choice of Law: The Restatement (First, Second) and Interest Analysis,* 45 Buff. L. Rev. 329, 359 (1997).

of interest analysis and provide a greater role for policy analysis than did the center of gravity method. Thus, the final version of § 145 calls for application of the law of "the state which. . . has the most significant relationship to the occurrence and the parties under the principles stated in § 6."[45] Correspondingly, the role of the enumerated contacts is diminished; they are simply "to be *taken into account* [emphasis added] in applying the principles of § 6."[46]

[g] Applying the Second Restatement: The Drafters' Intent

The Restatement gives no explicit directions on how its several disparate elements should be combined into a single choice–of–law methodology. More careful scrutiny, however, reveals what the drafters probably had in mind. In the absence of a statutory choice–of–law directive, a court should determine first whether a specific section covers the issue or claim before it. Most of the specific sections will be presumptive territorial references, but some will use other choice–of–law techniques.[47] Nearly all, however, will include some reference to § 6 and perhaps to one of the grouping–of–contacts sections, as well. If no specific section covers the issue or claim, the court should refer to the general grouping–of–contacts sections, which also include a reference to § 6. Thus, with either the specific sections or the general grouping–of–contacts sections, eventually the court will need to apply the factors of § 6(2).

Section 6 (2)(b) and (c) clearly contemplate performing some sort of interest analysis. Presumably if that analysis indicates a false conflict, the court should apply the law of the only interested state. If the case is a non–false conflict, the court should use the factors of § 6(2)(d)–(g) to resolve the true conflict or unprovided–for case. In no event, however, should the court use the grouping–of–contacts sections to justify a center–of–gravity or contact–counting approach. The contacts enumerated in the grouping–of–contacts sections have no independent significance and are relevant only insofar as they implicate the factors of § 6(2).

Even the early drafts of the grouping–of–contacts sections, however, went beyond the simple contact counting of the "center–of–gravity" approach; thus an early version of § 145 provided that "in determining the relative importance of the [enumerated] contacts, the forum will consider the issues, the character of the tort and the relevant purposes of the tort rules involved." Restatement (Second) of Conflict of Laws § 379 (Tent Draft No. 8, 1963). While not extremely specific, this provision at least injected content and policy analysis into the calculation.

[45] Restatement (Second) § 6.

[46] Comment (e) to § 145 demotes the contacts to mere presumptions, thus making the relative importance of policy analysis compared to contact enumeration even more clear:

> In applying the principles of § 6 to determine the state of most significant relationship, the forum should give consideration to the relevant policies of all potentially interested states and the relevant interests of those states in the decision of the particular issue. Those states which are most likely to be interested are those which have one or more of the following contacts with the occurrence and the parties.

[47] *See* subsection [e], *supra*.

[h] A Note on Escape Devices

The flexibility inherent in the most significant relationship test means that the escape devices so commonly employed under the vested rights theory have become more or less obsolete — at least for those who play the game by the rules of the Second Restatement. Renvoi plays but a small role in the Second Restatement; although the concept is generally available when uniformity of result is the goal, it is relegated to service in only a few areas.[48] Substance/procedure is a game which also has a reduced role because the focus has been shifted away from mechanical labeling and toward analysis of the policies (especially the forum's interest in judicial administration) that are involved with respect to each issue in the case.[49] Characterization, in general, still enjoys a significant status because the presumptive jurisdiction–selecting rules of the Restatement are organized by subject matter, an organization which necessarily requires characterization. At times, of course, selection of the correct label can be difficult, but the Restatement provides a partial solution to the problem by eliminating presumptive rules in some areas where characterization might be problematic. Vicarious liability, for example, has elements of tort, contract, and status, a combination which makes it an extremely difficult problem to characterize. The Restatement finesses the issue by referring vicarious liability questions to the law of the state with the most significant relationship to the issue.[50] That reference, of course, does not eliminate the problem, but at least rids it of the characterization overtones.

Public policy is the only escape device that retains a prominent role in the 1971 Restatement. Professor Reese and his Advisers, however, transformed it from a clumsy, post–hoc trump card into one of the general considerations of § 6. That treatment of public policy still leaves a good deal to the judge's discretion, but a stricter approach would probably do little except to drive the public policy consideration underground once again.

§ 72 The Second Restatement in the Courts

[a] Dominance

The Second Restatement is the dominant conflicts methodology in American courts today.[1] Twenty-two jurisdictions follow the Restatement's approach in tort conflicts, and twenty-four do so in contract cases.[2] Additionally several other jurisdictions follow the similar "significant contacts"

[48] *Id.* § 8(2). *See also* § 59, *supra.*

[49] *See also* § 58, *supra.*

[50] Restatement (Second) of Conflict of Laws § 174.

[1] *See* Patrick J. Borchers, *Courts and the Second Conflicts Restatement: Some Observations and an Empirical Note*, 56 Md. L. Rev. 1233, 1234 (1997), William L. Reynolds, *Legal Process and Choice of Law*, 56 Md. L. Rev. 1376, 1395 (1997).

[2] *See* Symeon Symeonides, *Choice of Law in the American Courts in 2000: As the Century Turns,* 49 Am. J. Comp. L. 1 (2001).

approach thus yielding a majority of American jurisdictions.[3] The next most popular American choice–of–law methodology, the traditional First Restatement approach, can claim less than half as many adherents.[4]

[b] Use and Abuse

The numerical count of jurisdictions that have adopted the Second Restatement may overstate somewhat its victory in the courts. As indicated in § 70, the Restatement adopts a layered approach that amalgamates much modern choice–of–law thinking as well as many traditional territorial presumptions. Further, the interaction of the presumptive references, the grouping–of–contacts sections, and the principles of § 6 is subtle and easy to misinterpret. A court that misunderstands the relationship among the three central elements might well believe that it has "adopted" the Second Restatement yet apply a very different, less sophisticated choice–of–law methodology.

Thus decisions in nominally Second Restatement jurisdictions often fail to identify the policies behind the competing states' laws, or even to identify the content of those states laws. Given these omissions, such a court, of course, has no hope of determining whether the case is a true or false conflict. Further some courts read § 6 to require only a "weighing" of state interests and rely heavily on the grouping of contacts sections to decide by crude contact counting.[5]

---

[3] *Id.* Even these numbers, however, understate the influence of the Second Restatement. Many federal courts use the Second Restatement in federal question cases, and several jurisdictions that follow other choice–of–law methodologies nevertheless use particular sections of the Restatement (Second). Thus, New York typically uses the "center–of–gravity" approach, but nevertheless follows § 188 in some contract cases. *Allstate Ins. Co. v. Stolarz*, 613 N.E.2d 936, 939 (N.Y. 1993). Likewise, many states that still use the traditional First Restatement system have adopted Restatement (Second) §§ 187, 193, and 203 to resolve party autonomy, insurance, and usury cases respectively. William M. Richman and David Riley, *The First Restatement of Conflict of Laws on the Twenty–fifth Anniversary of its Successor: Contemporary Practice on Traditional Courts*, 56 Md. L. Rev. 1196 1213–1217, 1226.

[4] *Richman and Riley, supra* note 3, at 1201. For speculation on the reasons for the Second Restatement's popularity, *see Symeonides, supra* note 1, at 1269–1277 ("it provides the judge with virtually unlimited discretion, does not require hard thinking,. . . . is not ideologically 'loaded,'. . . .is a complete 'system,'. . . . carries the prestige of the American Law Institute,. . . . and has 'momentum'."), *Borchers, supra* note 1, at 1233 (attributing the Restatement's popularity to its open–ended general provisions (§§ 6, 145, 188) as opposed to its many specific territorial jurisdiction–selecting sections, which, he claims, many courts ignore), *Reynolds, supra* note 1, at 1393, 1395 (user–friendly and well–written and with flexibility that guides decisions rather than controlling them, thus permitting the courts to avoid unjust results, compatible with the legal process tradition, in which most contemporary judges were trained). *See also* Harold G. Maier, *Finding the Trees In Spite of the Metaphorist: The Problem of State Interests in Choice of Law*, 56 Alb. L. Rev. 753, 771 (1993).

[5] A textbook example of each of these errors is Nationwide Mutual Ins. Co. v. Black, 656 N.E. 2d 1352 (1995). Rooted in an automobile accident in Ontario, the case was a subrogation claim by Nationwide, an Ohio corporation that insured Kay and William Black (both residents of Ohio) against an Ohio driver, Ruby Black, and her insurer State Farm (an Illinois corporation qualified to do business in Ohio). The court identified the content but not the motivating policies of Ohio's tort rule and Ontario's no–fault scheme and failed even to identify the content of the law of Illinois. Having failed to perform that most obvious preliminary step,

Abuse and misuse of the subtleties of the Second Restatement is not, however, ubiquitous. Other courts conscientiously locate the contacts in the grouping of contacts sections and then use the § 6 factors to perform an interest analysis. Thus they identify the policies behind the competing states' laws, classify the case as a false conflict, true conflict or unprovided–for case, and use the additional factors of § 6 to resolve non-false conflicts.[6]

Some of the fault for obtuse judicial interpretations belongs to the drafters of the Second Restatement. While § 6 requires an interest analysis, it does not do so in very explicit language, nor do the comments. Further, the comments *do* contain some language that easily can mislead an unsophisticated court. A frequently–quoted example is a hypothetical in the comments to § 146 that gives some courts the impression that they should override the place–of–injury rule only in cases where the parties stray unintentionally into the place of injury, whereas the principles of § 6 clearly justify the override in an ordinary, garden–variety false conflict.[7]

[c] Specific Versus General: In Practice

Another issue that has emerged in the interpretation of the Second Restatement is the role of the specific territorial presumptions. As indicated in § 70, the drafters intended that the court's choice–of–law calculation begin with the specific territorial presumptions, where applicable, and then proceed to the "most significant relationship" analysis under § 6 and the grouping–of–contacts sections. One might expect judges familiar with the traditional territorial system to be over–deferential to the presumptive references and reluctant to engage in the more free–form process required by § 6.

---

the court missed what was almost certainly a false conflict. Instead the court cited an inapposite Ohio Supreme Court case involving a defendant from a no–fault state and a plaintiff from a tort state. In that true conflict, the court had applied the law of the place of injury, and the *Black* court mistakenly read the decision as controlling the false conflict it faced.

Ignoring the guidance of § 6, the court said:

> In the case sub judice, Ontario could likely advance as many policy reasons for its no–fault insurance law as Ohio could for its fault–based system. Essentially, these considerations offset one another. Even when applying the law of another state would be contrary to the public policy of Ohio, Ohio law is not to be applied unless Ohio has a significantly greater interest in having its law applied.

[6] *See, e.g.,* Esser v. Mcintyre, 661 N.E.2d 1138 (1996) (departing from the place-of-injury rule of § 146 because the case was a common-domicile false conflict — the plaintiff and defendant from Illinois, injury in Mexico). Reviewing too many *Black*–style debacles and too-few *Esser*–style opinions easily could cause a Restatement critic to agree with Professor Kramer's recent remark, "one needs to read a lot of opinions in a single sitting fully to appreciate just how badly the Second Restatement works in practice." Larry Kramer, *Choice of Law in the American Courts in 1990: Trends and Developments*, 39 Am. J. Comp. L. 465, 486–487 (1990).

[7] On the unfortunate choice of this example, *see* Russell J. Weintraub, *"At Least, To Do No Harm": Does the Second Restatement of Conflicts Meet the Hippocratic Standard?* 56 Md. L. Rev. 1285, 1290 (1997). The court in *Black,* never missing an opportunity to misread the Restatement, relied heavily on the ill–chosen hypothetical.

In fact, however, the opposite approach seems to prevail. There is now some evidence that many Second Restatement courts skip the initial presumptive reference and proceed directly to the "most significant relationship" analysis. The evidence for this counter–intuitive development is a citation study conducted by Professor Borchers. He found in tort and contract cases that the citations to §§ 145 and 188 significantly outnumbered the total of citations to all the presumptive–reference sections combined.[8] Thus, he concludes:

> Over time, the Second Restatement has become something different from the document it appears to be. Even the courts that claim to adhere to the Second Restatement most likely do not look at it very often. . . . Instead, courts and the attorneys practicing before them look to cases quoting sections 6, 145, 188, or some of the other popular provisions. They content themselves with block quotations of those general sections and then proceed to solve the choice–of–law problem, considering only that general section. For judges and lawyers, the Second Restatement exists not as a handsome, two–volume book authored by the American Law Institute, but rather as a kind of chain letter consisting of selective block quotations.[9]

§ 73 The Second Restatement: Torts[1]

[a] Structure and Theory

[1] The Most Significant Relationship

Chapter 7 of the Second Restatement, denominated "Wrongs", contains one general grouping–of–contacts section for torts (§ 145) ten sections treating particular torts,[2] and twenty sections treating particular issues in tort cases.[3] Following the now familiar pattern, § 145 (1) calls for

[8] *Borchers, supra* note 1, at 1247–1249.

[9] *Id.* at 1249.

[1] *See generally* Robert A. Leflar, *The Torts Provisions of the Restatement (Second),* 72 Colum. L. Rev. 267 (1972).

[2] Restatement (Second) §§ 146–155. The defamation rules are perhaps the most interesting of the sections addressing specific problems, because the choice–of–law difficulties in a multi–state defamation action can be enormous. The initial focus is on the state of publication because that is where the harm to reputation (the interest protected by the defamation action) is most likely to occur. *Id.* § 149, comment c. When the publication is multi–state, the Second Restatement tracks the "single publication" rule of § 577A of the Restatement (Second) of Torts, which permits recovery in a single action for all harm done to the plaintiff, and treats the plaintiff as having but one cause of action even though the defamatory material has been distributed in several states. *Id.* § 150, comment c. Section 150 of the Restatement selects the domicile of natural persons and the principal place of business of corporations as the state whose law most likely will be applied. *Id.* 150. The Restatement approach to this problem is generally sound because it correlates the popular single publication rule with a plausible territorial answer to the choice–of–law problem.

[3] *Id.* §§ 156–174.

application of the law of the state of the most significant relationship, referring to § 6, and § 145(2) lists a group of contacts that will typically be relevant in tort cases.

(a) the place where the injury occurred,

(b) the place where the conduct causing the injury occurred,

(c) the domicil, residence, nationality, place of incorporation and place of business of the parties, and

(d) the place where the relationship, if any, between the parties is centered.

These contacts are to be evaluated according to their relative importance with respect to the particular issue.[4]

The combination of § 6 and § 145 gives a court a great deal of maneuvering room. The factors listed in § 6 direct attention to general policy concerns which should be considered in selecting a law, while § 145 focuses on contacts more directly related to tort problems. This combination of policy analysis and something resembling the old center of gravity test has proven popular.[5]

Further enhancing the popularity of the Restatement approach is the presence of over thirty sections addressing the specific types of torts and specific tort issues.

[2] Types of Torts

For most torts, the Restatement calls for the law of the place of injury "unless. . .some other state has a more significant relationship under the principles stated in § 6 to the occurrence and the parties. . . ."[6] That rebuttable presumption, for example, applies to personal injuries (§ 146), injuries to personal property (§ 147), and all sections dealing with wrongful death (§§ 175–180). Application of the place–of–injury presumption results in a reference to the law of the place of publication in single–state defamation (§ 149), invasion of privacy (§ 152), and injurious falsehood (§ 151)

---

[5] The presumptive selections have the advantage of focusing the court on the place which typically will have the greatest interest in the solution of the problem. The combination of these presumptive references with policy analysis helps to explain the popularity of the Restatement with the courts. Both are helpful to courts, the vast majority of which decide only a few choice–of–law cases every decade. Professor Kay, for example, writing a quarter century after the choice–of–law revolution had begun, found no "modern" cases in either Nevada or Montana. Herma H. Kay, *Theory into Practice: Choice of Law in the American Courts*, 34 Mercer L. Rev. 521 (1983). This paucity of decisional law, in an area where there are an enormous number of variables, necessarily leads to fragmented and inconsistent decision–making. The Restatement meets the judges' needs by giving them guidance (through the factors enumerated in § 6 and § 145), without artificially controlling their decision–making. To put the matter differently, the Restatement permits the court to combine the policy probing of interest analysis with a reassuring presumptive reference reminiscent of the territorial theory.

[6] *See* Robert A. Leflar, *The Torts Provisions of the Restatement (Second)*, 72 Colum. L. Rev. 266, 267 (1972).

cases; and in abuse of process cases (§ 155) to the law of the place where the proceeding occurred.

In fraud cases (§ 148), the presumption applies only when the place of the defendant's representation and the plaintiff's reliance is the same; otherwise, a grouping–of–contacts/most–significant–relationship provision controls. The place–of–injury presumption does not apply to three torts. In multi–state defamation (§ 150), invasion of privacy (§ 153), and injurious falsehood (§ 151) cases, the reference is to the plaintiff's domicile; and in interference with the marriage relationship (§ 154), the place of the defendant's conduct presumptively controls.

[3] Tort Issues

The place–of–injury presumption is weaker in the sections dealing with particular tort issues. For many issues, it does not operate at all; and the reference is simply to the rule of § 145, which thus controls defenses (§ 161), duty or privilege to act (§ 163), survival of actions (§ 167), charitable immunity (§ 168), damages (§ 171), contribution and indemnity (§ 173), and vicarious liability (§ 174).

In other sections, the place–of–injury presumption applies, but only weakly; these sections refer to the general rule of § 145 and merely *advise* that the choice will "usually" be the law of the place of injury. *See* § 156 (tortious character of conduct), § 157 (standard of care), § 158 (interest entitled to legal protection), § 159 (duty owed plaintiff), § 160 (legal cause), § 162 (conditions of liability), § 163 (duty or privilege to act), § 164 (contributory fault), § 165 (assumption of risk), § 166 (imputed negligence), § 170 (release or covenant not to sue), and § 172 (joint torts). For one issue, intra–family immunity, § 169 refers to the general rule of § 145, but advises that the "usually" applicable law will be that of the parties' domicile, rather than the place of injury.

[4] The Importance of the Place of Injury

A major controversy during the drafting of the torts provisions of the Second Restatement concerned the dominance of the place of injury rule. The Introductory Note to the Chapter explicitly abandons the vested rights approach and the last event rule, and one of the drafters believed that the most notable feature of the chapter is its abandonment of the place of injury rule.6 Nevertheless, the place of injury is still, by far, the most common territorial reference, appearing in 21 out of 35 sections, thus leading Professor Leflar to remark that it "hovers like a ghost over the entire chapter."[7] The Reporter for the Second Restatement offered this rationale for the place–of–injury presumption:

> To ignore the significance of territoriality is to ignore the basic reason for the existence of choice of law. Whether we like it or not, the world is composed of many states, each having its own system

[7] *Id.* at 269.

> of law, and it is customary for persons to travel freely from state to state. . . . The purpose of choice of law. . . is to provide a solution for the problems that inevitably arise. People naturally think in terms of territoriality, and so have the courts. To ignore its significance is to turn one's back on the past and to ignore a vital factor that underlies the field.[8]

Whether the presumption produces unfortunate results in the courts, depends upon how hard it is to rebut.[9] A more sensible approach would be to apply the presumption only in non-false conflict cases, using interest analysis to resolve false conflicts.[10] There is ample justification for such a strategy in the comments, which clearly incorporate interest analysis:

> In large part, the answer to this question [whether the presumption is rebutted] will depend upon whether some other state has a greater interest in the determination of the particular issue than the state where the injury occurred. The extent of the interest of each of the potentially interested states should be determined on the basis, among other things, of the purpose sought to be achieved by their relevant local law rules. . . .[11]

However, the comments also contain language supporting the less sensible strategy of trying to identify particular factual patterns that will and will not support the place of injury presumption. Comment d to § 146 unwisely adopts this approach by maintaining that the place of injury rule usually will apply when defendant's conduct and plaintiff's injury occur in the same state.[12] Worse, the comment suggests that the only exceptions will occur in truly unusual circumstances. (The example supplied is an airplane traveling from one point in state X to another point in state X, which passes briefly through the airspace of State Y. Over state Y, the pilot's negligence causes plaintiff, a passenger, severe fright and shock.)[13]

Unfortunately, however the common–place–of–conduct–and–injury rule will produce irrational results in a host of cases that are much more ordinary than the cited hypothetical. *Babcock v. Jackson*[14] is a classic

---

[8] Willis L. M. Reese, *The Second Restatement of Conflict of Laws Revisited*, 34 Mercer L. Rev. 501, 514 (1983). Comment c to Restatement (Second) § 146 (which applies the place–of–injury presumption to personal injuries) offers the additional rationale that it furthers the § 6 choice–of–law values of certainty, predictability, uniformity of result and, ease of application.

[9] *See* Michael S. Finch, *Choice–of–Law Problems in Florida Courts: A Retrospective on the Restatement (Second)*, 24 Stetson L. Rev. 653, 669 (1995).

[10] *See id.* at 669, Harold P. Southerland, *A Screaming Comes Across the Sky—Tort Choice–of–Law Doctrine in Florida Under the Second Restatement of Conflicts*, 40 Mercer L. Rev. 781, 800 (1989).

[11] Restatement (Second) § 146, comment c.

[12] *Id.*, comment d.

[13] *Id.*

[14] 12 N.Y.2d 473, 191 N.E.2d 279, 240 N.Y.S.2d 743 (1963). See § 78, *infra*.

example, as is any other common–domicile–false–conflict, where the conduct and injury occur in the non–domiciliary state.[15]

[b] Practice

When the laws of all states having contacts with a problem are identical, the Restatement provides that no conflict exists, and the case should be treated, for choice–of–law purposes, as if the contacts were grouped in a single state.[16] If the laws of at least two states do conflict, then the procedure is to apply the Restatement section addressing the specific problem (if there is one). Two cases illustrate the proper application of the presumptive reference and the check provided by the most significant relationship test.

The first, *Gordon v. Kramer*,[17] presents a very simple guest statute problem. Plaintiff and defendant, both Arizona residents, left that state on a vacation in a car driven by defendant.[18] The car crashed in Utah, injuring plaintiff. She sued in Arizona, and defendant pled the Utah guest statute in defense. The opinion began by noting that the law of the place of injury (here Utah) should be applied,[19] unless some other state had a more significant relationship to the liability question. The court then examined § 6 and § 145 to determine whether Arizona was such a state. The court discounted the tests of predictability and certainty as having little relevance in tort law; it also determined that ease of judicial administration was unimportant because the law of each state could easily be applied. The relevant factors for analysis were the basic policies underlying tort law; the court identified those as deterrence and compensation — purposes "not furthered by guest statutes." The court completed its analysis by comparing the relevant policies of the two states, as reflected in their liability laws, and evaluated those policies in terms of the interests each state had in seeing its law applied. The opinion concluded that Utah had "no interest"

---

[15] *See* Russell J. Weintraub, *"At Least To Do No Harm": Does the Second Restatement Meet the Hippocratic Standard?,* 56 Md. L. Rev. 1285, 1290 (1997). The limited available empirical evidence suggests that Second Restatement courts do not rely very heavily on the place–of–injury presumption. Professor Borchers examined over 800 trial and appellate tort choice–of–law cases decided after 1960. He then compared decisions by courts using the two Restatements, interest analysis, and Leflar's system according to three parameters: the extent to which the decisions (1) chose forum law, (2) favored recovery, and (3) favored forum residents. The results for courts using the three modern systems were statistically indistinguishable, but differed substantially from the results for courts using the First Restatement. *See* Patrick J. Borchers, *The Choice–of–Law Revolution: An Empirical Study*, 49 Wash. & Lee L. Rev. 357, 377–8 (1992). This suggests that courts using the Second Restatement were no more likely to defer to the territorial presumption than were courts using the other modern methods. It also suggests that the "hovering ghost" of the place–of–injury rule has not exerted the control over Second Restatement courts that the Restatement's critics feared it would.

[16] *Id.*, § 145, comment i. This, of course, refers to a "false conflict," discussed in § 78, *infra.*

[17] 124 Ariz. 442, 604 P.2d 1153 (1979).

[18] The court found it irrelevant that the car was garaged and insured in North Dakota, a state whose guest statute had been declared unconstitutional.

[19] *See* Restatement (Second) of Conflict of Laws § 146.

in having its law applied to the case, and hence the presumptive selection of the law of the place of injury had been overcome.

A somewhat more difficult problem is presented by *Johnson v. Spider Staging Corp.*,[20] a wrongful death action arising out of the collapse of a scaffold. The scaffold had been manufactured and sold in Washington; it collapsed in Kansas, the residence of plaintiff's decedent. The substantive issue was whether the Kansas limitation on recovery in a wrongful death action ($50,000) should be applied. The Washington court noted that § 175, the Second Restatement's wrongful death section, refers to the state most interested in the problem and requires examination of "the purpose sought to be achieved by [the] relevant local law rules."[21]

The court listed all of the contacts each state had with the transaction,[22] and noted that its job was "not merely to count contacts, but rather to consider which contacts were most significant." That step required analysis of the purposes behind the limitation on wrongful death damages, which the court found to be both protection of defendants from excessive financial burdens and speculative claims, and avoidance of difficult computation issues. Neither of those purposes applied in the case at bar because the limitation state was neither the forum nor defendants' residence; therefore, those purposes would not be furthered by applying the Kansas limitation on recovery. Moreover, the court found that the forum's policy of deterrence would be furthered by unlimited recovery.[23] Hence, Washington's law of unlimited recovery should be applied.

Gordon and *Johnson* are more or less typical of the better[24] decisions following the new Restatement. Both take a qualitative — as well as quantitative — look at contacts; both also use the references to policies in § 6 to inquire into the interests of the involved states, perhaps to a greater degree than originally foreseen. Nevertheless, in neither case does the decision–making reflect the potential lack of discipline that so worried the critics of the Restatement. Use of the Restatement, in other words, led to sound decisions.

---

[20] 87 Wash.2d 577, 555 P.2d 997 (1976).

[21] Restatement (Second) of Conflict of Laws § 175, comment d.

[22] The list included several contacts not mentioned in either § 6 or § 145 (*e.g.*, the place of shipping).

[23] The case presented, therefore, a false conflict.

[24] *See also* Esser v. Mcintyre, 661 N.E.2d 1138 (1996). Unfortunately, there are also abysmal examples of courts misusing the second Restatement to produce dysfunctional results. *See, e.g.*, Nationwide Mutual Ins. Co. v. Black, 656 N.E. 2d 1352 (1995). Both cases are discussed in § 72 [b], *supra*.

§ 74 The Second Restatement: Contracts[1]

[a] Structure of the Chapter

The Contracts chapter (Chapter Eight) of the Second Restatement resembles the torts chapter in structure. Like the torts chapter it frees the courts from the iron grip of tradition (in this case, the place–of–making rule). Instead, it contains, as might be expected, a general grouping–of–contacts section (§ 188) providing that (absent a choice–of–law clause) the controlling law is the "local law of the state which, with respect to that issue, has the most significant relationship. . .under the principles stated in § 6."[2] Section 188(2) then lists several factors peculiar to contract law that will help inform the § 6 choice.[3] Also like the torts chapter, the contracts provisions contain numerous presumptive references for particular types of contracts[4] and particular contract issues.[5] It also contains some substantivist provisions[6] as well as a massive departure from the First Restatement in the form of a strong commitment to party autonomy.[7]

[b] Party Autonomy

Section 187 provides that the parties can choose the law to govern "rights and duties" arising under the contract. Proponents of the vested rights theory did not like what we now call "party–autonomy": They believed that only the sovereign could convert the morally binding agreement into a legally enforceable "contract."[8] That kind of reasoning is, of course, inherently circular. A state, constrained only by the Constitution, can, if it wishes, make any promise binding. Thus, it can always choose to apply the law chosen by the parties to govern their agreement. Even before the promulgation of the First Restatement, an impressive array of case law had developed supporting the proposition that the proper choice of law in a contract case was the law that conformed with the parties' intentions.

[1] Background

The leading cases are *Pritchard v. Norton*[9] and *Siegelman v. Cunard White Star, Ltd.*[10] The Court in *Pritchard,* a suit against a surety, ignored

---

[1] *See generally* Robert Allen Sedler, *The Contracts Provisions of the Restatement (Second): An Analysis and a Critique,* 72 Colum. L. Rev. 279 (1972).

[2] Restatement (Second) § 188(1).

[3] *Id.*, § 188(2)

[4] *Id.* §§ 189–197.

[5] *Id.*, §§ 198–207.

[6] *See, e.g., id.*, § 203.

[7] *Id.*, § 187.

[8] *See* § 66, *supra.*

[9] 106 U.S. 124 (1882). *Pritchard* also is an example of substantivism, the choice of a law based on its substantive content, in that the decision favors the rule of validation.

[10] 221 F.2d 189 (2d Cir. 1955).

the law of the place of making (New York), where the contract was invalid (because it was not supported by consideration), and applied Louisiana law, where performance was to occur and where the agreement was binding. The Court reasoned in part that, although the contract had no express choice–of–law clause, "the obligation was entered into in view of the laws of Louisiana"; hence, it made an implied reference to Louisiana law. *Siegelman* upheld a provision designating English law for resolving questions concerning a "contract" (actually a ticket for passage) entered into by passengers on the *Queen Elizabeth*. The court went so far as to apply English law to the issue of whether a contractual provision had been waived, even though all acts relevant to the waiver had occurred in New York.

Siegelman and *Pritchard* illustrate what is sometimes called the Rule of Validation: Courts will strive to uphold the validity of contracts in choice–of–law cases. Both cases also support the notion of party autonomy (albeit implied in *Pritchard*), the policy from which § 187 is drawn.[11]

[2] Section 187(1)

Section 187 provides that the law chosen by the parties will be applied if the issue is one that could have been resolved by an express provision in the contract.[12] Properly speaking, § 187 does not specify a choice–of–law rule at all; rather, like *Pritchard* and *Siegelman,* § 187 provides a means by which the parties may incorporate by reference certain provisions from foreign law into their agreement.[13] An example would be a clause defining a particular term in accordance with the law of a designated state. In considering a choice–of–law provision, therefore, the first issue to address is whether under local law the issue is one which can be left in the control of the parties. If it is, it should not matter that they have expressed their intention on the issue in shorthand by incorporating foreign law instead of by including specific contractual language on that point. Incorporation by reference in those circumstances does not differ from any other form of drafting; if the included terms are otherwise permissible in the contract, the forum should not object merely because the parties' expression of the term took the form of reference to foreign law. Interpretation of contractual language, in other words, is what § 187(1) permits; and interpretation, no matter what form it takes, can always be controlled by the parties to the contract.[14]

---

[11] Party autonomy is also promoted by the general choice–of–law provision of the Uniform Commercial Code, § 1–105. *See* § 92, *infra.*

[12] Restatement (Second) of Conflict of Laws § 187(1).

[13] *Id.* comment c.

[14] There is one important difference between the provisions of § 187 and the holding of *Pritchard. Pritchard* inferred a reference to Louisiana law from the factual setting of the case; § 187, however, requires that the reference be "explicit." Hence, the Restatement does not really provide a rule of validation. To be sure, party autonomy is likely to validate an agreement, but the Restatement does not resort to implied intent to discern a law chosen by the parties, as the Court did in *Pritchard.*

[3] Section 187(2)

Section 187 also permits the parties to choose foreign law in circumstances that extend beyond its incorporation by reference for purposes of interpretation and construction. Thus, even if the issue is one which under forum law could not have been controlled by an express provision in the contract, the parties still may be able to choose the law which governs their agreement. There are two limits on their ability to choose: First, either the state whose law is chosen must have a "substantial" relation to the issue or else there must be some other reasonable basis for the parties' choice. Second, the designation will not be given effect if it would be "contrary to a fundamental policy" of another jurisdiction having "a materially greater interest than the chosen state in the determination of the particular issue," if that state would be the state with the most significant relationship on that issue. These limits are important, and their application can be difficult.

(i) *Express term not permitted.* Party autonomy partly hinges on the contract term which is referred to foreign law. Provisions that deal with construction, interpretation, quality of performance, and the like generally can be controlled by the parties.[15] Terms dealing with those kinds of problems are directly related to party expectations under the contract, and public policy is rarely involved. Expressed somewhat differently, the law that has grown up around such topics as conditions primarily serves to protect party expectations, real or implied. Because that law basically fills in gaps in express contractual language, there is little harm in permitting the parties to establish their own framework by referring to foreign law.

A different situation exists when the parties attempt to stipulate the applicable law with respect to an issue for which the state has formulated a strong policy in addition to the general protection of expectations. Areas such as capacity and validity often involve real policy judgments made by the sovereign. Consider a contract having substantial contacts with California and Oregon;[16] although valid in the former state, the contract is invalid in Oregon because one of the parties is a spendthrift. If suit is brought against the Oregon spendthrift, should the court give effect to a contractual term specifying that questions concerning a party's capacity to enter the agreement are to be governed by California law? Presumably, the spendthrift could not agree expressly to be bound despite his spendthrift status. If so, he should not be permitted to accomplish the same result via a choice–of–law clause referring the issue to California law; the policy behind the spendthrift statute should not be so easy to circumvent. Because an express provision on capacity would have been legally ineffective, in other words, the backdoor route of designation also should not be permitted.[17] As then–Judge Harlan wrote in *Siegelman,* "[to] permit parties to stipulate the law which should govern the validity of their agreement would afford them an

---

[15] *Id. See also* comment d.

[16] The hypothetical is based on Lilienthal v. Kaufman, 239 Or. 1, 395 P.2d 543 (1964).

[17] That does not mean that the court should necessarily hold for the spendthrift. California's interest in the matter may lead to the application of California law.

artificial device for avoiding the policies of the state which would otherwise regulate the permissibility of their agreement."

(ii) *Other reasonable basis.* Section 187 permits the parties to choose the law of a state with no substantial relation to a problem if a "reasonable basis" exists for doing so. The example provided in the Restatement is of a contract centered in a country whose legal system is both strange and "relatively immature."[18] In that situation, the parties' wish to use a sophisticated and known body of law[19] can be guaranteed by an effective choice–of–law provision.

(iii) *Contrary to a fundamental policy.* The designation of foreign law will not be accepted if it conflicts with the "fundamental policy" of the state with the most significant relationship to that issue. A fundamental policy must be substantial, and not merely a technical requirement (such as those relating to the Statute of Frauds) or one becoming obsolete.[20]

The Restatement is less helpful concerning what such a policy is, giving only the example of statutes that favor insureds over their insurers. Fortunately, the case law provides more guidance. Courts have readily ignored choice–of–law clauses when the parties have attempted to circumvent either a strong and long–standing common law policy (such as that limiting covenants not to compete), or a significant statutory policy (such as the regulation of an industry or the equalization of bargaining power).[21]

Indeed, one exhaustive survey of two decades of decisions involving party autonomy concluded that the courts have made "free–wheeling use" of the "fundamental policy" loophole in order to reject choice–of–law clauses.[22] Although that conclusion seems somewhat overstated,[23] the study reminds us that, despite the apparent uniformity of the contract law taught in the first year of law school, there are sometimes real policy differences among the states. Occasionally, social choices are made by a court or legislature in seeking to alleviate perceived problems in society. The parties may be able to designate a law designed to insure that their deal is not tripped

---

[18] Restatement (Second) of Conflict of Laws § 187, comment f.

[19] In The Bremen v. Zapata Off–Shore Co., 407 U.S. 1, 13 n.15 (1972), the Court gave as one reason for sustaining a jurisdiction–selection clause, the need "to obtain certainty as to the applicable substantive law," especially in a situation where the forum could easily be a relatively undeveloped nation. *See* § 30, *supra.*

[20] Restatement (Second) of Conflict of Laws § 187, comment g.

[21] *See* cases collected in Note, *Effectiveness of Choice–of–Law Clauses in Contract Conflict of Law: Party Autonomy or Objective Determination?* 82 Colum. L. Rev. 1659 (1982).

[22] *Id.* at 1676. More recent surveys have reached the same conclusion. *E.g.,* Larry Kramer, *Choice of Law in the American Courts in 1990: Trends and Developments,* 39 Am. J. Comp. L. 465, 480–86 (1991).

[23] The study found few reported cases involving the party autonomy rule — at least few given the frequency with which choice–of–law clauses are used in practice. A number of factors may limit litigation in this area; one is likely to be the parties' agreement on the efficacy of the designation. Another problem with the study's conclusion concerning judicial attitudes toward party autonomy is that many of the cases the study draws on are opinions of lower state courts or of federal courts applying state law — perhaps not the most authoritative sources.

up by some historical anachronism peculiar to one of the states touched by the deal; but the parties generally will not be permitted to avoid the duties imposed by law in response to significant current problems.[24]

Tele-Save Merchandising Co. v. Consumers Distrib. Co.,[25] illustrates litigation in this area. Consumers, a Canadian corporation, operated a large chain of catalog showrooms. It agreed to supply service and products to Tele-Save, an Ohio corporation, which would then operate as a retail catalog showroom. The agreement between the two provided that it would be "governed by, and construed in accordance with, the laws of the state of New Jersey." The agreement did not last long; Consumers terminated the franchise only a few months after it opened.

Tele-Save sued, alleging that Consumers had violated the Ohio Business Opportunity Plans Act. That Act provided certain rights to terminated franchisees like Tele-Save. Consumers moved for summary judgment, arguing that New Jersey law, rather than that of Ohio, governed the contract by the express wish of the parties. The district court granted the motion, and the Sixth Circuit affirmed.

That court first examined Ohio's choice–of–law "principles" which it found "receptiv[e] to contractual choice–of–law clauses." Those principles substantially replicated § 187 of the Restatement (Second) of Conflict of Laws. Tele–Save argued that the Ohio Business Opportunities Act represented a "fundamental policy" of Ohio and, therefore, that the parties could not eliminate its effect by contract. The court was not impressed. First, it found that the "contract was freely negotiated by aggressive and successful business executives, untainted by the suspicions and misgivings characteristic of adhesion contracts"; because the "fundamental policy" exception applied (at most) only to adhesion contracts, the parties' choice of law violated no fundamental policy of Ohio and should be upheld.[26] Second, even if the Ohio law were a "fundamental policy," the court found that no "significant differences" between New Jersey and Ohio law; New Jersey law also provided remedies for fraud and breach of contract claims which Tele-Save had alleged in its complaint. Thus, the contractual choice–of–law provision was upheld.

Dissenting, Judge Milburn wrote that Ohio had a "clearly expressed fundamental policy of protecting small, inexperienced purchasers of business opportunity plans. . . ." Moreover, Milburn argued that "Ohio has a clearly expressed fundamental policy of prohibiting [choice–of–law clauses] abrogating the protections offered by the Act." Because Milburn would have

[24] Even in areas of fundamental policy, if the difference between the designated law and forum law is not significant, party autonomy may be sustained. *E.g.,* Wilkinson v. Manpower, Inc., 531 F.2d 712 (5th Cir. 1976) (covenants not to compete).

[25] 814 F.2d 1120 (6th Cir. 1987).

[26] The importance of the unequal bargaining power argument is illustrated by Modern Computer Systems, Inc. v. Modern Banking Systems, Inc., 871 F.2d 734 (8th Cir. 1989) (en banc). There, the en banc court upheld the choice–of–law clause because there was no inequality of bargaining power. Both the trial judge and the panel majority had found inequality and refused, therefore, to enforce the clause. There were dissents in both appellate courts; all of the appellate opinions relied on one of the *Tele-Save* opinions.

found the choice–of–law clause invalid, he had to resort to more general choice–of–law rules to decide whether to apply Ohio law. This was a relatively easy chore; he would have applied Ohio law because Ohio had a "materially greater interest" in the problem.

[c] Presumptive Choices

The Restatement (Second) provides two general techniques for handling contracts cases in the absence of a valid choice–of–law clause. The first technique is a series of presumptive references in several specific categories of cases. The second is the old standby residual provision of the Restatement — the most significant relationship doctrine. This subsection and the next deal with those two techniques.

For most contracts, the Second Restatement presumes that a specific law will be applied unless the presumption is rebutted by "the principles of § 6." Nine sections deal with particular contracts: Land contracts apply the *lex sitae* (§§ 189–90); a sale of a chattel involves the law of the place of delivery (§ 191); insurance contracts generally apply the location of the risk (§§ 192–94), and other provisions presume application of the place of repayment of money lent (§ 195), the place where services will be rendered (§ 196), or the place of shipment in transportation contracts (§ 197).

The Restatement details nine rules for specific types of contracts (*e.g.*, the sale of a chattel, sale of an interest in land, etc.), and another nine for specific contract issues (*e.g.*, capacity, illegality). Characterization plays an important, albeit silent, role in the selection. Thus, the presumption in land contracts is the law of the situs[27] (treating the contract as an issue in real property), and the presumption concerning capacity runs to the party's domicile[28] (treating the issue as one of status). Still more interesting is the fact that several of these specific sections do not select a jurisdiction at all, but merely refer the court back to the Restatement's general contract choice–of–law sections, § 187 (party autonomy) and § 188 (most significant relationship). An example is § 201 which indicates that questions concerning the effect of mistake or duress in the formation of the agreement are to be determined by the law selected by §§ 6 and 188 — the general provisions of the Restatement.[29]

Where the Restatement sets forth a presumption concerning a specific problem, it usually maintains the most significant relationship test in reserve. The interplay of the sections is shown by a well–known Colorado case, *Wood Brothers Homes, Inc. v. Walker Adjustment Bureau.*[30] Defendant, a California resident, contracted with a Colorado builder to do carpentry work on an apartment complex owned by defendant in New Mexico. The contract was signed in Colorado following negotiations in all three

---

27 Restatement (Second) of Conflict of Laws §§ 189–90.

28 *Id.* § 198.

29 *Id.* § 201. Specific provisions are also provided for cases involving workers' compensation (§§ 181–85), assignment (§§ 208–11), discharge (§§ 212–13), and several other topics.

30 198 Colo. 444, 601 P.2d 1369 (1979).

states, and the builder began work. New Mexico officials halted the project, however, because the builder lacked a New Mexico contractor's license. When defendant cancelled the contract, the builder sued. The court began its analysis by examining § 196, which provides that:[31]

> The validity of a contract for the rendition of services and the rights created thereby are determined by the local law of the state where the contract requires that the services be rendered, unless, with respect to the particular issue, some other state has a more significant relationship.

The presumption in § 196, therefore, pointed toward New Mexico law on the issue of whether the absence of a license justified the termination. That presumption could be overcome, however, by a showing that Colorado had a more significant relationship to that issue. The court sustained the presumption. Although Colorado's interest in validating agreements and protecting party expectations is a "central policy" of contract law, giving Colorado a "strong" interest under § 6, it was not strong enough to overcome the presumption set up in § 196. The court pointed to New Mexico's policy of insuring quality construction and held that it "outweighed" the Colorado policy of protecting party expectations. That conclusion seems right if the court correctly identified New Mexico's policy:[32] A state's regulatory policy concerning the safety of construction certainly can limit more general interests, and Colorado's interest in the out–of–state performance of a contract which happened to be signed in Colorado is minimal. More troubling is the conclusory nature of the decision. After mentioning the interest of each state, the court seemed merely to put them on a balance and determined that the presumption had not been rebutted.

The most controversial of the Restatement's specific contract provisions involves the treatment of usury cases. Section 203 provides (emphasis added):

> The validity of a contract will be sustained against the charge of usury if it provides for a rate of interest that is permissible in a state to which the contract has a substantial relationship and is not greatly in excess of the rate permitted by the general usury law of the state of the otherwise applicable law under the rule of § 188.

Section 203 codifies a modified version of the rule of validation for usury cases, and thus constitutes a substantivist choice–of–law solution[33] but it also includes two important qualifications. The first requires that the interest rate be permissible under the law of a state having a "substantial relationship" to the transaction; this insures application of the law of an

[31] Copyright © 1971 by the American Law Institute. Reprinted with permission of the American Law Institute.

[32] It is plausible that the licensing requirement was designed simply to limit competition from foreign contractors.

[33] Section 203 can also be viewed as a modified form of the alternative reference rule which refers questions concerning contractual validity to the law of the interested jurisdiction which would sustain the contract. The alternative reference rule is usually associated with Seeman v. Philadelphia Warehouse Co., 274 U.S. 403 (1927).

interested jurisdiction. The second limitation is that the prescribed rate and the rate permitted by the law that otherwise would apply not be "greatly different." The Restatement explains that § 203 is designed to protect party expectations; hence, it can be viewed as merely a variation on the rule of validation that some have seen applied generally in contract cases.[34] Moreover, that protection can be extended without significantly offending the interests of any sovereign. Because legal interest rates "vary only slightly" among the states, validation of an agreement "can hardly affect adversely the interests of another state when the stipulated interest is only a few percentage points higher than [permitted by the other] state."[35] The Restatement, therefore, generally treats differences in interest rates as generally technical and assumes that states generally have only a limited interest in applying usury laws to upset party expectations.[36] The only limits placed upon the process by the Restatement are that the rate be legal in a state which has a "substantial relationship" to the problem; party autonomy, in other words, is limited only by the need to have a "normal" relation to the parties and to the contract.[37] A state with such a relation would be, for example, the domicile of lender or borrower, or the place where the loan was made or is to be repaid.[38]

The only problem with the scheme set up in § 203 is that it ignores the purposes behind usury laws.[39] Some states do feel strongly about at least some part of their usury laws; modification of usury laws is often the subject of strong legislative debate and, unlike a state's rule on concurrent conditions, for example, usury laws reflect a legislative tradeoff between creditor and debtor. Expressed somewhat differently, the policy of protecting party expectations (here, the contractual provisions concerning interest rates) is a weak reed to support non–application of a law specifically designed to frustrate those expectations. Thus, some differences between competing usury laws may be only technical, but others are not. Moreover, the Restatement's characterization of a difference of a few percentage points as a matter of detail is surely not shared by the person who must pay the extra money. By subordinating usury laws to a rule of validation, the Restatement has adopted a position favoring creditors as a class. No justification is offered in the Restatement for that choice, although it is one shared by scholars[40] and judges.[41] Distaste for limits on contractual

---

34 *See* § 82, *infra*.

35 Restatement (Second) of Conflict of Laws § 203, comment b.

36 If usurious everywhere, the Restatement commands application of the law of the state prescribing the "lightest penalty." *Id.*, comment d. This was the result reached in *Seeman, supra*, note 27.

37 Permitting express choice–of–law clauses in usury cases was thought to be unnecessary given the "liberality" of § 203. *Id.*, comment e.

38 *Id.*, comment c. The comment cautions that the relation between the state and the contract must be a normal one — not one manipulated for choice–of–law purposes.

39 Section 203 is trenchantly criticized by Sedler, *supra* note 1, at 315–27.

40 *E.g.*, Weintraub § 7.4A; *but see* Note, *Usury in the Conflict of Laws: The Doctrine of the Lex Debitoris*, 55 Cal. L. Rev. 123 (1967).

41 *See, e.g.*, Crisafulli v. Childs, 33 A.D.2d 293, 307 N.Y.S.2d 701 (1970). The contract there

freedom, however, may not be as widespread among legislators as it is among those who wrote the Second Restatement.

[d] The Most Significant Relationship

Section 188 lists a number of factors a court should consider, in combination with those mentioned in § 6, in determining the jurisdiction with the most significant relationship. These include:

(a) the place of contracting,

(b) the place of negotiation of the contract,

(c) the place of performance,

(d) the location of the subject matter of the contract, and

(e) the domicil, residence, nationality, place of incorporation and place of business of the parties.[42]

As in other areas, the most significant relationship test is a residual one, to be used in the absence of an effective choice–of–law by the parties or a specific section, or to override an applicable presumptive reference provision designed to deal with the specific problem.

[e] An Evaluation

One obvious observation is that the drafters of the Second Restatement's contracts provisions expected § 187 — party autonomy — to be of great importance. In drafting the clauses dealing with the residue of agreements (that is, those without choice–of–law clauses), the drafters chose to apply the law that most likely would be applied pursuant to the use of modern policy analysis. The faith in § 187 has been amply justified; it has long been a respected tool in the armory of the commercial lawyer

The result in non-party autonomy cases, however, has been more mixed. Professor Borchers found that the fate of the contract provisions mirrored that of the tort sections. In other words, most provisions received scant judicial attention, while a few attracted a larger number of citations.[43] Thus courts committed to the second Restatement have cited frequently and adopted explicitly § 192 (life insurance contracts), § 193 (fire, casualty, or surety insurance), § 196 (rendition of services), and § 203 (usury).[44] It may be that the Second Restatement has succeeded in identifying true rules in

---

was usurious under both New York and Pennsylvania law; the court refused to apply the harsher New York law, on the ground that this would give a "windfall" to the debtor. Of course, the idea behind the provision was to give a windfall in order to deter usurious agreements.

[42] Copyright © 1971 by the American Law Institute. Reprinted with the permission of the American Law Institute.

[43] Patrick J. Borchers, *Courts and the Second Conflicts Restatement: Some Observations and an Empirical Note*, 56 Md L. Rev. 1232, 1245 (1997).

[44] *Id.*

these sections since even courts otherwise committed to the First Restatement often apply them.[45]

§ 75 The Second Restatement: Property

[a] Generally

The Second Restatement closely resembles its predecessor in its treatment of property issues. There are some differences between the two works, however. An especially noticeable improvement is the willingness of Professor Reese's team to provide rationales for the choices that it made. Those rationales can be quite helpful in determining the application of particular rules. Another difference between the two, one which cuts through the entire Chapter, is the adoption by the later Restatement of a "general principle":[1]

> The interests of the parties in a thing are determined, depending upon the circumstances, either by the "law" or by the "local law" of the state which, with respect to the particular issue, has the most significant relationship to the thing and the parties under the principles stated in § 6.

Although most sections make a presumptive selection of the law of one state based on an important contact between that jurisdiction and the issue under consideration, the general reference to the state of the most significant relationship produces a flexibility unknown in the First Restatement and at least opens up possibilities of change in this area.[2]

Another important difference between the two Restatements concerns renvoi.[3] This doctrine was little used in the earlier work; its only application was to questions concerning title to land. In the property chapter of the current Restatement, however, the court is directed to refer to the whole law of a state, including its choice–of–law rules, when uniformity of result is the "primary objective."[4] This is more likely to be the goal in cases involving immovables, an area where uniformity of result is believed to be particularly important.

---

[45] *See* William Richman and David Riley, *The Restatement (First) of Conflict of Laws on the Twenty–fifth Anniversary of Its Successor: Contemporary Practice on Traditionalist Courts,* 56 Md. L. Rev. 1196 (1997). *See also* William Richman and William Reynolds, *Prologomenon to an Empirical Restatement of Conflicts,* 75 Ind. L.J. 417, 433 (2000).

[1] Restatement (Second) of Conflict of Laws § 222. Copyright © 1971 by the American Law Institute. Reprinted with permission of the American Law Institute.

[2] The courts have not embraced the possibility, however. *See* § 89, *infra.*

[3] Renvoi is discussed in § 59, *supra.*

[4] Restatement (Second) of Conflict of Laws § 222, comment e.

[b] Immovables

[1] The Situs Rule

The situs rule is probably the broadest and most rigid of all the choice–of–law provisions of the Second Restatement. It extends to all questions involving *inter vivos* conveyances (including validity as well as construction), transfers by operation of law encumbrances, powers, marital property, equitable interests, and succession on death.[5] Further, the drafters allow it to trump many of the values included in the principles of § 6. Thus, the law of the situs controls even when it thwarts powerful state interests,[6] or frustrates the parties' expectations.[7]

[2] Rationales for the Situs Rule

The drafters offer two principal justifications for the situs rule.[8]

The Situs State's Interest in Issues Involving Situs Land:[9] The comments following § 223 cite this reason for applying the situs rule to questions involving who may own the land, the conditions under which land may be held and the uses to which land may be put what restrictions, if any, are imposed upon the ownership of land by a corporation or by an alien and the period during which the power to alienate interests in land may be suspended.[10]

The drafters recognized, however, that a non–situs state might have the dominant interest with respect to some issues particularly when the land is "one item in an aggregate of things. . .which are situated in a number of states and which it is desirable to deal with as a unit." Thus the comments suggest that the situs courts might apply the law of the state of the marital domicile to issues involving the conveyance of interests in land between spouses.[11]

---

[5] See Restatement (Second) §§ 223–224, 226–234, 236–243. Note that the reference in each of the cited sections is to "the law that would be applied by the courts of the situs," i.e., the whole law of the situs, and thus each section calls for application of the doctrine of renvoi. The drafters give the dominant interest of the situs state in land issues as the rationale for the use of renvoi.

[6] *See id.*, §§ 237, 238 (legitimacy and adoption as affecting succession to land) and §§ 233, 234, 241, 242 (marital property and surviving spouse's interest in decedent's estate).

[7] *See id.*, §§ 224, 236, 240 (construction of wills and conveyances of land), and § 239 (intestate succession). The only exception to the situs rule concerns construction of a will devising real property; the testator may designate the law to be applied for purposes of construction. *Id.* § 240.

[8] In addition to the functional reasons for the situs rule, the drafters cite "sentimental and historical reasons." *See* Restatement (Second) Chapter 9, Topic 2 Immovables, Introductory Note.

[9] For commentary on this justification for the situs rule, see Russell Weintraub, Commentary on the Conflict of Laws 501 (4th ed. 2001); Moffatt Hancock, *Full Faith and Credit to Foreign Laws and Judgments in Real Property Litigation: the Supreme Court and the Land Taboo*, 18 Stan. L. Rev. 1299 (1966).

[10] *Id.*, § 223, comment b.

[11] *Id.*

Statements acknowledging the occasionally dominant interest of the non-situs state appear throughout the comments to the property sections, especially those governing issues where the interest of the non-situs state is obvious and compelling.[12] The result is that the Second Restatement's treatment of land issues has a schizophrenic quality. The comments to many sections feature subtle and nuanced interest–analytic discussions that are sensitive to the particular issue involved; by contrast, the black letter of section after section calls for the simple–minded application of the law of the situs. The ambivalence seems less likely to guide the courts than to confuse them. Perhaps, however, the ambivalence results from the inevitable conflict between the descriptive and prescriptive functions of a Restatement. In other words, the drafters recognized both the courts' universal application of the situs rule and the failure of the rule's interest–analytic justification.[13]

Recording Statutes:[14] The drafters use recording statutes to justify the situs rule even in cases where the situs does not have the dominant interest. The argument is that parties and their lawyers give considerable thought to the possible consequences of land transactions, so certainty, predictability, uniformity, ease in the determination and application of the law to be applied are important conflicts values. Thus situs law should apply whenever it is likely that a person relied on the record title before entering into the transaction. Furthermore, it is desirable that drafters and title searchers need consult only a single law — the one with which they are most familiar.[15]

This explanation will justify the black letter in many cases, but is inapposite in situations where the contest is between two sets of gratuitous transferees, none of whom has relied on the recording statutes.[16] Clearly,

[12] *See, e.g.*, §§ 233, 241 (rights of one spouse in other's land; state of marital domicile may have greater interest), § 236 (intestate succession; state of common domicile of decedent and heirs may have greater interest), § 240 (will construction; construction of will according to law of state of testator's domicile more likely to carry out testator's intentions).

[13] Thus it is not all that hard to think of cases where the non-situs state will have the dominant interest, but precedent for applying non–situs law is scarce. A few examples appear in the escape device cases that attempt to produce just results while keeping faith with the situs rule of the First Restatement. *See* § 67, *supra.* The Second Restatement does its best to eliminate the escape devices by addressing each with a specific section refering explicitly to situs law in an effort to remove the temptation to indulge in the ad hoc and inconsistent decision-making that mars many of the escape device cases. Thus, in § 223 a question concerning the validity and effect of a conveyance of land is referred to the law of the situs (treating the issue as one of property rather than contract); whether an equitable conversion has occurred is determined by reference to the situs (§ 225); and even the existence of marital property is determined by situs law (§ 233).

[14] For scholarly evaluation of this rationale for the situs rule see Russell Weintraub, Commentary on the Conflict of Laws 501 (4th ed. 2001); Moffatt Hancock, *Conceptual Devices for Avoiding the Land Taboo in Conflict of Laws: The Disadvantages of Disingenuousness*, 20 Stan. L. Rev. 1, 22–23 (1967), reprinted in Moffatt Hancock, Studies in Modern Choice of Law: Torts, Insurance, Land Titles 372 (1984).

[15] *See* Restatement (Second) § 223 comment b.

[16] *See In re Barrie's Estate*, § 67, *supra*.

application of non-situs law could not frustrate expectations of the parties in such a case. But could it lay a trap for unwary future purchasers of the land, who relied upon situs law in determining whether the grant to one set of gratuitous transferees was valid?

It is difficult to see how that could happen. The situation usually arises when a probate court orders the distribution of an estate (testate or intestate). Regardless of the law that it uses to determine the proper distribution, it typically orders the executor to make a deed, valid according to situs law, transferring the land to the prevailing contestant, who then records that instrument in the land records of the situs. A subsequent search would show the valid deed, and the searcher would not be misled. There would seldom, if ever, be an occasion for the searcher to consider the validity of the distribution itself, because the preclusive effect of the probate court's decision usually would settle that issue conclusively.

[c] Movables

[1] Intervivos Transfers

One purpose of the Uniform Commercial Code was to produce uniformity in commercial law among the states, and the Code's success has minimized choice–of–law problems involved in non-gratuitous transactions of movables.[17] Nevertheless, there are a few remaining issues because: the official version of the Code contains alternative choices for several sections; the official version has changed over time, and not all the states have adopted each set of changes; state legislatures have enacted variations in their own Codes; and judicial interpretation of uniform sections can vary from state to state. The variations, however, are relatively minor, and have not yet caused significant controversy.[18]

[2] Marital Property[19]

Sections 257–259 of the Second Restatement deal with choice–of–law problems between common law and community property states. In common law states, a spouse does not have an interest in property acquired during the marriage by the other spouse; rather, each spouse owns property individually subject only to a forced share for the other spouse at death and a divorce court's right to distribute the assets of both spouses equitably. In community property states, each spouse owns an undivided one-half interest in all assets acquired during the marriage.

For choice between the two regimes, § 258 calls for the application of the law of the state with the most significant relationship to the spouses and the property, and then specifies that the most important contact will

[17] The U.C.C. has been adopted in every state but Louisiana. Its choice–of–law provisions are discussed in § 92 *infra*.

[18] The Code deals with choice–of–law on the issues where there is interstate variation in two principal sections: § 1-105 and § 9-103. These sections are treated in § 92, *infra*.

[19] For more on choice–of–law and marital property, *see* § 89[c], *infra*.

usually be the state where the spouses were domiciled at the time the movable was acquired.[20] The rationale for the choice is state interest and uniformity. The state of domicile will have the greatest interest in the spouses and their rights in each other's property, and it is desirable that marital property interests in movables should be governed by a single law rather than the law of the situs of each movable.[21]

For reasons of fairness and convenience, § 259 provides that a spouse's interest in the other spouse's movable property is not affected by the mere removal of the property to a second state or a change in the spouses' common domicile.[22] Section 257 deals with the effect of a marriage on existing interests in movables owned by one of the spouses. This question arises only between American states and foreign nations because no state of the United States vests an interest in one spouse in the pre-existing movable property of the other on the occasion of the marriage.[23]

[3] Succession on Death

Sections 260 and 263 refer questions of descent and distribution of movable property to the law that would be applied by the state where the decedent died domiciled. The comments cite state interest, protection of justified expectations, certainty, predictability, uniformity of result, and ease in application as the rationale for the rule.[24]

Uniformity presumably is an important part of the rationale for the choice of the law of the decedent's domicile as well as for the use of renvoi.[25] An obvious alternative choice would be the place of the movable at the time of death, but that would result in a nonuniform distribution of the estate, not to mention a constant temptation to potential heirs to engage in self help by moving property as their loved ones lay dying.

The protection of party expectations also enters into the calculation. The case is clearest for the validity of a will. The testator probably expected the law of domicile to control and relied on the advice of counsel in that state. But expectations matter for intestacy, as well. A state's intestacy law fashions a will for a decedent who has neglected to do so. The legislature,

[20] Restatement (Second) § 258. For more on these issues, see Scoles, Hay, Borchers and Symeonides, Conflict of Laws 588–593 (3d ed. 2000).

[21] *Id.*, comment b.

[22] *Id.* § 259.

[23] *Id.* § 257. *See* Scoles, Hay, Borchers and Symeonides, Conflict of Laws 588 (3d ed. 2000).

[24] *See* Restatement (Second) of Conflict of Laws § 260, comment b.

[25] To see why renvoi produces uniformity, consider the following hypothetical. Suppose a citizen of the United States, dies domiciled in France, owning movable property in the United States and France. Suppose further that the French choice–of–law rule for intestacy selects the decedent's nationality and that the appropriate American state's rule selects the law of decedent's domicile. If the French courts will distribute the French property according to the American scheme, and the American court does not use renvoi, it will distribute the American property according to the French scheme, thus thwarting the goal of uniformity. If, instead, the American court follows § 260, it will distribute the American property according to the law that would be applied by the French court, i.e., the intestacy law of the appropriate American state; and the entire estate will pass as a unity.

with concern for local family customs and relations, selects a pattern of distribution that would coincide with the wishes of the "average testator." Presumably the legislature at the decedent's domicile is best situated to perform that task.[26]

Comment b to § 260 also cites state interest as a reason for the decedent's–domicile rule. Often the decedent's domicile will have the dominant interest, but not always. Typically the decedent's domicile will also be the situs of the movable and the domicile of many of those with competing claims to the estate.[27]

§ 76 The Second Restatement: Procedure

The drafters of the Second Restatement chose deliberately to abandon the terms "substantive" and "procedural," suggesting that they had led courts into mechanical decision–making. Instead the Second Restatement encourages courts to confront the question directly whether the forum's or some other state's law should apply. This approach should lead courts to consider directly the policies that call for the application of forum or foreign law in the variety of different circumstances in which courts have relied on the terms substance and procedure in the past.[1]

Section 122 announces the general rule that the forum usually will apply its own rules concerning the conduct of litigation even when it applies the law of another state to resolve other issues in the case.[2] The reasons for the rule are well known: the forum has a greater interest in the conduct of judicial proceedings in its courts than does any other state;[3] parties typically have no expectations with regard to rules of judicial administration, so nothing is gained by applying foreign law; and the forum courts avoid enormous burdens by applying forum law rather than having to learn the intricacies of pleadings discovery and evidence rules of a foreign state.[4]

---

[26] *See* Moffat Hancock, *Equitable Conversion and the Land Taboo in Conflict of Laws*, 70 Stan. L. Rev. 1095 (1965), reprinted in Moffat Hancock, Studies in Modern Choice of Law: Torts, Insurance, Land Titles 313 (1984).

[27] There are some cases where the decedent's–domicile rule will produce dysfunctional results. When the finding of domicile is based upon the special rules for students, prisoners, or military personnel or upon the technical rules for acquisition of a new domicile of choice (decedent's momentary presence in the new domicile sufficient), the state of domicile may have no strong interest. *See* Chapter 2, *supra,* especially §§ 4 and 5.

[1] Restatement Second § 1 22 comment b.

[2] In civil cases where state provides the rule of decision, Fed. R. Evid. 302, 501, 601, call for the federal court to apply state law on issues of presumption rebuttal, privilege, and competence of witnesses, thus treating these three issues as substantive for *Erie* purposes. For choice–of–law purposes, however, Restatement (Second) § 137 always, and §§ 134 and 139 often, apply the law of the forum to those issues. The inconsistency is not troublesome because the policy justifications for the *Erie* rule, on the one hand, and the use of forum law in choice–of–law cases, on the other, are sufficiently different to justify the discrepancy.

[3] This rationale, for example, explains the forum's application of its own shorter statute of limitations. *See* Restatement (Second) § 142(1) (1986).

[4] The "enormous burden" rationale is most apparent when the forum uses its own rules on pleading, discovery, evidence, and motion practice; consider how inconvenient it would be for

The Restatement characterizes the issues of persuasion and production burdens and presumptions as falling "into a gray area between issues relating primarily to judicial administration and those concerned primarily with the rights and liabilities of the parties." The Restatement's solution in §§ 133 and 134 is interest analytic in the sense that the purpose behind the relevant foreign rule is the deciding factor.[5]

The "enormous burden" rationale explains the Restatement's reference to forum law to control admissibility of evidence. The trial judge must rule promptly on evidentiary objections, so it makes sense for her to rely on the forum's familiar rules rather than having to learn a new set of rules whenever foreign substantive law applies. The argument applies *a fortiori* in areas where evidentiary doctrine is complicated, such as hearsay and the best evidence rule.[6]

The reference to forum law, however, does not control all evidence issues. For instance, although forum law supplies the standard for logical relevance, the otherwise applicable foreign substantive law necessarily controls which issues are material[7] by specifying the elements of the parties' claims and defenses.[8]

The Chapter provides an exception to the law–of–the–forum rule for privilege questions because privilege rules differ fundamentally from other rules of evidence.[9] The function of most evidence rules is to enhance the truth–seeking process, but privilege rules deliberately subordinate truth seeking to some other policy goal, usually the protection or fostering of a valued relationship. The hearsay rule, for example, excludes a category of evidence because it is typically unreliable, and thus harmful to the truth seeking process. The privilege for spousal communications, on the other hand, sacrifices whatever probative help the confidential communication could offer in order to protect marriage and foster confidential communications between spouses.[10]

The treatment of conflict of privilege rules is one of the Second Restatement's few "substantivist" provisions. Such rules, of which the principle of validation is an example, use the preference for a particular substantive

a Michigan court to learn Louisiana pleading and practice rules simply because a Louisiana tort found its way into a Michigan forum. Thus, the Restatement refers to forum law for issues relating to subject matter jurisdiction (§ 123), forms of action (§ 124), parties (§ 125) service of process (§ 126), pleadings (§ 127), mode of trial (§ 129), attachment garnishment and contempt (§ 130), and enforcement of judgments (§ 131). The lack of party expectations on these issues is also relevant. Note also that in these cases the reference to forum law is conclusive; there is no "most significant relationship" override.

[5] Note, however, that in the case of a true conflict, the Restatement, unlike Currie, defers to the law of the foreign state.

[6] *See* Restatement (Second) § 138, comment a.

[7] "[O]f consequence" in the language of Fed. R. Evid. 401.

[8] *See* Restatement (Second) § 138, comment b. Further the Restatement sensibly treats two pseudo-evidence issues, the parol evidence rule and the statute of frauds, as matters of contract law to be controlled by §§ 187 and 188. *See* §§ 140 and 141.

[9] *Id.* § 139.

[10] Christopher B. Mueller and Laird C. Kirkpatrick, Evidence §§ 5.1 and 5.34 (1995).

result as a choice–of–law device. The *substantive* preference of th Second Restatement in privilege cases is to favor truth–seeking. Thus, the Restatement chooses between the privilege rules of the forum and those of the state with the most significant relationship with the communication based upon which law will admit the evidence.[11]

This value preference, is consistent with the general principle of evidence law that privilege rules, because they deprive the court and the parties of probative evidence, should be strictly construed. In the words of the Supreme Court, "privileges contravene the fundamental principle that the public. . .has a right to every man's evidence." Thus they should be recognized "only to the very limited extent that permitting a refusal to testify or excluding relevant evidence has a public good transcending the normally predominant principle of utilizing all rational means for ascertaining truth."[12]

§ 77 Retrospective on the Second Restatement

Scholars have given the Second Restatement mixed reviews. The initial reaction was almost completely negative, criticizing the document as "too much of a compromise among conflicting philosophies, too vague, exceedingly elastic, unpredictable, directionless, and rudderless."[1] Recent commentary has been more measured, crediting the Second Restatement, at least, with helping to convince state courts to abandon the mechanical and dysfunctional lex loci rules[2] and with appealing to judges schooled in the legal process tradition.[3]

---

[11] *See* Restatement (Second) § 139

[12] *Trammel v. United States*, 445 U.S. 40, 50 (1980), *United States v. Nixon*, 418 U.S. 683, 710 (1974). *See also* Michael H. Graham, Handbook of Federal Evidence § 501.1 (4th ed. 1996). Interest analytic arguments also justify the value preference of § 139. The rule does not consider false conflicts because, in order to generate a false conflict, the forum must also be the state with the most significant relationship to the communication, and the result in such a case is so obvious as not to be treated as a choice–of–law problem at all. Section 139 (2) contemplates a true conflict between the forum's law admitting the evidence and the foreign law permitting the privilege. Interest analysis usually will not require the forum to sacrifice its own truth–seeking policy to the relationship–protecting policy of the foreign state.

Section 139 (1) contemplates an unprovided–for case where the evidence is privileged under forum law but not under the law of the place with the most significant relationship with the communication. Excluding the evidence will not advance the relationship–protecting policy of the forum, nor will admitting the evidence further the truth–seeking policy of the foreign state. However, the forum will have a residual truth–seeking policy in every case in its courts, and admission of the evidence will advance this policy.

[1] *See* Symeon C. Symeonides, *The Judicial Acceptance of the Second Conflicts Restatement: A Mixed Blessing*, 56 Md. L. Rev. 1248, 1249, n.3 and sources cited therein (1997).

[2] *Id.* at 1283.

[3] William L. Reynolds, *Legal Process and Choice of Law*, 56 Md. L. Rev. 1371 (1997). *See also* Russell Weintraub, *"At least, To Do No Harm": Does the Second Restatement of Conflicts Meet the Hippocratic Standard?*, 56 Md. L. Rev. 1284, 1315 (1997) (describing the Restatement as "an odd mixture of territorial gibberish and functional analysis ").

Some of the modern commentary, however, is every bit as harsh as the early critics were. *See, e.g.*, Larry Kramer, *Choice of Law in the American Courts 1990: Trends and Developments*, 39 Am. J. Comp. L. 465, 486–87 (1991) ("one needs to read a lot of opinions in a single sitting fully to appreciate just how badly the Second Restatement works in practice").

The courts, of course, have reacted differently, and the Second Restatement is the dominant choice–of–law methodology in United States today.[4] To say that most courts have adopted the Second Restatement, however, is not as clear an endorsement as it might seem; for it is not clear exactly what methodology many "Second Restatement" courts have adopted. Some apply the Second Restatement as it was intended by its drafters; others use a crude grouping–of–contacts analysis; others seem wedded to the Restatement's specific territorial references, ignoring the policy analysis required by § 6; and still others perform the general policy and contact analysis and seem to ignore the specific references entirely. Perhaps it is the Restatement's very flexibility and malleability that has made it so attractive to the courts.

It seems fair to say, then, that there is a town–gown split over the merits of the Second Restatement as well a fair amount of speculation about the reasons for that split.[5] Regardless, however, the Restatement's dominance in the courts assures that it will form the jumping-off place for any Third Restatement, or indeed any future choice–of–law reform with a serious chance of success.[6]

§ 78 Interest Analysis: The Theory

"Interest analysis" is a method of analyzing choice–of–law problems developed by the late Professor Brainerd Currie. His method has profoundly influenced both judges and scholars. The chronological coincidence of the development of interest analysis and of the Restatement (Second) provoked widespread re–examination of the choice–of–law problem and sparked the modern revolution in that area.

[a] Overview[1]

Currie based his system upon the observation that law is purposive in nature — that those who made the law sought to serve various social goals. Blind application of mechanical choice–of–law rules advances societal goals only fortuitously, because those mechanical rules were not designed to advance substantive goals. Thus, a non–mechanical approach must be sought. Although domestic law does seek substantive ends, it is normally designed

---

[4] Symeonides, *supra* note 1, 1250.

[5] Symeonides, *supra* note 1, Reynolds, *supra* note 1.

[6] *See Symposium: Preparing for the Next Century — A New Restatement of Conflicts?,* 75 Ind. L. J. 399-686 (2000) (articles and commentaries by Professors Juenger, Richman and Reynolds, Symeonides, Weinberg, Borchers, Dane, Hill, Maier, Peterson, Posnak, Reimann, Reppy, Sedler, Simson, Singer, Twerski, and Weintraub).

[1] A recent, sympathetic treatment of Interest Analysis is Bruce Posnak, *Choice of Law: Interest Analysis and Its "New Crits,"* 36 Am. J. Comp. L. 681 (1988); *see also* Lea Brilmayer, Conflict of Laws: Foundations and Future Directions 43–62 (1991); Larry Kramer, *More Notes on Methods and Objectives in Choice of Law,* 24 Cornell Int'l L. J. 245 (1991). Finally, the exchange on interest analysis between a critical Professor Friedrich Juenger and a sympathetic Professor Robert Sedler is well worth reading. The articles can be found in 21 U.C. Davis L. Rev. 515 (1988); 23 *id.* at 865 (1990); and 24 *id.* at 227 (1990).

to address purely domestic problems. As a result, rote application of domestic law to a choice–of–law problem may not optimally advance the various social goals implicated in a multi–state problem. Instead, Currie argued, in choice–of–law decision–making, the governmental interests of each jurisdiction in having its law applied should be considered. That procedure helps insure that a law will not be applied to a problem *unless applying the law would achieve a policy goal sought by the sovereign which promulgated the law.*

Forum law should normally supply the rule of decision; hence, the burden is on the party seeking to displace forum law to show that it would be proper to do so. When a party asks the court to displace forum law with foreign law, the court must examine the policies that the different laws seek to implement, using the "ordinary processes of construction and interpretation." The aim of that construction is to ascertain the policy of the law as it might be applied in a purely domestic case. If the policy of only one state would be furthered by applying it in the case at bar, then a *false conflict* exists. A false conflict should be resolved by applying the law of the only interested state.

A *true conflict* arises when the policies of each state would be furthered by the application of its law to the case. Currie suggested the following analysis for resolving true conflicts:

(i) First, the court should re–examine the laws of each state; it may be possible to avoid the conflict through a "more moderate or restrained interpretation of the policy or interest of one state."

(ii) If that reconsideration does not eliminate the conflict, then the forum should apply its own law.

(iii) If the forum has no interest of its own to further in the matter, but a true conflict exists between the laws of two other states, then Currie suggested two alternative methods for the *disinterested forum* to use: Apply forum law, at least if that law coincides with the law of one of the interested states; *or,* resolve the conflict as it would be resolved by a "supreme legislative body."

The final category analyzed by Currie is the *unprovided–for case.* That situation occurs when the policy of no state would be advanced by applying its law in the case at bar. Currie believed such cases to be rare, and he suggested that the forum apply its own law because there is no important policy reason to displace the normal presumption in favor of forum law.

[b] False Conflicts

The concept of the false conflict lies at the very heart of Currie's writing. The argument that a law should not be applied unless doing so would achieve some purpose[2] follows logically from the Legal Realism movement and that movement's rejection of mechanical jurisprudence, one aspect of

[2] This insight is not new, of course; compare the common law maxim, "*cessante ratione legis, cessat et ipsa lex*" (where the reason stops, there stops the rule).

which was the territorial approach of the First Conflicts Restatement.[3] Although Currie was by no means the first to argue that choice–of–law principles should concern themselves with substantive goals,[4] he certainly was the most influential. One reason for his influence was his exposure of the inane way in which traditional analysis handled the problem of the false conflict. Currie chose as his vehicle for that demonstration the well–known case of *Milliken v. Pratt*,[5] and the general problem of married women's contracts in multi–state transactions. The problem was created by laws in many states which made married (but not single) women legally incompetent to contract. How should a court handle a case which has contacts with a jurisdiction that has a statute protecting married women and also with a state which does not?

Currie began his analysis by identifying the policies served by the rule in each state (in *Milliken,* Massachusetts and Maine). One state (Massachusetts) sought to protect women from imprudent contracts by disabling them from entering into contracts. Currie then inquired into the scope of that protection. Clearly, married women would be "protected" by the Massachusetts law if the case were a wholly domestic one. But what of a case with foreign elements: Did the Massachusetts legislature intend to protect all married women, even those with no connection to Massachusetts? The answer, of course, is that the legislature sought to protect only "Massachusetts women." Having addressed the two polar situations (that is, the purely domestic and the purely foreign), Currie asked whether the Massachusetts statute was designed to address the in–between situations presented in the normal choice–of–law problem. Currie argued that statutes rarely provide for choice–of–law issues because the legislative focus is on the "normal" domestic case rather than on the "unusual" multi–state problem.

A similar analysis can be made of the policy of the second state (Maine), which generally upholds freedom of contract and does not place obstacles in the way of married women who wish to make contracts. Maine's policy of providing freedom of contract and protecting party expectations, however, was not designed for the protection of all contracting parties, but only for those having sufficient connections with Maine.

Currie then noted that four contacts had possible significance in a case involving a married woman's contract: the domiciles of the creditor and the woman, the place where the contract was made (or to be performed), and the forum. There are sixteen possible combinations of these four factors. Two of those possibilities are wholly domestic to one state or the other. Domestic law would be applied, of course, in those cases. In ten of the fourteen remaining cases there is no conflict between the two state policies

[3] *See* § 63, *supra.*

[4] *See, e.g.,* the Supreme Court's decisions in the workers' compensation cases from the 1930's discussed in § 96, *infra.*

[5] 125 Mass. 374 (1878). The discussion is in Brainerd Currie, *Married Women's Contracts: A Study in Conflict–of–Laws Method,* 25 U. Chi. L. Rev. 227 (1958), reprinted in Currie, Essays, Ch. 2. *Milliken* is also discussed *supra,* § 65. *See also* Vernon, Weinberg, Reynolds, and Richman at 301–06.

because only one state's policy can be furthered by the application of that state's law. Thus, for example, if the married woman lives in Maine, Massachusetts has no reason to refuse to enforce a contract she has made; if the state where she is domiciled (Maine) does not wish to protect her from improvident engagements, why should Massachusetts? To do so, Currie argued, would be "perverse." A similar analysis could be made of the other nine false conflict situations. To be sure, four of the fourteen possibilities (including *Milliken* itself) are true conflicts; but the magic of Currie's false conflict analysis is that it permits the court to dispose of most of the multi-state situations fairly easily and, at the same time, *further the policy of the only state interested in the transaction.*

It was not long before judges discovered interest analysis. The most commonly used illustrations involve the New York guest statute cases, beginning with *Babcock v. Jackson.*[6] There, both guest and host were New Yorkers; the accident occurred on a weekend trip to Ontario. That province had a guest statute which would have denied recovery to plaintiff. The Court of Appeals of New York rejected the vested rights doctrine and then examined the problem under various approaches, including a form of interest analysis. The court identified New York's policy as favoring compensation of tort victims; clearly, that interest could be furthered only if the guest statute were not applied. Ontario's interest was found to be the prevention of collusive suits which would defraud insurance companies. That interest was not involved in *Babcock* because the insured was not from Ontario. The case thus presented a false conflict because only New York's interest would be furthered by applying its law. Ontario's interest (as represented by the guest statute) would not be furthered, so its law was not applied. Interest analysis focuses on contacts, policies, and law. A convenient way to keep their relation straight is to represent the relation among those three groupings in a diagram.[7] A diagram of *Babcock,* for example, looks like this:

[6] 12 N.Y.2d 473, 191 N.E.2d 279, 240 N.Y.S.2d 743 (1963). *Babcock* is not expressly an interest analysis case; indeed, it deploys enough theories to satisfy everyone.

[7] *See generally* William M. Richman, *Diagramming Conflicts: A Graphic Understanding of Interest Analysis,* 43 Ohio St. L.J. 317 (1982). For more on diagramming conflicts, *see* Joseph W. Singer, *A Pragmatic Guide to Conflicts,* 70 B.U. L. Rev. 731 (1990).

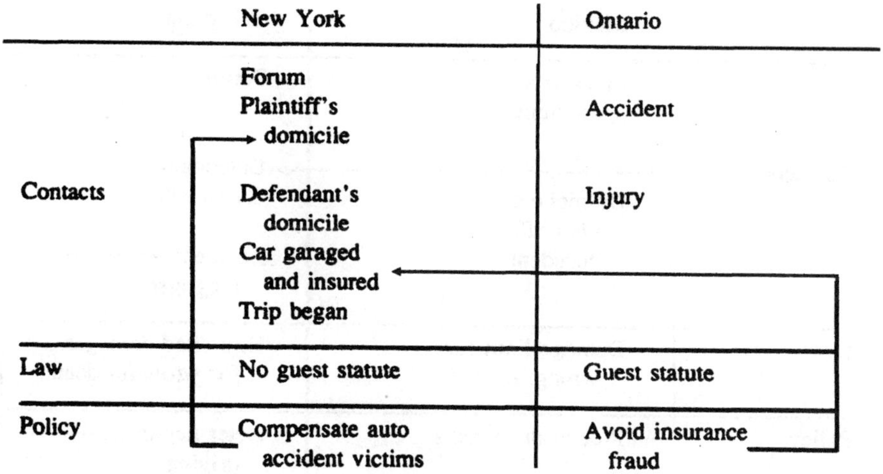

The diagram dramatically reveals Currie's insight into false conflicts. New York's policy of compensating tort victims points toward a New York contact — the domicile of the plaintiff. Ontario's policy of avoiding insurance fraud, however, does not point to an Ontario contact. Rather, it crosses the center line of the diagram and points to a New York contact — the "home" of the car. Because both policies point toward contacts in one state, the case presents a false conflict.

Hurtado v. Superior Court[8] provides a second example of a false conflict. The defendant in *Hurtado* was from California, while both the plaintiff and his decedent were Mexican domiciliaries. Following an accident in California, plaintiff brought a wrongful death action in that state. Mexican law at that time limited wrongful death recovery to about $2000, a limit apparently imposed to avoid impoverishing tortfeasors. California did not limit recovery; its policy was to deter tortious conduct. The case is a false conflict, as the diagram illustrates.

[8] 11 Cal.3d 574, 522 P.2d 666, 114 Cal. Rptr. 106 (1974).

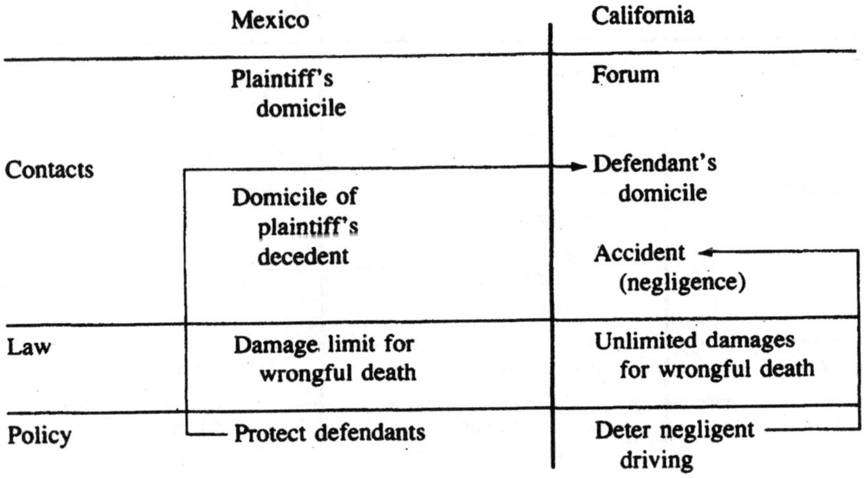

Mexico's interest would not be advanced by limiting the damages of a foreign tortfeasor. California's policy — encouraging safe driving — would be advanced, however, by choosing California law. Both arrows in the diagram point toward California, graphically illustrating *Hurtado's* classification as a false conflict.

False conflict analysis can also be used in cases like *Marie v. Garrison,*[9] where the law (as well as the policy) is the same in each jurisdiction. Interest analysis, therefore, would have avoided the inane result reached in *Marie,* where the court enforced an oral agreement despite the fact that the law (the Statute of Frauds) of the only two interested jurisdictions required that the agreement be written.[10]

[c] True Conflicts

A more difficult case arises when each state has a policy which would be advanced by the application of its law; that situation presents a true conflict. An example is *Lilienthal v. Kaufman.*[11] The defendant had been declared a spendthrift by an Oregon court, a status which substantially limited his capacity to contract. Nevertheless, he had entered into a joint venture with plaintiff, a Californian, to sell binoculars. The relevant dealings between the two had taken place in California, a state which does not have a spendthrift law. When defendant defaulted on a loan repayment, plaintiff sued in Oregon. The court found that a true conflict existed. California's policy was to protect its creditors as well as to protect anyone who enters into a contract in that state. Those policies would be advanced

[9] 13 Abb.N.Cas. 210 (N.Y. Sup. Ct. 1883), discussed in § 58, *supra.*

[10] *See generally* Comment, *False Conflicts,* 55 Cal. L. Rev. 74 (1967).

[11] 239 Or. 1, 395 P.2d 543 (1964).

if the agreement were upheld; doing so, however, would thwart Oregon's policy of protecting the estates of spendthrifts from dissipation. The relation between those policies and the contacts with each state can be diagrammed thus:

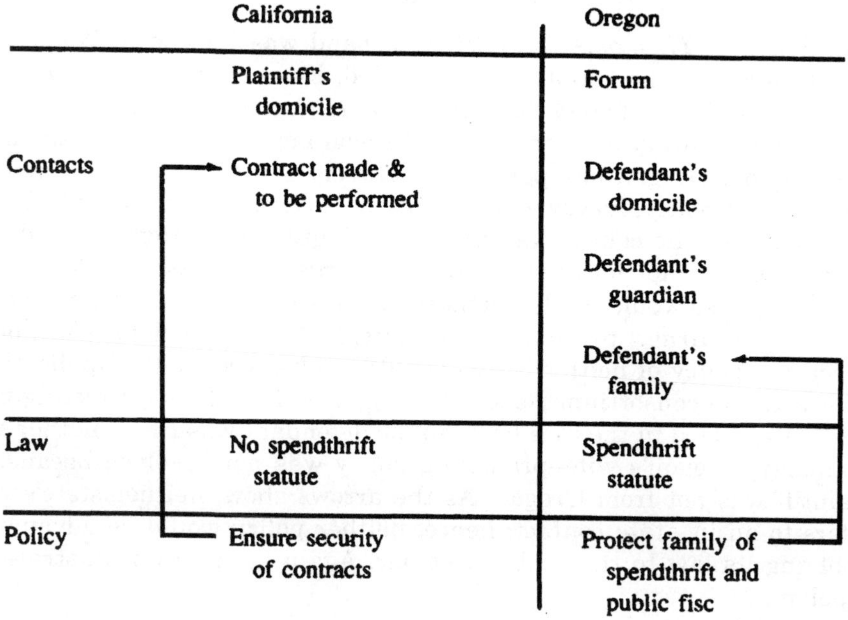

The diagram shows the true conflict. The policy of each state points to a contact in that state, which shows that each state's policy would be advanced if its law were applied in the case. Thus, a true conflict existed, which the court resolved, after some hesitation, by applying its own law.

Resolution of true conflicts provides advocates of interest analysis with their greatest challenge. It is discussed in the next section of this book, following an examination in the remainder of this section of the other components of interest analysis.

[d] The Disinterested Forum

A true conflict in a forum that has no interest of its own to advance raises the question of the law such a disinterested forum should choose. Cases of this sort seem to be quite rare,[12] perhaps because the problem of the disinterested forum is likely to arise only when defendant cannot be sued in an interested forum; modern long–arm statutes, however, generally make defendants amenable to jurisdiction in interested states. Currie suggested that the forum in such a case should dismiss on forum non

[12] The Restatement (Second) is written, however, from the perspective of a disinterested forum. *See* § 71, *supra*.

conveniens grounds; dismissal is appropriate if the action is not time–barred in both interested states, or if justice would not be frustrated by the dismissal.[13] If dismissal would be improper, Currie suggested that the forum either could choose the better law or the *lex fori.*

[e] The Unprovided–for Case

In *Erwin v. Thomas,*[14] Plaintiff's husband was injured in Washington, the state where the couple was domiciled, by an employee of an Oregon corporation. Plaintiff sued the corporation in Oregon for loss of consortium, a theory of recovery available under Oregon law, but not under the law of Washington. Oregon law permitted recovery in order to protect married women; that policy, however, would not be advanced in the case before the court because the couple was from Washington. Washington law did not permit recovery for loss of consortium in order to protect defendants, but that policy also would not be furthered because the defendant was not from Washington. *Erwin* presented, therefore, an unprovided–for case, one in which the policy of neither state would be advanced by the application of its law to the consortium issue. Washington's defendant–protecting policy was not involved in the case because the defendant was from another state. Similarly, Oregon's wife–protecting policy was not involved because the plaintiff was not from Oregon. As the arrows show, neither state's policy refers to an in–state contact; hence, neither policy would be advanced by applying its law to the problem at bar. Again, a diagram illustrates the problem:

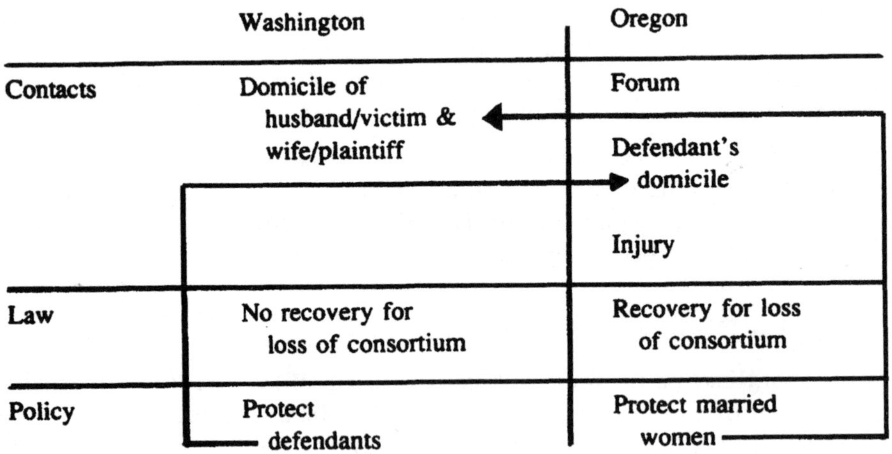

The Oregon court resolved the dilemma by adopting Currie's solution and applied its own law. Currie had argued that forum law should be followed

13 *See* Brainerd Currie, *The Disinterested Third State,* 28 Law & Contemp. Probs. 754 (1963).

14 264 Or. 454, 506 P.2d 494 (1973).

because no good reason existed for doing otherwise. He rejected an approach that would choose the better law, because it might place the court in the position of condemning the law of its own state.

§ 79 Interest Analysis: Resolving True Conflicts

The most difficult issue in interest analysis has proven to be the resolution of true conflicts. This section explores several methods of attacking the problem.

[a] Pure Interest Analysis

Currie originally took the position that courts should not weigh or balance competing state interests because "assessment of the respective values of the competing legitimate interests of two sovereign states is a political function of a very high order."[1] Courts should not assume that function in a democracy, Currie argued. Rather, that was a job best suited for the legislature. Forum law, therefore, should be applied, in the absence of a governing statute, to resolve a true conflict. Expressed differently, if interests do conflict, no reason exists to ignore the normal rule that forum law should not be displaced unless there is good ground for doing so.

Currie's position was strongly criticized, both on the practical ground that it leads to forum–shopping, and on the more theoretical ground that courts routinely balance competing interests when they make law in domestic cases.[2] Both objections make sense. Although Currie tended to minimize the possibility of forum–shopping, an attorney interested in fully protecting her client's rights will examine the choice–of–law regimes in each possible forum and, everything else being equal, use those options which benefit her client.[3]

More important is the theoretical objection: Currie recognized that courts, in domestic cases, always evaluate competing interests. That is the very nature of the common law. Even in cases involving statutes, courts routinely ask whether the legislature meant for a statute to be interpreted to override competing principles.[4] Thus, Currie's method for deciding true conflicts is inconsistent with judicial decision–making in ordinary domestic cases.[5]

---

[1] Brainerd Currie, *Notes on Methods and Objectives in the Conflict of Laws,* 1959 Duke L.J. 171, 176; Currie, Essays, 182.

[2] *See* Michael Traynor, *Conflict of Laws: Professor Currie's Restrained and Enlightened Forum,* 49 Calif. L. Rev. 845 (1961).

[3] Of course, everything else is seldom equal. Moreover, the possibility of forum–shopping is reduced somewhat by the unwillingness of some attorneys to refer a case to another attorney.

[4] The leading case is Riggs v. Palmer, 115 N.Y. 506, 22 N.E. 188 (1889) (the court interpreted a clear statute of descent and distribution as prohibiting inheritance by a murderer from his victim).

[5] An unrelated criticism of Currie's method can be found in Maurice Rosenberg, *The Comeback of Choice–of–Law Rules,* 81 Colum. L. Rev. 946 (1981). Professor Rosenberg's thesis is that courts use different reasoning in multi–state cases because they consider, *inter alia,* factors such as party expectations based on the locus of a relationship.

Currie responded by qualifying the rule that the forum should always apply its own law: When a court recognizes a true conflict, it should re–examine its own law to see if "a more moderate and restrained interpretation" of the policy behind the law will show that its purpose does not require application in a particular case.[6] That re–examination, in other words, might turn an "apparent true conflict" into a false conflict.

Currie used *Bernkrant v. Fowler*[7] as an example. Plaintiffs sought to enforce an oral contract made in Nevada to refinance a mortgage on Nevada real estate; the promisor died in California before he fulfilled his promise, and the promisees sued his estate in a California state court. The executrix set up the defense of the Statute of Frauds. The defense was good under California law, but not under that of Nevada. That difference appears to set up a true conflict between the California policy of protecting estates[8] and the Nevada policy favoring validation of commercial agreements.

Justice Traynor finessed the problem. He observed that California's general policy was to protect party expectations in contract cases. That policy was strong in *Bernkrant* because the contract was entered into in another state (where it was valid) and the parties could not know that the promisor might die in California (where his estate might be subject to the local Statute of Frauds). By finding an additional, more general, California policy, Traynor took what appeared to be a true conflict, involving the Statute of Frauds, and made it into a false one. He was able to do so by interpreting his state's Statute of Frauds in a "moderate and restrained way" — an interpretation which was also more consistent with party expectations. Construction of a statute in accordance with more general principles comports with good methods of statutory interpretation; the legislature is presumed to have worked against the backdrop of basic legal principles.[9] Moreover, such construction permits a court to reconcile local law with the needs of the interstate commercial system.

A similarly restrained and moderate examination of Oregon law would have led to a different result in *Lilienthal v. Kaufman,* discussed in the preceding section. Plaintiff in that case apparently had no way of knowing that he was dealing with a spendthrift because California law had no such status provision.[10] A person who enters into a contract without notice that his promisor is laboring under a disability is usually not penalized in contract law.[11] Surely one who is not even aware of the possibility of a

[6] Brainerd Currie, *The Disinterested Third State,* 28 Law & Contemp. Probs. 754, 757 (1963).

[7] 55 Cal.2d 588, 360 P.2d 906, 12 Cal. Rptr. 266 (1961).

[8] That policy would be implicated only if the promisor had been domiciled in California when he died, an issue that was neither clear nor necessary for the court to resolve.

[9] *See* William L. Reynolds, Judicial Process in a Nutshell 233–37 (2d ed. 1991).

[10] This would distinguish *Lilienthal* from Olshen v. Kaufman, 235 Or. 423, 385 P.2d 161 (1963) (involving the same spendthrift). *Olshen* involved a purely domestic transaction, and a domiciliary reasonably could be expected to be aware of the spendthrift statutes. Although the lender in *Lilienthal* apparently did run a credit check on the borrower in Oregon, the check did not disclose his status as a spendthrift. *See* Roger Cramton, *et al.,* Conflict of Laws 253 (4th ed. 1987).

[11] *Compare* Restatement (Second) of Contracts § 15(2) (1981) (lack of mental capacity to contract).

disability should not be penalized. Concern for the reasonable expectations of out–of–state contracting parties should have been an important consideration in construing the spendthrift statute in *Lilienthal,* the very consideration that Traynor employed so skillfully in *Bernkrant.*

[b] Comparative Impairment

In an important article written in 1963,[12] Professor William Baxter suggested a variation of Currie's notion of restrained and enlightened interpretation.[13] Baxter proposed a method for resolving true conflict cases based on his observation that state laws generally have, in addition to the domestic policy objectives identified by Currie, *external* objectives which are based on each state's need to have its own policies respected by other states. When the external objectives of each state conflict, Baxter argued that "the external objective of the state whose internal objective will be least impaired" should be subordinated to that of its competitor. Expressed somewhat differently, Baxter suggested that true conflicts could be resolved by comparing the extent of impairment of each state's policy and applying the law whose policy would be most impaired if it were not applied.

The California Supreme Court used comparative impairment to resolve a true conflict[14] in *Bernhard v. Harrah's Club.*[15] Plaintiff had been injured in California in a collision with a car driven by Fern Myers. Fern and her husband Phil were returning from a trip to defendant's casino where, it was claimed, they had been served drinks even though they were obviously drunk. Although located in Nevada, defendant advertised heavily in California. The California court had recently created a common law "dram shop" action holding a tavern keeper liable in those circumstances; the Nevada courts had refused to take a similar step, although serving a patron who was already inebriated was a crime under Nevada law. California's interest was in protecting drivers on its highways. Nevada's interest lay in protecting local taverns from excessive liability. That clash posed a true conflict for resolution by the court, as can be seen from the following diagram:

[12] William F. Baxter, *Choice of Law and the Federal System,* 16 Stan. L. Rev. 1 (1963).

[13] Baxter and Currie apparently developed their ideas independently and simultaneously. *See* Herma Hill Kay, *The Use of Comparative Impairment to Resolve True Conflicts: An Evaluation of the California Experience,* 68 Cal. L. Rev. 577, 584 n.52 (1980).

[14] Baxter developed this principle of comparative impairment for use by federal courts in full faith and credit and diversity cases; he rejected the notion that state judges could properly "allocat[e] spheres of legal control among states." Nevertheless, comparative impairment has found a home in the Supreme Court of California.

[15] 16 Cal.3d 313, 128 Cal.Rptr. 215, 546 P.2d 719, *cert. denied,* 429 U.S. 859 (1976).

	California	Nevada
Contacts	Forum Plaintiff's domicile Car driver's domicile Collision	Defendant tavern Drinking and tortious offering
Law	Tavern keeper liability	No tavern keeper liability
Policy	Protect citizens on highways	Protect gambling and tavern industry

The court resolved that conflict by re–examining each state's interest using comparative impairment (à la Baxter). The court found that California's interest would be "significantly impaired" if its dram shop law were not applied to defendant's conduct. When it solicited business in California, the tavern put itself "at the heart" of California's interest in preventing the sale of alcohol "to obviously intoxicated persons who are likely to act in California in the intoxicated state." Nevada's interest, on the other hand, would be less impaired. Nevada already imposed a duty on tavern owners (pursuant to a criminal statute) not to serve obviously drunk persons and, therefore, no new duty would be imposed on tavern owners if plaintiffs were to prevail. Moreover, Nevada's policy of protecting its innkeepers from the exposure to "ruinous" civil liability would not be significantly impaired because the liability would be placed only on those "who actively solicit California business." Comparative impairment thus was used to adjust the relationship between the competing interests of two sovereigns and to resolve a true conflict.

Comparative impairment has been developed more fully since *Bernhard.* In *Offshore Rental Co. v. Continental Oil Co.,*[16] the court stated that the goal of the comparative impairment test is "to determine the relative commitment of the respective states to the law involved." The analysis in *Offshore* to some extent resembles the "better law"[17] approach by inquiring into the current status of the particular state rule: How vigorously is it

[16] 22 Cal.3d 157, 148 Cal. Rptr. 867, 583 P.2d 721 (1978).

[17] *See* § 81, *infra.*

enforced,[18] and has it been adopted or rejected in other states? Finally, in a later federal case, the court, faced with a true conflict between the laws of two states which could not be resolved by comparative impairment, broke the "tie" by factoring into the equations the policies of a third jurisdiction — "the state with the next strongest relevant interest."[19] That policy was adopted because it coincided with the policy of one of the two most interested states.

California's use of comparative impairment has been criticized on the grounds of doctrinal impurity,[20] and the analysis in the decisions certainly can be questioned.[21] But those criticisms overlook the very real value of comparative impairment, which forces the court to examine closely exactly what is at stake in the case — how the decision will actually affect, interfere with, and advance relevant state policies. As Judge Sprecher observed in applying comparative impairment in a very complex case: "[T]he point is that the reviewing court must look behind an apparent conflict to the precise issue and the precise interest of each state."[22] Comparative impairment, in short, is a device for resolving a true conflict by fine–tuning the inquiry into state policy and interests.

[c] Other Ways to Resolve True Conflicts

This has hardly been an area lacking in scholarly activity, and a number of solutions have been advanced. Professor von Mehren once suggested the possibility of fashioning completely new rules for true conflicts.[23] In a case like *Lilienthal,* for example, the plaintiff might be permitted to recover half of his claim. This Solomonic proposal seems unlikely to be adopted; judicial resistance to cutting–the–baby–in–half type proposals seems to be too strong to overcome.[24]

Many other schemes have also been proposed. One example is Professor Weintraub's "functional" approach.[25] When a true conflict exists in a tort

[18] The intensity of enforcement inquiry builds around a suggestion in Arthur Taylor von Mehren & Donald T. Trautman, The Law of Multistate Problems 394 (1965).

[19] In Re Air Crash Disaster Near Chicago, Ill., 644 F.2d 594, 628 (7th Cir. 1981), *cert. denied,* 454 U.S. 878 (1981).

[20] *See, e.g.,* Kay, *supra* § 13, note 3.

[21] Especially vulnerable to criticism is *Offshore Rental;* there, the court found a true conflict by assuming — not deciding — what California law was on the problem at issue. Later, in I. J. Weinrot and Son, Inc. v. Jackson, 708 P.2d 682 (Cal. 1985), the court ruled, in effect, that California law was the same as the Louisiana law at issue in *Offshore Rental.*

[22] In Re Air Crash Disaster Near Chicago, Ill., 644 F.2d 594, 621 n.31 (7th Cir.), *cert. denied,* 454 U.S. 878 (1981).

[23] Arthur Taylor von Mehren, *Special Substantive Rules for Multistate Problems: Their Role and Significance in Contemporary Choice of Law Methodology,* 88 Harv. L. Rev. 347, 366–67 (1974).

[24] Compare the reluctance of courts to apportion losses in contracts discharged for impossibility. *See* Note, *Apportioning Loss After Discharge of a Burdensome Contract: A Statutory Solution,* 69 Yale L.J. 1054 (1960). On the other hand, judicial acceptance of fundamental changes such as comparative negligence augurs well for von Mehren's suggestion.

[25] Weintraub at 259–61, 397–98.

case, Weintraub would apply the law of the state favoring recovery, unless the particular rule favoring recovery is either aberrational or anachronistic. He reaches that conclusion because it is the "preferred national solution" to the problem. Why is it "preferred"? Weintraub argues that recovery by tort plaintiffs represents a national trend, that the presence of insurance makes unfair surprise of little relevance in tort law, and that recovery rules will limit the effect of anachronistic laws.

Weintraub's analysis has the virtue of ease of application, and, it might be argued that, in an increasingly pro–plaintiff legal world,[26] it will result in the application of the better rule of law. On the other hand, he denies a state the authority to impose its solution on a multi–state problem unless its views of the proper solution coincide with the national trend; that is hardly the essence of federalism. Moreover, Weintraub is not very concerned with the policies served by the rules in question (once a true conflict has been identified) and the impact on the functioning of those policies of a contrary holding. Finally, Weintraub's analysis does not deal well with the problem of unfair surprise (which does exist in some situations), as well as the problem that, in some areas of tort law, the trend favors the defendant (*e.g.,* the law of defamation).

Other attempts have been made to build a theoretical model that would resolve true conflicts. Professor Seidelson, for example, posits second and third levels of inquiry once a true conflict has been identified. Those inquiries would determine whether a state has a "minimal interest" in the litigation and then determine with an "enhanced degree of specificity" the exact impact of possible holdings.[27] Such attempts by scholars may help judges, other scholars, and students understand the difficulty of the task before the court. Because of their complexity, however, it is doubtful whether the practical impact of such models will be significant.

Other scholars have more or less given up the hunt and suggested a return to the *lex fori.* Professor Singer, for example, recommends a rebuttable preference on behalf of forum law.[28] That preference, he argues, would reflect both current practice and theory. Singer rejects a rigid forum preference in order to avoid a "race to the bottom among the states" and to avoid encouraging a race to the court house by sophisticated parties seeking declaratory judgments. And in deciding whether the forum presumption had been rebutted, the court would be able to consider multistate needs and fairness concerns.

Finally, Professor Weinberg has suggested that the forum faced with a true conflict in which it has an interest should "take unilateral responsibility for the enforcement of law."[29] That application of a strong *lex fori,*

---

[26] And the legal world arguably has become much more favorable to defendants since Weintraub advanced his thesis.

[27] David E. Seidelson, *Interest Analysis: The Quest for Perfection and the Frailties of Man,* 19 Duq. L. Rev. 207, 226–29 (1981).

[28] Joseph W. Singer, *Facing Real Conflicts,* 24 Cornell Int'l L.J. 197 (1991).

[29] Louise Weinberg, *Against Comity,* 80 Geo. L.J. 53, 94 (1991).

tempered by its limitation to true conflicts, reflects a wide feeling of unhappiness among judges and scholars with the even–handedness of modern conflicts law.[30] Nevertheless, as Professor Weinberg recognizes, her rule largely gives up the fight for choice–of–law rules which serve policy ends other than ease of administration. Whether that is worthwhile is the great debate in choice of law fight today.

[d] Balancing Interests: An Invitation to Heresy

A final word must be said on the balancing of interests. The notion that courts can balance interests is heretical to proponents of interest analysis, perhaps due to the still dominant influence of Brainerd Currie. Currie argued that accommodation of the interests of competing states was a "political" task to be entrusted to legislatures rather than to courts.

Surely that position is wrong. In ordinary domestic cases, courts constantly balance competing rules, both common law and statutory, in order to accommodate competing policy interests. The balancing task need not be entirely intuitive. The sophisticated judge knows that balancing is a shorthand way of describing a process which has many well–known, objectifiable components. When asked to choose between two competing common law rules, for example, courts examine such factors as the unfair surprise to litigants, the presence and intensity of the public policies involved, the trends in the area, the needs of the commercial world, and the relation of the competing rules to more deeply rooted principles drawn from more fundamental policy. Courts in domestic cases, in other words, use the same techniques suggested by interest analysts to resolve true conflicts. In domestic cases, however, judges rarely resort to the abstract theorizing seen in choice–of–law articles. The judge in the domestic case is familiar with the task of adjusting competing interests; she need not justify her use of craft techniques by elaborate theoretical modeling. Because resolution of choice–of–law cases does not differ materially from the problem of resolving domestic conflicts,[31] the judge with the choice–of–law problem should treat it, as indeed Currie suggested, in the same way she would treat an analogous domestic problem. Absent a controlling statute, she should ask which law should be applied and what reasons support that result. Her duty then is to explain the result as best she can. Undertaken in good faith and with a sensitivity for the concerns of other jurisdictions, resolution of competing interests should not be beyond the capacity of American courts.

§ 80 Interest Analysis In Practice

Brainerd Currie's method of analyzing choice–of–law problems has had great impact. Not only did interest analysis help shatter the vested rights

---

[30] *But see* Douglas Laycock, *Equal Citizens of Equal and Territorial States: The Constitutional Foundations of Choice of Law,* 92 Colum. L. Rev. 249, 311 (1992): "Eliminating forum preference altogether is the only constitutional solution."

[31] There would be a difference, however, if judges discriminated against foreign law.

theory, but all modern commentators on the subject must come to terms with Currie's work. Since Currie's untimely death in 1964, his disciples, notably Professors Kay,[1] Posnak,[2] and Sedler,[3] have borne the torch.

Interest analysis thus is alive and has strong adherents in the scholarly community. It also does well among judges. To be sure, according to Professor Borchers,[4] only four jurisdictions (California, Hawaii, Massachusetts, and New Jersey), purport to follow Currie's analysis directly. Nevertheless, it is clear that the influence of his method extends far beyond those two states. Many courts employ interest analysis either in conjunction with other theories or, indirectly, by reading interest analysis into the policies described in § 6 of the Second Restatement.[5] Indeed, both § 6 and Leflar's "choice–influencing considerations"[6] explicitly direct judicial attention to an analysis of state interests. Thus, it is apparent that interest analysis, in one form or another, continues to exert great influence on the judiciary and will do so for some time to come.

There is a final point to be made in connection with interest analysis. The old system of choice of law captured in the First Restatement combined apparently hard–and–fast rules with such escape devices as characterization, renvoi, and public policy.[7] Proponents of policy–based methods of analysis hoped that their systems, by encouraging open judicial consideration of policy, would eliminate the ad hoc and even cynical manipulation which marked the old system. The new systems do indeed focus concern — openly — on the policy–making role of judges. Nevertheless, judicial manipulation is still possible (many would say that it is easy) under interest analysis.[8]

The point can be illustrated by a simple guest statute case, *Kell v. Henderson.*[9] Plaintiff and defendant in *Kell* were both domiciled in Ontario where defendant's car was insured. On a trip from Ontario to New York, plaintiff was injured in an accident in New York. The case is a mirror image

[1] *E.g.*, Herma Hill Kay, *The Use of Comparative Impairment to Resolve True Conflicts: An Evaluation of the California Experience,* 68 Cal. L. Rev. 557 (1980).

[2] Bruce Posnak, *Choice of Law: Interest Analysis and its "New" Critics,* 36 Am. J. Comp. L. 681 (1988).

[3] Perhaps the most significant modification made by Sedler is the recognition that "real" interests of a jurisdiction must be identified before interest analysis comes into play. Robert Allen Sedler, *The Governmental Interest Approach to Choice of Law: An Analysis and a Reformulation,* 25 U.C.L.A. L. Rev. 181 (1977). Sedler also defends interest analysis with particular vigor against charges that it is difficult to apply; he challenges critics of the approach to demonstrate how it has led to "bad" results in actual cases, as opposed to hypotheticals unlikely to arise in practice. Robert Allen Sedler, *Interest Analysis and Forum Preference in the Conflict of Laws: A Response to the 'New Critics',* 34 Mercer L. Rev. 593 (1983).

[4] Patrick J. Borchers, *Choice–of–Law Revolution: An Empirical Study,* 49 Wash. & Lee L.Q. 349, 373 (1992).

[5] *E.g.,* Johnson v. Spider Staging Corp., 87 Wash.2d 577, 555 P.2d 997 (1976).

[6] *See* § 81, *infra.*

[7] *See* §§ 65–68, *supra.*

[8] *See* William M. Richman, *Diagramming Conflicts: A Graphic Understanding of Interest Analysis,* 43 Ohio St. L.J. 317 326–30 (1982).

[9] 47 Misc.2d 992, 263 N.Y.S.2d 647 (1965), aff'd, 26 A.D.2d 595, 270 N.Y.S.2d 552 (1966).

of *Babcock v. Jackson*,[10] and if the relevant policies are the same as those in that case, *Kell* presents a false conflict. New York has no interest in compensating Ontario plaintiffs. This can be seen readily in the following diagram:

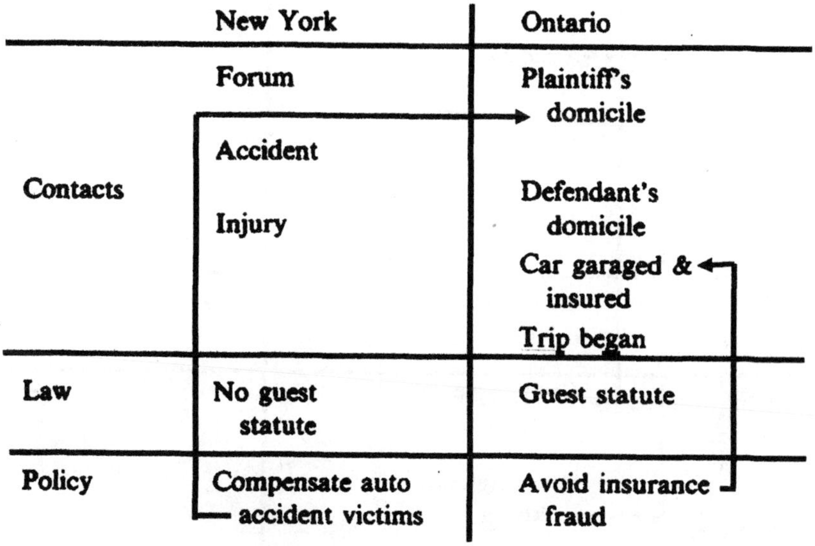

Because it is a false conflict, Ontario law will be applied.

In order to apply New York law (permitting the plaintiff to recover), all that is necessary is to characterize the case as a true conflict; Currie's system then would select forum law. That can be done by identifying a New York policy which points to a New York contact — not a difficult task. Professor Trautman, for example, has suggested that one reason New York does not have a guest statute is because it wishes to deter negligent driving on its roads.[11] That policy would be furthered by applying it to the *Kell* facts. Thus, with the deterrence policy added, the case becomes a true conflict, as can be seen in the following diagram:

[10] 12 N.Y.2d 473, 191 N.E.2d 279, 240 N.Y.S.2d 743 (1963). *Babcock* is discussed in § 78 *supra*.

[11] Donald T. Trautman, *Kell v. Henderson, A Comment,* 67 Colum. L. Rev. 465, 467 (1967).

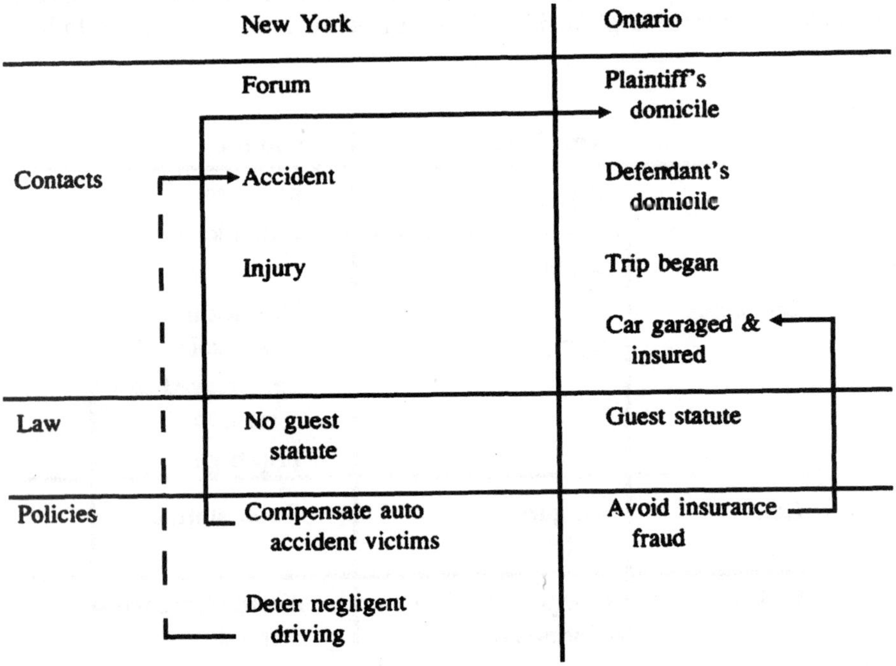

The point, of course, is that no system can escape completely the curse of characterization and manipulation. And perhaps scholars and judges have been too quick to identify a problem as a false conflict, as Professor Singer has demonstrated so ably.[12] In the end, however, the integrity and wisdom of the judges necessarily come into play. Nevertheless, some systems are better than others at structuring the decisionmaking process so as to discourage manipulation. Although interest analysis is not immune from the disease, its focus on identification of relevant interests represents a significant advance over the policy–blind system of the First Restatement.

§ 81 Choice–Influencing Considerations and the Better Law[1]

In a series of articles beginning in 1966, and later condensed in his treatise, Professor Robert Leflar identified five "choice–influencing considerations" that he perceived as providing a "working basis" for judicial decision–making. Leflar argued that his "considerations" embody the factors which actually motivate courts, and that public discussion of the considerations by judges in their opinions was an essential condition for proper decision–making. Moreover, this kind of open discussion is necessary

[12] Joseph W. Singer, *A Pragmatic Guide to Conflicts,* 70 B.U. L. Rev. 731 (1990) (developing sophisticated arguments on what state interests really are).

[1] *See generally* Leflar, McDougal & Felix §§ 95, 102–08. *See also Symposium, Leflar on Conflicts,* 31 S.C. L. Rev. 409 (1980).

to develop a workable body of precedent in the area of choice of law. Leflar was not the first to attempt this task;[2] his personal prestige and the clarity of his observations, however, have made his work especially influential. This section analyzes the five "considerations" Leflar focused upon; it then discusses his system in operation, both generally and in a specific case.

[a] The Considerations

[1] Predictability of Result

This is the first consideration listed by Leflar, although he states that the order of presentation is not significant.[3] Predictability is important because knowledge of the likely result encourages planning and reliance by parties to a consensual transaction and also discourages wasteful litigation and forum–shopping. Hence, predictability assumes special significance in cases involving contracts, wills, and marriages — situations styled by Leflar as "socially favored arrangements."[4] Conversely, the consideration of predictability will be less important in those areas of tort law where planning generally is of little or no importance.

[2] Maintenance of Interstate and International Order

A federal system of government strains relationships among its component sovereigns as each seeks to increase its influence over others. If another state has a strong interest in a matter, ignoring that interest, by applying the local law of the forum "unaccompanied by independent justification," improperly disregards the interest of the other state.[5] Again, this consideration assumes particular importance in commercial law where order is especially necessary to facilitate interstate business transactions.

[3] Simplification of the Judicial Task

Ease of judicial administration, Leflar argues, is not an end in itself, but it is certainly an important concern. The need to expedite litigation and conserve scarce judicial resources is the reason, for instance, for the rule which permits the forum to apply its own law of "procedure" even when it chooses the "substantive" law of another state.[6]

[4] Advancement of the Forum's Governmental Interests

This is an important objective in every case, but it should not be used by a court as "an unreasoning fallback" which it can substitute for

[2] *See, e.g.*, Elliot Cheatham & Willis Reese, *Choice of the Applicable Law,* 52 Colum. L. Rev. 959 (1952).

[3] Leflar, McDougal & Felix at 279.

[4] *Id.* at 291. The authors point out that this list resembles Ehrenzweig's "basic rules of validity," discussed *infra* § 82.

[5] Leflar, McDougal & Felix at 292.

[6] This problem is discussed in § 58, *supra*.

choice–of–law analysis.[7] Leflar especially cautions against reflexive application of forum law merely because a forum domiciliary is involved. He warns that basic policies (as opposed to rules) rarely oppose each other strongly in our society, and that adoption of a specific rule is often a matter of happenstance. Hence, a court, in using this fourth consideration, should be careful that it is not unthinkingly "justifying" the choice of forum law in a case where forum interests are not strongly implicated.

[5] The Better Rule of Law

The last consideration, application of "the better law," is surely the most famous and controversial of Leflar's five considerations. He does not claim to have been the first to notice that judges are influenced by a desire to apply the better law; indeed, he does not attach as much weight to this factor as some other commentators.[8] But scholarly consideration of Leflar's choice–of–law method has concentrated on the better law aspect.

Leflar writes that a law is better if it is "superior" to another law when considered in the light of "socioeconomic jurisprudential standards."[9] That definition, of course, merely reflects current thinking in jurisprudence that law is designed, and should be employed, to achieve societal goals.[10] Leflar believes that judges often apply the better law to a problem in their attempts to reach a just result. Unfortunately, they often do so covertly: by using escape devices, facile maneuvering around precedent, and other judicial "gimmicks." Open recognition of the desirability of applying the better rule eliminates the need to resort to such covert methods. It also helps achieve predictability and fairness in result and openly involves the parties in the decision–making process. Leflar, in short, would not change what courts actually have been doing over the years; rather, he merely wants to bring the process out of the closet. As Leflar puts it, "honesty is the best policy, even in judicial opinions."[11]

[b] The Better Law and Lex Fori

Discussion of the better law consideration tends to center on two concerns: How a court can determine the better rule and whether the approach will always lead to choice of forum law. Identifying the better law should be no more difficult in a conflicts case than in purely domestic litigation. A court asked to adopt strict liability in tort, for example, will examine the trend in other states, scholarly commentary, and the teachings of its own precedents to determine whether strict liability is the better rule. The same process should be followed in a multi–state transaction. An example is *Clark v. Clark*.[12] There, Chief Justice Kenison, using Leflar's method,

[7] Leflar, McDougal & Felix at 295.

[8] *E.g.*, Friedrich Juenger, *Choice of Law in Interstate Torts,* 118 U. Pa. L. Rev. 202 (1969).

[9] Leflar, McDougal & Felix at 297.

[10] *See* the comparable discussion in connection with interest analysis, § 75, *supra*.

[11] Leflar, McDougal & Felix at 300. *See also* Robert Leflar, *Honest Judicial Opinions,* 74 Nw. L. Rev. 721 (1979).

[12] 107 N.H. 351, 222 A.2d 205 (1966).

inquired whether a foreign guest statute was better law than the less restrictive forum rule which permitted the guest to recover on a showing of negligence only. Kenison noted that the pervasive nature of automobile insurance had made the modern world a far different place than it was in the 1920's when guest statutes had been adopted. Consequently, no state had adopted a guest statute for many years, and those which had adopted them "are today construing them much more narrowly, expressing their dissatisfaction with them." Such evidence easily convinced Kenison that the better law was the one based on negligence, and that a guest statute was "a drag on the coattails of civilization." Not all cases will be as easy as *Clark,* of course, but the same analytic technique will be available in each case where the better law approach is used.

The more serious problem in better law cases is whether *lex fori* will always turn out to be the better law. This really breaks down into two problems — one theoretical and one practical: Is it proper for a court ever to decide that forum law is not better, and will courts following Leflar's approach ever, in fact, choose non–forum law?

[1] The Theoretical Objection

One objection to the better law approach is that a court of the forum must decide whether forum law is the better law, a decision whose outcome is all too predictable. That concern is strongest when the forum law is enacted legislation. "It is not for us to consider which is the better law," wrote the Supreme Court of Iowa, "when the policymaking body of the state has spoken."[13] But surely that argument is specious. It is unlikely that the legislature ever considered the application of its rule in a case where another state has significant contacts; if forum law is archaic, the additional elements provided by the extra–forum contacts are sufficient reason not to apply forum law (at least when the legislature has not addressed specifically the choice–of–law problem). That certainly would be the case when the choice of foreign law is influenced by considerations in addition to better law.

Even a recent affirmation of an old rule should not preclude rejection of *lex fori* under the better law system. Consider a court which had recently rejected strict liability in tort for domestic cases on the ground that the negligence principle should not be overruled because too much reliance had been placed on it. Reliance on the old law might not be a factor in a case with foreign contacts, however, and it might be appropriate, therefore, for the courts to apply strict liability as the better law — even though that solution had been rejected domestically.

[2] The Practical Objection

Although scholarly commentary on the better law may exceed its use in the courts, several states have adopted Leflar's approach to choice–of–law

[13] Fuerste v. Bemis, 156 N.W.2d 831, 834 (Iowa 1968).

problems.[14] Critics have argued that the search for better law will serve merely as a cloak for choice of forum law. Experience, in fact, shows that the critics were mostly correct, as suggested by the *Milkovich* case discussed below. But there are examples in which courts using Leflar's approach have applied foreign rather than forum law,[15] suggesting perhaps that judges can be honest (at least sometimes) in their reasoning.

It is not surprising, in any event, that the law of the forum often turns out to be the better law. The forum courts and legislature, after all, have played an important role in developing their new law; presumably, a key factor in that development was determining that the doctrine which eventually became forum law was also the best law. There may have been reasons, of course, why the forum did not feel free to adopt *the* very best law (the pull of precedents in related areas, for example). Nevertheless, no one should be surprised if forum law generally is thought to be better.

[c] Leflar in Practice

Perhaps the leading case applying Leflar's approach is *Milkovich v. Saari*[16] — a guest statute case in which both parties were Ontario domiciliaries. They set out together from Thunder Bay, Ontario, for an evening on the town in Duluth, Minnesota. There was an accident in Duluth and the plaintiff, who had been hospitalized there, sued her host. Ontario, unlike Minnesota, has a guest statute, and the defendant employed it in his defense. The court followed Leflar's approach step by step.[17]

---

[14] Patrick J. Borchers, *The Choice–of–Law Revolution: An Empirical Study,* 49 Wash. & Lee L.Q. 349, 373 (1992), lists Arkansas, Minnesota, New Hampshire, Rhode Island, and Wisconsin as following Leflar's method.

[15] *E.g.,* Lichter v. Fritsch, 77 Wis.2d 178, 252 N.W.2d 360 (1977); Schneider v. Schneider, 110 N.H. 70, 260 A.2d 97 (1969). *See also* Offshore Rental Co. v. Continental Oil Co., 22 Cal.3d 157, 148 Cal.Rptr. 867, 583 P.2d 721 (1978) ("prevalent and progressive" foreign law applied rather than "unusual and outmoded" local statute; Leflar not cited, however).

[16] 295 Minn. 155, 203 N.W.2d 408 (1973).

[17] A diagram of the problem reveals it to be a false conflict; Minnesota's policy of protecting plaintiffs would not be advanced by applying Minnesota law.

The first three steps were easy (or so the court thought). The court believed *predictability* to be irrelevant in nonconsensual transactions, where planning is not important. The *needs of the interstate system* were satisfied as long as the law of a state with a substantial connection to the problem was selected. *Ease of judicial administration* was no concern given the issue before the court — the choice between applying the guest statute or not; either rule is equally easy to apply. That left two factors to resolve the conflict.

The *forum's interest* would be advanced by applying its law because of its "status as a justice–administering state." (The court did not note that, as defined, this interest gives double–weight to better law because justice is served, as the court observed, by applying the better law.) The court correctly found that its own rule was the *better law,* using reasoning similar to that used by Justice Kenison in *Clark v. Clark.* Thus, with its choice influenced by the only two relevant considerations, the court permitted plaintiff to proceed with her suit.

[d] A Final Word

Leflar has helped pinpoint the factors that influence judicial decision–making. The concern with his approach is that it does not really discipline judicial thinking; rather, it may tend to encourage ad hoc and unprincipled selection. In addition, his approach probably leans too far in the direction of *lex fori.* Its great merit, on the other hand, lies in forcing judges and scholars to consider openly the comparative merits of the underlying substantive laws. If they explain their choice honestly and carefully, the "considerations" Leflar has identified certainly can improve the quality of the judicial product.

§ 82 Ehrenzweig's "True Rules"[1]

Professor Albert Ehrenzweig developed an approach to choice–of–law questions based on what he styled a "proper law in a proper forum." At the heart of Ehrenzweig's thesis were "True Rules": statements formulated by his keen American Realist's appreciation of the need to analyze "the actual 'doing' of the courts rather than merely their language."[2] That analysis led Ehrenzweig to conclude that some jurisdiction–selecting rules of the First Restatement, such as the reference to the law of the place where the contract was made, masked what courts actually did in practice.

This observation of judicial behavior prompted Ehrenzweig to formulate a number of "true rules" to describe that actual practice. Among them were the following:[3] in family law, courts adopt rules which uphold a marriage ("favor matrimonii") and legitimacy ("favor legitimationis"); contract questions are controlled by party autonomy if the parties have chosen a law and,

[1] *See generally* Albert A. Ehrenzweig, *A Proper Law in a Proper Forum: A "Restatement" of the "Lex Fori Approach,"* 18 Okla. L. Rev. 340 (1965).

[2] Albert A. Ehrenzweig, Conflicts in a Nutshell 42 (3d ed. 1974).

[3] *See id.* at 329–36.

if not, by a "validating law" that would uphold the contract; the "lex situs" controls most land transactions as well as succession to immovables. Tort law, however, seems to lack true rules.

Once a court identifies a true rule as implicated in a particular case, it applies the rule to the facts and reaches a result. If no true rule exists, then Ehrenzweig believed the court generally should apply its own law — the lex fori. Thus, particularly in tort cases, the application of forum law (the law chosen by plaintiff, in other words) is quite likely.[4] Ehrenzweig argued that because most choice–of–law rules are based on precedent, statutory directions, and true rules, the need to resort to the residual category of forum law would not be great.[5]

Ehrenzweig recognized that a preference for forum law could lead to forum–shopping. He sought to ameliorate that possibility by having the forum exercise jurisdictional restraint. A court should exercise jurisdiction only if it is legitimately interested in seeing its law applied; if it is so interested then it is a "proper forum" and can apply a "proper law."[6]

Ehrenzweig's system has a number of appealing characteristics. His notion of true rules — and their identification — is very helpful in dissipating much of the fog created by choice–of–law rhetoric. Courts traditionally act with justice in mind, and recognition of true rules helps show the common perception of justice. That perception, in turn, should help guide judicial decision–making.

Perhaps of more importance, however, is his idea of a proper law in a proper forum. Ehrenzweig would restrain the crude preference for forum law seen in many cases by forcing the court to answer the jurisdictional question: Is it fair for the court to assert its power over this litigation? By recognizing that jurisdiction and choice of law are connected, Ehrenzweig hoped to avoid the unfair exercise of power. Although much can be said for that approach,[7] it has had little influence in the courts.[8] More lasting is his identification of rules that may truly guide judicial decision–making.[9]

§ 83 Counterattack: Neo–Territorialism

Interest analysis shifted the focus in choice–of–law cases away from the vested rights theory, a theory heavily dependent on territorial considerations. It was not long before a counter–revolution set in, and attempts were

[4] *See id.* at 333.

[5] *See id.* at 48–50. A corollary of Ehrenzweig's method is the notion that states have little real interest in having their substantive law applied in most situations. Albert A. Ehrenzweig, Private International Law 350 (2d ed. 1962).

[6] *See id.* at 350–52.

[7] *See* the discussion in § 94, *infra,* of the relation in constitutional law between jurisdiction and choice of law.

[8] *See* Robert Leflar, *Ehrenzweig and the Courts,* 18 Okla. L. Rev. 366 (1965).

[9] Not everyone has accepted Ehrenzweig's formulation of individual "true rules." *See, e.g.,* Brainerd Currie, *Ehrenzweig and the Statute of Frauds: An Inquiry into the "Rule of Validation,"* 18 Okla. L. Rev. 243 (1965).

made to restore primacy — in some form — to territorialism in choice–of–law. Professors Cavers[1] and Twerski[2] led the early "neo–territorialist" attack; their flagship case was *Cipolla v. Shaposka.*[3]

Plaintiff and defendant in *Cipolla* attended the same school in Delaware. After classes one day, defendant started to drive plaintiff to his home in Pennsylvania. An accident occurred in Delaware, and plaintiff later sued in Pennsylvania; defendant set up the Delaware guest statute as a defense. Defendant and his father (in whose name the car was registered) were Delaware residents.

The *Cipolla* court first examined the problem under interest analysis and found that Delaware's contacts were "qualitatively greater," and that Delaware had the "greater interest."[4] The court then added that:

> [I]t seems only fair to permit a defendant to rely on his home state law when he is acting within that state. Inhabitants of a state should not be put in jeopardy of liability exceeding that created by their state's law just because a visitor from a state offering higher protection decides to visit there.

The court concluded that "as a general approach a territorial view seems preferable to a personal view." Application of that approach to the "true conflict" presented by the case showed that Delaware "has the greater interest" in seeing its law applied.

The *Cipolla* court relied heavily on Professor Cavers' work as authority.[5] Cavers had argued that choice–of–law decisions should be influenced substantially by territorial considerations, both because governments (which have the responsibility for regulating conduct within their borders) are organized along territorial lines, and because party expectations have a strong territorial cast. Expectations, in other words, derive largely from the territory in which the activity takes place. Thus, a driver in a guest statute state, as in *Cipolla,* expects that his standard of liability will not change merely because he comes in contact with someone from a liability state; the intruder, on the contrary, has "exposed himself" to the possibility that the laws of the visited state will differ from those of his home state.

Cavers derived a set of seven "Principles of Preference" from his analysis of common choice–of–law problems. These principles, which specifically address only a limited number of problems in tort and contract law, emphasize "fairness" to the parties and deference to their territorially justified expectations. Yet the focus is not exclusively on territorialism, for Cavers

---

[1] David F. Cavers, The Choice–of–Law Process (1965).

[2] Aaron D. Twerski, *Enlightened Territorialism and Professor Cavers — The Pennsylvania Method,* 9 Duq. L. Rev. 373 (1971).

[3] 439 Pa. 563, 267 A.2d 854 (1970).

[4] The case was a true conflict, according to the court, because Pennsylvania's policy of compensating injured residents would be furthered by applying Pennsylvania law. Similarly, Delaware's policy, lower insurance rates, was also involved.

[5] In Broome v. Antlers' Hunting Club, 595 F.2d 921 (3d Cir. 1979), the court, applying Pennsylvania law, found the influence of Cavers on the Cipolla court so strong that the case was decided by referring to a discussion, within Cavers' treatise, of a hypothetical problem.

also tried with his principles to take into account the policies sought to be achieved by the laws of the competing states. Thus, he would deploy his principles only if there were a true conflict. Expressing all of this somewhat differently, Cavers tried to determine, in light of the policies normally implicated in certain common situations, which jurisdiction's law to select in order to protect territorially based party expectations. Normally, for example, a defendant acting in his non–liability home state will not be subject to the higher standard of care of an interested foreign jurisdiction; conversely, protection will be accorded a plaintiff injured in his state of higher care.

A good deal can be said in favor of Cavers' combination of policy, party expectations, and territorialism.[6] That combination helps the court achieve predictable results; at the same time, the deliberately narrow focus of the principles means they are more likely to advance relevant substantive policies than the broad rules of the First Restatement. The Principles should be of particular interest, therefore, to those who wish to temper the flexibility of policy analysis with a measure of predictability.[7]

§ 84 Counterattack: The Search for Rules

[a] The Problem[1]

The decisions applying modern choice–of–law analysis have not met with universal acclaim. There are many critics of the new systems and their complaints are often telling. The complaints have focused on two areas: a lack of predictability in decision–making and a strong tendency for judges to favor forum residents.

[1] Predictability

Certainly, judicial consistency in some areas has not been impressive. Professor Rosenberg's comment on the New York experience that "[a] New York lawyer with a guest statute case has more need of an ouija board than a copy of Shepard's citations"[2] could be made regarding a number of courts. Lack of predictability imposes social costs by increasing the risk incurred in planning consensual transactions and in conducting and compromising litigation. Lack of predictability also increases the opportunity for (and perception of) arbitrary judicial decision–making. For these reasons, predictability is an important goal of the judicial process.[3]

---

[6] *See* James E. Westbrook, *A Survey and Evaluation of Competing Choice–of–Law Methodologies: The Case for Eclecticism,* 40 Mo. L. Rev. 407, 460 (1975).

[7] It is not surprising, therefore, that the rules adopted in Neumeier v. Kuehner, 31 N.Y.2d 121, 335 N.Y.S.2d 64, 286 N.E.2d 454 (1972), discussed in § 84, *infra,* resemble Cavers' Principles, and that Professor Reese, an advocate of rules in choice of law, has praised the Cavers method. Willis Reese, *Choice of Law: Rules or Approach,* 57 Cornell L. Rev. 315, 324 (1972).

[1] *See generally* Willis Reese, *Choice of Law: Rules or Approach,* 57 Cornell L. Rev. 315 (1972).

[2] Maurice Rosenberg, *Two Views on Kell v. Henderson,* 67 Colum. L. Rev. 459, 460 (1967).

[3] *See* William L. Reynolds, Judicial Process in a Nutshell 55–60 (2d ed. 1991).

Critics of modern forms of choice–of–law analysis assert that it does not lead to predictable results. Interest analysis, comparative impairment, the most significant relationship, or better law are premised — or so the critics argue — on inherently nebulous concepts; these can be covertly (or subconsciously) manipulated by judges to escape the result required by the method of analysis ostensibly applied. Modern choice–of–law methods, in short, may lead to some kind of rough "justice," but not to the American ideal of justice under law.

[2] Forum Favoritism

The second major objection to modern methods is that the results tend to favor forum residents. Perhaps the nadir (or the zenith, depending on your point of view) of forum favoritism was reached in *Rosenthal v. Warren.*[4] Plaintiff's decedent in that case had traveled to Boston to be operated on by a famous surgeon, but had died during the operation. The Second Circuit purported to apply New York's brand of interest analysis; but, despite the complete lack of contacts between New York and the problem (other than that the decedent lived in New York), the court chose New York law and refused to apply the Massachusetts statutory limit on wrongful death actions. Although such parochialism in modern choice of law may not be as common as some commentators suggest, there are enough examples of questionable decisions favoring forum residents to arouse caution.[5]

[b] The Academic Solution

One possible solution to these problems is to limit the range of judicial discretion in decision–making by fitting the decisions into a framework of rules. Two decades ago Professor Willis Reese, the Reporter for the Restatement (Second), wrote that "[t]he principal question in choice of law today is whether we should have rules or an approach."[6] He defined a "rule" as a "formula which once applied will lead the court to a conclusion." An "approach," on the other hand, is an expression of factors to be considered, such as Leflar's choice–influencing considerations or the factors listed in § 6 of the Restatement (Second).

Reese favored the increased use of rules. He began by proposing that a reaction to the misguided rules of the First Restatement should not lead to a rejection of all rules for choice of law. Reese's argument for a rules–oriented choice–of–law method is based on his belief that rules channel the application of policy in ways that achieve certainty and predictability. He believed that relatively narrow rules will develop under modern forms of choice–of–law analysis as courts acquire experience in dealing with specific

[4] 475 F.2d 438 (2d Cir. 1973).

[5] Other examples of forum favoritism are: Allstate Ins. Co. v. Hague, 449 U.S. 302 (1981) (better law) (discussed *infra,* § 97[a]); Lilienthal v. Kaufman, 239 Or. 1, 395 P.2d 543 (1964) (interest analysis) (discussed *supra,* § 78).

[6] Reese, *supra* note 1, at 315.

problems. The validity of the rules will then be tested in later cases and modified if appropriate. Reese added two thoughts which should give pause to those willing to embrace a rules approach: Rulemaking "would be aided immeasurably if the courts were always to give their real reasons" for a decision; and, a rule should be used in a case even if it "would lead to a result that might be thought unfortunate."[7] What worried Reese, of course, was that long experience has shown that judges will strive hard to avoid results they believe to be "unjust," even if the applicable rules call for those results. Judicial evasion of the discipline rules seek to impose is captured by the phrase "hard cases make bad law" and, in conflicts, by the use of "escape devices" to avoid the rules imposed by the vested rights theory. The reluctance of judges to follow rules that hinder the pursuit of justice suggests that a decision–making regime which encourages the giving of reasons in individual cases may be preferable in the long run to a system which encourages only fidelity to rules.

Professor Reese's article generated a great deal of debate. Some scholars have even attempted to formulate rules of their own.[8] Most proponents of more rules in choice of law, however, have been more hesitant. Perhaps their caution is occasioned by the disappointing products of judicial efforts at rule formulation.

[c] Judicially Created Rules

In *Neumeier v. Kuehner,*[9] Chief Justice Fuld addressed the problem of rules in choice–of–law decision–making. Ontario's guest statute was again before the Court of Appeals of New York. Defendant's intestate, a New Yorker, drove into Ontario and picked up a friend and his family, all Ontario residents. While they were on an outing in New York, a train struck the car, and the host and his guests were killed. Litigation then ensued in New York.

After briefly commenting on the New York cases in this area and the policies underlying the laws of both jurisdictions, Judge Fuld argued that,

> *Babcock [v. Jackson]* and its progeny enable us to formulate a set of basic principles that may be profitably utilized, for they have helped us uncover the underlying values and policies which are operative in this area of the law.[10]

He then persuaded the court to adopt a set of three rules which he had first advanced in a concurring opinion a few years earlier in *Tooker v. Lopez*:[11]

---

[7] *Id.* at 322–23.

[8] *E.g.,* Weintraub at 346; Robert Allen Sedler, *Rules of Choice of Law versus Choice–of–Law Rules: Judicial Method in Conflicts Torts Cases,* 44 Tenn. L. Rev. 975 (1977).

[9] 31 N.Y.2d 121, 335 N.Y.S.2d 64, 286 N.E.2d 454 (1972).

[10] 31 N.Y.2d at 127, 286 N.E.2d at 457, 335 N.Y.S.2d at 69 (*Babcock* is discussed *supra,* § 78).

[11] 24 N.Y.2d 569, 249 N.E.2d 394, 301 N.Y.S.2d 519 (1969).

1. When the guest–passenger and the host–driver are domiciled in the same state, and the car is there registered, the law of that state should control and determine the standard of care which the host owes to his guest.
2. When the driver's conduct occurred in the state of his domicile and that state does not cast him in liability for that conduct, he should not be held liable by reason of the fact that liability would be imposed upon him under the tort law of the state of the victim's domicile. Conversely, when the guest was injured in the state of his own domicile and its law permits recovery, the driver who has come into that state should not — in the absence of special circumstances — be permitted to interpose the law of his state as a defense.
3. In other situations, when the passenger and the driver are domiciled in different states, the rule is necessarily less categorical. Normally, the applicable rule of decision will be that of the state where the accident occurred but not if it can be shown that displacing that normally applicable rule will advance the relevant substantive law purposes without impairing the smooth working of the multi–state system or producing great uncertainty for litigants.

Fuld emphasized that the *Neumeier* rules were only to be applied in guest statute cases.

[d] A Criticism of *Neumeier*[12]

If interest analysis is applied to the three rules, it can readily be seen that the first rule deals with false conflicts, the second with two true conflicts, and the third is a residual category. The false conflict described in the first rule is handled properly, in that the law of what is almost surely the only interested state (that of the common domicile) is applied.

The wisdom of the second rule is more uncertain. First, New York had only decided one true conflict case involving a guest statute;[13] hence, it was misleading to assert that the second rule could be derived fully from the *Babcock* line of cases. Second, decisions in other states had split regarding the wisdom of the results proclaimed in Judge Fuld's second rule.[14] Most important, the second rule fails to take account of the different policies which might be served by foreign guest statutes. Although the second rule

[12] *See generally* David E. Seidelson, *Interest Analysis: The Quest for Perfection and the Frailties of Man,* 19 Duq. L. Rev. 207, 214–29 (1981); Harold L. Korn, *The Choice–of–Law Revolution: A Critique,* 83 Colum. L. Rev. 772, 886–903 (1983).

[13] This was Dym v. Gordon, 16 N.Y.2d 120, 209 N.E.2d 792, 262 N.Y.S.2d 463 (1965) (a guest statute case with facts very similar to *Tooker,* and whose result *Tooker* seriously questioned). *See* Sedler, *supra* note 8, for a discussion of the New York cases.

[14] Robert Allen Sedler, *Interstate Accidents and the Unprovided For Case: Reflections on Neumeier v. Keuhner,* 1 Hofstra L. Rev. 125, 135 (1973).

may achieve policy ends, it will do so only if the policy behind the foreign guest statute is the same as the policy behind Ontario's.[15]

The third rule applies the law of the place of the wrong, unless doing otherwise would further the law of another jurisdiction. This was the holding in *Neumeier* itself. The territorial focus in the third rule resembles the dysfunctional rules of the First Restatement, for it does not deliberately advance the policy of any interested jurisdiction. The escape clause contained at the end of the third rule is of uncertain impact. At worst, it can upset the predictability sought in the preceding portions of the *Neumeier* formula. Concern over the wild card in the last part of the third rule may be one reason why it has not found favor among other judges. Thus, when the Supreme Court of Rhode Island rejected the rule in *Labree v. Major,*[16] a case factually similar to *Neumeier,* the court was quite candid in expressing its dissatisfaction with a return to *lex loci delicti* — a return whose apparent certainty in New York is saddled with an internal exception which "may in practice require a case–by–case analysis of governmental interests." That kind of analysis, of course, is the antithesis of the goals Fuld sought in promulgating his rules.

The *Neumeier* rules, in any event, do not solve all guest statute problems, as later cases in New York clearly show. What happens, for example, when plaintiff/guest and defendant/host are from different states and the accident is in a third state — the only one of the three with a guest statute? This was the situation in *Chila v. Owens,*[17] a case decided immediately after *Neumeier.* By its terms, the third rule should be controlling, and, therefore, the guest statute of the place of wrong (Ohio) should have been applied. This result — clearly wrong in terms of policy when both guest and host are from liability states — was rejected by Judge Weinstein: "[L]ogic and fairness would suggest that New York would equate the New Jersey claimant's position to that of its own domiciliary, and apply the first principle." Although there is no reason to believe that Judge Fuld would have decided the case any differently, it is instructive to note that judicial tinkering with the rules began immediately after their adoption.

Another example of a problem with the *Neumeier* classifications occurs when plaintiff and defendant are both New Yorkers, and the car is registered in California, a guest statute state. None of the rules covers that situation, again highlighting the difficulty of proposing choice–of–law rules to handle problems which, although deceptively simple, contain a great number of permutations.[18]

The unsatisfactory nature of the *Neumeier* rules is borne out by the reluctance of academic commentators who favor rules, in theory, to endorse

---

[15] Even if the second rule only addresses the situation where New York is the liability state, the policy behind the foreign guest statute must be examined to be sure that the law of an interested jurisdiction is applied.

[16] 111 R.I. 657, 306 A.2d 808 (1973).

[17] 348 F.Supp. 1207 (S.D.N.Y. 1972).

[18] *See* Pahmer v. Hertz Corp., 32 N.Y.2d 119, 343 N.Y.S.2d 341, 296 N.E.2d 243 (1973), for a case presenting the fact situation mentioned in the text, but decided on the ground that the guest statute had been declared unconstitutional.

them. But the failure of the Fuldian trilogy should not be laid primarily at the door of the Court of Appeals. Although part of the *Neumeier* problem stems from its premature and incomplete classifications,[19] a more important part of the problem is that the complexity of choice–of–law cases and the possibility of so many variables make conflicts problems particularly difficult to nail down with rules promulgated in advance. The problem, thus, runs deeper than any particular set of rules, because the search for rules is basically a misguided quest. Imposing order on the common law is a very difficult task. Rather than hard–and–fast mechanical rules, our jurisprudence is based on the more flexible doctrine of precedent. As that doctrine is understood today, the precedential effect of a case turns upon the policies used by the court to justify its decision — policies which must be read in light of the dispute presented to the court for resolution.[20] It is the reasoning supported by factual analysis which is important in common law adjudication. Expressed differently, the court's reasoning explains why a case was decided as it was, and the manner in which like cases should be decided; that reasoning, however, must be closely tied to the facts presented in order to preserve the proper framework for judicial decision–making.

It was precisely this kind of reasoning that *Neumeier* lacked.[21] Although the *Neumeier* rules were based on New York's experience in guest cases, Judge Fuld did not analyze the situations in terms of the various policies which would lead either to the imposition of liability or to the bar of the guest statute, nor did his opinion recognize that sometimes guest statutes may be justified by different policies which might change the court's analysis of some of the fact situations.[22] Moreover, the trilogy is expressly limited to guest statute cases. The court failed to explain why the reasoning that might lead to the adoption of the trilogy in those cases should not be extended to charitable immunity cases, for example. This failure to explain violated the basic common law rule that like cases should be decided in like fashion.[23]

Commentators, as well as courts, have searched for a system of dispositive rules that will also serve policy goals. Professor Korn, for example, has chosen party *domicile* as the basis for a system of choice–of–law rules.[24]

---

[19] Ironically enough, *Neumeier* provides the classic example of the "unprovided–for" case, *see supra* § 78, and a proper result could have been reached under interest analysis by applying forum law. The rules, in the context of the case that adopted them, were much ado about nothing.

[20] *See* W. Reynolds, *supra* note 3, at 77–85.

[21] Of course, to the extent that the *Neumeier* rules were not compelled by precedent they are dicta — they represent a statement of law not needed to reach a decision in the case actually before the court.

[22] Indeed, the Court of Appeals of New York had expressly recognized in *Tooker* that guest statutes were based on different policies.

[23] *See* Karl Llewellyn, The Bramble Bush 157–58 (2d ed. 1951), and his pronouncement of the "double maxim" that he made famous: "The rule follows where its reason leads; where the reason stops, there stops the rule." If the court had extended the rule beyond guest cases, it would have been forced to deal with its apparently inconsistent decision in Miller v. Miller, 22 N.Y.2d 12, 290 N.Y.S.2d 734, 237 N.E.2d 877 (1968). *See* Sedler, *supra* note 14, at 989.

[24] Korn, *supra* note 12.

Korn's proposed rules are much more elaborate than those of the First Restatement. In addition, Korn attempts to justify his rules (one reason for choosing domicile, for example, is that it is a useful proxy for party expectations). Nevertheless, because all rules favor certainty over policy, they are always vulnerable to a policy–based attack. Thus, Korn's rules have been trenchantly criticized primarily because party domicile often does not serve as a good link to policies that many laws are designed to serve.[25]

Professor Reese's concern that judges might not follow the new rules if they led to "unfortunate" results captures the essence of the problem. Judges who are formally bound by rules that lead to unfortunate results resort to various escape devices. This has happened in many areas of the law and, of course, was widespread under the regime of the First Restatement.[26] There is no reason to suppose that any new set of rules will eliminate the problem. Judges do not like to reach "unfortunate" results. Rather than force their decision–making into the closet, as a system of rules would do, it would be better to encourage opinions that would explain why a result was "unfortunate," and how it should be avoided in future cases.

To be sure, well–crafted rules can reduce uncertainty for a time. Rules cast in the form of tentative generalizations that explain a body of law can prove useful. But a court must remember that the law is not static; tentative generalizations, as a result, must be re–examined constantly. It must be remembered that predictability is not the only goal of the law, particularly in choice–of–law situations where the strong desires of other sovereigns may be implicated. Rather, the law should seek predictability based on policy analysis — the heart of common law adjudication. Reliance on rules, Professor Singer writes, "is fundamentally misguided because it institutionalizes arbitrariness."[27] That, after all, was the major problem with the vested rights theory.

§ 85 Choice–of–Law Theory Today

[a] A State of Disarray

The preceding sections should make clear that choice–of–law theory today is in considerable disarray — and has been for some time. When the vested rights theory crumbled under sustained assault in the late 1950s, observers of the conflicts scene predicted confidently that a new theory (or possibly two) would emerge dominant from scholarly and judicial activity. That hope has proven forlorn. Instead, current choice–of–law theory is marked by eclecticism and even eccentricity. No consensus exists among scholars as to whether rules are desirable, whether the choice–of–law process should evaluate the substantive content of a rule, or whether courts can consider the merits of competing state policies. The scholars, in other words, have

---

[25] *See* Bruce Posnak, *Choice of Law: Interest Analysis and its "New Critics,"* 31 Am. J. Comp. L. 681 (1988).

[26] *See* §§ 64–68, *supra.*

[27] Joseph W. Singer, *Facing Real Conflicts,* 24 Cornell Int'l L.J. 197, 201 (1991).

destroyed the old order; but like revolutionaries who can unite only to eliminate the existing government, they cannot agree on the establishment of a new one.

The disarray in the courts may be worse. Four or five theories are in vogue among the various states, with many decisions using — openly or covertly — more than one theory.[1] Inconsistency between the theoretical underpinnings of decisions in the same jurisdiction is also common, with one case relying on the Second Restatement, perhaps, and the next on interest analysis. Robert Leflar, the dean of conflicts scholars, refers, not critically, to such decisions as employing a "mish–mash."[2]

A number of reasons contribute to this inconsistency in the case law. Two are pre–eminent, however: academic dispute and the realities of common law decision–making. Because very few courts decide a significant number of choice–of–law cases, it is difficult for any court to develop its own choice–of–law theories.[3] The judges must rely, instead, on academic developments. In most areas of the law (products liability or the parol evidence rule, for example), scholars present judges with a more or less unified criticism of existing law; the decision for the judge, then, is simply whether to overrule the old precedent. That decision does not usually entail choosing among half a dozen different parol evidence theories; the choices, instead, are closely related to one another and tend to differ only in degree. Consider now the plight of the poor judge who asks her law clerk, fresh from law school, about the latest developments in choice of law, and who then is told the tale of the two Restatements, of Currie, of Better Law, and of the attempted counter–revolution by the new territorialists. Not having time to sort through those theories properly for herself, the judge uses the ones that have some appeal in the case at bar. Thus, faced with a particularly obnoxious law (a guest statute, for example), Better Law must be a particularly appealing theory for the judge[4] faced with a clearly "bad" result under the vested rights theory, but one which Currie teaches to be a false conflict, interest analysis should prove attractive.[5] No doubt there is a tendency to indulge in overkill in the manner of common law judges everywhere; if the selected result is correct under several theories, why not tell that to the world?[6] What harm can there be in debasing a doctrine by rendering it impure in the decision — it is the bottom line that counts, after

---

[1] Particularly appealing is the marriage between the Second Restatement and some other modern theory, such as interest analysis. A first–rate analysis of the theory underlying choice–of–law decisions in the 50 states is Herma Hill Kay, *Theory Into Practice: Choice of Law in the Courts,* 34 Mercer L. Rev. 521 (1983).

[2] Robert Leflar, *The Nature of Conflicts Law,* 81 Colum. L. Rev. 1080, 1094 (1981).

[3] The experience of New York, the state with perhaps the greatest conflicts caseload and the earliest rebellion against the territorial theory, must prove especially disturbing to other courts. A perceptive and detailed examination of the New York experience is Harold L. Korn, *The Choice–of–Law Revolution: A Critique,* 83 Colum. L. Rev. 722 (1983).

[4] *E.g.,* Milkovich v. Saari, 295 Minn. 155, 203 N.W.2d 408 (1973) (discussed *supra* § 81).

[5] *See, e.g.,* Reich v. Purcell, 67 Cal.2d 551, 63 Cal. Rptr. 31, 432 P.2d 727 (1967).

[6] Not only does overkill add persuasive weight to the result, but it leaves the court free to choose a more specific path later on; why burn bridges until it is necessary to do so?

all, rather than fidelity to a particular theology.[7] And, as one exhaustive study has demonstrated, the results are pretty much the same no matter which modern theory is used.[8]

That observation leads to the second major reason why choice–of–law theory in case law is a mish–mash: Judges resist theory and distrust *a priori* reasoning. Both their legal training and the demands of their profession make judges very practical persons. The primary role of common law judges is to decide cases, and they make law only as an incidental part of that process. Judges make law in order to insure consistency and predictability in decision–making, but they do so only as a part of their duty to resolve disputes.[9] Theory does not precede decision–making, but rather arises from the natural process of fitting together case law as it develops — as part of the continual shaping and reformulation of the common law.[10] This is true in all areas of the law, as frequent judicial use of the phrase "we decide today only" indicates. Judges may use academic theory to explain a line of cases, or to justify the overruling of precedent, but it is unusual to see a mature theory adopted as such in the first case in a field. Judges prefer to be cautious when they can. The problem in choice of law is particularly acute, because the scholars in the area tell judges that they must have a theory. So the judges choose one, or more than one, but their commitment to that chosen theory does not run deep, for its selection did not result from the common law process of shaping doctrine by reasoned elaboration of case results over time. The theory may anchor a particular decision, but the judge's commitment is more to the result than to the implication of the theory in not yet litigated hypotheticals.[11]

---

[7] The melding of different theories may also occur in the conference room, where a judge, anxious to secure agreement, may agree readily to insert a "harmless" paragraph submitted by a colleague. The paragraph may be harmless in the case, but, if it introduces a different theory, may sow the seeds of later confusion.

[8] Patrick J. Borchers, *The Choice–of–Law Revolution: An Empirical Study,* 49 Wash, & Lee L. Rev. 349 (1992). Borchers notes that results under the First Restatement do differ from those reached by modern methods. *Id.* at 373. Anyone who believes, however, that today's courts which follow the First Restatement do not use escape devices should read a series of recent Maryland cases which do just that: *See, e.g.,* Hauch v. Connor, 453 A.2d 1207 (Md. 1983) (significant use of characterization "escape" to achieve "just" result under *lex loci* rules); Bethlehem Steel Corp. v. G.C. Zarnas & Co., 498 A.2d 605 (Md. 1985) (same, using "public policy"); Karmer v. Balley's Park Place, Inc., 535 A.2d 466 (Md. 1988) (not against public policy to enforce gambling contracts).

[9] *See* William L. Reynolds, Judicial Process in a Nutshell 107–08 (2d ed. 1991).

[10] Perhaps the most famous illustration of this process is Cardozo's opinion redoing the theory of privity in tort law. MacPherson v. Buick Motor Co., 217 N.Y. 382, 111 N.E. 1050 (1916).

[11] Compounding the problem is the fact that judicial aversion to theory is particularly strong when dealing with problems that cut across a number of fields. An example is the problem of statutory interpretation. Courts are averse to deciding construction questions by developing a framework in which to analyze relevant data; rather, the actual decisions, although often articulating a theory, seem to pick and choose among the various possibilities in order to justify a result otherwise deemed desirable. *See, e.g.,* Patricia M. Wald, *Some Observations on the Use of Legislative History in the 1981 Supreme Court Term,* 68 Iowa L. Rev. 195 (1983). Judicial practice in statutory interpretation, in other words, resembles that in choice of law.

Understanding why courts employ a mish–mash does not imply that they are right to do so. Certainly, it makes the task of lower courts more difficult, and increases the appearance of arbitrary or biased decision–making. Moreover, a lack of discipline in judicial method may lead the court to rely on intuition rather than on reasoning, diminishing the quality of the judges' work. Last, and by no means least, the confusion among those courts which have rejected traditional methods of analysis has discouraged other courts from doing so,[12] perpetuating the sometimes very real evils of the First Restatement and its built–in arbitrariness.

[b] Is Disarray Bad?

But are the decisions in the end so bad? In an important article written in 1977, Professor Leflar argued that choice of law in the courts today has risen "high above the sinkhole it once occupied" to a "well–watered plateau," and, although there are "vistas" on the horizon, choice of law today is at a "rest–stop."[13] To support that appealing image, Leflar cited the decline in reported choice–of–law decisions, despite a great increase in the number of reported cases generally; the decline, he argued, demonstrates that the law in this area has become more predictable and, therefore, less likely to engender litigation.[14] An examination of recent decisions confirmed that hypothesis. Leflar found that judicial reliance on several theories is not offensive, because the courts generally reach results consistent with "any or nearly all of the new non–mechanical approaches to conflicts law." More recent studies have confirmed the vitality of eclecticism in choice–of–law decision–making.

Leflar's paean to eclectic decision–making did not go unchallenged,[15] but it also had its defenders.[16] Several recent surveys are not so sanguine. Professor Kramer, for example, after reading all of the choice–of–law decisions handed down in 1990 was far more critical.[17] He found the analysis "unsophisticated, unthoughtful, and often unreasoned." Particularly troubling to Kramer was judicial "comfort" with that lack of quality, much of

[12] *E.g.,* McMillan v. McMillan, 219 Va. 1127, 1131, 253 S.E.2d 662, 664 (1979) ("[T]he uniformity, predictability, and ease of application of the [traditional] rule should [not] be abandoned in exchange for a concept which is so susceptible to inconstancy.").

[13] Robert Leflar, *Choice of Law: A Well-Watered Plateau,* 41 Law & Contemp. Probs. 10, 26 (Spring 1977).

[14] Another possibility is that the law of the several states is becoming more uniform, and, therefore, there is less room for conflict. Professor Juenger, for example, once predicted that as obsolete laws such as guest statutes were eliminated, choice–of–law cases would rapidly diminish. Friedrich Juenger, *Choice of Law in Interstate Torts,* 118 U. Pa. L. Rev. 202 (1969).

[15] *E.g.,* William A. Reppy, Jr., *Eclecticism in Choice of Law: Hybrid Method or Mishmash,* 34 Mercer L. Rev. 645 (1983).

[16] *E.g.,* Robert Allen Sedler, *Interest Analysis and Forum Preference in the Conflict of Laws: A Response to the "New Critics,"* 34 Mercer L. Rev. 593 (1983). *See also* James A. McLaughlin, *Conflict of Laws: The New Approach to Choice of Law: Justice in Search of Certainty,* 94 W. Va. L. Rev. 73 (1991).

[17] Larry Kramer, *Choice of Law in the American Courts in 1990: Trends and Developments,* 39 Am. J. Comp. L. 465 (1991).

which he blamed on the popularity of the Second Restatement, which he believes "invites post–hoc rationalizing of intuitions. . . ." Of course, academic criticism of judicial decisions invites the response that academics have done no better. The next sub–section describes some recent scholarly attempts to address the perennial disarray in choice of law.

[c] The Future of Choice of Law

Much speculation has centered on the course this body of law will take in the future. Some have argued that the task is to identify rules that can be drawn from the existing body of case law,[18] somewhat in the fashion of Ehrenzweig's "true rules"; others have argued for the identification of elaborate rules that can accommodate competing interests in sophisticated fashion.[19] Below we describe in detail some — but by no means all — contemporary theories about the proper direction for choice of law to take.

— *New True Rules.* Larry Kramer has attempted to formulate a set of "canons" that he believes will solve quickly and fairly many choice–of–law problems.[20] These canons resemble Ehrenzweig's "True Rules"[21] in that they are both normative and descriptive. An example is his Canon for Contract Cases: In a true conflict, the court should apply the law chosen by the parties; if they have chosen none, then the *lex validationis* should be applied. This canon has the virtues of simplicity and predictability. It suffers from a major defect, however, in that it simply ignores a strong policy interest a state may have in regulating conduct within its borders (as in the case of covenants not to compete). Nevertheless, Kramer's new canons are a serious effort to harness judicial discretion in choice of law by setting forth rules for decision in common situations. Moreover, those rules are less arbitrary than those of the First Restatement because Kramer' canons try to reflect commonly–held policies. As with all rules, however, they are not "true" all of the time; as a result, arbitrary decision making is built into the system.

— *Negative Rights.* Lea Brilmayer, in an important new book,[22] focused her attention on party "rights." These rights are mainly negative, in the sense that each of us has a general right to be free of state interference.

---

[18] *E.g.*, Maurice Rosenberg, *The Comeback of Choice–of–Law Rules,* 81 Colum. L. Rev. 946 (1981). *See* § 84, *supra.* It should not be surprising if courts which reject the territorial theory have reached more or less consistent results: A plaintiff in the days of long–arm statutes is likely to sue defendant in the jurisdiction with the most favorable substantive law; because modern theories of choice of law tend to favor either forum law or plaintiffs, agreement on a result which favors plaintiffs can easily be expected.

[19] *E.g.*, Luther L. McDougal, *Comprehensive Interest Analysis Versus Reformulated Governmental Interest Analysis: An Appraisal in the Context of Choice–of–Law Problems Concerning Contributory and Comparative Negligence,* 26 U.C.L.A. L. Rev. 439 (1979).

[20] Larry Kramer, *Rethinking Choice of Law,* 90 Colum. L. Rev. 277 (1990).

[21] Discussed in § 82, *supra.*

[22] Lea Brilmayer, Conflict of Laws: Foundations and Future Directions (1991). *See also* Harold G. Maier, *Baseball and Chicken Salad: A Realistic Look at Choice of Law,* 44 Vand. L. Rev. 827 (1991); Patrick C. Borchers, *Professor Brilmayer and the Holy Grail,* 1991 Wisc. L. Rev. 465.

This concept of "political rights" drives Brilmayer's notion of proper choice–of–law decision–making: A person's negative right to be left alone, however, can be overcome by consent[23] — either through domicile (a domiciliary has the ability to affect the forum's political processes and thus its law), or by physical presence (implied consent to abide by the forum's rules). Another way of saying this is that the choice–of–law decision must focus on the relation between a state whose law might be applied and the person who will benefit (or suffer) from the application of that law. Consent, therefore, should play a significant role in choice–of–law decision making. Brilmayer also believes mutuality is important; a state cannot expect its laws to be followed if it would not do the same if the situation were reversed.

This model of negative rights certainly captures much of the dissatisfaction with current choice–of–law practice. Party expectations *should* matter, and modern theories *do* pay too little attention to them. "Negative rights," however, is not a complete choice–of–law theory; states also have interests (or "rights") and the interplay between the two has to be carefully thought out. Moreover, domicile and presence alone do not describe accurately enough the relation which justify a state's assertion of legislative jurisdiction. Nevertheless, it is a work full of insight and brilliance which surely will help shape the choice–of–law debate.[24]

— *Game Theory.* These two scholars have also turned their attention to "game theory" to help understand how judges may best use choice–of–law to achieve policy goals. Both Brilmayer[25] and Kramer[26] have developed sophisticated variations of this approach based on recognizing that states do have legitimate policy differences. Both authors suggest instead that states should cooperate in order to achieve those goals in multi–state problems, rather than engage in a no–win, forum–preference choice–of–law war. Brilmayer would accomplish this goal by using a forum such as the American Law Institute. Kramer's more radical suggestions is the greater use of renvoi in choice–of–law cases. Because renvoi implicitly recognizes another state's interest in the problem by asking how that state would decide the matter, Kramer argues, it is a good vehicle for accommodating competing state interests.

Brilmayer's disinterested central forum has much to recommend it. Nevertheless, the American Law Institute has been notably unsuccessful at imposing order in choice of law,[27] and there really is no reason to believe that that will change. Kramer's advocacy of renvoi is interesting and provocative, but judges have had available for many years tools that would

[23] *See* Maier, *supra* note 22 at 835–36.

[24] For an argument that Brilmayer's real complaint is with *judicial* jurisdiction, *see id.* at 845.

[25] Lea Brilmayer, *supra* note 22.

[26] Larry Kramer, *The Return of the Renvoi,* 66 N.Y.U.L. Rev. 979 (1991).

[27] The Second Restatement of Conflicts has been around in draft form for over a quarter century and yet has been adopted by only half of the states. That relative lack of success should be contrasted with the almost universal adoption of most of the provisions of the Second Restatements of Contracts and Torts.

recognize other state's legitimate interests. And yet those tools have been largely ignored. Why should game theory/renvoi make things different?

— *The ALI Complex Litigation Project.* The American Law Institute has been working since the late 1980's on finding solutions to the enormous problems created by today's massive complex litigation caseload.[28] The Complex Litigation Project has made many far–reaching recommendations; among the most prominent are choice–of–law rules for mass contract and tort actions.[29] The result in tort cases is a hybrid involving the policy consideration found in § 6 of the Restatement (Second) of Conflict of Laws, and, in certain specific situations, some or all of the *territorial* preferences of *Neumeier v. Kuehner,*[30] Professor Korn's common domicile approach,[31] and amazingly, as a residual factor, "the law of the state where the conduct causing the injury occurred."[32] The drafters, "in the interests of justice" would permit the court to ignore the preferences and select the law of another jurisdiction.[33] The solutions ultimately proposed by the Complex Litigation Project promise to be influential, whether they really will work an improvement on § 6, of course, is another matter.

— *Hybrid Law.* Finally, some scholars have argued that substantive decisions should reflect the substantive policies of the larger communities of which the interested states form a part. This approach, said by Luther McDougall to resemble the old Roman concept of *ius gentium,*[34] rejects the use of forum or other law designed only to achieve internal policy goals. Rather, it seeks to achieve those goals which transcend jurisdictional boundaries. This transnational approach has an obvious appeal to any serious student of interest analysis, and is reminiscent of the directive in § 6(2)(e) of the Restatement (Second) of Conflict of Laws to consider "the basic policies underlying the particular field of law." The real question, of course, is how a modern *ius gentium* possibly could work in practice.

. . . .

We believe that the future of choice of law will contain continued protection by the judiciary of the sovereign power exercised by the governments of each state; no choice–of–law theory can ignore that reality. Further, any attempt to formulate rules in specific areas will probably run into the difficulty that Judge Fuld's rules for guest statutes encountered;[35]

[28] This Project is also discussed in § 54, *supra.*

[29] The Co–Reporter for the Project has commented on the choice–of–law problem in Mary Kay Kane, *Drafting Choice of Law Rules for Complex Litigation: Some Preliminary Thoughts,* 10 Rev. of Litig. 309 (1991).

[30] *See* § 84, *supra.*

[31] *See* § 84, *supra.*

[32] American Law Institute, Complex Litigation Project § 6.01(c)(4) (tent. draft no. 3, March 31, 1992).

[33] *Id.* § 6.01(d).

[34] Luther L. McDougall III, *"Private" International Law: Ius Gentium versus Choice of Law Rules or Approaches,* 38 Am. J. Comp. L. 521 (1990).

[35] Judicial rule–based solutions are discussed in the preceding section.

the number of variables in multi–state problems may be too great to be anticipated by rules formulated before the fact. Courts, instead, will treat problems in choice of law as they treat other problems; they are issues to be thought about, discussed, and decided in an opinion which explains (to the litigants and to the public) why a particular decision was reached and how that decision can be used in similar cases arising in the future. Perhaps the theory most likely to succeed is one that tells the judges that there is nothing wrong with coming to rest on a well–watered plateau — at least if the judges also learn that attempts to reach the vistas on the horizon may lead, instead, to disaster in the sinkholes which lie in ambush at the foot of the plateau.

[d] Are Legislative Solutions Desirable?

There have been sporadic attempts by legislatures over the years to deal with choice–of–law problems. By and large, the efforts have not been so successful as to create optimism about future statutory solutions to choice–of–law problems. To be sure, the legislatures have attacked, with some success, a few conflicts problems; borrowing statutes are a good example of a partial solution.[36] And there is much to be said for Uniform Acts, especially those which curb the worst excesses of federalism.[37] But choice–of–law problems generally are too complex to be susceptible of effective legislative direction beyond the specification of a single contact jurisdiction–selecting rule;[38] thus, it is not surprising that the no–fault statutes rely on a single contact (either plaintiff's domicile or the place of injury) to select the governing law.[39]

Legislative direction is necessarily clumsy, and, therefore, arbitrary, and even policy–defeating; statutory solutions for that reason, do not seem to be the answer. On this point something of a scholarly consensus has emerged.[40] That consensus is surprising, given its absence in conflicts scholarship generally; it is perhaps even more surprising given the emphasis Brainerd Currie (and others) have placed on Congressional action to resolve choice–of–law problems.[41] In any event, significant legislative action in this area seems unlikely; courts will simply have to muddle through on their own. Because neither legislatures nor scholars seem to

---

[36] *See* § 93, *infra.*

[37] *E.g.,* The Uniform Child Custody Jurisdiction Act, discussed *infra,* § 130.

[38] Louisiana presents a notable exception. That state has recently codified its torts choice–of–law rules in a manner resembling the ALI proposals described in the preceding section. *See generally* Symeon C. Symeonides, *Louisiana's New Law of Choice of Law for Torts Conflicts: An Exegesis,* 66 Tulane L. Rev. 677 (1992).

[39] *See* § 87, *infra.*

[40] The participants in Symposium, *Reflections on Conflict-of-Laws Methodology: A Dialogue,* 32 Hastings L.J. 1609 (1981), agreed that statutory solutions were not the answer. This group included some who liked current choice–of–law theories, and some who did not.

[41] *See* Brainerd Currie, *Notes on Method and Objectives in the Conflict of Laws,* 1959 Duke L.J. 171; Currie, Essays, Ch. 4; William F. Baxter, *Choice of Law and the Federal System,* 16 Stan. L. Rev. 1 (1963).

have developed a sure–fire way to leave the choice–of–law plateau, conflicts law must gather its breath as it waits for the next breakthrough.

Part D

CHOICE OF LAW TODAY

§ 86 Introduction

The discussion of choice–of–law so far in this Chapter has focused on different analytic theories and techniques which can be used in approaching choice–of–law problems. This Part of the Chapter examines choice–of–law problems in seven discrete subjects. Although some of what is said here is either drawn or can be readily inferred from preceding sections, much of the material in this part is new. Here we present an overview of each of these areas, a perspective which will be helpful in tying down some of the abstractions covered in the preceding sections. The discussion also illustrates the value of the different approaches in various areas of substantive law.

The first three sections of this Part cover some familiar ground: torts, contracts, and property. The remaining four sections deal with discrete legal areas not really touched on elsewhere, but whose practical importance should be clear.

§ 87 Torts

Choice of law in tort litigation is the most unsettled part of modern choice–of–law practice. This is due both to the nature of the substantive law of torts and to divergent theory in conflicts. This section examines both problems and concludes with a look at the problem of no-fault law.

[a] Substantive Problems

The substantive law of torts, in contrast to property or contract law, has been in a state of flux in this country for quite some time. The changes have included the elimination of obstacles impeding the creation of a completely fault-based system of liability (*e.g.*, guest statutes), as well as a shift away from fault and toward strict liability. We have exhausted two Torts Restatements in the past six decades, and a third is well under way. Given the dynamic nature of the field, it is not surprising that much of the ferment in choice of law during the past quarter century has centered on judicial efforts to avoid anachronistic tort rules. Thus, Professor Reese, writing in 1977, observed that the major torts conflicts decisions have involved such obsolete areas as guest statutes and limitations on recovery in wrongful death actions; he regarded most other choice–of–law problems in torts as "settled."[1]

---

[1] Willis Reese, *Choice of Law in Torts and Contracts and Directions for the Future*, 16 Colum. J. Trans. L. 1, 12 (1977). A similar view is expressed in Friedrich Juenger, *Choice of Law in Interstate Torts*, 118 U. Pa. L. Rev. 202, 222 (1969).

As the states eliminate such unpopular laws (unpopular at least in foreign courts), Reese believed that the likely result would be the elimination of significant tort choice–of–law problems. Any remaining uncertainty in conflicts cases then primarily would involve "tangential" issues.[2]

But Reese's prediction seems unlikely to come true. The diversity and change which mark today's tort law cannot fail to create many difficult choice–of–law problems in the future. Thus, although large chunks of the common law of torts are being overthrown today, the trend is being resisted in some states in many areas of law.

Medical malpractice provides an easy example. Some states, in an effort to deal with burgeoning malpractice costs, dramatically changed traditional rules. We now see mandatory arbitration, limits on recovery for pain and suffering, and elimination of the collateral source rule. Other states, in contrast, have retained the common law. The obvious tension between the different regimes will lead to many choice–of–law problems.[3] *Kaiser-Georgetown Community Health Plan, Inc., v. Stutsman*[4] illustrates the area. Plaintiff, a Virginia resident, worked in the District of Columbia and had an employee health plan with a District of Columbia HMO. She sued defendant for malpractice allegedly committed by its agents in Virginia. Suit was brought in the District of Columbia for $10 million. Virginia, unlike the District, limits malpractice damages to $750,000. Using interest analysis, the court applied District law. Not surprisingly, that law was also forum law and favored plaintiff.

Cases like *Stutsman* show that the always-changing substance of the law will constantly create choice–of–law problems. Eventually, of course, those problems will be resolved, (as indeed is more or less true today with respect to guest statute cases), but new problems will arise. Even when the general solution to an issue has been agreed upon, differences in "detail" among those solutions may be sufficiently significant to raise serious choice–of–law questions. A prime example is products liability.[5] Although the notion that a producer should be responsible for the ultimate safety of its products has been widely adopted, much disagreement still exists over the scope of the liability: Should contributory negligence be a defense? Should a court consider the "state of the art"? Does § 402A of the Restatement (Second) of Torts correctly adumbrate the standard of liability? Such issues, in a major products liability case, can be of enormous monetary importance and are likely to provide great challenges to the courts that must address them.[6]

[2] Reese, *supra* note 1, at 14.

[3] *See generally,* David E. Seidelson, *Choice of Law Problems in Medical Malpractice Actions: Legislative Prescriptions and Judicial Side Effects*, 28 Duq. L. Rev. 41 (1989).

[4] 491 A.2d 502 (D.C. 1985).

[5] *See, e.g.,* Scoles et al. § 17-41. *See also* Russell J. Weintraub, *A Proposed Choice of Law Standard for International Products Liability Disputes*, 16 Brook. J. Int'l L. 225 (1990).

[6] *See generally* David F. Cavers, *The Proper Law of Producer's Liability*, 26 Int'l & Comp. L.Q. 703 (1977).

[b] Theoretical Problems

The theory to be applied in tort choice–of–law cases is also unsettled. Indeed, it is hard to say very much at all about the area with any confidence. In the first place, the vested rights theory espoused by the 1934 Restatement retains surprising vitality today. A recent survey identified ten American jurisdictions which still follow that approach.[7] Second, courts that have rejected the traditional method have been unable to agree upon a replacement. Many have embraced policy-based systems, using some kind of false conflict analysis (although perhaps under a different name).[8] But even those courts do not seem to agree on how to resolve conflicts having significant contacts with more than one state. Finally, some courts have embraced the "better law" view. Despite the current diversity in theory, a practical trend is evident:[9] The decisions often favor forum residents and plaintiffs, a not surprising result, given the possibilities for forum-shopping created by modern long-arm statutes.

[c] No–Fault Statutes[10]

Legislation providing reimbursement for automobile accidents without regard to fault has become increasingly common in the past two decades. This basis of compensation is often called "no–fault." There are, however, significant differences among no–fault statutes and little agreement concerning the best approach.

Because no–fault significantly changes the common law rules regarding automobile liability, the scope of coverage can be quite important. The two basic choices are to extend no-fault protection to all persons injured in the state (no matter where they may reside), or to protect all persons domiciled within the state (no matter where they may have been injured). The latter solution has proven somewhat more popular than the former.

Needless to say, perhaps, choice–of–law problems of great complexity are possible here. Because no-fault law is statutory in origin, judicial adjustment is particularly difficult. This is one area which could benefit from the uniformity provided by federal intervention. Some no–fault bills have been introduced in Congress, but passage seems doubtful.

§ 88 Contracts

Contract law has been a relatively stable area. The primary goal of contract law is to protect the expectations of the parties as they engage in private ordering of their affairs, although the past few decades have also seen an increase in judicial limitation on freedom of contract in order to

---

[7] Scoles, et al. at 13 (Supp. 2001).

[8] *See* Willis Reese, *The Second Restatement of Conflict of Laws Revisited*, 34 Mercer L. Rev. 501, 510 (1983).

[9] Reese, *supra* note 1, at 12–16, discusses some judicial approaches.

[10] An excellent general discussion is Scoles, et al. § 17.42–.44. *See also* John Kozyris, *No–Fault Auto–Insurance in the Conflict of Laws*, 1972 Duke L.J. 333, and 1973 Duke L.J. 1009.

protect individuals (*e.g.*, contracts of adhesion) or state interests (*e.g.*, covenants not to compete). The goal of facilitating private ordering which does not impinge on other strongly held interests exerts a major influence on choice–of–law in contracts.

Sophisticated contracting parties often provide a choice–of–law clause in their contracts. These provisions, which reflect a policy generally styled "party autonomy" (a policy endorsed by both the Uniform Commercial Code[1] and the Restatement (Second) of Conflict of Laws,[2] are usually effective,[3] absent over reaching by one of the parties or disregard of an important state policy. An example of overreaching is *General Electric Co. v. Keyser*,[4] a usury case, where the court disregarded a contractual provision specifying New York law. The court refused to apply that law because the only connection between the parties and New York was that the lender was incorporated there; the borrower, however, was located in West Virginia, and the loan was to be repaid in California. An example of a choice–of–law clause invalidated because it offended a strongly held public policy is *DeSantis v. Wackenhut Corp.*[5] The Texas court in *DeSantis,* basing its decision on Texas policy, refused to enforce a covenant not to compete, although the covenant was enforceable under the law stipulated by the parties.

Most of the decisions, however, are receptive to choice–of–law clauses, even in areas where a state's policy runs strong. Thus, party autonomy has been upheld in usury cases when the existence of a "normal" relation with the chosen state shows that the parties are not deliberately attempting to evade the state's proscription of excess interest.[6] Where the substantive policy is held less strongly, judicial invalidation of a choice–of–law provision is unlikely indeed. Even if a state may be hostile to a specific choice–of–law clause, good drafting may overcome that obstacle. Wise counsel will include a forum–selection clause in their contracts, referring all disputes to a jurisdiction generally receptive to choice–of–law clauses and specifically not hostile to provisions that may become the subject of dispute.[7]

When the parties do not stipulate a governing law, courts seem to follow one of two approaches. First, eleven jurisdictions still apply the rules of the First Restatement[8] ; by judicious use of escape devices, however, courts often can protect party expectations by validating the contract. Second,

[1] *See* § 92, *infra.*

[2] *See* § 75, *supra.*

[3] Willis Reese, *Choice of Law in Torts and Contracts and Directions for the Future*, 16 Colum. J. Trans. L. 1, 22 (1977). This is true even in jurisdictions which otherwise follow the traditional theory embodied in the First Restatement, a theory not hospitable to choice–of–law clauses. *See, e.g.*, Kronovet v. Lipchin, 288 Md. 30, 415 A.2d 1096 (1980).

[4] 275 S.E.2d 289 (W. Va. 1981).

[5] 793 SW.2d 670 (Tex. 1990).

[6] *E.g.*, Continental Mortgage Investors v. Sailboat Key, 395 So.2d 507 (Fla. 1981).

[7] *See* George F. Carpinello, *Testing the Limits of Choice–of–Law Clauses: Franchise Contracts as a Case Study*, 74 Marq. L. Rev. 57 (1990).

[8] Scoles, et al. at 13 (Supp. 2001).

there seems to be, as Professor Weintraub suggests, an "emerging consensus" that the center of gravity or most significant relationship test should be employed to resolve cases of true conflict.[9] It is easy to justify that consensus, because application of those tests should help conform judicial opinion to the probable expectations (if any) of the contracting parties. Protecting those expectations achieves the primary goal of contract law. At the same time, the most significant relationship test is flexible enough to permit the courts to protect those who need protection, and also to advance important governmental interests (*e.g.*, limitations on covenants not to compete), which the contracting parties sometimes seem willing to ignore.

The apparent paucity of case law concerning choice of law in contracts should not be surprising; substantive contract law tends to be more or less the same everywhere in the nation.[10] Moreover, it is difficult and expensive to ferret out differences between the decisional laws of two states. As a result, we suspect commercial litigation typically treats forum law as controlling B; and that law, in turn, is heavily influenced by "general" contract law. The few reported decisions involving choice–of–law problems in contracts, therefore, are likely to arise from the "pathological" case, the case involving a strongly held public policy reflected in clear case law or statute. Anyone working with the decisional law in this area must be careful, therefore, when generalizing only from the published decisions.

§ 89 Property[1]

[a] Immovables: The Situs Rule

There is still one area of choice of law where the territorial ideas of the First Restatement clearly hold sway: Questions concerning real property are determined by the law of the situs.[2] That was the position of the First Restatement;[3] it is the essential position of the Second Restatement;[4] and it is the rule in contemporary case law. Indeed, so strong is its hold that a reader only of opinions dealing with property matters would be unaware of the revolution in choice–of–law thinking, for very few of those opinions

[9] Weintraub § 7.3D.

[10] And, perhaps through the industrial world. *See* T. W. Bennett, *Choice of Law Rules in Claims of Unjust Enrichment*, 39 Int'l & Comp. L.Q. 137 (1990).

[1] Traditional theory distinguishes between movable and immovable property, a distinction which corresponds closely to the difference between real and personal property. The major difference involves a leasehold estate, which conflicts law characterizes as an immovable.

[2] The situs rule is, of course, much older than the First Restatement in American jurisprudence, going back to the work of Joseph Story. For a criticism of Story's adoption of the situs rule, *see* Moffatt Hancock, *Conceptual Devices for Avoiding the Land Taboo in Conflict of Laws: The Disadvantage of Disingenuousness*, 20 Stan. L. Rev. 1, 810 (1967).

[3] *See* § 67, *supra.*

[4] The 1971 Restatement softens the impact of the situs rule by referring such questions to the whole law of the situs, opening up the possibility of renvoi. Renvoi, however, has seen little use. In any event, the courts of the situs will generally apply local law. Restatement (Second) of Conflict of Laws, Ch. 9, Topic 2, Introductory Note.

even mention modern approaches to choice of law.[5] Why that should be so is difficult to determine. Certainly, the situs rule B; at least as an invariable rule of natural law, is vulnerable to criticism.[6]

The first justification usually offered on behalf of the situs rule is that only the courts of the situs have power over the land.[7] That, of course, is true, but the same could be said of any property located within the state: Only the courts of that state can act directly (in rem) on land or goods located there.[8] This justification, in other words, goes to judicial jurisdiction rather than to choice–of–law; it provides an explanation (although an unsatisfactory one) of why non-situs courts cannot hear a case involving land,[9] but it fails to explain why situs law should always be applied. Explained somewhat differently, even if jurisdiction to hear a problem properly exists only in a court of the situs, it does not follow necessarily that the law of the situs should be applied.

A second justification for the situs rule in choice of law centers on the strong interest that the situs has in the sanctity of its land records. This argument is based on the title-searcher's need for certainty concerning the entries in those records. Preserving confidence in the reliability of those records is an extremely strong interest. A question concerning those records should be decided according to lex sitae. But most cases involving real property have little or nothing to do with land records or title searches.[10]

Consider the simple case of *Strang v. Strang*,[11] a divorce proceeding between Arkansas domiciliaries. One question in the case concerned whether the husband's separately owned property in Oklahoma could be considered in making a support order. The court, with no apparent reflection on the issue, ruled that the issue should be determined by situs (Oklahoma) law. It is hard to justify that decision. Certainly, the question of support should be determined by one law (the parties' common domicile), and it is very difficult to see how a support decision based on Arkansas (non-situs) law could possibly affect Oklahoma's (situs) land records.

Confirmation of the argument that choice of non-situs law in cases involving immovables will not harm the legitimate interests of the situs is not hard to come by. The proof lies in the ready acceptance of "escape devices" (such as equitable conversion and characterization) to avoid the iron hand of the situs rule.[12] Their widespread use has not been

---

[5] A rare example is Williams v. Williams, 390 A.2d 4 (D.C. 1978).

[6] The best analysis is found in Weintraub §§ 8.18-22, and in a series of articles by Professor Moffett Hancock in the Stanford Law Review in the mid–1960's. The last of those articles is cited in note 2, *supra*.

[7] Weintraub § 8.2.

[8] Restatement (Second) of Conflict of Laws, Ch. 9, Topic 2, Introductory Note.

[9] The argument limiting jurisdiction to decide questions about land is no more persuasive than the argument concerning choice of law. The jurisdictional problem, and its full faith and credit connotations, are discussed *infra*, § 115.

[10] Weintraub § 8.2.

[11] 258 Ark. 139, 523 S.W.2d 887 (1975). There was a strong dissent, however.

[12] *See* § 67, *supra*.

accompanied by outraged cries that the land records of the situs are being irreparably damaged. On this issue, silence perhaps is more eloquent than language.

The third commonly advanced explanation of the situs rule centers on the interest of the situs in the proper use of its land.[13] This, too, is a legitimate interest. Protection of the interest of the situs in land use, however, does not require application of situs law in all situations. A decision of a court considering whether a will disposing of land has been executed properly is not likely to upset the environmental balance of the situs, no matter what law it applies to the execution problem. That is not to say that situs policy never has a role to play in such a case; the will, for example, may restrict the alienation of land for a period longer than that permitted by the perpetuities rule of the situs. Because the situs has a strong interest (as shown by its Rule Against Perpetuities) in protecting the alienability of its land,[14] situs law should be considered by the forum for use in this situation.

All three explanations for the situs rule B; the jurisdictional justification, the need to protect land records, and the interest of the situs B; fail to justify its routine application in property cases. This failure can be demonstrated graphically by the well–known case of *In re Barrie's Estate*.[15] The issue there was whether a will had been revoked properly. The decedent had been an Illinois domiciliary; real property left to charity by the will was located in Iowa. The Supreme Court of Iowa held that the revocation had to be tested under Iowa law[16] (the law of the situs); by that standard, the revocation was ineffective. This result was at odds with an earlier decision of the Illinois Supreme Court (concerning property located in Illinois), holding that the will had been properly revoked. The result in Iowa cannot be justified on policy grounds. Even if we assume that the Illinois finding of revocation should not have been accorded full faith and credit, Iowa had no reason to apply its own law to the issue of revocation. The decision would not affect land use at all,[17] and the sanctity of Iowa's land records was assured by the fact that the decision would be rendered by a court of the situs. In short, blind application of lex sitae advanced no interest of the situs and was strongly opposed to modern, policy-based methods of looking at problems in choice of law.[18]

Unfortunately, there are few signs of a change in judicial attitude to favor a careful analysis of the reasons which might justify application of non-situs

[13] *See* Restatement (Second) of Conflict of Laws, Ch. 9, Topic 2, Introductory Note.

[14] *See* Weintraub § 8.12.

[15] 240 Iowa 431, 35 N.W.2d 658 (1949). *See also* § 67, *supra*. The case is criticized in Hancock, *supra* note 2, at 18.

[16] The court found inapplicable an apparently controlling Iowa statute which would have referred the problem to Illinois law; the reasoning on this issue was ludicrous.

[17] The opinion does not indicate any hostility in Iowa towards charitable ownership of real estate. If such a policy existed, then Iowa would have an interest.

[18] *See* Weintraub §§ 8.6–8.22 for an examination of a number of issues involving immovables, using a functional choice–of–law analysis.

law.[19] We can only hope that courts will eventually see the virtues of modern choice–of–law approaches for real property cases.[20]

[b] Movables

The near–universal adoption of the Uniform Commercial Code rendered obsolete much of the traditional learning on choice–of–law questions involving movable property.[21] The U.C.C., however, does not reach all transactions, leaving some room for the operation of common law principles. Perhaps the most important choice–of–law problem in this area today is the gratuitous transfer (either inter vivos or testamentary) of personal property; the outlines of that system are sketched in the next section.[22]

[c] Marital Property

Questions concerning marital property can arise in a number of different settings (*e.g.* succession, divorce, bankruptcy), and some cases may involve both community and common law marital property regimes. Complicating the problems are a range of new statutory rights created by both the state[23] and federal[24] governments. Nevertheless, there are a few general rules that work in this area. First, the law of the situs determines a spouse's interest in real estate, including whether the marriage creates an interest in land[25] and the scope of interests in real estate acquired after the wedding.[26] Interests in personal property usually are determined by the law of the marital domicile.[27] Marital rights are not modified or eliminated if the property is moved to another state, or if it is sold and the proceeds used to acquire other property.[28] Finally, questions concerning a surviving spouse's rights in marital property are usually treated as questions of "succession" for choice–of–law purposes.

A well–drafted pre-marital contract can solve many problems in this area. Pre–marital contracts are generally treated the same as other contracts;[29]

---

[19] *But see* Judge McGowan's excellent discussion in Mazza v. Mazza, 475 F.2d 385 (D.C. Cir. 1973).

[20] For a contrary view, *see* Willis Resse, *A Suggested Approach to Choice of Law*, 14 Vt. L. Rev. 1 (1989).

[21] *See* § 67, *supra*.

[22] *See* Leflar, McDougall & Felix §§ 175–179.

[23] Among these rights are the recent equitable apportionment statutes. The problems presented by divorce are discussed in § 129, *infra*.

[24] *See* Louise Graham, *State Marital Property Laws and Federally Created Benefits: A Conflict of Laws Analysis*, 29 Wayne L. Rev. 1 (1982).

[25] Since the virtual elimination of dower and curtesy rights, each spouse keeps the rights in property acquired before the marriage. Leflar, McDougall & Felix § 233.

[26] Restatement (Second) of Conflict of Laws § 234.

[27] *Id.*, at § 258.

[28] *See* Leflar, McDougall & Felix §§ 233–34; Weintraub § 8.14.

[29] *See* Leflar, McDougall & Felix § 236. One important difference is that pre-marital contracts are said not to arise by implication, but only by the express will of the parties.

one important result of that treatment is that the parties will be permitted to designate the governing law.[30]

§ 90 Estates and Trusts

Estate and trust problems comprise one of the most complex fields in the whole area of conflicts. That complexity is reflected by the observation that about one–third of the sections of the Second Restatement involve estate and trust matters.[1]

Several factors, including the highly mobile nature of our society, the different treatment accorded personal and real property, and the hostility toward foreign personal representatives, make this a confusing area. Nevertheless, some order can be imposed on this vast body of law, and the Uniform Probate Code (U.P.C.).[2] has improved the situation.[3]

[a] The Validity of the Instrument

Questions concerning the validity (or construction) of a will or trust instrument that conveys an interest in realty are controlled by the law of the situs.[4] The situs rule has been criticized in the preceding section, a criticism which applies with equal force to its routine application in this area. Cases employing escape devices to avoid the situs rule are not hard to find, including a renvoi case or two.[5] The U.P.C. substantially softens the situs rule by recognizing the validity of a will if it was valid in a foreign jurisdiction having any one of seven contacts with the testator.[6]

Wills that dispose of movables are controlled by the law of the testator's domicile at death.[7] Trust instruments conveying movables are generally controlled by the law of the testator's domicile at death, if the trust is testamentary,[8] and probably by that of her domicile, if the trust is created inter vivos.[9] The domicile rule makes good sense, because it permits a uniform disposition of assets which may be located in several jurisdictions.[10]

---

[30] *See* Wyatt v. Fulrath, 16 N.Y.2d 169, 211 N.E.2d 637, 264 N.Y.S.2d 233 (1965).

[1] The Associate Reporter of the Conflicts Restatement, Professor Austin Scott, was also the Reporter for the Restatement (Second) of Trusts (1959).

[2] 8 U.L.A. Pts 1-2. The UPC has been adopted as a whole in 16 states and, in part, in nearly all of the other states. *See generally* Lawrence H. Averill, The Uniform Probate Code in a Nutshell (5th ed. 2000).

[3] *See also* Jeffrey Schoenblum, *Choice of Law and Succession to Wealth: A Critical Analysis of the Ramifications of the Hague Convention on Succession to Decedents' Estates*, 32 Va. J. of Int'l L. 83 (1991).

[4] Restatement (Second) of Conflict of Laws §§ 239, 278.

[5] *E.g.*, In Re Schneider's Estate, 198 Misc. 1017, 96 N.Y.S.2d 652 (N.Y.Sup.Ct. 1950), discussed *supra*, § 59.

[6] U.P.C. § 2-506. Comparable provisions are found in a number of states which have not adopted the U.P.C.

[7] Restatement (Second) of Conflict of Laws § 263.

[8] *Id.* § 269(a).

[9] Leflar, McDougall & Felix § 188.

[10] *See id.*

The settlor can also designate the law to be applied to the instrument;[11] and, even if the settlor has not designated a governing law, the courts may still apply a rule of validation and choose the law that she "intended" to control the transaction.[12]

Finally, questions involving intestate succession[13] and election for or against the will[14] are treated in the same general way as trusts and wills. Here again, the situs rule dominates when land is involved, and the domicile rule generally controls other situations.

[b] Administration

The real difficulties in the trusts and estates areas center on questions of administration. Our concern is with the trust or decedent's estate which has connections with several states.

[1] Trusts

Administration of trusts of movables (both testamentary and inter vivos) is governed, in the absence of an effective choice–of–law clause in the trust instrument, by the place where the trust is to be administered.[15] In the case of real property, situs law will control questions of administration unless the settlor has designated otherwise.[16]

[2] Estates

Administration of a decedent's estate is considered to be an in rem proceeding, a treatment which explains the traditional and complicating restriction that a personal representative[17] has no authority to act outside

---

[11] The designated state should have a "substantial relation" to the trust. Restatement (Second) of Conflict of Laws § 270(a). Comment b cautions that the designation will not be honored if it would offend "a strong public policy" of the state having the most significant relationship to that issue. A cynic might observe that public policy is more likely to be offended when the assets of the trust are located in the forum. *See, e.g.*, Nat'l Shawmut Bank of Boston v. Cumming, 325 Mass. 457, 91 N.E.2d 337 (1950), Matter of Bauer, 14 N.Y.2d 272, 251 N.Y.S.2d 23, 200 N.E.2d 207 (1964). The U.P.C. provision on party autonomy (*see* Lawrence Averill, *supra* note 2, at 256) is probably less restrictive than that of the Restatement.

[12] Leflar, McDougall & Felix §§ 188–89. A trust valid under the law of the settlor's domicile or the place where it is to be administered will almost surely be validated. Willis Reese, *American Choice of Law*, 30 Am. J. Comp. L. 135, 144–45 (1982). In order to sustain the trust, a court may test the validity of a testamentary trust separately from the validity of the will. John Ester & Eugene Scoles, *Estate Planning and Conflict of Laws*, 24 Ohio St. L.J. 270, 271 (1963).

[13] *See* Restatement (Second) of Conflict of Laws §§ 236, 260.

[14] See Annot., *Conflict of Laws Regarding Election For Or Against the Will, and Effect in One Jurisdiction of Election in Another*, 69 A.L.R.3d 1081 (1976).

[15] Leflar, McDougall & Felix § 191; 5 Austin Scott, The Law of Trusts §§ 604–12 (3d ed. 1967).

[16] *Id.* at § 659.

[17] An "executor" is named in the will; an "administrator" is named by the court. The term "personal representative," which we use, is often used to denote either capacity.

the jurisdiction that appointed her. This rule can be justified only by the need to protect local creditors,[18] a justification which has been long since rendered obsolete by modern theories of judicial jurisdiction, and long-arm statutes reaching acts causing harm within the forum. The "local estate" rule which results from the in rem classification has an expensive and unfortunate consequence: A personal representative can neither sue nor be sued in a jurisdiction in which she has not been appointed. To be sure, the effect of that consequence is ameliorated by the fact that the representative can probably be appointed as an ancillary administrator in every relevant jurisdiction, but doing so is a costly proposition.[19]

Dissatisfaction with the local estate concept has led to a number of legislative reforms[20] that are milestones on the road to a unified administration of estates.[21] An example of those reforms is § 4205 of the U.P.C., which substantially eases the ability of the domiciliary representative to act without the need for local administration. The U.P.C. provisions on ancillary administration and the representative's capacity to sue and be sued mark a significant advance on the road to unified administration, a road which will also ease the choice–of–law problems in the area.[22]

§ 91 Corporations[1]

Choice–of–law questions involving corporations are governed by two general rules: If the question involves the internal management of corporate affairs (such as a director's duty of care), then the law of the place of incorporation controls;[2] if the problem centers around corporate responsibility to others (a breach of contract claim, for example), then the normal or otherwise applicable choice–of–law rules govern.[3]

Difficulties rarely arise in practice. When the corporation, behaving like any other party, becomes embroiled in a legal dispute, it is treated as if it were a natural person. Thus, when a corporation makes a contract, commits a tort, or buys property, the law applied to that transaction will be the same law that would be applied in the case of a non-corporate party. If, on the other hand, application of different and inconsistent laws would interfere unduly with the "internal affairs" of the corporation, then the law of the state of incorporation is applied. Thus, problems such as the issuance

[18] Banks McDowell, Foreign Personal Representatives 171 (1957). A cynic might also suspect that the rule protects the local probate bar.

[19] Some states do not permit a foreign corporation to act as a representative.

[20] B. McDowell, *supra* note 18, at 172.

[21] *See id.* at 170–93, for a discussion of this concept.

[22] *See generally* Lawrence Averill, *supra* note 2, ch. 26. The Restatement (Second) of Conflict of Laws, Chapter 14, Topic 1, Introductory Note, mentions that the Restatement emphasizes the "unitary character" of estate administration in light of recent trends in the area.

[1] *See generally* Phaedon John Kozyris, *Corporate Choice of Law*, 1985 Duke L.J. 1; J. Thomas Oldham, *Regulating the Regulators: Limitations Upon a State's Ability to Regulate Corporations with Multi–State Contacts*, 57 Den. L.J. 345 (1980).

[2] Restatement (Second) of Conflict of Laws § 302. *See also* U.C.C. § 8-106 (1977).

[3] Restatement (Second) of Conflict of Laws § 301.

of corporate stock, a director's liability, and the method of choosing directors are referred to the law of only one state; that where the corporation was chartered.[4]

The Supreme Court captured the essential difference between these two ways of dealing with corporations in a case involving the question of what law determined whether a bank incorporated under Cuban law was amenable to suit in this country:[5]

> As a general matter, the law of the state of incorporation normally determines issues relating to the *internal* affairs of a corporation. Application of that body of law achieves the need for certainty and predictability of result while generally protecting the justified expectations of parties with interests in the corporation. Different conflicts principles apply, however, where the rights of third parties *external* to the corporation are at issue. (citations omitted; emphasis in original.)

Only a handful of cases (and statutes) have resisted these two dominant rules. The exceptions have been reactions to the exploitation by both states and corporations of the internal affairs rule.[6]

Loose state regulation of a corporation's internal affairs naturally attracts corporate business; because of the widespread choice–of–law reference to the state of incorporation, a corporate move to a laissez–faire state will help insulate the company from regulation of its internal affairs, even by a state which may have a substantial interest in the problem. Business, therefore, flows from states of significant regulation to states (like Delaware) with less regulation. To paraphrase Gresham's law on the quality of money, less regulation drives out more. Occasionally, states resist this trend and apply forum law instead of the law of the state of incorporation when the corporate activity results in palpable harm in the forum. Thus, a sale of stock in Iowa might violate Iowa's Blue Sky law, even though the transaction was legal in Delaware, the state of incorporation. Because Iowa has a strong interest in protecting its citizens, the internal affairs rule may be disregarded by an Iowa court.[7]

A few states have gone even further and adopted statutes which seek to regulate "pseudo–foreign" corporations.[8] California, for example, regulates certain aspects of governance when the corporation's California business exceeds one–half of its total activities and more than half the stock

---

[4] A court, however, may still exercise judicial jurisdiction over the affairs of a foreign corporation. Scoles, et al. §§ 9.4-9.10.

[5] First National City Bank v. Banco Para el Comercio, 462 U.S. 611, 621 (1983).

[6] Daniel Boorstein has written that when states use the opportunity to manipulate the federal system to their advantage, they trade in the "federal commodity." Daniel J. Boorstin, The Americans: The Democratic Experience 414–16 (1973). A federal law of corporations would solve the "federal commodity" problem in this area. *see* William L. Cary, *Federalism and Corporate Law: Reflections Upon Delaware*, 83 Yale L.J. 663 (1974).

[7] Restatement (Second) of Conflict of Laws § 302, illustration 1. *See also* Louis Loss, *The Conflict of Laws and the Blue Sky Laws*, 71 Harv. L. Rev. 209 (1957). The leading case is Western Air Lines, Inc. v. Sobieski, 191 Cal. App. 2d 399, 12 Cal.Rptr. 719 (1961).

[8] Elwin R Latty, *Pseudo-Foreign Corporations*, 65 Yale L.J. 137 (1955).

in the corporation is held by Californians.[9] In contrast, other states and the Model Business Corporation Act prohibit internal regulation of foreign corporations.[10] Although this is an area where serious problems are possible, the extreme reluctance of American courts to intervene in a corporation's internal affairs, absent an overwhelming reason for doing so, makes it unlikely that those potential problems will often occur. Indeed, given the quasi-constitutional status of the internal affairs rule, it may be impossible for a state to regulate the internal affairs of a foreign corporation.[11]

§ 92 The Uniform Commercial Code[1]

The Uniform Commercial Code was designed to produce uniformity in several areas of commercial law. Its adoption in 49 states (the exception is Louisiana), the District of Columbia, and Puerto Rico has largely accomplished that objective. Over time, however, the uniformity has been eroded somewhat. There are a number of reasons for this: The official version of the Code contains alternative choices for several sections; the official version has been changed several times, and not all changes have been unanimously adopted among the states; state legislatures tinker with their own codes; and judicial interpretation can and does vary from court to court. As a result, choice–of–law issues can arise under the Code, although they have not as yet created significant controversy.

[a] Generally

The Code attempts to handle choice of law in three ways, using a framework established in § 1-105. The first rule is that forum law controls any transaction covered by the Code if there is sufficient contact between the forum and the problem; thus, "this Act applies to transactions bearing an *appropriate relation* to this state."[2]

Although the Code does not define the phrase "appropriate relation," the Official Comment states that "the mere fact" that suit is brought in a particular state does not create an "appropriate" relation with the forum. More helpfully, the Comment suggests that party expectations may also bear on determining whether an appropriate relation exists, at least within the general goal of promoting uniformity in Code cases.[3]

---

[9] Cal. Corp. Code § 2115(a) (West 1990).

[10] Model Business Corp. Act § 15.05(c) (1991). *See also* N.Y. Bus. Corp. Law § 1320 (McKinney 2001). Such regulation raises questions concerning constitutional limitations on choice of law. *See* §§ 96–99, *infra*.

[11] *See* § 99, *infra*. Because the constitutional nature of the internal affairs rule turns on the possibility of inconsistent state regulation, a state may be able to regulate a foreign corporation's internal affairs in some circumstances. *See, e.g.*, Sandler v. NCR Corp., 928 F.2d 40 (2d Cir. 1991).

[1] *See generally* Weintraub §§ 8.27–8.45, Robert Leflar, *Conflict of Laws Under the U.C.C.*, 35 Ark. L. Rev. 87 (1981).

[2] U.C.C. § 1-105(1) (emphasis added).

[3] *Id.*, comment 2.

Although the appropriate relationship test seems to be a less demanding standard for the exercise of legislative jurisdiction than the test of "most significant relationship" established by Section 188 of the Restatement (Second),[4] it is possible that judicial familiarity with the Restatement will bring the two standards into harmony. Further, the Code permits the parties to stipulate the law that will govern their transaction if the stipulated law "bears a reasonable relation" to the transaction. That test, the comment states,[5] "is similar to the one laid down by the Supreme Court in *Seeman v. Philadelphia Warehouse Company*."[6] The comment expects the parties ordinarily will choose a jurisdiction "where a significant portion of the making or performance of the contract" will take place.[7] The choice of such a jurisdiction is not required, however, for the comment also states that the parties may sometimes choose the law of a jurisdiction "even though the transaction has no significant contact with the jurisdiction chosen."[8] Although the reasonable relation test is not a very helpful formulation, at least as amplified by the comment, it is again likely to be construed in a fashion similar to the comparable Restatement (Second) provisions on party autonomy.[9]

Section 1-105 was substantially revised by the drafters of the Code in 2001.[10] The new provision permits the parties to choose the applicable law, "regardless of whether or not the transaction bears a relation to the State designated. . . ."[11] If the parties do not designate the governing law, then the court should apply forum law, including the forum's "conflict of laws principles."[12] Thus, the default rule is the whole law of the forum.

A different rule applies, however, if one of the parties is a consumer. Three rules apply to consumer transactions. First, the parties may still stipulate a governing law, but that jurisdiction must bear a "reasonable relation" to the transaction.[13] Second, the parties "may not deprive the consumer of any rule of law. . .which is both protective of consumers and may not be varied by agreement. . . ." Third, the "protective" laws referred to in the second rule are those of the consumer's principal residence unless, the contract involves a sale of goods; then the parties may stipulate the law of the place where the contract was made and where she takes delivery of the goods. New Article 1, in other words, does not permit the consumer

[4] *See* § 74, *supra*.

[5] U.C.C., § 1-105, comment 1. *See generally* Thomas G. Ryan, *Reasonable Relation and Party Autonomy Under the Uniform Commercial Code*, 63 Marq. L. Rev. 219 (1979).

[6] 274 U.S. 403 (1927). *Seeman* applied the doctrine of "alternative reference" discussed *supra*, § 73.

[7] U.C.C. § 1-105, comment 1.

[8] *Id.*

[9] *See* § 74, *supra*.

[10] No state has yet adopted the new version of Article 1, perhaps because it was supposed to be joined with a new Article 2-a revision which has not yet received official approval. The new Articles 1 and 2 are discussed in a Symposium, 54 SMU L. Rev.469 (2001) (contributions by many, many professors).

[11] U.C.C. § 1-105 (c) (1). The rule applies to both domestic and international transactions.

[12] U.C.C. § 1-105 (d).

[13] U.C.C. § 1-105 (e) contains the rules governing consumer transactions.

to waive the consumer protection laws of her home state through the back door of stipulating the law of a state which does not recognize those protections.

[b] Secured Transactions Under the Present Code

The first two parts of the § 1-105 model permit the parties to choose their own law, with a residual reference to forum law in the absence of a choice–of–law clause. Because Article 1 applies to the entire Code, these two provisions of § 1-105 control choice of law in the sale of goods, commercial paper, letters of credit, secured transactions, and virtually everything else covered by the Code. The final part of the § 1-105 framework, however, creates six exceptions to the two general rules.[14] The most significant of these exceptions involves the provisions of Article 9, dealing with the perfection of security interests. Perfection is very important to lenders who secure their loans with some form of collateral; if their interest in the collateral is "perfected," the creditor has some sort of priority over unsecured creditors if the debtor defaults.

Article 9 was thoroughly revised in 2000, and the revised version has been adopted in all 50 states. Among the most important changes were those involving the perfection of security interests, a subject which had been complex and confusing under the old Article 9. The new rules are very simple: First, the creditor must perfect its interest where the debtor is located.[15] That place, for an individual, is her habitual residence; a corporation is located in the jurisdiction where it is incorporated.[16] Third, the mechanics of filing — which office, what forms to use, etc. — are governed by the law of the place where filing takes place.[17] These changes should eliminate much of the litigation involving multi-state security interests.

§ 93 Statutes of Limitations[1]

[a] Analysis

Limitations periods traditionally have been characterized as procedural for choice of law purposes. This pigeon–holing stems from the odd notion that limitations periods are "remedial" (and, therefore, procedural) because they affect only the remedy available, but do not affect the underlying right. As a result, the forum applies its own law to limitations questions. This

[14] U.C.C. § 1-105(2).

[15] U.C.C. § 9-301.

[16] *Id.* § 9-307.

[17] *Id.* § 9-401.

[1] *See generally* Louise Weinberg, *Choosing Law: The Limitations Debate*, 1991 U. Ill. L. Rev. 683; Michael D. Green, *The Paradox of Statutes of Limitations in Toxic Substances Litigation*, 76 Cal. L. Rev. 965 (1988); Margaret Rosso Grossman, *Statutes of Limitations and the Conflict of Laws: A Modern Analysis*, 1980 Ariz. St. L.J. 1.

characterization was carried over into the Second Restatement,[2] even though that work generally frowns on the substance/procedure classification process.[3] Before the 1988 revisions, the Restatement applied the procedural classification with a vengeance in the area of limitations; even if the claim was time–barred under otherwise applicable foreign law, the forum was directed to hear the claim if it was not barred by the forum's limitations period.[4]

No good reason exists for the procedural characterization of limitations issues. The two main reasons for appending that label to a problem[5] apply only minimally in this area. The first reason, the difficulty of ascertaining foreign law, should rarely be a factor, for it should be relatively easy to find and interpret a foreign statute of limitations. The second basis for labeling a problem procedural is the forum's interest in the control of litigation in its own courts. In the limitations field, however, that justification exists only when the forum has a *shorter* limitations period. In that situation, the forum's policy against entertaining stale claims may be relevant. Where the forum's limitation period is longer, however, there is no good reason to use the procedural label to apply forum law. Instead of mechanically labeling limitations "procedural," therefore, a court should analyze each case in light of generally applicable conflicts principles to determine if there is any good reason to use the forum statute in a case where foreign "substantive" law otherwise governs.

That kind of policy–oriented approach to limitations problems would not only eliminate the routine procedural classification, but would also lead to consideration of the legitimate interests of the foreign state in the litigation. A policy approach to limitations problems might also curtail much of the forum–shopping associated with the current approach. Unfortunately, such analysis has been relatively rare, and courts have matter–of–factly applied the forum's statutory period. Thus, Professor Weinberg notes a "surprising judicial tolerance"[6] for forum shopping in the limitations area. Traditionally, only two escape devices were available; one created by courts and the other (borrowing statutes) by legislatures. There have been recent developments, however, which might lead to more use of modern choice–of–law analysis in this area. These developments will be considered after a brief review of the escape devices.

[b] Substantive Limitations

The procedural classification depends on the notion that the running of the limitations period affects only the remedy and not the right. If the foreign right and limitations period are found to be closely linked, however,

[2] Restatement (Second) of Conflict of Laws § 142.

[3] *See id.* § 122, comment b.

[4] *Id.* § 142(2). This rule is perfectly constitutional, of course. Sun Oil Co. v. Wortman, 486 U.S. 717 (1988), discussed in § 97, *infra*.

[5] *See* § 58, *supra*.

[6] Weinberg, *supra* note 1, at 686.

then the limitations period will be styled "substantive," and foreign law will be applied to determine if the claim is time–barred.

The difficulty inheres in determining when the necessary connection is present. This is relatively easy with some statutes; the limitations period is "built–in" to the right and the two go together hand–in–glove. The best examples are those statutes, such as wrongful death acts, where the limitations period and the right are created by the same legislative pronouncement. In those situations, it can readily be argued that the limitations period was adopted as a device to limit the sweep of the substantive right created by the statute. When the right and limitations period are not found together, courts apply a variety of tests to determine whether a particular provision is substantive.

An old example is *Davis v. Mills.*[7] Justice Holmes established in that case what has become known as the "specificity" test: The limitation provision is treated as substantive when it is "directed to the newly created liability so specifically as to warrant saying that it qualified the right."

Such tests are necessarily vague. They permit partial escape from the procedural classification, but at a cost of reduced certainty and possibly increased judicial manipulation. A well–known example is *Bournias v. Atlantic Maritime Co.*,[8] an opinion written by Judge (later Justice) Harlan. Plaintiff, a Panamanian seaman, sued for wages he claimed were due under the Panamanian Labor Code. The suit was time–barred under a provision of that Code which specified a one–year limitations period; the law of the forum (New York), however, would have held the suit timely filed. After canvassing great masses of authority (and lamenting its vagueness), Harlan decided to apply the test of *Davis v. Mills*. Naturally, the Labor Code flunked the test. Nothing in the record showed that the Panamanian legislature "gave special consideration" to the interplay between the limitations period and the substantive rights created by the Labor Code which formed the basis of plaintiff's claim. Hence, the one–year provision lacked the requisite "specificity" to be declared "substantive," and, therefore, the court applied the forum's limitations period. One can only wonder what policy, other than protecting a seaman, Harlan thought he was advancing by applying the longer statute of limitations of the forum; certainly the opinion gives no clue concerning the reasons for upsetting the clearly expressed policy of Panama on this issue.

[c] Borrowing Statutes[9]

Most state legislatures have adopted the more comprehensive, but still far from perfect, solution B; the enactment of "borrowing" statutes. Those statutes provide that a cause of action is barred in the forum if it is also barred in another state B; typically, the state where the claim arose or

[7] 194 U.S. 451, 454 (1904).

[8] 220 F.2d 152 (2d Cir. 1955).

[9] *See generally* John Ester, *Borrowing Statutes of Limitation and Conflict of Laws*, 15 U. Fla. L. Rev. 33 (1962).

where the parties reside. The foreign period is borrowed only if the claim would be barred in the foreign state. If the claim is time–barred in the forum, on the other hand, the borrowing statute will not be used. The effect, therefore, is to apply the shorter of the foreign or local limitations period.[10]

[d] Recent Developments

The Uniform Conflict of Laws Limitations Act[11] provides that the applicable limitations period should be that set by the state whose substantive law will be used to decide the case. The Act also provides an out if it would be "unfair" to apply that law. The Act is a step forward in treating limitations as a substantive issue. The difficulty with its approach, however, is that it fails to address the forum's legitimate interests as a forum B; that is, the forum's interest in keeping out stale litigation, if it wishes.[12]

The American Law Institute also addressed the limitations problem recently in amending § 142 of the Restatement (Second) of the Conflict of Laws. Under new § 142, a court will choose a limitations period by applying the general principles of § 6.[13]

The drafters of the new provision noted that "[i]n general" the forum will apply its own limitations period barring the claim, a choice that makes good sense according to modern policy analysis. The forum-state's shorter limitation period is designed to protect its courts from stale claims, and that interest justifies barring the out–of–date suit, even if it would be permitted in the courts of the claim–state. When the forum's limitation's period is longer than that of the claim–state, § 142's provisions are more complicated: If maintenance of the claim would serve no significant interest of the forum, and the claim is barred where it arose, the forum should not apply its own longer limitations period.

The focus in new § 142 on the § 6 policy guidelines to determine limitations is correct; it forces the court to think about what policies and expectations (including those of the forum) are involved in deciding what period to choose. The new section avoids the use of the substance/procedure distinction entirely, directing the court away from characterization and toward analysis of the relevant choice–influencing considerations of § 6.

---

[10] This too is perfectly constitutional. Wells v. Simonds Abrasive Co., 345 U.S. 514 (1953), discussed *supra*, § 101.

[11] 12 U.L.A. 61 (Supp. 1992) [adopted in five states]. *See generally* Robert A. Leflar, *The New Conflicts–Limitations Act,* 35 Mercer L. Rev. 461 (1984).

[12] *See* Weinberg *supra* note 1, at 703–05. An example of the application of the Act is Perkins v. Clark Equipment Co., 823 F.2d 207 (8th Cir. 1987) (North Dakota federal court applied Iowa limitation law to a case governed by Iowa tort law).

[13] *See* § 71, *supra*.

Part E

THE CONSTITUTION AND CHOICE OF LAW

§ 94 Legislative Jurisdiction[1]

A state is not free to apply any law it wishes to solve a particular problem; that choice is limited by several provisions of the United States Constitution. Historically, the most important provisions in this area have been the Due Process Clause of the Fourteenth Amendment and the Full Faith and Credit Clause of Article Four. Several anti-discrimination provisions B; the Commerce Clause, the Equal Protection Clauses, and the Privileges and Immunities clause also are relevant.

The question presented in this part is whether a state possesses legislative jurisdiction; in other words, whether the Federal Constitution permits the state to apply its law (jurisdiction to "legislate") to a legal problem. "Judicial jurisdiction" concerns the authority of a state's court to hear a case; legislative jurisdiction, by contrast, involves the authority of a state to apply its law statutory or judge–made. The law of legislative jurisdiction has paralleled the development of choice–of–law generally. In the early years of this century, it looked as if the Supreme Court would impose a constitutionally derived territorial rule on the states, but inquiry today focuses largely on whether the state has sufficient contacts with or interest in the problem to justify the imposition of its law. Current analysis of the constitutional limits on legislative jurisdiction, in short, resembles modern thought concerning constitutional limitations on the exercise of judicial jurisdiction.

This part analyzes the cases involved in that development. The first several sections trace the historical development of the Court's approach to questions of legislative jurisdiction, culminating in a trilogy of recent cases, *Allstate Ins. Co. v. Hague*,[2] *Phillips Petroleum Co. v. Shutts*,[3] and *Sun Oil Co. v. Wortman*.[4]

Next is a section discussing the possible impact of different constitutional provisions on choice–of–law, followed by a summary of that law today. Finally, §§ 97 and 98 analyze two related problems: the ability of a state to keep out foreign litigation, and the power of a state to keep certain litigation at home.

---

[1] *See generally* Willis Reese, *Legislative Jurisdiction*, 78 Colum. L. Rev. 1587 (1978).

[2] 449 U.S. 302 (1981).

[3] 472 U.S. 797 (1985).

[4] 486 U.S. 717 (1988).

§ 95 Prelude: The Early Cases

The history of Supreme Court intervention in state choice of law dates only from the beginning of this century. The Court's entry into choice of law coincided with a more general trend in that tribunal toward constitutional protection of property and contract rights against increasing state regulation. Because limiting state regulation in interstate transactions was one way of protecting property rights, the Court's imposition of constitutional limits in choice of law was hardly surprising. The vehicle used, the Due Process Clause (although perhaps not as obvious a choice as the Full Faith and Credit Clause), also was not surprising, given the emphasis the Supreme Court placed on due process protection of economic rights in the generation before the New Deal.[1]

Constitutional intervention came at a time of great formalism in substantive areas, such as the law of contract.[2] The result was a clutch of cases that came close to engraving in the Constitution the vested rights theory associated with Professor Beale and the First Restatement.[3] The two leading cases, both involving insurance, illustrate the Court's approach. The earlier of the two, *New York Life Insurance Co. v. Dodge,*[4] involved a Missouri resident who applied for a life insurance policy with New York Life, a company incorporated in New York, where it had its main office. The policy was issued in Missouri. Dodge later obtained a loan from the company. When he defaulted on loan payments, the company applied the reserve value of the policy to the repayment of the loan. That course of action was permitted by both the policy itself and by New York law; a Missouri non-forfeiture statute, however, forbade the procedure. After Dodge died, his named beneficiary sued on the policy in a Missouri state court.

The Supreme Court reversed the state court judgment in favor of plaintiff. The Court viewed the loan contract as one made in New York, as the policy expressly stated. Because it was a "New York" contract, Missouri lacked power to regulate it. "To hold otherwise," the opinion argued, "would sanction the impairment of that liberty of contract guaranteed to all by the Fourteenth Amendment." Thus were wedded the vested rights theory and the law of the place of making with the protection of liberty of contract under the Due Process Clause.[5]

A similar approach was followed a dozen years later in *Home Insurance Co. v. Dick,*[6] an action brought in a Texas court to recover on a fire

[1] *See generally* Robert Allen Sedler, *Constitutional Limitations on Choice of Law: The Perspective of Constitutional Generalism*, 10 Hofstra L. Rev. 59, 62–68 (1981).

[2] *see* Grant Gilmore, The Death of Contract (1974).

[3] *See* §§ 63–68, *supra*, for a discussion of the vested rights theory.

[4] 246 U.S. 357 (1918).

[5] There is an interesting dissent by Justice Brandeis in *Dodge*, arguing that the policy was a "Missouri contract," and that Missouri law could be applied. Brandeis' reasons in part resemble those of the center of gravity test, discussed *supra*, § 70.

[6] 281 U.S. 397 (1930).

insurance policy on a tugboat. The policy had been issued in Mexico by a Mexican company to a Mexican national, and it covered the tug only in Mexican waters. Payment was to be made in Mexican currency. The policy was later assigned to plaintiff, a Texan temporarily living in Mexico. After the tug burned, plaintiff sued defendant, a New York company which had entered into a reinsurance agreement with the original Mexican insurer. The defendant asserted that the action had not been filed according to a clause in the insurance contract which provided a one year statute of limitations on claims. To that defense plaintiff demurred, arguing that the policy limitations period was invalid under a Texas statute forbidding limitations provisions shorter than two years. The Texas state courts agreed with plaintiff, rejecting the New York company's constitutional challenge to the application of the Texas legislation. The Supreme Court reversed. Justice Brandeis' majority opinion relied on the absence of contacts between Texas and the policy in issue:

> All acts relating to the making of the policy were done in Mexico. All acts in relation to the making of the contracts of reinsurance were done there or in New York. The fact that Dick's permanent residence was in Texas is without significance. Hence, Texas lacked "power to affect the terms of contracts so made." Because it lacked that power it could not, consistent with the Due Process Clause, impose on the parties "a greater obligation than that agreed upon."[7]

Both *Dick* and *Dodge*, therefore, suggest that the Court was approaching a constitutionalization of the vested rights theory. Other cases reinforce that observation.[8] Perhaps the most striking illustration of that trend is *Mutual Life Ins. Co. v. Liebing*,[9] which presented virtually the same facts as *Dodge*, except that in *Liebing* the plaintiff prevailed. The difference between the two was that in *Liebing*; the Court, speaking through Justice Holmes, found the insurance contract contained "a positive promise to make the loan if asked"; hence, the "offer" contained in the policy was "accepted" when the insured applied for a loan. Because the application had been delivered to a company agent in Missouri, the contract had been made in Missouri "and the first principles of legal thinking allow the law of the place where the contract was made to determine the validity and consequences of the act." The Missouri non-forfeiture statute, therefore, could be applied to protect the plaintiff in Liebing. The apparent inconsistency between *Liebing* and *Dodge* thus vanishes, and both cases can be seen to turn on the question of where the contract was made. By forbidding regulation by any jurisdiction other than the state where the contract was completed, the Court elevated the rule of *lex loci contractus* to constitutional status.

[7] Brandeis' opinion in *Dick* can also be read as a precursor to modern forms of choice–of–law analysis.

[8] Other Supreme Court opinions during this period also embraced the territorial view of choice of law embodied in the vested rights theory. In Western Union Telegraph v. Brown, 234 U.S. 542 (1914), for example, Justice Holmes seemed to suggest that the place of injury rule was required by the Constitution. Allgeyer v. Louisiana, 165 U.S. 578 (1897), apparently viewed the *lex locus* rule in contracts as part of the "liberty" guaranteed by the 14th Amendment.

[9] 259 U.S. 209 (1922).

§ 96 Intermezzo: The New Deal Cases and Their Progeny

The Court's apparent constitutionalization of the vested rights theory, however, could not withstand the economic hardship of the 1930s and the increased state regulation of business which the legislatures adopted in response to the Depression. The seeds of the demise had been sown in the *Dick* case, for the language quoted in the preceding section could be read easily as adopting a test which took into account the interests of the involved states; Texas, lacking any interest in the insurance contract at issue, lacked authority under the Constitution to regulate it. Not until the Court decided two workers' compensation cases in the 1930s, however, did it become clear that a New Deal in constitutional choice of law had begun.

The first of these decisions, the *Alaska Packers case*,[1] upheld an award of compensation by California to a non–resident alien, hired in that state but injured in Alaska. The opinion clearly shows a Court in transition. Much of the opinion refers back to the *Dick–Dodge* line of cases (the Court in *Alaska Packers* described the problem as one of contract rather than tort, thereby emphasizing the law of the place of employment, rather than the law of the place of injury), but there is also language looking forward to interest analysis.[2] The Court found that both Alaska and California had a "legitimate public interest" in the resolution of the problem. The solution devised was to balance those interests "by appraising the governmental interests of each jurisdiction, and turning the scale of decision according to their weight." Because California's interest was "greater than that of Alaska," the Court upheld the California award of compensation against both due process and full faith and credit challenges.

The Supreme Court's budding romance with interest analysis blossomed fully three years later in *Pacific Employers Ins. Co. v. Industrial Accident Comm'n.*[3] That case involved a Massachusetts employer who sent his Massachusetts employee to a "branch factory in California to act temporarily as its technical adviser"; while in California, he was injured. The California worker's compensation board made an award to the employee. The employer challenged that award under the Full Faith and Credit Clause, on the ground that the Massachusetts statute controlled all employment contracts entered into in that state. If it did, then the award was improper, because the Massachusetts act required a written notice, which the employee had not sent.

The question thus involved a direct conflict between the statutes of two states, both of which were seriously interested in the problem. Justice Stone's opinion recognized that each state could have applied its law to the problem constitutionally, but he did not balance the interests of the two states, as he had in *Alaska Packers*. Instead, he asked whether the forum (California) had a substantial interest in the dispute. After determining that it did, Stone concluded that the Full Faith and Credit Clause does not permit

1 Alaska Packers Ass'n v. Industrial Acc. Comm'n., 294 U.S. 532 (1935).

2 For a discussion of interest analysis, *see* § 78, *supra*.

3 306 U.S. 493 (1939).

Massachusetts "to legislate across state lines so as to preclude [California] from prescribing for itself the legal consequences of acts within it."

Pacific Employers clearly reveals how much had changed since *Dick* and *Dodge.*[4] The court had progressed from requiring the application of the *lex loci delicti* or the *lex loci contractus* to the point of requiring only that the law applied be the law of a state with some substantial interest in the dispute.

The Court's concern with states' interests was confirmed by later cases, particularly *Watson v. Employers' Liability Ins. Corp.*[5] and *Clay v. Sun Ins. Office, Ltd.*[6] The plaintiff in *Watson* alleged injury resulting from her use in her home state of Louisiana of a "Toni Home Permanent," a product made by an Illinois subsidiary of a Massachusetts corporation. Suit was brought in Louisiana under a Louisiana statute permitting a "direct action" against insurance companies.[7] The contract between the insurance company and Toni, however, contained a clause that prohibited direct actions, a clause which was valid under the laws of Massachusetts and Illinois. In rejecting defendant's due process and full faith and credit attacks on the Louisiana statute, the Court emphasized that the case at bar had important contacts with Louisiana; Louisiana, therefore, had sufficient "interests" in the "multistate transaction" so that it could "regulate to protect the interests of its own people." Such regulation, unlike that in *Dick* (which the Court expressly distinguished), was not "mere intermeddling in affairs beyond her borders which are no concern of hers." The focus on the forum's interests obviously foreshadows modern choice–of–law theory, with its emphasis on the advancement of state policy.

In *Clay*, the plaintiff, while a resident of Illinois, had purchased from defendant in Illinois an insurance policy which covered plaintiff's personal property. Several months later, plaintiff established a new residence in Florida where the insured property was lost two years later. The problem arose over the one–year limitations period provided in the contract; Florida law nullified internal limitations clauses if the stated period was less than five years. The Supreme Court sustained the Florida courts' application of Florida law. The opinion emphasized the "ambulatory nature" of the contract, and the insurer's knowledge that the property, according to the terms of the policy, could be taken anywhere in the world. Thus, Florida had the requisite contact with the problem.[8] Moreover, it was foreseeable to defendant that the property would move into states such as Florida (the policy was styled a "Personal Property Floater Policy B; World Wide") where

[4] There had been harbingers of this new approach in addition to *Dick. E.g.*, Union Trust Co. v. Grosman, 245 U.S. 412 (1918) (married woman's contract made in another state held unenforceable).

[5] 348 U.S. 66 (1954).

[6] 377 U.S. 179 (1964).

[7] Ordinarily, suit is not brought against the insurance carrier but against the insured. Direct action statutes, such as that in Louisiana, permit the carrier to be named as defendant in some circumstances.

[8] *Dick* was distinguished on the ground that Texas contacts had been wholly lacking in that case.

the policy limitations period would be held invalid. For those reasons, the choice of Florida law was both fair to the company and a constitutional exercise of Florida's jurisdiction to legislate.

Thus, the thirty years between *Alaska Packers* and *Clay* provided strong evidence that the Court had embraced a test for legislative jurisdiction which required only a significant state contact with the dispute or a legitimate state interest in the outcome.[9]

That conclusion was to be tested in a trilogy of cases decided during the 1980s.

§ 97 The Eighties' Trilogy: *Allstate, Shutts,* and *Wortman*

Although the line of Supreme Court cases ending with *Clay* seemed to lay to rest any notion that the Constitution substantially limits a state's autonomy in choice of law, modern developments in choice–of–law theory were putting pressure on the Court to recognize such limits. The growth of policy–based choice–of–law analysis brought with it actual and theoretical problems that led many to believe that effective constitutional restraints in the choice–of–law area would be necessary.[1]

The actual problems arose in a few well–publicized cases that purported to apply some form of interest analysis, but which seemed in fact to be so irrational in result, and so lacking in natural justice, as to warrant Supreme Court intervention.[2] The theoretical problem concerned the propriety of a disinterested forum applying its law in the event of a true conflict. Analysis of those problems suggested that free–wheeling choice of law, permitted by modern approaches, required the imposition of constitutional limits by that most disinterested forum; the Supreme Court. By the mid–1970s, a number of scholars had begun arguing forcefully for recognition of such constitutional limits.[3] During the 1980's, the Court responded to those concerns in a trilogy of decisions which both confused and clarified.

[9] Only one case gives any cause for caution about that conclusion. In Order of United Commercial Travelers of America v. Wolfe, 331 U.S. 586 (1947), the Court followed a long line of precedent, holding that the Full Faith and Credit Clause requires that the law of the state where a fraternal benefit society is incorporated be applied to all cases involving a claim of benefits due from that society. *Wolfe* represents constitutional recognition of the internal affairs doctrine, which is based on the overwhelming need to insure that a corporation's (or a mutual benefit society's) internal affairs be regulated by the law of only one state; inconsistent decisions by different states on such questions could well lead to economic chaos. That need, however, is a limited one, although, as the Court's discussion of the internal affairs doctrine has shown, it is still very much alive. *see* § 91, *supra*; Restatement (Second) of Conflict of Laws § 302.

[1] Although this section focuses on judicial development of constitutional limits, some scholars have argued forcefully that the Congressional power to implement the Full Faith and Credit Clause should be used to prescribe statutory limits in choice of law. *See, e.g.*, Currie, Essays.

[2] Perhaps the "worst" case was Rosenthal v. Warren, 475 F.2d 438 (2d Cir. 1973), discussed *supra*, § 84[a].

[3] *E.g.*, James A. Martin, *Constitutional Limitations on Choice of Law*, 61 Cornell L. Rev. 185 (1976); Frederic L. Kirgis, *The Roles of Due Process and Full Faith and Credit in Choice of Law*, 62 Cornell L. Rev. 94 (1976).

[a] *Allstate*

The first of the trilogy, *Allstate Insurance Co. v. Hague*,[4] lacks a majority opinion but still suggests the Court's approach to the Constitution in choice of law.[5] Plaintiff's husband, Ralph Hague, was killed in Wisconsin when a motorcycle on which he was a passenger was hit by a car. Both drivers were Wisconsin residents, as were plaintiff and her husband. The husband had worked in Red Wing, Minnesota, just across the state line from his Wisconsin home. After the accident, plaintiff moved to Minnesota, where she remarried. A Minnesota probate judge named her administrator of Ralph's estate. She then sued Allstate in a Minnesota state court, seeking to recover on the uninsured motorist coverage in the policies Ralph had purchased from Allstate. There were three such policies, one for each car Ralph had owned, each providing $15,000 in uninsured motorist coverage. Plaintiff sought to recover $45,000 by "stacking" (combining) the policies, a practice permitted in a number of states, including Minnesota; Wisconsin, which did not permit stacking, would have limited recovery to the $15,000 coverage provided in one policy. The Minnesota Supreme Court, purporting to employ Leflar's "Choice–Influencing Considerations," applied Minnesota law.

[1] The Plurality Opinion

A sharply divided Supreme Court affirmed. Justice Brennan's opinion (joined by three Justices) analyzed a number of precedents, and concluded that the lesson to be drawn from the cases is that the Constitution requires that the "state must have a significant contact or significant aggregation of contacts, creating state interests, such that choice of its law is neither arbitrary nor fundamentally unfair." Justice Brennan found three such contacts: Ralph had been employed in Minnesota for 15 years before he died; Allstate at all times did business in Minnesota; and plaintiff had moved to Minnesota before filing suit. Brennan determined that "Minnesota had a significant aggregation of contacts with the parties and the occurrence," and thus concluded that Minnesota's application of its own law did not violate the Constitution. An examination of each contact, however, displays the gossamer nature of Brennan's web.[6]

[i] Employment. The substantive question in *Allstate* was one of contract interpretation. Although the plurality argued that Minnesota had police power responsibilities to its non–resident employees, it is difficult to see the relevance of that point to the issue at hand; the legal effect of an automobile insurance policy. It would have been different, for example, if the case had involved some problem related to employment; without such

---

[4] 449 U.S. 302 (1981).

[5] *Allstate* was the first decision by the Court reviewing a decision which turned on modern choice–of–law theory. It was also the Court's first full-blown foray into the field since the *Clay* case, decided almost twenty years earlier.

[6] Brennan also mentioned that Ralph Hague commuted to Red Wing every day to work. Brennan does not explain, however, why Ralph's commute was worth mentioning.

a relation, however, Ralph's employment in Minnesota has no connection to the issue of insurance contract interpretation.

[ii] **Doing Business.** Brennan also argued that, because Allstate was doing business in Minnesota, it could "hardly claim unfamiliarity with the laws of the host jurisdiction and surprise that the state courts might apply forum law in litigation in which the company is involved." Brennan seems to have missed the point here, for his reasoning would permit a court in any state in which Allstate does business to assert legislative jurisdiction. Again, Allstate's business operations in Minnesota had nothing to do with a policy sold in Wisconsin to a resident of that state. Thus, this contact also is irrelevant.

[iii] **Change of Residence.** The former Mrs. Hague moved to Minnesota before filing suit, although there was no suggestion that the move was litigation–motivated. Brennan argued that the move gave Minnesota an interest in fully compensating residents who were harmed by accidents and keeping them "off welfare rolls." Brennan carefully noted, however, that a post–occurrence change of residence was insufficient, standing alone, to confer legislative jurisdiction on the state,[7] but he argued that the move might be part of an aggregation of contacts. Nevertheless, it is very difficult to see what plaintiff's move adds to Brennan's analysis.[8] It is, to be sure, a contact on Minnesota's side, but a meager one, unrelated to the legal question posed by the case.

[iv] **Aggregation.** Although each contact relied on by Brennan is either irrelevant or trivial, perhaps the whole is greater than the sum of the parts. Certainly, the opinion suggests that "aggregation" was important. And yet a close look at the contacts reveals virtually no connection between the legal issue before the Court (stacking) and the contacts. There are several connections with Minnesota, but none that is significantly related to the stacking issue. Hence, Brennan's cumulative approach to the problem suggests that any time a state has some connections with a problem, it also has legislative jurisdiction, even when the connections are unrelated to the choice–of–law issue.

[2] The Concurring Opinion

Justice Stevens concurred in the result, but wrote an opinion markedly different from the plurality's. Stevens' starting point was that the Full Faith and Credit and Due Process Clauses impose different restraints upon choice of law. Each, therefore, must be examined separately. Stevens believed an "arbitrary or fundamentally unfair" choice of law would violate due process.

---

[7] The plurality carefully expressed "no view" as to whether either of the first two contacts, standing alone, would sustain the choice of Minnesota law.

[8] A number of courts have resisted the impulse to consider post–event moves to the forum as relevant to interest analysis. *E.g.*, Reich v. Purcell, 67 Cal.2d 551, 432 P.2d 727, 63 Cal. Rptr. 31 (1967).

That did not occur in *Allstate* because the forum almost always is justified in using its own law; in addition, because the stacking rule is followed in a majority of states, its application raises no "serious question of fairness"or frustrated expectations.

As for full faith and credit, Stevens wrote that its purpose in this context is to insure that all states "respect the legitimate interests of other States." But the forum has legitimate interests as well; hence, a choice of law is constitutional unless it "threatens the federal interest in national unity." Wisconsin's interests were not impermissibly threatened in *Allstate* because, at the time of contracting, it was clear that other states might exercise legislative jurisdiction over the insurance policy. Wisconsin, therefore, had no interest in ensuring that questions of construction would be answered in accordance with its law.[9] For those reasons, Stevens voted to affirm the decision below, even though he thought the use of Minnesota law "was plainly unsound as a matter of normal conflicts law."

[3] The Dissent

Justice Powell's dissenting opinion (joined by Burger and Rehnquist) began by noting that his "disagreement with the plurality is narrow." Powell believed the Constitution imposes only a "modest check on state power," that applies "only when there are no significant contacts between the State and the litigation." Thus, there was little disagreement between plurality and dissent over the black letter law; the dispute lay in the application of that law to the facts.

Powell believed that application of Minnesota law did not upset reasonable expectations, because Hague's proximity to Minnesota made the application of Minnesota law reasonably foreseeable. But Powell concluded that use of Minnesota law would not further "a legitimate state interest." First, plaintiff's post–accident change of residence was "irrelevant" and unrelated to the legal problem in the case; a contrary rule would encourage forum–shopping and defeat Allstate's expectations. Second, Minnesota had no interest in regulating Allstate except with respect to events within the state. Finally, Powell thought it irrelevant that Ralph had worked in Minnesota, because the problem at bar had nothing to do with his employment.[10]

[4] *Allstate* in Perspective

The lessons of *Allstate* are both clear and unclear. Although it is difficult to draw any conclusion from a plurality decision, it seems fairly apparent that a majority of the Court (Brennan's plurality plus Stevens) was willing to uphold an exercise of legislative jurisdiction on a *very* skimpy set of facts,

[9] Here, Stevens was plainly wrong. Although Wisconsin could foresee that a Minnesota court might apply its own law, that does not mean Wisconsin was not interested in the interpretation question; the state might have rejected stacking, perhaps, in the hope of lowering insurance rates, a hope that would be partially frustrated by the decision.

[10] Powell also trenchantly criticized Brennan's use of precedent.

an exercise that many commentators believe unconstitutional. Perhaps the willingness of the Justices to do so merely reflects the plaintiff-orientation of American courts in choice–of–law matters.[11] That position assumes added importance with the recognition that seven of the eight sitting Justices agreed that the test to be applied in constitutional choice–of–law cases is whether the state has sufficient contact with, and interest in, the dispute so that the application of its law is neither arbitrary nor patently unfair. Thus, it seemed fairly safe after *Allstate* to predict that the Court would generally adopt a hands-off attitude in this area; it would be a rare case, indeed, that would attract the necessary majority to overturn a state's choice–of–law decision.

Allstate certainly established the ground rules for choice of law: Legislative jurisdiction cannot be exercised unless there are significant contacts creating state interests so that the choice of law is neither arbitrary nor fundamentally unfair. Because this test can be satisfied by very minimal contacts (as demonstrated by the facts of *Allstate* itself), it is apparent that the principal constitutional limits on choice–of–law are the more stringent restrictions upon judicial jurisdiction. They prevent a forum, which is unconnected to the parties and the transaction, from hearing the case, and thus they render a completely arbitrary choice–of–law decision unlikely.

Before despairing too much over the outcome in *Allstate*, a final word should be added on the happenstance of the litigation. The actual decision led to the application of what arguably was the better law and certainly was the majority position among state courts; if an aberrational substantive rule had resulted from the Minnesota choice–of–law decision, the outcome in the Supreme Court might have been different. Finally, a widow was suing an insurance company on an arguably correct reading of an automobile insurance policy. Widows and orphans (just like hard cases) often produce bad law in exchange for rough justice. In sum, the peculiarities of this litigation made affirmance easy in *Allstate* despite the absence of contacts between Minnesota and the problem. The facts of another case, however, might push the Court in a different direction. The *Allstate* "only a little" test is not a serious limitation on state power.

[b] *Shutts*

Four years after *Allstate*, the Court provided a much–needed example of a situation where the forum state's contacts *were* insufficient for the constitutional exercise of legislative jurisdiction. In *Phillips Petroleum Co. v. Shutts*,[12] the Court, for the first time in its modern era, invalidated a state's choice–of–law decision. That case involved a class action brought in Kansas state court by lessors of gaslands in Kansas state court against Phillips and other lessees for interest allegedly due on royalty payments. The class of lessors, consisting of 28,100 members, owned land in 11 states; fewer than 3% of the plaintiffs and 1% of the leases had any "apparent

---

[11] *See, e.g.*, Weintraub § 6.4.

[12] 472 U.S. 797 (1985). The jurisdictional holding of *Shutts* is discussed *supra*, § 30[c][3].

connection with the State of Kansas. . . . "Nevertheless, the Kansas state courts "applied Kansas contract and Kansas equity law to every claim in this case . . .," an application whose constitutionality Phillips challenged in the Supreme Court.

[1] The Test

Justice Rehnquist, speaking for a seven–Justice majority,[13] began by making two things clear: First, he observed that if the dispute were over substantively similar laws there would be no problem; the Constitution is only implicated, in other words, by a true conflict: "There can be no injury in applying Kansas law if it is not in conflict with that of any other jurisdiction connected to this suit." Rehnquist also confirmed that the test stated by the *Allstate* plurality controlled his analysis. He quoted with approval the following passage from that opinion: "[F]or a state's substantive law to be selected in a constitutionally permissible manner, that State must have a significant contact or significant aggregation of contracts, creating state interests such that choice of its law is neither arbitrary nor fundamentally unfair."

The Court then found that the contacts in the case at bar were not "significant" enough to satisfy that test. It first found that application of Kansas law could not be supported by the fact that hundreds of Kansas plaintiffs were affected by the litigation, nor by the fact that "gas extraction is an important business in Kansas." Unfortunately, there were thousands of lessors located elsewhere and there was no "common fund" located in Kansas. The Court also gave "little credence" to plaintiffs' argument that they wanted Kansas law to govern; giving effect to that contention effectively would have eliminated any constitutional restraints on choice–of–law. Similarly, Rehnquist also rejected what he called the "bootstrap" argument by the Supreme Court of Kansas that it needed more latitude to apply its own law to a nationwide class action, an action which requires the presence of a common question of law or fact: Obviously a state may not apply forum law in order to satisfy the procedural requirement that there be a "common question of law." Finally, Rehnquist had no trouble in concluding that a state cannot apply its law to a transaction in which the state has no interest:

> Given Kansas' lack of "interest" in claims unrelated to that State, and the substantive conflict with jurisdictions such as Texas, we conclude that application of Kansas law to every claim in this case is sufficiently arbitrary and unfair as to exceed constitutional limits.

[2] A Perspective on *Shutts*[14]

Shutts provided a great service by confirming the test for legislative jurisdiction adopted by the *Allstate* plurality. The opinion does have some

[13] Justice Stevens dissented on the ground that the case presented a false conflict. Justice Powell did not sit.

[14] *See generally* Louise Weinberg, *The Place of Trial and the Law Applied: Overhauling Constitutional Theory*, 59 U. Colo. L. Rev. 67 (1988).

troubling aspects, however. The most important of these involves the aggregation of contacts; those contacts could have been "aggregated," as they had been in *Allstate*, to support legislative jurisdiction. Defendant Phillips, after all, *was* doing business in Kansas, some plaintiffs *were* located there, and the state did have *some* regulatory interest in gaslands located within its borders.[15] Nevertheless, this aggregation, unlike the one in *Allstate*, failed to satisfy constitutional standards. Unfortunately, the Court neglected to explain the difference between the two.

On the other hand, the decision seems fairly clear that de minimis contacts will not be sufficient; a constitutional exercise of legislative jurisdiction requires contacts of some substance. Moreover, *Shutts* also holds that the residual application of forum law is not constitutional; the court specifically rejected the argument that the forum could apply its own law absent some "compelling interest" in applying some other law. Of course, the contrast between the "not quite enough" facts of *Shutts* and the "just barely enough" facts of *Allstate*, is not very great. Nevertheless, *Shutts* does make clear that there are, indeed, *some* limits to a state's freedom to choose what law to apply to a problem before it.

The holding of *Shutts* led some commentators to believe that interest analysis perhaps had been constitutionalized; that is, a state could not apply its own law to a problem unless it had some "interest" (or purpose) in doing so.[16] If so, significant changes in choice of law might have resulted; among those changes might have been an end to those *lex loci* rules which occasionally require the application of the law of a disinterested state. The Supreme Court, however, soon would make clear that interest analysis was not a constitutional requirement.

[c] *Wortman*

The Kansas Oil Royalty litigation came back before the Supreme Court three years after *Shutts* in *Sun Oil Co. v. Wortman.*[17] The *Wortman* litigation involved the same problem of payments for gas royalties that had been at issue in *Shutts*; the decision below in *Wortman* had been vacated and remanded to the Kansas Supreme Court in light of *Shutts*. That court then finessed the substantive law questions by holding that all states with an interest in the royalty litigation would apply the same liability rules and interest rates that Kansas did. That finding obviously created a false conflict and, as a result, deftly avoided the constitutional issues seen by the Supreme Court of the United States in *Shutts*. Also at issue in *Wortman* was the applicable statute of limitations. The Kansas courts had applied that state's five year statute of limitations to all claims, although almost all of them would have been time-barred in the states where the gas properties were located. The Kansas Supreme Court had reasoned that because the limitations question was a procedural issue, it was free to apply its own law. The Supreme Court of the United States affirmed.

[15] *See* Vernon, Weinberg, Reynolds, & Richman at 438–39.

[16] *E.g.*, Gene R. Shreve, *Interest Analysis as Constitutional Law*, 48 Ohio St. L.J. 51 (1987).

[17] 486 U.S. 717 (1988).

Justice Scalia's majority opinion sustained the Kansas ruling against challenges made under both the Full Faith and Credit and the Due Process Clauses. Scalia's focus in each instance was both on "the tradition in place when the constitutional provision was adopted," as well as on "subsequent practice." As to Full Faith and Credit, Scalia wrote that the "historical record shows conclusively, we think, that the society which adopted the Constitution did not regard statutes of limitations as substantive provisions, akin to the rules governing the validity and effect of contracts, but rather as procedural restrictions fashioned by each jurisdiction for its own courts." Because "the procedural rules of its courts are surely matters on which a state is competent to legislate, it follows that a State may apply its own procedural rules to actions litigated in its courts." Kansas, therefore, was free to treat the limitations question as "procedural" and apply its own law.

Scalia refused an invitation to treat the limitations question as "substantive," or, as he put it, to "update our notion of what is sufficiently 'substantive' to require full faith and credit," because he could not "imagine what would be the basis for such an updating." After all: "If we abandon the currently applied, traditional notions of [substance and procedure] we would embark upon the enterprise of constitutionalizing choice–of–law rules, with no compass to guide us beyond our own perceptions of what seems desirable." Even though some modern scholars might think it unwise to treat limitations invariably as procedural, the Court stated that it was not its job to make such "departures from established choice–of–law precedent and practice constitutionally mandatory."[18]

Scalia's rejection of the Due Process challenge of the application of Kansas' own statute of limitations was equally straight–forward. He first observed that the forum's use of its own limitation period was well–established at the time the Fourteenth Amendment was adopted. Moreover, at that time the "practice had gone substantially unchallenged," and it has been "essentially unchallenged since." Because both the "tradition" and "subsequent practice" tests were satisfied, the defendant could not "have been unfairly surprised by . . . a rule as old as the Republic." Tradition and lack of surprise, therefore, validated the application of the forum's limitations period.

Justice Brennan, in a concurring opinion joined by Justices Marshall and Blackmun, agreed that "the contact a State has with a claim simply by virtue of being the forum creates a sufficient procedural interest to make the application of limitations period to wholly out-of-state claims consistent with the Full Faith and Credit Clause." Justice Brennan, however, disagreed with Scalia's emphasis on history and the argument that a choice–of–law practice that is "long–established and still subsiding" is necessarily constitutional.[19]

---

[18] The Court also rejected an argument that the Kansas Supreme Court had denied the defendants due process by misconstruing the laws of Texas, Oklahoma, and Louisiana.

[19] Justice O'Connor dissented in an opinion which Chief Justice Rehnquist joined. O'Connor argued that Kansas had violated the Full Faith and Credit Clause in construing the laws of Texas, Oklahoma, and Louisiana.

[d] A Perspective on the Trilogy

Allstate and *Shutts* can be read together and still make good sense. Both teach that there must be *some* relation between the law to be applied and the litigation for the exercise of legislative jurisdiction to pass constitutional muster. *Allstate* shows that not much is needed to satisfy the Court, at least as long as there is some "real" connection with the litigation. *Shutts* confirms that real contacts do matter, and that judicial convenience will not carry the day. It also confirms the common sense proposition that only a true conflict implicates the Constitution. Finally, *Shutts* showed that there were some choice–of–law results that even the Supreme Court would not tolerate.

Does *Wortman* upset that analysis? Probably not, especially if it is read in light of the Court's later decision in *Burnham v. Superior Court.*[20] Both *Wortman* and *Burnham* emphasize the need to use history in making constitutional inquiries: A practice will not violate due process if it has a solid historical base and it has not been widely repudiated. Traditional choice–of–law methods of analysis such as the First Restatement, in other words, may be used with little fear of offending the Constitution. Newer methods, however, must leap the additional hurdle of minimal state contacts and interests established by *Allstate* and *Shutts*. That may be a very low hurdle, but it is still something that adherents of modern methods of analyzing choice–of–law problems must reckon with.

Nevertheless, the chances that the Court will upset a state's choice of law are remote. The basis for the Court's reluctance to do so should not be hard to identify.[21] The Supreme Court, faced with an impossible caseload, simply lacks the time to fashion the necessary decisional law to elaborate a significant constitutional theory to deal with choice of law; more important matters demand the limited attention of the nation's highest court. Moreover, many choice–of–law matters involve what traditional constitutional analysis identifies as social and economic legislation; and the Court has shown, ever since the New Deal, great deference to decisions in those areas made by the states. To be sure, choice–of–law decisions occasionally involve competing claims by sovereigns, but the rights at stake in those cases, with rare exceptions, are those of the litigants, not of the states.[22] For that reason, there is little prospect of the Balkanization among the states so feared by Framers and Justices alike. If that Balkanization ever appears likely, the Court (or Congress)[23] could intervene and

[20] 495 U.S. 604 (1990), discussed in § 28, *supra*.

[21] *See generally* Louise Weinberg, *Choice of Law and Minimal Scrutiny*, 49 U. Chi. L. Rev. 440 (1982).

[22] Even in cases where interests of the sovereign *qua* sovereign clearly are involved, the Supreme Court has been reluctant to intercede. In Nevada v. Hall, 440 U.S. 410 (1979), for example, the Court upheld a California decision imposing $1,150,000 in damages on the University of Nevada for an accident that occurred in California; it did so despite a statutory limit in Nevada of $25,000 for liability in tort by a governmental agency.

[23] Congress clearly would have legislative jurisdiction under either the Commerce Clause or the Full Faith and Credit Clause.

formulate detailed constitutional (or statutory) restrictions on choice of law. Until then, however, the Court will satisfy its perceived duty by laying down general ground rules and trust that state courts will restrain their most parochial impulses.[24]

§ 98 Another Look at Full Faith and Credit and Due Process

Commentators on the problems of legislative jurisdiction have debated recently whether the proper constitutional foundation for choice–of–law restrictions is the Due Process Clause or the Full Faith and Credit Clause. Although the Supreme Court has been ambivalent at times,[1] the three recent opinions just discussed do provide a rather clear answer: there is little that is different in how the Court approaches questions under either clause. Thus, in *Allstate* the analysis by seven of the eight Justices surely is the same under either provision. The *Shutts* majority clearly does not differentiate between the two Clauses. Finally, although Scalia's majority opinion in *Wortman* discusses the Due Process and Full Faith and Credit questions separately, it does not make clear how the two might differ, if at all.[2] The opinion examines both in light of tradition and later developments. The Court, obviously enough, views the two provisions as synonymous.

Nevertheless, there may be good reasons to differentiate between the two. Only Justice Stevens in his concurring opinion in *Allstate* sharply distinguished between the purposes of the two clauses in his analysis. He was correct in doing so, for the clauses do indeed serve different ends. This section, therefore, examines the role of each clause, as well as the part played in choice–of–law litigation by several other constitutional provisions.[3]

The Due Process Clause basically protects persons against procedural unfairness.[4] In choice of law, therefore, the focus is on foreseeability and unfair surprise. Those concerns have greater weight in some cases (*e.g.*, problems involving interpretation of a contract entered into by parties of equal bargaining power), and less weight in others (*e.g.*, problems involving the law of contributory negligence in an auto accident). Failure to recognize and give proper scope to those concerns may result in sufficient unfairness to amount to a violation of the Due Process Clause. That is why Scalia's

---

[24] *See* Linda Silberman, *Can the State of Minnesota Bind the Nation?: Federal Choice–of–Law Constraints after Allstate Insurance Co. v. Hague*, 10 Hofstra L. Rev. 103, 110–11 (1981).

[1] *See, e.g.*, Home Ins. Co. v. Dick, 281 U.S. 397 (1930) (due process); Bradford Elec. Light Co. v. Clapper, 286 U.S. 145 (1932) (full faith and credit).

[2] Indeed, footnotes in both the majority and concurring opinions suggest that analysis is the same under either Clause. *See* 486 U.S. at 729 n. 3 and 735 n.2.

[3] *See generally* Frederic L. Kirgis, *The Roles of Due Process and Full Faith and Credit in Choice of Law*, 62 Cornell L. Rev. 94 (1976); James A. Martin, *A Reply to Professor Kirgis*, at 151.

[4] Although the Court has imparted, at times, a substantive component to due process, "substantive due process" is not today a generally favored concept.

due process analysis in *Wortman* notes that there could have been no "unfair surprise" to the defendants in that case.

The Due Process Clause should not be used as a device for accommodating competing state interests. Persons, not states, have a right to due process.[5] It is better, therefore, to analyze a problem involving governmental interests in terms of the opposing state interests, rather than by using the parties as surrogates for their sovereigns. The appropriate device for that analysis is the Full Faith and Credit Clause[6] — called "the Lawyer's Clause" by Justice Jackson[7] because it is little noticed or understood by anyone else. Nevertheless, the Clause is crucial, because it helped mold a group of minimally united states into a single nation. Its function was, and is, to ensure that each member of the Union gives proper respect to the interests of the others.[8] Thus, it is the Full Faith and Credit Clause that should control when the Court wishes to determine whether the forum's application of its own law imposes upon the concerns of a sister state.

Proper separation of the constitutional limitations on choice of law surely will help focus and sharpen the inquiry. Due process analysis should center on the parties and ask questions about fairness, surprise, and expectations. Full faith and credit analysis should focus on the role of the states as sovereigns and inquire into the proper relations among sovereigns in a federal union. Unfortunately, the Supreme Court views things differently, and it tacitly has abandoned the use of any provision other than the Due Process Clause to limit the exercise of legislative jurisdiction.

§ 99 Choice of Law and Discrimination Against Non-Citizens

Several constitutional provisions prevent a state from discriminating against persons who live in other states. Those provisions include the Commerce Clause, the Equal Protection Clause, and the Privileges and Immunities Clause. All choice–of–law analysis, of course, requires some differentiation of result based on where a litigant lives (or works). This was true even under the First Restatement where questions of status, for example, depended on the state of domicile. Modern choice–of–law methods, especially interest analysis, focus much more heavily on questions of domicile and other factors turning on the location of parties and enterprises.

---

[5] *But see* the discussion of Alton v. Alton, 207 F.2d, 667 (3d Cir. 1953), *infra* § 121. *Alton* held that the Due Process Clause required one divorcing party to be domiciled in the forum for that court to have subject matter jurisdiction; the requirement of domicile insured that the forum had a sufficient interest to grant the divorce.

[6] U.S. Const., art. IV, § 1.

[7] Robert H. Jackson, *Full Faith and Credit — The Lawyer's Clause of the Constitution*, 45 Colum. L. Rev. 1 (1945).

[8] For a powerful argument that the Full Faith and Credit Clause was designed to achieve that end, *see* Douglas Laycock, *Equal Citizens of Equal and Territorial States: The Constitutional Foundations of Choice of Law*, 92 Colum. L. Rev. 249 (1992). Laycock argues that the Constitution "precludes choice–of–law rules that prefer local litigants or local law. . . ." *Id.*. at 315.

The possibility of discrimination, therefore, looms as a theoretical possibility in many decisions.

The last several decades have seen not only the growth of modern choice–of–law analysis but also significantly heightened scrutiny by the Supreme Court of all state laws and regulations which discriminate against noncitizens. The resulting possibilities for conflict between the Constitution and modern choice–of–law analysis have dazzled some commentators.[1] The courts, however, have largely ignored the tension between choice–of–law theory and the constitutional anti-discrimination provisions.

[a] The Commerce Clause[2]

The Constitutional grant of power to Congress to regulate interstate commerce has long been read as a limitation on the power of states to interfere with such commerce (this is often called the "dormant Commerce Clause"). The Supreme Court currently uses a balancing test to resolve Commerce Clause problems: If the statute does not discriminate against other states and has only an incidental effect on commerce, and if the burden imposed does not clearly exceed the local benefits, the statute will be sustained.[3] When state regulation overreaches, substantially interfering with commerce, the law is invalid. Although the Commerce Clause has significant potential implications for choice of law, the Supreme Court has never used it to decide a case in that area.

The absence of case law can be explained by thinking of the dormant Commerce Clause as not being concerned as much with "extraterritoriality" as it is with discrimination. The Commerce Clause forbids state classifications which interfere with the flow of commerce by undue discrimination against out–of–state parties. Thus, in *Bendix Autolite Corp. v. Midwesco Enterprises, Inc.*,[4] the Court held invalid on Commerce Clause grounds an Ohio law that made it harder for non-residents to toll the Ohio statute of limitations. In contrast, a discrimination based on "a reasonable distinction between residents and nonresidents,"[5] is not unconstitutional; the state must possess sufficient power to make *reasonable* distinctions.

In *Edgar v. MITE Corp.*,[6] the Court suggested that the Commerce Clause may be used to limit a state's choice of law. The problem in *Edgar* concerned an attempt by Illinois to regulate take–over offers directed at any corporation in which 10% of the stock was held by Illinois residents. Part of the

[1] *See, e.g.*, Lea Brilmayer, Conflict of Laws: Foundation and Future Direction, ch. 5 (1991).

[2] *See generally* Louise Weinberg, *Choosing Law: The Limitations Debate*, 1991 U. Ill. L. Rev. 683; Harold W. Horowitz, *The Commerce Clause as a Limitation On State Choice–of–Law Doctrine*, 84 Harv. L. Rev. 806 (1971).

[3] Pike v. Bruce Church, Inc., 397 U.S. 137 (1970).

[4] 486 U.S. 888 (1987). The Court had found the burden on commerce too great even though a few years earlier a similar statute had been able to withstand an equal protection challenge. G.D. Searle & Co. v. Cohn, 455 U.S. 405 (1982).

[5] Louise Weinberg, *Against Comity*, 80 Geo. L. J. 53, 80 (1991).

[6] 457 U.S. 624 (1982).

state's proffered justification for the regulation was its interest in regulating the internal affairs of domestic corporations. Although the Court recognized the general validity of the internal affairs doctrine,[7] the opinion stated that this doctrine was of "little use" in the case at bar, because the Illinois regulation was not limited to take–overs of domestic corporations: "Illinois has no interest in regulating the internal affairs of foreign corporations."

The Court revisited state anti–takeover legislation in *CTS Corp. v. Dynamics Corp. of America*,[8] and confirmed the relation between the Constitution and the internal affairs doctrine. The legislation in question there was challenged in part because it burdened interstate commerce by making hostile take–overs more difficult, and in part because it favored local corporations by effectively insulating them from corporate raiders. The Court rejected those arguments, in large measure because the "firmly established" authority of a state to regulate the internal affairs of a domestic corporation meant that there was little risk of inconsistent regulation. In other words, the Commerce Clause did not forbid non–discriminatory regulation by the only state which could, as a practical matter, regulate the problem. If the Court had supplied a contrary answer, it is difficult to understand how *any* state could regulate a corporation's internal affairs without running a severe risk of inconsistent overlapping regulation — the very result the Commerce Clause seeks to avoid. After *Edgar* and *CTS* therefore, the Commerce Clause may well act to limit the ability of states to apply their own law to regulate the internal affairs of foreign corporations. The national interest in the free flow of commerce requires the application of only one law to govern the conduct of a corporation's internal affairs.

[b] Privileges and Immunities

Article IV, Section 2 of the Constitution states that a citizen "shall be entitled to all Privileges and Immunities of Citizens in the several states." Arguably, that Clause provides a basis for invalidation of a state court's choice–of–law decisions if it denies a "privilege" to a person simply because she is a citizen of another state. If the state has a valid reason for that denial, however, the clause has not been violated. Thus, the Privileges and Immunities Clause "is a specialized type of equal protection provision,"[9] insuring comity within the federal union. Some commentators have found in the clause (and its attendant case law) a prohibition of discrimination in choice of law based on the domicile of the parties.[10] Because so much of modern choice–of–law practice is domicile-driven, that prohibition could have a profound impact.

---

[7] *See* § 91, *supra*; Restatement (Second) of Conflict of Laws § 302.

[8] 481 U.S. 69 (1987). *See generally* Donald C. Langevoort, *The Supreme Court and the Politics of Corporate Takeovers: A Comment on CTS Corp. v. Dynamics Corp. of America*, 101 Harv. L. Rev. 96 (1987).

[9] John Nowak and Ronald Rotunda, Constitutional Law 335 (5th ed. 2001).

[10] *E.g.*, Laycock, *supra* note 8; John Hart Ely, *Choice of Law and the State's Interest in Protecting its Own*, 23 Wm. & Mary L. Rev. 173 (1981); *see* Austin v. New Hampshire, 420 U.S. 656 (1975).

Such a development is unlikely. The Privileges and Immunities Clause has seen little use outside the area of state restrictions on access to natural resources and other state benefits (and it has never been employed by the Supreme Court in a choice–of–law case). Moreover, the Privileges and Immunities Clause is not offended if a rational basis exists for the challenged distinction.[11] Because modern choice–of–law analysis is all about "rational bases" (at least, in theory), this clause should not prove to be a difficult problem. It is unlikely, therefore, that the Privileges and Immunities Clause will be held to limit significantly state decisions in choice of law.

[c] Equal Protection

The Equal Protection Clause of the Fourteenth Amendment also has seen virtually no service in choice–of–law cases. Modern equal protection analysis generally employs a rational basis test to determine the constitutionality of state-imposed classifications. A classification satisfies the rational basis standard unless it is "patently arbitrary"; virtually no legislation fails that test. A classification based on race or alienage, or one which interferes with the exercise of a fundamental right is subject to "strict scrutiny," a very difficult test to satisfy. An equal protection challenge to a choice–of–law decision is likely to fail, therefore, unless strict scrutiny is applied. A choice of law based on race, for example, would be highly vulnerable, but such a choice seems most unlikely. More plausible, perhaps, is a challenge to a choice–of–law rule that impedes the exercise of a fundamental right (*E.g.*, travel, voting, free speech). In such circumstances, the Equal Protection Clause would subject the choice to strict scrutiny and probably invalidate the selection. Although the Equal Protection Clause has never been the basis of a Supreme Court choice–of–law decision, the possibility of its use, albeit in a limited number of situations, is much more real than the use of the Privileges and Immunities Clause.

§ 100 A Partial Summing Up

The opinions in *Allstate*, when coupled with the decision to validate Minnesota's exercise of legislative jurisdiction, make it clear that it will be a rare case with multi–state elements where the forum cannot apply its own law to a problem. Perhaps the only limitation on that statement which can be identified confidently is that there must be some connection with the dispute, in addition to a post–occurrence change of residence. As *Allstate* illustrates, that extra connection may be quite minimal. But, as *Shutts* demonstrates, there must be *some* connection; the Court, after all, did strike down the application of Kansas law to those leases and lessors lacking any contact with Kansas. The administrative convenience of using one law to control a massive state–court class action was not enough. Finally, *Wortman* shows that tradition may validate a state choice–of–law decision even in the absence of a modern functional justification based on contacts and

[11] *See* John Nowak & Ronald Rotunda, *supra* note 9, at 323.

state interests. The net result is constitutional validation of the plaintiff–orientation of contemporary American choice–of–law methodology; a plaintiff in any multi–state transaction is likely to be able to bring her action in the involved state whose law is most favorable to her.[1]

In short, constitutional limitations on state choice of law decisions are likely to be minimal in the foreseeable future. With its "hands off" or minimal scrutiny strategy, the Supreme Court has given constitutional validation to the plaintiffs' orientation of contemporary American choice–of–law methods. If the plaintiff can find favorable law in an interested forum, the meager constitutional limitations on state choice–of–law decisions will not stand in its way. Thus, the only constitutional restraints on choice of law will be indirect, based on due process jurisdictional requirements. Once a state has assumed jurisdiction of a problem, only its own sense of justice is likely to restrain its freedom to apply whatever law it wishes.[2] Nevertheless, the limits imposed by the jurisdictional decisions — both judicial and legislative — ensure, at least, minimal fairness to the defendant and to other states.[3]

§ 101 Forum Closing I: Can a State Keep Out Foreign Litigation?

Two additional problems involving the Constitution and choice–of–law can be identified. Both deal with a state's attempts to insulate itself from problems created by contact with other states. These questions are addressed in this section and the one following. The first issue is: Can a state court refuse to hear a cause of action because it arose under a foreign statute, or does such a refusal violate the Full Faith and Credit Clause? The Court's response to this question has been fairly definite: with limited exceptions, a court must entertain a transitory cause of action that arises elsewhere. The leading case is *Hughes v. Fetter.*[1]

Hughes arose out of an automobile accident in Illinois. Suit was brought in Wisconsin under the Illinois wrongful death statute. The Wisconsin

[1] Indeed, the underlying transaction may not have to be multi-state. Consider the case of a plaintiff, who suffered a loss in X, where she resided, and then changed her residence to Y following the loss. She then sues her national insurance company in Y. If Y should apply its own law, that choice might be constitutional under *Allstate*. This hypothetical, a common enough possibility, clearly illustrates the tilt toward plaintiffs in today's choice of law.

[2] Some might argue that as long as there are limits on the state's ability to act unfairly and without any interest of its own to vindicate, it does not matter whether the limits come labeled as jurisdictional or choice of law. And yet the difference might be very real. No doubt there are instances where there will be the expense of traveling to an inconvenient forum, but it is much more likely that a defendant will suffer from an "inconvenient" choice of law.

[3] Gerling Global Reinsurance Corp. of Am. V. Gallagher, 267 F. 3d 1228 (11th Cir. 2001), provides an interesting reminder of the need for some relevant contact. Florida required certain insurers to file reports concerning insurance transactions which took place in Germany during the Nazi era between Holocaust victims and the German affiliates of the insurance companies. The court held that Florida lacked legislative jurisdiction even though the insurance companies themselves were doing business in Florida; there simply was no connection between Florida and the wholly German insurance transactions.

[1] 341 U.S. 609 (1951).

courts refused to hear the case, arguing that Wisconsin statutory law established a policy against entertaining suits brought under wrongful death acts of another state. Justice Black, writing for a 5-4 majority, held the Illinois statute to be a "public act" entitled to full faith and credit. The majority ruled for the plaintiff because Wisconsin had "no real feeling of antagonism" with respect to wrongful death actions and regularly provided a forum for them (there was a Wisconsin wrongful death statute similar to that of Illinois). Wisconsin's interest in not hearing the "Illinois" claim, therefore, was slim. Black recognized that the forum did not have to subordinate its own interests in every case,[2] stating that it was the function of the Supreme Court to insure that the forum struck a proper balance between the unifying principle of the Full Faith and Credit Clause and the forum's policy of not entertaining foreign wrongful death actions.[3] Although *Hughes* can be criticized for its result,[4] the case makes good sense in light of the unifying object of that clause. Surely a refusal to hear a case merely because it arose under the law of a different state poses a serious threat to interstate harmony. In the absence of substantive forum law to the contrary,[5] the sovereign interest of the law–giving state should not be so lightly disregarded. Thus, *Hughes* is a sound decision.[6]

There are, however, important limitations to the *Hughes* rule. First, the opinion did not purport to deal with the choice–of–law problem. It dealt with the forum's refusal to hear a case based on foreign law, not with the forum's choice of its own law to govern a case with multi–state contacts. Thus, it has had little influence upon the Supreme Court's later constitutional choice–of–law decisions. Second, the *Hughes* opinion expressly preserved the right of the forum to refuse to hear a case based on the doctrine of forum non conveniens. Third, Justice Black left a loophole of undetermined dimensions when he noted that Wisconsin had "no real feeling of antagonism" toward wrongful death actions. Left unanswered was what would happen if a state did have such a "feeling."[7] Although that question has not been addressed by the Court, it is likely that in practice the "antagonism" would take the form of a divergent legal rule; and, hence, the issue would be framed as a choice–of–law problem, not as a refusal of jurisdiction. Thus, the issue would be resolved in accordance with the *Allstate* line of cases.

---

[2] If the forum did have to subordinate its interest, then plaintiff would have great leeway in determining both which court should hear the case and which law should be applied.

[3] Black emphasized that the problem was not one of choice of law, but rather one where the forum refused to hear a case based on foreign law.

[4] *E.g.*, Weintraub § 9.3A.

[5] Then, of course, the problem would be one of choice of law.

[6] *Hughes* was also in line with precedent. *E.g.*, Broderick v. Rosner, 294 U.S. 629 (1935); Milwaukee County v. M. E. White Co., 296 U.S. 268 (1935).

[7] A related problem arises if the foreign law includes mandatory procedures not required by forum law. In Bledsoe v. Crowley, 849 F.2d 639 (D.C. Cir. 1989), a case applying Maryland substantive law, the court held that Maryland law requiring pre–trial "arbitration" of malpractice claims had to be followed even though the case was pending in the courts of the District of Columbia.

The way in which lower courts have expressed their "antagonism" toward another state's law is illustrated in *Pearson v. Northeast Airlines, Inc.*[8] A New Yorker was killed when a flight originating in New York crashed in Massachusetts. Using New York choice–of–law rules, the Second Circuit applied Massachusetts' wrongful death statute, but refused to honor the Massachusetts limitation on the amount of damages. The court rejected the defendant's constitutional argument that once New York accords any faith and credit to Massachusetts law, it must give full faith and credit to that law. The court emphasized New York's strong opposition to limitations on wrongful death recovery (expressed by a state constitutional provision), and concluded that Massachusetts had no right, in light of interstate needs, to impose its policy in full on New York when the latter state had expressed a strong policy to the contrary.[9]

The final limitation on the *Hughes* rule is provided by *Wells v. Simonds Abrasive Co.*[10] After plaintiff's decedent had been killed in Alabama, plaintiff brought a wrongful death action in Pennsylvania. The Court dismissed the action, based on the Pennsylvania wrongful death statute of limitations. Under the Alabama wrongful death statute, the action would not have been time–barred. The Supreme Court held that the forum could apply its own, shorter, limitations period. In an opinion notably bereft of reasoning, Chief Justice Vinson merely ruled that full faith and credit did not compel a forum to adopt a limitations period other than its own[11] . *Hughes* was inapposite, Vinson wrote, because the problem in that case was one of discrimination against foreign actions; in *Wells* on the other hand, Pennsylvania's limitations period was applied to all wrongful death actions, foreign and domestic.

That result seems plausible enough from both a constitutional and a conflicts perspective. The forum has a significant interest in not hearing stale claims, and it did not discriminate against out–of–state cases. Those two factors certainly support the forum's refusal to hear the case.

§ 102 Forum Closing II: Can a State Keep Litigation to Itself?

Occasionally, state law provides that a certain cause of action can be maintained only if brought in the courts of that state. Such legislation is probably unconstitutional. The leading case on this topic is *Crider v. Zurich Ins. Co.*[1] The Court there affirmed a judgment rendered by a federal court

[8] 309 F.2d 553 (2d Cir.1962).

[9] The Second Circuit also justified its holding by noting that the Massachusetts damage limitation was more procedural than substantive in nature, and thus, New York could apply Massachusetts substantive law and New York procedural law.

[10] 345 U.S. 514 (1953).

[11] Vinson distinguished cases in which "a limitation is so intimately connected with the right that it must be enforced in the forum state along with the substantive right." *See* § 93, *supra*, for a discussion of those cases.

[1] 380 U.S. 39 (1965).

in Alabama in favor of a resident of that state injured there in the course of his employment for a Georgia company. Plaintif sued under the Georgia Workmen's Compensation Act, and defendant objected on the ground that a remedy under the Georgia Act could only be awarded by the Georgia Compensation Board. The Court had little difficulty with the case. Justice Douglas' majority opinion[2] emphasized Alabama's interest in protecting its residents and its workers; and, hence, it could make an award under the Georgia act "consistent with constitutional requirements."

The *Crider* holding follows hoary precedent[3] and generally has met with favorable critical commentary. Like *Hughes v. Fetter, Crider* reinforces the strong national interest in making sure that transitory causes of action are heard.[4] The two cases together make clear the strength of that policy in the Supreme Court.

[2] The dissent believed the Court should not reach the constitutional issue, because Alabama law had been improperly applied by the courts below.

[3] *E.g.*, Tennessee Coal, Iron, & R. R. Co. v. George, 233 U.S. 354 (1914) (case involved the converse of *Crider*; Georgia's application of Alabama law upheld).

[4] *See* Brainerd Currie, *The Constitution and the "Transitory" Cause of Action*, 73 Harv. L. Rev. 36, 268 (1959), reprinted in Currie, Essays, 283.

Part F

SPECIAL PROBLEMS IN FEDERAL COURTS

§ 103 Introduction to *Erie*

We have deliberately treated the *Erie* problem briefly. The subject matter is covered in two law school courses other than conflicts — civil procedure and federal jurisdiction. Accordingly, because of time and credit hour constraints, many conflicts teachers omit detailed treatment of *Erie*, even though it is part of the conceptual problem of choice of law. We have adopted a compromise solution. We treat the problem, but only in its broadest outlines. For those with more interest and time, several exhaustive discussions of the whole range of *Erie* problems are listed below.[1]

§ 104 Federal Law or State Law — The *Erie* Doctrine

Most of the choice–of–law discussions in conflicts center on the question of which state's law the forum court should apply. When a federal court exercises diversity jurisdiction, however, there is an additional problem: Should the federal court apply state or federal law?[1] The answer to the question requires consideration of two Acts of Congress — The Rules of Decision Act[2] and the Rules Enabling Act[3] — and four major Supreme Court opinions — *Erie Railroad Co. v. Tompkins,*[4] *Guaranty Trust Co. v. York,*[5] *Byrd v. Blue Ridge Rural Electric Cooperative, Inc.,*[6] and *Hanna v. Plumer.*[7] The remainder of this section treats those sources.

---

[1] *See generally* Erwin Chemerinsky, Federal Jurisdiction § 5.3.5 (3d ed.1999). Charles Alan Wright, Law of Federal Courts, ch.9 (5th ed.1994); Weintraub ch. 10; Henry J. Friendly, *In Praise of Erie and of the New Federal Common Law*, 39 N.Y.U. L. Rev. 383 (1964). For a very challenging discussion of *Erie*, more for the expert than the beginner, see the following four articles in volume 87 of the Harvard Law Review: John Hart Ely, *The Irrepressible Myth of Erie*, 87 Harv. L. Rev. 693 (1974); Abram Chayes, *Some Further Last Words on Erie — The Bead Game*, 87 Harv. L. Rev. 741 (1974); John Hart Ely, *Some Further Last Words on Erie — The Necklace,* 87 Harv. L. Rev. 753 (1974); Paul J. Mishkin, *Some Further Last Words on Erie — The Thread*, 87 Harv. L. Rev. 1682 (1974).

[1] For interesting treatments of *Erie* as a choice–of–law problem, *see* John R. Leathers, *Erie and its Progeny as Choice of Law Cases*, 11 Hous. L. Rev. 791 (1974), and Joseph P. Bauer, *The Erie Doctrine Revisited: How a Conflicts Perspective Can Aid the Analysis*, 74 Notre Dame L. Rev. 1255 (1999).

[2] The Act is now codified at 28 U.S.C. § 1652.

[3] As revised, the Act is codified at 28 U.S.C. § 2072.

[4] 304 U.S. 64 (1938).

[5] 326 U.S. 99 (1945).

[6] 356 U.S. 525 (1958).

[7] 380 U.S. 460 (1965).

[a] The Great 1938 Flip-Flop

The federal courts underwent a profound change in 1938. Before that date, they applied state rules of procedure and federal general common law on questions of substantive law not covered by state statute. After 1938, the situation was reversed: Federal courts applied the newly enacted Federal Rules of Civil Procedure and the substantive law of the state where they sat.

[1] Procedure

The Conformity Act of 1872[8] governed procedure in Federal Courts before 1938. That Act provided that "the practice, pleadings, and forms and modes of proceeding" in civil cases in the district courts "shall conform, as near as may be, to the practice, pleadings, and forms and modes of proceeding" in similar cases in the courts of record of the state in which the district court sits. The laudable idea behind the Act was to require a practitioner to know only one procedural system which would be used in both the federal and state courts where he practiced. Over time, however, the Act became riddled with exceptions, and it was difficult to know whether on a particular issue a federal court was bound to conform to state practice or was free, under an exception, to use a federal rule. The Conformity Act did not apply to actions in equity, so federal procedure in equity cases was governed by separate federal equity rules promulgated by the Supreme Court.[9]

The cure for this unsatisfactory state of procedural law in the federal courts was the Federal Rules of Civil Procedure. Congress passed the Rules Enabling Act[10] in 1934, authorizing the Supreme Court to draft procedural rules; after great effort the Rules became effective in 1938. The Rules united law and equity and provided a simple, modern, and uniform system of procedure for all federal district courts.

[2] Substance

The substantive law applied by the federal courts before 1938 was determined by the Rules of Decision Act[11] and a key interpretation of that Act by the Supreme Court. The Act provided that "the laws of the several states, except where the Constitution, treaties, or statutes of the United States shall otherwise require or provide, shall be regarded as rules of decision in trials at common law in the courts of the United States in cases where they apply." The interpretation came in the famous case of *Swift v. Tyson*,[12] where the Court held, in an opinion by Justice Story, that the words "laws of the several states" meant the statutory law of the several

[8] Act of June 1, 1872, ch. 255 § 5, 17 Stat. 196, 197. For a crisp discussion of the Conformity Act, *see* Charles Alan Wright, Law of Federal Courts § 61 (5th ed. 1994).

[9] The Court promulgated equity rules in 1822, 1842 and 1912. Congress' granted rule-making authority in the Act of May 8, 1792, ch. 36, 1 Stat. 275.

[10] Subsequently revised and codified at 28 U.S.C. § 2072.

[11] Subsequently revised and codified at 28 U.S.C. § 1652.

[12] 41 U.S. (16 Pet.) 1 (1842).

states and did not include state decisions on matters of general common law.

Swift meant that the federal courts were free to develop their own federal general common law.[13] It made possible, in other words, a federal law of torts, of contracts, of commercial paper, and so on.[14] The reasons motivating that decision are not altogether clear. Perhaps the point of the decision was to encourage uniformity of workable legal rules among the several states, the idea being that a federal stand on an issue might persuade the states to adopt a similar position.[15] Thus, national legal uniformity, so important to the developing nation, might be fostered.[16] In fact, interstate uniformity did not materialize; rather, a serious *intra*state discrepancy resulted. Because the federal courts in a state applied substantive law different from that used in the state courts, a litigant could often obtain a change of law merely by choosing to sue in federal court rather than in the state court across the street. This led to significant discrimination in favor of the out–of–state litigant who, because of diversity jurisdiction, could engage in forum shopping between state and federal courts.[17]

The Supreme Court's decision in *Erie Railroad Co. v. Tompkins*;[18] overruled *Swift* and put an end to the possibility of forum shopping by the out–of–state litigant. It requires a federal court sitting in diversity to apply the substantive law (statute and case law) of the state where it sits. Thus, the great 1938 flip–flop was completed.

[b] *Erie*: The Bases for the Decision

Erie began as a quite ordinary case. Harry Tompkins was injured in Pennsylvania by a train belonging to the Erie Railroad while he was walking along the tracks. He sued the railroad in a federal court in New York. The railroad argued that under Pennsylvania law Tompkins was a trespasser; therefore, it owed him no duty of care. Tompkins countered that

[13] This is an over–simplification. Under *Swift*, federal courts also used a local law/general law distinction. On questions of general law, they were free to follow their own lights. On matters of local law, they followed the state courts. Ordinarily questions of real property were deemed local, as were questions of state statutory or constitutional construction.

[14] *Swift* originally applied only to questions of contract and commercial law. In the late 19th and early 20th centuries, the federal courts expanded the *Swift* doctrine so as to embrace almost all of what we now think of as "common law."

[15] One historian has argued that Story believed that state courts could not be trusted to resist popular pressure against the protections commercial law properly offered creditors. By giving federal courts wide authority in commercial matters, that pressure could be resisted, at least partially, and the young United States would be better able to prosper. *See* Morton Horwitz, The Transformation of American Law 1770–1860, 196–7 (1977).

[16] *See* Weintraub § 10.2.

[17] Black and White Taxicab & Transfer Co. v. Brown and Yellow Taxicab & Transfer Co., 276 U.S. 518 (1928), was one of the most egregious examples. Plaintiff, a Kentucky corporation, sought to enforce a contract which was unenforceable under Kentucky law. It dissolved and reincorporated itself under the laws of Tennessee and brought a diversity action in the district court. The Supreme Court held that the federal court was free to apply general federal law, rather than Kentucky law, and that it could enforce the contract.

[18] 304 U.S. 64 (1938).

the federal court was not bound to follow Pennsylvania law; under the general federal common law, he was a licensee; and, therefore, the railroad did owe him a duty of care.

When the case got to the Supreme Court, Justice Brandeis posed the issue in stark terms — "whether the oft–challenged doctrine of *Swift v. Tyson* shall now be disapproved." Brandeis, of course, answered in the affirmative and rested his conclusion on three arguments. First, he cited the research of Professor Charles Warren[19] into the legislative history of the Rules of Decision Act. Warren had uncovered an earlier draft of the Act in which the words "the laws of the several states" did not appear. Instead, the early draft spoke of "the Statute law of the several States in force for the time being and their unwritten or common law now in use." Warren reasoned, and Brandeis agreed, that the language of the statute ("the laws of the several states") was simply shorthand for the earlier version. Accordingly, *Swift's* interpretation of the Act as applying only to state statutory law had been wrong.[20]

Second, Brandeis relied on the practical failure of the *Swift* doctrine. National legal uniformity had not resulted from the development of general federal common law because of the "[p]ersistence of state courts in their own opinions on questions of common law." Further, the rule of *Swift* permitted "grave discrimination by non–citizens [of the state] against citizens." In other words, it permitted the out–of–state litigant to choose in a diversity case between federal and state court and to gain by that choice the advantage of picking the substantive law most favorable to his claim. It fostered forum shopping and "rendered impossible equal protection of the law."

Brandeis' third and most controversial[21] argument against *Swift* was that its result was unconstitutional. He argued that the Constitution gave neither the Congress nor the federal courts the right to declare the law for the states. General law–making authority in our country — except where the Constitution expressly grants legislative authority to the federal government — rests with the states. In Brandeis' words: "Congress has no power to declare substantive rules of common law applicable in a State. And no clause in the Constitution purports to confer such a power upon the federal courts."

---

[19] Charles Warren, *New Light on the History of the Federal Judiciary Act of 1789*, 37 Harv. L. Rev. 49, 51–52, 81–88, 108 (1923).

[20] Not all have agreed with Warren's inference. *See, e.g.*, Henry Friendly, *In Praise of Erie — And of the New Federal Common Law*, 39 N.Y.U. L. Rev. 383, 389–391 (1964). Warren's inference does seem to provide little support for overruling such a strong and old precedent.

[21] *Compare* Charles Clark, *State Law in the Federal Courts: The Brooding Omnipresence of Erie v. Tompkins*, 55 Yale L.J. 267, 278–280 (1946), *with* Henry Friendly, *In Praise of Erie — And of the New Federal Common Law*, 39 N.Y.U. L. Rev. 383, 392–398 (1964).

[c] *Guaranty Trust Co. v. York* and the Outcome Determinative Test

The scope of the *Erie* Doctrine clearly depends upon how much state law the federal courts must apply. Although federal courts can apply their own law of procedure, *Erie* requires them to apply state substantive law. Accordingly, a crucial problem after *Erie* was cast in terms of how to distinguish substance from procedure.[22] The way to avoid confusion is to keep constantly in mind the reasons why the classification is used in each different context.

Guaranty Trust Co. v. York,[23] an early solution to the problem, significantly expanded the scope of the Erie Doctrine. It held that a federal court exercising diversity jurisdiction must apply the state statute of limitations to an action in equity. Far more important than the holding, however, was the test the Court announced for distinguishing matters of substance from matters of procedure for *Erie* purposes. The test, known as the "Outcome–Determinative Test," instructs the district court to apply state law to any issue that could affect the result of the action:

> In essence, the intent of [*Erie*] was to insure that, in all cases where a federal court is exercising jurisdiction solely because of the diversity of citizenship of the parties, the outcome of the litigation in the federal court should be substantially the same, so far as legal rules determine the outcome of a litigation, as it would be if tried in a State court.

The Outcome–Determinative Test was strong medicine, indeed. Applied literally, it might have required the abandonment of the Federal Rules of Civil Procedure for diversity cases, for nearly every legal rule — no matter how clearly "procedural"— can affect the outcome of the suit.[24] To take only one of many possible examples, consider Rule 15(b) of the Federal Rules:[25] It permits amendments of the pleadings to conform to the evidence and radically reduces the impact of a variance between pleading and proof. Under common law pleading rules, a significant variance between pleading and proof — say, pleading contract and proving quantum meruit — could be fatal. Clearly then, for a federal court to apply Rule 15(b) when a state

---

[22] "Substance" and "procedure" come up often in conflicts law. It is important to understand, however, that they come up in different contexts and that the words may have different meanings in the different contexts. The Supreme Court in *York* showed sensitivity to the problem of classification:

> Matters of "substance" and matters of "procedure" are much talked about in the books as though they defined a great divide cutting across the whole domain of law. But, of course, "substance" and "procedure" are the same key–words to very different problems. Neither "substance" nor "procedure" represents the same invariants. Each implies different variables depending upon the particular problem for which it is used. 326 U.S. 99, 108 (1945).

[23] 326 U.S. 99 (1945).

[24] *See* Edward L. Merrigan, *Erie to York to Ragan — A Triple Play on the Federal Rules*, 3 Vand. L. Rev. 711 (1950).

[25] Fed. R. Civ. P. 15(b).

court would apply a stricter common law rule of variance could affect the result of the litigation, and thus violate the Outcome–Determinative Test.

[d] *Byrd* and the Balancing Test

Perhaps to avoid such anomalies, the Court began chiseling away at the Outcome–Determinative Test. *Byrd v. Blue Ridge Rural Electric Cooperative, Inc.*,[26] was the first step. Plaintiff, an employee of defendant's sub-contractor, sued defendant for work–related injuries in a federal court in South Carolina. Defendant contended that plaintiff was an "employee" under the South Carolina Workmen's Compensation Act, and, therefore, that his sole remedy was an administrative proceeding under that Act. The issue treated by the Supreme Court was whether plaintiff's status as an "employee" was a question to be decided by the judge (as South Carolina required) or by the jury (as would be done in a purely federal case). The Court noted that the issue might be outcomev determinative, because plaintiff's status as an "employee" might be viewed one way by the judge and the opposite way by the jury. The Court saw, however, an "affirmative countervailing" consideration, the preference in the federal system "under the influence — if not the command — of the Seventh Amendment," for jury determination of factual disputes. The question, said the Court, was "whether the federal policy favoring jury decisions of disputed fact questions should yield to the state rule in the interest of furthering the objective that the litigation should not come out one way in federal court and another way in state court."

The Court held that it should not. The outcome–determination objective did not weigh heavily in the decision, because the identity of the decision maker — while conceivably outcome determinative — was not nearly as likely to affect the result as the statute of limitations issue in *York*. On the other hand, the federal policy concerning jury trials weighed quite heavily. "It cannot be gainsaid that there is a strong federal policy against allowing state rules to disrupt the judge–jury relationship in the federal courts." Thus, in *Byrd*, the Court indicated that the *Erie/York* principle, while strong, might have to yield in a proper case to other important principles.

[e] *Hanna* and the Presumptive Validity of the Federal Rules

In *Hanna v. Plumer*,[27] the Court effectively insulated the various federal rules dealing with procedure from any *Erie*–based attack. Plaintiff, injured in an auto accident by decedent, sued decedent's executor in federal court in Massachusetts. Process was served by leaving copies of the summons and the complaint with the executor's wife at his home. Service made in this manner was permissible under Federal Rule 4(d)(1),[28] but not under the relevant Massachusetts rule on service.

[26] 356 U.S. 525 (1958).

[27] 380 U.S. 460 (1965).

[28] Fed. R. Civ. P. 4(d)(1).

In the Supreme Court, the executor argued that the Outcome-Determinative Test required application of the state rule because, if service had been made improperly, the action would have to be dismissed. The Court attacked the argument along two lines. First, the Court found that the executor's argument overstated the Outcome–Determinative Test. Process had already been served according to Federal Rule 4(d)(1), and in the Supreme Court the only remedy for a defect in service would have been dismissal. Virtually every procedural variation is outcome determinative in that sense. The Court suggested, however, that outcome determination must be viewed in light of the goal of discouraging forum shopping. The difference between rule 4(d)(1) and the Massachusetts service rule is not the sort of discrepancy that would have caused the plaintiff to choose one forum over the other. Thus reformulated, the Outcome–Determinative Test might best be renamed the "Forum–Choice Determinative Test": It counsels use of state law when a difference between state and federal law would prompt a litigant to choose one forum rather than the other.

The Court found an even more significant flaw in the executor's argument. The argument assumed that *Erie* and its progeny furnish the proper test for determining the validity of a Federal Rule of Civil Procedure. They do not. The correct test for measuring a Federal Rule, articulated in a separate line of cases,[29] is whether the rule is within the authority granted to the Supreme Court by the Enabling Act, and within the Congressional power to regulate procedure in the federal courts. If the Rule passes muster under those tests, it represents a valid exercise of federal power; the Supremacy Clause of the Federal Constitution requires that it take precedence over any conflicting state law.

> When a situation is covered by one of the Federal Rules, the question facing the court is a far cry from the typical, relatively unguided *Erie* choice: the court has been instructed to apply the Federal Rule, and can refuse to do so only if the Advisory Committee, this Court, and Congress erred in their prima facie judgment that the Rule in question transgresses neither the terms of the Enabling Act nor constitutional restrictions.[30]

The Court could scarcely have been more plain; the Federal Rules are no longer vulnerable to an *Erie*–based challenge.[31]

---

[29] The most influential decision was Sibbach v. Wilson, 312 U.S. 1 (1941).

[30] Hanna v. Plumer, 380 U.S. 460 (1965).

[31] Professor Ely has argued, however, that the second sentence of the Enabling Act contains a meaningful limitation on the scope of the Federal Rules. It says, "Such rules shall not abridge, enlarge or modify any substantive right." Ely argued that a Federal Rule might be disqualified by this second sentence. An example is Rule 35, permitting mental and physical examinations. If state practice excluded such a provision out of concern for bodily privacy, then arguably, application of Rule 35 would "abridge" a substantive right granted by the state and thus violate the second sentence of the Act. *See* John Hart Ely, *The Irrepressible Myth of Erie*, 87 Harv. L. Rev. 693, 718–734 (1974). The Supreme Court, however, has ignored the Act's second sentence.

[f] *Woods* and *Ricoh*: *Hanna* Reaffirmed

Two recent cases have made it quite clear that the *Hanna* approach controls all *Erie* questions where either a federal statute or Rule is involved. First, the Court addressed a conflict between a Federal Rule and state law. In *Burlington Northern RR. Co. v. Woods*,[32] the Court was faced with a conflict between an Alabama penalty of 10% imposed on all unsuccessful appeals of money judgements and Rule 38 of the Federal Rules of Appellate Procedure, which penalized only frivolous appeals. After finding that Rule 38's "discretionary mode of operation unmistakably conflicts with the mandatory provision" of the Alabama statute, the Court held that Rule 38 controlled:

> Federal Rule 38 regulates matters which can reasonably be classified as procedural, thereby satisfying the constitutional standard for validity. Its displacement of the Alabama statute also satisfies the statutory constraints of the Rules Enabling Act.

Because Rule 38 was a validly adopted "Rule," in other words, the Supremacy Clause required that it displace the conflicting Alabama rule. That holding, certainly consistent with *Hannah* and other cases, is only remarkable for its failure to construe the Federal Rule narrowly, as the Court had done in other cases, to avoid a conflict with the state rule.[33]

The second key decision in recent years is *Stewart Organization, Inc. v. Ricoh Corp.*[34] That case involved a dealership agreement between an Alabama corporation and a national manufacturer whose principal place of business was in New Jersey. The contract between the two provided that any dispute arising out of the agreement could be brought only in a court located in Manhattan. Petitioner, however, sued for breach of contract in the United States District Court for the Northern District of Alabama; jurisdiction there was based on diversity of citizenship. The defendant, relying on the forum–selection clause, moved for a transfer to the Southern District of New York under 28 U.S.C. § 1404(a) or for dismissal under 28 U.S.C. § 1406. The district court denied the motion, on the ground that Alabama law controlled the motion and Alabama law was quite hostile to forum–selection clauses. A badly divided Court of Appeals reversed.

The Supreme Court affirmed. The opinion by Justice Marshall makes quite clear the analysis to be followed in *Erie* cases where a federal statute is involved:

> Our cases indicate that when the federal law sought to be applied is a Congressional statute, the first and chief question for the district court's determinations is whether the statute is "sufficiently broad to control the issue before the Court." This question involves

---

[32] 480 U.S. 1 (1987).

[33] *See, e.g.*, Ragan v. Merchants Tfr. & Whse. Co., 330 U.S. 539 (1949).

[34] 487 U.S. 22 (1988). For commentary, *see* Walter Heiser, *Forum Selection Clauses in Federal Courts: Limitations on Enforcement After Stewart and Carnival Cruise*, 45 Fla. L. Rev. 553 (1993).

> a straightforward exercise in statutory interpretation to determine if the statute covers the point in dispute. . . .
>
> Thus a District Court sitting in diversity must apply a federal statute that controls the issue before that court and that represents a valid exercise of Congress' constitutional powers.

In other words, when a federal statute arguably conflicts with state law, there is no need for fancy judicial footwork. Rather, the focus is on ordinary Supremacy Clause analysis: If a "straightforward exercise in statutory interpretation shows that this statute" covers the point, then the federal law prevails.

This led the court to an easy resolution of *Ricoh* itself. Under § 1404(a), construed by the Court to require "a flexible and multifacted analysis," the forum selection clause should play a role — but not a "dispositive" role — in the district court's exercises of the "broad discretion" granted to it by the statute. The forum–selection clause, therefore, is entitled to play some undefined role in the decision whether to transfer.

Justice Scalia dissented.[35] He found § 1404(a) inapplicable. The real question in the case to him was whether the forum-selection clause was valid, an issue about which § 1404(a), which "is simply a venue provision," simply has nothing to say. Hence, neither a federal statute nor Rule was properly involved. That conclusion forced him to consider the "twin–aims" *Erie* test, and, in the end, to find that state law must prevail.

[g] *Gasperini*: *Byrd* Revived?

The Court's most recent *Erie* decision is also its most confusing in some time. *Gasperini v. Center for Humanities, Inc.*,[36] involved a New York law which sought to restrain jury verdicts. The law required both trial and appellate courts in New York to determine whether a jury award was excessive or inadequate. That law had been applied by the Second Circuit in *Gasperini* to overturn a jury verdict in a diversity case that the court found to be excessive. The Supreme court reversed, in a kind of *Erie* split–decision. Justice Ginsburg's opinion for the Court first held the New York law to be "substantive" under the Outcome Determinative Test; the federal trial court, therefore, should have applied the New York law, rather than federal law, to review the verdict. The difference is important because federal law is quite deferential to jury verdicts and, on appeal, to the trial judge's review of the award; the New York law, on the other hand, was expressly designed to impose a less deferential standard.

Although the Court held that the trial court should apply the New York law to its review of the jury verdict, it held that the Second Circuit had erred when it applied a less deferential standard. The problem was that in doing so, that court had run up against the Reexamination Clause of

[35] Justices Kennedy and O'Connor concurred in a brief opinion emphasizing the importance of forum-selection clauses; they concluded that a "valid" clause should be "given controlling weight in all but the most exceptional cases." 487 U.S. 22, 33 (1987).

[36] 515 U. S. 415 (1996).

the Seventh Amendment — a clause which Ginsburg read as prohibiting a federal court from engaging in non–deferential review of a jury verdict.[37] The upshot was that the federal trial court could apply the New York law, but the Circuit Court could not.

Ginsburg's exasperating opinion–exasperating because the basis for the decision is obscure — makes it difficult to know what weight to give it for *Erie* purposes. The problem is that the opinion relies not only on the "twin–aims" test of *Hanna*, but also on the *Byrd* balancing test — a case cited by the Court for the first time in 38 years.[38] Moreover, it is not clear whether the Court believed the Seventh Amendment to be controlling or whether it was merely "influenced" by it. In those circumstances, all that can be said is that the *Byrd* balancing test is alive — if not well — in cases involving judge–jury relations, an area where the federal interest is strong.[39]

[h] Analytical Summary

Hanna and *Ricoh* make clear how the Supreme Court expects a district court to handle an *Erie* problem. First, the court must determine if a federal statute, a Federal Rule of Civil Procedure, or some other federal rule[40] covers the issue. If it does, it almost surely must be applied; the rules are presumptively valid.[41] If the issue is not covered by a statute or rule, the court is left with "the typical relatively unguided *Erie* choice," and should apply the now–familiar "twin aims" test. Two questions then become relevant: (1) Is the issue forum–choice determinative, that is, would a ruling one way or another upon the issue affect a party's choice of forum? and (2) Is there some countervailing federal policy? An affirmative answer to the first question and a negative answer to the second call for application of

[37] The Reexamination Clause states that "no fact tried by a jury, shall be otherwise reexamined in any Court. . .than according to the rules of the common law."

[38] Richard D. Freer, *The State of Erie After Gasperini,* 76 Tex. L. Rev. 1637 (1996)

[39] Scoles, *et al.* at 186. *See also* Wendy Perdue, *The Sources and Scope of Federal Procedural Common Law: Some Reflections on Erie and Gasperini,* 26 U. Kan. L. Rev. 751 (1998).

[40] Since *Hanna*, the Federal Rules of Evidence have taken effect. They also are presumptively valid. Note however, that the Rules defer to state law on several issues: rebuttal of presumptions, Fed. R. Evid. 302; competence of witnesses, Fed. R. Evid. 601; privilege, Fed. R. Evid. 501.

[41] This is not to say that a particular Federal Rule will always prevail against a state rule which seems to conflict with it. The Supreme Court has tended to construe the Rules narrowly to avoid a direct collision. In Walker v. Armco Steel Corp., 446 U.S. 740 (1980), plaintiff filed his complaint before the Oklahoma statute of limitations had run, but defendant was served after the limitations period expired. Fed. R. Civ. P. 3 provides that a civil action is commenced by filing the complaint; the Oklahoma statute, by contrast, provided that service must be accomplished before the action is commenced for limitations purposes. The Court read Rule 3 narrowly to avoid the problem: "Rule 3 governs the date from which various timing requirements of the Federal rules begin to run, but does not affect state statutes of limitations." *Walker* is remarkable because the identical issue was raised in 1949 — just after *York*, but before *Hanna* — in Ragan v. Merchants Transfer & Warehouse Co., 337 U.S. 530 (1949). *Ragan* also held that state law must be applied, but many thought that *Hanna* overruled *Ragan*. *Walker* puts that speculation to rest.

state law. Opposite answers call for federal law. Affirmative answers to both questions require the court to balance the strength of the *Erie* policy against the strength of the countervailing federal policy. Finally, in cases involving judge–jury relations, the riddle of *Gasperini* must be wrestled with.[42]

Perhaps the most prominent *Erie* issue today requiring the "twin–aims" test to be applied is forum non conveniens in federal courts.[43] A few states are much more hostile to forum non conveniens than are the federal courts. Although there is some split in authority, the lower courts have generally applied the federal rule; the emphasis in the opinions has been on the strong federal interest in the orderly administration of justice.[44]

§ 105 Ascertaining State Law[1]

Erie enjoins the federal courts to apply state decisional law in diversity cases, but that injunction raises a difficult question: What is "state law"? Surely the most recent decisions of the state's highest court are "state law," but what of high court decisions a generation old which have not been recently reexamined? And what about the decisions of state intermediate appellate courts and state trial courts? The first Supreme Court decisions following *Erie* seemed to require federal courts to adhere, almost mechanically, to the decisions of state courts at every level. Four decisions in volume 311 of the U.S. Reports illustrate the trend. Three of them[2] held that federal courts are bound by the decisions of a state's intermediate appellate courts, unless there is strong evidence that the state's highest court would rule differently. The fourth, *Fidelity Union Trust Co. v. Field*,[3] went even further and held a federal court bound by the decisions of the New Jersey Court of Chancery — a court of original jurisdiction.[4] These decisions were not well received. Judge Friendly referred to them as "the excesses of 311 U.S.,"[5] and Judge Frank complained that the federal courts were being required to "play the role of ventriloquist's dummy" to the state courts.[6]

---

[42] Also to be examined is a cryptic dictum in Semtek Int'l Inc. v. Lockheed Martin Corp., 531 U. S. 497 (2001), suggesting that the "twin aims" test should apply to decisions involving the Federal Rules of Civil Procedure. That dictum, of course, starkly contrasts with language to the contrary in *Hanna* itself.

[43] Forum non conveniens is discussed in § 47, *supra*.

[44] *See* the separate opinions in In Re Air Crash Disaster Near New Orleans, La., 821 F.2d 1147 (5th Cir. 1987) (en banc), *vacated on other grounds*, 490 U.S. 1032 (1988). *See generally* William L. Reynolds, *The Proper Forum for a Suit: Transnational Forum Non Conveniens And Antisuit Injunctions in the Federal Courts*, 70 Tex. L. Rev. 1663 (1992); Allan R. Stein, *Erie and Court Access*, 100 Yale L.J. 1935 (1991).

[1] *See generally* Charles Alan Wright, The Law of Federal Courts § 58 (5th ed. 1994); Marian O. Boner, *Erie v. Tompkins: A Study in Judicial Precedent*, II, 40 Tex. L. Rev. 619 (1962).

[2] Six Companies v. Joint Highway Dist., 311 U.S. 180 (1940); West v. A.T.& T. Co., 311 U.S. 223 (1940); Stoner v. New York Life Ins. Co., 311 U.S. 464 (1940).

[3] 311 U.S. 169 (1940). The embarrassing tale of the *Field* case is related in Charles Alan Wright, The Law of Federal Courts 370–71 (5th ed. 1994).

[4] The Chancery court was, however, the equitable equivalent of an intermediate appellate court on the legal side.

[5] Henry Friendly, *In Praise of Erie And of the New Federal Common Law*, 39 N.Y.U. L. Rev. 383, 400 (1964).

[6] Richardson v. Commissioner of Internal Revenue, 126 F.2d 562 (2d Cir. 1942).

Later cases have taken a more flexible view of the fidelity that federal courts owe to state court decisions. In *King v. Order of United Commercial Travelers of America*,[7] for example, the Supreme Court held that a federal court was not bound by decisions of Ohio trial courts. The Court distinguished *Field* on the ground that the New Jersey Chancery Court was an intermediate court of appeals in equity matters and that it had statewide jurisdiction. Further indication of a change in approach came in *Bernhardt v. Polygraphic Co. of America*.[8] There, although the Court required the federal courts to follow a forty–five year old decision of the Supreme Court of Vermont, it explained:

> That case was decided in 1910. But it was agreed on oral argument that there is no later authority from the Vermont courts, that no fracture in the rules announced in those cases has appeared in subsequent rulings or dicta, and that no legislative movement is under way in Vermont to change the result of those cases.

The obvious implication is that a federal district court is free to consider "fractures," "dicta," and "legislative movement" in determining state law and, thus, that it need not adhere mechanically to state court decisions. Another revealing dictum comes from *Commissioner v. Estate of Bosch*:[9]

> If there be no decision [from the state's highest court] then federal authorities must apply what they find to be the state law after giving "proper regard" to relevant rulings of other courts of the State. In this respect, it may be said to be, in effect, sitting as a state court.

Modern commentators have relied on these more recent decisions to conclude that federal courts are no longer bound to follow mechanically the decisions of lower state courts, nor even the decisions of the state's highest courts, if these decisions are old and eroded. Rather, a district judge must consider all relevant expressions of state "law" in order to predict how the state's highest court would rule on a particular issue.[10]

This position, of course, makes good sense. The Supreme Court's earlier decisions requiring lockstep obedience to state court decisions could produce a problem of reverse forum shopping. State trial courts often do not consider themselves bound by other trial courts, by intermediate appellate courts of other appellate districts, or even by older high court decisions whose present authority is questionable. If the federal courts were so bound, a litigant relying on such questionable authority would prefer the hamstrung federal court (where his legal cripple was guaranteed strict obedience) to the state court which is free to make an informed prediction about the ruling of the state's highest court.

An alternative solution to the problem of unclear state law is the Uniform Certification of Questions of Law Act.[11] It permits a federal court to certify

---

[7] 333 U.S. 153 (1948).

[8] 350 U.S. 198 (1956).

[9] 387 U.S. 456 (1967).

[10] C. Wright, *supra* note 1, § 58.

[11] 12 U.L.A. 49.

a question of state law to the highest court of the state and removes the need for judicial guesswork.

§ 106 Door Closing Rules

One of the farthest extensions of the *Erie* Doctrine allows the states to control indirectly the jurisdiction of the federal courts. When a state closes the doors of its own courts to certain kinds of cases, *Erie* may require the federal courts in that state to close their doors as well. *Angel v. Bullington*[1] is the key case. Plaintiff, a citizen of Virginia, sold land in Virginia to defendant, a citizen of North Carolina. Defendant paid part of the purchase price and executed notes for the remainder. The notes were secured by a deed of trust on the land. When defendant defaulted, the land was sold, but the proceeds were not sufficient to cover the full amount of the notes. Accordingly, plaintiff sued defendant for the deficiency in a North Carolina court. Defendant relied on a North Carolina statute which prohibited a holder of notes secured by a deed of trust from recovering a deficiency judgment. The Supreme Court of North Carolina held that the statute barred plaintiff's suit. It rejected his argument that closing North Carolina's courts to the suit violated the United States Constitution. Plaintiff did not seek review by the Supreme Court. Instead, he brought a second action for the deficiency in a federal court in North Carolina. The second suit ultimately arrived at the Supreme Court by writ of certiorari.

The Supreme Court first dealt with the question of whether North Carolina could constitutionally close its courts to actions for deficiency judgments. The Court did not decide that question, however, because it had already been decided by the state court in plaintiff's first action. The state court's decision on the constitutionality of the court–closing statute precluded relitigation of the issue in a subsequent action. The Court was then faced with the *Erie* issue: If the North Carolina state courts were prohibited from hearing an action for a deficiency judgment, could a federal court in North Carolina nevertheless entertain such an action? The Court held it could not:

> If North Carolina has authoritatively announced that deficiency judgments cannot be secured within its borders, it contradicts the presuppositions of diversity jurisdiction for a federal court in that State to give such a deficiency judgment. North Carolina would hardly allow defeat of a State–wide policy through occasional suits in a federal court. What is more important, diversity jurisdiction must follow State law and policy. A federal court in North Carolina, when invoked on grounds of diversity of citizenship, cannot give that which North Carolina has withheld.

At first glance, the rule might appear anomalous, since it permits a state indirect control over the jurisdiction of the federal courts. Yet the result is required by the *Erie* Doctrine. A state may express its substantive policies in several ways. One way, of course, is for it to promulgate (by statute or

[1] 330 U.S. 183 (1947).

decision) a substantive rule of law for the decision of cases. Such rules must be applied by the federal courts, according to the *Erie* interpretation of the Rules of Decision Act. But state policy may also be expressed by jurisdictional statutes. An emphatic way for a state to assert its opposition to a particular cause of action, for instance, is not only to disallow it as a matter of substantive law, but also to deprive its courts of jurisdiction to hear it. The federal courts should be bound by such a statute because it expresses substantive state policy, and the central thrust of the *Erie* Doctrine is that state policy should control in federal diversity actions. Not every state jurisdictional statute expresses substantive state policy, however. Some court–closing rules are based only on policies relevant to the administration of justice — for instance, rules of forum non conveniens and rules prohibiting actions for declaratory relief. Arguably, *Erie* does not require that the federal courts be bound by such statutes.[2]

§ 107 *Klaxon* — Choice of Law in Federal Courts[1]

Erie requires federal courts to apply state substantive law in diversity cases. When a dispute touches more than one state, however, the federal court must determine which state's law to apply. What choice–of–law principles should it use to make that decision? The Supreme Court answered that question in *Klaxon Co. v. Stentor Electric Manufacturing Co.*[2] Plaintiff contracted in New York to sell its entire business to defendant. Several years later, plaintiff sued on the agreement in a diversity action in the federal court in Delaware. After plaintiff recovered a jury verdict, it requested interest from the date the action was commenced. The district court, without considering Delaware's choice–of–law rules, held that New York law should apply to the question of interest and granted plaintiff's request. The case reached the Supreme Court by writ of certiorari after the Court of Appeals affirmed. The Supreme Court reversed and held on *Erie* grounds that a federal court sitting in diversity must apply the choice–of–law rules of the state where it sits. The Court's treatment of the issue was brief and conclusory:

> We are of the opinion that the prohibition declared in *Erie R. Co. v. Tompkins* against such independent determinations by the federal courts, extends to the field of conflict of laws. The conflict of laws rules to be applied by the federal court in Delaware must conform to those prevailing in Delaware's state courts. Otherwise, the accident of diversity of citizenship would constantly disturb equal administration of justice in coordinate state and federal courts sitting side by side. Any other ruling would do violence to the principle of uniformity within a state, upon which the *Tompkins* decision is based.

Thus, federal courts must treat conflicts problems exactly as they do any other problem of substantive law.

---

[2] The argument is Professor Weintraub's. *See* Weintraub § 10.6.

[1] *See generally* Scoles, et al.Ch. 3. IV; Weintraub §§ 10.2–10.6.

[2] 313 U.S. 487 (1941).

In *Day & Zimmerman, Inc. v. Challoner*,[3] the Supreme Court reaffirmed the *Klaxon* principle and made quite clear that the modern revolution in choice–of–law theory does not authorize the federal courts to ignore state conflicts law — however outmoded.[4] In that case, one American soldier was killed and another severely injured when an artillery shell manufactured by defendant in Texas exploded prematurely in Cambodia. The action was brought in a federal court in Texas. The Fifth Circuit affirmed the district court's refusal to apply Texas choice–of–law principles, which would have referred to the substantive law of Cambodia — the place of injury. The court based its decision upon interest analysis, reasoning that Cambodia had no interest in the resolution of a products liability action between American servicemen and an American arms manufacturer.

The Supreme Court reversed. In a short per curiam opinion, it rejected the Fifth Circuit's contention that the federal courts are free to ignore a state conflicts rule which refers to the law of a state with no policy interest in the case. Said the Court:

> A federal court in a diversity case is not free to engraft onto those state rules exceptions or modifications which may commend themselves to the federal court, but which have not commended themselves to the State in which the federal court sits. The Court of Appeals in this case should identify and follow the Texas conflicts rule.

Thus, a federal court may opt for a modern choice–of–law system, but only if it does so in an attempt to predict the action of the state's courts.[5]

Klaxon has been the subject of considerable discussion among scholars.[6] Several strong arguments have been made against its holding. First, it has been suggested that the constitutional and statutory arguments which compel *Erie* do not support *Klaxon*. *Erie's* premise is that the federal government lacks the constitutional authority to make common law rules to control intra–state cases. But surely in a conflicts case the Congress and the federal courts have authority under the Full Faith and Credit Clause to make rules for choosing among competing states' substantive laws;[7] the federal government, after all, should have authority to deal with the problems created by a federal system.[8] Nor does the Rules of Decision Act[9]

---

[3] 423 U.S. 3 (1975). The Fifth Circuit's opinion is reported at 512 F.2d 77 (5th Cir. 1975).

[4] For a time it appeared that the federal courts, under the influence of the modern revolution in choice–of–law methodology, might attempt to exercise some independent judgment. In Lester v. Aetna Life Insurance Co., 433 F.2d 884 (5th Cir. 1970), *cert. denied*, 402 U.S. 909 (1971), the Fifth Circuit refused to apply Louisiana's lex loci rule in a contract case. The court held the *Klaxon* principle inapplicable to a case which presents only a false conflict; the decision reasoned that if there was a false conflict there was no choice–of–law problem. See § 78, *supra*, for a discussion of the concept of a false conflict.

[5] *See* § 105, *supra*, for a discussion of the federal courts' duty to predict the view of the state's highest court.

[6] *See generally* Scoles, *et al.* § 3.36; Weintraub § 10.5A–D.

[7] *See* William Baxter, *Choice of Law and the Federal System*, 16 Stan. L. Rev. 1, 23 (1963).

[8] *See* Douglas Laycock, *Equal Citizens of Equal and Territorial States: The Constitutional Foundations of Choice of Law*, 92 Colum. L. Rev. 249, 282 (1992).

[9] Now codified at 28 U.S.C § 1652. The Act is discussed in § 104, *supra*.

compel the *Klaxon* holding. It directs federal courts to employ state rules of decision only "in cases where they apply." The last phrase arguably leaves open for federal courts the question of which state's law "applies" — the choice–of–law question.[10]

Another argument against *Klaxon* focuses on its practical effects. *Erie's* central goal is to eliminate *intra*state forum–shopping between the federal and state courts in a particular state. In choice–of–law cases, there is a greater possibility of *inter*state forum–shopping — choosing one state forum rather than another because its substantive law and choice–of–law principles are more favorable. The holding of *Klaxon* does nothing to avoid this problem, because it compels the local federal court to mimic the possibly parochial state court.[11]

If the federal courts were free to develop a set of federal rules for choice of law, a good deal of *inter*state forum-shopping could be avoided. A check would exist on the plaintiff's ability to choose a state forum because of its favorable choice–of–law rules — the possibility that defendant would remove the case to a federal court which would then apply federal choice–of–law principles. The result, however, is that the intrastate uniformity that *Erie* sought would be at least partially sacrificed.

Both interstate and intrastate uniformity could be achieved if the federal courts were authorized to develop federal choice–of–law principles, and those principles were then held binding on the state courts under the Supremacy Clause.[12] The argument for that solution is that the responsibility for determining competing state claims to legal control over a multi-state problem is a uniquely federal function in our system, and cannot be left to the individual states.[13] Adoption of such a radical remedy, however, would require a major constitutional upheaval; not only would *Klaxon* have to be overruled,[14] but the Court also would have to discard the very long line of cases that hold that the states do have the freedom (within quite broad constitutional limits) to fashion their own choice–of–law rules.[15]

Although this radical solution is not likely to be adopted, its focus on the dangers of interstate and intrastate forum shopping suggests a more

---

[10] Baxter, *supra* note 7, at 41.

[11] According to Professor Weintraub, *Klaxon* may also encourage a perverse sort of intrastate forum shopping. A litigant who wished to rely on a state's old territorial choice–of–law rules might sensibly prefer federal court to state court, since the federal court, straight–jacketed by *Klaxon*, would not feel as free as the state court to embrace one of the new choice–of–law methodologies. Weintraub § 10.5B.

[12] *See* Scoles, et al. § 3.36. Judge Weinstein tried a variation of this approach in In Re Agent Orange Products Liability Litigation, 580 F. Supp. 690 (E. D. N.Y. 1984). That action involved a huge class of Vietnam veterans; the court found that each state whose law might be applied would choose "a form of national consensus law or of federal law itself."

[13] *See* Baxter, *supra* note 7, at 23.

[14] Professor Cavers opposed overruling *Klaxon*. His most impressive argument suggested that if the avowed purpose for doing so were the hope of generating interstate uniformity in choice–of–law rules, the federal courts, charged with developing uniform principles, might naturally sink into the First Restatement's mechanical system, which modern scholars have struggled to overthrow. *See* David F. Cavers, The Choice of Law Process 222 (1965).

[15] *See* §§ 97–100, *supra*.

modest alteration of the *Klaxon* rule. When the possibility of intrastate forum shopping between state and federal courts does not exist, and the chance of interstate forum shopping is great, the *Klaxon* rule should not apply.[16] The situation arises when the personal jurisdiction of the federal court is wider than that of the corresponding state court. In interpleader actions, for example, federal courts have nationwide jurisdiction[17] and state courts do not. Thus, when claimants are from several different states, the possibility of intrastate forum shopping may not exist, because the federal court may be the only one with jurisdiction over all claimants. There may, however, be a substantial opportunity for interstate forum shopping. A claimant can sue the stakeholder in federal court and be reasonably confident that the stakeholder will file a bill of interpleader in that court,[18] joining all other claimants — including those who would be beyond the personal jurisdiction of the local state courts. Because of *Klaxon*, there is a great incentive for that first claimant to sue in the federal court of a state that has substantive law rules and choice–of–law principles favorable to his claim.[19] Thus, in federal interpleader actions, the application of the *Klaxon* rule is unjustified.[20] Avoidance of intrastate forum–shopping (the principal *Klaxon* goal) is not a worry, and encouragement of interstate forum–shopping (*Klaxon's* principal drawback) is. Nevertheless in *Griffin v. McCoach*,[21] the Supreme Court held that the *Klaxon* rule *does* apply in federal interpleader actions. A sensible and modest modification of the *Klaxon* doctrine would be the overruling of *Griffin*.

§ 108 Federal Common Law[1]

In *Erie*,[2] Justice Brandeis proclaimed that "[t]here is no federal general common law." By that statement, he meant that there is no federal common law which exists side by side with state law, and which generally applies in the manner of state common law. Federal courts have developed, however, a more specialized federal common law to decide cases where, although there is no applicable Congressional enactment, the subject matter is one that must be governed by federal law. A federal court not

---

16 For more complete statements of the argument, *see* Weintraub § 10.7; Scoles et al. § 3.42.

17 28 U.S.C. § 2361.

18 Weintraub suggests that the bill of interpleader will be filed in the district where the first claimant sues "as a reflex action." Weintraub § 10.7A.

19 There are, of course, venue restrictions on the ability to forum shop. An interpleader action can be filed only in a district "in which one or more of the claimants reside." 28 U.S.C. § 1397.

20 There are other circumstances where the federal court's personal jurisdiction may exceed that of the state courts — the one hundred mile bulge provision of Fed. R. Civ. P. 4(f), for instance. Weintraub argues that *Klaxon* should not apply in any of these circumstances. *See* Weintraub § 10.8.

21 313 U.S. 498 (1941).

1 *See generally* Scoles, et al. §§ 3.49–3.55; Alfred Hill, *The Law–Making Power of the Federal Courts: Constitutional Preemption*, 67 Colum. L. Rev. 1024 (1967); Henry Friendly, *In Praise of Erie — And of the New Federal Common Law*, 39 N.Y.U. L. Rev. 383 (1964).

2 Erie Railroad Co. v. Tompkins, 304 U.S. 64 (1938).

bound by a particular act of Congress, and not bound to follow state law, must fashion a rule from national policy. When it does so, it makes federal common law.

The area of federal common law is clouded in considerable uncertainty. The source of federal judicial authority to fashion federal common law is not clear, nor is it certain what exact circumstances justify its creation. But before considering these difficult questions, it is best to determine what is clear about the area: First, if federal common law applies, there is no *Erie* problem. By virtue of the Supremacy Clause, federal common law (just like federal statutory law) binds federal and state courts, regardless of state law provisions to the contrary. Second, the federal courts' role in making federal common law is very different from their role as interpreters of the Constitution. When they interpret the Constitution, their rulings bind Congress; by contrast, when they make federal common law, they "legislate" interstitially in areas where Congress has authority to speak but has not addressed the issue before the court. Should Congress later choose to address the issue, the statute supersedes the earlier federal common law rule. Third, a federal common law rule will support "arising under" jurisdiction under 28 U.S.C. § 1331; a case based on federal common law is, in other words, a federal question case. As with most such cases, there is concurrent jurisdiction in the state courts, but those courts must apply the federal rule.

The first area of considerable uncertainty is the appropriate source for the federal courts' authority to make federal common law.[3] Clearly, Congress could delegate some of its law–making authority to the federal courts in the form of a command to fashion federal common law in certain areas. In *Textile Workers Union of America v. Lincoln Mills*,[4] the Supreme Court concluded that Congress had done just that. The Court interpreted a statute[5] establishing jurisdiction in the federal courts over disputes involving collective bargaining agreements as a grant of authority to fashion a set of rules to decide those disputes. Even more clearly, a direct grant of power in the Constitution could authorize the federal courts to make federal common law. Some commentators[6] have concluded that the Constitution contains such more or less direct grants of judicial law–making authority in admiralty,[7] foreign relations,[8] and interstate boundary and water disputes.[9] A final possible source for the federal courts' common

[3] Two conflicting articles illustrate the debate. Louise Weinberg, *Federal Common Law*, 83 Nw. U. L. Rev. 805 (1989), argues forcefully that a federal common law should be fashioned on the basis of "carefully considered national substantive policy." Martin Redish, *Federal Common Law, Political Legitimacy, and the Interpretive Process: An "Institutionalists Perspective,"* 83 Nw. U. L. Rev. 761 (1989), contends that the Rules of Decision Act precludes the development of federal common law.

[4] 353 U.S. 448 (1957).

[5] 29 U.S.C. § 185(a).

[6] *See, e.g.*, Hill, *supra* note 1; Friendly, *supra* note 1.

[7] Southern Pac. Ry. Co. v. Jensen, 244 U.S. 205 (1917).

[8] Banco Nacional de Cuba v. Sabbatino, 376 U.S. 398 (1964).

[9] Hinderlider v. La Plata Co., 304 U.S. 92 (1938).

law–making power is their authority, independent of specific constitutional or statutory grant, to legislate on issues that Congress has not specifically treated, but which Congress intended to pre–empt from state control.[10]

In contrast to the uncertainty over the source of the federal courts' authority, the general standard for exercising that authority is fairly clear. Federal courts should make federal common law when they are faced with an issue which: (1) is within the federal law–making competence, (2) has not been specifically dealt with by Congress, and (3) should not be left to state regulation because of important federal interests. Several examples illustrate the point. In *Clearfield Trust Co. v. United States*,[11] the Supreme Court held that federal common law must govern the obligations of the United States on commercial paper which it issues. The important federal interest that prohibited state control was the federal government's interest in a uniform rule to govern its obligations. Said the Court: "The application of state law would subject the rights and duties of the United States to exceptional uncertainty. It would lead to great diversity in results by making identical transactions subject to the vagaries of the laws of the several states. The desirability of a uniform rule is plain."

In *Banco Nacional de Cuba v. Sabbatino*,[12] the relationship between the executive and judicial branches of the federal government, in the context of foreign relations, supplied the key federal interest. The case involved a challenge to the expropriation by the Cuban government of property of American–held companies. The Supreme Court held that the act–of–state doctrine precluded the federal court from questioning the validity of the acts of a foreign sovereign effective within its own territory.[13] The reason for the doctrine is that foreign relations are particularly within the authority of the executive branch of the national government; judicial interference is likely to frustrate, rather than advance, national goals. New York law incorporated the act–of–state doctrine in terms virtually identical to the federal decisions. Nevertheless, the Supreme Court made it clear that the area must be governed by federal rather than state law. The relations between the executive and judicial branches of the federal government and the responsibility of each in the area of foreign relations are issues that cannot be subject to state control.

In *Illinois v. City of Milwaukee*,[14] Illinois sought to invoke the Supreme Court's original jurisdiction to abate a nuisance (pollution of Lake

[10] *See* Scoles, *et al.* § 3.50.

[11] 318 U.S. 363 (1943).

[12] 376 U.S. 398 (1964).

[13] Congress, responding to public reaction following *Sabbatino,* substantially modified the scope of the act–of–state doctrine in American courts. 22 U.S.C. § 2370(e)(2). For a concise discussion of the doctrine, *Sabbatino*, and the Congressional response, *see* Leflar, McDougal & Felix § 68.

[14] 406 U.S. 91 (1972). The lifespan of the rule announced in Illinois v. City of Milwaukee was brief. Shortly after the decision, Congress passed the Federal Water Pollution Control Act Amendments of 1972. In City of Milwaukee v. Illinois, 451 U.S. 304 (1981), the Court ruled that the Act occupied the field of national pollution control and left no room for a federal common law of nuisance. Later, in International Paper Co. v. Ouellette, 479 U.S. 481 (1987),

Michigan) caused by several cities and sewerage treatment facilities in Wisconsin. The Court refused to entertain the action under its original jurisdiction, but held that Illinois could file an action in the district court based on federal common law. Federal common law was necessary, because a dispute between states (or governmental subdivisions) could not sensibly be referred to any single state's law. The Court analogized the problem of interstate nuisance to other disputes between states involving boundaries and apportionment of interstate streams.

These three examples demonstrate the Court's use of federal common law when, because of a strong federal interest, the issue is not appropriate for state control. Although the general standard is relatively clear, its application has generated considerable uncertainty. For instance, although the national interest in uniformity requires federal common law to govern the obligations of the United States on commercial paper which it issues, state law governs disputes among private parties concerning such commercial paper.[15] Contracts between the United States and private parties pursuant to federal regulatory programs have been held sometimes to be governed by state law and other times by federal common law.[16] Another area of uncertainty is the tort liability and privilege of federal officers.[17]

Because of this uncertainty, predicting the future creation of federal common law has been a difficult chore. To the extent that trends are useful, the Court has been reluctant in recent years to find the sort of strong federal interest which justifies the application of federal common law. Recent decisions have indicated that federal common law is appropriate "only in such narrow areas as those concerned with the rights and obligations of the United States, interstate and international disputes implicating the conflicting rights of States or our relations with foreign nations, and admiralty cases."[18] The primary source of the Court's reluctance seems to be deference to Congress as the primary federal law–making authority.[19]

---

the Court read the Act as requiring application of the law of the state of the pollution. (Apparently, *lex loci* is like a toxic waste site: no matter how hard you try, you can never get rid of it.)

[15] Bank of America v. Parnell, 352 U.S. 29 (1956).

[16] *Compare* United States v. Yazell, 382 U.S. 341 (1966), *with* United States v. Carson, 372 F.2d 429 (6th Cir. 1967).

[17] *Compare* Wheeldin v. Wheeler, 373 U.S. 647 (1963), *with* Howard v. Lyons, 360 U.S. 593 (1959).

[18] Texas Industries, Inc. v. Radcliff Materials, Inc., 451 U.S. 630, 641 (1981).

[19] *Id.;* City of Milwaukee v. Illinois, 451 U.S. 304 (1981); Northwest Airlines, Inc. v. Transport Workers Union of America, 451 U.S. 77 (1981).

Chapter 5
JUDGMENTS

Part A

BASIC PRINCIPLES

§ 109 Finality in F-1 — Res Judicata

Conflict of laws has been concerned traditionally with the interstate recognition and enforcement of judgments. The focus of that concern has been this question: What effect does a judgment rendered in one state (Forum #1, usually called F–1), have *in a sister state* (Forum #2 or F–2)? Before investigating this question in detail, however, it makes sense to consider what effect a judgment has *in the state where it was rendered* (F–1). The effect of a judgment in F–1 is controlled by the law of res judicata or former adjudication. A full exposition of that topic is beyond the scope of this book; it is well treated in books[1] and courses in civil procedure. Nevertheless, a brief treatment is warranted here because so much of the law of full faith and credit depends upon the policies and doctrines embodied in the law of res judicata.

[a] The Policies Behind Finality

The policies behind the law of res judicata are easy to articulate.[2] For the litigant, finality is an important goal; the purpose of litigation is dispute resolution, and the parties want a resolution that they can rely on. A certain and final resolution permits the parties to order their affairs and plan in a sensible way; otherwise, they cannot. Society is no less interested in finality than are the litigants. Resolving a single dispute more than once wastes limited societal resources. There are, of course, countervailing policies of justice. Enforcing broad and strict rules of finality may occasionally deprive a litigant of her rights, merely because she failed to assert them at the proper time. These two goals — judicial economy and justice — have been the principal forces which have forged the doctrine of res judicata.

---

[1] Excellent treatments are: §§ 4301-4500 Charles A. Wright, Arthur R. Miller, & Edward H. Cooper, Federal Practice and Procedure (1981,2002); Shreve & Raven–Hansen, Ch. 15; Fleming James, Jr., Geoffrey C. Hazard, Jr. & John Leubsdorf, Civil Procedure, Ch. 11 (5th ed. 2001); Larry L. Teply & Ralph U. Whitten, Civil Procedure, Ch. 13 (2d ed. 2000); Jack H. Friedenthal, Mary K. Kane & Arthur R. Miller, Civil Procedure, Ch. 14 (3d ed. 1999). *See also* Restatement (Second) of Judgments, Ch. 3 and 4, *Developments in the Law — Res Judicata,* 65 Harv. L. Rev. 818 (1952).

[2] *Developments in the Law — Res Judicata, supra* note 1, at 820.

The modern trend in American courts has been to emphasize the policy of judicial economy and thus to expand the scope of res judicata.[3] One reason for the trend is the advent of modern procedural rules permitting, and in some cases requiring, joinder of claims and parties to produce larger litigation packages.[4] Another probable cause is the modern perception that courts are becoming dangerously overloaded. The American Law Institute has endorsed the trend; thus the Restatement (Second) of Judgments provides for a broader scope to the finality doctrines than did its predecessor.

[b] Claim Preclusion and Issue Preclusion

The law of res judicata is composed of two major branches: claim preclusion (in older terminology, "bar and merger") and issue preclusion (in older terminology, direct and collateral estoppel).[5] Claim preclusion prohibits a second suit on a *claim* or *cause of action* which was asserted in a prior suit, which proceeded to a final judgment on the merits. The judgment in the first action precludes not only all questions which were actually litigated, but also all issues which might have been litigated. Issue preclusion, more limited in scope, prohibits relitigation of *factual issues* actually decided in a prior proceeding, regardless of whether the second proceeding is based upon the same claim or cause of action.[6]

A series of three examples illustrates the distinction. Suppose that plaintiff has been injured twice in two entirely unrelated accidents by ambulance drivers, who are both employees of defendant hospital. Further, suppose that the jurisdiction where the litigations occur has a rule of charitable immunity. The following chart shows three possible sequences of litigation. In each case, assume that litigation #1 occurs before litigation #2.

[3] *See* Shreve and Raven–Hansen, *supra* note 1.

[4] *See, e.g.*, Fed. R. Civ. P. 13, 14, 18–24.

[5] For a famous rendition of the distinction, *see* Cromwell v. County of Sac, 94 U.S. 351 (1876). *See also* Restatement (Second) of Judgments § 17, comments a, b, and c.

[6] Courts and commentators are not always consistent on terminology. Some use the term "res judicata" to refer to the entire topic (claim preclusion and issue preclusion); others use it to refer only to claim preclusion. *See* Teply & Whitten, *supra* note 1 at 898–899.

	Litigation	Cause of Action	Issue Litigated	
I.	1. P. v. Hospital	Accident #1	Issue A:	Did ambulance #1 run the stop sign?
	2. P. v. Hospital	Accident #1	Issue B:	Did ambulance #1 exceed the speed limit?
II.	1. P. v. Hospital	Accident #1	Issue C:	Is the hospital a charitable institution?
	2. P. v. Hospital	Accident #2	Issue C:	Is the hospital a charitable institution?
III.	1. P. v. Hospital	Accident #1	Issue A:	Did ambulance #1 run the stop sign?
	2. P. v. Hospital	Accident #2	Issue C:	Is the hospital a charitable institution?

In example I, claim preclusion will prohibit the second suit entirely. Because both suits are on the same cause of action (Accident #1), the second suit is precluded, even though it raises an issue that was not litigated in the first suit (ambulance's speed). That issue *might have been litigated* in the first suit. In example II, issue preclusion will prohibit relitigation of the charitable immunity issue in the second suit, even though the two suits are on different causes of action. That issue was already litigated between the parties in the first suit. Finally, in example III, neither doctrine applies; claim preclusion does not apply because the two suits are on different causes of action (different accidents), and issue preclusion does not apply because the charitable immunity issue was not litigated in the first suit.

[c] The Dimensions of a Claim or Cause of Action

A comparison of claim preclusion and issue preclusion illustrates the importance of determining the dimensions of a single claim or cause of action. If two suits are based upon the same cause of action, the second is precluded entirely, even though new issues are raised; by contrast, if the two suits are on different causes of action, only issues actually litigated in the first suit are precluded in the subsequent action. So the question is: What constitutes a single claim or cause of action?[7]

[7] *See generally* James, Hazard & Leubsdorf, *supra* note 1 at § 11.9, Shreve & Raven–Hansen, § 15.02.

There are several answers to the question, but two predominate. The primary right theory holds that a single cause of action consists of the violation of a single primary right. Suppose, for instance, defendant negligently drives his car into plaintiff's car and then batters plaintiff in an ensuing argument. According to the primary right theory, plaintiff has two causes of action — one to vindicate his right not to have his property damaged negligently, and another to vindicate his right not to have his person injured intentionally. The transactional theory defines a cause of action as a single transaction or occurrence, or an interlocked series of transactions or occurrences. In the example posed above, the transactional theory would indicate only one cause of action because the auto accident and the battery constitute one interlocked series of occurrences.[8]

[d] Persons Affected by Res Judicata — Parties and Privies

Who is bound by a judgment, and who may benefit from a judgment?[9] The answer typically given is: the parties to the action and those in privity with them. Determining the parties to a suit seldom presents a problem; they are usually the people named in the action and subject to the jurisdiction of the court. The concept of privity is more difficult. The term is really a conclusory one; it is shorthand for the conclusion that a person is so closely related to a party that it is fair to bind him to the results of a litigation. The question, then, is: What relationships suffice to establish privity?

A person may be considered a privy of a party if the party is her legal representative. Thus, if a trustee sues defendant and loses, the beneficiary of the trust will be precluded from suing defendant on the same cause of action.[10] Another classic privity situation involves successive owners of property. Suppose *O* owns a piece of land over which *D* claims an easement. *O* sues *D* to quiet his title in the land free of the easement, but loses. Subsequently *O* conveys to *O2*. *O2* is precluded from claiming the land free of the easement because *O2* is considered a privy of *O*.[11] A final example of privity concerns persons who control the litigation, even though they are not parties.[12] Suppose *P* sues *D* for negligence. *D*'s insurer assumes the defense of the action. A judgment against *D* will also bind *D*'s insurer because, although not a party, it controlled the defense of the first action.

---

[8] These two views of cause of action, and two others, as well, are discussed in Restatement (Second) of Judgments § 24, comment a. The Restatement adopted the transactional theory.

[9] *See generally* Shreve & Raven–Hansen, § 15.08; James, Hazard & Leubsdorf, *supra* note 1, at §§ 11.23-11.30; Teply & Whitten, *supra* note 1, at 930–945; Friedenthal, Kane & Miller, *supra* note 1, at §§ 14.13–14.14.

[10] Restatement (Second) of Judgments § 41.

[11] *Id.* § 43.

[12] *Id.* § 39.

[e] Strangers to the Litigation — Mutuality of Estoppel[13]

The Due Process Clause prohibits depriving a person of important rights without affording him notice of a claim against him and an opportunity to be heard in his defense. The implication of this principle is that a court may not apply the doctrines of claim preclusion or issue preclusion to the detriment of strangers to the litigation. The principles of res judicata are constitutional as long as they bind only those who have had a day in court. Suppose, for example, *D* drives his car into a car containing *P1* and *P2*. *P1* sues *D*, contending *D* was negligent, and loses. In the later negligence action by *P2* against *D*, *D* may not use the results of the first suit against *P2* because *P2* has not yet had a day in court on the issue of *D*'s negligence.

An entirely different question is whether a stranger to the litigation may *benefit* from the doctrines of claim and issue preclusion. The stranger cannot be bound by findings in the litigation, but can she use those findings (in a subsequent action) against one who was a party? Once again, suppose *D* drives his car into a car containing *P1* and *P2*. *P1* sues *D*, contending that *D* was negligent, and this time she wins. Can *P2* now use that determination in a subsequent action against *D*? The older cases, relying on the doctrine of mutuality of estoppel, said *P2* could not.[14] Because *P2* would not have been bound by the result in *P1 v. D* (because *P2* was not a party), she could not benefit from the result either.

Commentators[15] have had harsh words for the doctrine of mutuality, and many courts[16] have abandoned it. Some have rejected it completely, permitting a stranger to use the results of a prior litigation in nearly all circumstances. Others have been more cautious and have permitted a stranger to the litigation to benefit only to the extent that he wishes to use the result defensively — to protect himself from recovery by one who was a losing party in the first action.

---

[13] *See generally* sources cited in note 9, *supra*.

[14] *See, e.g.*, Ralph Wolff & Sons v. New Zealand Ins. Co., 248 Ky. 304, 58 S.W.2d 623 (1933).

[15] Fleming James, citing Brainerd Currie and Jeremy Bentham, said:

> Here as elsewhere in the law a requirement of mutuality as an independent principle of justice has been aptly described as a "tinkling cymbal, an empty and fatuous formula productive of more harm than good." It is indeed a notion more appropriate to the gaming table than to the bench.

Fleming James, Jr., Civil Procedure § 11.31 (1965).

[16] *See* Parklane Hosiery Co. v. Shore, 439 U.S. 322 (1979); Bernhard v. Bank of America Nat'l. Trust & Sav. Ass'n, 19 Cal.2d 807, 122 P.2d 892 (1942).

§ 110 Interstate Finality — Full Faith and Credit[1]

[a] Generally

The Framers included the Full Faith and Credit Clause in the Constitution as part of their effort to form one nation out of the thirteen separate states. The Clause provides that:

> Full Faith and Credit shall be given in each State to the public Acts, Records, and judicial Proceedings of every other State. And the Congress may by general Laws prescribe the Manner in which such Acts, Records and Proceedings shall be proved, and the Effect thereof.[2]

The Clause is not wholly self–executing,[3] its second sentence contemplating implementation by federal legislation. Congress first exercised its authority under the Clause in 1790.[4] The statute, provides that:

> The Acts of the legislature of any State, Territory, or Possession . . . shall be authenticated by affixing the seal of such State thereto.
>
> The records and judicial proceedings of any court of any such State, Territory, or Possession . . . shall be proved . . . by the attestation of the clerk . . . together with a certificate of a judge of the court that the said attestation is in proper form.
>
> Such Acts, records and judicial proceedings or copies thereof, so authenticated, shall have the same full faith and credit in every court within the United States . . . as they have by law or usage in the courts . . . from which they are taken.

The statute (now codified as 28 U.S.C. § 1738) exceeds the constitutional mandate by requiring full faith and credit for the judgments of territories and possessions, and by requiring that *federal* courts give full faith and credit to state court judgments.[5] Neither the Constitution nor the statute specifically addresses the recognition of federal court judgments in state

---

[1] *See generally* Charles A. Wright, Arthur R. Miller & Edward H. Cooper, Federal Practice and Procedure §§ 4466–4472 (1981 & 2000 Supp.); Larry L. Teply & Ralph U. Whitten, Civil Procedure 949–963 (2d ed. 2000); Shreve & Raven-Hansen § 15.10.

[2] U.S. Const. art. IV, § 1. The Clause is the first section of Article IV of the Constitution. The Article's function is to adjust the relations among the several states. Thus it provides, *inter alia*, for extradition of fugitives from justice and from slavery, and the admission of states; it also contains the Privileges and Immunities Clause. The Full Faith and Credit Clause is modeled on provisions found in several state constitutions and in the Articles of Confederation. On the history of the Clause, *see* Douglass Leycock, *Equal Citizens of Equal and Territorial States: The Constitutional Foundation of Choice of Law*, 92 Colum. L. Rev. 249 (1992); Ralph U. Whitten, *The Constitutional Limitation on State–Court Jurisdiction: A Historical–Interpretive Reexamination of the Full Faith and Credit and Due Process Clauses*, 14 Creighton L. Rev. 499 ((1981); Kurt H. Nadelmann, *Full Faith and Credit to Judgments and Public Acts: A Historical–Analytical Reappraisal*, 56 Mich. L. Rev. 33 (1957).

[3] *See* Leflar, McDougal & Felix § 73.

[4] Act of May 26, 1790, Ch. 11, 1 Stat. 122.

[5] The preclusive effect of state judgments in federal courts is discussed in § 113, *infra*.

courts. Nevertheless, the Supreme Court consistently has required that state courts grant full faith and credit to federal court judgments.[6]

Because Congress has made only minimal efforts to implement the Full Faith and Credit Clause,[7] the courts have had the primary responsibility for developing the law in this area. Their strategy has been to apply the common law principles of res judicata "as though they were embodied in the constitutional provision."[8] Thus, the governing law of full faith and credit might be described as the interstate application of the doctrines of claim preclusion and issue preclusion.

One final point is worth noting about the Clause and the implementing statute. Although both refer to state *acts*, as well as judgments, the Supreme Court has not read either provision as having much effect on state court choice–of–law decisions. The states, subject only to minimal restrictions under the Due Process and Full Faith and Credit Clauses, remain free to apply their own law to litigation brought in their courts.[9]

[b] Enforcing the F–1 Judgment in F–2

A helpful way to begin a discussion of the enforcement of an F–1 judgment in F–2 is with a short review of how an F–1 judgment is enforced in F–1. An F–1 money judgment is enforced by a writ of execution[10] — typically, an order to a sheriff or other proper official to seize defendant's property, sell it at a judicial sale, and apply the proceeds to plaintiff's judgment. The natural and simple way, therefore, for F–2 to recognize the F–1 judgment would be for its courts to issue a writ of execution directly on the F–1 judgment. The Supreme Court, however, has never read the Full Faith and Credit Clause to require F–2 to enforce an F–1 judgment by so direct a procedure.[11] Instead, plaintiff must bring an action in F–2 based on the F–1 judgment.[12] The result of this action in F–2 is an F–2 judgment which may then be enforced by a writ of execution in F–2 by appropriate F–2 officials. This procedure is slow and clumsy, and the commentators have

---

[6] *See, e.g.*, Stoll v. Gottlieb, 305 U.S. 165 (1938). The preclusive effect of federal judgments in state courts is discussed in § 113, *infra*.

[7] Several commentators have advocated a stronger role for Congress in implementing the Clause. *See, e.g.*, Brainerd Currie, *Full Faith and Credit, Chiefly to Judgments: A Role for Congress,* 1964 Sup. Ct. Rev. 89; William Tucker Dean, Jr., *The Conflict of Conflict of Laws,* 3 Stan. L. Rev. 388 (1951). In one specialized area, Congress has been more active, specifying in the Parental Kidnapping Prevention Act, 28 U.S.C. 1738A, the preclusive effect of child custody decrees. *See* 130, *infra*.

[8] Leflar, McDougal & Felix § 73.

[9] §§ 97–100, *supra*, for a discussion of those limits.

[10] Some non–money judgments are self–executing; examples are a decree granting a divorce and a decree quieting title in a piece of property. Other non–money judgments — decrees ordering the doing of an act, for instance — are enforced by the contempt power of the court. *See generally* Fleming James, Jr., & Geoffrey C. Hazard, Jr. & John Leubsdorf, Civil Procedure § 1.20 (5th ed. 2001).

[11] M'Elmoyle v. Cohen, 38 U.S. (13 Pet.) 312 (1839).

[12] The F–1 judgment makes the F–1 defendant a judgment debtor of the F–1 plaintiff. Thus, the suit in F–2 for enforcement is basically an action in debt.

condemned it.[13] Plaintiff must file a complaint; defendant may answer and raise a defense;[14] even if the case can be disposed of via summary judgment, it could languish on the motion calendar in an F–2 court for several months. By the traditional enforcement procedure, therefore, there's many a slip twixt the cup (a valid F–1 judgment) and the lip (execution of a resultant F–2 judgment).

In the federal courts, a victorious plaintiff need not go through this clumsy exercise to enforce a money judgment in another district. Congress enacted a statute in 1948 which provides that a judgment of one district court may be "registered" in any other district.[15] The statute further provides that a "judgment so registered shall have the same effect as a judgment of the district court of the district where registered and may be enforced in like manner." In other words, the registered F–1 judgment becomes essentially an F–2 judgment, which can be enforced directly like any other F–2 judgment. There is no need for a separate suit, nor is there a requirement that the F–1 judgment debtor be notified.[16]

Congress probably has power under the Full Faith and Credit Clause to provide for a similar registration procedure for state court judgments, but it has not done so. The Conference of Commissioners on Uniform State Laws, however, has suggested a procedure which is analogous to the federal act. The Uniform Enforcement of Foreign Judgments Act (UEFJA)[17] provides for the "filing" of an F–1 judgment in the F–2 court. The Act (§ 2) then indicates:

> A judgment so filed has the same effect and is subject to the same procedures, defenses and proceedings for reopening, vacating, or staying as a judgment of a (District Court of any city or county) of this state and may be enforced or satisfied in like manner.

Although generally similar to the federal statute, the Uniform Act differs from the federal legislation in a few respects. First, it provides (§ 3) for notice to the F–1 judgment debtor. Further, it seems to contemplate litigation in F–2 of defenses to the F–1 judgment. Under the federal act, F–2 district courts typically have refused to hear defenses and instead have referred disputes concerning the judgment back to the court which rendered it. The differences between the federal act and the UEFJA are relatively

[13] *See, e.g.,* Leflar, McDougal & Felix § 78; Currie, *supra,* note 7; Robert H. Jackson, *Full Faith and Credit — The Lawyer's Clause of the Constitution,* 45 Colum. L. Rev. 1 (1945).

[14] Defenses to an action on an F–1 judgment are discussed in Part B of this Chapter.

[15] 28 U.S.C. § 1963. *See generally* Charles A. Wright, Arthur R. Miller, & Mary K. Kane, Federal Practice and Procedure §§ 2787 and 2865 (2d ed. 1995). *See also* Hershel Shanks & Steven A. Sandiford, *Schizophrenia in Federal Judgment Enforcement: Registration of Foreign Judgments Under 28 U.S.C. § 1963,* 59 Notre Dame L. Rev. 851 (1984).

[16] Wright, Miller & Kane, *supra* note 15.

[17] 13 U.L.A. 149 (1964). The Uniform Reciprocal Enforcement of Support Act (URESA), 9B U.L.A. 381 (1968), provides for a similar enforcement process for sister–state support orders. The Uniform Interstate Family Support Act 9 U.L.A. (PartIB) 235 (1996), successor to URESA and RURESA, retains the registration option, but also provides several mechanisms for the direct (i.e., without need for registration) enforcement of a support order in a sister state. *See* § 125, *infra.*

minor. Their collective effect has been a significant move toward the modernization of the enforcement procedures for F–1 judgments. The entire federal district court system is covered by 28 U.S.C. § 1963, and the UEFJA has been adopted in forty–one states.[18]

[c] Whose Law of Finality?

F–2 must give full faith and credit to the judgments of F–1's courts, but exactly how much faith and credit is required? The answer to the question is to be found in the law of res judicata — claim preclusion and issue preclusion. That answer, however, in turn raises another question: Whose law of res judicata — F–1's or F–2's? The law of claim preclusion and issue preclusion is not identical from state to state. The states differ on several questions: the dimensions of a cause of action (what counts as splitting a cause of action), the kinds of dismissals which are "on the merits," the persons who are considered to be parties and privies, and the rule of mutuality. Different positions on these issues will generate significantly different preclusive effects for the F–1 judgment.

[1] At Least as Much Preclusive Effect

If the preclusion law of F–2 is less preclusive than that of F–1, can F–2 apply its own law to the F–1 judgment, or do the Full Faith and Credit Clause and the implementing statute (§ 1738) compel it to apply the more preclusive law of F–1? Concrete examples of differences in preclusion law help to focus the question. Suppose Ohio has adopted the transactional theory of cause of action and thus requires an automobile accident plaintiff to bring all claims arising out of a particular incident in a single action. In contrast, Indiana, adhering to the older primary right theory, permits splitting the claim into one action for property damage and another for personal injury. If plaintiff sues first in Ohio for property damage and later in Indiana for personal injuries, what is Indiana's obligation under the Full Faith and Credit Clause? Must it apply Ohio's law precluding the personal injury claim or can it apply its own less preclusive rule?[19]

Issue preclusion also furnishes examples. Suppose that Maryland has abandoned the mutuality rule, but that Delaware has not.[20] After an airline accident in Delaware, A, a Marylander, sues the airline, a Delaware corporation, in Maryland and wins on the issue of the airline's negligence. Subsequently, B, a domiciliary of Delaware, sues the airline in Delaware and wants to use the result from the Maryland case to preclude the airline from re–litigating the negligence issue. Is Delaware free to use its own law,

---

[18] One additional state has adopted an earlier version of the act, 13 U.L.A. 189 (1948). Both acts are treated in greater detail in Leflar, McDougal & Felix § 78. *See also* Note, *Full Faith and Credit — Procedures for Enforcement of Foreign Money Judgments*, 17 Vand. L. Rev. 652 (1964). William C. Sturm, *Enforcement of Foreign Judgments*, 95 Com. L.J. 200 (1990).

[19] The example is suggested by Rush v. City of Maple Heights, 167 Ohio St. 221, 147 N.E.2d 599, *cert. denied*, 358 U.S. 814 (1958). The two different theories of cause of action are discussed in § 109[c], *supra*.

[20] The problem of mutuality is discussed in 109[e], *supra*.

to permit re–litigation of the airline's negligence; or must it apply Maryland's more preclusive law and thus preclude the issue?

The Supreme Court's answer in both hypotheticals is derived from a "plain meaning" analysis of the Full Faith and Credit Clause and statute (§ 1738), which requires that state–court judgments be given "the same faith and credit . . . as they have . . . in the courts of such state . . . from which they are taken."[21] The Court consistently has held that F–2 must give the F–1 judgment "at least the res judicata effect which the judgment would be accorded in the State which rendered it."[22] In other words F–2 must use F–1's law of judgments when that law is *more preclusive* than its own. Only by using the more preclusive law of F–1 can F–2 give the judgment as much effect as it would have in F–1.

Some commentators approve of the Court's rigid adherence to the law–of–the–rendering–state rule.[23] Others, however, use interest analysis to argue that F–2 should be able to use its own preclusion law in some situations.[24] Consider again the airline crash hypothetical and suppose that Delaware has retained the mutuality rule to protect its common carriers from serial litigation and ruinous liability in mass accident cases. Also suppose that Maryland's reason for abandoning the mutuality rule is to protect its courts from repetitive litigation and thus conserve judicial resources.[25] A diagram of the case[26] shows it to be — in interest analysis terminology[27] — a false conflict.

---

[21] 28 U.S.C. § 1738. The Court's use of the plain meaning analysis is discussed in detail and criticized in Sanford N. Caust–Ellenbogen, *False Conflicts and Interstate Preclusion: Moving Beyond a Wooden Reading of the Full Faith and Credit Statute*, 58 Fordham L. Rev. 593 (1990).

[22] Durfee v. Duke, 375 U.S. 106, 109 (1963). *See also* Restatement (Second) of Conflict of Laws §§ 94 & 95 (issues and persons affected by the judgment determined by the law of the rendering state).

Despite the apparent rigidity of this rule, it has at least one settled exception. The forum can apply its own statute of limitations barring an action to enforce the judgment when the suit would not be time–barred in the rendering state. M'Elmoyle v. Cohen, 38 U.S. (13 Pet.) 312 (1839). *See also* Watkins v. Conway, 385 U.S. 188 (1966).

Other exceptions are more controversial; the Supreme Court has limited the effect of the Full Faith and Credit Clause in worker's compensation and domestic relations cases. *See* § 117, *infra*.

[23] *See e.g.*, Ronan E. Degnan, *Federalized Res Judicata*, 85 Yale L. J. 741 (1976). *See also* Restatement (Second) of Conflict of Laws §§ 94 and 95. *But see* Paul Carrington, *Collateral Estoppel and Foreign Judgments*, 24 Ohio St. L.J. 381 (1963); Wright, Miller & Cooper, *supra* note 1, § 4467 (On issues at the "central core" of finality policy, F–2 must follow F–1's law, but need not with regard to "every last variation of preclusion policy.") For more on their suggestion, *see* Vernon, Weinberg, Reynolds & Richman 590–591.

[24] *See* Teply & Whitten, *supra* note 1, at 951–952; Caust–Ellenbogen, *supra* note 21.

[25] The hypothetical is adapted from Teply & Whitten, *supra* note 1, at 952.

[26] The diagrams of state contacts, law, and policy are explained in § 78, *supra*. *See also* William M. Richman, *Diagramming Conflicts: A Graphic Understanding of Interest Analysis*, 43 Ohio St. L.J. 317 (1982).

[27] Interest analysis is discussed at length in §§ 78–80, *supra*.

	Delaware	Maryland
	F–2	F–1
Contacts	Domicile of B (plaintiff #2) Domicile of Defendant airline	Domicile of A (plaintiff #1)
Law	Mutuality Rule	No Mutuality Rule
Policy	Protect common Carriers	Conserve judicial resources

Maryland's judicial resource conserving policy is not implicated because the second claim was brought in Delaware. Thus, applying Maryland law will not reduce the load on Maryland courts. Delaware's policy, however, is applicable. Applying Delaware law will protect a Delaware carrier. The analysis shows that Delaware is the only interested state. Thus, the case is a false conflict, and interest analysis would call for the application of Delaware law. Despite arguments of this type, the Supreme Court seems committed to the law–of–the–rendering–state rule.[28] That rule is required to implement the *national* policy of full faith and credit, which supersedes any analysis based only on the competing policies of the interested states.[29]

[2] More Preclusive Effect

What is the obligation of the enforcing state when its law of res judicata is *more* preclusive than that of the rendering state. If F–2 applies its own law, it will give the F–1 judgment more faith and credit than it would receive at home. Can F–2 do that, or do the Full Faith and Credit Clause and statute (§ 1738) require it to give the judgment as much effect as it would have at home *and no more*?

The airplane crash hypothetical again offers a useful example, but this time, reverse the order of the two suits. Suppose, in other words that A sues the defendant airline in Delaware and prevails on the issue of the defendant's negligence. Now B sues the defendant in Maryland and wants to use the Delaware result to preclude the negligence issue. Recall, that Delaware (F–1) has retained the mutuality rule and that Maryland (F–2) has abandoned it. Can the Maryland court apply its own law permitting non–mutual preclusion and thus give the Delaware judgment more faith and credit than it would receive at home? Or, is the Maryland court

[28] *See, e.g.*, Marrese v. American Academy of Orthopaedic Surgeons, 470 U.S. 373 (1985); Migra v. Warren City School District Board of Education, 465 U.S. 75 (1984); Allen v. McCurry, 449 U.S. 90 (1980); Durfee v. Duke, 375 U.S. 106 (1963).

[29] *See* Fauntleroy v. Lum, 210 U.S. 230 (1908).

constrained by the full faith and credit requirement to give the Delaware judgment no more faith and credit than a Delaware court would?[30]

Arguments can be marshalled on both sides. On the one hand, it is hard to see how giving the Delaware judgment more faith and credit than it would receive in Delaware could possibly offend that state or jeopardize national unity, the goal of the Full Faith and Credit Clause. The clause and § 1738 were designed to prevent under–recognition of sister–state judgments, not over–recognition. Further it makes no sense to allow Delaware to force a Maryland court to expend judicial resources adjudicating an issue that Maryland law considers settled.[31]

On the other hand, § 1738 requires F–2 to give the judgment "the *same* full faith and credit" it would receive in F–1, and "the same" could be read literally to mean "as much and no more." Further, in some cases it might be seriously unfair to give a judgment more preclusive effect than it would receive in the rendering state. Suppose, for instance, in the airplane crash case that the first plaintiff's injuries were slight, and her damage demand low. The defendant might rely on Delaware's mutuality rule and mount only a limited defense, confident that other more seriously injured plaintiffs could not use the results from the first suit against it. In a subsequent suit by one of those plaintiffs in Maryland, it would be unfair for the Maryland court to apply its own law permitting non–mutual issue preclusion.[32]

These nicely balanced arguments notwithstanding, the Supreme Court may have settled the issue in *Marrese v. American Academy of Orthopedic Surgeons*,[33] the Court held that § 1738 prohibits a federal court from giving a state judgment more preclusive effect than it would receive in the state's own courts. Might the holding apply only when the second forum is a federal court and thus leave state courts free to grant more preclusive effect to a sister–state judgment? Certainly the Court's most forceful statements on the more–faith–and–credit issue all have involved federal courts,[34] but

[30] The hypothetical is modeled on Hart v. American Airlines Inc., 61 Misc.2d 41, 304 N.Y.S.2d 810 (Sup.Ct. 1969). The New York (F–2) court applied New York law and gave non–mutual issue preclusion effect to a Texas judgment even though Texas retained the mutuality rule and would not have precluded the issue. *See also* Finley v. Kesling, 105 Ill. App.3d 1, 433 N.E.2d 1112 (1982)(Same; F–1 was Indiana; F–2, Illinois). *But see* Columbia Casualty Co. v. Playtex FP, Inc., 584 A.2d 1214 (1991)(Delaware (F–2) would not apply its own law to give Kansas judgment more faith and credit than would Kansas; instead Delaware should apply Kansas' mutuality rule.)

[31] *See* Robert C. Casad, *Intersystem Issue Preclusion and the Restatement (Second) of Judgments*, 66 Cornell L. Rev. 510, 523 (1981), Jeffrey E. Lewis, *Mutuality in Conflict—Flexibility and Full Faith and Credit*, 23 Drake L. Rev. 364 (1974).

[32] These arguments appear in Barbara A. Atwood, *State Court Judgments in Federal Litigation: Mapping the Contours of Full Faith and Credit*, 58 Ind. L.J. 59, 70 n. 54 (1982). The hypothetical assumes that preclusion law affects the behavior of litigants; on that question, *see* Howard M. Erichson, *Interjurisdictional Preclusion*, 96 Mich. L. Rev. 945, 992–993 (1998).

[33] 470 U.S. 373 (1985). For commentary on *Marrese*, *see* Shreve & Raven–Hansen, § 15.11[1]; Gene R. Shreve, *Preclusion and Federal Choice of Law*, 64 Tex. L. Rev. 1209 (1986); Stephen B. Burbank, *Afterwards: A Response to Professor Hazard and a Comment on Marrese*, 70 Cornell L. Rev. 659 (1985).

[34] *See* Parsons Steel Inc. v. First Alabama Bank, 474 U.S. 518 (1986); Migra v. Warren City School District Board of Education, 465 U.S. 75 (1984).

nothing in the law of full faith and credit supports such a limitation on the holding in *Marrese*. Section 1738 binds state courts as well as federal courts. The Full Faith and Credit Clause binds state courts and not federal courts, but that distinction cuts in the wrong direction. It cannot support an argument that state courts should be more free than federal courts to give greater preclusion effect to the F–1 judgment.[35]

§ 111 Full Faith and Credit for In Rem Proceedings

When a court exercises some form of in rem jurisdiction over property within the state, are the proceedings entitled to full faith and credit in the courts of sister states? As posed, the question is too broad and thus confusing. In fact it encompasses at least three constituent questions: First, what effect must the forum give to a sister–state judgment that purports to create or destroy interests in the property? Second, what if the rendering state exceeds its limited authority and issues a judgment that purports to create or destroy personal obligations? Is the judgment entitled to full faith and credit? Finally, what respect does the forum owe to the findings made by the rendering court on contested issues of fact?[1]

[a] Recognition of Interests in the Property

An F–1 in rem, quasi–in–rem, or attachment judgment is entitled to full faith and credit in F–2.[2] To understand what full faith and credit means in this context, recall that the effect of a property based judgment *in F–1* is very limited. A court that has only property–based jurisdiction cannot order defendant to perform an act, nor can it decree that defendant is a judgment debtor of plaintiff. All that it can do is adjudicate the rights of persons in the thing over which it has jurisdiction.[3] Its judgment can do no more than create or destroy interests in the *res*. F–2's obligation under the Full Faith and Credit Clause, then, is simply to recognize as valid the interests created by the F–1 judgment.

Suppose, for instance, a probate proceeding in Iowa validates *T*'s will and, pursuant to its terms, gives *A* title to *T*'s car. *A* takes the car into Illinois, where *B* sues him for it. *B* is an heir of T's who was not subject to the personal jurisdiction of the Iowa probate court, but who did receive adequate notice of the Iowa probate action. The Illinois court must dismiss *B*'s action because the Iowa court had in rem jurisdiction over the assets of *T*'s estate located in Iowa (including the car). Illinois must accord the Iowa decree full faith and credit and recognize *A*'s title to the car, even though Iowa lacked personal jurisdiction over *B*.[4]

---

[35] *See* Shreve & Raven–Hansen, § 15.11[2].

[1] *See generally* Charles A. Wright, Arthur R. Miller, Edward A. Cooper, Federal Practice and Procedure § 4431, Restatement (Second) of Judgments § 30. The organization of the topic here parallels that of the Restatement.

[2] Restatement (Second) of Conflict of Laws, Ch. 5, Topic 2, Introductory Note.

[3] *See* § 41, *supra,* for the distinction between the powers of a court with in personam jurisdiction and one with in rem jurisdiction.

[4] *See* Restatement (Second) of Judgments § 30(1).

[b] Binding the Parties Personally

If an F–1 court with only property–based jurisdiction exceeds its limited powers and purports to issue a personal judgment against defendant, that judgment is not entitled to full faith and credit in F–2.[5] Suppose, for example, creditor lends money to debtor and receives as security a mortgage on land in F–1. Upon debtor's default, creditor sues her in F–1 to foreclose the mortgage. The F–1 court, of course, has jurisdiction over the F–1 land and can foreclose the mortgage, but, unless it has personal jurisdiction over debtor, the F–1 court cannot issue a deficiency judgment. If it purports to do so, that judgment will not be entitled to full faith and credit in F–2.

The well known case of *Combs v. Combs*[6] is a variation of the last hypothetical case. Debtor owed creditor a considerable sum of money and, to secure that debt, gave creditor a lien on debtor's land in Arkansas. Creditor sued debtor in Kentucky (F–2) on the debt. Before process could be served on debtor, however, he sued creditor in Arkansas (F–1) to remove the lien on the F–1 land. Creditor was not subject to the in personam jurisdiction of the Arkansas court. Debtor alleged that he was indebted to creditor, that creditor had a lien on his land, and that he had paid a part of the debt. Debtor asked the court to permit him to pay the remainder into court and to cancel the lien as a cloud on his title. The Arkansas court granted debtor's request; it fixed the sum he owed creditor (the original debt less the amount he claimed to have paid), ordered debtor to pay the balance into court, and extinguished the lien. Debtor then appeared in the Kentucky (F–2) action and argued that the findings of the Arkansas court precluded litigation of the amount of the debt in Kentucky. The Kentucky court rejected the argument. It held that the Arkansas court, because it had in rem jurisdiction over the land, could extinguish creditor's interest in it. But absent personal jurisdiction over creditor, Arkansas could not extinguish the underlying obligation.

The lesson to be drawn from the hypothetical case and *Combs* is really quite simple. An F–1 in rem judgment is entitled to full faith and credit in F–2, but its effect is limited by the authority of the court that rendered it. That authority consists only of the power to adjudicate the interests of persons in the *res*. If the F–1 court exceeds that authority and purports to adjudicate the personal rights of parties over whom it lacks jurisdiction, its *ultra vires* act is not entitled to full faith and credit in F–2.

[c] Preclusion of Litigated Issues

The preceding subsections indicate the very limited effect that an F–1 in rem *judgment* can have on a subsequent suit in F–2. There is, however, another way in which an in rem proceeding can affect later litigation. The doctrine of issue preclusion may prohibit relitigation in F–2 of *issues* actually litigated in F–1 regardless of the basis of the F–1 court's jurisdiction. Thus, in some circumstances, the *findings* of the F–1 court may be

[5] *Id.*, § 30(2).

[6] 249 Ky. 155, 60 S.W.2d 368 (1933).

entitled to full faith and credit. Often, no issues will be actually litigated in an in rem, quasi–in–rem, or attachment action, because defendant will default. If the court permits defendant to make a limited appearance, however,[7] the parties will litigate the issues essential to an adjudication of their interests in the res. The court's findings on those issues may preclude subsequent relitigation of them in F–2.

The leading case is *Harnischfeger Sales Corp. v. Sternberg Dredging Co.*[8] There, seller sold a dredge to buyer and received in return a series of notes for the purchase price and a chattel mortgage on the dredge. Buyer defaulted, and seller sued in Louisiana. He sought to foreclose the chattel mortgage and to obtain a personal judgment as well. Both parties appeared in the action and litigated the merits, the principal issue being whether the dredge fulfilled seller's warranty that it would handle a "two–yard bucket." The trial court found for seller, foreclosed the chattel mortgage, and ordered the dredge sold; it also issued a personal judgment against buyer for the amount of the debt. On appeal, however, the Louisiana Supreme Court held that the trial court lacked in personam jurisdiction over buyer; accordingly, it affirmed the trial court's foreclosure order, but reversed its in personam judgment. The effective result of the appellate court's action was that buyer had been allowed to make a *limited appearance:* He was permitted to litigate the merits of the action without being bound by the in personam jurisdiction of the court.

Seller next sued buyer in Mississippi for the remainder of the debt (the original amount less the proceeds from the sale of the dredge). Buyer again set up the "two–yard bucket" defense, but this time he claimed that seller's representations constituted fraud. Seller argued that the defense was precluded by the findings in the Louisiana action. The Mississippi Supreme Court held that the "two–yard bucket" issue, whether styled a "fraud" or a "breach of warranty," was precluded by the full litigation of the question in Louisiana.

To understand precisely the holding of *Harnischfeger,* it is important to note that seller did not sue buyer in Mississippi *to enforce the Louisiana judgment.* The limited effect of that in rem judgment had already been exhausted by the sale of the dredge. Rather, seller sued buyer in Mississippi *on the original debt.* The effect of the Louisiana proceeding on the subsequent action in Mississippi was simply to preclude relitigation of a particular defense. Thus, *Harnischfeger* stands for this proposition: If, in an in rem, quasi–in–rem, or attachment action in F–1, defendant makes a limited appearance and the parties litigate the merits, the F–1 court's *findings* on issues *actually litigated* will preclude subsequent relitigation of those issues in F–2, even though the F–1 court lacked personal jurisdiction over defendant.

---

[7] *See* § 43, *supra,* for a description of the limited appearance.

[8] 189 Miss. 73, 191 So. 94 (1939). For a detailed, if dated, discussion of *Harnischfeger, see* Charles W. Taintor II, *Foreign Judgment In Rem: Full Faith and Credit v. Res Judicatea In Personam,* 8 Pitt. L. Rev. 221 (1942).

The argument in favor of the *Harnischfeger* principle relies on the policies that favor issue preclusion generally.[9] There has been one determination of the issue, and that determination cost the parties and the court valuable resources. Another determination will expend more resources without any reason to believe that a more just result will ensue. Moreover, the defendant, by choosing to make a limited appearance, showed that he could litigate effectively in F–1. Absent a showing that defendant's opportunity or incentive[10] to litigate the issue in F–1 was not sufficient to produce a fair adversarial determination, issue preclusion should apply.

The argument against *Harnischfeger*[11] is that it destroys the value of the limited appearance. The point of that device is to permit defendant to defend his interest in the property without requiring him to submit to the personal jurisdiction of the F–1 court. If the F–1 court's findings are entitled to issue preclusion effect, the result for defendant is nearly as damaging as an in personam judgment.[12]

On balance, the *Harnischfeger* principle is justified. The limited appearance is a device for mitigating the unfairness to defendant which existed under traditional attachment jurisdiction practice. *Shaffer v. Heitner*[13] and *Rush v. Savchuk*[14] eliminate that unfairness. No forum can exercise jurisdiction over defendant's interest in a piece of property, absent an adequate connection among the defendant, the forum, and the litigation. There may still be cases where the limited appearance prevents unfairness at the margin, but concern for the integrity of that device easily can be overstated in the post–*Shaffer* era. That concern ought not be permitted to outweigh the policies of finality and judicial economy that underlie the doctrine of issue preclusion.

---

[9] The arguments for and against the *Harnischfeger* rule are carefully analyzed in Wright, Miller, and Cooper, *supra* note 1, § 4431. The American Law Institute has adopted the *Harnischfeger* principle. Restatement (Second) of Judgments §§ 30(3) and 32(3).

[10] Such a showing might be made by demonstrating that F–1 was a terribly inconvenient forum for defendant and that his defense was significantly hampered. Or defendant might show that the value of the property at issue in F–1 was too low to prompt a really spirited defense. *See* Eugene F. Scoles, *Interstate Preclusion by Prior Litigation*, 74 Nw. U. L. Rev. 742, 755 (1979).

[11] Not all states adhere to the *Harnischfeger* principle; some permit re–litigation of issues determined in a prior in rem action in which defendant has made a limited appearance. Suppose plaintiff brings an attachment action against defendant in such a state; defendant makes a limited appearance, litigates the merits, and loses. Plaintiff now brings an in personam action against defendant in a state that adheres to the *Harnischfeger* rule? Can the second state preclude defendant from re–litigating the issues even though the first state would not? This is just a specialized example of the "more faith and credit" problem discussed in § 110[c][2], *supra*. *See* Michael H. Hoffheimer, *Mississippi Conflict of Laws*, 67 Miss. L.J. 175, 198 (1997), Robert C. Casad, *Intersystem Issue Preclusion and the Restatement (Second) of Judgments*, 66 Cornell L. Rev. 510, 530 (1981).

[12] Nearly, but not quite. Issue preclusion applies only to issues actually litigated, so defendant would be permitted to raise new defenses in the F–2 action — defenses that were not litigated in F–1. Thus, in *Harnischfeger,* buyer could not litigate the "two–yard bucket" issue in Mississippi, but he could litigate some other defense, such as payment of the note.

[13] 433 U.S. 186 (1977), discussed in § 45, *supra*.

[14] 444 U.S. 320 (1980), discussed in § 46, *supra*.

§ 112 Recognition of Foreign Nation Judgments[1]

The Full Faith and Credit Clause does not apply to the judgments of foreign nations. Rather, courts in the United States recognize those judgments based on the principle of comity. Comity is the "recognition which one nation allows within its territory to the legislative, executive or judicial acts of another nation, having due regard both to international duty and convenience, and to the rights of its own citizens or of other persons who are under the protection of its laws."[2] The principle is not compelled by the Constitution; rather, the states of the United States are free to interpret it as they will.

An early interpretation by the Supreme Court clouded the issue considerably. In *Hilton v. Guyot,*[3] plaintiff, a French citizen, sued two New Yorkers in France and recovered a judgment against them. He then sued in a federal court in New York on the French judgment. The Supreme Court held that the judgment was not entitled to conclusive recognition. It distinguished among foreign national judgments based on the parties to the action. In the following three cases, the foreign judgment is entitled to recognition subject only to ordinary defenses:[4] (1) both parties are citizens of the foreign state; (2) defendant is a citizen of the foreign state, but plaintiff is not; (3) plaintiff is a citizen of the foreign state, defendant is not, and judgment is for defendant. However, where a citizen of the foreign state recovers a judgment against a non–citizen, the Court injected an additional requirement — the requirement of reciprocity. Because the Court found that a judgment from an American court against a French citizen would not be conclusive in a French court, it denied conclusive effect to the French judgment against the American citizen.

This tit–for–tat principle of retaliation has been criticized by the commentators,[5] and with good reason. It makes little sense to penalize a private person (the foreign plaintiff) for the acts of his country's courts. The policies that control the law of res judicata generally — fairness, repose, and judicial economy — should govern here as well.[6]

---

[1] A fine short treatment of this topic appears in Leflar, McDougal & Felix § 84. For a much longer and more detailed treatment, *see* Scoles, Hay, Borchers & Symeonides §§ 24.33–24.45.

[2] Hilton v. Guyot, 159 U.S. 113 (1895).

[3] *Id.* Before *Hilton*, early English and American case law held that a foreign nation judgment was only *prima facie* evidence of the justice of the underlying claim. Thus all defenses that could have been raised to the original claim could also be interposed in the suit on the foreign judgment. Isolated examples of this view survived until very late; *see* Svenska Handelsbanken v. Carlson, 258 F. Supp. 448 (D. Mass 1966)(a federal court read 150–year–old Massachusetts case law to give only prima facie effect to a Swedish judgment). For a discussion of the early cases, *see* Courtland H. Peterson, *Foreign Country Judgments and the Second Restatement of Conflict of Laws*, 72 Colum. L. Rev. 220, 224–227 (1972).

[4] *See* text at note 11, *infra*, for a discussion of defenses.

[5] *See* Leflar, McDougal & Felix § 84; Scoles, Hay, Borchers & Symeonides§ 24.34; Restatement (Second) of Conflict of Laws § 98, comment e. Arthur Lenhoff, *Reciprocity and the Law of Foreign Judgments: A Historical–Critical Analysis*, 16 La. L. Rev. 465 (1956).

[6] A more complete discussion of the policies relevant to the recognition of foreign–nation judgments appears in Robert C. Casad, *Issue Preclusion and Foreign Country Judgments: Whose Law?*, 70 Iowa L. Rev. 53, 61 (1984).

Fortunately, *Hilton* has had relatively little influence. Because the Court's holding was not based on the Constitution or federal legislation, it does not bind state courts, and many have rejected it.[7] Further limiting the influence of *Hilton* is the holding of federal courts that the *Erie* decision compels them to apply state rather than federal law on the issue.[8] Thus, in a diversity case, federal courts do not follow the reciprocity rule if it has been rejected by the courts of the state where the federal court sits.

The modern trend among American courts is toward giving the judgments of foreign nations the same respect that is given the judgments of sister states.[9] Thus, most courts will recognize a foreign nation judgment as conclusive unless there is some adequate defense. The Restatement (Second) of Conflicts is somewhat more cautious, requiring recognition only when the foreign–nation judgment resulted from a "fair trial in a contested proceeding" and only "so far as the immediate parties and the underlying transaction are concerned."[10]

The defenses against a foreign nation judgment generally parallel those which are available against a sister state judgment.[11] Thus, a foreign court judgment may be attacked on the ground that the rendering court lacked jurisdiction, or that it was procured by fraud, or that it is a penal judgment. One defense, however, operates very differently in the two different contexts. Against interstate judgments, the public policy of F–2 (the recognizing court) is rarely a useful defense.[12] In the international context, by contrast, this concept has far greater impact, as it should. There are nations whose legal systems and judgments incorporate concepts which an American court could not recognize — for instance, slavery, *de jure* racism, or

[7] A prime example is Johnston v. Compagnie Generale Transatlantique, 242 N.Y. 381, 152 N.E. 121 (1926).

[8] *See, e.g.*, Somportex, Ltd. v. Philadelphia Chewing Gum Corp., 453 F.2d 435 (3d Cir. 1971). The *Erie* decision is discussed in § 104, *supra*.

[9] *See* Scoles, Hay, Borchers & Symeonides § 24.35. An example of the trend is Somportex Ltd. v. Philadelphia Chewing Gum Corp., 453 F.2d 435 (3d Cir. 1971), *cert. denied,* 405 U.S. 1017 (1972), in which the court held an English default judgment was entitled to recognition in a federal court in Pennsylvania.

[10] Restatement (Second) of Conflict of Laws § 98. The "contested proceeding" language seems to disqualify default judgments, but comment e is more generous. It suggests that a default judgment should be recognized provided that the court had jurisdiction and the defendant received adequate notice and an opportunity to be heard. Jurisdiction should be measured by American due process standards, *i.e.,* the minimum contacts standard of International Shoe v. Washington, 326 U.S. 310 (1945). *See* § 20[a], *supra*. For commentary, *see* Peterson, *supra* note 3, at 245–247.

[11] *See* §§ 114–117, *infra,* for a discussion of the defenses to sister state judgments. In the interstate context F–2 must apply the law of judgments (including defenses to judgments) of F–1. Thus the law of F–1 will control such questions as the extent of claim and issue preclusion, whether the judgment is on the merits, what counts as fraud, whether the judgment is modifiable, etc. In the international context, however, an American state *is not* required to apply the foreign's state's law of judgments and may apply its own instead. Whether an American state *should* apply the law of the foreign nation is another question. The authorities are in conflict. For an excellent discussion of the relevant case law, and the position of the American Law Institute, *see* Casad, *supra*, note 6.

[12] *See* § 117, *infra*.

caste or tribal distinctions.[13] But for the judgments of most countries, the scope given to the public policy defense should be quite narrow — nearly as narrow as it is in the interstate context.

As indicated in the discussion of *Hilton*, the recognition to be accorded to a foreign–nation judgment is governed largely by state law.[14] The area has not been pre–empted by federal statute, treaty or common law. That is unfortunate because uniformity is quite crucial and where the national interest is strong because of the impact on foreign relations and foreign trade.[15] One possible way to produce uniformity would be by entering mutual recognition treaties with our principal trading partners.

The members of the European Economic Community along with the members of the European Free Trade Association have concluded mutual recognition agreements,[16] providing nearly all of Western Europe with the practical equivalent of a full faith and credit clause.

The prospects that the United States will adopt a similar strategy are improving. Until recently, there seemed little likelihood that the United States would participate in an international judgments recognition regime. After extensive negotiations between the United States and the United Kingdom between 1974 and 1976, the parties initialed a draft convention, but there was resistance in Britain based on unwillingness to recognize "excessive" American tort damage awards and treble–damage antitrust judgments. In 1980, the negotiations were suspended indefinitely.[17]

---

[13] *See* Restatement (Third) of Foreign Relations Law of the United States § 482(1)(a), (2)(d), requiring non–recognition if the foreign judicial system does not provide impartial tribunals or fair procedures, and permitting non–recognition of a judgment based on a cause of action "repugnant to the public policy" of an American jurisdiction.

[14] *See* Aetna Life Ins. Co. v. Tremblay, 223 U.S. 185 (1912), in which the Supreme Court held that Maine's refusal to recognize a Canadian judgment did not raise a federal question.

[15] Thus many commentators prefer a uniform federal solution. *See, e.g.*, Scoles, Hay, Borchers & Symeonides § 24.38; Casad, *supra* note 6, at 77. *But see* Peterson, *supra* note 3, 238 (most issues concerning recognition and effect of judgments — priority, mutuality, jurisdiction and even public policy — can be left safely to the states without fear of disrupting foreign policy). Those favoring a uniform national solution were encouraged by Zschernig v. Miller, 389 U.S. 429 (1968), in which the Supreme Court struck down an Oregon law that prohibited distributions from Oregon estates to claimants who resided in foreign countries unless (1) American citizens enjoyed the reciprocal right to take from decedent's estates in those countries, and (2) the foreign claimant had the right to receive the proceeds "without confiscation." The Court held the statute "an intrusion in the federal domain" of foreign policy. *Zschernig*, however, seems to have been an isolated occurrence; a federal common law of recognition of foreign nation judgments does not seem to be forthcoming from the Supreme Court.

[16] The Brussels Convention on Jurisdiction and the Enforcement of Judgments in Civil and Commercial Matters, September 27, 1968, applies to the EEC, and the parallel Lugano Convention on Jurisdiction and Enforcement of Judgments in Civil and Commercial Matters, September 16, 1988 includes the six additional nations of the European Free Trade Association. *See* Scoles, Hay, Borchers & Symeonides 24.38. For commentary on the two conventions, see Robert Reuland, *The Recognition of Judgments in the European Community: The Twenty-Fifth Anniversary of the Brussels Convention*, 14 Mich. J. Int'l L. 559 (1993); Patrick J. Borchers, *Comparing Personal Jurisdiction in the United States and the European Community: Lessons for American Reform*, 40 Am. J. Comp. L. 121, 131–2 (1992).

[17] *See* Andreas Lowenfeld, Conflict of Laws 732–734 (2d ed. 1998).

In 1992, however, the United States proposed that the Hague Conference on Private International Law prepare a convention on jurisdiction and the recognition of judgments in civil and commercial matters. The member states of the Hague Conference took up the challenge and produced a draft convention in 1999.[18]

Another possibility is the adoption by the states of uniform legislation recognizing foreign judgments. The Conference of Commissioners on Uniform State laws has made such a proposal, and the Uniform Foreign Money Judgments Recognition Act has been adopted in thirty–one states.[19]

The most obvious way to produce uniformity and national control in this area would be for Congress to enact a statute specifying the extent to which American courts must recognize foreign nation judgments, but that proposal does not seem to be near the top of anyone's legislative agenda.[20]

§ 113 Full Faith and Credit and Federal Courts

The application of full faith and credit law to federal courts generates many of the same questions that inter–state application does. There are, however, enough differences to warrant separate consideration of the problem. This section first considers the unique problems generated when the federal court is the rendering court (F–1) and then treats those that arise when the federal court is the recognizing court (F–2).

---

[18] A preliminary draft of a convention was adopted by the Special Commission in October of 1999, *see* www.hcch.net/e/conventions/draft36e.html, Scoles, Hay, Borchers & Symeonides § 24.39; the most recent development was an experts meeting to discuss the intellectual property implications of the convention. *See* www.hcch.net/e/workprog/wipo.html. When a final convention will appear and whether the United States will ratify it are, of course, uncertain. For commentary on the project, see Symposium, *Enforcing Judgments Abroad: The Global Challenge*, 24 Brook. J. Int'l L. 1–221 (1998) (articles by Mary Ellen Fullerton, Peter Pfund, Arthur von Mehren, Louise Lussier, Paul Beaumont, Friedrich Juenger, Ronald Brand, Patrick Borchers, and Russell Weintraub). *See also* Kevin Clermont, *Jurisdictional Salvation and the Hague Treaty*, 85 Cornell L. Rev. 89 (1999). From the perspective of the United States, a crucial issue will be whether the provisions of the Convention can trump the United States Supreme Court's rulings on the jurisdictional limitations imposed by the due process clause. *See* Symposium, *"Could a Treaty Trump Supreme Court Jurisdictional Doctrine?"* 61 Alb. L. Rev. 1159–1309 (1998) (articles by Professors Patrick Borchers, Stanley Cox, Harold Maier, Andrew Strauss, Russell Weintraub, and Joachim Zekoll).

Although the United States has not yet entered into mutual judgment recognition treaties, it is a party to the United Nations Convention on the Recognition and Enforcement of Foreign Arbitral Awards, 21 U.S.T. 2517, T.I.A.S. No. 6997, 330 U.N.T.S. 38. It requires American courts to enforce agreements to arbitrate and to recognize arbitral awards. For extensive commentary on the Convention, the American implementing legislation, and practice under both, *see* Comment, *International Commercial Arbitration Under the United Nations Convention and the Amended Federal Arbitration Statute*, 47 Wash. L. Rev. 441 (1972).

[19] 13 U.L.A. 261 (2000 Supp.).

[20] The American Law Institute is in the process of drafting such a statute to recommend to Congress. *See* International Jurisdiction and Judgments Project, Discussion Draft (March 29, 2002).

[a] Recognition of Federal Court Judgments

Neither the Full Faith and Credit Clause nor the implementing statute (28 U.S.C. § 1738) require that state or federal courts give full faith and credit to federal court judgments. The clause and the statute address in terms only state–court judgments.[1] Nevertheless it is clear that federal court judgments are entitled to full faith and credit; any other result would be "unthinkable."[2]

There remains, however, a choice–of–law issue for the recognizing court. What set of preclusion principles must the recognizing court apply to the federal court judgment — its own, the law of the state where the federal court sits, or a set of federal common law rules of preclusion?[3] The source of preclusion law when federal courts adjudicate questions of federal law has long been clear; principles of federal common law govern and must be applied in all recognizing courts, state or federal.[4]

For many years, however, there was no equal clarity on the preclusion principles to be applied to the judgment of a federal court sitting in diversity jurisdiction.[5] The Supreme Court settled the issue in *Semtek International, Inc. v. Lockheed Martin Corp.*[6] After plaintiff sued the defendant in California state court, defendant removed to the proper California federal court, which granted the defendant's motion to dismiss the claim as barred by federal court, which granted the defendant's motion to dismiss the claim as barred by California's two-year statute of limitations. The plaintiff also sued the defendant in state court in Maryland where its claims were not barred by the applicable three-year statute of limitations. The Maryland court dismissed on grounds of res judicata, and the Maryland appellate

[1] *See* Restatement (Second) of Judgments § 87, comment a; Shreve & Raven–Hansen § 15.10[4]; Ronan E. Degnan, *Federalized Res Judicata*, 85 Yale L.J. 741, 744 (1976).

[2] Charles A. Wright, Arthur R. Miller & Edward H. Cooper, Federal Practice and Procedure § 4468.

[3] This question has attracted substantial attention from the commentators. *See, e.g.*, Wright, Miller & Cooper, *supra* note 2; Degnan, *supra* note 1; Stephen B. Burbank, *Interjurisdictional Preclusion, Full Faith and Credit and Federal Common Law: A General Approach*, 71 Cornell L. Rev. 733 (1986).

[4] Deposit Bank v. Frankfort, 191 U.S. 499 (1903); Wright, Miller & Cooper, *supra* note 2, at 656. An example of the Supreme Court's fashioning of federal common law to control the preclusive effects of federal court judgments in federal question cases is Parklane Hosiery v. Shore, 439 U.S. 322 (1979)(offensive use of non–mutual issue preclusion is permissible in most cases).

[5] The Supreme Court has not settled the issue, *see* Heiser v. Woodruff, 327 U.S. 762 (1945)(issue expressly left open); and the lower courts have disagreed. *Compare* Lane v. Sullivan, 900 F.2d 1247 (8th Cir. 1990)(law of the state where the federal court sits); Hunt v. Liberty Lobby, Inc., 707 F.2d 1493 (D.C. Cir. 1983)(same); *with* Hauser v. Krupp Steel Producers, Inc., 761 F.2d 204 (5th Cir. 1985)(federal law governs); Kern v. Hettinger, 303 F.2d 333 (2d Cir. 1962)(same). A recent update on the issue is Gene R. Shreve, *Judgments From a Choice–of–Law Perspective,* 40 Am. J. Comp. L. 985 (1992). For commentary on the decision, see Gene R. Shreve, *Judgments From a Choice–of–Law Perspective,* 40 Am. J. Comp. L. 985 (1992).

[6] 531 U.S. 497 (2001). For commentary on the decision, see Stephen B. Burbank, *Semtek, Forum Shopping, And Federal Common Law,* 77 Notre Dame L. Rev. 1027 (2002); *Leading Cases*, 115 Harv. L. Rev. 467 (2001).

court affirmed, holding that federal principles of res judicata determined the preclusive effect of the California federal court judgment.[7] The Supreme Court granted certiorari.

In a short unanimous opinion by Justice Scalia, the Supreme Court reversed. The opinion first rejected the defendant's contention that the preclusion effect of a federal diversity judgment was settled by *Dupasseur v. Rochereau,*[8] which held that state law applied. *Dupasseur,* however, was decided under the Conformity Act, which required federal courts to apply the procedural law of the forum state. Since the Conformity Act had been superseded by the Federal Rules of Civil Procedure, *Dupasseur* was no longer controlling precedent.

The court next rejected the defendant's argument that federal rule 41(b),[9] required dismissal of the plaintiff's claim because the California federal judgment was "upon the merits" according to its terms. In a strained interpretation, Justice Scalia held that rule 41(b) controlled only the plaintiff's ability to refile the dismissing court, not the preclusive effect of the dismissal upon litigation elsewhere.

Having disqualified *Dupasseur* and federal rule 41(b), Justice Scalia also noted that neither the constitutional clause nor the full faith and credit statute addressed in terms the preclusive effect due federal court judgments in state court. That left the Court free to devise a federal common law rule to govern the issue. The need for national uniformity might have counseled a rule requiring the application of federal preclusion law, but there was no such need since the substantive law controlling diversity cases is state and not federal law. Further, Justice Scalia concluded that the policies against intrastate forum shopping—the rationale for the *Erie* decision.[10] —applied. Accordingly, the Court fashioned a federal common law rule that determines the preclusive effect of a federal court diversity judgment by referring to the preclusion law of the state in which the federal court sits.[11]

Notwithstanding the convoluted discussion of Rule 41(b), the decision is a good one.[12] Preclusion rules can be substantive for *Erie* purposes; a clear

---

[7] 128 Md. App. 39, 736 A.2d 1104 (1999).

[8] 21 Wall. 130 (1875).

[9] Fed. R. Civ. P. 41(b).

[10] *See* § 104[b], *supra.*

[11] The Restatement (Second) of Judgments § 87 agrees: "Federal law determines the effects under the rules of res judicata of a judgment of a federal court." In comment b, however, the Restatement suggests that for diversity judgments the federal law of res judicata should incorporate state–law principles dealing with substantive legal relationships resulting in preclusion.

[12] Before *Semtek* the dominant view, associated with Professor Ronan Degnan, had been that federal law controls the preclusive effects of all federal–court judgments regardless of whether the rendering court was excercising federal question or diversity jurisdiction. The argument was that "determining the scope of its own judgments" is "[o]ne of the strongest policies a court can have. *See* Kern v. Hettinger, 303 F.2d 333, 340 (2d Cir. 1962). According to Professor Degnan, a court that lacks power is "less than a court," and the Constitution clearly contemplated that the federal courts be courts "in the fullest historical sense of the word."

Some more recent comentators disagreed. Before *Semtek* they argued that the many varying example is a state that retains the mutuality of estoppel rule in airplane disaster cases based on its desire to protect airlines from repetitive and ruinous liability. Second, differences between federal and state preclusion law could encourage forum shopping. If, for instance a state has retained the mutuality rule but the federal courts have abandoned it, an attorney for the victims of an air diaster would be wise to choose the federal court. If she wins the first case, her other clients will be able to use the result against the airline in successive cases. By contrast, victory in the state court would not have that added benefit.

[b] Recognition of State Judgments in Federal Courts

[1] In General

As a general matter federal courts must give full faith and credit to state–court judgments. The source of the requirements is not the Full Faith and Credit Clause, which, in terms, applies only when the recognizing court is a state court. Instead the obligation is based on the full faith and credit statute (28 U.S.C. § 1738), which requires "every court within the United States"[13] to give full faith and credit to state–court judgments.

Although statutory and not constitutional, the full faith and credit obligation of federal courts is rigorous, as is illustrated by the Supreme Court's decision in *Parsons Steel Inc. v. First Alabama Bank.*[14] Parsons brought a fraud action against the Bank in Alabama state court and a simultaneous action against the Bank in Alabama federal court based on federal legislation.[15] The federal action went to trial first; the Bank prevailed, and then pled the judgment as res judicata in the state case. The state court held the doctrine inapplicable and issued judgment in favor of Parsons.

---

substantive and procedural state and federal policies implicated by preclusion issues cannot be comprehended by a single rigid choice–of–law principle (federal law controls). Rather, specific rules should be crafted to deal with the particular policy balances required by individual preclusion issues. *See* Larry L. Teply & Ralph U. Whitten, Civil Procedure 963-968 (2d ed. 2000); Wright, Miller & Cooper, *supra* note 2, § 4472; Burbank, *supra* note 3.

[13] For further discussion of the statute, *see* § 110, *supra*. A number of decisions also locate the state-federal preclusion requirement in the limitations on the subject matter jurisdiction of the lower federal courts. The Rooker-Feldman Doctrine prohibits a lower federal court from reexamining state court proceedings because the authority to review such proceedings on appeal is located exclusively in the United States Supreme Court, see 28 U.S.C. § 1257. The doctrine gets its name from Rooker v. Fidelity Trust Co., 263 U.S. 413 (1923), and District of Columbia Court of Appeals v. Feldman, 460 U.S. 462 (1983). It is unclear what, if anything, is to be gained from recasting preclusion principles into rules of subject matter jurisdiction; further the attendant doctrinal confusion may produce mischief out of proportion to any possible gain. For detailed commentary, see Wright, Miller & Cooper § 4469.1.

[14] 474 U.S. 518 (1986). Plaintiffs were Parsons Steel Inc. and Jim and Melba Parsons; defendants were the Bank and one of its officers. For ease of discussion, the text refers to the plaintiffs as "Parsons" and, the defendants as "the Bank." The case is discussed further in Vernon, Weinberg, Reynolds & Richman 664–666.

[15] The Bank Holding Company Act, 12 U.S.C. §§ 1971–1978.

The Bank, having lost in the state case, filed a third action in Alabama federal court seeking to enjoin the Parsons from further prosecuting the state action. The district court held that the Alabama state court should have given claim preclusion effect to the original federal judgment and then granted the injunction. The Eleventh Circuit affirmed, holding the injunction proper under the "re–litigation exception" to the anti–injunction statute[16] which prohibits a federal court from enjoining state court actions except to protect or effectuate its (the federal court's) judgment.

The Supreme Court reversed unanimously, holding that the circuit court erred in failing to give the state court judgment the full preclusive effect it would have in Alabama state courts:

> We hold, therefore, that the Court of Appeals erred by refusing to consider the possible preclusive effect, under Alabama law, of the state-court judgment. Even if the state court mistakenly rejected respondents' claim of res judicata, this does not justify the highly intrusive remedy of a federal–court injunction against the enforcement of the state–court judgment. Rather, the Full Faith and Credit Act requires that federal courts give the state-court judgment, and particularly the state court's resolution of the res judicata issue, the same preclusive effect it would have had in another court of the same State. Challenges to the correctness of a state court's determination as to the conclusive effect of a federal judgment must be pursued by way of appeal through the state–court system and certiorari from this Court.

The Court scarcely could have found a more impressive way to make the point. The federal courts' general obligation under the full faith and credit statute to respect state–court judgments is every bit as rigorous as the constitutional obligation of a state to reorganize the judgments of another state. The obligation prevails even when the state–court judgment fails to give full faith and credit to a prior federal–court judgment. Thus, *Parsons* strongly re–enforces the Iron Law of Full Faith and Credit decreed by the Supreme Court in *Fauntleroy v. Lum*[17] and *Treines v. Sunshine Mining Co.*[18]

[2] Exceptions

The fact that the full faith and credit obligation on federal courts comes from the statute and not the constitution has one important implication. The statute, like all federal statutes, and unlike constitutional provisions, can be repealed or modified by Congress. In other words, Congress, by later legislation, could provide for exceptions to the full faith and credit statute and thus to the full faith and credit obligation of federal courts.[19] Indeed Congress has done so explicitly in the federal habeas corpus statute, which

16 28 U.S.C. § 2283.

17 210 U.S. 230 (1908), discussed in § 114[a], *infra*.

18 308 U.S. 66 (1939), discussed in § 114[b], *infra*.

19 *See* Shreve & Raven–Hansen § 15.10[2]; Gene R. Shreve, *Preclusion and Federal Choice of Law*, 64 Tex. L. Rev. 1209, 1223–4 (1986).

permits collateral attack in the federal district courts on state–court criminal convictions.[20]

It has been suggested that other federal legislation has modified or partially repealed the statute implicitly, thus leaving federal courts free to disregard state court proceedings in civil rights cases[21] and cases within the exclusive jurisdiction of federal courts.[22]

[3] Exclusive Jurisdiction

Suppose plaintiff sues defendant in state court based on state antitrust law. Plaintiff also has a federal antitrust claim against the defendant, but cannot pursue it in the state court because federal courts have exclusive jurisdiction over claims based on the federal antitrust laws.[23] Can the plaintiff later sue on the federal antitrust claim in federal court, or is that claim precluded by the prior state court action?

There are arguments against preclusion in such a case. First it is unfair to preclude plaintiff's federal claim when she could not have asserted that claim in the prior proceeding in state court. The rules of claim preclusion are designed in part to avoid piecemeal litigation; but if the splitting of the claim is required by jurisdictional rules, plaintiff ought not suffer.[24] Second precluding the federal claim might diminish the effectiveness of the federal legislative regime of which the claim is a part.

Based on considerations like these, the Restatement (Second) of Judgments concludes that plaintiff's exclusive jurisdiction antitrust claim should not be precluded by the prior state action.[25] But what if state law does not concur and provides for no such limitation on claim preclusion. Must the federal court apply state preclusion law and preclude the federal antitrust action or is it free — because of an implied exception to § 1738 — to hear the claim?

The Supreme Court had a chance to settle the issue in *Marrese v. American Academy of Orthopaedic Surgeons.*[26] On facts very similar to the hypothetical antitrust case posed above, the Court refused to determine whether the exclusive antitrust jurisdiction statutes worked an implied

---

[20] 28 U.S.C. § 2254.

[21] *See* text and footnotes in subsections [4] & [5], *infra.*

[22] *See* text and footnotes in subsection [3], *infra.*

[23] The example is suggested by Marrese v. American Academy of Orthopaedic Surgeons, 470 U.S. 373 (1985).

[24] *See* Restatement (Second) of Judgments § 26(1)(C) & comment c (1982). There is a counter–argument. Plaintiff could have pursued both claims in federal court if that court were willing to exercise supplemental jurisdiction over that state–law claim. *See* 28 U.S.C. § 1367. Thus it is not unfair to penalize the plaintiff for suing in a forum where her claim must be split because she could have chosen a forum where no split was required.

[25] *Id.*

[26] 470 U.S. 373 (1985). *Marrese* and the general problem of exceptions to the full faith and credit statute based on exclusive federal jurisdiction statutes are the subject of excellent commentary. *See* Wright Miller & Cooper, *supra* note 2, § 4470.1; Shreve & Raven–Hansen § 15.10[2]; Teply & Whitten, *supra* note 9, at 953–954; Shreve, *supra* note 16, at 1222 *et seq.*

partial repeal of the full faith and credit statute (§ 1738). Instead, the Court mandated a two–step analysis for such cases. First the federal court must examine state preclusion law to determine whether it would preclude a claim that (because of the exclusive jurisdiction statues) could not have been asserted in the prior proceeding.[27] Only if State law would preclude the claim is there a need to determine whether the exclusive jurisdiction statutes effect an implied partial repeal of § 1738 and permit the federal court to hear the claim in spite of state preclusion law.

The second question, said the Court, depends entirely on the intent of Congress in passing the exclusive jurisdiction statutes. To infer that intent, the court should consider the particular federal statute, the nature of the federal claim and issue, and the concerns underlying the particular grant of exclusive jurisdiction.

The Supreme Court in *Marrese* did not reach the second step of the required analysis. The lower courts had not followed step one and thus had not determined the preclusive effect of the state judgment under state law. If state law did not preclude the exclusive jurisdiction claim, there would be no need to consider whether the exclusive jurisdiction statute worked a partial repeal of § 1738. Accordingly, the Court remanded the case, instructing the lower courts to determine the preclusive effect of the state–court judgment under state law.

In *Matsushita Electrical Industrial Co. Ltd. v. Epstein,*[28] the Supreme Court applied both steps of the *Marrese* analysis. After Matsushita made a tender offer for the common stock of MCA, Inc., shareholders of MCA brought a class action in Delaware state court against MCA, its directors and Matsushita, stating various state–law claims. While that action was pending, members of the plaintiff class commenced a California federal–court class action against Matsushita based on the exclusive jurisdiction provisions of the Securities Exchange Act of 1934. After the district court dismissed the case and while it was on appeal to the Ninth Circuit, the parties to the Delaware action negotiated a settlement providing for a global release of all federal and state claims in return for the defendants' payment of $2 million into a settlement fund to be distributed to the class members. The California federal court plaintiff's did not opt out of the settlement. Matsushita then invoked the Delaware settlement as a bar to the federal court action, but the Ninth Circuit rejected the argument.

---

[27] The Court recognized that there was likely to be no state law on the precise issue of preclusion of exclusive federal jurisdiction claims:

> To be sure a state court will not have occasion to address the specific question whether a state judgment has issue or claim preclusion effect in a later action that can be bought only in federal court.

Nevertheless there would likely be state preclusion law on the general question whether a claim could be precluded by a prior proceeding even though it could not have been asserted in that proceeding.

[28] 516 U.S. 367 (1996). For more complete treatment of the case see Teply & Whitten, *supra* note 9, 955–958. For critical commentary on the decision see Wright, Miller & Cooper, *supra* note 2, § 4470 (2000 Supp.), Mollie A. Murphy, *The Interstate Class Settlement: Of Comity, Consent, And Collusion*, 47 U. Kan. L. Rev. 41 3 (1999).

The Supreme Court reversed. Initially the court held that the *Marrese* analytical framework was not inapplicable merely because the Delaware judgment flowed from a class action settlement. In step one of the analysis, the court concluded that, under Delaware law, a judgment based on a class action settlement would preclude subsequent claims even though they could not have been asserted in the class action proceeding.[29]

That left the question of an implied partial repeal of § 1738, which the Court had concluded in *Marrese* was entirely dependent upon the intent of Congress. Of course the Court found nothing in the language or legislative history of the Securities Exchange Act that was directly relevant to an exclusive–jurisdiction exception to § 1738. The opinion determined that the purpose of the exclusive–jurisdiction provision of the Act was "to achieve greater uniformity of construction and more effective and expert application of that law." Those purposes, it concluded, did not require an exception to the general rule of preclusion.

> When a state court upholds a settlement that releases claims under the Exchange Act, it threatens neither of these policies. There is no danger that state–court judges who are not fully expert in federal securities law will say definitively what the Exchange Act means and enforce legal liabilities and duties thereunder. And the uniform construction of the Act is unaffected by a state court's approval of a proposed settlement because the state court does not adjudicate the Exchange Act claim but only evaluates the overall fairness of the settlement . . .[30]

Marrese and *Epstein* do not settle completely the question of implied partial repeal of § 1738 by subsequent exclusive jurisdiction statutes. *Marrese*, of course, did not address the issue, and the settlement and class action complications of *Epstein* prohibit a completely confident prediction of the Court's ultimate resolution of the issue. Nevertheless, both cases suggest that the Court rarely will find sufficient evidence of congressional intent in an exclusive-jurisdiction statute to limit the full faith and credit command of § 1738.

The issue of implied exceptions to the full faith and credit statute based on subsequent exclusive jurisdiction statutes can arise in the context of issue preclusion, as well. Suppose seller sues buyer in state court on a contract claim. Buyer responds with the federal defense that the contract

---

[29] The Court acknowledged that state preclusion law rarely will consider explicitly the question of a state court judgment's preclusive affect in a subsequent federal court exclusive jurisdiction action for the simple reason that such an action cannot be brought in state court. Nevertheless, the Court found sufficient indications in Delaware's general preclusion law to extrapolate. This portion of the Court's opinion is inconsistent with its treatment of state law in *Marrese,* where it remanded to the lower federal courts to interpret and apply state preclusion law in the first instance. Justices Stevens Ginsberg and Soutar dissented upon that ground, preferring to remand the case to the Ninth Circuit for an initial interpretation of Delaware law. *Id.* at 388. The dissent also suggested that Delaware law might well deny preclusive effect to the class action settlement based on collusion and inadequate representation of class interests by the named representatives. *Id.* at 395–399.

[30] *Id.* at 383.

is illegal because it violates the federal antitrust laws. The state court hears the issue and determines that the contract did not violate the federal legislation. Subsequently buyer sues seller in a federal antitrust action seeking treble damages.[31] Does the prior determination in state court that the contract did not violate federal antitrust laws preclude buyer from re–litigating the issue in the federal court? The decisions in *Marrese* and *Epstein*, of course, do not resolve this question conclusively because those cases involved claim preclusion, not issue preclusion. However, the Court has made it clear that the same two–step analysis would apply, and further that it will be reluctant to find that an exclusive-jurisdiction statute has worked an implied partial appeal of § 1738.[32]

[4] Civil Rights — § 1983 Cases

In several recent cases, the Supreme Court has considered whether the federal civil rights statutes work an implied partial repeal of the full faith and credit statute. If they do, federal courts hearing civil rights claims would not have to give full claim and issue preclusion effect to prior state proceedings. The cases that have considered the issue have dealt principally with two civil rights statutes; (1) the Ku Klux Klan Act, 42 U.S.C. § 1983, and (2) Title VII of the Civil Rights Act of 1964;[33] and the discussion in this subsection and the next treats them one at a time.

In *Allen v. McCurry*,[34] plaintiff brought a § 1983 action against the City of St. Louis, its police department, and several individual police officers, claiming that the officers had violated his Fourth Amendment rights by illegally searching his house. Plaintiff's action followed his conviction in Missouri state court for possession of heroin and assault with intent to kill. During the state prosecution, plaintiff had made a motion to suppress evidence seized by the police from his home, and after a hearing, the trial court denied the motion in part and ruled that plaintiff's Fourth Amendment rights had not been violated.

In plaintiff's subsequent § 1983 action, the defendants argued that the Fourth Amendment issue was precluded by the litigation and decision of the question during the suppression hearing. The Supreme Court ruled in their favor, holding that § 1983 did not alter the federal courts' obligation to give full faith and credit to state–court proceedings; thus these proceedings would have issue preclusion effect in subsequent § 1983 cases.

Plaintiff had argued that part of the legislative impetus for § 1983 was Congress' distrust of southern state courts, and the court of appeals had

---

[31] The hypothetical case is based on Lyons v. Westinghouse Electric Corp., 222 F. 2d 184 (2d Cir. 1955).

[32] *See also* Kremer v. Chemical Construction Corp., 456 U.S. 461 (1982)(the two–step approach applied in issue preclusion cases). The case would be on all fours with the issue preclusion hypothetical in the text except that it was not clear in *Kremer* that the subsequent federal action was within the exclusive jurisdiction of the federal courts.

[33] 42 U.S.C. § 2000c *et seq.*

[34] 449 U.S. 90 (1980).

relied on "the special role of the federal courts in protecting civil rights."[35] The Supreme Court countered that these arguments might support an exception to the normal rule of issue preclusion when the state court had not provided for "a full and fair opportunity to litigate the claim."[36] But there was nothing in the language or history of § 1983 that would support a routine exception to issue preclusion even though a litigant had had such an opportunity in state court.

In *Migra v. Warren City School Dist. Bd. of Education*[37] the Court extended the rule of *Allen* to cover cases of claim preclusion. Plaintiff, the supervisor of elementary education in the Warren city school district, also had the task of designing a social studies curriculum and fashioning a voluntary desegregation plan for the district's schools. The Board offered plaintiff a renewal of her contract, and she accepted it. Subsequently, however, the Board reconsidered the issue and voted not to renew plaintiff's contract.

She brought a breach of contract and wrongful interference with contract action against the Board and some of its members in state court. After she won, she brought a § 1983 action in federal court, claiming that the Board had fired her because it objected to her social studies curriculum and desegregation plan. The Board's actions, she alleged, violated her First Amendment rights and deprived her of due process and equal protection. The Board argued that the federal claim was precluded by the prior state–court judgment.

The Supreme Court upheld the Board's defense, holding that the full faith and credit statute required a federal court to give a prior state court judgment the same claim preclusive effect it would receive in state court. There would be no exception for § 1983 actions. The holding, argued Justice

---

[35] McCurry v. Allen, 606 F.2d 795, 799 (8th Cir. 1979).

[36] The "full and fair opportunity" exception is required, of course, by the Due Process Clause and applies regardless of the substantive law basis of the subsequent federal action. Whether there should be a broader exception for § 1983 cases is a question that has provoked substantial commentary. *See, e.g.*, Robert H. Smith, *Full Faith and Credit and Section 1983: A Reappraisal*, 63 N.C.L. Rev. 59, 62 (1984). Proponents of a more flexible approach were heartened by Haring v. Prosise, 462 U.S. 306 (1983). Plaintiff had been convicted in a Virginia state court after a guilty plea. He later brought a § 1983 action in federal court, alleging that the police officers who arrested him had violated his Fourth Amendment rights by illegally searching his apartment. Defendants argued that plaintiff's conviction collaterally estopped him from litigating the legality of the search in the § 1983 action.

The Court rejected the defense and held that plaintiff's § 1983 claim was in no way precluded by his guilty plea. The Court's unanimous decision was easy and obviously correct. Issue preclusion could not possibly apply because the legality of the search had not been litigated in the Virginia court. Virginia's law did not permit issue preclusion in such circumstances and thus the full faith and credit statute did not require or permit the federal court to preclude the unlitigated issue.

On the way to this easy result, Justice Marshall's opinion suggested that there might be "additional exceptions" to issue preclusion in § 1983 actions beside the *Allen* Court's "full and fair opportunity" restriction. Subsequent cases, however, have not picked up on the theme and the "additional exceptions" language probably should be disregarded as harmless dictum. *See* Wright, Miller & Cooper, *supra* note 2, § 4471.

[37] 465 U.S. 75 (1984).

Blackmun was compelled by the reasoning in *Allen*. If distrust of state courts was not sufficient to deny their results issue preclusion effect in § 1983 cases, how could it be enough to deny them claim preclusion effect?[38]

The Court's most recent decision — *University of Tennessee v. Elliott*[39] — concerns the issue preclusion effect of state administrative proceedings on subsequent § 1983 actions in federal court. Plaintiff, an African–American employee of the University of Tennessee, was informed he would be fired for job–related reasons. He requested a hearing pursuant to Tennessee administrative law and also filed a Title VII and § 1983 action in federal court.

At the hearing an assistant to a University vice president, acting as an administrative law judge, heard extensive evidence,[40] and found that some of the charges were valid, that they were not racially motivated, and that discharge was too severe a penalty. He recommended a transfer instead. Plaintiff appealed the findings to a University vice president who affirmed, but Plaintiff did not seek review in the state courts. Instead he pursued his § 1983 and Title VII claims in the federal court. The University argued that the state administrative findings precluded re–litigation of the issues in the federal court.

The Supreme Court upheld the University's preclusion defense to the § 1983 claim.[41] Preliminarily, the Court held that issue preclusion was not required by the full faith and credit statute, which applies only to state *judicial* proceedings. Nevertheless, the Court found that strong policies favored preclusion. The parties need repose and the judicial system needs to conserve its resources. Moreover preclusion furthers federalism.[42] These policies, said the Court, apply with the same force regardless of whether the state factfinder is a court or an administrative agency. Accordingly, the Court chose to fashion a rule of federal common law to govern the issue: "[W]hen a state agency 'acting in a judicial capacity . . . resolves disputed issues of fact . . . which the parties have had an adequate opportunity to

38 Plaintiff made an interesting argument based on the relative expertise of the state and federal courts. She contended that giving state results issue preclusion, but not claim preclusion effect, permitted a plaintiff to sue on the state claims in state court and the federal claim in federal court, getting an expert decider in each case. The court was not impressed, and its answer was terse.

> Although such a division may seem attractive from a plaintiff's perspective, it is not the system established by § 1738 [the full faith and credit statute]. That statute embodies the view that it is more important to give full faith and credit to state–court judgments than to insure separate forums for federal and state claims.

39 478 U.S. 788 (1986).

40 The hearing involved 100 witnesses, 150 exhibits and 5,000 pages of transcript.

41 The Court's holding on the Title VII claim is discussed in subsection [5], *infra*.

42 The Court cited its decision in Thomas v. Washington Gas Light Co., 448 U.S. 261 (1980), in which all the opinions agreed that the Full Faith and Credit Clause required state courts to give issue preclusion effect to the fact findings sister–states' administrative agencies. *Thomas* is discussed in § 117[c], *infra*.

litigate,' federal courts must give the agency's factfinding the same preclusive effect to which it would be entitled in the State's courts."[43]

It is unusual in our law — particularly our conflicts law — when a string of Supreme Court cases spanning more that a decade is relatively consistent in approach and result. It is far more unusual when the string can be condensed into a single, clear, arguably correct rule, but even low probability events occur sometimes. The Court has held uniformly that there is no exception for § 1983 cases to the federal courts' full faith and credit obligation; the federal court must give state judicial and administrative proceedings the same faith and credit that a state court would.

[5] Civil Rights — Title VII Cases

In *Kremer v. Chemical Construction Corp.*,[44] the Supreme Court considered whether there is an exception in Title VII (employment discrimination) cases to the federal courts' obligation to give full faith and credit to state proceedings. Plaintiff filed charges with the Equal Employment Opportunity Commission claiming that defendant, his employer, discriminated against him because of his religion and national origin. Title VII requires that the EEOC give state anti–discrimination agencies 60 days to resolve such disputes, so it referred plaintiff's charge to the New York State Division of Human Rights. After an investigation the NYHRD concluded that the defendant had not discriminated against plaintiff. Plaintiff then sought judicial review of the administrative decision in the appropriate New York court, which upheld the agency's decision.

After the EEOC also ruled against plaintiffs, he brought a Title VII action in federal court. Defendant argued that the discrimination issue was precluded by the prior New York administrative and judicial proceedings. The Supreme Court agreed, and rejected plaintiff's argument that Title VII worked an implied repeal of the full faith and statute. Nothing in the language or history of Title VII suggested a congressional intent to insulate Title VII cases from the preclusive effect of prior state court proceedings. The Court also rejected plaintiff's attempt to use the preclusion exception provided by the Court in *Allen v. McCurry* for cases where a party has not had a "full and fair opportunity" to litigate the issue in the state proceedings;[45] New York had not denied the plaintiff such an opportunity. The Court held that the "full and fair opportunity" proviso required only that the state factfinding "satisfy the minimum procedural requirements of the Fourteenth Amendment's Due Process Clause,"[46] and the New York proceedings easily met that test.

---

[43] The Restatement (Second) of Judgments § 83 (1982) provides relatively strong support for administrative preclusion, but there is another point of view. *See* Marjorie A. Silver, *In Lieu of Preclusion: Reconciling Administrative Decision Making and Federal Civil Rights Claims*, 65 Ind. L. J. 367 (1990).

[44] 456 U.S. 461 (1982).

[45] 449 U.S. 90 (1980), discussed in subsection [4], *supra*.

[46] *Kremer* thus seems to suggest that the language in Haring v. Prosise, 462 U.S. 306 (1983), suggesting a broader issue preclusion exception should not be taken too seriously. *See* note 32, *supra*.

Kremer dealt with the full faith and credit due an administrative factfinding that had been reviewed by a court. But what of an unreviewed state agency proceeding; should it also receive issue preclusion effect in a subsequent Title VII action in federal court? The Supreme Court answered this question in *University of Tennessee v. Elliott.*[47] The full faith and credit statute, said the Court, applied to state "judicial proceedings," not to unreviewed administrative agency findings.

Further, the Court refused to fashion a federal common law rule of preclusion. Such a rule would not fit in the statutory scheme of Title VII. It requires that the Equal Employment Opportunity Commission give only "substantial weight" to state anti–discrimination agency factfindings; "it would make little sense for Congress to write such a provision if state agency findings were entitled to preclusive effect in Title VII actions in federal court."

Together *Kremer* and *Elliott* define the respect owed state administrative proceedings in subsequent federal Title VII cases: An administrative agency finding reviewed by a state court is entitled to issue preclusion effect, but an unreviewed agency finding is not.[48]

[47] 478 U.S. 788 (1986). *Elliott* also involved a § 1983 claim. The preclusive effects of state administrative agency determinations in subsequent § 1983 cases is discussed in subsection [4], *supra*.

[48] For commentary on *Elliott* and *Kremer*, *see* Wright, Miller & Cooper, *supra* note 2, § 4471.3; Silver, *supra* note 43.

Part B

THE REACH AND LIMITS OF FULL FAITH AND CREDIT

The Full Faith and Credit Clause demands rigorous obedience. Nevertheless, its rule is not absolute, and some exceptions to the regime do exist. This Part first explores the source of the Iron Law of Full Faith and Credit. Next, it examines the two main types of exceptions: those involving problems with the decree itself and those which may permit an enforcing state to deny credit to a valid decree. This Part concludes with a discussion of public policy in the enforcement process.

§ 114 The Iron Law of Full Faith and Credit

If the F–1 court has jurisdiction over both the person and the subject matter, its judgment is entitled to full faith and credit in F–2, even though that judgment is based upon a mistake of fact or law.[1] If the losing litigant wishes to correct such an error, she must do so in F–1's courts — either on appeal or through some other type of direct attack (such as a motion to vacate or a motion for relief from judgment).[2] Once the F–1 judgment is final according to the law of F–1, however, the Full Faith and Credit Clause prohibits collateral attack in F–2. This might be called the "Iron Law" of Full Faith and Credit.[3]

[a] *Fauntleroy v. Lum*

A striking example of this principle is *Fauntleroy v. Lum*.[4] Plaintiff and defendant, both residents of Mississippi, entered into a "futures" commodities contract; such contracts were illegal (as a form of gambling) in Mississippi. The parties disputed the effect of the contract and submitted their differences to an arbitrator, who made an award to plaintiff. Plaintiff then sued defendant in a Mississippi court to recover upon the award. When the court's attention was drawn to the illegality of the contract, plaintiff dismissed the case. Plaintiff later sued defendant in Missouri. The Missouri court rejected defendant's evidence on the illegality issue and rendered judgment for the plaintiff on the arbitrator's award. Plaintiff assigned the judgment to his attorney, who sued defendant in Mississippi to enforce the Missouri judgment. The Mississippi courts refused to grant full faith and credit to the Missouri judgment. The Supreme Court reversed in emphatic language: "A judgment is conclusive as to all the media concludendi; and

---

[1] Restatement (Second) of Conflict of Laws § 106.

[2] *See, e.g.*, Fed. R. Civ. P. 60(b).

[3] *See* Vernon, Weinberg, Reynolds, and Richman at 605.

[4] 210 U.S. 230 (1908).

it needs no authority to show that it cannot be impeached either in or out of the State by showing that it was based upon a mistake of law."

The Court could scarcely have picked a more striking case to illustrate the principle. Not only did the Missouri court err, but it erred on a question of Mississippi law, and the error frustrated an important social policy of Mississippi. Nevertheless, the Missouri judgment was entitled to full faith and credit in Mississippi — the very state whose law was misconstrued. *Fauntleroy*, then, clearly indicates that the Full Faith and Credit Clause means exactly what it says: a federal union requires that the doctrines of repose and finality be given interstate effect.

[b] Inconsistent Judgments[5]

Strong as the requirement for full faith and credit to judgments is, it is not absolute; a judgment need not be given preclusive effect, for example, if the rendering court lacked personal jurisdiction over the defendant. If the second court refuses to give full faith and credit to the F–1 judgment and then reaches a different result on the merits inconsistent judgments will be the outcome. The question then becomes, which of those judgments is entitled to full faith and credit in a later action?

That was the issue in the case of *Treinies v. Sunshine Mining Co.*,[6] a dispute between stepfather and daughter over the ownership of mining stock. A Washington state court first held for the stepfather; when he introduced that decree in a suit in Idaho between the same parties, the Idaho court found that the Washington court had lacked jurisdiction over the subject matter. The Idaho court then entered a decree for the daughter. When more litigation ensued, the company filed a bill of interpleader, an action that eventually reached the Supreme Court, where the daughter's Idaho victory finally prevailed. The Court adopted a "last–in–time" rule:[7] The second (or last, if more than two) of two inconsistent judgments must be given full faith and credit.

One advantage of the *Treinies* rule is that it generally simplifies the task of judicial administration. If a third court, for example, is asked to enforce the F–2 judgment, all it need inquire into is whether the court had jurisdiction. If it did — and if the F–2 judgment is later in time than F–1's — then the F–2 judgment must be enforced. Thus, F–3 has been spared the need to choose between the F–1 and F–2 results in terms of "rightness."[8]

Another advantage is that the rule fits well in the conceptual scheme of full faith and credit. If F–2 errs in refusing full faith and credit to an F–1

[5] *See generally* Ruth Bader Ginsburg, *Judgments in Search of Full Faith and Credit: The Last–in–Time Rule for Conflicting Judgments*, 82 Harv. L. Rev. 798 (1969).

[6] 308 U.S. 66 (1939).

[7] *See also* Restatement (Second) of Conflict of Laws § 114; Restatement (Second) of Judgments § 15.

[8] We do not address the questions created when F–2 enjoins an action in F–1: At present, the injunction may issue, but the Supreme Court has not required that such an order be obeyed in the sister state. *See generally* Ginsburg, *supra* note 5, at 823–30.

judgment, it has committed an error of law and issued an erroneous judgment. Wrong judgments, so says the basic rule of *Fauntleroy v. Lum*,[9] are nevertheless entitled to full faith and credit. Correction must occur by appeal in F–2, not by collateral attack.

A possible problem with the *Treinies* rule is that it might permit F–2 to ignore its constitutional responsibility to respect F–1 judgments. Of course, in our federal system, proper adherence to the mandate of the Full Faith and Credit Clause is a federal question, and correction is always possible by way of a writ of *certiorari*[10] from the Supreme Court. Given the Court's workload,[11] however, and the large number of state cases involving full faith and credit, review by *certiorari* is really a forlorn hope.[12] The real reason why the *Treinies* rule is not a major cause for worry is that there is little evidence today of the sort of parochialism that could cause state courts to ignore systematically the constitutional mandate of full faith and credit.

Although the last–in–time rule is simplicity itself, a problem in its application has arisen when F–3 is also F–1 — when, in other words, the later decree is taken back to F–1 to be enforced. The logic of *Treinies* suggests that F–1 must give full faith and credit to the F–2 decree, a result several state courts have resisted.[13] The Supreme Court, however, has indicated strongly that that refusal is improper.[14]

§ 115 Exceptions to the Iron Law I — Problems with the F–1 Decree

[a] Judgments Not on the Merits

The Full Faith and Credit Clause requires that each state accord a judgment of another state as much respect and credit as it would receive in the rendering state.[1] A judgment that does not have preclusive effect in F–1, therefore, need not be given such effect by F–2.

Judgments not on the merits make up one large class of judgments without claim–preclusive effect.[2] What is meant by "on the merits" differs,

[9] 210 U.S. 230 (1908).

[10] In *Treinies* itself, the Court noted the failure of the stepfather to petition for certiorari from a final Idaho decree.

[11] *See* Vernon, Weinberg, Reynolds, and Richman at 609 n. 3 for a discussion of the workload problem.

[12] *See* Restatement (Second) of Conflict of Laws § 114, comment b (it may be inappropriate to give conclusive effect to second judgment when Supreme Court has denied review of that judgment).

[13] *See, e.g.*, Porter v. Porter, 101 Ariz. 131, 416 P.2d 564 (1966), *cert. denied*, 386 U.S. 957 (1967); Kessler v. Fauquier Nat'l Bank, 195 Va. 1095, 81 S.E.2d 440 (1954).

[14] *See* Sutton v. Leib, 342 U.S. 402 (1952) (dictum). *See also* Ginsburg, *supra* note 5, at 806–11. In Colby v. Colby, 78 Nev. 150, 369 P.2d 1019, *cert. denied*, 371 U.S. 888 (1962), however, the Nevada Supreme Court recognized as valid an earlier Nevada divorce decree that a Maryland court had declared invalid.

[1] *See* § 110[c], *supra*.

[2] Restatement (Second) of Conflict of Laws § 110; Scoles, Hay, Borchers & Symeonides § 24.24.

of course, from state to state, but several general observations can be made. A judgment is typically said to be on the merits when it rests upon a determination of the validity of the parties' claims and defenses under the applicable substantive law. In nearly all jurisdictions, certain classes of judgments are held to be not on the merits — judgments based upon lack of subject matter jurisdiction, lack of jurisdiction over persons or property, improper venue, or misjoinder or nonjoinder of parties.[3] Such judgments indicate only that plaintiff chose to sue in the wrong court or to sue the wrong parties; they say nothing about the substantive validity of the case. Similarly, a dismissal by F–1 on the ground that plaintiff's case is time–barred does not reach the merits of plaintiff's case; because it does not, F–2 is free to permit plaintiff to sue later on the same cause of action.[4]

A situation which produces more ambiguity is the judgment based upon a demurrer or motion to dismiss for failure to state a claim. Often such dismissals result simply from pleading errors which do not preclude a subsequent well–pleaded complaint. In other cases, a dismissal on demurrer may be regarded as preclusive because the complaint reveals a central and irreparable defect in plaintiff's case. In those cases, therefore, the dismissal should be accorded full faith and credit in later litigation.

[b] Lack of Finality in F–1

A judgment not final under the law of the state which rendered it is not entitled to full faith and credit.[5] In many jurisdictions this rule embraces judgments on appeal or subject to appeal. Similarly, a judgment vacated in F–1 is not entitled to full faith and credit in F–2.[6] A judgment subject to modification in F–1 is not considered a final judgment and, therefore, need not be enforced by F–2.[7] In most jurisdictions, for example, awards of custody and alimony are modifiable both prospectively and retrospectively. Those possibilities raise difficult full faith and credit issues.

Consider a case where a wife has been awarded alimony of $1000 per month. The husband pays for a while, but then moves to F–2 and stops paying. After six months the wife returns to the F–1 court and obtains a judgment which directs husband to pay a sum certain ($6000 — arrearages which have accrued since his last payment) and to continue to pay to the wife $1000 per month. Three months later, the wife, unable to satisfy the F–1 judgment in that state, sues husband in F–2. What the wife now wants is an order from the F–2 court which directs husband to: (1) pay the wife $6000 — the accrued alimony, liquidated by the F–1 lump sum judgment;

[3] *See, e.g.*, Fed. R. Civ. P. 41(b).

[4] *E.g.*, Warner v. Buffalo Drydock Co., 67 F.2d 540 (2d Cir. 1933). Of course, the case may be time–barred by the F–2 statute of limitations; or F–2, because of a borrowing statute or some other choice–of–law rule, may apply F–1's statute of limitations and refuse to hear the claim. *See* § 93, *infra*, for a discussion of the choice–of–law problems posed by statutes of limitations.

[5] Restatement (Second) of Conflict of Laws § 107; Scoles, Hay, Borchers & Symeonides § 24.28.

[6] Restatement (Second) of Conflict of Laws § 112.

[7] *Id.* § 107.

(2) pay the wife $3000 — alimony accrued between the date of the F–1 judgment and the present F–2 proceeding; and (3) pay the wife $1000 per month in the future.

The question posed then is: Which of those requested orders does the Full Faith and Credit Clause require the F–2 court to issue? First, F–2 must issue the first order.[8] The wife seeks full faith and credit for a final F–1 judgment. Because the judgment cannot be modified in F–1, it must be granted full faith and credit in F–2. That jurisdiction, however, need not make the third requested order. The request there is that F–2 grant full faith and credit to F–1's award of future alimony. In most jurisdictions, however, an award of future alimony can be modified prospectively, and the Supreme Court has held that the national policy of full faith and credit does not require the F–2 court to enforce a judgment still modifiable in the state that rendered it.[9]

The second request of wife raises a more difficult question. There she seeks the alimony that accrued between the date of the F–1 judgment and the F–2 proceeding. The amount while accrued has not been reduced to judgment. In some jurisdictions, alimony awards are modifiable only prospectively; the court may modify the alimony award, but only with respect to payments that have not yet accrued. In other jurisdictions, alimony awards are modifiable retrospectively as well; in those states, a court may also review the propriety of the alimony award with regard to payments that have already accrued.

Once the complication of prospective and retrospective modification is removed, the application of the general rule of full faith and credit becomes clear. F–2 must issue the wife's second requested order if alimony awards are not retrospectively modifiable in F–1.[10] F–2 need not issue the order if alimony awards are retrospectively modifiable in F–1. This case, then, can be seen to be simply a more complicated example of the general rule that F–2 need not grant full faith and credit to F–1 judgments which are modifiable under F–1 law.

Although F–2 need not enforce a modifiable judgment, it is not precluded from doing so. In *Worthley v. Worthley*,[11] Justice Traynor indicated that an F–2 court should generally be willing to enforce modifiable alimony awards. After all, as long as the defendant has been given an opportunity to litigate the question of modifiability, he has not been disadvantaged. Moreover, if the second state will not enforce modifiable orders, the F–1 plaintiff must periodically reduce accrued and unpaid alimony to an F–1 judgment, and then sue in F–2 on the final and unmodifiable judgment.

[8] Barber v. Barber, 323 U.S. 77 (1944); Lynde v. Lynde, 181 U.S. 183 (1901).

[9] Sistare v. Sistare, 218 U.S. 1 (1910).

[10] *Id.*; Barber v. Barber, 323 U.S. 77 (1944).

[11] 44 Cal.2d 465, 283 P.2d 19 (1955).

The cost and delay involved in such a cumbersome procedure considerably reduce the benefit which the support order was designed to produce.[12]

[c] Fraud in Obtaining the F–1 Judgment[13]

F–2 need not grant full faith and credit to an F–1 judgment that was procured by fraud. Because "fraud" is a very slippery term, the question really is: What counts as the sort of fraud that will justify F–2 in refusing full faith and credit? Here, as is true of any discussion of foreign judgments, it is useful to return to basic principles. One of those principles is that F–2 must give at least as much effect to an F–1 judgment as would an F–1 court;[14] thus, an F–2 court may permit collateral attack on an F–1 judgment based on fraud only in cases where an F–1 court would permit such an attack.

Fortunately, there is considerable agreement among the state courts on those types of fraud that justify a collateral attack and those that do not. First, it is quite clear that an issue of fraud (such as a suit based on the tort of misrepresentation), which was raised and adjudicated in F–1, is subject to the same issue preclusion effect as any other adjudicated issue. Second, many courts distinguish between extrinsic and intrinsic fraud; the former is a sufficient ground for denying full faith and credit to a sister state judgment, while the latter is not.

Extrinsic fraud refers to a fraud that could not have been ruled on by the F–1 tribunal — a fraud that deprived defendant of his opportunity to appear and defend. A classic example is *Levin v. Gladstein.*[15] There, plaintiff seller (from Maryland) and defendant buyer (from North Carolina) had a dispute over the quality of the goods sold. Defendant visited plaintiff in Maryland and was served with process from the Maryland court. Plaintiff and defendant then met and resolved their differences, with plaintiff assuring defendant that the suit would be withdrawn. Relying upon that representation, defendant returned to North Carolina and did not defend the Maryland action. Plaintiff did not dismiss, however, but instead obtained a default judgment. He then sued defendant in North Carolina upon the Maryland judgment. The North Carolina court refused to enforce the Maryland judgment. The fraud involved was extrinsic because it could never have been raised in the Maryland court; indeed, the fraud deprived defendant of the opportunity of making any defense in the Maryland court.

[12] The problem of interstate enforcement of support decrees has produced legislative as well as judicial solutions. The Uniform Reciprocal Enforcement of Support Act, 9A U.L.A. 643 (1968 Revised Act) has been adopted in some form in every state. In the 1958 version of the Act as well as in the 1968 revision, provision was made for the enforcement and registration of foreign alimony awards. *See* 9A U.L.A. 749. Earlier versions (including the version available in California at the time of *Worthley*) did not include such a provision. For a more detailed treatment of the Act, *see* § 128, *infra.*

[13] *See generally* Michael Charles Pryles, *The Impeachment of Sister State Judgments for Fraud*, 25 Sw. L.J. 697 (1975).

[14] *See* § 110[c], *supra.*

[15] 142 N.C. 482, 55 S.E. 371 (1906).

Intrinsic fraud, by contrast, is fraud that the F–1 court did have the opportunity to rule on, such as perjured testimony or fabricated documentary evidence. Because the losing litigant had an opportunity to reveal the fraud to the F–1 tribunal, she is not permitted a second opportunity by collateral attack in F–2. Some modern authorities[16] have rejected this position on intrinsic fraud. The argument is that a litigant's knowing use of fraudulent evidence may deprive his opponent of a fair hearing just as effectively as tricking him into a default judgment. Further, if the defrauded litigant could not have known of the fabricated evidence, she really had no opportunity to reveal the fraud to the F–1 court, and thus should not be precluded from raising the issue in a collateral attack in F–2. For these reasons, the Restatement (Second) of Judgments discards the intrinsic/extrinsic distinction; instead, it permits a party to obtain relief from a judgment based on fraudulent evidence if she can show that she "made a reasonable effort in the original action to ascertain the truth of the matter."[17] Moreover, Rule 60(b) (3) of the Federal Rules of Civil Procedure now permits verdicts to be set aside if they were procured by "fraud (whether heretofore denominated intrinsic or extrinsic), misrepresentation, or other misconduct of an opposing party." Rule 60 and the Restatement promise to make the fraud exception more readily available in enforcement actions.

[d] Lack of Jurisdiction in F–1

[1] Lack of Jurisdiction Over the Person

When a court lacks jurisdiction over the subject matter or jurisdiction over the person, its judgment is void and, therefore, not entitled to full faith and credit in F–2.[18] That rule, perhaps as basic as the Iron Law of Full Faith and Credit, is subject to an important qualification. A court's findings on questions of jurisdiction, like its findings on any other relevant issue, may preclude re–litigation of that issue. Thus, a determination by an F–1 court that it has jurisdiction, even though in fact it does not, may preclude the parties from relitigating the jurisdictional question in F–1 or anywhere else.[19]

If the asserted defect in the judgment is a lack of jurisdiction over the person, the situation is relatively simple. When defendant appears in F–1 and fails to object to the court's jurisdiction, she waives any jurisdictional defect involving her person; she has consented to the F–1 court's exercise of jurisdiction over her. Of course, instead of appearing generally (and consenting to jurisdiction), defendant may make a special appearance for the sole purpose of challenging the F–1 court's jurisdiction. If defendant

[16] *See, e.g.*, Restatement (Second) of Judgments § 70, comment c; Vernon, Weinberg, Reynolds, and Richman at 612–13; Scoles, Hay, Borchers & Symeonides § 24.17.

[17] Restatement (Second) of Judgments § 70(c).

[18] Restatement (Second) of Conflict of Laws §§ 104, 105.

[19] Restatement (Second) of Judgments §§ 10, 12; Restatement (Second) of Conflict of Laws §§ 96, 97.

does appear specially, and the F–1 court rules that it has jurisdiction, can she relitigate the issue of F–1's jurisdiction when she is sued in F–2 upon the F–1 judgment? The Supreme Court, in *Baldwin v. Iowa State Traveling Men's Ass'n*,[20] ruled that she may not. Defendant's appearance in F–1 was precisely for the purpose of litigating the jurisdictional question. Her remedy for an unsatisfactory decision on that issue is to appeal within the F–1 judicial system and, ultimately, to the Supreme Court. She may not, however, reopen the jurisdictional issue in F–2; one complete judicial determination of the matter is enough.

A mere recitation in the F–1 judgment that the court had jurisdiction is not, of course, the sort of "litigation" that would preclude the issue in F–2.[21] If it were, such a recitation could be included in every judgment, and defendant would be forced to appear in F–1, rather than being able to default and litigate the F–1 court's jurisdiction in F–2.

[2] Lack of Jurisdiction Over the Subject Matter

If the asserted defect in the F–1 proceeding is a lack of jurisdiction over the subject matter, the foreclosure of collateral attack is more problematic. Questions of subject matter jurisdiction implicate public interests extending beyond those of the litigants themselves; defendant cannot consent to the lack of subject matter jurisdiction, nor can the parties confer subject matter jurisdiction on the court by agreement. Federal courts are especially sensitive to defects involving subject matter jurisdiction,[22] because a federal court which exceeds its limited subject matter jurisdiction may be acting unconstitutionally.

Nevertheless, the Supreme Court has held that litigation and adjudication (whether correct or not) of subject matter jurisdiction issues in F–1 may preclude their relitigation in F–2. In *Durfee v. Duke*,[23] plaintiff sued defendant in a Nebraska court to quiet title to a parcel of land adjacent to the Missouri River, the main channel of which forms the boundary between Missouri and Nebraska. The Nebraska court had jurisdiction over the land only if it was in Nebraska. That question, in turn, depended upon a factual determination of whether a shift in the course of the river had been the result of avulsion or accretion. Defendant appeared in the Nebraska court and vigorously litigated the question of its jurisdiction. The Nebraska court determined that it had jurisdiction and quieted title in plaintiff. Defendant later sued the Nebraska plaintiff in a Missouri court to quiet title to the same land. To plaintiff's contention that the Nebraska

---

[20] 283 U.S. 522 (1931).

[21] Thompson v. Whitman, 85 U.S. (18 Wall.) 457 (1873).

[22] *See, e.g.*, Fed. R. Civ. P. 12(h), which permits lack of subject matter jurisdiction to be raised by anyone at any time, and requires, in any event, that it be raised by the court *sua sponte*. In the state courts, a mistake of competence is not always treated as a "jurisdictional" error. In other words, some errors of competence may not furnish a ground for collateral attack. If according to the law of F–1, the error is not "jurisdictional," F–2 must grant full faith and credit.

[23] 375 U.S. 106 (1963).

judgment was entitled to full faith and credit, defendant responded that the Nebraska court lacked subject matter jurisdiction. The question posed then was whether the Nebraska court's determination that it had jurisdiction precluded relitigation of that issue in a later action. The Supreme Court held that it did, and laid down the following principle:

> From these decisions there emerges the general rule that a judgment is entitled to full faith and credit — even as to questions of jurisdiction — when the second court's inquiry discloses that those questions have been fully and fairly litigated and finally decided in the court which rendered the original judgment.

It would be tempting to conclude that the rule of *Durfee* (subject matter jurisdiction issues are precluded if "fully and fairly litigated" in F–1) ended the inquiry.[24] The rule is straightforward, succinct, and arguably correct.[25] Unfortunately, however, the Supreme Court has decided cases which cannot be squared with the *Durfee* principle. In *Kalb v. Feuerstein*,[26] for example, the Court indicated that subject matter jurisdiction issues may furnish a ground for collateral attack, even after they have been once fully and fairly litigated. The situation in *Kalb* involved a state court's erroneous conclusion that it had jurisdiction over a matter which Congress (in federal bankruptcy legislation) had assigned to the exclusive jurisdiction of the federal courts. The need to protect the integrity of the federal policy from a possibly hostile (or, at least, less than sympathetic) state judiciary was considered strong enough to overcome the general rule of issue preclusion. That result makes good sense; if the rule were otherwise, the parties to an action could cause — negligently or deliberately — important federal policies to be ignored or under–valued.

To complicate matters further, the Court has occasionally indicated that issues of subject matter jurisdiction are foreclosed from collateral attack even though they have not once been fully litigated. In *Sherrer v. Sherrer*,[27] "litigation" of the jurisdictional issue (wife's domicile in F–1) consisted only of the husband's denial of jurisdiction in his answer; he did not offer proof on the question, nor did he cross–examine his wife. Nevertheless, the Court held that the issue could not be reopened by collateral attack in F–2. In

---

[24] The rule has been applied by the Supreme Court in a wide variety of contexts: Stoll v. Gottlieb, 305 U.S. 165 (1938) (bankruptcy jurisdiction); Dowell v. Applegate, 152 U.S. 327 (1894) (federal question jurisdiction); Des Moines Nav. & R.R. Co. v. Iowa Homestead Co., 123 U.S. 552 (1887) (diversity jurisdiction).

[25] The rule has been termed the " 'Bootstrap Principle" by one commentator. *See* Dan B. Dobbs, *The Validation of Void Judgments: The Bootstrap Principle*, 53 Va. L. Rev. 1003 (1967). Restatement (Second) of Judgments § 12(1) provides, however, that full faith and credit is not required when the "subject matter of the action was so plainly beyond the court's jurisdiction that its entertaining the action was a manifest abuse of authority. . . ." The authority supporting the section is doubtful, however.

[26] 308 U.S. 433 (1940). *See generally* Bennett Boskey and Robert Braucher, *Jurisdiction and Collateral Attack*, 40 Colum. L. Rev. 1006 (1940). *Cf.* Consolidated Rail Corp. v. Illinois, 423 F. Supp. 941 (Regional Rail Reorg. Ct. 1976), *cert. denied*, 429 U.S. 1095 (1977) (no preclusive effect should be given an earlier *federal* district court decision when Congress had reserved certain issues for a special court on railroad reorganization.)

[27] 334 U.S. 343 (1948).

Chicot County Drainage Dist. v. Baxter State Bank[28] (decided in the same Term as *Kalb*), there was no litigation of the jurisdictional question at all. The Court, nevertheless, precluded collateral attack upon the ground that the jurisdictional issue could have been raised in the first proceeding.[29]

The Court, then, has given different and at times confusing signals on the question of collateral attack based on lack of subject matter jurisdiction. *Durfee* holds that issues of subject matter jurisdiction are precluded if they have been fully litigated in F–1; *Sherrer* and *Chicot County* indicate preclusion may occur in some cases even when there is little or no litigation of the issues in F–1; and *Kalb* indicates that in other cases preclusion is impermissible despite full and fair litigation in F–1. The apparent difficulty in reconciling those cases[30] indicates a conflict between two fundamental principles.[31] On the one hand, courts must not act beyond their subject matter competence; when they do, their actions are void; on the other hand, final judgments should not be reopened. The difficulty, however, may be more apparent than real. Two observations are useful. When the policies behind the subject matter limitation are strong (*e.g.*, the balance between federal and state power at issue in *Kalb*), courts will tend to permit relitigation. By contrast, when the policies supporting finality are especially pressing (full, fair, and vigorous litigation in F–1, as in *Durfee*), collateral attack will be prohibited.[32]

[e] The Land Taboo

The preceding section discussed the requirement that F–1 have jurisdiction in a case if its judgment is to be recognized in F–2. A specialized aspect of that requirement involves the problem of a foreign judgment that affects real property located in the forum. The law can be stated simply: An F–1 judgment that purports to affect directly title to land located in F–2 need not be respected by F–2. The leading decision is *Fall v. Eastin.*[33] That case began with a divorce decree in Washington, accompanied by an order directing the husband (over whom the Washington court had personal jurisdiction) to convey Nebraska real property to his wife. When the

[28] 308 U.S. 371 (1940).

[29] Even if the case could have been removed to federal court, the parties may not have done so, either out of choice or ignorance, and state courts may not provide adequate protection for federal policies. The state judge who hears the case may not appreciate federal policies the way a federal judge might; indeed, a state judge might not even be aware of those policies. For an example of this problem *see* Blue Cross & Blue Shield of Md., Inc. v. Weiner, 868 F.2d 1550 (4th Cir. 1989), *cert. denied*, 493 U.S. 892 (1990). (One of the authors was counsel in the case.)

[30] For an attempt at reconciliation, *see* Dobbs, *supra* note 25.

[31] These two principles are articulated in Restatement (Second) of Judgments § 12, comment a; Restatement (Second) of Conflict of Laws § 97, comment d.

[32] Restatement (Second) of Judgments § 12 takes the position that the policy of finality typically should prevail and that a judgment in a contested action (default judgments are excepted) should not be vulnerable to collateral attack based on lack of subject matter jurisdiction. Section 12 provides three limited exceptions to this rule.

[33] 215 U.S. 1 (1909).

husband did not comply with the order, the Washington court appointed a commissioner to execute a deed in favor of the wife. Later, the wife brought an action in Nebraska to quiet title to the land in question, the defendant in that action being a grantee of the husband. The Nebraska court held that because the Washington court lacked jurisdiction to affect title to land in Nebraska, the deed and decree need not be recognized.

The Supreme Court affirmed. The majority opinion in *Fall*[34] stands for the principle that one state cannot directly affect title to land located in another state. In order to appreciate the reach of that rule, it is useful to consider two variations on the facts of the case itself.

The first variation supposes that the husband, threatened by the Washington court with contempt, had himself executed a deed conveying the Nebraska land to his wife.[35] The majority in *Fall* stated that such a conveyance — although executed under duress — would have been effective. Although the actions of the Washington court in this variation would have affected title to land located elsewhere, the conveyance by the husband would have been effective in Nebraska. The difference between the first hypothetical situation and *Fall* itself is, simply, that in the actual case the Washington court attempted directly to affect title to Nebraska land by making (through the commissioner) its own conveyance; in the hypothetical situation, title is not directly affected.

The second variation on *Fall* assumes that the wife had asked the Nebraska court to enforce the Washington order to the husband to convey the land in question. In other words, what would have happened if the wife had sued him on the Washington equity decree itself rather than suing his grantee based on the commissioner's deed? Would that decree have been entitled to full faith and credit? Today, the answer is most likely yes — although when *Fall* was decided, the answer perhaps was less than clear, for at the time it was thought that a decree of an equity court need not be recognized by another state.[36] There is, however, scant functional reason to treat such decrees, as a class, differently from legal judgments. Commentators today agree that equity decrees should be accorded full faith and credit,[37] and there is little reason to believe that the Supreme Court would differ.[38]

The two variations just explored suggest that the *Fall* rule, that only the situs has jurisdiction over its own real property, is really quite limited.

---

[34] Justice Holmes concurred. He believed the Washington decree to be entitled to full faith and credit, but that the Nebraska court could refuse, as a matter of local law, to deny rights to the husband's grantee, even if she was not a bona fide purchaser.

[35] *See* Note, *Validity of Deed Given Under Compulsion of "Foreign" Court*, 12 Mont. L. Rev. 59 (1951).

[36] The distinction arose from the early belief that equity decrees acted only on the person and on the defendant's conscience. *See generally* Willis Reese, *Full Faith and Credit to Foreign Equity Decrees*, 42 Iowa L. Rev. 183 (1957).

[37] *E.g.*, Scoles, Hay, Borchers & Symeonides § 24.9; Leflar, McDougal & Felix § 174. This is also the position of Restatement (Second) of Judgments § 43.

[38] The Supreme Court has required that a non-modifiable equity decree for support be given full faith and credit. Sistare v. Sistare, 218 U.S. 1 (1910).

Nevertheless, the rule is of long standing[39] and has not yet been repudiated by the Supreme Court. Whether it can be justified today is less clear.

One possible justification for the rule is that because the situs is deeply concerned over the reliability of its land records, it must have the authority to insure that those records are not confused by foreign decrees. The trouble with that argument is that it is hard to see why a state cannot protect its land records without discriminating against foreign judgments. Nebraska could easily require registration of foreign decrees affecting local land in a way that would preserve the integrity of its land records.

A second justification for the situs rule centers on the need of the situs — the most interested jurisdiction — to insure that questions involving its realty are answered as the situs deems proper. There are several flaws with that argument, however. First, it runs distinctly counter to the teaching of *Fauntleroy v. Lum*,[40] that full faith and credit requires the enforcement of judgments rendered by other American courts, no matter how wrong they may be. Second, it is difficult to understand why a state's interest in its land is sufficiently greater than its interest in its residents to justify different treatment of the two under the Constitution. Finally, the premise that the situs will be the most concerned jurisdiction will often prove false. As *Fall* itself illustrates, a decree concerning land may only be incidental to litigation (divorce) of far greater interest to another jurisdiction. In order for that court to resolve those questions properly, it needs power to act effectively on the issues before it. Doing so should not materially offend the situs. An increasing number of courts have come to appreciate the weaknesses of the arguments in favor of the *Fall* rule and have chosen to follow the more basic principles associated with the Full Faith and Credit Clause. Those courts have recognized foreign decrees affecting land on the basis of either comity[41] or full faith and credit.[42]

What then of Mrs. Fall? Why did she lose? If, at the time of *Fall*, equity decrees had been entitled to full faith and credit (as they seem to be today), she lost because she misconceived her remedy; instead of suing on the deed, she should have sued her husband or his grantee[43] in Nebraska on the decree.[44] Put that way, the rule in *Fall v. Eastin* is indeed limited. F–1's orders concerning F–2 land are entitled to full faith and credit, provided only that they do not purport to transfer title directly.

---

[39] It can be traced back to Livingston v. Jefferson, 15 F. Cas. 660 (C.C.D. Va. 1811) (No. 8,411).

[40] 210 U.S. 230 (1908), discussed in § 114, *infra*.

[41] *E.g.*, Weesner v. Weesner, 168 Neb. 346, 95 N.W.2d 682 (1959). Note that *Weesner* was decided by the same state court that decided Fall v. Eastin.

[42] *E.g.*, Varone v. Varone, 359 F.2d 769 (7th Cir. 1966).

[43] It may have been that the husband's grantee was a bona fide purchaser. If so, she may not have been bound by the equity decree against her brother.

[44] For a discussion of methods of avoiding *Fall*, *see* Brainerd Currie, *Full Faith and Credit to Foreign Land Decrees*, 21 U. Chi. L. Rev. 620 (1954).

§ 116 Exceptions to the Iron Law II: F–2's Ability to Ignore a Valid F–1 Judgment

[a] The Lack of a Competent Court in F–2

The law is well settled that a state may not refuse to enforce a sister state judgment on the ground that the original action could not have been brought in the state in which enforcement is sought. That is the lesson of *Fauntleroy v. Lum*,[1] where F–2 was required to give full faith to an F–1 judgment involving a contract made in F–2 and illegal in that state.

Any doubts about that conclusion should have been laid to rest in *Kenney v. Supreme Lodge*.[2] There, Illinois was asked to enforce a judgment for wrongful death rendered in Alabama. The Illinois court held that, because the original action could not have been brought in Illinois, its courts lacked jurisdiction over a suit upon the judgment. The Supreme Court reversed, with Justice Holmes writing: "It is plain that a State cannot escape its constitutional obligations by the simple device of denying jurisdiction in such cases to courts otherwise competent." Thus, a claim that has been reduced to judgment must be enforced by another state even though the claim is one that could not have been brought there originally.[3] That policy is strongly in accord with the principles established in *Fauntleroy v. Lum*.

There seem to be only two limits on the *Kenney* doctrine. First, a state need not permit a suit to enforce a judgment by one who lacks capacity to sue under forum law.[4] In *Anglo-American Provision Co. v. Davis Provision Co.*,[5] for example, the Supreme Court upheld the refusal of the New York courts to entertain a suit between foreign corporations based on a foreign judgment. Second, the judgment creditor must seek relief of a type ordinarily available in the forum. That requirement ordinarily presents no problem; most judgment creditors seek to recover a money judgment, and all states provide such a mechanism for the collection of a debt. The Constitution does not require a state to provide procedures for enforcement not available in domestic actions.[6]

[b] Penal Judgments

Discussions of penal judgments customarily begin by quoting Chief Justice Marshall: "The courts of no country execute the penal laws of another."[7] Marshall's words come up in two contexts in conflict of laws: (1) May a court refuse to hear a case based on a sister state statute which is

---

[1] 210 U.S. 230 (1908).

[2] 252 U.S. 411 (1920).

[3] *See also* Restatement (Second) of Conflict of Laws § 117, comment d.

[4] *Id.*; Scoles, Hay, Borchers & Symeonides § 24.22; George Stumberg, Principles of Conflict of Laws 119–20 (3d ed. 1963).

[5] 191 U.S. 373 (1903).

[6] G. Stumberg, *supra*, note 4, at 118.

[7] The Antelope, 23 U.S. (10 Wheat.) 66, 123 (1825).

penal? and (2) May a court of F–2 refuse to grant full faith and credit to an F–1 judgment which is based upon a penal statute? In this section, only the second question is treated.[8]

Valid F–1 judgments based upon purely penal claims are not entitled to full faith and credit in F–2.[9] The Supreme Court in *Huntington v. Atrill*,[10] however, considerably restricted the scope of this exception to the Full Faith and Credit Clause by assigning a narrow meaning to the word "penal." The Court in *Huntington* required enforcement of a judgment, unless it was based upon a statute that is penal in the "international sense." The Court then noted that whether a statute is penal in the international sense "depends upon the question whether its purpose is to punish an offense against the public justice of the State, or to afford a private remedy to a person injured by the wrongful act." That language seems to set up a two part test. In order for a judgment to be penal in the international sense, its purpose must be to punish, rather than to compensate, and the recovery must be in favor of the state, not a private individual.

Applying that test, judgments of double or treble damages are not penal so long as recovery is in favor of a private individual; neither are wrongful death judgments (even where defendant's fault is the measure of recovery). A judgment in favor of the state for tortious conduct against the state's proprietary interests is not penal, since its purpose is compensation, not punishment. Similarly, judgments for taxes are entitled to full faith and credit. Although recovery is in favor of the state, the purpose of tax statutes is to generate revenue, not to punish tax payers; therefore, such judgments do not fall within the *Huntington* definition.[11]

§ 117 The Public Policy of F–2: The Problem of Restatement (Second) Section 103

F–2 may not refuse full faith and credit to an F–1 judgment simply because that judgment is based upon a claim which violates the public policy of F–2.[1] This part of the Iron Law has been applied rigorously. Thus, in *Fauntleroy v. Lum*,[2] the Supreme Court required Mississippi to give full faith and credit to a Missouri judgment, even though that judgment was based upon a "futures" contract — a transaction that Mississippi had outlawed as against its public policy.

---

[8] *See* § 49, *supra*, for a discussion of the first question.

[9] Leflar, McDougal & Felix § 46.

[10] 146 U.S. 657 (1892).

[11] Milwaukee County v. M. E. White Co., 296 U.S. 268 (1935). This includes administrative tax determinations. Scoles, Hay, Borchers & Symeonides § 24.23. For a more complete list of cases classified as penal or non–penal, *see* Restatement (Second) of Conflict of Laws § 89, Reporter's Note. *See also* Scoles, Hay, Borchers & Symeonides § 24.23, where the authors argue that all penal judgments are entitled to full faith and credit. This conclusion, they argue, is an important one in light of the modern trend to subject business entities to substantial regulatory penalties for toxic pollution, antitrust and securities violations, and other corporate misdeeds.

[1] Restatement (Second) of Conflict of Laws § 117.

[2] 210 U.S. 230 (1908), discussed in § 114, *supra*.

[a] Section 103 and *Yarborough v. Yarborough*

But are there situations where F–2 may refuse full faith and credit to a valid F–1 judgment because recognition of that judgment would entail too great a sacrifice of F–2's important interests? The Restatement (Second) takes the position that there are such cases. Section 103 addresses the issue:

> A judgment rendered in one State of the United States need not be recognized or enforced in a sister State if such recognition or enforcement is not required by the national policy of full faith and credit because it would involve an improper interference with important interests of the sister State.[3]

Section 103, in other words, takes the quite controversial position that there are some F–1 judgments which are perfectly valid under the Due Process Clause, yet which are not entitled to full faith and credit in F–2.

Much of the inspiration for § 103 came from Justice Stone's dissent in *Yarborough v. Yarborough*.[4] In *Yarborough*, defendant, pursuant to a Georgia judgment, made a lump sum child support payment to his daughter; that payment, according to Georgia law, exhausted his obligations to the child. She later sued him in South Carolina (her domicile) for additional support for her education and maintenance. The Supreme Court ruled that the Georgia judgment was entitled to full faith and credit in South Carolina and that the judgment precluded the daughter's subsequent action for support.

Justice Stone wrote a sharp dissent based upon the "intent" of the Georgia order and the strong interest of South Carolina in the child. He first argued that the Georgia order was rendered with the purpose only of regulating the relationship of the parties in Georgia, and, therefore, that the Georgia court had not intended to control the parties' rights and duties in South Carolina. Stone's next argument was far more radical. He suggested that South Carolina had an important interest in the maintenance and support of its children and that a sister state judgment ought not be permitted to jeopardize that interest. Stone did not suggest that the Georgia judgment was invalid; rather, he argued that the judgment was not entitled to recognition in South Carolina because the Full Faith and Credit Clause does not authorize "such control by one state of the internal affairs of another." The basic thrust of his argument and the dominant theme behind § 103 is suggested by this passage from Stone's dissent:

> Between the prohibition of the due process clause, acting upon the courts of the state from which such proceedings may be taken, and the mandate of the full faith and credit clause, acting upon the state to which they may be taken, there is an area which federal authority has not occupied. In the assertion of rights, defined by a judgment of one state, within the territory of another, there is often an inescapable

[3] Restatement (Second) of Conflict of Laws § 103. Copyright © 1971 by the American Law Institute. Reprinted with permission of the American Law Institute.

[4] 290 U.S. 202 (1933).

> conflict of interest of the two states, and there comes a point beyond which the imposition of the will of one state beyond its own borders involves a forbidden infringement of some legitimate domestic interest of the other.

Despite Stone's eloquence and the prestige of the American Law Institute, it is quite doubtful whether § 103 provides an accurate general statement of the law.[5] Advocates of § 103 can look to Supreme Court cases in two areas for support:[6] domestic relations and worker's compensation. The domestic relations cases are discussed fully elsewhere[7] in this book; this section only summarizes them. The worker's compensation cases are treated here in detail.

[b] The Domestic Relations Cases

Williams v. North Carolina (II)[8] provides the least ambiguous support for § 103. An earlier decision, *Williams I*,[9] had held that the domicile of a deserting spouse (F–1) has jurisdiction to grant a valid divorce. In *Williams II*, however, the Court held that the state of the matrimonial domicile (F–2) could re-examine F–1's jurisdictional finding of domicile. If, after according F–1's finding "respect and more," F–2 finds the deserting spouse had no bona fide F–1 domicile, it may prosecute for bigamous cohabitation. The holding in *Williams II* supports § 103, because it permits F–2 to deny full recognition to an F–1 judgment based on F–2's strong interest in the marriage:

> [T]he decree of divorce is a conclusive adjudication of everything except the jurisdictional facts upon which it is founded, and domicil is a jurisdictional fact. To permit the necessary finding of domicil by one State to foreclose all States in the protection of their social institutions would be intolerable.

The "divisible divorce" cases, *Estin v. Estin*[10] and *Vanderbilt v. Vanderbilt*,[11] hold that F–2 (the wife's domicile) need not give full faith and credit to an F–1 (husband's domicile) order cutting off the wife's right to alimony. Those holdings provide only equivocal support for § 103, however. Although there is language in the opinions indicating concern for the important

---

[5] *See* Scoles, Hay, Borchers & Symeonides § 24.21.

[6] There is another group of cases which provides support for § 103, but none from this group has reached the Supreme Court. Imagine that an F–1 court with in personam jurisdiction over plaintiff enjoins him from bringing an action in F–2. Plaintiff, however, disobeys the injunction and files suit in F–2. Does the Full Faith and Credit Clause compel F–2 to recognize the F–1 order and dismiss the suit? The cases have held that F–2 need not grant full faith and credit. They rely on the notion that F–1 ought not be able to control the workings of the F–2 court. *See, e.g.*, James v. Grand Trunk W. R.R. Co., 14 Ill. 2d 356, 152 N.E.2d 858 (1958). *See generally* Comment, *Extraterritorial Recognition of Injunctions Against Suit*, 39 Yale L.J. 719 (1930).

[7] *See* §§ 117, 123, 127, *infra*.

[8] 325 U.S. 226 (1945).

[9] Williams v. North Carolina, 317 U.S. 287 (1942).

[10] 334 U.S. 541 (1948). For a thorough discussion of *Estin* and *Vanderbilt*, *see* § 126, *infra*.

[11] 354 U.S. 416 (1957).

interests of F–2 (the § 103 theory), each opinion also contains language suggesting that the holdings are based on the wife's right not to have property taken from her without due process.

May v. Anderson,[12] a custody case, is also ambiguous in its support for § 103. *May* held that F–2 (the wife's domicile) need not give full faith and credit to an F–1 (the husband's domicile) order giving custody of the couple's children to the husband. Once again, the case may be explained on two different grounds: concern either for the policy interests of F–2 or for the wife's due process right not to be deprived of custody by a court that lacked personal jurisdiction over her. Given the tenor of the Court's other decisions, especially *Fauntleroy v. Lum,*[13] however, the more likely reading of the domestic relations cases is that the Court was concerned about protecting the property rights of the absent litigant, the "stay–at–home" spouse or parent. That reading becomes even more compelling in light of the failure of the Court in domestic cases since *Williams I ever* to permit F–2 to refuse to recognize an F–1 decree on the grounds of the public policy of F–2.

[c] The Workers' Compensation Cases

[1] *Magnolia*

Magnolia Petroleum Co. v. Hunt[14] was the first of the workers' compensation cases to discuss the conflict between the mandate of full faith and credit and the important interests of F–2 — the issue posed by § 103. The employee, a Louisiana resident, normally worked in Louisiana, but, in the course of his employment, he travelled to Texas where he was injured. He received a compensation award from the Texas Industrial Accident Board, and employer began making payments as required by the award. The employee later sought to collect worker's compensation under the Louisiana statute.[15] The employer pled the Texas award as res judicata, but the Louisiana courts rejected his contention. The Supreme Court reversed in an opinion by Justice Stone and ruled that, because the Texas award was entitled to full faith and credit, there could be no higher award under the Louisiana statute.

In separate dissents, Justices Douglas and Black made the same arguments Justice Stone had found so convincing in *Yarborough*. Both argued that the Texas award was not intended to bind the parties in Louisiana and that, regardless of the "intent" of the Texas award, it could not bind Louisiana in a matter so important to its social policy and interests.

---

[12] 345 U.S. 528 (1953). For a detailed discussion of *May, see* § 130, *infra.*

[13] *Fauntleroy v. Lum,* 210 U.S. 230 (1908), it will be recalled, originated the Iron Law of Full Faith and Credit. *See* discussion *supra* at § 114.

[14] 320 U.S. 430 (1943).

[15] The issue here in the workers' compensation cases is not whether the worker can get a double recovery. If a second suit is allowed and F–2's measure of compensation is higher than F–1's, the F–2 tribunal credits the employer for the amount of the F–1 award and then awards the employee the difference. The result is that the employee gets two awards from two states, but the total amount of compensation is the amount proper under the statutory scheme of the state allowing the higher award.

[2] *McCartin*

Four years later, in *Industrial Commission of Wisconsin v. McCartin*,[16] the Supreme Court relied heavily on the "not intended" argument and substantially overruled *Magnolia*. Employer and employee, both residents of Illinois, contracted there for employee to work in Wisconsin, where he was injured in the course of his employment. The employee sought workers' compensation benefits in both states. The Illinois proceeding occurred first, and the award (a product of a settlement contract) provided that it "did not affect any rights that [employee] may have under the Workmen's Compensation Act of the State of Wisconsin." Subsequently, employee received a larger award from the Wisconsin Commission. The award was set aside by the Wisconsin courts on the authority of *Magnolia*. The Supreme Court reversed.

The Court relied heavily on language in the Illinois award which expressly stated that the award would not affect any rights under Wisconsin law. The opinion indicated, however, that even absent such language, courts should be reluctant to construe a workers' compensation award in F–1 to preclude a subsequent (higher) award in F–2:

> But there is nothing in the statute or in the decisions thereunder to indicate that it is designed to preclude any recovery by proceedings brought in another state for injuries received there in the course of an Illinois employment. . . . [W]e should not readily interpret such a statute so as to cut off an employee's right to sue under other legislation passed for his benefit. Only some unmistakable language by a state legislature or judiciary would warrant our accepting such a construction.

Predictably, "unmistakable language" in workers' compensation statutes is quite rare, because state legislatures ordinarily give little thought to the compensation schemes of other states. Thus, by relying on the "not intended" argument, the Supreme Court carved a substantial exception out of the Full Faith and Credit Clause for workers' compensation awards. The exception, while analytically suspect,[17] had at least this to recommend it: It was easy to apply and narrowly circumscribed; it appeared to apply to workers' compensation awards, and nothing else.

[3] *Thomas*: The Plurality Opinion

This cautious treatment of the § 103 issue was abandoned by the plurality opinion in *Thomas v. Washington Gas Light Co.*[18] The facts follow the now familiar pattern. Employee, a resident of the District of Columbia, worked for employer in the District, Maryland, and Virginia. In the course of his employment in Virginia, he sustained a back injury. He received an award (pursuant to a settlement agreement) under the Virginia Workmen's Compensation Act, and later sought to receive a supplemental award under

[16] 330 U.S. 622 (1947).

[17] The criticisms of the *McCartin* rule are summarized, *infra*, in the next subsection.

[18] 448 U.S. 261 (1980).

the District of Columbia Act. The administrative tribunals in the District granted the supplemental award; but the Court of Appeals for the Fourth Circuit reversed, holding that the Virginia award was entitled to full faith and credit. A badly fractured Supreme Court reversed.

The plurality opinion by Justice Stevens (joined by Justices Brennan, Stewart, and Blackmun) rejected both the "unmistakable language" formulation of *McCartin* and the strict full faith and credit view of *Magnolia*. The plurality rejected the *McCartin* rule precisely because *McCartin* relied on the "not intended" argument. A state, Stevens wrote, does have indirect control over the recognition of its judgments; it can determine the effect of a judgment by prescribing its effects within the state. Once it has done so, however, the Full Faith and Credit Clause, as interpreted by the Supreme Court, determines the judgment's extraterritorial effect. Thus, according to the plurality, the *McCartin* rule, by focusing on the extraterritorial intent of the rendering state, improperly delegated to that state a power properly exercised only by the Supreme Court. Once a state (through its judiciary and legislature) has determined the domestic effect of a judgment, it cannot, by use of "unmistakable language" indicating its intentions, expand or contract the judgment's extraterritorial effect.

The plurality next rejected the *Magnolia* rule because it was not consistent with settled practice. Before *Magnolia*, the states had not granted preclusive effect to sister state workers' compensation awards. Further, *McCartin* had substantially overruled *Magnolia*. In the thirty years since *McCartin*, only one state had included "unmistakable language" in its statute.[19] Thus, the practice of most courts, both before *Magnolia* and after *McCartin*, was not to give full faith and credit to workers' compensation awards.

Having rejected the approaches of both *Magnolia* and *McCartin*, the plurality took a fresh look at the problem and based its solutions on the kind of interest balancing suggested by § 103. The opinion identified three relevant state interests: (1) Virginia's interest in placing limits on the liability of employers and their insurers; (2) the interests of both jurisdictions in compensating the injured worker; and (3) Virginia's interest in the integrity of its administrative proceedings.

The first two interests were quickly dismissed. The common interest of Virginia and the District in compensating an injured worker could not be harmed by permitting a supplemental award. Virginia's interest in limiting liability did not get much weight, because an employee could choose initially to proceed under the compensation scheme of either Virginia or the District of Columbia. Thus, employers and their insurers would have to measure their potential liability by the more generous of the two systems. Further, giving strong preclusive effect to a workers' compensation award would place a premium on an injured worker's ability to make the correct choice of forum. The plurality reasoned that such an emphasis on forum shopping was inappropriate in an area where proceedings are initiated informally and often without advice of counsel.

[19] *See* Nev. Rev. Stat. § 616.525 (1979).

With these two interests discounted, it remained for the plurality to consider Virginia's interest in the integrity of its quasi–judicial proceedings. In assessing that interest, the opinion relied on an argument originally made by proponents of § 103.[20] The plurality drew a sharp distinction between a court of general jurisdiction and an administrative tribunal. Although the plurality believed that the factual findings of both are entitled to extraterritorial recognition, the claim–preclusive effect of an administrative award should not be the same as that of an ordinary judgment. In a court of general jurisdiction in F–1, the parties can argue that the law of F–2 should control, and the court can decide this issue. When it does so, it has before it the important interests of F–2 embodied in F–2's law. An F–1 administrative tribunal, by contrast, can apply only the law that its statutory authorization permits — the law of F–1. Accordingly, it makes sense to distinguish between an ordinary judgment and an administrative award when it comes to full faith and credit. Because F–2's interests can be raised before an F–1 court, F–2 may not deny full faith and credit based on those interests. By contrast, because F–2's interests cannot be raised before an F–1 administrative tribunal, F–2 may consider those interests when determining whether to recognize the F–1 award. The plurality summarized its argument toward the end of the opinion:

> Thus, whether or not the worker has sought an award from the less generous jurisdiction in the first instance, the vindication of that State's interest in placing a ceiling on employers' liability would inevitably impinge upon the substantial interests of the second jurisdiction in the welfare and subsistence of disabled workers — interests that a court of general jurisdiction might consider, but which must be ignored by the Virginia Industrial Commission.

The plurality's argument, then — which for convenience can be labelled "the limited choice of law" argument — appears to be a limited resurrection of Justice Stone's (and § 103's) notion of an exception to full faith and credit based on the important interests of F–2.

[4] *Thomas*: The Concurrence and the Dissent

Justice White concurred in an opinion in which Chief Justice Burger and Justice Powell joined. White challenged the "limited choice of law" argument with a powerful *reductio ad absurdum* hypothetical. He suggested that the argument might apply just as well to an ordinary tort action in which the F–1 court was constrained to apply F–1 law by a strong statutory or judge–made forum–favoring choice–of–law rule.[21] If the plurality's

[20] *See* Willis Reese & Vincent Johnson, *The Scope of Full Faith and Credit to Judgments*, 49 Colum L. Rev. 153, 176–177 (1949); Elliot Cheatham, *Res Judicata and the Full Faith and Credit Clause: Magnolia Petroleum v. Hunt*, 44 Colum L. Rev. 330, 341–346 (1944). Although the plurality opinion cites both articles, it does not credit either for originating this particular argument. The dissent, in footnote 2, noticed that omission and credited the commentators for the plurality's argument. The argument, in fact, may have appeared even earlier, for there is at least a hint of it in Justice Black's dissent in *Magnolia*.

[21] An apt example is provided by Semler v. Psychiatric Institute of Washington, D.C. 575

argument applies in such a case (and it is difficult to distinguish the hypothetical case from *Thomas*), it proves too much, for it seems to require a wholesale re–evaluation of the Full Faith and Credit Clause. In Justice White's words:

> Hence the plurality's rationale would portend a wide–ranging reassessment of the principles of full faith and credit in many areas. Such a reassessment is not necessarily undesirable if the results are likely to be healthy for the judicial system and consistent with the underlying purposes of the Full Faith and Credit Clause. But at least without the benefit of briefs and arguments directed to the issue, I cannot conclude that the rule advocated by the plurality would have such a beneficial impact.

Justice White advocated the retention of the *McCartin* approach. While he thought it rested on "questionable foundations," he nevertheless favored it over the plurality's approach as more narrowly limited to workers' compensation cases and less likely to have untoward ramifications elsewhere.

Justice Rehnquist's dissenting opinion, in which Justice Marshall joined, also rejected the "limited choice of law" argument. Rehnquist thought the plurality radically under–estimated Virginia's interest in the finality of its determination. Virginia had invested time and money in the resolution of the dispute and, accordingly, had an interest in seeing that its resources were not wasted by relitigation. Rehnquist's fundamental dispute with the plurality transcended these points, however. He objected to the whole notion of "interest balancing" as a technique for interpreting the Full Faith and Credit Clause. Although the balancing of interests has a role in the choice–of–law inquiry, it has no place in the discussion of the interstate recognition of judgments:

> The Full Faith and Credit Clause did not allot to this Court the task of "balancing" interests where the "public Acts, Records, and judicial Proceedings" of a State were involved. It simply directed that they be given the "Full Faith and Credit" that the Court today denies to those of Virginia.

Justice Rehnquist rejected the *McCartin* rule as well as the plurality's "balancing" approach. Instead, he favored a return to the rule of *Magnolia*, which gave the same faith and credit to worker's compensation awards as to all other state court judgments.

F.2d 922 (D.C. Cir. 1978). That case involved a successful wrongful death action in Virginia followed by an attempt to recover survivor's benefits under the law of the District of Columbia. The court rejected that effort, in part because the plaintiff could have sued originally in either the District of Columbia or in Virginia. Plaintiff attempted to analogize her case to *McCartin* because the District of Columbia, unlike Virginia, distinguished between wrongful death and survivor's recovery and would have permitted the later action. The Court of Appeals, however, found it easy to distinguish *McCartin* and *Magnolia Petroleum* on the simple ground that they do not apply in "ordinary choice–of–law cases."

[5] *Thomas*: An Evaluation[22]

Justice White's solution to the worker's compensation problem is the most practical. It is quite clear that *McCartin* rests on a "questionable foundation." All nine members of the Court agree on that score. Yet it may be an adequate answer to the narrow question of the interstate recognition of compensation awards. Surely that is an issue which is more important to settle than to settle correctly. On this narrow view of the problem, *McCartin* is an almost perfect answer. It is limited in scope, easy to understand, and difficult to over–generalize (unlike the plurality opinion in *Thomas*). Further, unlike the dissent in *Thomas*, it does not entail the dislocations which typically accompany the overhaul of a thirty–year–old rule.[23]

As a solution to the broad problem of the conflict between full faith and credit and the important interests of F–2, *McCartin* is totally inadequate. It may be, however, that a solution to the larger problem is not so crucial. The question has arisen so far in only a few areas, and the individual solutions in those areas seem to be adequately understood and narrowly limited.[24] Perhaps it is better to settle for such individual solutions than to search for a broad subsuming principle which can be easily misunderstood or over–generalized.

Section 103 is, of course, an ambitious attempt to solve the larger problem, and today its stock is higher than it was before the plurality opinion in *Thomas*. Still, its advocates can look for unequivocal support from the Supreme Court to only one majority opinion[25] and one plurality opinion. The majority opinion (*Williams II*) was written half a century ago, and its authority has been severely undercut by subsequent cases, which radically restrict the opportunity for collateral attack upon an F–1 divorce.[26] Furthermore, many of the cases[27] that seem to support the interest–balancing language in *Williams II* can be explained by the Supreme Court's concern for the interests of absent parties, rather than by its concern for the interests of F–2. Finally, it is tempting (and easy) to dismiss the workers' compensation cases (*McCartin* and *Thomas*) as result–oriented decisions born of the Court's desire to protect the injured worker at all costs. Thus, although the case for § 103 is today stronger than it was before *Thomas*, it is still based on two isolated, atypical lines of authority.[28]

---

[22] For more commentary on *Thomas, see* Stewart Sterk, *Full Faith and Credit, More or Less, to Judgments: Doubts about Thomas v. Washington Gas Light Co.*, 69 Geo. L.J. 1329 (1981).

[23] It is doubtful, however, whether overruling the *McCartin* rule would cause any dislocations simply because it is unlikely that anyone ever relied upon it.

[24] *See* these domestic relations cases: Williams v. North Carolina (Williams II), 325 U.S. 226 (1945); Estin v. Estin, 334 U.S. 541 (1948); Vanderbilt v. Vanderbilt, 354 U.S. 416 (1957); May v. Anderson, 345 U.S. 528 (1953); the workers' compensation case: Industrial Commission of Wisconsin v. McCartin, 330 U.S. 622 (1947); and the injunction cases, note 6, *supra*.

[25] Williams v. North Carolina (Williams II), 325 U.S. 226 (1945).

[26] *See* Cook v. Cook, 342 U.S. 126 (1951); Johnson v. Muelberger, 340 U.S. 581 (1951); Sherrer v. Sherrer, 334 U.S. 343 (1948).

[27] *E.g., Estin, Vanderbilt*, and *May*. *See* notes 10–13, *supra*.

[28] Once again, the injunction cases (*see* note 6, *supra*) may furnish another line of authority, but none of these cases has been to the Supreme Court.

To formulate an entire theory of full faith and credit based upon such limited authority seems to be a classic case of allowing the tail to wag the dog. The Iron Law of Full Faith and Credit, in other words, still stands.

[d] *Baker v. General Motors*

In *Baker v. General Motors*,[29] the Supreme Court gave the § 103 theory a much narrower range of operation than did the plurality in *Thomas*. Ronald Elwell, an engineer employed by General Motors sued the company in Michigan for wrongful discharge, and GM counterclaimed for breach of fiduciary duty. The dispute involved Elwell's testimony against GM in a Georgia product liability action based on the design defects of certain GM fuel systems. The parties settled the Michigan action, with Elwell receiving an undisclosed sum of money and the parties' agreeing to an injunction prohibiting Elwell from testifying against GM in any future product liability actions. The settlement agreement contained an exception permitting Elwell to testify in such actions if ordered by the court.

Later in Missouri, the Bakers brought a wrongful death product liability action against GM based on the defective design of a fuel pump. After GM removed the action to federal court, the Bakers sought to depose Elwell and call him as a witness at trial. When GM objected, arguing that the Michigan injunction barred Elwell's testimony, the Baker's countered that the Michigan injunction could not override the Missouri subpoena. The district court ruled in favor of the Bakers,[30] and Elwell testified at trial. The Eighth Circuit reversed,[31] holding that Elwell's testimony should not have been admitted.

In a unanimous decision supported by three different opinions, the Supreme Court reversed the Eighth Circuit. Justice Ginsberg, writing for a five–vote majority, reinforced the Iron Law of full faith and credit and made short work of the *Thomas* plurality's expansive version of the public policy exception:

> Our decision support no roving "public policy exception" to the full faith and credit due judgments. . . . We are "aware of [no] considerations of local policy or law which could rightly be deemed to impair the force and effect which the full faith and credit clause and the act of Congress require to be given to [a money] judgment made outside the state of its rendition."[32]

Further she laid to rest any lingering suspicion that equity decrees are entitled to less faith and credit than law judgments. "We see no reason why the preclusive effects of an adjudication on parties and those 'in privity'

---

[29] 522 U.S. 222. For commentary, see Stewart E. Sterk, *The Muddy Boundaries Between Res Judicata and Full Faith and Credit,* 58 Wash. & Lee L. Rev. 47 (2001).

[30] 159 F.R.D. 519.

[31] 86 F.3d 811 (8th Cir. 1996).

[32] 522 U.S. at 233.

with them. . .should differ depending solely upon the type of relief sought a civil action."[33]

Nevertheless, the majority opinion did permit a very limited scope of operation for the § 103 principle. Citing *Fall v. Eastin*[34] and the state court anti–suit injunction cases,[35] Justice Ginsberg stated that state court judgments have been "denied enforcement when they purported to accomplish an official act within the exclusive province of. . .[a sister] State or interfered with litigation over which the ordering State had no authority."

The precedential value of even this pared–down version of the § 103 principle is unclear, however; it is after all dictum in the case. The actual holding rested on the simpler and uncontroversial preclusion principle that a stranger to a litigation is not bound by its results. Because the Bakers had not been parties to the Michigan action, the injunction could not bind them.[36]

Justice Scalia based his short concurring opinion[37] on the general principle that the full faith and credit clause does not require an F–2 court to enforce an F–1 judgment directly. Just as the F–2 court need not issue execution upon an F–1 money judgment (the F–1 plaintiff first must sue in F–2 and obtain an F–2 judgment, which then can be enforced by execution), it need not enforce directly an F–1 injunction. To obtain full faith and credit for its Michigan injunction, GM would have had to sue Elwell in Missouri on the Michigan judgment and obtain a Missouri injunction, which it then could have enforced to prevent Elwell's testimony. Because GM had not gone through this proper procedure, Scalia was not faced squarely with § 103 issue: whether Michigan, *by any device*, could control the admissibility of evidence in a Missouri proceeding.

Justice Kennedy, joined by Justices O'Connor and Thomas, concurred in a separate opinion.[38] He refused to join the majority opinion because of doubts about even the pared-down version of the § 103 exception to full faith and credit. He argued–and the majority conceded as much–that the Court had not yet considered whether the full faith and credit clause permitted an F–2 court to ignore an F–1 antisuit injunction purporting to control litigation in F–2. Since *Baker* did not require a decision of that issue, he saw no reason to resolve it, or to generalize from its resolution the majority's pared–down version of the § 103 principle. He also expressed

[33] *Id.* at 234. For discussion of the lower-court cases that had considered this issue, see Polly J. Price, *Full Faith and Credit and the Equity Conflict*, 84 Va. L. Rev. 747, 757–761 (1998).

[34] 215 U.S. 1 (1909). *See* § 115[e], *supra*.

[35] *See, e.g.*, James v. Grand Trunk W. R. R., 14 Ill. 2d 356, 152 N.E. 2d 858 (1958), discussed supra at note 6. For discussion of this portion of Justice Ginsberg's opinion, see Earl M. Maltz, *The Full Faith and Credit Clause and the First Restatement: The Place of* Baker v General Motors Corp. *in Choice of Law Theory*, 73 Tul. L. Rev. 305, 310 (1998).

[36] In response to a hypothetical posed by Justice Kennedy, 522 U.S. 245–246, Justice Ginsberg acknowledged that had the Bakers been parties to the Michigan proceeding, they would have been precluded from litigating the privileged character of Elwell's testimony in Missouri. 522 U.S. at 238.

[37] 522 U.S. at 241.

[38] *Id.* at 243.

doubt about whether the majority's articulation of the exception ("accomplish an official act" or "interfere with the litigation over which the ordering state had no authority") gave the lower courts adequate guidance on when and how the exception should apply.

Justice Kennedy would have resolved the case by applying the first step of the *Marrese–Matsushita*[39] analysis. When granting full faith in credit to a state–court judgment, a federal court must first consider what preclusive effect the judgment would have under law of the issuing state. Justice Kennedy reviewed Michigan preclusion law, and concluded that it would not give the judgment preclusive effect against the Bakers, and therefore that there was no need to consider the second step of the analysis: whether there was any applicable exception to the iron law full faith and credit.

The opinions in *Baker* add a modicum of clarity to the law full faith and credit and repair the damage done by the *Thomas* plurality's opinion. The court unanimously rejected a "roving public policy exception" to the iron law full faith in credit. Five justices still believe that there should be some minimal § 103–type exception to full faith and credit, but that it should be limited to anti–suit injunctions and settled Supreme Court precedents such as *Fall v. Eastin.*[40] Even the anti–suit injunction exception is not certain, all the justices agreeing that the Supreme Court has never affirmed the principle with a clear holding. Nevertheless dictum in *Baker* and numerous state–court cases suggest that the exception should exist. Apparently however the Supreme Court is in no hurry to settle the issue; anti–suit injunction cases arise frequently, and if the Supreme Court wanted to, it could grant certiorari and decide a case directly on point.

---

[39] Marrese v. American Academy of Orthopedic Surgeons, 470 U.S. 373 (1985), Matsushita Electrical Industrial Co. Ltd. v. Epstein, 516 U.S. 367 (1996), both discussed *supra* at § 113[b][3].

[40] For favorable commentary on the majority's minimalist interpretation of § 103, see Katherine C. Pearson, *Common–law Preclusion, Full Faith and Credit, and Consent Judgments: The Analytical Challenge*, 48 Cath. U. L. Rev. 419, 463 (1999).

Chapter 6

FAMILY LAW

§ 118 Introduction to Family Law and Conflicts

Family law presents unique problems in the field of conflicts. Although family legal problems are sometimes treated in the same fashion as any other personal legal problem encountered in tort or contract law, the law also treats the relationship among family members as creating a status *res* (or thing) in whose existence and dissolution the state has an interest. Thus, the partners to a marriage may not divorce without at least some form of approval by the state, nor may they ignore their children without a great deal of state intervention. The peculiar nature of the family's legal status, in other words, creates special conflicts problems.

Further problems are created by the continuing need for adjustments to the family's legal arrangements; support payments may have to be modified or custody arrangements altered, and, if the parties cannot agree, a judge must intervene. Because the parties involved often have moved to other states, the new jurisdiction is also interested in the situation. The interest of several states in the supervision and adjustment of continuing arrangements among family members makes problems in domestic relations particularly knotty.

This unique nature of family law problems provides an interesting and instructive contrast with the rest of conflicts law. We have chosen, for that reason, to conclude this book with a chapter on those problems. There are three Parts in this Chapter. The first discusses the opposite problems of marriage and divorce; in these sections the major concern is jurisdiction to marry or to divorce, with choice of law having a supporting role. The second Part of the Chapter addresses the after–effects of separation and divorce, alimony and support; once again, the primary concern is jurisdiction. The third Part of the Chapter examines conflict of laws and children; here, choice of law and jurisdiction are both important.

Part A

MARRIAGE AND DIVORCE

§ 119 The Validity of the Marriage

[a] Generally[1]

American law regulates both the creation and dissolution of marital ties. The overwhelming tendency in American conflicts cases is to validate the marriage. Courts usually accomplish this result by deciding questions about the validity of the marriage under the law of the place where the marriage was celebrated. Use of the *lex celebrationis* can be rationalized under either traditional or modern approaches to choice of law. The First Restatement used the law of the celebrating state because marriage creates a status between the celebrants; hence, questions concerning the validity of the marriage were referred to the law of the place that created the status.[2] The net effect of that reference, of course, is to validate the marriage.[3]

The rationalization of the general rule of validation under modern approaches to choice of law is also easy to understand, although the desire to validate may be misplaced. A famous illustration is *In Re May's Estate.*[4] That case involved an uncle and niece, both New York residents, whose marriage was forbidden by New York law. The two traveled to Rhode Island (where such marriages were legal), returned to New York shortly after the ceremony, and lived there together for 35 years. When Mrs. May died, one of their children objected to the appointment of Mr. May as the administrator of her estate, asserting the invalidity of the Rhode Island marriage. The Court of Appeals of New York rejected that challenge, referring to the general rule concerning marital validity.

Powerful reasons support that result: the validation rule confirms the parties' expectations, it provides stability in an area where stability (because of children and property) is very important, and it avoids the potentially hideous problems that would arise if the legality of a marriage varied from state to state.[5] Yet, the validation of the Rhode Island marriage

---

[1] *See generally* Scoles, et al. ch. 13; Weintraub § 5.1.

[2] Restatement (First) of Conflict of Laws § 121.

[3] The tendency to validate is so strong that Professor Ehrenzweig identified this as one of his "True Rules." Albert A. Ehrenzweig, Treatise on the Conflict of Laws 138 (1962). *See* § 81, *supra*. The tendency to validate includes overlooking problems with procedural formalities. Scoles, et al. § 13.6. Common law marriages are generally validated unless the connection with the common law jurisdiction is tenuous. *Id.*

[4] 305 N.Y. 486, 114 N.E.2d 4 (1953).

[5] *See* Leflar, McDougal & Felix § 220; Restatement (Second) of Conflict of Laws § 283.

in *May's Estate* sacrifices New York's legitimate, strong, and legislatively expressed interest in preventing incestuous relations among its residents.[6]

Courts faced with choice of law problems involving the validity of a marriage, however, typically are more concerned with personal than with governmental interests. Hence, it is not surprising that even under policy–based analysis the general approach to choice–of–law in this area parallels the approach followed in contracts cases. There, too, courts often choose the law which validates the parties' agreement, unless doing so would offend a strongly held policy of an interested state.[7]

[b] The Exceptions

The rule of celebration can be upset in rare cases if the state has a sufficiently strong interest. The opinion in *May's Estate* suggests two possibilities for upsetting the marriage: Either the legislature must "clearly" express that the general rule of validity should not be applied,[8] or the prohibited union must be so "offensive to the public sense of morality" as to be regarded as abhorrent and a violation of "natural law."

Instances of clear statutory rules are rare. Perhaps the best examples are provided by the old "paramour's statutes" which prohibited remarriage within a specified period following a divorce.[9] Examples of prohibited abhorrent relations include polygamy and incest. A polygamous marriage of a domiciliary probably would not be validated by an American court, even if valid where celebrated. A marriage of a minor, however, is likely to be recognized, although not all jurisdictions agree.[10] Marriage involving some incestuous relations (*e.g.*, first cousins) probably will be recognized, but marriage of others clearly will not (*e.g.*, mother–son); and some marriages (*e.g.*, uncle–niece) are a toss–up.

[c] The Incidental Question[11]

A final problem in this area concerns what has come to be known as the "incidental question" a question concerning the validity of a marriage that arises incidentally in the resolution of another question (such as whether a claimant is a spouse under the workers' compensation laws). Although the incidental question can arise in any area of the law,[12] American

[6] Viewed solely in terms of modern interest analysis, *May's Estate* arguably presented a false conflict.

[7] *See* § 88, *supra*. Perhaps the closest analogy is to the law applied in usury cases.

[8] The New York legislature had forbidden the celebration of the marriage in New York, but had not expressly stated that all uncle–niece marriages by New York domiciliaries were invalid.

[9] *See* Scoles, et al. § 13.9.

[10] *See* Leflar, McDougal & Felix § 221.

[11] *See generally* Willis Reese, *Marriage in American Conflict of Laws*, 26 Int'l & Comp. L.Q. 952 (1977).

[12] *See generally* A. E. Gotlieb, *The Incidental Question Revisited, Theory and Practice in the Conflict of Laws*, 26 Int'l & Comp. L.Q. 734 (1977).

conflicts literature usually limits the discussion to marriage. The incidental question arises often in this area because many statutes attach important legal consequences to marital status. A compensation statute, for example, may provide benefits only to a "spouse." In determining whether a claimant is a "spouse," should a court apply the same test that it would use in an action brought by one of the partners to set aside his own marriage? Expressed differently, did the legislature, by using the term "spouse," mean to incorporate the law (including the choice–of–law rules) that would govern a dispute between the two parties to the purported marriage? The usual answer is that "spouse" (or "husband" or "wife") has a fixed meaning that remains the same everywhere it is used. That answer has the enormous advantage of certainty, bringing with it a large body of case law and commentary on difficult questions.

It is by no means clear, however, that the usual answer is correct. A workers' compensation statute, for example, is designed to protect those who depended on the wage earner, a statutory goal unaffected by the policies that led to the prohibition of incestuous marriages. Hence, the answer to the incidental question should focus on the purposes to be achieved by the particular statute in issue. Rote referral to the general law dealing with marital validity only fortuitously address the questions the court should ask in cases dealing with problems like survivor's benefits.

An example is *In Re Estate of Lenherr.*[13] The Lenherrs each had been divorced; each divorce was grounded on adultery committed by the Lenherrs with each other. The Lenherrs, Pennsylvania domiciliaries, were forbidden by a Pennsylvania statute to marry during the lives of their former spouses. They married in West Virginia where their union was legal, and returned to Pennsylvania to live. When Mr. Lenherr died, Mrs. Lenherr sought the tax exemption available to widows under Pennsylvania inheritance law. The Supreme Court of Pennsylvania held that she was entitled to the exemption. It found that the purpose behind the remarriage prohibition was to protect "the sensibilities" of the injured spouse, a purpose that would not be advanced significantly by denying a tax exemption designed to ameliorate financial hardship. Because the purpose behind the exemption would be frustrated by its denial to the "widow," the court would not apply Pennsylvania law to invalidate the marriage.[14] This sensible result illustrates nicely how the "incidental question" should be analyzed when marital status is at issue.

[d] The Defense of Marriage Act

Congress adopted the Defense of Marriage Act ("DOMA") in 1996.[15] It did so in response to a decision by the Hawaii Supreme Court that the

---

[13] 455 Pa. 225, 314 A.2d 255 (1974).

[14] The court's analysis bears a marked resemblance to comparative impairment. *See* § 79, *supra*. But note that in *Lenherr* the two rules that must be tested for "comparative impairment" are from the same jurisdiction, Pennsylvania.

[15] 1 U.S.C. § 7 and 28 U.S. C. § 1738C (1996). DOMA has spawned a vast literature. *See,*

Hawaiian Constitution forbade discrimination against same–sex couples who wanted to marry. Congress, worried that states would be compelled constitutionally to recognize a same–sex marriage valid in one state, used its legislative power under the Full Faith and Credit Clause to make clear that recognition may not be required:

> No state . . . is required to give effect to any public act, record, or judicial proceeding of any other state . . . respecting a relationship between persons of the same sex that is treated as a marriage under the laws of such state . . .

DOMA was, of course, unnecessary if *In Re May's Estate*[16] is constitutionally sound[17] — a proposition of which there was little doubt until the furor over DOMA erupted. *May's Estate* states the widely accepted rule: Each state is free to accept or reject a marriage celebrated elsewhere. That rule is part of a larger rule, of course: The Full Faith and Credit Clause generally does not require recognition of *statutes* (as apposed to *judgments*) of another state.[18]

§ 120 Jurisdiction to Divorce: Domicile

The basis for the exercise of divorce jurisdiction in American law today is domicile. Not only is domicile the overwhelming basis in state law, but it also may be constitutionally required. The requisite domiciliary connection may be that of either spouse, and it need not be the marital domicile — the place where the parties lived together as husband and wife. The leading case is *Williams v. North Carolina*.[1]

[a] *Williams I*

Petitioners in *Williams* each had been married previously to another partner in the small town of Granite Falls, North Carolina.[2] In 1940, they traveled to Nevada, where they stayed for six weeks at the Alamo Auto Court. Each petitioner then filed for divorce through the same lawyer. Service on the absent spouses was made by publication, by mail, and by

---

e.g., Symposium, *Inter–jurisdictional Marriage Recognition*, 32 Creighton L. Rev. 3 (1998) (contributions by many professors); Larry Kramer, *Same–Sex Marriage, Choice of Law, and Public Policy*, 106 Yale L.J. 1965 (1997); Joseph W. Hovermill, *A Conflict of Laws and Morals: The Choice of Law Implications of Hawaii's Recognition of Same-Sex Marriages*, 53 Md. L. Rev. 450 (1994).

[16] *See* § 119[a], *supra*.

[17] DOMA, of course, might run afoul of other constitutional provisions, such as equal protection or due process. Those problems are beyond the scope of this book. *See generally* Mark Strasser, *Loving the Romer out for Baehr: On Acts in Defense of Marriage and the Constitution*, 58 U. Pitt. L. Rev. 279 (1997).

[18] *See* § 97, *supra*.

[1] 317 U.S. 287 (1942). This opinion is usually referred to as *Williams I* because the case was the subject of another landmark Supreme Court decision in 1945, reported at 325 U.S. 226 (1945), and known as *Williams II*.

[2] The official report of the case is supplemented in memorable detail in Thomas Reed Powell, *And Repent at Leisure*, 58 Harv. L. Rev. 930 (1945).

personal service. The Nevada court found that the petitioners were domiciled in Nevada and granted the divorces. The two were then married in Nevada and returned to North Carolina to live. Despite an apparently quiet life, they were prosecuted and convicted of bigamous cohabitation and sentenced to the state prison. The Supreme Court reversed.

Justice Douglas' majority opinion recognized that the basic issue was the extent to which the Nevada decree was entitled to full faith and credit. If the court that rendered the divorce had jurisdiction to do so, then North Carolina was required to give effect to the decree. Thus, the following constitutional question was posed: Is the domicile of one spouse a sufficient jurisdictional basis for divorce? Douglas answered that it was, referring to the "rightful and legitimate concern" of each state with its domiciliaries. "Domicil," he wrote, "creates a relationship to the state which is adequate for numerous exercises of state power," including adjusting a status (marriage) that affects children, property interests, and responsibilities to the spouse.

The lesson of *Williams I* is that F–2 must give full faith and credit to an F–1 divorce if F–1 was the domicile of one of the spouses — even the deserting spouse. F–1 need not be the domicile of both spouses, nor need it be the marital domicile. Douglas found it irrelevant that the state of the matrimonial domicile might not have its interests fully represented or even considered by the decree. Citing *Fauntleroy v. Lum,*[3] Douglas commented sententiously that, "Such is part of the price of our federal system."

[b] *Williams II*

On remand, the unhappy defendants were retried and convicted again. The case once again came before the Supreme Court. The issue the second time around was the relevance of the finding by the North Carolina courts that petitioners had lacked a "bona fide" domicile in Nevada, a finding not before the Supreme Court in *Williams I.* This time, the Court affirmed the convictions.[4]

At the heart of the majority opinion is the notion that if divorce may be based on domicile in F–1, it would be "intolerable" to prevent F–2 from challenging that jurisdictional fact in a collateral proceeding. Justice Frankfurter wrote that "the decree of divorce is a conclusive adjudication of everything except the jurisdictional facts upon which it is founded, and domicil is a jurisdictional fact." To hold otherwise would mean "the policy of each State in matters of most intimate concern could be subverted by the policy of every other State." Because North Carolina had not been a party to the Nevada litigation, it should not be foreclosed from challenging the jurisdictional facts necessary to the grant of a valid divorce.[5]

---

[3] 210 U.S. 230 (1908), discussed *supra*, § 114.

[4] Williams v. North Carolina (II), 325 U.S. 226 (1945).

[5] Justice Frankfurter did not explain whether the applicable law of domicile should be determined by federal or state law. The requirement that North Carolina need only give "great deference" to Nevada's finding of domicile suggests, however, that Frankfurter had in mind

Justice Frankfurter, in short, recognized that the practical effect of *Williams I* was to enshrine a variant of Gresham's Law in the Constitution — lenient divorce laws drive out strict ones. In order to reduce the ability of a divorce mill like Nevada to undermine the legitimate concerns of the marital domicile, it was necessary to permit F–2 to re–examine the jurisdictional finding of domicile to insure that it was something more than a legal fiction. "Divorce," Frankfurter observed, "like marriage, is of concern not merely to the immediate parties." A state (in this case, Nevada) must have its own interest in the res before it can effectively interfere with the interests of another state (North Carolina) in that same *res*. Whether any interest other than domicile gives a state a sufficient interest is discussed in the next section.

§ 121 Jurisdiction to Divorce: Other Bases[1]

In *Williams I*, the Supreme Court held that the domicile of one spouse provides a sufficient jurisdictional basis for the divorce to be recognized under the Full Faith and Credit Clause. The Court, however, has never approved or disapproved a basis other than domicile for jurisdiction to divorce; it is possible, therefore, that other affiliating factors will satisfy the constitutional demand of due process, and that decrees based on those factors will be entitled to full faith and credit.[2]

The most likely candidate is residence. The Uniform Marriage and Divorce Act[3] permits divorce of armed forces personnel based only on 90 days' residence in the state, a result also reached by some state courts without benefit of a statute. Relaxing the requirement of domicile in this situation makes sense: Soldiers and sailors, because of the compulsory and ambulatory nature of their work, have problems not easily solved under the nebulous rubric of domicile.[4]

There has been little judicial discussion of the domicile requirement in other contexts. The leading case, *Alton v. Alton*,[5] involved a divorce in the Virgin Islands of a couple domiciled in Connecticut. The decree was

---

a universal notion of domicile which all states must follow. In any event, the relevant definition should be provided by federal law; because of the holding in *Williams I* that the *federal* constitution required domicile as a jurisdictional nexus, no other result would be plausible. In note 7 of its opinion, the Court noted that "the proper criteria for ascertaining domicile, should these be in dispute, become matters for federal determination." That is clearly correct; if domicile is constitutionally required in order to obtain subject matter jurisdiction, then the contours of that requirement must be subject to Supreme Court delineation.

[1] *See generally* Helen Garfield, *The Transitory Divorce Action: Jurisdiction in the No–Fault Era*, 58 Tex. L. Rev. 501 (1980); Rhonda Wasserman, *Parents, Partners, and Personal Jurisdiction*, 1995 U. Ill. L. Rev. 813.

[2] *See* Restatement (Second) of Conflict of Laws § 72, Reporter's Note.

[3] 9A U.L.A. § 302 (a)(1).

[4] It is especially difficult for service personnel to demonstrate the "intent" necessary to establish a domicile of choice. *See generally* Note, *Conflict of Laws: Limitations on the "Domicile of Choice" of Military Servicemen*, 31 Okla. L. Rev. 167 (1978).

[5] 207 F.2d 667 (3d Cir. 1953), *vacated as moot*, 347 U.S. 610 (1954).

rendered solely on the basis of the residence of the wife and personal jurisdiction over the husband. The territorial statute permitting the divorce was held unconstitutional by the Third Circuit in an opinion written by Judge Goodrich, a formidable conflicts scholar.[6]

Goodrich wrote that the question of whether domicile was indispensable for divorce jurisdiction forced the court to "go out beyond where legal trails end." That journey led him to conclude that the traditional requirement of domicile was necessary "if our states are really to have control over the domestic relations of their citizens." If domicile were not required, a divorce mill would find it all too easy to intervene in those relations without any legitimate interest in them; only domicile can supply the requisite nexus between petitioner and the forum to insure that the forum is protecting its own interests and not simply meddling in the affairs of a sister state. Because the Virgin Islands divorce statute did not require domicile as a jurisdictional basis, it violated the due process component of the Fifth Amendment.[7]

Judge Hastie, dissenting, found the historical basis for the domicile requirement flimsy. More important, he argued that a "highly technical concept" such as domicile was "elusive and very unsatisfactory," and, therefore, not a good basis for a constitutional test for jurisdiction. To Judge Hastie, "the due process question in divorce jurisdiction is whether it is fair for a state and its courts to adjudicate the merits of a petition for [divorce]." The focus on fairness led Hastie to conclude that any court possessing personal jurisdiction over the parties could properly hear the claim. Finally, Hastie recognized that if personal jurisdiction were a sufficient basis for divorce, then choice of law would become a live issue in divorce cases as, of course, it is in other areas of the law.[8]

Choosing between the two positions is not easy. Bolstering Hastie's position is the argument that failure of the Virgin Islands court to hear a divorce claim arising in Connecticut would violate the rule in *Hughes v. Fetter* requiring state courts to hear transitory causes of action.[9] Reinforcing that argument further is the fact that almost all states now permit divorce on no–fault grounds,[10] a development which shows that divorce has changed in the years since *Williams I*, from an area in which the sovereign

---

[6] The Virgin Islands statute was later held unconstitutional by the Supreme Court because it conflicted with the enabling act for territorial legislation. Granville–Smith v. Granville–Smith, 349 U.S. 1 (1955).

[7] Goodrich did not explain how due process could be violated given that the respondent husband had entered a general appearance. The protection of the Due Process Clause expressly runs only to "persons," but the parties had not been deprived of anything, because the parties *wanted* the divorce. Hence, the use of the Due Process Clause to protect "states' rights" in *Alton* is curious.

[8] If the forum choice–of–law rule were retained in divorce cases, a divorce system based on personal jurisdiction might make a spouse reluctant to travel to Nevada to gamble! In the case at bar, Judge Hastie believed the law of Connecticut, the marital domicile, would most likely be applied.

[9] *See* § 49, *supra*, for a discussion of the difference between local and transitory actions.

[10] Homer Clark, The Law of Domestic Relations in the United States 700–701 (2d ed. 1987).

had an important substantive policy interest to one where the state's interests are in ensuring that the marriage is really "dead" and in securing procedural regularity in its dissolution. Those interests may not be strong enough to need the protection afforded by the requirement of domicile for divorce jurisdiction.[11] On the other hand, it can be argued in support of Goodrich that the peculiar nature of divorce proceedings, especially in states which have established unusual administrative machinery such as mediation and conciliation,[12] should divest the Virgin Islands of jurisdiction unless it has acquired a legitimate interest in the marital res — such as becoming the domicile of one of the spouses.

Despite such interesting problems, the issue remains little discussed today. Judge Hastie's forward–looking opinion, although well known to conflicts students, has not been followed.[13] Jurisdiction based on domicile, or its first cousin, residence, remains the universal order of the day.[14] Nor has there been any movement away from automatic choice of forum law in divorce cases, another concern of Judge Hastie in *Alton*, and the topic examined in the next section.

§ 122 Choice of Law in Divorce[1]

American courts have almost always applied forum law to determine the grounds for divorce.[2] That practice is not surprising in light of the constitutional requirement of domicile for divorce jurisdiction. Choice of forum law is justified because "[t]he state of a person's domicile has the dominant interest in that person's marital status."[3] Modern choice–of–law theories have not changed traditional practice in this area. To the extent that the divorce petitioner has a "real" domicile in the forum, the forum is interested in the outcome of the case. If the divorce laws of the respondent's home state differ from those of the forum, the case presents a "true conflict." In

[11] *See* Garfield, *supra* note 1, at 522–26. Professor Garfield also argues that recent developments in constitutional law, which establish a "right to freedom of choice in marriage" may limit the ability of a state to deny a divorce to non–domiciliaries. *Id.* at 517–22. *See also* Developments in the Law, *The Constitution and the Family*, 93 Harv. L. Rev. 1156, 1308–13 (1980).

[12] Adjustment of marital property under the new equitable apportionment statutes also falls in this category.

[13] In Sosna v. Iowa, 419 U.S. 393 (1975), which upheld a one–year residency requirement for divorce, the opinion noted that "this Court has often stated that 'judicial power to grant a divorce — jurisdiction strictly speaking — is founded on domicile.'" To be sure, that statement is dictum, and the holding in *Sosna* is unrelated to a domicile requirement for divorce. Nevertheless, there has been no sign in the Supreme Court that Judge Hastie's opinion will prevail in the near future.

[14] Restatement (Second) of Conflict of Laws § 72 finesses the question by permitting a non-domiciliary state to divorce when it is "reasonable" to do so.

[1] *See generally* Leflar, McDougal and Felix § 222.

[2] *Id.* § 225. Restatement (Second) of Conflict of Laws § 285 agrees.

[3] Restatement (Second) of Conflict of Laws § 285, comment a. The major exception is the requirement in some states that the acts which form the basis of the divorce either must have occurred in the forum or constitute grounds for divorce in the state where the plaintiff was domiciled when the acts took place. *Id.* comment b.

that situation, Brainerd Currie argued for the application of forum law.[4] Other modern choice–of–law theorists, such as Leflar who argued for choice–influencing considerations,[5] also tend to favor the application of forum law. Hence, the universal choice of forum law in a divorce action seems likely to continue undisturbed, despite the revolution in general choice–of–law theory.

That result is not objectionable. Under the system of "divisible divorce," the divorcing court, unless it has personal jurisdiction over the absent spouse, can affect only the marital status of the parties; it cannot determine alimony and support questions.[6]

Nevertheless, the universal satisfaction with forum law for divorce cases depends upon the continued requirement of domicile for divorce jurisdiction. If domicile loses its position as the sole basis for divorce jurisdiction, significant choice–of–law problems may arise. Their resolution would prove quite interesting.

§ 123 Recognition and Collateral Attack[1]

Williams I and *II* held that domicile of one spouse is sufficient to permit F–1 to grant a divorce, but that F–2 can re-examine F–1's finding of domicile. Although the Court in *Williams II* stated that the assailant of the F-1 decree bore a heavy burden, the holding in that case dramatically increased the possibility of collateral attack upon the F–1 decree in a later proceeding in F–2. The attack can take a number of forms. *Williams II*, for example, permitted a state — in the guise of a prosecution for bigamous cohabitation — to question the validity of a foreign divorce; fortunately, this rarely — if ever — happens today. This section examines when others may attack the divorce.

[a] Attack by the F–1 Petitioner

Normally, the person who sought the divorce is estopped from challenging its validity.[2] This principle derives from basic notions of fairness and res judicata. It is not a principle of constitutional law; but, rather, one of local law, and may vary from state to state.[3]

---

[4] An example might occur in a state which uses some form of interest analysis. A spouse newly domiciled in that state might seek divorce for mental cruelty, a ground not available under the law of the state where the spouse was formerly domiciled with her husband. *See* § 113, *supra*.

[5] *See* § 81, *supra*.

[6] *See* § 125, *infra*.

[1] *See generally* David Currie, *Suitcase Divorce in the Conflict of Laws: Simons, Rosenstiel, and Borax*, 34 U. Chi. L. Rev. 26 (1965).

[2] *See* Homer Clark, *Estoppel Against Jurisdictional Attack on Decrees of Divorce*, 70 Yale L.J. 45 (1960).

[3] The estoppel doctrine has been applied against third parties, such as someone who persuades another to obtain a divorce and then marries that person; the Restatement (Second) of Conflict of Laws § 74, comment b, cautions that the cases are "divided" on the use of estoppel against third parties.

[b] Attack by the F–1 Respondent

This is a more fertile source of attack. If the F–1 divorce was awarded in an ex parte proceeding, the F–1 respondent can always attack it collaterally. If the F–1 divorce was bilateral, that is, if the F–1 respondent took any part in the action, the situation is more complicated. The leading decision, *Sherrer v. Sherrer*,[4] involved a couple whose marital domicile had been Massachusetts. The wife left the Bay State for Florida. After she had been there for the statutory minimum residence period (90 days), she sued for divorce. Her husband retained counsel, who entered a general appearance.[5]

He offered evidence on the question of child custody, but did not contest jurisdiction (based on the wife's domicile) or the grounds for divorce. The court granted the divorce. Later, the putative wife returned to Massachusetts where her former husband sued her to have his land in that state declared free of her dower rights. Under Massachusetts's law, his right to that remedy depended upon the invalidity of the Florida decree.

Before turning to Chief Justice Vinson's opinion, a review of a basic principle of res judicata and jurisdiction will prove helpful. The "bootstrap" principle provides that a person who has had a chance to contest the issue of jurisdiction (either personal or subject matter) is bound by the court's finding that jurisdiction exists, even if, in fact, it did not.[6] Applying that principle to *Sherrer*, one would expect that the husband's general appearance in Florida — while represented by counsel — would render the Florida decree immune from attack, even if the wife had not in fact been domiciled in Florida. The Court agreed. The opinion of the Chief Justice treated the problem as a routine application of res judicata law, emphasizing the importance of finality. Indeed, he argued that because divorce affects "vital interests," it is "a matter of greater rather than lesser importance that there should be a place to end such litigation." *Sherrer*, therefore, represents a strong vote against special rules for collateral attack in divorce litigation.

[c] The Effect on Third Parties

Three years later, in *Johnson v. Muelberger*,[7] the Court applied the *Sherrer* rule to bar collateral attack by a third party the daughter of the F–1 respondent. The challenger in *Johnson* attacked her father's Florida divorce in New York. The father had appeared through an attorney in the challenged proceeding in Florida (F–1), although he had not contested his wife's domicile there. The Court held that because there had been full opportunity to contest the jurisdictional issues the decree was not subject

[4] 334 U.S. 343 (1948).

[5] The husband actually appeared (through his attorney) in *Sherrer*. Some courts have been willing, when respondent's only appearance is by counsel, to inquire into the adequacy of that representation.

[6] *See* § 114, *supra*.

[7] 340 U.S. 581 (1951).

to attack, despite the "undisputed" fact that the wife had not complied with Florida's jurisdictional residency requirement.

The reasoning behind this holding is less than clear. Justice Reed's opinion centers on the fact that the daughter could not attack the decree under Florida law, although the Court did not believe it necessary to ascertain exactly what Florida law on this subject was:

> If the laws of Florida should be that a surviving child is in privity with its parent as to that parent's estate, surely the Florida doctrine of res judicata would apply to the child's collateral attack as it would to the father's. If, on the other hand, Florida holds, as New York does in this case, that the child of a former marriage is a stranger to the divorce proceedings, late opinions of Florida indicate that the child would not be permitted to attack the divorce, since the child had a mere expectancy at the time of the divorce.

The daughter lost, therefore, either because she was in privity with her father, or because she lacked standing under Florida law to challenge the decree. In either event, her lack of a claim in F–1 meant that she had no grounds for her collateral attack in F–2. By emphasizing that the state law of collateral attack can bar strangers to the divorce proceedings from challenging the F–1 decree, the Court indicated that attacks by third persons could be barred if collateral attack by the parties could be.[8] *Johnson*, in short, is more potent medicine even than *Sherrer*.[9]

[d] How Much is Needed for a Bootstrap?

Johnson makes clear the Court's willingness to foreclose attack, even though jurisdiction has never been litigated and probably did not exist. It is at least arguable that *Johnson* and *Sherrer* go further than ordinary full faith and credit principles.[10] Some state cases have attempted to limit the damage by refusing to preclude collateral attack unless there was at least some pretense of an adversarial proceeding in F–1, but those cases are probably inconsistent with *Sherrer*.[11] On the other hand, the decree is not entitled to more recognition than it would receive in the home state. Thus, in one case where the wife's consent to a Nevada divorce proceeding was obtained by fraudulent means, a Maryland court permitted her to challenge the decree.[12] Nevada has attempted to limit the vulnerability of its divorces to such forms of attack by holding that perjury as to domicile is intrinsic

---

[8] *Accord* Cook v. Cook, 342 U.S. 126 (1951).

[9] The Court did not discuss the due process implications of *Johnson*. Although cutting off the daughter's "rights" without giving her a hearing may seem unfair, it is difficult to imagine how the divisible divorce system could function if *Johnson* had gone the other way, and strangers to the action were permitted to attack the decree.

[10] *See* § 114, *supra*.

[11] *See* Restatement (Second) of Conflict of Laws § 73, Reporter's Note. Dicta in *Sherrer, Johnson*, and other cases are pretty explicit that a spouse who has appeared in F–1 — even if only through an attorney — cannot later contest jurisdiction.

[12] Day v. Day, 237 Md. 229, 205 A.2d 798 (1965).

fraud and, therefore, not subject to collateral attack.[13] The Supreme Court has not yet faced that issue; but prohibiting a challenge based on fraudulent proof of jurisdiction raises serious constitutional questions, for on that question due process and full faith and credit meet head on.

[e] Does *Sherrer* Make Sense?

Much can be said for the strong rule of finality laid down in *Sherrer*. The rule certainly enhances the ordering of very important private affairs. There are problems, however. *Williams II* allowed a bigamous cohabitation prosecution in the state of the marital domicile in order to permit that state to vindicate its interest in the integrity of its divorce laws. But it is extremely unlikely that the risk of prosecution will ever be serious enough to dent the trade in quickie out–of–state divorces. The only realistic way that a home state's interest in its citizens' marriages is likely to be raised is through an attack by the respondent spouse. But *Sherrer* forecloses that possibility completely if the F–1 proceeding was bilateral.

Sherrer provides a way for sophisticated divorce litigants to insulate their divorce from collateral attack by parties and privies; all that is necessary is an appearance by the respondent in the forum. In addition, many commentators believe that *Sherrer* effectively overrules *Williams II*[14] because no state is likely to prosecute in a situation where collateral attack by private parties has been foreclosed. If so, the run on the national scene of *Williams II* was short, indeed.

[f] Recognition of Foreign Nation Divorces

The Full Faith and Credit Clause does not require a state to recognize a divorce awarded by a foreign country. Other nations vary widely in their approach to both the jurisdictional bases for divorce and the substantive law to be applied. When a divorced spouse asks a court of an American state to recognize a divorce granted on a basis unknown in this country, what should it do?

The first question concerns jurisdiction. Generally, if the foreign country had jurisdiction based on domicile, an American court is likely to recognize the divorce, obtained unless it was granted on some ground which offends a strongly held policy of that state.

The most difficult problem involves a "quickie" bilateral divorce obtained in a nearby foreign country which requires only presence (and not domicile) to exercise jurisdiction and imposes no significant impediment to a speedy rendition of a decree. Most states refuse to recognize these divorces,[15]

[13] Colby v. Colby, 78 Nev. 150, 369 P.2d 1019 (1962).

[14] *E.g.*, Albert A. Ehrenzweig, Treatise on the Conflict of Laws 253 (1962).

[15] In recent years, a number of states have recognized such divorces, often on the ground of estoppel. The cases are collected in Homer Clark, The Law of Domestic Relations in the United States 432 (2d ed. 1987). The status of foreign non-judicial divorces is discussed in Scoles, et al. § 15.24.

taking the position that although *Williams I* and the Full Faith and Credit Clause prevent a state from interposing its own divorce policies between a domiciliary and a sister–state divorce decree, no such prohibition exists when the decree comes from a foreign nation. Thus, a state court is free to protect domestic policies by permitting collateral attack upon the foreign nation divorce, and most cases do so.

The leading exception is *Rosenstiel v. Rosenstiel.*[16] There, the Court of Appeals of New York refused to permit a collateral attack upon a consensual divorce rendered in Juarez, Mexico, based on one day's presence in that city by each spouse. The decision is unfortunate. The basic problem stems from the court's failure to respect the public policy of New York, embodied at the time in New York's own, very strict, divorce laws. The court's failure to further those strong domestic policies, especially when the rendering state was completely disinterested, is difficult to justify.[17]

§ 124 The Impact of the *Williams* Litigation

The decision in *Williams I* helped contribute to a revolution in divorce law. Today, nearly every state has no–fault divorce. We do not know, of course, whether the Justices saw that development as a possible outcome. Nevertheless, the ability of a New Yorker, say, to travel to Nevada and obtain a divorce good throughout the United States no doubt played a significant role in the easing of restrictions on divorce.

Liberalized divorce has not been cost–free; much human misery is associated with the end of a marriage, and the marked increase in single–parent families and the increasing feminization of poverty surely can be traced to some extent to the result in *Williams I*. Nevertheless, a return to the law that existed before that decision would be unthinkable today.

§ 125 Annulment[1]

Divorce dissolves a marriage based on events which occur after celebration; an annulment, in contrast, is based on events existing at the time of celebration, and its effect is to nullify the marriage; that is, to treat the marriage as if it never had taken place. Those differences between the two proceedings lead to somewhat different treatment in conflicts cases.

---

16 16 N.Y.2d 64, 209 N.E.2d 709, 262 N.Y.S.2d 86 (1965).

17 David Currie, *Suitcase Divorce in the Conflict of Laws: Simons, Rosenstiel and Borax*, 36 U. Chi. L. Rev. 26, 5764 (1966), criticizes *Rosenstiel* at some length. A less sweeping opinion, emphasizing the estoppel aspects of the case, would have been easier to square with New York policy. Although the Court of Appeals of New York may take a relaxed view of foreign divorce, the Internal Revenue Service does not. The Service has long taken the position that it can ignore a colorable divorce and assess taxes based on the realities of the situation. *See* Rev. Rule 76255 (1976); Borax' Estate v. C.I.R., 349 F.2d 666 (2d Cir.1965); *but cf.* Lee v. Commissioner, 550 F.2d 1201 (9th Cir.1977). Those looking for a quick fix to the so–called "marital penalty" problem in tax should be very careful.

1 *See generally* Scoles, et al. §§ 15.15, 15.16.

[a] Choice of Law

Because the decision whether to grant an annulment decree turns on the validity of the marriage, the law of the state of celebration is usually applied, instead of the law of the forum.[2] The rule makes sense; the state of celebration will typically have the greatest interest in defects in the ceremony and the events which lead up to it. But that is not always so. The contacts between the celebrating state and the parties may be ephemeral, reducing the intensity of that state's interest. At the same time, another state may have a strong interest in seeing that its policy concerning permissible marriage is not thwarted, especially when that policy is strongly held. Thus, when a marriage between two New Jersey domiciliaries, celebrated in Indiana, was challenged in New Jersey on the ground that the wife was too young to marry, the court upheld the challenge, notwithstanding the fact that she had been old enough to marry in Indiana.[3] The Second Restatement approves of this result, at least if the invalidating state has the most significant relationship with the problem.[4]

[b] Jurisdiction

A state has jurisdiction to annul a marriage whenever it would have jurisdiction to grant a divorce (that is, if either spouse is a domiciliary).[5] But, can an annulment be rendered in other circumstances? In *Whealton v. Whealton,*[6] Justice Traynor suggested, in the context of an annulment action brought by a serviceman against his wife (who had entered a personal appearance), that personal jurisdiction alone should be a sufficient jurisdictional basis. Traynor distinguished divorce from annulment based on the different choice–of–law rules that would be applied in the two situations. In a divorce action, forum law is always applied; hence, requiring domicile as a jurisdictional basis insures that the law of an interested jurisdiction will always be applied. In contrast, because courts in annulment cases typically apply the law of the state of celebration, there is no need for a strong connection between the forum and the parties in order to ensure that a proper law will be applied. Traynor concluded that the interests of the state of celebration were protected by the choice–of–law rule, and, therefore, that an annulment can be granted by a court with only personal jurisdiction over the parties.

The Second Conflicts Restatement does not go quite so far, but would permit jurisdiction to be exercised if the forum is the state of celebration and if it has personal jurisdiction over the respondent spouse.[7] As justification, the comment emphasizes the interest that the state of celebration has

---

[2] Leflar, McDougal, & Felix § 231.

[3] Wilkins v. Zelichowski, 26 N.J. 370, 140 A.2d 65 (1958).

[4] Restatement (Second) of Conflict of Laws § 283(2). The invalidating policy, however, must be a "strong" one.

[5] Restatement (Second) of Conflict of Laws § 76(a).

[6] 67 Cal.2d 656, 432 P.2d 979, 63 Cal.Rptr. 291 (1967).

[7] Restatement (Second) of Conflict of Laws § 76(b).

in the matter, and the likelihood that it will prove the most convenient forum in those circumstances.[8]

[8] *Id.* comment c.

Part B

ALIMONY AND SUPPORT

§ 126 Divisible Divorce[1]

Williams I held that a state could grant a divorce entitled to full faith and credit, even though only one spouse was domiciled in the forum.[2] That holding briefly opened the possibility that the absent spouse could be divested of property rights in the marriage without having had a day in court. Such a result would undoubtedly violate the basic test of fairness embodied in the Due Process Clause; and so the Court held six years after *Williams I,* in *Estin v. Estin.*[3]

The parties in *Estin* had their marital domicile in New York. The wife obtained a decree of separation and an award of permanent alimony in 1943; the court making that award had jurisdiction over the husband. The next year he went to Nevada, however, where he sued for divorce. Although the wife was notified by mail of the Nevada proceedings, she did not enter an appearance there. The Nevada court granted the husband a divorce in 1945; no provision for alimony was made in that decree and the husband stopped paying alimony. The wife then sued in New York for arrearages due under the 1943 New York order. The husband set up the Nevada decree as a defense. When he lost, he sought review by the Supreme Court.

The Court affirmed. Justice Douglas' opinion recognized the New York judgment as a "property interest" of the wife created by a state which also had a legitimate concern for her well–being. Because the award was a "property interest," it could not be extinguished by a court lacking personal jurisdiction over her. Nevada could not "wipe out" the wife's claim, because that would be "an attempt to exercise in personam jurisdiction over a person not before the court." Although the divorce decree effectively dissolved the marriage and was entitled to full faith and credit, its validity did not mean that every other legal incidence of the marriage was necessarily affected or that a state concerned about the wife could not use its law to protect her. Douglas concluded that "the result in this situation is to make the divorce divisible."

Despite Justice Jackson's snide comment in dissent that the "Court reaches the Solomon–like conclusion that the Nevada decree is half good and half bad under the full faith and credit clause," the result makes perfect sense. *Estin* minimizes the damage done by *Williams I* to the rights of the absent spouse. Although *Williams I* deprives the stay–at–home spouse of

[1] *See generally* David Currie, *Suitcase Divorce in the Conflict of Laws: Simons, Rosenstiel, and Borax*, 34 U. Chi. L. Rev. 26 (1966).

[2] *See* § 119, *supra.*

[3] 334 U.S. 541 (1948).

the ability to prevent the dissolution of her marital status in a foreign state, *Estin* keeps her from being deprived in an ex parte proceeding of the economic interests generated by her marriage in an ex parte proceeding. Her husband must sue in a court having personal jurisdiction over her if he wishes to adjust those interests, a step which would have been necessary under the Due Process Clause if he wished to deprive her of any other economic interest. Divisible divorce, to be sure, only protects economic rights; and it can be argued that the marital *res*, at least to some persons, has a spiritual value transcending its economic worth.[4] But that argument points out a flaw in *Williams I. Estin* and the concept of divisible divorce at least limit the damage.

Cases after *Estin* refined the concept. *In Vanderbilt v. Vanderbilt*,[5] the Court permitted New York to enter a support order after the entry of the Nevada decree. In *Estin*, the Court had emphasized New York's interest in protecting one of its residents; it did not matter, therefore, that the New York order in *Vanderbilt* was entered after the Nevada decree. Nor did it matter that New York had not been the marital domicile of the Vanderbilts; the wife had moved there before the Nevada decree dissolved the marriage. Thus, at the time of the divorce, New York had a sufficient interest in Mrs. Vanderbilt to create a property right for her.[6] It has been held that such an interest does not exist when the wife moves to the state after the divorce, and a court should not be able to award alimony based on that post–divorce connection alone.[7] That holding seems dubious; residence in the new state surely gives that state an interest in awarding support to the spouse who had not participated in the divorce.

Thus, the divisible divorce concept insures that the absent spouse need not travel to an inconvenient forum in order to protect her interest in marital property.[8] This result also accords with more general notions of due process in jurisdiction. The economic protection afforded the stay–at–home spouse, however, was curtailed somewhat in the Supreme Court's most recent foray into the divisible divorce problem, *Simons v. Miami Beach First National Bank*.[9] The ex parte divorce in that case had been rendered by a Florida court. After the husband's death in that state, the wife appeared in the probate proceedings and claimed her dower rights under Florida law. The Florida courts denied her claim, and the Supreme Court affirmed.

The Court pointed out that dower rights under Florida law are "inchoate" and, therefore, could be extinguished in an ex parte proceeding. But that argument misses the point. All property "rights" at issue in a divorce could

[4] *See, e.g.*, Robert F. Drinan, *What are the Rights of the Involuntary Divorcee? Reflections on Divisible Divorce*, 53 Ky. L.J. 209 (1965).

[5] 354 U.S. 416 (1957).

[6] Weintraub at 241.

[7] *Loeb v. Loeb*, 4 N.Y.2d 542, 152 N.E.2d 36 (1958), *cert. denied*, 359 U.S. 913 (1959).

[8] The question whether the court in an ex parte divorce can terminate custody rights is discussed *infra* § 130.

[9] 381 U.S. 81 (1965).

be styled "inchoate," at least until there is an award from a court. A court, for example, could dissolve the marriage and decline to award any alimony. Dower rights, to be sure, do not survive dissolution; but that should not be significant. The wife, after all, could have contested the divorce on the merits, and, if she had prevailed, she would have preserved her dower rights. *Simons*, therefore, forces on her an unattractive choice: She can stay home and lose her right to dower; or, if she wishes to protect that right, she must travel to Florida (an inconvenient forum), make a general appearance, and oppose the divorce on the merits. That option exposes her to all sorts of possible adverse rulings (such as the termination of alimony). Forcing such a choice on the stay–at–home spouse is just the sort of harsh dilemma that the Due Process Clause otherwise forbids.[10]

Although *Simons* is something of a retreat from the *Estin* principle, its effect should not be overstated.[11] The concept of divisible divorce still provides substantial protection in most cases to the economic interests of the stay–at–home spouse.

§ 127 Jurisdiction to Make an Award

A court must have personal jurisdiction over a spouse in order to make an award of alimony or support against her. Personal jurisdiction, of course, can be obtained if the spouse is present in the state, but what if one spouse has deserted the other and fled to another state? It seems clear that personal jurisdiction cannot be asserted based simply on the fact that the other spouse (and perhaps a child) now live in the forum; that much is made clear by *Kulko v. Superior Court.*[1] *Kulko* involved a custody agreement, entered into in New York, that gave the father custody of his two daughters. The children lived briefly with their father in New York, but, with his permission, moved to California to live with their mother. Eventually, she brought an action in California state court seeking to increase the father's child support obligation. The California state courts asserted personal jurisdiction over the father, but the Supreme Court of the United States reversed. Justice Marshall, speaking for the Court, applied the "minimum contacts" test and found that the exercise of jurisdiction was not proper. Two factors stand out from his opinion: First, Marshall emphasized that the cause of action arose "not from the defendant's commercial transactions in interstate commerce, but rather from his personal, domestic relations." Second, he observed that California had not "attempted to assert any particularized interest in trying such [child support] cases in its courts. . . ." Both arguments are troubling. Certainly, the father's failure to support children in California can lead to serious, adverse consequences there; that harm is eminently foreseeable and easily could have been found

---

[10] *See* the discussion of Shaffer v. Heitner, 433 U.S. 186 (1977), § 44, *supra.*

[11] *Simons* may have been a necessary retreat from *Estin.* If the dower rights had been protected, there could have been two widows with rights in Mr. Simons' property. The resulting mess could well have undermined the Supreme Court's efforts to establish a satisfactory accommodation of state and individual interests in divorce law.

[1] 434 U.S. 84 (1978).

to satisfy the minimum contacts test. On the other hand, as Marshall observed, the father only "acquiesced" in the children going to California; perhaps it could then be said that he had not purposefully "availed himself" of the benefits of California law. The second point is also troubling, especially given the Court's later decisions in cases such as *Helicopteros* which minimized any particularized interest the forum might have in the transaction.[2] In any event, the holding in *Kulko* has proven to be a serious obstacle to enforcing support orders against parents who no longer live with their children.

But typically the deserting spouse can be reached (at least if her address is known). A majority of states have adopted long–arm statutes providing jurisdiction over the absent spouse for the express purpose of entering a support or alimony order based on a number of different contacts. The exact list varies from state to state, but may include living as a couple in the forum, fathering a child there, failing to follow the forum's support order, and so forth. The constitutional question is whether those contacts are sufficient to provide the minimum necessary under *Kulko*. Clearly most of them are; fathering a child or deserting a family should give the state enough interest in the problem to satisfy constitutional requirements. Moreover, the father or absent spouse certainly could foresee that harm would be caused in the forum by his acts there.

More problematic, perhaps, is long–arm jurisdiction based on the mere fact of separation at a time when the forum was the matrimonial domicile. But again, the defendant should have foreseen the consequences of leaving a spouse without providing adequate financial arrangements for support, and certainly the forum has a sufficient interest in seeing that the deserted partner is cared for.[3] In addition, the cause of action (alimony or support) arises out of the defendant's connection with the forum (living in the marital relationship). Thus, the contacts required by the domestic long–arm statutes should satisfy the minimum contacts test as, indeed, state courts have held.[4]

Finally, jurisdiction may be exercised on the basis of a more traditional long–arm statute. Thus, it has been held that the execution of a separation agreement in the forum will support jurisdiction based on the "transacting any business" language of many long–arm statutes.[5] Non-support has also been held to be a tort within the "causing injury to the person or property" clause.[6]

---

[2] *Helicopteros* is discussed *infra,* § 25.

[3] A state may constitutionally enter a support decree even after a divorce has been granted. Vanderbilt v. Vanderbilt, 354 U.S. 416 (1957).

[4] *See, e.g.,* Scott v. Hall, 203 Kan. 331, 454 P.2d 449 (1969).

[5] Van Wagenberg v. Van Wagenberg, 241 Md. 154, 215 A.2d 812 (1966), *cert. denied*, 385 U.S. 833 (1966) (enforcing New York judgment).

[6] In re Miller, 86 Wash. 2d 712, 548 P.2d 542 (1976). It is unlikely that this result would be reached after *Kulko*. *See* § 33, *supra* for a discussion of these clauses in modern long–arm statutes. *See generally* Anne Bradford Stevens, *Is Failure to Support a Minor Child in the State Sufficient Contact to Justify In Personam Jurisdiction*, 17 So Ill. U.L. Rev. 491 (1993).

§ 128 Recognition of Alimony and Support Decrees[1]

A court with personal jurisdiction over the spouses may award alimony or order support for a child. Other states must recognize the award to the same extent that it would be recognized in the rendering state. Thus, a decree, which cannot be modified in F–1, must be accorded full faith and credit in F–2 without modification.[2] Until quite recently, all child support decrees, however, were modifiable, at least as to future payments, and, therefore, enforcement was not required as to those sums. Nevertheless, courts generally will recognize those awards, modifying them where appropriate.[3] Recognition of alimony and support decrees, in other words, closely followed the law developed in other areas involving full faith and credit. A decree, which cannot be modified, must be enforced; a decree, which can be modified, may be recognized, but F–2 will generally modify the order if that is thought to be the appropriate action.

The major problem with the traditional model was a practical one: enforcement. How does a spouse enforce a support order in another jurisdiction? Beginning in 1950 with the promulgation of the Uniform Reciprocal Enforcement of Support Act[4] ("URESA"), the state and federal governments adopted legislation to make enforcement easier. URESA provided the framework for enforcing child support orders until quite recently. Its great innovation was to permit the state where the custodial parent lived to ask for enforcement of an order by the state where the obligor lived. This mechanism made it possible, at least in theory, for poor and middle class parents to obtain relief from deadbeat obligors.

The experience with URESA was not an altogether happy one, however; bureaucratic delay and indifference in a large number of states have led to significant federal involvement in the collection of child support. Moreover, URESA permitted the existence of multiple orders, an occurrence that led to a great deal of confusion.

The federal government eventually took an interest in the problem. It did so for three reasons: benevolence, to save money (on child welfare payments), and because the enforcement of judgments across state lines is a job properly done by Congress. As a result, Title IV-D of the Social Security Act[5] contains a number of provisions designed to make collection of support payments easier. These include mandatory withholding in original support orders, interception of tax refunds, and federal monitoring. Perhaps the most important requirement is that child support payments which are in arrears must be treated as final judgments for enforcement purposes;[6] as

---

[1] *See generally* Margaret C. Haynes & G. Diane Dodson (eds.), Interstate Child Support Remedies (1989).

[2] Barber v. Barber, 323 U.S. 77 (1944). *See generally* Weintraub 245–46.

[3] Worthley v. Worthley, 44 Cal. 2d 465, 283 P.2d 19 (1955) (Traynor, J.) is the leading case.

[4] 9A U.L.A. 647 (eventually, the Act was adopted in form from in every state).

[5] 42 U.S.C. §§ 651-62. Title IV-D provides federal monetary assistance for state child welfare programs. As a condition to receiving this money, the states must agree to adopt certain federal laws, including the ones mentioned in the text.

[6] *See* 42 U.S.C. § 666(b)(9) (the "Bradley Amendment").

a result, back payments can be enforced under the Full Faith and Credit Clause. Moreover, in 1992 a federally–sponsored Child Support Commission made sweeping recommendations for improving the payment of child support.

The enforcement of support orders across state lines today is controlled by a web of statutory law. The most important of these laws is the Uniform Interstate Family Support Act ("UIFSA"); all fifty states have now adopted UIFSA. The guiding principle of UIFSA is that there should be only one outstanding order at one time for any support obligation.[7] In order to achieve the goal of "one controlling order," UIFSA establishes a hierarchy of child support orders.

A court with jurisdiction over the subject matter and the parties[8] first checks to see whether any other court with proper jurisdiction has entered an order concerning the dispute. The forum must recognize that order, known as the "controlling order." If no controlling order exists, then the forum may enter its own controlling order. *Only* the court which entered the controlling order, may modify that order. To use the terms found in UIFSA itself, there is "continuing exclusive jurisdiction" to modify that order in the court which issued it — and *only in that court.* That court *only* loses jurisdiction if both parents and the child have moved to another state (or if all consent to the entry of a controlling order by another court).

It is difficult to over–state the importance of a law that makes it easier for custodial parents to collect child support payments. By simplifying the process, with its one controlling order concept, UIFSA makes it more likely that payment will be collected.[9] Congress has recognized the importance of UIFSA by adopting the Full Faith and Credit Clause to Child Support Orders Act ("FFCSOA").[10] FFCSOA requires that full faith and credit be given to orders entered by a state, which has adopted UIFSA. The federal law may be redundant because each state has adopted UIFSA; nevertheless, it puts the imprimatur of the Constitution and the federal government behind the enforcement of child support decrees.

UIFSA also aids enforcement by simplifying procedures. Thus, the petitioner does not have to appear in person in the foreign tribunal, the rules of evidence are relaxed, and the hearing can be conducted by phone or video conference. State officials are authorized to help the petitioner collect on the award.

One might expect enforcement of support orders entered by the court of another country to be governed by federal law. One would be wrong. In fact,

[7] This one "controlling order" rule is borrowed from the UCCJA, *see* § 130, *infra*, and deliberately replaces the multiple orders possible under URESA, the predecessor Uniform Act. The following discussion does not cover the rules governing the transition between UIFSA and URESA (warning: the transitional rules are really complicated).

[8] UIFSA tacitly "over–rules" *Kulko* by providing for personal jurisdiction over the absent parent merely because the child lives in the forum.

[9] That process has also been helped greatly by other federal statutes, such as the Bradley Amendment and new ways to locate deadbeat obligors and collect arrearages from them.

[10] 28 U.S.C. § 1738B.

the federal government has been remarkably unwilling to deal with the problem of enforcing foreign support orders. As a result, a number of states, with the tacit blessings of the State Department, at least, entered into "arrangements" with foreign countries concerning the actual enforcement of child support orders. (Is it constitutional for a state to have "foreign relations" with other countries?)[11] In 1996, however, the federal government expressly authorized the states, under certain conditions, to enter into reciprocal support agreements with foreign countries.[12] Federal law now mirrors UIFSA which authorizes enforcement of an order from a foreign country whose own enforcement procedures resemble those of UIFSA.

§ 129 A Note on Marital Property

Division of the property owned by divorcing parties can present extraordinarily difficult choice–of–law problems.[1] The most difficult issues involve the fundamental split between equitable distribution laws, present in varying form in most states; community property laws; and the common law concept of separate property.

Equitable distribution statutes are designed to divide marital property in a manner similar to that achieved by community property regimes. In community property states, the court has power to award the domiciliary spouse a one–half interest in marital property, defined generally as all property acquired by either husband or wife during their marriage except that acquired by gift, devise or descent.[2] Issues in equitable division states often center on what is "marital property" subject to division between the spouses. Traditionally, courts in equitable distribution states made a major distinction between personality and realty; personality acquired during marriage was generally governed by the law of the marital domicile at the time of acquisition, but realty was governed by situs law.[3]

Today, a court's ability to resolve all aspects of a divorce, including out–of–state property, depends on whether it has personal jurisdiction over both spouses. If only one party is subject to the personal jurisdiction of the court, the court may take out–of–state property into consideration when dividing property within the state, but still cannot change title to personality or realty outside its jurisdiction.[4] However, if the record owner of the property

---

[11] *See generally* Gloria DeHart, *Comity, Conventions, and the Constitutions: State and Federal Initiatives in Recognition and Enforcement of Judgments and Child Support Obligations in United States and Canadian Courts*, 34 Tex. Int'l L.J. 361 (1999).

[12] 42 U.S.C. § 659a (d).

[1] *See generally*, J. Thomas Oldham, *Conflict of Laws and Marital Property Rights*, 39 Baylor L. Rev. 1255 (1987).

[2] *See, e.g.*, Ariz. Rev. Stat. § 25-211 (1989).

[3] Restatement (Second) of Conflicts of Law § 9(2) explains the same distinction in terms of movables and immovables.

[4] Fall v. Eastin, 215 U.S. 1 (1909) (holding that the Full Faith and Credit Clause did not compel Nebraska to give effect to a deed of Nebraska land made by a court commissioner as part of a Washington divorce decree) discussed in § 115, *supra*; *but see* Furman v. Macitti, 714 F.2d 299 (4th Cir. 1983) ("equitable" relief available in some circumstances).

is before the court, most states permit the court to order the owner to convey title to the property to another, subject to the court's contempt power if he or she refuses to comply.[5] A few states still consider this kind of court-ordered transfer invalid,[6] but generally the situs state will recognize and enforce such an order under either the Full Faith and Credit Clause or under the principle of comity.

A related problem involves conflict of laws over time: when property moves from state to state, which state's laws control its disposition upon divorce? If the state has no statute–authorizing jurisdiction over out–of–state realty, common law rules apply. The courts have focused to a large extent on party expectations. Even absent a choice–of–law clause in a valid marriage contract,[7] the parties' expectations play a significant role in judicial decision making.[8]

Federal laws also can complicate the state court's power to distribute property in divorce. While there is a federal presumption that state law controls in divorce cases, federal benefits that are considered marital property raise the question of federal preemption. The property at issue is usually pension benefits of federal employees. Some federal statutes, such as ERISA, explicitly state that they supersede state law regarding division of benefits at divorce.

[5] *See* Sylvester v. Sylvester, 723 P.2d 1253 (Alaska 1983); Dority v. Dority, 645 P.2d 56 (Utah 1982); Wanberg v. Wanberg, 664 P.2d 568 (Alaska 1983) (dividing Arizona land); and Egle v. Egle, 715 F.2d 999 (5th Cir. 1983) (Canal Zone law applied to Maryland land). *But cf.* Cottman v. Cottman, 418 So.2d 1241 (Fla. App. 1981) (applying D.C. law to divide money obtained on the sale of D.C. realty sold earlier).

[6] *See, e.g.* Sammons v. Sammons, 479 So.2d 223 (Fla. Dist Ct. App.1985), and Ralske v. Ralske, 445 N.Y.S. 2d 9 (App. Div.1981).

[7] *See* Scoles, et al. Ch. 14. *See also* J. Thomas Oldham, *Premarital Contracts Are Now Enforceable, Unless . . .*, 21 Hous. L. Rev. 757 (1984).

[8] Those provisions are generally deferred to. *E.g.,* Wyatt v. Fulrath, 264 N.Y.S. 2d 233 (1964).

Part C

CHILDREN AND THE CONFLICT OF LAWS

§ 130 Custody[1]

Divorce often is a messy process that adversely affects all those whom the proceedings touch. The greatest tragedy in divorce cases takes place when the battle spills over into a bitter custody dispute. Bad as that problem may be, when it takes on interstate elements, its adverse effects can be greatly exacerbated. Historically, this area has been marked by parochial courts, injunctions and counter–injunctions, conflicting custody orders, and parental kidnapping. Judges, in recent years, have attempted to avoid such problems. Greatly aiding judicial efforts has been the adoption of the Uniform Child Custody Jurisdiction Act (the UCCJA),[2] and the Parental Kidnaping Prevention Act (PKPA). This section explores the problem of interstate custody within the framework provided by the UCCJA; it then examines the impact of the PKPA[3] on that framework.

[a] Jurisdiction

The jurisdictional sections of the Uniform Act were designed so that custody problems will be resolved by "that state which can best decide the case in the interest of the child"[4] — the state which, at the same time, can avoid judicial conflict and deter parental misbehavior. Those ends are accomplished by overlapping jurisdictional provisions, which are subject to judicial adjustment.

The basic jurisdictional concept is the "home state." That state is the state where the child lived with a parent or guardian for "at least six consecutive months" before the action began.[5] The home state always has subject matter jurisdiction in custody cases. The home state provision is designed to locate jurisdiction in the state with the greatest concern for the child. Determining the home state may be a difficult problem at times, for it is quite possible that each parent (although located in different states) can advance plausible claims that the child "lived" with him or her for the six

---

[1] *See generally* Anne B. Goldstein, *The Tragedy of the Interstate Child: A Critical Reexamination of the Uniform Child Custody Jurisdiction Act and the Parental Kidnaping Prevention Act*, 25 U.C. Davis L. Rev. 845 (1992); Russell M. Coombs, *Interstate Child Custody: Jurisdiction, Recognition, and Enforcement*, 66 Minn. L. Rev. 711 (1982).

[2] 9 U.L.A. 116 (1979).

[3] 28 U.S.C. § 1738A.

[4] Uniform Child Custody Jurisdiction Act, § 1(a)(2), 9 U.L.A. 117 (1979).

[5] *Id.* § 2(5). A state retains its status as home state if the child is absent "because of his removal or retention by a person claiming his custody and a parent or person acting as parent continues to live in this State." *Id.*, § 3(a)(1).

months before the action began. A jurisdiction's status as the home state is a continuing status, and it is not lost merely because the child moves to another state. Thus, the "home state" provision minimizes the effect of an unauthorized removal of the child by one parent by ensuring that the child's removal does not automatically divest the home state of jurisdiction. Jurisdiction may be exercised by a *new* home state, however, after the child has lived there for six months.

Besides the "home state" provision, the UCCJA contains two additional jurisdictional bases; unfortunately these bases create the possibility of overlapping jurisdiction. Both require that the child be physically present in the forum. One also requires that there be an "emergency" where the child needs protection.[6] The other basis requires a "significant connection" between the state and the child, or between the state and at least one parent.[7] "Significant connection" jurisdiction should not be used where there is "home state" jurisdiction.[8]

The emergency jurisdictional provision should cause few problems. Professor Bodenheimer, who helped draft the Act, illustrated the application of this section with an example of a child visiting a parent who threatens the child with violence.[9] A court in that parent's state surely should be able to address such a problem. The effect of the "significant connection" provision on the orderly functioning of the Act, however, may be more problematic, because the whole jurisdictional scheme of the Act will be undermined if a state exercises jurisdiction when its connection with the problem is weak. The self–restraint of each state, therefore, is vital to the smooth working of the UCCJA.[10]

Still, the Act's overlapping jurisdictional provisions open up the possibility of multiple custody contests. This problem becomes particularly acute when the decree was made by a "home state" which has lost that status because the child has moved elsewhere; nevertheless, the decree–rendering state can retain jurisdiction if it still has a "significant connection" with the child.[11] The UCCJA addresses that problem by permitting a court to

[6] *Id.* § 3(a)(3).

[7] *Id.* § 3(a)(2). There must also be "substantial evidence" within the jurisdiction concerning the child's well being. A residual jurisdictional provision permits a case to be heard when no other court can or is willing to exercise jurisdiction, and doing so would be in the best interests of the child. *Id.* § 3(a)(4). *See* Leonard G. Ratner, *Procedural Due Process and Jurisdiction to Adjudicate*, 78 Nw. U. L. Rev. 363, 406–10 (1980).

[8] 9 U.L.A. 144, Commissioner's Note.

[9] Brigitte Bodenheimer, *Progress Under the Uniform Child Custody Jurisdiction Act and Remaining Problems: Punitive Decrees, Joint Custody, and Excessive Modifications*, 65 Cal. L. Rev. 978, 993 (1977).

[10] Two examples of self–restraint are Rexford v. Rexford, 631 P.2d 475 (Alas.1980) (although Alaska was the home state and California lacked even a significant connection, Alaska trial court did not abuse discretion by deferring to pending proceedings in California); In Re Marriage of Ben–Yehoshua, 91 Cal. App. 3d 259, 154 Cal. Rptr. 80 (1979)(no significant connection to California when children had grown up in Israel and had only been in California for two weeks; mother's and grandmother's residence in the state insufficient to establish jurisdiction).

[11] *E.g.*, Harris v. Melnick, 314 Md. 539, 552 A.2d 38 (1989) (significant connection found in Maryland because child visited his father there, and witnesses in Maryland could testify to the relation between father and son).

declare itself an "inconvenient forum" and then either refuse to hear the case or to enter a stay pending satisfaction of appropriate conditions (such as a party's consenting to the jurisdiction of another court).[12] In the event that two courts are appropriate forums, the Act establishes a priority–in–time rule and a consultative process:[13] The state in which the second action is filed should stay its own proceeding and communicate with the other court to determine the more appropriate forum.

Again, judicial self–restraint is called for to ensure the effectiveness of the Act's priority–in–time rule for resolving conflicts.[14] Finally, a court has authority to deny jurisdiction if the petitioner "has wrongfully taken the child from another state or has engaged in similar reprehensible conduct."[15] This codification of the "clean hands doctrine" is designed to limit forum–shopping as well as parental kidnaping; its application is discretionary.[16]

[b] Enforcement

A custody decree made under the UCCJA by a state with subject matter jurisdiction must be recognized in other states, which have adopted the Act.[17] Because the UCCJA does not require personal jurisdiction over the parents, a custody award can raise due process issues. When the rendering court has personal jurisdiction over both contestants, recognition should not be a problem. A decree entered by a court without one of the contestants before it, however, may present constitutional problems under *May v. Anderson*.[18] *May* involved a Wisconsin divorce decree, entered ex parte, which awarded custody to the father. He took the decree to Ohio, where his children were living with their mother, and sought to have it enforced. When the Ohio courts accorded the Wisconsin decree full faith and credit, the mother sought review in the Supreme Court. That tribunal, speaking through Justice Burton, reversed.

That reversal creates concern about enforcement of ex parte orders under the UCCJA. The exact nature of the holding in *May* is not clear. The Court may have held that a custody determination is like the adjudication of other "property" rights, which cannot be terminated without personal jurisdiction over the respondent.[19] Or, it may have held simply that Ohio could, but was not required to, recognize the Wisconsin decree. Burton's opinion

---

[12] UCCJA § 7, 9 U.L.A. 137 (1979).

[13] *Id.*

[14] *See* Vanneck v. Vanneck, 49 N.Y. 2d 602, 427 N.Y.S. 2d 735, 404 N.E. 2d 1278 (1980) (New York court ordered to stay its own proceedings and consult with Connecticut court, even though jurisdictional basis of that court was questionable).

[15] UCCJA § 8(a).

[16] One study has found that the "clean hands" idea often plays a role in custody decisions, but that it is rarely mentioned in those cases where it is important. *See* Goldstein, *supra* note 1, at 910.

[17] UCCJA §§ 13.

[18] 345 U.S. 528 (1953). *See generally* Helen Garfield, *Due Process Rights of Absent Parents in Interstate Custody Conflicts*, 16 Ind. L.J. 445 (1983).

[19] *See* § 130, *supra*.

provides ammunition for devotees of both holdings, which we may conveniently label the "property rights" holding and the "permissive" full faith and credit holding.

The property rights argument finds support in *Burton's* characterization of the issue as the ability of a state court to terminate petitioner's "right" to custody "without having jurisdiction over her in personam." A rhetorical flourish near the end of his opinion also supports the property rights interpretation of *May*: "Rights far more precious to appellant than property rights will be cut off if she is to be bound by the Wisconsin award of custody." Other parts of the opinion, however, suggest that *May* merely meant that Ohio (F–2) was not required to recognize the Wisconsin order. Although this argument comes out most clearly in Justice Frankfurter's concurring opinion, Justice Burton did not discuss the Due Process Clause, the provision which would have been the source of the mother's property rights. Moreover, he also seemed to frame the issue in terms of the wisdom of giving Wisconsin the right, "as against Ohio," to decide the mother's custody rights.

Since the *May* decision, the Supreme Court has not directly addressed the issues raised by that case. Later developments in jurisdictional jurisprudence, especially the grand dictum in *Shaffer v. Heitner*;[20] extending the minimum contacts requirement to all exercises of jurisdiction, suggest that custody decrees rendered without jurisdiction over all concerned may present serious constitutional concerns.[21] No longer can the argument be made that, because a custody hearing adjusts status, it is merely an in rem proceeding and, therefore, not subject to the minimum contacts standard.[22]

Some have argued that status adjudications, or at least those involving children, will escape testing under the *Shaffer* standard;[23] indeed, that issue was apparently left open in a footnote in the Court's opinion in *Shaffer*.[24] The argument is strengthened by the analogy to the continued survival of the in rem characterization of jurisdictional issues in divorce, as well as by the state's strong need as a sovereign to serve the best interests of the child. Nevertheless, it is possible that the minimum contacts standard will be applied to custody cases. "Minimum contacts," however, is a flexible standard which depends to a large degree upon context; it is quite likely that the standard will not be applied as rigorously in custody

---

[20] 433 U.S. 186 (1977).

[21] *See* § 28, *supra*. This statement may have to be modified in light of Justice Scalia's opinion in Burham v. Superior Court, 495 U.S. 604 (1990), suggesting that the *Shaffer* dictum was limited to attachment cases. This reading of Shaffer could not be used to support a "property rights" interpretation of *May*.

[22] *See* Coombs, *supra* note 1, at 735–64. *But see* Rhonda Wasserman, *Parents, Partners, and Personal Jurisdiction*, 1995 U. Ill. L. Rev. 813.

[23] *See, e.g.*, Brigitte Bodenheimer & Janet Neeley–Kvarme, *Jurisdiction Over Child Custody and Adoption After Shaffer and Kulko*, 12 U.C.D. L.Rev. 229 (1979).

[24] 433 U.S. at 208, n.30. Footnote 30, which states that "status" questions may not be covered by the *Shaffer* rule, does not cite *May*, an omission which led one commentator to ask whether "the Court does not consider a custody case to involve status?" Homer Clark, The Domestic Relations Law of the United States 462 n. 53 (2d ed. 1987). That question seems a bit rhetorical.

cases as in, say, products liability litigation.[25] Moreover, the UCCJA permits jurisdiction to be exercised only when the forum has a strong interest. Those factors suggest that it will be unusual for a UCCJA order to raise significant due process claims.[26]

[c] Modification

The basic rule under the UCCJA is continuing jurisdiction. A custody decree made under the UCCJA cannot be modified by a court of another state (F–2) unless the rendering court (F–1) has lost or refuses to exercise jurisdiction under the Act and there is jurisdiction in the new court.[27] In other words, a modification can be made in F–2 only if F–1 no longer has jurisdiction.

[d] The PKPA

In 1980, Congress responded to public concern over interstate custody problems by enacting the Parental Kidnapping Prevention Act. This law has a number of interesting provisions,[28] but for our purposes the most important sections deal with the enforcement of custody decrees. The Act (codified as 28 U.S.C. 1738A) supplements the existing full faith and credit statute (28 U.S.C. 1738) by requiring enforcement of custody decrees if the awarding court had jurisdiction. The definition of jurisdiction in the PKPA closely parallels that in the UCCJA,[29] illustrating the success of the Uniform Act since its promulgation. The PKPA, of course, also makes the UCCJA more effective. Modification of a custody decree is permitted under the PKPA only by a court in F–1, unless that court has lost subject matter jurisdiction. That limitation on modification strongly confirms the priority–in–time rule and the modification provisions of the UCCJA. Finally, the Act requires a court to give contestants notice of the proceeding and an opportunity to be heard.[30]

Although the PKPA tracks rather closely the jurisdiction and recognition sections of the UCCJA, the federal law is by no means redundant. First,

---

[25] *See* § 37, *supra.*

[26] Barbara Ann Atwood, *Child Custody Jurisdiction and Territoriality*, 52 Ohio St. L.J. 369–402 (1991), argues that personal jurisdiction is necessary in custody cases, but that power over the absent parent "can arise from child–centered contacts with the forum."

[27] UCCJA § 14(a).

[28] One provision of the PKPA provides for the use of the Parent Locator Service, which is provided for in the Social Security Act. 42 U.S.C. § 653. The Service provides information for locating a parent or child in order to enforce certain state or federal laws. Hence, the Service may be used in order to enforce a law regarding the "unlawful taking or restraint of a child," or to make or enforce a custody determination. The last provision of the Act makes 18 U.S.C. § 1073, the federal kidnapping statute, applicable to "cases involving parental kidnapping and interstate or international flight to avoid prosecution under applicable state felony statutes." A state which makes parental kidnapping a crime may seek the help of the FBI in locating the abducting parent. This is the only section of the Act with international implications — the other sections only apply to states and United States territories and possessions.

[29] *See* Coombs, *supra* note 1, at 713 n.

[30] 28 U.S.C. § 1738A(e).

it throws the judgment of Congress behind a restrictive interpretation of *May v. Anderson* and the conclusion that ex parte custody decrees issued by a court having substantial contact with the problem do not present due process problems. Second, it confirms the need to avoid parochialism in custody matters. Third, it favors the "home state" over a state that has jurisdiction based on a significant connection. Finally, it makes the UCCJA effective in those states that have not adopted a complete version of it.

Custody cases present a constant tension between two fundamental and inconsistent goals — "preventing or punishing 'child–snatching' and promoting well informed decisions",[31] this, of course, is merely a specialized version of the age–old conflict between certainty of decision and achieving justice in the case at bar. Although it has been suggested that the PKPA and UCCJA really are not working well,[32] it is unlikely that courts, at least without strong legislative prodding, will be able to resist the urge to "do justice" to a case involving a child and a resident parent.

The final significant activity in interstate custody problems was the adoption of the Uniform Child Custody Jurisdiction and Enforcement Act[33] — ("UCCJEA"). The main purpose of that Act was to reconcile the UCCJA with the PKPA, although the new law also provides a host of novel enforcement mechanisms.

§ 131 International Custody[1]

Custody disputes are bad enough in domestic litigation; when the dispute turns international, the problems are magnified enormously. Jurisdiction and enforcement, the difficulty in locating absent parents, and the tendency to favor forum residents all become much more difficult when the battle includes different countries. Fortunately, the Hague Convention on the Civil Aspect of International Child Abduction (1980) provides some relief. The Convention was ratified by Congress in 1988 and implemented by statute shortly thereafter.[2] The Convention provides for strict enforcement of custody orders. Any valid order issued by a court in a country which signed the order must be enforced by every other signatory to the Convention. The American implementing legislation requires both state and federal courts to do so without question. So far, the Convention seems to work reasonably well. This statute is the first legislation requiring federal courts to hear family law disputes, and it codifies sound policy. The resolution of problems created by our system of federalism should fall to both state *and* federal courts.

---

[31] Goldstein, *supra* note 1, at 851.

[32] *Id.* at 942–43.

[33] U.L.A. *See generally* Patricia M. Hoff, *The ABC's of the UCCJEA: Interstate Child Custody Practice Under the New Act*, 32 Fam. L.Q. 267 (1998).

[1] *See generally* Linda Silberman, *Hague International Child Abduction Convention: A Progress Report*, 57 L. & Contemp. Probs. 210 (1994); Adair Dyer, *The Internationalization of Family Law*, 30 U.C. Davis L. Rev. 625 (1997).

[2] 42 U.S.C. §§ 11601 *et seq.*

§ 132 Adoption and Legitimacy

A court has jurisdiction to issue a decree in an adoption case if the parties (that is, the child and all parents) are domiciled in that state. If there is no common domicile, there is good authority that the domicile of the adopting parents has jurisdiction;[1] and if the child is homeless, the state where the child is living may provide for his future by issuing an adoption decree.[2] The reasoning is that a state should be able to act in the best interests of the child, and that the adoption only burdens the adopting parents. Nevertheless, it is quite possible that an effective adoption will require personal jurisdiction over the biological parents, at least if they are known. The adoption, after all, will terminate their interests in something they may find extremely important. By analogy to divisible divorce, important rights cannot be terminated in the absence of personal jurisdiction. Support for this argument comes from the fact that the forum must accord the biological parents notice concerning the adoption and an opportunity to be heard.[3] Finally, the forum will apply its own law.[4]

An adoption decree is entitled to full faith and credit to the same extent and with the same limits as other court orders. The only real issue concerning the effect of a foreign decree of adoption centers on the incidents of adoption, especially the right of the adopted child to inherit. The Restatement (Second) treats the inheritance problem as a question involving the succession to land or to movables, which leads, in turn, to a resolution of the problem by the law of the situs when land is involved, and by the law of the decedent's domicile at death in the case of personal property.[5] Probably the most frequent fact situation involves the construction of the word "child" in a will or trust: Does that term include someone who was adopted? The answer, however, is usually provided not as a matter of law, but by considering the "intent" of the testator or settlor (as well as by looking at equitable factors).[6] By applying what might be called general principles of construction in this way, courts are able to bypass the choice-of-law questions.

The legitimation of children is usually done pursuant to a statute which establishes necessary formalities.[7] Generally, if the legitimation was effective in the state where accomplished, the child's new status will be recognized by other jurisdictions. Although there may be exceptions, the clear propensity of judges is to treat the child as fully legitimate for all purposes. Recent Supreme Court decisions holding that discriminatory

---

1 Leflar, McDougal & Felix § 239; Scoles, et al. § 16.5.

2 Restatement (Second) of Conflict of Laws § 78.

3 Armstrong v. Manzo, 380 U.S. 545 (1965). *See also* Lehr v. Robertson, 463 U.S. 248 (1983).

4 Restatement (Second) of Conflict of Laws § 289. *But see* Herma Hill Kay, *Adoption in the Conflict of Laws: The UAA, Not the UCCJA is the Answer*, 84 Cal. L. Rev. 703 (1996) (arguing for the adoption of the Uniform Arbitration Act to resolve interstate adoption disputes).

5 *See id.* §§ 238, 262.

6 *See* Matter of Griswold, 140 N.J. Super. 35, 354 A.2d 717 (1976).

7 *See generally* John Ester, *Illegitimate Children and Conflict of Laws*, 36 Ind. L.J. 163 (1961).

treatment of illegitimate children may violate the Equal Protection Clause can only enhance that tendency.[8]

[8] *See, e.g.,* Trimble v. Gordon, 430 U.S. 762 (1977).

TABLE OF CASES

[References are to page numbers and/or note numbers.]

C

D

E

F

G

H

P

Q

R

S

T

U

V

W

X

Y

Z

TABLE OF AUTHORITIES

[References are to page numbers and/or note numbers.]

C

D

G

H

I

J

K

L

M

N

O

P

R

W

Y

Z

INDEX

[References are to pages.]

[References are to pages.]

[References are to pages.]

[References are to pages.]

[References are to pages.]

R

S

T

U